The Solicitor's Ha
2015

Related titles from Law Society Publishing:

Anti-Bribery Toolkit
Amy Bell

Anti-Money Laundering Toolkit
Alison Matthews

COFAs Toolkit
Jeremy Black and Florence Perret du Cray

COLPs Toolkit
Michelle Garlick

Complaints Handling Toolkit
Vicky Ling and Fiona Westwood

In-house Lawyers' Toolkit
Richard Tapp and Ann Page

Outcomes-Focused Regulation
Andrew Hopper QC and Gregory Treverton-Jones QC

SRA Handbook (October 2014)
Solicitors Regulation Authority

THE SOLICITOR'S HANDBOOK 2015

By

Andrew Hopper QC

and

Gregory Treverton-Jones QC

The Law Society

ISBN 978-1-78446-008-2

First edition published in 2008
Second edition published in 2009
Third edition published in 2011
Fourth edition published in 2012
Fifth edition published in 2013

This sixth edition published in 2014 by the Law Society
113 Chancery Lane, London WC2A 1PL

Typeset by Columns Design XML Ltd, Reading
Printed and bound in the UK by Hobbs the Printers Ltd, Totton, Hants

FSC
www.fsc.org
MIX
Board from responsible sources
FSC® C020438

The paper used for the text pages of this book is FSC certified. FSC (The Forest Stewardship Council) is an international network to promote responsible management of the world's forests.

Contents

Foreword to the 2008 edition

The authors have asked me to write a short foreword to this book. I am delighted to do so because I entirely agree with the views expressed in the Preface. Although I quite understand that it may be necessary to use the Internet in order for practitioners to be fully up to date at any given moment, many people (and not only the very old like me) like to have a book which sets out the basic principles and which they can readily consult. *The Solicitor's Handbook* is precisely that. It concisely sets out the relevant position under a number of different headings and is very user friendly.

The authors express the hope that the book will prove to be a valuable resource for regulator and regulated alike and that it will contribute to good regulation by identifying and explaining areas of particular concern and risk, especially where practitioners have, in the past, made innocent mistakes which have nevertheless had serious consequences.

I know that hope springs eternal, but in this case I am confident that the authors' hopes will be fulfilled. I wish it well.

Sir Anthony Clarke

Master of the Rolls
Royal Courts of Justice
October 2007

Preface to the 2008 edition

For generations of solicitors *The Guide to the Professional Conduct of Solicitors* (first published in 1960 and always provided free of charge) was the source of all knowledge in relation to the rules that controlled the profession. If you could not find it in the Guide, or if the available published guidance still left you in a quandary, you could always 'ring Redditch' – the Law Society's ethics helpline. Looking it up in the Guide and seeking the Law Society's advice was a total solution. After all; how could you be criticised for following the Law Society's own advice?

The Guide is no more. The eighth edition, published in 1999, was the last. We have moved into the modern era; the paperless age. The Solicitors' Code of Conduct 2007 (which henceforth we will refer to as 'the Code') appears on the website of the Solicitors Regulation Authority (SRA); so do the Solicitors' Accounts Rules 1998, and the Financial Services Rules and other rules. Diligent searching on the Law Society website will reveal much in the way of published guidance, pronunciations and edicts. Information about how clients can complain about you, and what will happen when they do, can be found on the website of the Legal Complaints Service (LCS).

Only in the two thick volumes of the mighty *Cordery on Solicitors* will practitioners find in written form all the law and professional rules relating to solicitors.

But the paperless age and rapidly changing regulatory rules carry with them real dangers for practitioners who may find it difficult or impossible to discover what rules were in force when they did things which later become the subject of regulatory concern. This Handbook, which will be updated annually, seeks to remove those problems.

This Handbook brings together all the professional rules governing the conduct and regulation of solicitors in a manner that is convenient and inexpensive. We hope that we have added much more of value, by drawing upon our professional experience to explain how the rules and the regulatory machinery work in practice.

We have addressed our book to 'you' the practitioner: it has been written from the perspective of the practitioner, to whom it is intended to provide information and guidance. We have included material that we consider relevant and important to the practitioner but which is not included within the formal rules (for example, how money laundering, mortgage fraud and investment scams work), so that independently of the published guidance you can spot problems before they develop into loss to clients and others, damage to reputation, and regulatory interest.

We have included guidance on the workings of the Solicitors Disciplinary Tribunal, on the powers of intervention available to the SRA and the regime for the imposition of conditions on practising certificates.

And we have included a section on where you can obtain further specialist advice and help if all else fails.

It is unlikely that any practitioner currently feels that the profession is under-regulated; the weight of regulation, and dealings with the SRA, can be daunting. The Solicitors' Practice Rules 1936 (made by virtue of section 1 of the Solicitors Act 1933) comprised seven rules (in reality only four) and could be printed on one page.[1] The latest Code, if printed on A4, occupies 253 pages (and 190 pages of this book). We also live in a rapidly changing regulatory environment. The Code came into force on 1 July 2007: one month later it was amended for the first time. An updated version of the Accounts Rules to be incorporated into the Code by amendment is already in contemplation. We now have two regulators – the LCS, dealing with client complaints and redress for poor service, and the SRA, dealing with everything else. Under the previous system, if a complaint engaged both conduct and service issues it was a 'hybrid' and both aspects were dealt with together. Now, all consumer complaints and redress will be dealt with first by the LCS and if any conduct issues are considered to arise they will be referred to the SRA to be dealt with subsequently (although, if very serious concerns are raised and the interests of the public require it, more urgent action will no doubt be taken).

You can still 'ring Redditch' for advice on issues of professional conduct, but the official and published position of the SRA is that for the purpose of any investigation or adjudication it is 'not bound' by any opinion or advice given by its own staff on the ethics helpline. In other words, you can follow the advice of the regulator, but – in theory at least – the regulator can nevertheless find you guilty of misconduct and impose sanctions. It is also not clear to what extent, if at all, information provided for the purposes of seeking such advice will be regarded as confidential, as opposed to being useful intelligence for regulatory purposes about the person making the enquiry.

The Legal Services Act 2007 maintains the division between conduct and service, hiving off consumer complaints and redress to the independent Office for Legal Complaints, which will succeed the LCS. The Act grants significant new powers to the SRA (which we have touched upon in Chapter 2) and sweeps away significant parts of the current statutory regime, for example in relation to conditions on practising certificates. Where changes will occur, we explain what the future holds.

We hope that this book will prove to be a valuable resource for regulator and regulated alike, and that it will contribute to good regulation in identifying and explaining areas of particular concern and risk – especially where practitioners have in the past made innocent mistakes that have nevertheless had serious consequences.

We would welcome feedback from practitioners, and particularly any requests and recommendations for the inclusion of material in areas we have not covered in this first edition.

We are grateful to the following for their drafting and other suggestions: Euros Jones of James Saunders & Co., who conducted extensive research and provided considerable input for the money laundering chapter; Mike Calvert of the SRA and Che Odlum of the Law Society, who shared their practical experience of money laundering and investment fraud issues; Iain Miller of Bevan Brittan for his substantial contributions to the chapter on the Code; and Geoffrey Williams QC for reviewing and suggesting amendments to Chapter 14. Many other members of the SRA and SDT, notably Sue Elson and Liz Aldred, answered our queries constructively and with unfailing courtesy. All provided invaluable assistance, although the responsibility for any errors and omissions is ours alone. Others deserve particular thanks. Michael Hoyle was the inspiration for Andrew Hopper's original interest in solicitors' regulatory law and practice. When legal complications arose after we finished the writing, we received matchless assistance from Nick Gardner and David Mayhew at Herbert Smith, and valuable advice from Tony Grabiner at 1 Essex Court, and Sean Wilken and Ben Williams at 39 Essex Street. Finally, we are both deeply grateful to our respective wives, Ros and Tamsin, for their support and forbearance while their otherwise apparently sane husbands buried themselves in some of the more esoteric material contained in this book.

1 In brief – Rule 1: no touting; Rule 2: no charging under the published scale fees; Rule 3: no fee sharing; Rule 4: no association with ambulance chasers; Rule 5: provision for waivers; Rule 6: definitions; Rule 7: commencement.

Preface to the 2015 edition

When we embarked upon the first edition of this book in 2007, we had only a limited appreciation of the revolution that was about to engulf the legal profession. Both the Solicitors' Code of Conduct 2007 and the Legal Services Act 2007 were hot off the presses, and the Solicitors Regulation Authority (SRA) had been newly created, but the future shape of the profession was far from clear. Since then, we have had the creation of the Legal Services Board, the demise of the 2007 Code and its replacement by the concept of outcomes-focused regulation enshrined in the SRA Code of Conduct 2011, and the advent of alternative business structures (ABSs). There have been a host of other changes, some caused by external events such as the financial crisis and subsequent recession. But at last the pace of change has started to slow, and we have been able to allow a year to pass since the 2013 edition of this book, although we may be about to enter another period of upheaval based on another raft of SRA consultations and proposed changes, which we shall try to anticipate.

The effects of the revolution over the last seven years will continue to play out in the months and years ahead. There have been the first failures of ABSs. Although the Solicitors Disciplinary Tribunal (SDT) has been constituted as an appellate tribunal since 2011, it has not yet actually decided any appeals. Likewise, although the SRA is now the designated disciplinary body for ABSs and those who work in them, it has not yet decided any cases. All of this will change in the months and years ahead. Much of the SRA's focus over the last 18 months has been upon the financial stability of firms in the wake of the recession. Investigations seem to have been put on hold, or have been proceeding very slowly. Prosecutions in the SDT in 2013 numbered fewer than 100 in contrast to an average of more than 200 per annum in the several years prior to that. There are signs that this is changing, and that enforcement action is becoming more vigorous once again. We can look forward to a period of more litigation, as the decisions made under the new regulatory structures are tested in the courts.

That is not to say that yet further revolution can be ruled out. The present Government has pursued an agenda that seeks to reduce regulatory burdens on professions and businesses. Politically, we may see pressure for the abolition of the Legal Services Board, and consolidation of legal regulation under one regulator. There have been signs too that some Members of Parliament are unhappy with the response to the referral fee ban imposed in personal injury cases with effect from 1 April 2013, and further primary legislation cannot be ruled out.

All in all, we continue to live in interesting times, and we hope that this edition helps to guide our readers through the maze of rules and regulations which bind them. There have been various amendments to the SRA Code of Conduct 2011 since the last edition, and the courts have been busy hearing appeals and clarifying and developing the law. In particular, the level of fines imposed by the SDT has been examined on two occasions, in the *Fuglers* and *Andersons* appeals. The first few challenges to decisions of the Legal Ombudsman (LeO) have been determined by the High Court. The SDT has issued Standard Directions, which supplement the Solicitors (Disciplinary Proceedings) Rules 2007, and plug important gaps. Solicitors' relationship with the consumer credit legislation has changed. We have incorporated all of this, and a great deal more, in the current edition. In particular, we have substantially rewritten **CHAPTER 4**, as the 2011 Code is no longer the shining new jewel it was when we last published, and its predecessor, the 2007 Code, is slowly slipping away from memory.

In the preparation of this edition, we are grateful to Ian Ryan of Howard Kennedy FSI for his work on **CHAPTERS 26** and **27**, and to Andrew Blatt and Robert Forman of Messrs Murdochs, who contributed the section on voluntary closure in **CHAPTER 16**. As ever, we are indebted to our editors, Stephen Honey and Sarah Foulkes at Law Society Publishing, for ensuring that the finished product is as impressive as usual.

The law is stated as at 1 September 2014.

Table of cases

Table of statutes

Paragraph references printed in **bold type** indicate where the Enactment is set out in part or in full.

Table of statutory instruments

Paragraph references printed in **bold type** indicate where the Enactment is set out in part or in full.

Table of European legislation and other international materials

Primary legislation

Conventions

Secondary legislation

Directives

Table of other enactments

Paragraph references printed in **bold** type indicate where the Enactment is set out in part or in full.

PART 1
Overview

CHAPTER 1

The regulatory and disciplinary landscape

1.1

In the earliest times only the courts exercised disciplinary jurisdiction over solicitors, as officers of the court. When Mr Brounsall was struck off the roll of attorneys in 1778, having been convicted of stealing a guinea, for which he had been sentenced 'to be branded on the hand, and to be confined to the house of correction for nine months' the question was raised as to whether the striking off would amount to a second, and unlawful, penalty. Lord Mansfield announced that as this raised issues concerning the dignity of the profession, 'a solemn opinion should be given' and that the matter should be mentioned 'to all the judges'. On 27 June 1778, a Saturday, Lord Mansfield announced:

> 'We have consulted all the judges upon this case, and they are unanimously of opinion, that the defendant's having been burnt in the hand, is no objection to his being struck off the roll. And it is on this principle; that he is an unfit person to practise as an attorney.'[1]

By the nineteenth century, and by virtue of the Solicitors Act 1888, applications against solicitors were made to a Committee of the Incorporated Law Society, whose members were appointed by the Master of the Rolls. The Committee made findings which were embodied in a report to the court, but the court continued to exercise the disciplinary jurisdiction. No report from the Society's Committee was necessary however; the court could still act on its own motion.[2]

1 *Ex parte Brounsall* [1778] 2 Cowp 829.
2 Sections 12, 13 and 19 of the Solicitors Act 1888; and see *Re Weare* [1893] 2 QB 439, CA.

1.2

The Solicitors Act 1919 granted the powers of the court, to strike solicitors from the roll and to impose other penalties, to the Disciplinary Committee of the Law Society, but preserved the court's inherent jurisdiction. The Disciplinary Committee was not a committee of the Council of the Law Society, but a separate statutory body whose members continued to be appointed by the Master of the Rolls. The Disciplinary Committee was replaced by the Solicitors Disciplinary Tribunal ('the Tribunal' or SDT) in 1975, by the Solicitors Act (SA) 1974. Section 50 of SA 1974 continues to preserve the court's parallel and inherent jurisdiction. The functions of the investigator and prosecutor have remained with the Law Society throughout, as they still do (in the sense that although the Solicitors Regulation Authority (SRA) operates independently of the Society through its own Board, it has no separate legal existence).

1.3

In January 2007 the Law Society split into three organisations:

(1) the Society itself, based in Chancery Lane, which remains the representative body for solicitors; their 'trade union' – though not in the fullest sense of that phrase. It remains impossible, for example, for the Law Society to assist directly in the defence of any individual solicitor in dealings with the SRA;

(2) the Solicitors Regulation Authority (SRA), which since October 2012 is based in Birmingham, with a satellite City of London office, and which is the professional regulator; and

(3) the Legal Complaints Service (LCS) which between 2007 and October 2010 dealt with client complaints.

The functions of the LCS were brought to an end in respect of all complaints made on and after 6 October 2010 and it has now ceased to exist. Consumer or client complaints were removed by the Legal Services Act (LSA) 2007 from the existing regulators altogether[1] and vested in the Office for Legal Complaints (which uses the title of Legal Ombudsman). Part 6 of LSA 2007 established a comprehensive ombudsman scheme for the handling of complaints by consumers. For the Legal Ombudsman see **CHAPTER 13.**

The SRA is run by its own Board. As the statutory powers remain vested in the Council of the Law Society, under SA 1974 as amended, those powers are delegated by the Council to and through the Board, to enable the SRA to operate independently of the Law Society.

1 Section 157 of LSA 2007.

1.4

Under LSA 2007, the Legal Services Board (LSB) is established to promote and maintain regulatory objectives relating to the provision of legal services, namely:

(1) protecting and promoting public interest;

(2) supporting the constitutional principle of the rule of law;

(3) improving access to justice;

(4) protecting and promoting the interests of consumers;

(5) promoting competition in the provision of legal services;

(6) encouraging an independent, strong, diverse and effective legal profession;

(7) increasing public understanding of the citizen's legal rights and duties; and

(8) promoting and maintaining adherence to professional principles.[1]

The professional principles are:

(1) acting with independence and integrity;

(2) maintaining proper standards of work;

(3) acting in the best interests of clients;

(4) complying with the duty to the court to act with independence in the interests of justice in relation to litigation and advocacy; and

(5) keeping the affairs of clients confidential.[2]

The LSB regulates the regulators, delegating the primary role to approved regulators (including the Law Society/SRA) but maintaining oversight. A detailed consideration of the Board's powers is outside the parameters of this book.

1 Section 1(1) of LSA 2007.
2 Section 1(3).

1.5

Part 5 of LSA 2007 is concerned with alternative business structures (ABSs) – the licensing of bodies, not owned or controlled by lawyers, to provide legal services. The Council for Licensed Conveyancers began licensing ABSs from 6 October 2011, providing legal services restricted to conveyancing and probate, and the SRA began taking applications in January 2012.

When the ABS regime is fully in force, any legal disciplinary partnership with a non-lawyer manager (see **CHAPTER 2**) will have to re-register as an ABS. The transitional period is set by the LSB and the end date has not yet been specified.

In order to ensure that the existing suite of rules was appropriate for the changed landscape that would exist when ABSs became licensed, the SRA undertook the mammoth task of amending it. The result is the 'SRA Handbook', which brings together the new Principles and Code of Conduct, the relevant Accounts Rules, now reconstituted as the SRA Accounts Rules 2011, and the various rules covering authorisation and practising requirements, discipline and costs recovery, and specialist services. The SRA Handbook is available in hard copy but is updated more regularly online. It has been regularly amended and the print copy (the third) is already out of date. The SRA Handbook reached its tenth version or iteration on 1 July 2014.

Duties of approved regulators

1.6

Under section 28 of LSA 2007, approved regulators are under a statutory duty to act in a way that is compatible with the regulatory objectives (see **1.4**) and in a way most appropriate for the purpose of meeting those objectives. Those objectives require, of course, regulation in the public interest, but a strong and independent profession is in the view of Parliament an essential requirement in the public interest. It is therefore part of the function of the SRA to work towards improving access to justice, promoting competition in the provision of legal services, encouraging an independent, strong, diverse and effective legal profession, and increasing public understanding of the citizen's legal rights and duties, all of which involve support for the profession.

Approved regulators must also have regard to the principles under which regulatory activities should be transparent, accountable, proportionate, consistent and targeted only at cases in which action is needed.[1] It has not always been the case (so it has seemed to informed commentators and so it may have seemed to the profession following encounters with the SRA) that these principles have been rigorously applied in practice, although they are officially adopted as SRA policy. A whole-hearted commitment to outcomes-focused regulation as intended by the SRA (see **CHAPTER 14**), but which cannot be said to have become a reality some three years after it was formally adopted, should result in the aspiration becoming reality.

In April 2014 the Better Regulation Delivery Office of the Department for Business, Innovation and Skills issued a 'Regulators' Code' (see **APPENDIX 10**), which sets out six principles each with accompanying detailed requirements. The general principles are:

1. Regulators should carry out their activities in a way that supports those they regulate to comply and grow.
2. Regulators should provide simple and straightforward ways to engage with those they regulate and hear their views.
3. Regulators should base their regulatory activities on risk.
4. Regulators should share information about compliance and risk.
5. Regulators should ensure clear information, guidance and advice is available to help those they regulate meet their responsibilities to comply.
6. Regulators should ensure that their approach to their regulatory activities is transparent.

The Regulators' Code is not fully applicable to the SRA but does apply to the LSB and is likely to be adopted in principle by the SRA or to be imposed on all the approved regulators by the LSB.

1 Section 28(3) of LSA 2007.

CHAPTER 2

The regulation and authorisation of business entities

Entity or firm-based regulation

2.1

The year 2009 saw the beginning of a series of substantial changes in the way that the profession is regulated. The Solicitors Regulation Authority (SRA) moved to firm-based regulation, although the first signs of this happening in practice did not emerge until the third quarter of 2010. The intention was that the focus of investigation and regulatory action would more frequently be the business within which solicitors practise, rather than individual practitioners. Explanations were to be sought from the firm, in relation to matters perceived to have gone wrong, and less from individual solicitors. The business entity became liable to rebukes, fines and controls on the way it is permitted to operate, although individual solicitors, or other managers or employees of the business, may also be targeted. For a consideration of the practical consequences of this, see **14.7** and **14.8**.

Secondly, the Legal Services Act (LSA) 2007 created an environment in which businesses that provide legal services may have a choice as to which of the available approved regulators is to regulate the firm. For example, the Council for Licensed Conveyancers (CLC) can regulate those who supply conveyancing and probate services; the Institute of Chartered Accountants of Scotland and the Association of Chartered Certified Accountants are approved to regulate the supply of probate services in England and Wales, though it appears that they are not actually authorising or regulating anyone at present. The Institute of Chartered Accountants in England and Wales (ICAEW) has also more recently been granted approved regulator status in respect of probate services and is expected to become an active regulator. Furthermore, it is evident that the CLC proposes to expand its role so as to be able to regulate the supply of litigation services and advocacy. If that expectation becomes reality, it will become a direct rival to the SRA. The regulatory arm of the Chartered Institute of Legal Executives (formerly ILEX, now CILEx), which is still named ILEX Professional Standards or IPS, also intends to expand its role.

Since 31 March 2009, firms of solicitors have been able to become legal disciplinary partnerships and, if they limit the services they provide to conveyancing and probate, may choose to be regulated by the CLC in place of the SRA.

2.2

In consequence, individual solicitors may find themselves subject to two different regulatory regimes simultaneously. For example, the business by which they are employed may be an entity regulated by the CLC or ICAEW, while the solicitors as individuals may be regulated by the SRA. LSA 2007 provides[1] that if a conflict arises between the regulations that apply to the entity and those that apply to an employee or manager of the entity, the regulations applying to the entity prevail. Thus, a solicitor who is a manager of or employed by a business regulated by the CLC must comply with the rules of the CLC or ICAEW in relation to, for example, referral fees and deposit interest. However, the SRA Principles apply to a solicitor who is practising as such, whether or not the entity through which the individual practises is subject to the Principles.[2] The SRA asserts that the whole of the SRA Code of Conduct 2011 also applies to solicitors practising in this way, but this has to be read as being subject to section 52(4) of LSA 2007 as last mentioned.[3] Chapters 10 (You and your regulator), 12 (Separate businesses) as well as the application, waivers and interpretation sections – Chapters 13 to 15, of the 2011 Code apply to a solicitor who is a manager or employee of a legal services provider authorised by a regulator other than the SRA, or one who is an owner of such a firm.[4] Solicitors are also subject to the requirement to have a practising certificate issued by the SRA, even if employed by a legal services provider regulated by another regulator, or if they are managers of such a body, if the solicitor's involvement in the firm, or the work undertaken, depends on the individual being a solicitor, or the individual is employed or held out explicitly or implicitly as a solicitor.[5]

Nevertheless, a publication concerned with the regulation of solicitors can no longer focus exclusively on the rules promulgated by the SRA. Therefore, a brief consideration of the CLC rules is contained in **CHAPTER 12** and the CLC Code of Conduct is reproduced at **APPENDIX 7**.

1 Section 52(4) of LSA 2007.
2 SRA Principles – Application provisions, para 3.1(a).
3 SRA Code of Conduct 2011, Chapter 13, para 13.1(a). The effect of section 52(4) is expressly acknowledged in rule 11 of the SRA Authorisation Rules for Legal Services Bodies and Licensable Bodies 2011.
4 SRA Code of Conduct 2011, Chapter 13, para 13.2(a) and (b).
5 Rule 9.2 of the SRA Practice Framework Rules 2011.

Authorisation

2.3

'Authorisation' is one of the three strands of regulation covered by the SRA Handbook, the other two being supervision and enforcement.

Authorisation as an area of regulation covers the processes whereby individuals may be permitted to provide legal services, including the process of being admitted as a solicitor – and thus includes the SRA Training Regulations, Admission Regulations, Qualified Lawyers Transfer Scheme Regulations – and also covers any additional qualification needed to provide specific services, currently limited to the SRA Higher Rights of Audience Regulations and the SRA Quality Assurance Scheme for Advocates (Crime) Notification Regulations (all of which are outside the scope of this book), and the SRA Suitability Test which, as well as being relevant to the enrolment of students and admission to the roll, is applicable in relation to the approval of non-lawyer managers of law firms (within legal disciplinary partnerships and alternative business structures), of compliance officers for legal practice and for finance and administration (COLPs and COFAs; see **CHAPTER 6**), and of non-lawyers who own a material interest in a law firm.

Authorisation also encompasses the procedures regulating firms and individuals in the manner in which they provide legal services, through the SRA Authorisation Rules for Legal Services Bodies and Licensable Bodies 2011, the SRA Practice Framework Rules and the SRA Practising Regulations.

SRA Authorisation Rules for Legal Services Bodies and Licensable Bodies 2011

2.4

These rules[1] are the core of the SRA's control mechanism for all forms of practice. They apply to alternative business structures (ABSs) ('licensable bodies' or 'licensed bodies' depending on the context) and to all other more traditional forms of practice ('legal services bodies' or 'recognised bodies'), including legal disciplinary partnerships. At a date yet to be set in the near future the concept of sole practitioner recognition will cease and sole practitioners will be authorised as all other practices, and the Authorisation Rules will apply to them too.[2]

'Recognition' of an existing recognised body or sole practitioner has or shortly will have effect as if it is authorisation under the Authorisation Rules and all managers and owners of such practices shall be deemed to be approved for the purposes of the Authorisation Rules.[3]

There are four key elements to the Authorisation Rules:

- the process of authorisation, including applications and conditions;
- the approval process for managers, owners and compliance officers;
- information requirements; and
- the role of compliance officers – the compliance officer for legal practice (COLP) and the compliance officer for finance and administration (COFA).

There are also provisions relating to the duration, suspension and revocation of authorisation; the effect of unforeseen breaches in relation to the requirements for authorisation; appeals and transitional arrangements.

'Authorisation' is used to describe the recognition process for recognised bodies, *and* the licensing process for ABSs. Once authorised a firm will not need to renew its authorisation (recognition or licence); it will continue in force until withdrawn or revoked, although there will be a requirement to make annual returns with specified information and to pay annual fees.

1 We will refer to them throughout as the Authorisation Rules.
2 Consequently, that part of the SRA Practising Regulations 2011 which deals with sole practitioner recognition is expected to have a short life from the date of publication of this book, and although there are differences between them and the 2009 Regulations of the same name, contained and explained in *The Solicitor's Handbook 2011*, the differences are not substantial. We have therefore elected not to deal with sole practitioner recognition in this edition.
3 Rule 28 of the Authorisation Rules.

Applications

2.5

The SRA must make a decision on an application that has been duly made, using the correct form and accompanied by all the required information, within six months unless an extension notice is served, which may be done only once, so as to bring the maximum period for any decision to nine months.[1] This is plainly intended to provide for the most complex ABS authorisation applications which require extensive investigation. More routine applications are dealt with far faster, although the process may still take months for even the most straightforward application, particularly if one factors in the time needed to complete the complex and demanding application forms. It had not initially been appreciated, in the context of ABS licence applications, that the period of six months does not start to run until the SRA has satisfied itself that it has all the information it requires, a process which itself can take many months.

The SRA may only grant an application for authorisation if the applicant satisfies, in terms of the business structure, the statutory requirements for a legal services body (non-ABS) or a licensable body (ABS); if it is a partnership, the body must have adopted a name under which it is to be registered, and which complies with Chapter 8 (Publicity) of the SRA Code of Conduct 2011; and upon authorisation, the body must be in compliance with the SRA Indemnity Insurance Rules and Compensation Fund Rules.

The applicant will also have to satisfy the requirements as to the appointment of compliance officers, and obtain the SRA's approval; demonstrate that all managers and owners of the business are approved as necessary, and not disqualified (for example, as a result of having been struck off); that there is compliance with rule 12 of the SRA Practice Framework Rules in relation to persons who must be 'qualified to supervise' (see **2.26**); and with rules 15 and 16 of those Rules as to formation, registered office, practising address and composition of the body.[2]

The SRA may refuse an application even though these conditions are satisfied:

- if it is not satisfied that the applicant body's managers and interest holders are suitable, as a group, to operate or control a business providing regulated legal services;
- if it is not satisfied that the applicant body's management or governance arrangements are adequate to safeguard the regulatory objectives;
- if it is not satisfied that if the authorisation is granted, the applicant body will comply with the SRA's regulatory arrangements including the Authorisation Rules and any conditions imposed on the authorisation;
- if the applicant body has provided inaccurate or misleading information in its application or in response to any requests by the SRA for information;
- if the applicant body has failed to notify the SRA of any changes in the information provided in the application; or
- if for any other reason, the SRA considers that it would be against the public interest or otherwise inconsistent with the regulatory objectives to grant authorisation.[3]

1 Rule 5 of the Authorisation Rules.
2 Rule 6.2 of the Authorisation Rules.
3 Rule 6.3.

Conditions

2.6

All authorisations will be subject to standard conditions (under rule 8 of the Authorisation Rules) as well as any specific conditions the SRA decides to impose (under rule 9; these are broadly comparable with the purposes for which conditions may be imposed currently on recognitions and practising certificates; see **15.5**).

The standard conditions impose duties as to regulatory compliance; as to making suitable arrangements to ensure compliance; as to the payment of periodical fees; as to any limits on the activities that may be carried out; as to the appointment of compliance officers; as to those permitted to have management responsibilities and control; and as to the provision of information, including information requirements specific to partnerships, recognised bodies and licensed bodies.[1]

1 Rules 8.1 to 8.10 of the Authorisation Rules.

2.7

Under rule 8.1 an authorised body and its managers must ensure that any obligations imposed from time to time on the authorised body, its managers, employees or interest holders by or under the SRA's regulatory arrangements, and any other statutory obligations imposed on the authorised body, its managers, employees or interest holders, in relation to the body's business of carrying on authorised activities, are complied with. Interest holders are, broadly speaking, shareholders. An authorised body and its managers must agree to be subject to the SRA Disciplinary Procedure Rules 2011 and in particular the power of the SRA to impose a written rebuke and publish details of a written rebuke or a decision to impose a penalty, in accordance with rule 3 of those rules.

The effect of this widely drawn provision is that compliance with the whole of the SRA Handbook is a condition of the authorisation and thus a condition on the licence of an ABS. A failure to comply with any SRA rule is therefore a breach of a condition of authorisation and of the licence.

By rule 8.2 an authorised body must at all times have suitable arrangements in place to ensure that the body, its managers and employees, comply with the SRA's regulatory arrangements as they apply to them; and that the body and its managers and employees, who are authorised persons, maintain the professional principles.[1] A licensed body must at all times have suitable arrangements in place to ensure that the employees and managers and interest holders of that body who are non-authorised persons do nothing which causes or substantially contributes to a breach by the licensed body or its employees or managers of the SRA's regulatory arrangements.[2]

By rule 8.3 every authorised body must pay to the SRA the prescribed periodical fees by the prescribed date, and there are provisions as to applications to vary the fees by reference to mergers, splits, successions and the apportionment of turnover on which fees are based.

Rule 8.4 specifies that an authorised body may only carry on a regulated activity if that is done through a body and individual who is authorised to carry on that activity.

Rule 8.5 is concerned with COLPs and COFAs and is considered in more detail in **CHAPTER 6**.

Rule 8.6 requires that an authorised body must ensure that any manager or owner of the authorised body, or any manager of a body corporate which is a manager or owner of the authorised body, has been approved by the SRA. Solicitors with a current practising certificate and an existing authorised body are deemed to be approved.[3] No manager of a licensed body may be a person who is disqualified from being a manager. An authorised body (or manager or employee of such a body) and a recognised body (or manager or employee) must not employ or remunerate a person without the written permission of the SRA if they are in certain categories, for example, struck off or suspended solicitors or persons subject to an order under section 43 of the Solicitors Act (SA) 1974. Nor may such a person be permitted to be a manager or owner of the body.

Rule 8.7 deals with information requirements. As there are numerous reporting obligations in various places throughout the SRA Handbook (and not just in the Authorisation Rules) a summary of all of them can be found at **APPENDIX 19**.

Rules 8.8 to 8.10 deal with the matters that must be addressed by, respectively, partnerships, recognised bodies and licensed bodies where the last remaining individual whose presence ensures that there is a valid partnership, or that a recognised body meets the requirements for a legal services body, or that a licensed body remains a licensable body, ceases to be able to fulfil that role, through imprisonment, illness, loss of mental capacity, abandonment or the imposition of regulatory conditions. In any such case the body must inform the SRA within seven days and must within 28 days ensure that the body regularises the position or (in the case of a recognised body or licensed body) ceases to practise.

By rule 8.9(a) an interest holder of a recognised body must not create any charge or other third party interest over his or her interest in the recognised body except by means of a permitted nominee arrangement in favour of another who is able to hold an interest in the firm having regard to the terms of rule 8.6 (that is, one who is approved and not disqualified).

1 This is a restatement of the requirements of section 176 of LSA 2007.
2 This is a restatement of the requirements of section 90 of LSA 2007.
3 Rule 13.2 of the Authorisation Rules – unless there are conflicting practising certificate conditions, and provided the SRA has been notified in advance and has not withdrawn approval.

Additional conditions and modifications

2.8

Under rule 9.1(a) the SRA may at any time impose further conditions.

> 9.1 The *SRA* may at any time impose one or more further conditions on an *authorisation* if it considers:

(a) that:

(i) the condition would limit, restrict, halt or prevent an activity or activities on the part of the body, or of a *manager, employee*, or *interest holder* of the body, which is putting or is likely to put at risk the interests of *clients*, third parties or the public;

(ii) the condition would prevent or limit the activities of a *manager* or *employee* of the body who is considered unsuitable to undertake a particular activity, either at all or save as specified in the condition;

(iii) the condition would limit, halt or prevent a risk to *clients*, third parties or the public arising from a business agreement or association which the body has or is likely to enter into, or a business practice which the body has or is likely to adopt;

(iv) a *relevant insolvency event*[1] has occurred in relation to the body but the *SRA* does not propose at that time to suspend or revoke the *authorisation* under Rule 22;

(v) the condition is necessary to facilitate effective monitoring by the *SRA* of compliance with its *regulatory arrangements* on the part of the body, its *managers*, *employees* or *interest holders*;

(vi) the *SRA* considers that imposing the condition will require the body concerned to take specified steps conducive to the proper, effective or efficient carrying on of a *legal activity* by that body; or

(vii) the *SRA* considers that imposing a condition is necessary in order to ensure compliance with the *regulatory objectives*;

and

(b) that it is in the public interest to impose the condition.

A condition imposed under rule 9 takes effect from the date on which the condition is imposed unless otherwise specified by the SRA.

Under rule 10 the SRA may at any time modify the specified reserved legal activities which the authorised body is authorised to carry out, either on the application of the body or if it considers it appropriate to do so.

1 This occurs if there is a resolution to wind up a company without a declaration of solvency; the company enters administration or an administrative receiver is appointed, or a meeting of creditors converts a members' voluntary winding up into a creditors' voluntary winding up, or the company is ordered to be wound up by the court; or all the managers of an unincorporated body are adjudicated bankrupt; or an event occurs in relation to a foreign company which is analogous to one of these.

Approval

2.9

As part of the authorisation process express approval is required by the SRA of an authorised body's managers, owners and compliance officers. Solicitors who hold a current practising certificate and existing authorised bodies will be deemed to be approved to be owners or managers of an authorised body, provided that there are no practising certificate conditions or conditions on the body's authorisation which would be inconsistent with approval, and provided that the SRA has been notified in advance of the intention that the person or body should be a manager or owner, and has not withdrawn approval.[1]

It should be noted that there is no such deeming provision in relation to the appointment of compliance officers. The position of COLPs and COFAs is considered in more detail in **CHAPTER 6**.

1 Rule 13.2 of the Authorisation Rules.

SRA Suitability Test

2.10

Those who are not deemed to be approved for their roles must be expressly approved by the SRA which will apply its 'Suitability Test'. This is largely designed to exclude those who have been convicted of criminal offences of varying degrees of seriousness, and those with other serious lapses in their history.

Those with a conviction which resulted in a custodial or suspended sentence; or involved dishonesty, fraud, perjury and/or bribery; or resulted in the applicant being included on the Violent and Sex Offender Register; or was associated with obstructing the course of justice; or demonstrated behaviour showing signs of discrimination towards others; or was associated with terrorism; or was racially aggravated; or was motivated by any of the 'protected' characteristics defined within the Equality Act 2010; or which in the SRA's judgement is otherwise sufficiently serious as normally to prevent approval; and those who have been convicted by a court of more than one criminal offence, would not be approved save in exceptional circumstances.

Applications are more likely than not to fail if the applicant has been convicted of an offence that is less serious but is one which has an impact on the character and suitability of the applicant, or if the applicant has been included on the Violent and Sex Offender Register but without being convicted of a criminal offence; or has accepted a caution for an offence involving dishonesty.

An application may still fail, but has some prospect of success, if the applicant has received a local warning from the police; accepted a caution from the police for an offence not involving dishonesty; received a Penalty Notice for Disorder from the police; received a final warning or reprimand from the police (youths only); and/or received a referral order from the courts (youths only).

Any failure to disclose any material information is treated as prima facie evidence of dishonest behaviour.

2.11

It is not only criminal convictions that are relevant. Unless there are exceptional circumstances, there will be no approval for those who have been responsible for behaviour which is dishonest or violent, or where there is evidence of discrimination towards others; or where the individual has misused his or her position to obtain pecuniary advantage, abused a position of trust in relation to vulnerable people; or been responsible for other forms of behaviour which demonstrate that he or she could not be relied upon to comply with regulatory responsibilities.

Similarly, those who have committed or have been adjudged by an education establishment to have committed a deliberate assessment offence which amounts to plagiarism or cheating to gain an advantage, whether for the individual or others, will not be approved save in exceptional circumstances.

Past financial failings are relevant. Unless there are exceptional circumstances the SRA will not approve applicants where there is evidence that finances have not been managed properly and carefully; or there is evidence that the applicant has deliberately sought to avoid responsibility for his or her debts; or if there is evidence of dishonesty in relation to the management of finances.

If the applicant has been declared bankrupt, entered into any individual voluntary arrangement (IVA) or had a county court judgment issued against him or her it will raise a presumption that there has been evidence that the applicant cannot manage finances properly and carefully.

2.12

A poor regulatory history is relevant. Unless there are exceptional circumstances the SRA will refuse an application from anyone who has been made the subject of a serious disciplinary finding, sanction or action by a regulatory body and/or any court or other body hearing appeals in relation to disciplinary or regulatory findings; or who has failed to disclose information to a regulatory body when required to do so; or who has provided false or misleading information or significantly breached the requirements of a regulatory body; or who has been refused registration by a regulatory body; or who has failed to comply with the reasonable requests of a regulatory body.

The SRA may also refuse an application where the applicant has been rebuked, reprimanded or received a warning about his or her conduct by a regulatory body, unless there are exceptional circumstances.

2.13

All the above considerations apply to those seeking to be admitted as a solicitor, but additional provisions apply to those seeking approval of any role covered by the Authorisation Rules: that is, any COLP, COFA, owner or manager.

Unless there are exceptional circumstances the SRA may refuse to approve anyone who has been removed from the office of trustee for a charity by an order under the Charities Act 1993; or who has been removed and/or disqualified as a company director; or where any body corporate of which the applicant is or was a manager or owner has been the subject of a winding up order, an administrative order or an administrative receivership, or has otherwise been wound up or put into administration in circumstances of insolvency; or if the applicant has a previous conviction, which is spent, for a criminal offence relating to bankruptcy, IVAs or other circumstances of insolvency; or if the applicant is a corporate person or entity subject to a relevant insolvency event;[1] or the applicant is a corporate person or entity and other matters that call its fitness and propriety into question are disclosed or come to light; or if the applicant has committed an offence under the Companies Act 2006.

The SRA is obliged by LSA 2007 to consider the associates of those to be approved as owners of material interests in ABSs,[2] and has extended the same requirement to all covered by the Authorisation Rules. Applications for approval may be refused if the SRA has evidence reflecting on the honesty and integrity of a person the applicant is related to, affiliated with, or acts together with, where there is reason to believe that the person may have an influence over the way in which the applicant will exercise his, her or its authorised role.

1 See the footnote to **2.8**.
2 Paragraph 6 of Schedule 13 to LSA 2007.

2.14

It is important to bear in mind that the onus is on applicants to satisfy the regulator. There is no entitlement to an appointment. The law and the relevant tests to be applied are considered in the context of appeals to the Solicitors Disciplinary Tribunal ('the Tribunal' or SDT) in relation to licensing matters; see **22.14**.

Withdrawal of approval

2.15

The SRA may withdraw approval where approval, including deemed approval, has been granted if it is not satisfied that the person continues to meet the criteria for approval; or if it is satisfied that a condition imposed on the body's authorisation has not been or is not being complied with; or if there has been a breach of a duty or obligation imposed upon the approved person under the SRA Handbook or any statute, or if information or documentation is not promptly supplied in response to a request made by the SRA.[1]

Where withdrawal of approval relates to a director of a company, the SRA may set separate dates for that individual ceasing to be a director and disposing of his or her shares.[2]

1 Rule 17.1 of the Authorisation Rules.
2 Rule 17.2.

Revocation and suspension of authorisation

2.16

The SRA may revoke or suspend a body's authorisation where, in the case of an authorised body (that is, any practice that the SRA has authorised, ABS or non-ABS):

- authorisation was granted as a result of error, misleading or inaccurate information, or fraud;
- the body is or becomes ineligible to be authorised in accordance with the criteria set out in the Authorisation Rules;
- the SRA is satisfied that the body has no intention of carrying on the legal activities for which it has been authorised;

- the body has failed to provide any information required by the SRA under the Authorisation Rules;
- the body has failed to pay any fee payable to the SRA under the Authorisation Rules;
- a relevant insolvency event[1] has occurred in relation to the body;
- the body makes an application to the SRA for its authorisation to be revoked or suspended;
- the SRA has decided to exercise its intervention powers;
- the body, or an owner, interest holder, manager or employee of the body fails to comply with the duties imposed by or under the Authorisation Rules or under any statutory obligations in relation to the body's business of carrying on authorised activities, including payment of any fine or other financial penalty imposed on the body by the SRA, the Solicitors Disciplinary Tribunal, or the High Court;
- in the case of a licensed body (applicable to ABSs alone), the body fails to comply with the prohibition on appointing disqualified managers; or in the case of any authorised body, the body fails to comply with the prohibition on employing disqualified persons (struck off solicitors and the like) if the manager or employee concerned was disqualified as a result of breach of the duties imposed upon the manager or employee by sections 176 or 90 of LSA 2007 (the general duties imposed to comply with all regulatory arrangements for ABSs);
- the body does not comply with the requirements in relation to compliance officers;
- the body fails to comply with the management and control requirements (to ensure that those requiring approval are approved and that no disqualified person is employed without permission); or
- for any other reason it is in the public interest.

The SRA may also revoke or suspend a body's authorisation where, in the case of a *licensed* body (applicable to ABSs alone), a non-authorised person holds an interest in the licensed body:

- as a result of the person taking a step in circumstances where that constitutes an offence under paragraph 24(1) of Schedule 13 to LSA 2007 (whether or not the person is charged with or convicted of an offence under that paragraph) – this is failing to give notice as to the proposed or actual acquisition of a material interest in an ABS;
- in breach of conditions imposed on the owners of material interests in the ABS; or
- the person's holding of which is subject to an objection by the licensing authority.

1 See the footnote to **2.8**.

2.17

Before the SRA can revoke or suspend an authorisation it must first give the authorised body an opportunity to make representations to it on the issues that have led the SRA to consider this course, and it must also give at least 28 days' notice of its intention to make the decision to revoke or suspend.[1]

Guidance notes to rule 22 emphasise that the SRA is unlikely to revoke or suspend authorisation if to do so would present any risk to clients, the public, the protection of public money or to any SRA investigation.

1 Rule 22.2 of the Authorisation Rules.

Unforeseen temporary breach

2.18

Rule 23 of the Authorisation Rules provides for a variety of situations in which authorised bodies (ABSs and non-ABSs) could cease to be eligible to be authorised; for example, if an ABS no longer has a manager who is a qualified lawyer, or a recognised body no longer has one manager who is a solicitor. If the development could not reasonably have been foreseen, the SRA is notified within seven days, and the problem is resolved within 28 days, the firm will not be regarded as being in default or liable to have its authorisation revoked. If a limited liability partnership (LLP) has only one member in unforeseen circumstances but is otherwise compliant and the situation is remedied within six months the same applies.[1]

There are specific provisions relating to the death of a shareowner (because the personal representatives would not automatically be approved as interest holders) or where a member or shareowner ceases to be approved, or becomes insolvent, or has a Court of Protection deputy appointed under the Mental Capacity Act 2005, all of which provide short-term solutions deeming the firm to remain in compliance.[2]

1 Rules 23.1 and 23.2 of the Authorisation Rules.
2 Rules 23.3 to 23.6.

Partnership changes and temporary emergency authorisation

2.19

A change in composition of a partnership does not generally affect the firm's authorisation. However, if the change in composition results in there being no individual who is a partner after the change who was also a partner before the change, this is not a change in composition at all, but the cessation of one firm and the creation of another. The new firm cannot adopt the authorisation of the old firm.[1]

If a partnership change results in there being only one solicitor left (or a registered European lawyer) the firm may continue to practise provided this could not reasonably have been foreseen, the SRA is notified within seven days, the individual is granted temporary emergency authorisation and commences a substantive application for authorisation within 28 days, either as a sole practitioner or as a partnership with a new partner.[2]

In the same way, if there is a partnership split which results in there being a new firm comprising some of the partners of the original authorised firm, the new firm may continue to practise subject to essentially the same conditions (lack of foreseeability, prompt notification, emergency authorisation, and a substantive application within 28 days), provided the new firm also complies with the SRA Indemnity Insurance Rules.[3]

1 Rule 24.2(a) of the Authorisation Rules.
2 Rule 24.2(b).
3 Rules 24.2(c) and 25.

Reconsideration and appeals

2.20

The SRA reserves to itself the right to review or have 'reconsidered' any decision made by a decision-maker. Historically, this power has been used in disciplinary investigations when adjudicators have made decisions which the SRA staff had not expected or did not like (see **19.11**). Rule 29.2 of the Authorisation Rules makes it clear that decisions will only be reconsidered on the initiative of the SRA. It is in the nature of a 'prosecutor's appeal'.

This may be done if it appears to someone with the necessary authority that the decision-maker was not provided with material evidence that was available to the SRA; or was materially misled; or failed to take proper account of material facts or evidence; or took into account immaterial facts or evidence; or made a material error of law; or made a decision which was otherwise irrational or procedurally unfair; or made a decision which was otherwise ultra vires; or failed to give sufficient reasons.[1]

1 Rule 29.1 of the Authorisation Rules.

2.21

The appeal provisions vary depending on whether the authorised body is or is not an ABS, because the licensing and appeal decisions for an ABS are dictated by LSA 2007.

An ABS may appeal to the Solicitors Disciplinary Tribunal against a refusal of authorisation, a decision to impose a condition on an authorisation, a decision to revoke or suspend an authorisation, a refusal to approve a step which under a condition requires prior approval, a decision to modify, or to refuse to modify the conditions of an authorisation, but must first invoke the SRA's own appeal procedure.[1]

An ABS or the person affected may appeal to the Tribunal against a refusal to approve a person as a manager or compliance officer, to impose conditions on an approval or to withdraw approval, but must first invoke the SRA's appeal procedure.[2]

There are also ABS-specific provisions concerning financial penalties, disqualification and ownership issues, dealt with in **CHAPTERS 24** and **25**.

1 Rule 31.1 of the Authorisation Rules.
2 Rule 31.2.

2.22

Traditional firms (legal services bodies/recognised bodies) do not have any right of appeal to the Tribunal, nor do individuals within them affected by authorisation or approval decisions. The statutory background to the process of approval of recognised bodies is the Administration of Justice Act 1985 as amended by LSA 2007, and under Schedule 2 to that statute[1] appeal lies where relevant to the High Court.

A legal services body may appeal to the High Court against a refusal of authorisation, a decision to impose a condition on an authorisation, a refusal to approve a step which under a condition requires prior approval, or a decision to revoke or suspend an authorisation. In the case of a revocation or suspension of authorisation the aggrieved body must first invoke the SRA's own appeal procedure. In all other cases it may choose to but is not obliged to.[2]

A legal services body or the person affected may appeal to the High Court against the refusal of the SRA to approve a person to be a manager of the body or a decision to withdraw that approval, but must first invoke the SRA's own appeal procedure.[3]

If the body is not an ABS, but a legal services body/recognised body, there is no external right of appeal at all, and only the prospect of an appeal to a different decision-maker in the SRA[4] in relation to decisions:

- to refuse to approve a person to be an owner of the body;[5]
- to withdraw approval of an owner;
- to refuse to approve a person as a compliance officer – COLP or COFA;
- to withdraw approval of a compliance officer;
- to approve a manager, owner or compliance officer subject to conditions;
- to modify or to refuse to modify terms and conditions of authorisation.

1 See **APPENDIX 16**.
2 Rules 30.1(b) and 30.3 of the Authorisation Rules.
3 Rule 30.4.
4 Rules 30.1(a) and 30.2.
5 If a non-authorised person has an interest in a regulated firm that is equivalent to 10 per cent or more the firm is licensable as an ABS and the interest holder must be expressly approved (see **24.1** and **24.3**). If a non-authorised person has an interest that is less than 10 per cent, the body does not qualify as an ABS but the SRA still has to be satisfied that the body's managers and interest holders are suitable, as a group, to operate or control a business providing regulated legal services; see rule 6.3(a) of the Authorisation Rules.

2.23

The SRA's decision to adopt the same authorisation principles for all practices regardless of the statutory background has therefore created serious anomalies. A decision, for example, to impose conditions on a manager, to refuse approval of a compliance officer or to withdraw approval of a compliance officer where the individual's role is in an ABS is subject to an internal appeal process but is also subject to external review by the Tribunal, potentially with costs consequences if the SRA got it wrong.

Exactly the same decisions, made under the same rules applying the same principles and the same procedures, but where the individual's role is within an authorised practice that is not an ABS, can only be appealed internally. If the SRA decision-maker on appeal endorses the decision of the SRA first instance decision-maker there is no further right of appeal, leaving only the unsatisfactory remedy of judicial review.

2.24

The time limit for internal appeals is 28 days from notification of the decision and reasons. The SRA specifies that unless otherwise provided in rules of the High Court or the Tribunal appeals to the court or Tribunal must be made within 21 days.[1] Appeals to the High Court are governed by Part 52 of the Civil Procedure Rules and should be entered in the Administrative Court within 21 days of the decision, or of receipt of the reasons for the decision if later.[2] The Tribunal has set the time for appeal as 28 days from receipt of the decision in all cases; see **22.5**.

1 Rule 32.2 of the Authorisation Rules.
2 CPR Part 52.4; Part 52 Practice Direction 52D, paragraphs 3.3A and 27.1.

The SRA Practice Framework Rules 2011

2.25

The Practice Framework Rules mainly comprise lists of the various ways in which solicitors, registered European lawyers (RELs), registered foreign lawyers (RFLs) and authorised bodies may practise when regulated by the SRA, in offices in England and Wales and elsewhere, and the reserved legal activities for which they are authorised by the SRA. Limitations on the work that can be done by non-lawyer managers and employees are explained, and the fundamental legal criteria for recognised bodies and licensed bodies are set out.

Matters considered likely to be relevant in everyday practice are in part considered elsewhere in this book; for RELs and RFLs see **Chapter 11**; for in-house and overseas practice see **4.121** to **4.127**.

Two particularly relevant and important issues are dealt with in these rules – the circumstances in which practising certificates are required and the requirement for someone 'qualified to supervise'.

All solicitors require practising certificates (unless they are in the privileged group exempted by section 88 of SA 1974, such as those employed in central government) if:

- they are involved in 'legal practice'. This includes not only the provision of legal advice or assistance, or representation in connection with the application of the law or resolution of legal disputes, but also the provision of other services such as are provided by solicitors,[1] and:
- the involvement in the firm or the work depends on the individual being a solicitor; or
- the individual is held out explicitly or implicitly as a practising solicitor; or
- the individual is employed explicitly or implicitly as a solicitor; or
- section 1A of SA 1974 applies.[2]

Section 1A of SA 1974 states that a person who has been admitted as a solicitor and whose name is on the roll shall be taken to be acting as a solicitor (if this would not otherwise be so) if he or she is employed in connection with the provision of any legal services by any person who is qualified to act as a solicitor, by a partnership at least one member of which is qualified to act as a solicitor, by a recognised body, or by any other person or body who is authorised under LSA 2007 to provide reserved legal services.

Thus by section 1A any solicitor employed in what may be loosely termed private practice must always have a practising certificate. Solicitors employed by other bodies, for example, in industry or local government or by charities, will need to consider whether their employment depends on them being solicitors, whether they are employed on that basis, or whether they are held out as practising solicitors.

Rule 9.4 of the SRA Practice Framework Rules 2011 provides that if you are a solicitor who was formerly an REL, and you are practising from an office in the United Kingdom as a lawyer of an Establishment Directive[3] profession, you must have in force a practising certificate issued by the SRA, even if you are not practising as a solicitor.

1 Rule 9.3 of the SRA Practice Framework Rules 2011.
2 Rule 9.2.
3 European Communities and Council Directive 98/5/EC to facilitate practice of the profession of lawyer on a permanent basis in certain states other than the state in which the professional qualification was obtained.

2.26

To be qualified to supervise a person must have been entitled to practise as a lawyer for at least 36 months within the last ten years and to have completed the training specified from time to time by the SRA for this purpose, and to be able to demonstrate this if asked. The training currently specified involves attendance at or participation in a course on management skills for at least 12 hours.

The persons required to be qualified to supervise include sole practitioners, one lawyer manager of an authorised body, one solicitor or REL in a law centre, and one in-house solicitor or REL where solicitors or RELs undertake publicly funded work, advocacy, the supervision of advocacy or the conduct of proceedings for members of the public before a court or immigration tribunal as part of their employment.

PART 2

The Principles and the SRA Code of Conduct 2011

CHAPTER 3

The Principles and overview of the 2011 Code

Introduction

3.1

The rather modest regulatory impact of the 1936 Solicitors' Practice Rules has been mentioned in the Preface to the 2008 edition of this book. The Practice Rules changed very little in subsequent decades. A new rule was made in 1967, requiring that only solicitors with practising certificates should be listed on notepaper and the office nameplate. Rule 2 (which prohibited the sin of charging less than scale fees) was replaced in 1972 with a rule against acting for both parties in conveyancing transactions subject to familiar exceptions. A comprehensive new set of Rules was made in 1987, which are recognisably the precursor to the Solicitors' Practice Rules 1990 and very little different from the 1990 Rules in their original form. The 1990 Rules were amended and supplemented extensively after they were implemented; not all the changes were readily accessible.

The Law Society embarked on the preparation of a new comprehensive set of rules in and before 2004, and the resulting Solicitors' Code of Conduct 2007 (2007 Code) came into force on 1 July 2007. The 2007 Code abandoned the historical approach of relatively narrow practice rules and wider but non-exclusive (official and published) guidance. Instead, it created a comprehensive regulatory framework for all aspects of a solicitor's conduct. The 2007 Code comprised 25 individual rules and was supplemented by guidance produced by the Solicitors Regulation Authority (SRA) which amplified and explained its provisions. The guidance was not mandatory and did not form part of the 2007 Code; however, the SRA added a note to the preamble to the 2007 Code with effect from 31 March 2009 to the effect that if solicitors did not follow the guidance they could be required to demonstrate (i.e. prove) how they nevertheless complied with the rules.

The 2007 Code's life was short. Because of its all-encompassing nature, the 2007 Code and the guidance associated with each rule had to be amended regularly, which caused problems for solicitors who found it difficult to pinpoint what rule or guidance was in force at a given time. This was accompanied by an approach to regulation by the SRA which appeared to concentrate on minutiae – for example, precisely what needed to be said to clients about referral arrangements, and when it had to be said, about which it was not difficult to make mistakes, even when solicitors were doing what they thought was entirely proper.

3.2

The passing of the Legal Services Act (LSA) 2007, the inevitable need to create a regulatory environment which would work for both traditional law firms and alternative business structures (ABSs) and strong guidance from the Legal Services

Board, created the need to move to a different basis and style of regulation. Principles-based regulation had been pioneered by the financial services profession, and was then introduced to the legal profession in October 2011 under the title 'outcomes-focused regulation' (OFR). Instead of professionals being bound, and often hamstrung, by a prescriptive set of rules, the onus shifts to the regulated individual or entity to deliver satisfactory outcomes for consumers based upon an overarching set of ethical principles. The regulated individual, the solicitor, is (or should be) trusted to think for him- or herself in order to achieve satisfactory outcomes for clients.

3.3

OFR is designed to move away, both in the form of rules and by the way in which they are policed, from the tick-box, strict liability, 'every breach is a breach' approach described above, which had seriously damaged the relationship between the profession and the regulator. The problem with that former approach was that it was too easy to hit the wrong target – the solicitor trying to get it right but making mistakes, as opposed to the one who does not care, or deliberately breaks the rules.

In an open and healthy manner, during the consultation process before the introduction of the SRA Code of Conduct 2011 (2011 Code), the SRA announced that:

> 'We know that the current rule book is too prescriptive. OFR will give firms the flexibility to do new and better things for consumers. It will lead to a more grown-up relationship between the SRA and the regulated community.'

and:

> 'The introduction of OFR will give a simplified rulebook and freedom to practise innovatively, which will be good for consumers and providers of legal services alike. OFR is risk-based regulation; firms will have to comply with broad principles rather than detailed rules. Firms will be able to comply with the principles in the ways which best suit their businesses. Formal rules will still apply in important areas including accounts and indemnity, where they are necessary. …
>
> The SRA's enforcement of OFR will be effective, fair and proportionate. We will focus on the things which really matter to consumers; for example risks which may lead to a loss of their money, justice, or social or economic wellbeing.'[1]

This was profoundly welcome as it turned the clock back to a time when the consequence of something going wrong – whether there was in fact any mischief or prejudice caused, as opposed to being a 'bare breach' – was an important if not determinative factor in how the regulator treated the solicitor concerned.

Accordingly, we anticipated that we would see a refreshingly different approach to enforcement of the 2011 Code by the SRA. The experience of practitioners since October 2011 has been mixed. Many have found the relationship with their regulator easier than it had been in the past, but others have reported little change. In 2013, there was a very significant fall in the number of SRA prosecutions commenced in the Solicitors Disciplinary Tribunal ('the Tribunal' or SDT), but although the new style of regulation was a factor in this, it was not the only one: much of the attention and resources of the SRA were directed at issues of financial stability which had been caused by the financial crash in 2008 and the subsequent recession, and the SRA itself was in the throes of much organisational and geographical change.

1 'Freedom in practice: better outcomes for consumers. A passport to regulatory reform' issued by the SRA in April 2010.

3.4

The 2011 Code is built around ten core principles – defined in detail in the SRA Principles 2011 – four more than the core duties set out in rule 1 of the 2007 Code. It is divided into five sections comprising 15 chapters in all (with Chapters 13 to 15 dealing with the application of the Code, waivers, interpretation, commencement and repeals):

- The section 'You and your client' contains client care, equality and diversity, conflicts, confidentiality and disclosure, the client and the court, and introductions of clients to third parties;
- 'You and your business' contains business management, publicity, and fee sharing and referrals;
- 'You and your regulator' is Section 3 and Chapter 10;
- 'You and others' covers relations with third parties and separate businesses.

Each chapter contains mandatory 'outcomes' rather than prescriptive rules, and non-mandatory 'indicative behaviours', both positive – consistent with compliance, and negative – indicative of non-compliance. There are some, very limited, notes, and no published guidance at all. This is a deliberate policy by the SRA: there is always a danger that non-mandatory guidance becomes seen as a rule, and that the solicitor stops thinking for him- or herself.

3.5

The Principles and 2011 Code apply, as did their predecessors, to every person and body regulated by the SRA; solicitors of course, but also registered European lawyers, registered foreign lawyers (RELs and RFLs), the business entity itself; partnerships, LLPs, limited liability companies, recognised sole practitioners, legal disciplinary practices, ABSs and ABSs in the form of multi-disciplinary practices, and everyone employed by a regulated entity. Although this book is written principally for solicitors, the reach of regulation should not be overlooked.

The ten Principles

3.6

There are ten mandatory Principles which apply to all those regulated by the SRA.

You must:

1. uphold the rule of law and the proper administration of justice;

2. act with integrity;
3. not allow your independence to be compromised;
4. act in the best interests of each *client*;
5. provide a proper standard of service to your *clients*;
6. behave in a way that maintains the trust the public places in you and in the provision of legal services;
7. comply with your legal and regulatory obligations and deal with your regulators and ombudsmen in an open, timely and co-operative manner;
8. run your business or carry out your role in the business effectively and in accordance with proper governance and sound financial and risk management principles;
9. run your business or carry out your role in the business in a way that encourages equality of opportunity and respect for diversity; and
10. protect *client* money and *assets*.

3.7

Solicitors, RELs and RFLs must comply with principles 1, 2 and 6 even in relation to activities which fall outside their legal practices, including activities conducted in a private, as well as a business, capacity.

You must comply with the Principles at all times, but the extent to which you are expected to implement their requirements will depend on your role in the firm, or your way of practising. For example, those who are managing a business will be expected to have more influence on how the business is run than those practising in-house but not managing a legal department, or those practising as employees of a firm.

3.8

General guidance on the application of the Principles is set out within the 2011 Code in the following terms:

> 'They define the fundamental ethical and professional standards that we expect of all firms and individuals (including owners who may not be lawyers) when providing legal services. You should always have regard to the Principles and use them as your starting point when faced with an ethical dilemma.
>
> Where two or more Principles come into conflict the one which takes precedence is the one which best serves the public interest in the particular circumstances, especially the public interest in the proper administration of justice. Compliance with the Principles is also subject to any overriding legal obligations.'

3.9

Principles 1 to 6 repeat the core duties set out in rule 1 of the 2007 Code, with virtually no change. In relation to the standard of service the word 'good' in the 2007 Code is replaced with 'proper', which is sensible in setting the standard at what is reasonably required, in place of phraseology which implied that something better than reasonable was necessary. However, this is not to be taken as a relaxation in standards, as opposed to a better choice of language. Solicitors have always been liable to disciplinary action in respect of work carried out to a poor standard.

Principle 6 is phrased to create a positive obligation to maintain the public trust rather than to avoid behaviour which would tend to diminish that trust, but this is again simply a change of language rather than a change in the nature of the professional obligation. It remains a 'catch all' upon which to base allegations of professional fault which may not be the subject of an express prohibition or requirement.

Principles 7 and 8 are imported from the former rules 20 and 5 of the 2007 Code, without material change, and principle 10 reflects the obligations imposed by the Solicitors Accounts Rules (renamed the SRA Accounts Rules) but extends to other assets such as documents and anything else entrusted to the solicitor.[1] It is questionable whether this adds anything substantive to the duty to act in the client's interests.

1 Assets are defined in the SRA Handbook Glossary 2012: 'assets includes money, documents, wills, deeds, investments and other property'.

3.10

The one principle which differs from the comparable obligation imposed by the 2007 Code is principle 9 on equality and diversity. Equality and diversity are also the subject of a specific set of outcomes in Chapter 2 of the 2011 Code. While the guidance notes to Chapter 2 (see further below) assert that the professional duties 'mirror' legal obligations this is not strictly true. The legal obligation is negative – not to discriminate by reference to any 'protected characteristic'.[1] Principle 9 and Chapter 2 of the 2011 Code go further in imposing a positive obligation to *encourage* equality of opportunity and respect for diversity as well as a negative obligation to avoid discrimination, and to adopt policies for these purposes.

The SRA's statement about the result of its October 2010 consultation on the draft principles,[2] in reaffirming the form that principle 9 now takes, contradicts the explanatory notes. In this statement it is asserted that the principle '[goes] beyond mere statutory obligations, without imposing a duty to discriminate positively'.

It must follow that the SRA expects firms to go beyond their statutory obligations in a way that currently remains entirely unexplained.

The guidance note to principle 9 takes this important point no further: 'Whether you are a manager or an employee, you have a role to play in achieving the outcomes in Chapter 2 (Your clients and equality and diversity) of the Code. Note that a finding of unlawful discrimination outside practice could also amount to a breach of Principles 1 and 6'.

This will be considered in more detail in the context of a consideration of Chapter 2 of the 2011 Code; see **4.21** to **4.24**.

1 See generally Chapters 1 and 2 of Part 2 of the Equality Act 2010.
2 SRA 'Policy statement on our October 2010 Consultation', March 2011, para 50.

Overview of the 2011 Code

3.11

The SRA Handbook contains an overview of the 2011 Code including this:

> 'Outcomes-focused regulation concentrates on providing positive outcomes which when achieved will benefit and protect clients and the public. The SRA Code of Conduct (the Code) sets out our outcomes-focused conduct requirements so that you can consider how best to achieve the right outcomes for your clients taking into account the way that your firm works and its client base. The Code is underpinned by effective, risk-based supervision and enforcement.
>
> Those involved in providing legal advice and representation have long held the role of trusted adviser. There are fiduciary duties arising from this role and obligations owed to others, especially the court. *No code can foresee or address every issue or ethical dilemma which may arise. You must strive to uphold the intention of the Code as well as its letter.*' (emphasis added)

There is nothing new in the second paragraph quoted. The professional rules and codes have never been able to cover every eventuality (though the 2007 Code sought to do so, which was why it had to be amended so frequently during its relatively short life).

The key to the first paragraph is the SRA itself – freedom to interpret the rules and to apply them proportionately to the needs of your own clients and style of practice has to be accompanied by a style of policing which permits that flexibility and understands it. The SRA must therefore have and if necessary acquire an understanding of the way that, for example, niche practices or those with particularly sophisticated clients work in ways that are different from, say, a bulk claimants personal injury practice.

3.12

The specified outcomes are mandatory; the accompanying indicative behaviours and notes are not mandatory. The indicative behaviours specify, but do not constitute an exhaustive list of, the kind of behaviour which may establish compliance with, or contravention of, the Principles.

However, there is something of a sting in the tail, and unless there is a very substantial change in the attitude of the SRA (which has emphatically been promised) there is a danger that the indicative behaviours and notes may gradually acquire the status of rules, despite an absolute disavowal that they have that force. This is because the SRA states that the indicative behaviours:

> 'may help us to decide whether an outcome has been achieved in compliance with the Principles. We recognise that there may be other ways of achieving the outcomes. *Where you have chosen a different method from those we have described as indicative behaviours, we might require you to demonstrate how you have nevertheless achieved the outcome.* We encourage firms to consider how they can best achieve the outcomes, taking into account the nature of

the firm, the particular circumstances of the matter and, crucially, the needs of their particular clients.' (emphasis added)

This is capable of being interpreted to mean: 'Comply with the outcomes *and* the indicative behaviours or the onus will be on you to prove, if you have chosen an innovative approach, how you comply with the outcomes'. If that does happen it will be contrary to the principles of OFR and will undermine the slogan that the SRA has used to promote its vision of OFR: 'Freedom in Practice'. It is still too early to say whether this fear will be realised.

Private lives

3.13

Before considering the 2011 Code chapter by chapter it may be convenient to note those parts of it that apply to solicitors and registered European lawyers outside practice – that is, those that apply to practitioners in their private lives.

Principles 1, 2, 3 and 6 may clearly be breached outside the work environment. For instance a conviction for a serious criminal offence which has nothing to do with a solicitor's practice is likely to result in the solicitor being struck off the roll.

Paragraph 13.7 of Chapter 13 (application and waivers provisions) of the 2011 Code specifies that in relation to activities which fall outside practice, whether undertaken as a lawyer or in some other business or private capacity, outcomes 11.1 and 11.2 apply to solicitors and RELs. These are the obligations not to take advantage of third parties when acting in either a professional or personal capacity, and to comply with undertakings.

CHAPTER 4

The SRA Code of Conduct 2011

4.1

The SRA Code of Conduct 2011 (2011 Code) came into force on 6 October 2011. There are therefore now three separate regulatory codes which are relevant when considering a solicitor's past professional conduct.

Until 1 July 2007, solicitors were governed by the Solicitors' Practice Rules 1990 as amended from time to time, and wider non-codified provisions which might be described as the common law of conduct. The Law Society issued *The Guide to the Professional Conduct of Solicitors* periodically free of charge to the profession. The final edition, the 8th, was published in 1999, and so was considerably out of date by July 2007, although attempts had been made to keep it current by postings on the SRA website under the style of the 'Guide Online'.

The Solicitors' Code of Conduct 2007 (2007 Code) came into force on 1 July 2007, but both the rules and the associated guidance were regularly amended thereafter. By paragraph 15.1 of Chapter 15 of the 2011 Code: 'For the avoidance of doubt, where a breach of any provision of the Solicitors' Code of Conduct 2007 comes to the attention of the Solicitors Regulation Authority (SRA) after 6 October 2011, this shall be subject to action by the SRA notwithstanding any repeal of the relevant provision'.

The 2011 Code governs the conduct of solicitors from 6 October 2011. Solicitors continue to be prosecuted for breaches of the 2007 Code as well as the 2011 Principles and Code, as some of the alleged misconduct brought before the Solicitors Disciplinary Tribunal ('the Tribunal' or SDT) occurs over a significant period of time.

In this chapter, we examine the 2011 Code chapter by chapter, comparing it to what went before, and making practical suggestions as to how solicitors can best achieve compliance with the Principles, outcomes and indicative behaviours that are at the core of the post-2011 regime.

The SRA Handbook, of which the 2011 Code is part, has been been regularly amended since the first version appeared in October 2011.

- Version 2 was dated 23 December 2011.
- Version 3 was dated 18 April 2012.
- Version 4 was dated 21 June 2012.
- Version 5 was dated 1 October 2012.
- Version 6 was dated 1 January 2013.

All of these versions were incorporated into *The Solicitor's Handbook 2013*. Since that volume was published, there have been three further amendments:

- Version 7 was dated 1 April 2013, and contained amendments to Chapters 6 and 9 of the 2011 Code to reflect the coming into force on that day of the relevant sections of the Legal Aid Sentencing and Punishment of Offenders Act (LASPOA) 2012 which contained the referral fee ban in personal injury cases.
- Version 8 was dated 1 October 2013 and made significant changes to the rules governing those practising overseas. The outcomes which referred to overseas practice were removed, and a new Chapter 13A, with a new set of outcomes, added in order to cover the conduct requirements when a regulated individual or entity is practising temporarily overseas: the new rules are summarised at **4.127**.
- Version 9 was dated 1 April 2014, without further changes to the 2011 Code.
- Version 10 was dated 1 July 2014 and also left the 2011 Code untouched.

The text below reflects the latest version.

Chapter 1: Client care

4.2

This chapter is about providing a proper standard of service, which takes into account the individual needs and circumstances of each *client*. This includes providing *clients* with the information they need to make informed decisions about the services they need, how these will be delivered and how much they will cost. This will enable you and your *client* to understand each other's expectations and responsibilities. This chapter is also about ensuring that if *clients* are not happy with the service they have received they know how to make a *complaint* and that all *complaints* are dealt with promptly and fairly.

Your relationship with your *client* is a contractual one which carries with it legal, as well as conduct, obligations. This chapter focuses on your obligations in conduct.

You are generally free to decide whether or not to accept instructions in any matter, provided you do not discriminate unlawfully (see Chapter 2).

The outcomes in this chapter show how the *Principles* apply in the context of client care.

Outcomes

You must achieve these outcomes:

O(1.1) you treat your *clients* fairly;

O(1.2) you provide services to your *clients* in a manner which protects their interests in their matter, subject to the proper administration of justice;

O(1.3) when deciding whether to act, or terminate your instructions, you comply with the law and the Code;

O(1.4) you have the resources, skills and procedures to carry out your *clients'* instructions;

O(1.5) the service you provide to *clients* is competent, delivered in a timely manner and takes account of your *clients'* needs and circumstances;

O(1.6) you only enter into fee agreements with your *clients* that are legal, and which you consider are suitable for the *client's* needs and take account of the *client's* best interests;

O(1.7) you inform *clients* whether and how the services you provide are regulated and how this affects the protections available to the *client*;

O(1.8) *clients* have the benefit of your *compulsory professional indemnity insurance* and you do not exclude or attempt to exclude liability below the minimum level of cover required by the *SRA Indemnity Insurance Rules*;

O(1.9) *clients* are informed in writing at the outset of their matter of their right to complain and how *complaints* can be made;

O(1.10) *clients* are informed in writing, both at the time of engagement and at the conclusion of your *complaints* procedure, of their right to complain to the *Legal Ombudsman*, the time frame for doing so and full details of how to contact the *Legal Ombudsman*;

O(1.11) *clients' complaints* are dealt with promptly, fairly, openly and effectively;

O(1.12) *clients* are in a position to make informed decisions about the services they need, how their matter will be handled and the options available to them;

O(1.13) *clients* receive the best possible information, both at the time of engagement and when appropriate as their matter progresses, about the likely overall cost of their matter;

O(1.14) *clients* are informed of their right to challenge or complain about your bill and the circumstances in which they may be liable to pay interest on an unpaid bill;

O(1.15) you properly account to *clients* for any *financial benefit* you receive as a result of your instructions;

O(1.16) you inform current *clients* if you discover any act or omission which could give rise to a claim by them against you.

Indicative behaviours

Acting in the following way(s) may tend to show that you have achieved these outcomes and therefore complied with the *Principles*:

Dealing with the client's matter

IB(1.1) agreeing an appropriate level of service with your *client*, for example the type and frequency of communications;

IB(1.2) explaining your responsibilities and those of the *client*;

IB(1.3) ensuring that the *client* is told, in writing, the name and status of the person(s) dealing with the matter and the name and status of the person responsible for its overall supervision;

IB(1.4) explaining any arrangements, such as fee sharing or *referral arrangements*, which are relevant to the *client's* instructions;

IB(1.5) explaining any limitations or conditions on what you can do for the *client*, for example, because of the way the *client's* matter is funded;

IB(1.6) in taking instructions and during the course of the retainer, having proper regard to your *client's* mental capacity or other vulnerability, such as incapacity or duress;

IB(1.7) considering whether you should decline to act or cease to act because you cannot act in the *client's* best interests;

IB(1.8) if you seek to limit your liability to your *client* to a level above the minimum required by the *SRA Indemnity Insurance Rules*, ensuring that this limitation is in writing and is brought to the *client's* attention;

IB(1.9) refusing to act where your *client* proposes to make a gift of significant value to you or a member of your family, or a member of your *firm* or their family, unless the *client* takes independent legal advice;

IB(1.10) if you have to cease acting for a *client*, explaining to the *client* their possible options for pursuing their matter;

IB(1.11) you inform *clients* if they are not entitled to the protections of the SRA Compensation Fund;

IB(1.12) considering whether a *conflict of interests* has arisen or whether the *client* should be advised to obtain independent advice where the *client* notifies you of their intention to make a claim or if you discover an act or omission which might give rise to a claim;

Fee arrangements with your client

IB(1.13) discussing whether the potential outcomes of the *client's* matter are likely to justify the expense or risk involved, including any risk of having to pay someone else's legal fees;

IB(1.14) clearly explaining your fees and if and when they are likely to change;

IB(1.15) warning about any other payments for which the *client* may be responsible;

IB(1.16) discussing how the *client* will pay, including whether public funding may be available, whether the *client* has insurance that might cover the fees, and whether the fees may be paid by someone else such as a trade union;

IB(1.17) where you are acting for a *client* under a fee arrangement governed by statute, such as a conditional fee agreement, giving the *client* all relevant information relating to that arrangement;

IB(1.18) where you are acting for a publicly funded *client*, explaining how their publicly funded status affects the costs;

IB(1.19) providing the information in a clear and accessible form which is appropriate to the needs and circumstances of the *client*;

IB(1.20) where you receive a *financial benefit* as a result of acting for a *client*, either:

(a) paying it to the *client*;

(b) offsetting it against your fees; or

(c) keeping it only where you can justify keeping it, you have told the *client* the amount of the benefit (or an approximation if you do not know the exact amount) and the *client* has agreed that you can keep it;

IB(1.21) ensuring that *disbursements* included in your bill reflect the actual amount spent or to be spent on behalf of the *client*;

Complaints handling

IB(1.22) having a written *complaints* procedure which:

(a) is brought to *clients'* attention at the outset of the matter;

(b) is easy for *clients* to use and understand, allowing for *complaints* to be made by any reasonable means;

(c) is responsive to the needs of individual *clients*, especially those who are vulnerable;

(d) enables *complaints* to be dealt with promptly and fairly, with decisions based on a sufficient investigation of the circumstances;

(e) provides for appropriate remedies; and

(f) does not involve any charges to *clients* for handling their *complaints*;

IB(1.23) providing the *client* with a copy of the *firm's complaints* procedure on request;

IB(1.24) in the event that a *client* makes a *complaint*, providing them with all necessary information concerning the handling of the *complaint*.

Acting in the following way(s) may tend to show that you have not achieved these outcomes and therefore not complied with the *Principles*:

Accepting and refusing instructions

IB(1.25) acting for a *client* when instructions are given by someone else, or by only one *client* when you act jointly for others unless you are satisfied that the *person* providing the instructions has the authority to do so on behalf of all of the *clients*;

IB(1.26) ceasing to act for a *client* without good reason and without providing reasonable notice;

IB(1.27) entering into unlawful fee arrangements such as an unlawful contingency fee;

IB(1.28) acting for a *client* when there are reasonable grounds for believing that the instructions are affected by duress or undue influence without satisfying yourself that they represent the *client's* wishes.

4.3

The chapter, which is the successor to rule 2 of the 2007 Code, enables and encourages an approach that takes account of different kinds of practice and client, from the vulnerable to the powerful, from the ignorant to the sophisticated. This could and probably should result in firms not adopting a 'one size fits all' approach to client care, and particularly to client care letters, depending on the nature of the practice.

The provisions of Chapter 1 are fundamental to practice as a solicitor. Failures of compliance can lead to a complaint to the Legal Ombudsman or, in the case of more serious failures of client care, to disciplinary proceedings.

Outcome 1.16 was amended in version 2 (23 December 2011) to clarify that the requirement to disclose to clients an act or omission that could give rise to a claim applies only in relation to current clients.

4.4

The chapter includes matters concerned with retainers, such as when instructions can or should be refused, and limitation of liability by contract.

It is not permissible to exclude or to attempt to exclude all liability to clients, but liability may be limited to the minimum level of cover required by the SRA Indemnity Insurance Rules – outcome 1.8. If this is done, it should be brought to the client's attention in writing – indicative behaviour 1.8.

Solicitors are generally free to decide whether or not to accept instructions, but must refuse to act or cease to act when acting for the client would involve a breach of the law or professional rules, or when the solicitor has insufficient resources or competence (outcomes 1.4 and 1.5, and indicative behaviour 1.7). Rule 2.01 of the 2007 Code provided that the solicitor must be satisfied that instructions given by a third party, or by one client on behalf of others, represented the true intentions of the client or all clients, and that instructions are not affected by undue influence or duress. Much the same provisions are found in indicative behaviours 1.25 and 1.28.

4.5

Rule 2.01(1)(b) of the 2007 Code, which required solicitors to decline to act or to cease to act when they had insufficient resources or lacked the competence to deal with the matter (see now indicative behaviour 1.7, in different terms), was considered by the Court of Appeal in *R v Ulcay*.[1] In a criminal trial the judge had refused an adjournment for the amount of time requested by defence counsel and solicitors who had been instructed in place of the original defence team at the end of the prosecution case. The new solicitors had withdrawn on the basis that the time allowed did not enable them to prepare their client's case to the necessary standard. It was held that they were wrong to do so and that the rule did not allow a solicitor to refuse to act or to cease to act where an order of the court creates difficulties and makes it harder for him to discharge his professional duties. Those difficulties arose because of the judge's ruling, and not as a result of the absence of appropriate resources or competence.

1 [2007] EWCA Crim 2379.

4.6

The familiar requirement in indicative behaviour 1.26 (reproducing the common law position) that solicitors must not cease acting for a client except for good cause and on reasonable notice was considered in *Richard Buxton (Solicitors) v Mills-Owens*[1] in a situation in which the client was persisting in a course that his solicitors and counsel considered unwise. He insisted on points being advanced and argued on his behalf that his lawyers considered to be wholly unarguable. They considered their position to be untenable, obtained supportive advice to this effect from the Law Society and ceased to act on reasonable notice. It was held at first instance that they were not entitled to do so (at [21]):

> 'if a client who is prepared to pay for a case to be advanced, and who wants the claim advanced on a particular basis, which does not involve impropriety on the part of the solicitor or counsel, then it is no answer for the solicitor to say that he believes it is bound to fail therefore he will not do it.'

In consequence, a claim for costs by the solicitor for the work done up to the date the retainer was terminated was disallowed on the basis that he was required to complete the retainer: to carry on the action to the end. This was (fortunately) reversed by the Court of Appeal[2] which held that the solicitors had good reason to terminate the retainer, and were entitled to be paid their costs to date. The Law Society intervened in the appeal in support of the firm. The court noted (at [32]) that rule 11.01(3) of the 2007 Code provided:[3]

> 'you must not construct facts supporting your client's case or draft any documents relating to any proceedings containing … any contention which you do not consider to be properly arguable.'

Dyson LJ (with whom Sir Mark Potter P and Maurice Kay LJ agreed) stated (at [41]):

> 'There is no comprehensive definition of what amounts to a good reason to terminate in the Solicitors' Practice Rules or the Code of Conduct (although examples are given in both documents), or in any of the authorities that have been cited to us. That is not surprising, since whether there is a good reason to terminate is a fact-sensitive question. I accept the submission of Mr Drabble [for the Law Society] that it is wrong to restrict the circumstances in which a solicitor can lawfully terminate his retainer to those in which he is instructed to do something improper.'

And at [43]:

> 'I am in no doubt that even before the point was spelt out in the 2007 Code, it would have been understood by all solicitors that, as officers of the court, they were under a professional duty (i) not to include in the court documents that they drafted any contention which they did not consider to be properly arguable and (ii) not to instruct counsel to advance contentions which they did not consider to be properly arguable. That duty was reinforced by CPR 1.3.'

1 [2008] EWHC 1831 (QB).
2 [2010] EWCA Civ 122.
3 See now indicative behaviour 5.7.

4.7

Rule 2 of the 2007 Code, in so far as it related to the provision of information about costs and in relation to complaints handling, underwent two additional changes in August 2009 and March 2010 as a result of the revocation of the Solicitors' (Non-Contentious Business) Remuneration Order 1994 and its replacement by the 2009 Order of the same name (SI 2009/1931) with effect from 11 August 2009. This abolished the remuneration certificate procedure. In August 2009 an emergency rule was introduced to require solicitors, before bringing any action on a bill or immediately on deducting sums for costs from funds held on behalf of clients, to inform clients of their entitlement to seek detailed assessment of costs. After a proper consultation process this was replaced on 1 March 2010 with a rather more proportionate requirement that, when clients were given the information required by rule 2.05 about complaints handling, they also had to be informed that any issue raised with the firm could include a complaint about the firm's bill; that there might also be a right to object to the bill by making a complaint to the Legal Complaints Service (LCS) or (post-October 2010) the Legal Ombudsman (LeO), and/or by applying to the court for detailed assessment; and that if all or part of a bill remained unpaid, the firm might be entitled to charge interest. These provisions have not been carried forward into the 2011 Code. However, the requirements to inform of the right to complain to LeO and the time limits (in the Scheme Rules, in order to take advantage of those time limits) have much the same effect.

4.8

In one material respect rule 2 of the 2007 Code changed the common law and curtailed the right of solicitors to exercise a lien for their unpaid fees. Rule 2.03(1)(e) required that clients were notified of circumstances in which a lien may be exercised. A failure to do so would seemingly remove the right. This provision has not been incorporated into the 2011 Code. It may therefore be that the traditional unfettered right to exercise a solicitor's lien in accordance with the common law has been reinstated, perhaps inadvertently by the move to outcomes-focused regulation. It would nevertheless be prudent to make an express reference in the client care letter to the right to exercise a lien as it might be argued to be a necessary function of the obligation to treat clients fairly (outcome 1.1) as clients might not otherwise be aware of the possibility.

4.9

There are four material changes from the 2007 Code, regarding:

- contingency fees;
- information to clients;
- complaints procedures;
- commissions and financial benefits.

Contingency fees

4.10

There is no longer any reference, at all, to contingency fees, either in relation to the solicitor/client retainer (rule 2.04 in the 2007 Code), or in relation to associations with other organisations who charge such fees (rule 9.01(4) of the 2007 Code). The only provision is outcome 1.6: 'you only enter into fee agreements with your clients that are legal, and which you consider are suitable for the client's needs and take account of the client's best interests'. In other words, to the extent that contingency fees are lawful, they no longer raise any regulatory concern *per se* (but suitability and the best interests of the client need still to be considered).

The provisions of the 2011 Code follow the law without any 'add-on' obligation or constraint. The relevant law can be summarised as follows.

Contingency fees in non-contentious work

4.11

It has always been lawful for solicitors to charge contingency fees in non-contentious work. This is currently enshrined in section 57 of the Solicitors Act (SA) 1974.[1] Solicitors can (and always have been able to) enter into a retainer in respect of non-contentious business whereby the solicitor can be remunerated by way of a cut of any spoils, or conditional on the result. To be enforceable a non-contentious business agreement must be in writing and signed by the person to be bound by it 'or his agent in that behalf' (section 57(3)). Section 87 of SA 1974 defines contentious business:

> ' "contentious business" means business done, whether as solicitor or advocate, in or for the purposes of proceedings begun before a court or before an arbitrator, not being business which falls within the definition of non-contentious or common form probate business contained in section 128 of the Senior Courts Act 1981.'

Any business that is not within that definition is non-contentious. In order to fall within the definition, proceedings must actually have been commenced before a court or arbitrator. Thus, work undertaken in relation to a claim which might be litigated, but which is in fact resolved without the issue of proceedings, remains outside the definition of contentious business.

Similarly, in 'proceedings' which bear all the attributes of contentious work, such as those in employment tribunals, but which are not proceedings before a court or an arbitrator, solicitors have been able to charge clients on a contingency fee basis. Contingency fee agreements in relation to employment and other matters are now subject to express regulation.[2]

Otherwise there is no statutory or regulatory limit on what a solicitor may charge by way of a contingency fee in non-contentious work. Outcome 1.6 of course requires that the fee agreement is not only legal, but also suitable for the client's needs and that it takes account of the client's best interests. It has, in short, to be fair.

Outcome 1.14 requires that clients are informed about their right to challenge or complain about bills, and, where applicable, their right to complain to LeO. Costs due under a non-contentious business agreement are liable to detailed assessment and the costs judge/officer may enquire into the facts and if appropriate certify for the court that the agreement should be set aside or the amount payable reduced, and the court may so order.[3]

Solicitors need also to have one eye on the doctrine of unconscionable bargain,[4] although there is no reported example of a contingency fee agreement in non-contentious work between solicitor and client being struck down as unconscionable. If such an agreement were found to be an unconscionable bargain, not only would the agreement be unenforceable, but the solicitor would be at risk of a finding of a breach of principle 6, which requires him or her to 'behave in a way that maintains the trust the public places in you and in the provision of legal services'.

1 '(1) Whether or not any order is in force under section 56, a solicitor and his client may, before or after or in the course of the transaction of any non-contentious business by the solicitor, make an agreement as to his remuneration in respect of that business. (2) The agreement may provide for the remuneration of the solicitor by a gross sum or by reference to an hourly rate, or by a commission or percentage, or by a salary, or otherwise.'

2 Section 58AA of the Courts and Legal Services Act 1990 (introduced into that Act by section 154 of the Coroners and Justice Act 2009) and the Damages-Based Agreements Regulations 2010 (SI 2010/1206). See now the 2013 Regulations of the same name (SI 2013/609).

3 Section 57(5) of SA 1974.

4 See **4.75**.

Contingency fees in contentious work: CFAs and DBAs

4.12

For centuries, contingency fees in contentious work were outlawed on public policy grounds as offending the rule against champerty. The scope of the law of champerty has become attenuated in the light of shifting public policy perceptions.[1] The funding revolution of the 1990s brought an end to the absolute prohibition by permitting conditional fee agreements (CFAs), and CFAs are now permitted in all types of proceedings save for family and criminal proceedings, provided that they comply with formalities imposed by delegated legislation. As from November 2005, most of the burdensome formalities imposed by the Conditional Fee Agreements Regulations 2000 (SI 2000/692) were removed.

Following the coming into force of the relevant provisions of LASPOA 2012 on 1 April 2013, the law relating to CFAs fundamentally changed again. Henceforth, the success fee was no longer recoverable from the losing party, and a cap was imposed upon the amount of the success fee that the client would have to yield up to the solicitor out of damages in personal injury cases. At the same time, damages-based agreements (DBAs) became lawful in a wide range of cases (hitherto, they had been restricted to employment law cases). These are true contingency fees, the solicitor's remuneration ordinarily being calculated as a percentage of the client's damages, subject to statutory maxima. At the time of writing there is considerable uncertainty surrounding the commercial advisability of entering into DBAs, partly due to the extremely poor drafting of the relevant Regulations. Ethical issues are, however, likely to arise in relation to the amount agreed as the solicitor's remuneration, and whether this is properly justifiable.

A detailed consideration of the legal framework for CFAs and DBAs is beyond the scope of this book, and that framework is not affected by changes in the SRA's rules.

1 See *R v Secretary of State for Transport, ex p Factortame* [2003] QB 381. The issue of contingency fees and the reach of the modern law on champerty was revisited by the Court of Appeal in *Sibthorpe and Morris v Southwark LBC* [2011] EWCA Civ 25. For a fuller discussion, see Andrew Hopper and Gregory Treverton-Jones, *Outcomes-Focused Regulation: A Practical Guide*, Law Society, 2011.

Introducers operating on a contingency fee basis

4.13

This issue is now largely historical, in that the 2011 Code abolished a rule that had caused difficulty and controversy for many years. Rule 9.04 of the 2007 Code re-enacted Rule 9 of the Solicitors' Practice Rules 1990 and provided that:

> 'You must not, in respect of any claim arising as a result of death or personal injury, either: (a) enter into an arrangement for the referral of clients with; or (b) act in association with, any person whose business, or any part of whose business, is to make, support or prosecute (whether by action or otherwise, and whether by a solicitor or agent or otherwise) claims arising as a result of death or personal injury, and who, in the course of such business, solicits or receives contingency fees in respect of such claims.'

The controversy arose from the fact that the 2007 Code, in all its draft forms up to the beginning of 2007, did not contain any such provision. The policy decision had been made to abolish the rule, not least because claims management companies were to become regulated under the Compensation Act 2006. In the event, the provision was saved, and became rule 9.01(4) of the 2007 Code.

Many solicitors have found themselves before the SDT as a result of arrangements made with introducers who have charged on a contingency fee basis in both contentious and non-contentious work. A large number of solicitors handling miners' compensation cases under the claims handling agreements relating to vibration white finger and pulmonary disease claims were disciplined between 2006 and 2010 because introducers (whether commercial entities or trades unions) had agreed to take a slice of the miners' compensation. The courts eventually ruled that these were contentious proceedings.[1] There was also a handful of successful prosecutions arising out of solicitors' arrangements with an organisation known as Justice Direct, which introduced employment tribunal and personal injury claims to solicitors in return for a 'broker's fee' calculated as 25 per cent of any sum recovered plus a percentage of the fees charged by its panel solicitors.[2]

Finally, in 2011, the rule was abolished. That is not the end of the matter, however. The focus now is upon whether the solicitor can properly maintain independence if he or she has an arrangement with an introducer who operates on a contingency fee basis, and whether the agreement between the introducer and the client by which the client agrees to yield up a slice of the damages is in the client's best interests. The Tribunal decision in *Tilbury* remains highly relevant, and solicitors must ask themselves when taking on a new client whether a contingency fee arrangement between the client and the introducer was an unconscionable bargain or otherwise not in the best interests of the new client. This is considered in greater detail in relation to the outcomes required by Chapter 9 of the 2011 Code; see **4.92** to **4.94**.

1 *Beresford and Smith v SRA* [2009] EWHC 3155 (Admin).
2 *Tilbury* 9880–2008; *Kelsall* 10352–2009.

Information to clients

4.14

Outcome 1.7 provides: 'you inform clients whether and how the services you provide are regulated and how this affects the protections available to the client'. This was introduced to cater for the advent of alternative business structures – ABSs – which can provide both regulated legal services *and* other services (funeral services, for example) which will not be regulated by the SRA. Clients need to be informed which is which, and what the consequences will be.

An additional obligation to give information to clients appeared to have arisen by reason of outcome 1.16 which requires that clients be informed when it is discovered that the client may have a claim (in negligence or otherwise) against the firm. That did not appear to change the existing law. However, 'client' is not defined in the same language as that used in section 87 of SA 1974; there is a specific definition for the purposes of the SRA Handbook, including the Code, in the SRA Handbook Glossary 2012, and a client 'where the context permits, includes prospective and former clients'. This would have required solicitors to notify former clients whose retainers had been concluded if a mistake was subsequently discovered, and would have changed the law. The SRA later confirmed that this was not the intention and the Code was rapidly amended to read 'current clients'.

It is relevant to note that the Legal Ombudsman has reported that costs are the single largest reason for client dissatisfaction, an indication that the profession could do much more to keep clients informed, particularly as the matter progresses and circumstances change, so that initial information needs to be updated. Most firms are well organised in giving adequate information at the outset; it is much more difficult to manage the situation and to keep clients informed about changes in costs estimates as matters proceed, frequently at a fast pace.

Complaints procedures

4.15

There are requirements in the 2011 Code concerning information for clients about complaints procedures. Outcomes 1.9 and 1.10 impose requirements that all clients are informed at the outset, in writing, of their right to complain and how to do so, and of their right to complain to the Legal Ombudsman and how to do so. This is more burdensome than the equivalent provisions in the 2007 Code. Under those provisions practitioners could elect not to provide some or all of the information under the general heading of 'client care' if it could be demonstrated that it was inappropriate in the circumstances to do so;[1] in other words, if there were repeat clients or sophisticated clients who evidently knew their rights and did not need to be informed or reminded, it was possible to avoid providing basic client care information. This is no longer the case. It would seem that client care letters are now required when they were not previously needed. It may not even be possible for the client to waive the requirement. However, the compulsory elements relate only to LeO, and so to be compliant, a client care letter could be very limited.

Note (i) to Chapter 1 of the 2011 Code confirms:

> 'The information you give to clients will vary according to the needs and circumstances of the individual client and the type of work you are doing for them, for example an individual instructing you on a conveyancing matter is unlikely to need the same information as a sophisticated commercial client who instructs you on a regular basis.'

This approach is not, however, maintained logically when the Chapter 1 outcomes are considered, in requiring complaints information to be given even where the client plainly does not need it.

Moreover, outcome 1.10 fails altogether to take into account that many clients have no right to complain to the Legal Ombudsman. In general terms only individuals and small businesses may do so. Larger corporate clients have no such remedy.[2]

As the outcome requires solicitors to inform clients of 'their right' to complain to LeO, it follows that initial letters may need in appropriate cases to state that the client does not have that right. It would not be appropriate to use the same formula across the board, thus potentially misleading some clients into believing that there is a further remedy when there is not. In some cases it might be that solicitors would not know at the outset, or even at the conclusion of the retainer, whether a business client is able to complain to LeO, because this is a question determined by the number of staff, turnover, balance sheet value, net asset value or annual income. One could envisage situations in which advice on a specific point might be sought without the need for disclosure of that level of information.

In those cases it will be necessary to inform the client of the possibility of the existence of a right to complain to LeO, with the relevant time limits and contact details, subject to the client being within the Legal Ombudsman Scheme Rules 2013 (as amended).

Firms will have to adapt their standard documentation to match their client base and the specific needs of clients.

1 Rules 2.03(7) and 2.05(2) of the 2007 Code.
2 See rules 2.1 to 2.5 of the Legal Ombudsman Scheme Rules 2013 (**APPENDIX 11**), and **CHAPTER 13**.

Commissions and financial benefits

4.16

The requirement in respect of commissions (outcome 1.15) has been simplified in comparison to what went before: 'you properly account to clients for any financial benefit you receive as a result of your instructions'. There is no longer a *de minimis* £20 figure below which the provisions do not apply (as there was in the Solicitors' Practice Rules 1990 and the 2007 Code), and the word 'commission' does not appear in the relevant outcome, being replaced with 'financial benefit' which is defined thus: 'financial benefit includes any commission, discount or rebate, but does not include your fees or interest earned on any client account'.[1]

This, on the face of it, brings the professional rules into line with the law. Under the general law, a solicitor as a fiduciary must not make a secret profit, and must inform his client of all relevant issues concerning the client's matter. The general law is satisfied if the fiduciary obtains the informed consent of the client at the outset of the retainer to retention of a financial benefit. The £20 *de minimis* exception has not been reproduced in the 2011 Code, and no longer exists; a secret profit is a secret profit, whether of £20 or £20 million, and it is arguable as a matter of legal principle that the Law Society should never have created the *de minimis* exception in the first place.

1 The distinction between a commission, and a discount or rebate, had caused difficulty in practice: see *Law Society v Adcock and Mocroft* [2006] EWHC 3212 (Admin), [2007] 1 WLR 1096. Hence the move to the wider phrase 'financial benefit'.

4.17

So far so good: the general law and outcome 1.15 appear to be entirely consistent. Regrettably, however, confused non-mandatory guidance accompanies the stated outcome, which repeats similar contradictory guidance to rule 2.06 of the 2007 Code – but crucially still without any explanation.[1]

Indicative behaviour 1.20 refers to 'keeping [a financial benefit] only where you can justify keeping it, you have told the client the amount of the benefit … and the client has agreed that you can keep it'.

Indicative behaviours are not mandatory. There is no explanation as to how a solicitor may 'justify' retaining the benefit. This cannot be because, for example, he could charge an amount equal to it by way of fees. If that were the case the solicitor would not be receiving, or retaining, any benefit – the client would be receiving it as a reduction in the charges he would otherwise be liable to pay. This was the essence of the error in the guidance notes to the 2007 Code. On the one hand, the SRA was saying (in the rule) that solicitors could retain commission if the client gave informed consent; but on the other, the SRA was also saying, in the non-binding guidance, that consent was not enough and the client had to receive some benefit, one way or the other (so that the solicitor could not really benefit at all).

This error has been carried through into indicative behaviour 1.20. If the SRA intends to prevent solicitors receiving income from any source but their legal costs, and intends that solicitors should pay all financial benefits received as a result of acting for clients to those clients, it has the power so to decide. But it should make this both explicit and mandatory. Such an important restriction on a solicitor's freedom to obtain commission income should not be imposed by way of a non-mandatory indicative behaviour.

If, on the other hand, solicitors are simply subject to the law on fiduciaries and secret profits, solicitors can 'justify' keeping a financial benefit including commission whenever they have been transparent from the outset about receipt of that sum, and the client has provided informed consent to its retention. A fiduciary is under no obligation in law to account for benefits which he is authorised to take under the terms of the agreement under which he acts as a fiduciary.[2]

Commissions and payments for introductions are a normal part of business life. Clients are generally, in our experience, unconcerned with the business arrangements solicitors make with third parties provided that they are transparent and cause no prejudice to the clients. The fact that solicitors may take a commission raises no eyebrows. There is no reason or justification for taking a puritanical stance inimical to the receipt of secondary sources of income by solicitors – or if that is intended it needs, in our view, to be by way of express prohibition so that solicitors may know where they stand.

No explanation has ever been given as to what the SRA would perceive as appropriate justification – indeed our enquiries at a high level indicated an acceptance that the guidance in the 2007 Code was wrong.

If nevertheless 'justification' is needed, it could be provided by demonstrating the administrative responsibility that may fall on the firm in its dealings, for example, with a third party, but may also be justified by the firm's business model – that it relies on certain income streams in planning its business and the services it is able to give to clients.

1 For a full discussion of the relevant provisions of the 2007 Code, see *The Solicitor's Handbook 2011* (at 3.10) and Andrew Hopper and Gregory Treverton-Jones, *Outcomes-Focused Regulation: A Practical Guide*, Law Society, 2011.
2 The liability to account arises if there is no such authority: 'If the person in a fiduciary position does gain or receive any financial benefit arising out of the use of the property of the beneficiary he cannot keep it unless he can show such authority'; *Brown v Inland Revenue Commissioners* [1965] AC 244, HL per Lord Reid at 256G.

4.18

Solicitors should also be aware, however, that financial benefits received from third parties in the personal injury field are prohibited under section 56(2) of LASPOA 2012, which provides that a regulated person is also in breach of section 56 if, while providing legal services in the course of prescribed legal business, the regulated person arranges for a third party to provide services to the client and is paid or has been paid for making that arrangement. This is likely to be relevant, for example, where the solicitor arranges for the client to be examined by a medical practitioner who is on the books of a medical agency, and/or helps the client obtain after the event insurance, and/or helps to arrange car hire for the injured claimant following a road traffic accident. Such arrangements are caught by the referral fee ban, and outlawed if the solicitor is paid for the referral.[1]

1 See also outcome 6.4 of the 2011 Code.

Indicative behaviours

4.19

There is little here that is new; the section on fees, in particular, reproduces very familiar principles (indicative behaviours 1.13 to 1.19). It is not clear why indicative behaviours 1.9 and 1.12 appear here rather than in Chapter 3 on conflicts of interests.

Indicative behaviour 1.21 reflects the widespread problems over the misdescription of telegraphic transfer fees, now likely to be only of historical interest as firms will have reacted to the publicity associated with this issue. The (hopefully past) problem was that firms developed a practice of making a charge for undertaking routine telegraphic transfers in conveyancing. There was nothing wrong with that, but what tended to happen was that if the bank charged the firm, say, £10, the firm would make a charge to the client of £20 – but still describe the fee as a disbursement, as if it had all been paid to the bank. The mischief was neither in passing on the bank's charge, nor in charging a fee for the work entailed, but rather in misdescribing a charge as a disbursement. This misled the client and hid the fact that the firm was making an extra modest profit.

Indicative behaviour 1.11 supports outcome 1.7 to deal with the situation in which the firm is providing regulated and unregulated services.

Some indicative behaviours look very like rules, rather than unenforceable guidance, for example, indicative behaviour 1.4 on disclosing fee sharing and referral arrangements; indicative behaviour 1.8 on limitation of liability; indicative behaviour 1.9 on refusing gifts unless there is independent advice; and indicative behaviour 1.12 on conflicts of interests.

Provision of Services Regulations 2009

4.20

It is convenient to deal with the Provision of Services Regulations 2009 (SI 2009/2999) at this point because they require certain information to be provided to clients, but these requirements go beyond what is required by the 2011 Code: specifically, the firm's VAT number, details of compulsory professional indemnity insurance cover, details as to how to access professional rules and details of complaint resolution procedures.[1] Not all the information has to be provided in the same way. The VAT number and insurance information – which must include the contact details of the insurers and the territorial coverage of the insurance – may optionally be given in writing at the outset, in a client care letter or terms of business, or made easily accessible to clients in hard copy at the firm's offices or on the firm's website.

Information about professional rules, which requires a reference to the SRA Code of Conduct and a link to the Code on the SRA website, must be provided in a clear and unambiguous manner in good time before the conclusion of the contract or, if there is no written contract, before the service is provided. It must also be provided on request. Making the information and link available on the firm's website and including a reference to where the information could be found (or including the information itself) within the client care letter would suffice.

Information about complaint resolution procedures involves telling clients about the role of the Legal Ombudsman and where further information can be obtained. Similarly, this must be provided in a clear and unambiguous manner in good time before the conclusion of the contract or, if there is no written contract, before the service is provided, but must also be provided in any information document in which the firm gives a detailed description of the service provided. This could therefore also be provided through a website and/or the client care letter. However, the LeO provides a service only to individuals and small businesses (see **13.8**), so that telling all clients including large corporate clients that there is a complaint resolution service through the LeO when they will not, in fact, be able to take advantage of it would be misleading and unhelpful.

1 Regulation 8(1)(g) covers VAT; 8(1)(n), insurance; 9(1)(d), professional rules; 10, complaint resolution; and 11, manner of providing information.

Chapter 2: Equality and diversity

4.21

This chapter is about encouraging equality of opportunity and respect for diversity, and preventing unlawful discrimination, in your relationship with your *clients* and others. The requirements apply in relation to age, disability, gender reassignment, marriage and civil partnership, pregnancy and maternity, race, religion or belief, sex and sexual orientation.

Everyone needs to contribute to compliance with these requirements, for example, by treating each other, and *clients*, fairly and with respect, by embedding such values in the workplace and by challenging inappropriate behaviour and processes. Your role in embedding these values will vary depending on your role.

As a matter of general law you must comply with requirements set out in legislation – including the Equality Act 2010 – as well as the conduct duties contained in this chapter.

The outcomes in this chapter show how the *Principles* apply in the context of equality and diversity.

Outcomes

You must achieve these outcomes:

O(2.1) you do not discriminate unlawfully, or victimise or harass anyone, in the course of your professional dealings;

O(2.2) you provide services to *clients* in a way that respects diversity;

O(2.3) you make reasonable adjustments to ensure that disabled *clients*, *employees* or *managers* are not placed at a substantial disadvantage compared to those who are not disabled, and you do not pass on the costs of these adjustments to these disabled *clients*, *employees* or *managers*;

O(2.4) your approach to recruitment and employment encourages equality of opportunity and respect for diversity;

O(2.5) *complaints* of discrimination are dealt with promptly, fairly, openly, and effectively.

Indicative behaviours

Acting in the following way(s) may tend to show that you have achieved these outcomes and therefore complied with the *Principles*:

IB(2.1) having a written equality and diversity policy which is appropriate to the size and nature of the *firm* and includes the following features:

- (a) a commitment to the principles of equality and diversity and legislative requirements;
- (b) a requirement that all *employees* and *managers* comply with the outcomes;

(c) provisions to encompass your recruitment and interview processes;

(d) details of how the *firm* will implement, monitor, evaluate and update the policy;

(e) details of how the *firm* will ensure equality in relation to the treatment of *employees*, *managers*, *clients* and third parties instructed in connection with *client* matters;

(f) details of how *complaints* and disciplinary issues are to be dealt with;

(g) details of the *firm's* arrangements for workforce diversity monitoring; and

(h) details of how the *firm* will communicate the policy to *employees*, *managers* and *clients*;

IB(2.2) providing *employees* and *managers* with training and information about complying with equality and diversity requirements;

IB(2.3) monitoring and responding to issues identified by your policy and reviewing and updating your policy.

Acting in the following way(s) may tend to show that you have not achieved these outcomes and therefore not complied with the *Principles*:

IB(2.4) being subject to any decision of a court or tribunal of the *UK*, that you have committed, or are to be treated as having committed, an unlawful act of discrimination;

IB(2.5) discriminating unlawfully when accepting or refusing instructions to act for a *client*.

4.22

Equality and diversity were first made the subject of regulatory requirements by the Solicitors' Anti-Discrimination Rules 2004. These were replaced by rule 6 of the 2007 Code, which simply imposed obligations not to discriminate in a way that would be unlawful, and to have a written policy. The language in the 2011 Code has wholly changed.

The introduction to Chapter 2 of the 2011 Code states that it 'is about encouraging equality of opportunity and respect for diversity, and preventing unlawful discrimination'. The requirements apply in relation to age, disability, gender reassignment, marriage and civil partnership, pregnancy and maternity, race, religion or belief, and sex or sexual orientation. The SRA intends that everyone should contribute to compliance with these requirements by embedding appropriate values in the workplace and by challenging inappropriate behaviour and processes. The individual's responsibility for embedding these values will vary depending on the role in the organisation. It is plainly intended that the rules of conduct should supplement rather than merely restate the general law.

As noted above in the context of principle 9, the SRA's statement about the result of its October 2010 consultation on the draft principles,[1] in reaffirming the form that principle 9 now takes, asserts that the principle '[goes] beyond mere statutory obligations, without imposing a duty to discriminate positively', and it follows that the SRA expects firms to go beyond their statutory obligations in a way that currently remains unexplained.

- Principle 9 requires you to run your business or carry out your role in the business in a way that *encourages* equality of opportunity and respect for diversity.
- The introduction to Chapter 2 states that it is about *encouraging* equality of opportunity and respect for diversity.
- The policy statement asserts that professional obligations *go beyond* 'mere statutory obligations'.
- Only one outcome, concerned with recruitment and employment, uses the word 'encourages'.
- The guidance notes state that the obligations in this chapter *closely mirror* the relevant legal obligations, and suggest further information be obtained (as a matter of necessary inference about those legal obligations) from the Equality and Human Rights Commission.
- The Law Society's response to the SRA's consultation expressed concern that this requirement appeared to go beyond statutory obligations, that it was unclear to what extent firms will be required to take positive action to promote equality and diversity. The Law Society asked the SRA to clarify what is to be expected of the regulatory community. This has not been done.

Despite the change of language from that used in rule 6 of the 2007 Code, the outcomes in the 2011 Code largely restate what would have been necessary to comply with the former rule, with the sole exception of the vexed issue of 'encouraging' equality and respect for diversity, in relation to recruitment and employment.

1 SRA 'Policy statement on our October 2010 Consultation', March 2011, para 50.

CHAPTER 4
SRA CODE OF CONDUCT 2011

Practical suggestions

4.23

There is nothing in the indicative behaviours which is of assistance in interpreting the one requirement to 'encourage' behaviour which goes beyond the statutory requirements. Firms will already have a written policy because it was a requirement of rule 6 of the 2007 Code. That should be checked for consistency with indicative behaviour 2.1. Firms should also ensure that issues of training are addressed in the document.

In the absence of anything more by way of guidance from the SRA, the word 'encourage' is probably to be treated as a regulatory obligation to approach issues of equality and diversity in a positive frame of mind; to be alive to opportunities and, in a manner falling short of positive discrimination, seek to ensure that issues of equality and diversity remain at the forefront when decisions are made.

In short, Chapter 2 is about having the right attitude of mind.

Looking at the matter from a defensive perspective – how do you ensure that the SRA will be satisfied – ask yourself the question: 'How do I/does the firm encourage equality of opportunity and respect for diversity?' and, having determined the answer, write it into your policy document.

More positive assistance is available from the Law Society, which promotes a Diversity and Inclusion Charter, the signatories to which make a commitment to:

> 'Strive to achieve best practice in our recruitment, retention and career progression practices as employers.
>
> Support the development of good diversity practice by collecting and sharing with other signatories examples of practical activities that contribute to progress.
>
> Assign responsibility for meeting our Charter commitments to a named, senior level individual.
>
> Work together to develop and adopt future protocols that support the practical implementation of the aims of this Charter.
>
> Publish annually the diversity profile of our UK employees and details of our work on equality, diversity and inclusion.
>
> Publish a joint annual report on the basis of a monitoring exercise to measure the impact of this Diversity and Inclusion Charter and its protocols. These reports will form the basis of regular dialogue with stakeholders, employees and clients.'

4.24

The Law Society makes available, free of charge to those who commit to the Charter, its 'Equality and diversity standards and toolkit' designed to help the legal profession to promote successfully and implement best practice in equality, diversity and inclusion – as employers, as providers of legal services, as purchasers of goods and services and in its wider role in society.

For further details visit www.lawsociety.org.uk/practicesupport/equalitydiversity.

Chapter 3: Conflicts of interests

4.25

This chapter deals with the proper handling of *conflicts of interests*, which is a critical public protection. It is important to have in place systems that enable you to identify and deal with potential conflicts.

Conflicts of interests can arise between:

1. you and current *clients* ("*own interest conflict*"); and
2. two or more current *clients* ("*client conflict*").

You can never act where there is a conflict, or a significant risk of conflict, between you and your *client*.

If there is a conflict, or a significant risk of a conflict, between two or more current *clients*, you must not act for all or both of them unless the matter falls within the scope of the limited exceptions set out at Outcomes 3.6 or 3.7. In deciding whether to act in these limited circumstances, the overriding consideration will be the best interests of each of the *clients* concerned and, in particular, whether the benefits to the *clients* of you acting for all or both of the *clients* outweigh the risks.

You should also bear in mind that *conflicts of interests* may affect your duties of confidentiality and disclosure which are dealt with in Chapter 4.

The outcomes in this chapter show how the *Principles* apply in the context of *conflicts of interests*.

Outcomes

You must achieve these outcomes:

Systems

O(3.1) you have effective systems and controls in place to enable you to identify and assess potential *conflicts of interests*;

O(3.2) your systems and controls for identifying *own interest conflicts* are appropriate to the size and complexity of the *firm* and the nature of the work undertaken, and enable you to assess all the relevant circumstances, including whether your ability as an individual, or that of anyone within your *firm*, to act in the best interests of the *client(s)*, is impaired by:

(a) any financial interest;

(b) a personal relationship;

(c) the appointment of you, or a member of your *firm* or family, to public office;

(d) commercial relationships; or

(e) your employment;

O(3.3) your systems and controls for identifying *client conflicts* are appropriate to the size and complexity of the *firm* and the nature of the work undertaken, and enable you to assess all relevant circumstances, including whether:

(a) the *clients'* interests are different;

(b) your ability to give independent advice to the *clients* may be fettered;

(c) there is a need to negotiate between the *clients*;

(d) there is an imbalance in bargaining power between the *clients*; or

(e) any *client* is vulnerable;

Prohibition on acting in conflict situations

O(3.4) you do not act if there is an *own interest conflict* or a significant risk of an *own interest conflict*;

O(3.5) you do not act if there is a *client conflict*, or a significant risk of a *client conflict*, unless the circumstances set out in Outcomes 3.6 or 3.7 apply;

Exceptions where you may act, with appropriate safeguards, where there is a client conflict

O(3.6) where there is a *client conflict* and the *clients* have a *substantially common interest* in relation to a matter or a particular aspect of it, you only act if:

(a) you have explained the relevant issues and risks to the *clients* and you have a reasonable belief that they understand those issues and risks;

(b) all the *clients* have given informed consent in writing to you acting;

(c) you are satisfied that it is reasonable for you to act for all the *clients* and that it is in their best interests; and

(d) you are satisfied that the benefits to the *clients* of you doing so outweigh the risks;

O(3.7) where there is a *client conflict* and the *clients* are *competing for the same objective*, you only act if:

(a) you have explained the relevant issues and risks to the *clients* and you have a reasonable belief that they understand those issues and risks;

(b) the *clients* have confirmed in writing that they want you to act, in the knowledge that you act, or may act, for one or more other *clients* who are *competing for the same objective*;

(c) there is no other *client conflict* in relation to that matter;

(d) unless the *clients* specifically agree, no individual acts for, or is responsible for the supervision of work done for, more than one of the *clients* in that matter; and

(e) you are satisfied that it is reasonable for you to act for all the *clients* and that the benefits to the *clients* of you doing so outweigh the risks.

Indicative behaviours

Acting in the following way(s) may tend to show that you have achieved these outcomes and therefore complied with the *Principles*:

IB(3.1) training *employees* and *managers* to identify and assess potential *conflicts of interests*;

IB(3.2) declining to act for *clients* whose interests are in direct conflict, for example claimant and defendant in litigation;

IB(3.3) declining to act for *clients* where you may need to negotiate on matters of substance on their behalf, for example negotiating on price between a buyer and seller of a property;

IB(3.4) declining to act where there is unequal bargaining power between the *clients*, for example acting for a seller and buyer where a builder is selling to a non-commercial *client*;

IB(3.5) declining to act for *clients* under Outcome 3.6 (*substantially common interest*) or Outcome 3.7 (*competing for the same objective*) where the *clients* cannot be represented even-handedly, or will be prejudiced by lack of separate representation;

IB(3.6) acting for *clients* under Outcome 3.7 (*competing for the same objective*) only where the *clients* are sophisticated users of legal services;

IB(3.7) acting for *clients* who are the lender and borrower on the grant of a mortgage of land only where:

(a) the mortgage is a standard mortgage (i.e. one provided in the normal course of the lender's activities, where a significant part of the lender's activities consists of lending and the mortgage is on standard terms) of property to be used as the borrower's private residence;

(b) you are satisfied that it is reasonable and in the *clients'* best interests for you to act; and

(c) the certificate of title required by the lender is in the form approved by the *Society* and the Council of Mortgage Lenders.

Acting in the following way(s) may tend to show that you have not achieved these outcomes and therefore not complied with the *Principles*:

IB(3.8) in a personal capacity, selling to or buying from, lending to or borrowing from a *client*, unless the *client* has obtained independent legal advice;

IB(3.9) advising a *client* to invest in a business, in which you have an interest which affects your ability to provide impartial advice;

IB(3.10) where you hold a power of attorney for a *client*, using that power to gain a benefit for yourself which in your professional capacity you would not have been prepared to allow to a third party;

IB(3.11) acting for two or more *clients* in a *conflict of interests* under Outcome 3.6 (*substantially common interest*) where the *clients'* interests in the end result are not the same, for example one partner buying out the interest of the other partner in their joint business or a seller transferring a property to a buyer;

IB(3.12) acting for two or more *clients* in a *conflict of interests* under Outcome 3.6 (*substantially common interest*) where it is unreasonable to act because there is unequal bargaining power;

IB(3.13) acting for two buyers where there is a *conflict of interests* under Outcome 3.7 (*competing for the same objective*), for example where two buyers are competing for a residential property;

IB(3.14) acting for a buyer (including a lessee) and seller (including a lessor) in a transaction relating to the transfer of land for value, the grant or assignment of a lease or some other interest in land for value.

4.26

This chapter, which is the successor to rule 3 of the 2007 Code, involves in part a restatement of current principles and rules and in part fairly radical changes: in emphasis, particularly on the need for systems to avoid conflicts of interests; in brevity and relative simplicity (the former rule was the longest and most complex in the 2007 Code); and in its practical consequences, particularly for conveyancing.

It also gives a more proportionate prominence to conflicts of interests between solicitor and client (defined as an 'own interest conflict'), which was mentioned almost as an afterthought in the former rule.

It is constructive and to be welcomed that 'conflict of interests' is treated not as one subject, but as two, separating 'own interest conflict' from 'client conflict'.

Rule 3 of the 2007 Code was in many ways exceptional in that it was substantially concerned with the protection of solicitors rather than their regulation, and imposed limitations on the extent of a solicitor's duties when acting for lenders when the firm also acted for the borrower in routine conveyancing transactions. The rule prevented lenders from imposing onerous obligations and strictly limited the scope of the retainer. That protection survives to a limited extent, in that only a certificate of title in the form approved for the time being by the Law Society and the Council of Mortgage Lenders should be given in these circumstances, although this is no longer a rule, but non-binding guidance.

Indicative behaviour 3.1 provides a helpful emphasis on training. Qualified lawyers have a fairly well-ingrained instinct about conflicts of interests. As new business models develop in an ABS environment these instincts cannot be taken for granted.

Own interest conflict

4.27

Indicative behaviours 3.8, 3.9 and 3.10 provide unexceptionable and unsurprising examples of 'own interest conflicts'.

As is made clear in the introduction to Chapter 3, the prohibition on acting in an 'own interest conflict' is absolute. While it could be said that this has always been so, there has also always been an understanding that not every dealing between solicitor and client which has the potential for conflict, in fact involves a conflict or a significant risk of one. Examples are an unsecured interest-free loan from solicitor to client, as an act of humanity; or bridging finance on standard terms, or a modest gift to a solicitor by a client in a will, as distinct from a gift which is 'significant' in the terms of the former rule 3.04.

Guidance to the equivalent rule in the 2007 Code made it clear that solicitors could take security for their costs by a charge over the client's property, and that independent legal advice 'would not normally be essential unless the terms of the proposed charge are particularly onerous or would give you some unusual benefit or profit'. So was that not a conflict, or was it a conflict that was exceptionally permitted? It would be difficult to argue that it was not, strictly speaking, a conflict of interests (what were the terms of the legal charge to be?).

Are these historic indications still valid? In our view they are. Save in respect of conveyancing, on which there is a plain shift in policy, there are no indications that the former regime is intended to be subjected to material change. Much of the former rule, particularly as to the exceptions enabling the firm to act in 'client conflict' situations, is reproduced without substantive change.

The SRA's position may also be gauged from another quotation from its policy statement:[1]

> 'The position under OFR is that we now expect firms to exercise their own judgement as to whether it would be proper to act in a particular situation, rather than the Handbook specifying the circumstances where it is appropriate to do so.'

That suggests not a change in 'the rules', as such, but a change in the form of regulation, placing the onus on practitioners, in effect, to think and make judgements. That is indeed the OFR approach, and in our view in the situations described above by way of historic example there would be no failure to comply with the 2011 Code, because there would be perceived to be no genuine 'own interest conflict'.

Where, however, there is a genuine 'own interest conflict', the prohibition against a solicitor acting where his or her personal interests actually conflict with those of a client is absolute. Many solicitors continue to believe that merely informing a client that independent advice should be taken is sufficient to discharge their duties to the client. This is not so and normally, if the client does not in fact take independent advice, the solicitor must not proceed with the transaction (whether it be the purchase of an asset from the client, the drafting of a will containing a significant bequest in favour of the solicitor, or as the case may be).

1 At para 75.

Client conflict

4.28

As to 'client conflicts', *The Guide to the Professional Conduct of Solicitors 1999* (8th edn) contained a valuable commentary which remains valid and the substance of which is reproduced here: where a solicitor is acting for two or more clients, whether they are husband and wife, business partners or companies embarking on a joint venture, the solicitor always owes a duty to each individual person or body and he or she must advise each individual in accordance with that individual's interests. A practical initial test to apply to assist in identifying whether a conflict exists is to ask: what would occur if the solicitor was only acting for one of the parties? In particular, would any advice be different?

A conflict between clients must involve current retainers from two or more relevant clients. Chapter 3 does not prohibit a solicitor from acting for a client against a former client. In this situation, Chapter 4 will be in play in relation to any confidential information that may be held about the former client. Chapter 3 does not permit a client to consent to a solicitor acting in a conflict of interests situation unless one of the specified exceptions applies. It is not possible to erect an information barrier (or Chinese wall) to 'cure' a client conflict.

4.29

The exceptions in outcomes 3.6 and 3.7, enabling firms to act despite a client conflict – particularly when read together with the relevant indicative behaviours (3.11, 3.12 and 3.13), and the reference to sophisticated clients in this context – reflect the provisions of the 2007 Code, expressed rather more economically. The former phrase: 'substantially common interest' is repeated verbatim, and now helpfully defined in SRA Handbook Glossary 2012:

> 'a situation where there is a clear common purpose in relation to any matter or a particular aspect of it between the clients and a strong consensus on how it is to be achieved and the client conflict is peripheral to this common purpose.'

The former provision relating to 'competing for the same asset' becomes 'competing for the same objective' and is also defined in the Glossary:

> 'any situation in which two or more clients are competing for an "objective" which, if attained by one client, will make that "objective" unattainable to the other client or clients and "objective" means, for the purposes of Chapter 3, an asset, contract or business opportunity which two or more clients are seeking to acquire or recover through a liquidation (or some other form of insolvency process) or by means of an auction or tender process or a bid or offer which is not public.'

Outcome 3.5 was amended in version 3 (18 April 2012) to clarify that the exceptions to the prohibition on acting in a conflict of interests, as set out in outcomes 3.6 and 3.7, apply in the alternative.

The importance of making a judgement

4.30

As noted above, the 2011 Code challenges solicitors to make judgements, rather than setting out in prescriptive rules how they must behave. The exercise of judgement is nowhere more important than in a solicitor's assessment of whether it is proper to act in a situation where there may be a conflict of interests. If the matter is properly and conscientiously addressed by the solicitor, an error of judgement will not amount to professional misconduct. However, this does not mean that a solicitor's professional obligations are discharged merely by giving careful thought to the matter. If a solicitor does not honestly and genuinely address the matter he may be guilty of a disciplinary offence. And if his decision is one that no reasonably competent solicitor could have made, it may be inferred that he had not (or could not have) properly addressed the issue. This inference may well be appropriate where the reason given for the solicitor's professional decision is manifestly unsustainable.[1]

1 See *Connolly v Law Society* [2007] EWHC 1175 (Admin).

Conveyancing

4.31

The wholly new approach to conveyancing and to acting for buyer and seller in the 2011 Code can be discerned from the removal of any equivalent to rules 3.07 to 3.22

of the 2007 Code, from the indicative behaviours and from the policy document quoted above. The potential for upheaval can be seen in indicative behaviour 3.14 whereby acting for seller and buyer 'may tend to show that you have not achieved' the Chapter 3 outcomes.

Much of the former rule was concerned with domestic conveyancing, and the circumstances in which a firm could act for both buyer and seller, as well as for lender and borrower. That part of the rule, and its many predecessors, imposed limitations on the ability of a firm to act for both parties, even if no conflict of interests existed. In other words, it was accepted that there was no inherent conflict of interests in acting for buyer and seller, but by regulation going beyond the requirements of the common law, solicitors were prevented from acting for both parties in most circumstances, even when there was no conflict. Solicitors were permitted to act for both parties, by exception to the general rule, in limited circumstances (for example, where both were established clients and gave written consent), but the exceptions did not apply if there was a conflict of interests.

A rule having this effect was first made in 1972 but the earliest commentary on the subject, in the 1960 *Guide to the Professional Conduct and Etiquette of Solicitors*, stated firmly:[1]

> 'there are a good many conveyancing transactions in which the possibility of a conflict of interest between vendor and purchaser is remote and is rarely experienced in practice. There is thus nothing inherently improper in a solicitor acting for both vendor and purchaser ... The complete cessation of the practice of acting for both parties would cause hardship and inconvenience to the public, particularly where both parties are already established clients of the same solicitor.'

1 At p 114.

4.32

The new rule reflects the view of the SRA that this is no longer correct. In its policy statement on its October 2010 consultation the SRA stated its view in diametrically opposite terms:[1]

> 'the circumstances in which either there is no conflict of interests nor a significant risk of a conflict of interests as between buyer and seller must be extremely limited ... There may, of course, be some conveyancing situations where there are no conflicts of interests, although, for example, as between a seller and a buyer we expect that these will be rare. Our intention was not to prohibit acting in such cases, but rather to put the onus on firms to make the assessment as to whether a conflict exists.'

It may be noted that the Council for Licensed Conveyancers does not take the same view, and those it regulates may act for both parties in circumstances broadly comparable with rule 3 of the 2007 Code, though the CLC rules are somewhat less restrictive.

The SRA has not yet explained why and on what evidential basis it came to the conclusion that something that has always in the past been thought not to involve an inherent or overwhelmingly likely conflict, now does.

1 At paras 74 and 75.

4.33

The SRA's change of stance will have had a profound effect on conveyancing practice, the extent of which will depend on the attitude of firms to regulatory risk. Some will have decided that indicative behaviour 3.14 is in effect a rule against acting for buyer and seller bearing in mind that it is unqualified in terms. Such firms will have also noted the assertions by the SRA quoted above that:

> 'the circumstances in which either there is no conflict of interests nor a significant risk of a conflict of interests as between buyer and seller must be extremely limited ... There may, of course, be some conveyancing situations where there are no conflicts of interests, although, for example, as between a seller and a buyer we expect that these will be rare'

and may have decided that the SRA's use of 'extremely limited' and 'rare' is a pretty broad hint that it will need a great deal of persuading that it is proper for a firm to act, ever, for buyer and seller and that its 'default' position is that it cannot be done.

The rest of the quotation however may also be noted:

> 'Our intention was not to prohibit acting in such cases, but rather to put the onus on firms to make the assessment as to whether a conflict exists.'

Practical suggestions

4.34

Firms which have conscientiously applied the exceptions in rule 3.02 of the 2007 Code (Exceptions to the duty not to act) can confidently continue on the basis that there is no material change.

Firms of all sizes must be able to demonstrate appropriate systems and controls to identify and assess potential conflicts, including staff training.

The historic approach to what is now called 'own interest conflict' still applies.

Practice has had to change in relation to acting for buyer and seller in conveyancing transactions. Whether firms take the safest line and simply cease to act rather than risk-assess each case, and be prepared to justify departure from a perceived norm, or whether cases will be assessed individually, it is not an option to carry on as before.

One of the former factors relevant to a firm's decision to act for both parties continues to be relevant to an assessment of risk and the identification of a conflict: that the transaction is not at arm's length. Others are plainly not relevant at all. The fact that both parties are established clients or that they are represented by two separate offices of the firm cannot be relevant to the presence or the absence of a conflict of interests.

Another problem is that because the SRA's 'default position' is that only rarely will there not be a conflict of interests, a conveyancing practitioner who genuinely believes that in a particular case there is no conflict, but that there is nothing out of the ordinary about the transaction, may struggle to convince the SRA that it is in the narrow category where it is proper to act. The SRA is in the process of developing a written 'supervision and enforcement strategy' for conveyancing, having published drafts in April and November 2011, which stress the risks of conflicts of interests in conveyancing. This process has proved to be very slow.

It is highly desirable to make a note of the decision and the reasoning.

4.35

Finally, indicative behaviour 3.7 preserves the status quo in relation to acting for lender and borrower in domestic conveyancing transactions, save that the reinforcement on the limitations of the retainer and the obligations a lender could impose, expressed in rule 3.19 of the 2007 Code, do not survive; though the requirement to use only the approved form of certificate of title, formerly the Annex to rule 3 of the 2007 Code, is maintained, but of course not in rule form, rather as unenforceable guidance.

Chapter 4: Confidentiality and disclosure

4.36

This chapter is about the protection of *clients'* confidential information and the disclosure of material information to *clients*.

Protection of confidential information is a fundamental feature of your relationship with *clients*. It exists as a concept both as a matter of law and as a matter of conduct. This duty continues despite the end of the retainer and even after the death of the *client*.

It is important to distinguish the conduct duties from the concept of law known as legal professional privilege.

Bear in mind that all members of the *firm* or *in-house practice*, including support staff, consultants and locums, owe a duty of confidentiality to your *clients*.

The duty of confidentiality to all *clients* must be reconciled with the duty of disclosure to *clients*. This duty of disclosure is limited to information of which you are aware which is material to your *client's* matter. Where you cannot reconcile these two duties, then the protection of confidential information is paramount. You should not continue to act for a *client* for whom you cannot disclose material information, except in very limited circumstances, where safeguards are in place. Such situations often also give rise to a *conflict of interests* which is discussed in Chapter 3.

The outcomes in this chapter show how the *Principles* apply in the context of confidentiality and disclosure.

Outcomes

You must achieve these outcomes:

O(4.1) you keep the affairs of *clients* confidential unless disclosure is required or permitted by law or the *client* consents;

O(4.2) any individual who is advising a *client* makes that *client* aware of all information material to that retainer of which the individual has personal knowledge;

O(4.3) you ensure that where your duty of confidentiality to one *client* comes into conflict with your duty of disclosure to another *client*, your duty of confidentiality takes precedence;

O(4.4) you do not act for A in a matter where A has an interest adverse to B, and B is a *client* for whom you hold confidential information which is material to A in that matter, unless the confidential information can be protected by the use of safeguards, and:

- (a) you reasonably believe that A is aware of, and understands, the relevant issues and gives informed consent;
- (b) either:
  - (i) B gives informed consent and you agree with B the safeguards to protect B's information; or
  - (ii) where this is not possible, you put in place effective safeguards including information barriers which comply with the common law; and
- (c) it is reasonable in all the circumstances to act for A with such safeguards in place;

O(4.5) you have effective systems and controls in place to enable you to identify risks to *client* confidentiality and to mitigate those risks.

Indicative behaviours

Acting in the following way(s) may tend to show that you have achieved these outcomes and therefore complied with the *Principles*:

IB(4.1) your systems and controls for identifying risks to *client* confidentiality are appropriate to the size and complexity of the *firm* or *in-house practice* and the nature of the work undertaken, and enable you to assess all the relevant circumstances;

IB(4.2) you comply with the law in respect of your fiduciary duties in relation to confidentiality and disclosure;

IB(4.3) you only outsource services when you are satisfied that the provider has taken all appropriate steps to ensure that your *clients'* confidential information will be protected;

IB(4.4) where you are an individual who has responsibility for acting for a *client* or supervising a *client's* matter, you disclose to the *client* all information material to the *client's* matter of which you are personally aware, except when:

(a) the *client* gives specific informed consent to non-disclosure or a different standard of disclosure arises;

(b) there is evidence that serious physical or mental injury will be caused to a person(s) if the information is disclosed to the *client*;

(c) legal restrictions effectively prohibit you from passing the information to the *client*, such as the provisions in the money-laundering and anti-terrorism legislation;

(d) it is obvious that privileged documents have been mistakenly disclosed to you;

(e) you come into possession of information relating to state security or intelligence matters to which the Official Secrets Act 1989 applies;

IB(4.5) not acting for A where B is a *client* for whom you hold confidential information which is material to A unless the confidential information can be protected.

Acting in the following way(s) may tend to show that you have not achieved these outcomes and therefore not complied with the *Principles*:

IB(4.6) disclosing the content of a will on the death of a *client* unless consent has been provided by the personal representatives for the content to be released;

IB(4.7) disclosing details of bills sent to *clients* to third parties, such as debt factoring companies in relation to the collection of book debts, unless the *client* has consented.

4.37

This chapter is the natural successor to rule 4 of the 2007 Code[1] and although it is drafted in a different style consistent with OFR the underlying philosophy and regulatory requirements are largely unaltered, though it is significantly simplified in relation to situations in which client consent and information barriers may be employed to prevent the misuse of confidential information. The only wholly new matter is a reference to outsourcing and the protection of confidentiality in that context. Outsourcing is considered in more detail in relation to Chapter 7 of the 2011 Code; see **4.60** to **4.67**.

The duty of confidentiality continues beyond the end of the retainer. Chapter 4 is, and its predecessor was, mainly concerned in practice with situations in which confidential information is held relating to a *former* client. If a situation arose in relation to two or more *current* clients the principles likely to be applicable will be found in Chapter 3 on conflicts of interest. Nevertheless, Chapter 4 refers throughout to 'clients' and makes no reference to former clients. This is because a client is defined in the SRA Handbook Glossary 2012 as including: 'where the context permits … prospective and former clients'. It should be borne in mind that this definition applies to the SRA Handbook, but it is not consistent with the statutory definition in section 87 of the Solicitors Act 1974, so that it should not be used or taken to be relevant for other purposes.

The importance of systems is again emphasised (outcome 4.5 and indicative behaviour 4.1).

1 Rule 4 replaced Rule 16E of the Solicitors' Practice Rules 1990, which came into force on 25 April 2006. Before that date there had been no specific Practice Rule dealing with the duty of confidentiality – although such a duty had long been recognised by the courts and in the guidance provided by the Law Society.

Informed consent and information barriers

4.38

The provisions and guidance relevant to information barriers (Chinese walls or ethical walls) have been redrawn and have been simplified, but without material change from the position under rule 4 of the 2007 Code when fully analysed. However, it is necessary to have regard to the explanatory notes to Chapter 4 to obtain the full picture (see further below, including **4.40**). In substance: there are exceptional circumstances in which it is possible to act for one client, to whom a duty would be owed to disclose material information, when there is a contemporaneous duty of confidentiality to a second client (or former client) which would prevent such disclosure. It is possible to continue to act, on the basis that confidentiality to the second client is absolutely maintained, subject to various combinations of informed consent, adequate and effective information barriers, reasonableness, and the common law. It is important to recognise that this is an exception to the normal absolute rule that continuing to act in these circumstances would be bound to put a solicitor in breach of one or other duty, and therefore impossible.[1]

1 See e.g. *Hilton v Barker Booth & Eastwood (a firm)* [2005] UKHL 8, [2005] 1 WLR 567.

4.39

As for informed consent, if practicable both clients must give such consent and it must in all the circumstances be reasonable for the matter to proceed in this way. Solicitors will need to justify their approach should questions be raised by the SRA or the courts. A detailed written record of all aspects of the matter, including the informed consent of the clients, will therefore be all but essential. Particular caution should be exercised where the clients or former clients are not sophisticated users of legal services.

Outcome 4.4(b)(ii) provides that where it is not possible to obtain the consent of the person on behalf of whom the confidential information is held, the firm may nevertheless act if an information barrier is put in place – if the current client consents and if it is reasonable in all the circumstances to act in this way.

4.40

As for information barriers, guidance note (ii) is important and an aid to interpretation of the outcomes. An understanding of the law is also required. The leading case is *Bolkiah v KPMG*,[1] particularly the speech of Lord Millett. The principles are helpfully extracted and summarised in *Koch Shipping Inc v Richards Butler*,[2] in the following terms (at [24]):[3]

'(1) The court's jurisdiction to intervene is founded on the right of the former client to the protection of his confidential information (per Lord Millett at p.234).

(2) The only duty to the former client which survives the termination of

the client relationship is a continuing duty to preserve the confidentiality of information imparted during its subsistence (per Lord Millett at p.235).

(3) The duty to preserve confidentiality is unqualified. It is a duty to keep the information confidential, not merely to take all reasonable steps to do so (per Lord Millett at p.235).

(4) The former client cannot be protected completely from accidental or inadvertent disclosure, but he is entitled to prevent his former solicitor from exposing him to any avoidable risk. This includes the increased risk of the use of the information to his prejudice arising from the acceptance of instructions to act for another client with an adverse interest in a matter to which the information may be relevant (per Lord Millett at pp.235–236).

(5) The former client must establish that the defendant solicitors possess confidential information which is or might be relevant to the matter and to the disclosure of which he has not consented (per Lord Millett at pp.234–235).

(6) The burden then passes to the defendant solicitors to show that there is *no risk* of disclosure. The court should intervene unless it is satisfied that there is no risk of disclosure. The risk must be a real one, and not merely fanciful or theoretical, but it need not be substantial (per Lord Millett at p.237).

(7) It is wrong in principle to conduct a balancing exercise. If the former client establishes the facts in (5) above, the former client is entitled to an injunction unless the defendant solicitors show that there is no risk of disclosure.

(8) In considering whether the solicitors have shown that there is no risk of disclosure, the starting point must be that, unless special measures are taken, information moves within a firm (per Lord Millett at p.237). However, that is only the starting point. The Prince Jefri case does not establish a rule of law that special measures have to be taken to prevent the information passing within a firm: see also *Young v Robson Rhodes* [1999] 3 All ER 524, per Laddie J at p.538. On the other hand, the courts should restrain the solicitors from acting unless satisfied on the basis of clear and convincing evidence that all effective measures have been taken to ensure that no disclosure will occur (per Lord Millett at pp.237–238, where he adapted the test identified by Sopinka J in *MacDonald Estate v Martin* (1991) 77 DLR (4th) 249 at p.269). This is a heavy burden (per Lord Millett at p.239).'

And at [25]:

'It is to my mind important to emphasise that each case turns on its own facts.'

In *Gus Consulting GmbH v LeBoeuf Lamb Greene & Macrae*, the 'ethical wall' involved three main steps: software preventing access to any electronic documents relating to restricted matters; allocation of a matter number used in archive management software to prevent given lawyers from being able to retrieve any files; and the files were physically stamped as being restricted. In addition instructions were disseminated internally to draw attention to the importance of the confidential material not coming to the attention of anybody, particularly those in the team working on the arbitration. The sensitive material related to transactions which had taken place and been concluded some years previously. It was only upon the basis of these arrangements and the undertakings that the court was persuaded not to restrain the firm from acting by injunction.

1 [1999] 2 AC 222, HL. See also *Marks & Spencer plc v Freshfields* [2004] EWCA Civ 741.
2 [2002] EWCA Civ 1280, [2003] PNLR 11.
3 A useful example of the practical measures necessary to be taken can be seen from the undertakings given by the solicitors in *Gus Consulting GmbH v LeBoeuf Lamb Greene & Macrae* [2006] EWCA Civ 683, [2006] PNLR 32 at [20].

4.41

It follows that although the issue will remain fact sensitive, arrangements that are less effective and wide-ranging would be unlikely to be sufficient, and it would not be lawful for a firm to continue acting, unless it were to be possible – on the basis of informed consent by the affected client – to impose safeguards which were less than is required by the common law.

It is unsurprising in the circumstances that the guidance notes to Chapter 4 emphasise the difficulty of implementing effective safeguards and information barriers if the firm is small; if the physical structure or layout of the firm means that it will be difficult to preserve confidentiality; or if the clients are not sophisticated users of legal services. While this is not a 'City firm only' rule or '20+ partner only' rule, in reality it is unlikely in the extreme that any small firm would be able to achieve the necessary protections and effective barriers.

It is also noted that the protection of confidential information may be at particular risk where two or more firms merge, or any lawyers leave one firm and join another, resulting in a team acting against one of its former clients.

A practical checklist

4.42

In outcome 4.4 both parties are referred to as clients but it may be easier to think of A as the current client who would be interested in receiving information, and B as the former client whose right to confidentiality is in play. Although the outcome refers to A having an interest adverse to B this is not strictly the position in law (though it is likely to be the case in practice). The important point is not whether they have contrary interests in a litigation sense, but whether A would want to receive the information, because it is 'material'; that is, potentially of value, and whether B would agree to release it or would want the confidential information to remain so.

If this situation arises and B does not consent to disclosure – or plainly cannot be expected to consent if asked – the default position is that the firm must cease to act for A. If the firm wishes to use the exception provided by outcome 4.4 the following need to be considered:

- Would it be reasonable, in principle, for the firm to continue to act for A if sufficient safeguards to protect B could be put in place? Would this be in A's interests? One could envisage a situation in which those acting for A within the firm might have been compromised by learning of the confidential information so that, as a minimum, a new team would have to take over immediately, and it might on balance be better if A instructs a new firm. If nevertheless the answer is yes:

- A must give informed consent; that is, he/she/they must be informed that the firm has information of potential value that it cannot disclose. The firm would almost certainly not be in a position to identify B as the source of that information or to say anything more about it, although, for example, as a result of a protest by B, A may otherwise learn something of this. A must be content, without knowing more, for the firm to continue acting on the basis that the information will never be disclosed. This would require a sophisticated thought process and an enlightened individual or body, well able to understand among other things that there will be 'no cheating'. Although the outcome refers to the position where you 'reasonably believe' that A understands and gives informed consent, there is little room here for uncertainty. If A does give informed consent, either:
- B is consulted, agrees that the firm may continue to act and agrees the safeguards to be put in place to protect the confidential information, which could be to a standard sufficient to meet the common law requirements, or something less; or
- In the absence of B's informed consent, which could be because of an unreasonable refusal or because B cannot be contacted, for example, safeguards are put in place sufficient to meet the firm's obligations at law.

Chapter 5: Your client and the court

4.43

This chapter is about your duties to your *client* and to the *court* if you are exercising a right to conduct litigation or acting as an advocate. The outcomes apply to both litigation and advocacy but there are some indicative behaviours which may be relevant only when you are acting as an advocate.

The outcomes in this chapter show how the *Principles* apply in the context of your *client* and the *court*.

Outcomes

You must achieve these outcomes:

O(5.1) you do not attempt to deceive or knowingly or recklessly mislead the *court*;

O(5.2) you are not complicit in another *person* deceiving or misleading the *court*;

O(5.3) you comply with *court* orders which place obligations on you;

O(5.4) you do not place yourself in contempt of *court*;

O(5.5) where relevant, *clients* are informed of the circumstances in which your duties to the *court* outweigh your obligations to your *client*;

O(5.6) you comply with your duties to the *court*;

O(5.7) you ensure that evidence relating to sensitive issues is not misused;

O(5.8) you do not make or offer to make payments to witnesses dependent upon their evidence or the outcome of the case.

Indicative behaviours

Acting in the following way(s) may tend to show that you have achieved these outcomes and therefore complied with the *Principles*:

IB(5.1) advising your *clients* to comply with *court* orders made against them, and advising them of the consequences of failing to comply;

IB(5.2) drawing the *court's* attention to relevant cases and statutory provisions, and any material procedural irregularity;

IB(5.3) ensuring child witness evidence is kept securely and not released to *clients* or third parties;

IB(5.4) immediately informing the *court*, with your *client's* consent, if during the course of proceedings you become aware that you have inadvertently misled the *court*, or ceasing to act if the *client* does not consent to you informing the *court*;

IB(5.5) refusing to continue acting for a *client* if you become aware they have committed perjury or misled the *court*, or attempted to mislead the *court*, in any material matter unless the *client* agrees to disclose the truth to the *court*;

IB(5.6) not appearing as an advocate, or acting in litigation, if it is clear that you, or anyone within your *firm*, will be called as a witness in the matter unless you are satisfied that this will not prejudice your independence as an advocate, or litigator, or the interests of your *clients* or the interests of justice.

Acting in the following way(s) may tend to show that you have not achieved these outcomes and therefore not complied with the *Principles*:

IB(5.7) constructing facts supporting your *client's* case or drafting any documents relating to any proceedings containing:

- (a) any contention which you do not consider to be properly arguable; or
- (b) any allegation of fraud, unless you are instructed to do so and you have material which you reasonably believe shows, on the face of it, a case of fraud;

IB(5.8) suggesting that any *person* is guilty of a crime, fraud or misconduct unless such allegations:

- (a) go to a matter in issue which is material to your own *client's* case; and
- (b) appear to you to be supported by reasonable grounds;

IB(5.9) calling a witness whose evidence you know is untrue;

IB(5.10) attempting to influence a witness, when taking a statement from that witness, with regard to the contents of their statement;

IB(5.11) tampering with evidence or seeking to persuade a witness to change their evidence;

IB(5.12) when acting as an advocate, naming in open *court* any third party whose character would thereby be called into question, unless it is necessary for the proper conduct of the case;

IB(5.13) when acting as an advocate, calling into question the character of a witness you have cross-examined unless the witness has had the opportunity to answer the allegations during cross-examination.

4.44

There is nothing in Chapter 5 of the 2011 Code that is substantively different from the obligations imposed by rule 11 of the 2007 Code and any practitioner familiar with the proper standards of behaviour of litigators and advocates need have no concern that the outcomes or indicative behaviours in the 2011 Code present any traps.

Rule 11 of the 2007 Code replaced the Law Society's Code for Advocacy and those principles that were previously contained in Chapter 21 of *The Guide to the Professional Conduct of Solicitors 1999* (8th edn). Rule 11 imposed on all solicitors who conduct litigation some of the obligations that had previously been imposed only on advocates – for example, that a solicitor could not draft documents containing any allegation that he or she did not consider properly arguable.[1] Rule 11 was considered by the Court of Appeal in *Richard Buxton (Solicitors) v Mills-Owens*[2] in which it was held that solicitors could lawfully determine their retainer when required by a client to advance an argument which they considered to be untenable.

1 Rule 11.01(3)(a) – this has not been specifically included in the 2011 Code.
2 [2010] EWCA Civ 122.

4.45

The opportunity was taken in promulgating the 2011 Code to clarify one situation. Both rule 11 of the 2007 Code and the first drafts of the present Chapter 5 included references to the court being misled by others: in rule 11: 'You must never … knowingly allow the court to be misled' and in the draft Chapter 5: 'You do not knowingly allow another person to deceive or mislead … the court'.

Both could have been interpreted to mean that in the well-known situation in which, in the criminal courts, the prosecution fails to identify that the defendant had previous convictions, a defence advocate would have been under a regulatory obligation to correct the misunderstanding. The former rule was never interpreted in that way because it was well understood that in this respect the 2007 Code served to codify existing principles and guidance and not to change them.

The 2011 Code is to be interpreted as it stands without assistance from the legislative background, as it is part of a complete new regulatory system. An outcome which required defence advocates to prevent the court being innocently misled by the prosecution would, among other things, have required different standards to be applied by barristers and solicitors.

The law has always been that:

> 'A barrister must not wilfully mislead the court as to the law nor may he actively mislead the court as to the facts; although, consistently with the rule that the prosecution must prove its case, he may passively stand by and watch the court being misled by reason of its failure to ascertain facts that are within the barrister's knowledge.'[1]

By changing outcome 5.2 to its present form, prohibiting a solicitor from being 'complicit' in another person misleading the court the status quo is maintained.

1 *Saif Ali v Sydney Mitchell & Co* [1980] AC 198, per Lord Diplock at 220.

Solicitor advocates

4.46

For solicitors who appear as advocates, it is worth repeating some of the contents of rule 11 of the 2007 Code, which were included in earlier editions of *The Solicitor's Handbook* but which have not found their way into the 2011 Code, as there can be no doubt that they still hold good. Rule 11.05 provided that:

> 'If you are appearing as an advocate:
>
> (a) you must not say anything which is merely scandalous or intended only to insult a witness or any other person;
>
> (b) you must avoid naming in open court any third party whose character would thereby be called into question, unless it is necessary for the proper conduct of the case;
>
> (c) you must not call into question the character of a witness you have cross-examined unless the witness has had the opportunity to answer the allegations during cross-examination; and
>
> (d) you must not suggest that any person is guilty of a crime, fraud or misconduct unless such allegations:
>
> (i) go to a matter in issue which is material to your client's case; and
>
> (ii) appear to you to be supported by reasonable grounds.'

Rule 11.08 provided that:

> 'If you are acting in the defence or prosecution of an accused and you have in your possession a copy of an audio or video recording of a child witness which has been identified as having been prepared to be admitted in evidence at a criminal trial in accordance with the relevant provisions of the Criminal Justice Act 1991 or the Youth Justice and Criminal Evidence Act 1999, you must:
>
> (a) not make or permit any person to make a copy of the recording;
>
> (b) not release the recording to the accused;
>
> (c) not make or permit any disclosure of the recording or its contents to

any person except when, in your opinion, it is necessary in the course of preparing the prosecution, defence or appeal against conviction and/or sentence;

(d) ensure that the recording is always kept in a locked, secure container when not in use; and

(e) return the recording when you are no longer instructed in the matter.'

The solicitor as potential witness

4.47

The essence of indicative behaviour 5.6 is not new and the wording is very similar to the wording of rule 11.06 of the 2007 Code. The principle has caused difficulties in the past because it has not seemed to be wholly logical. It was first expressed as guidance in successive editions of *The Guide to the Professional Conduct of Solicitors*, and appeared in the 1999 edition as principle 21.12. There the principle was:

> 'A solicitor must not accept instructions to act as advocate for a client if it is clear that he or she or a member of the firm will be called as a witness on behalf of the client, unless the evidence is purely formal.'

It will be noted that the focus is not only on advocacy, but on the sequence of events. The question was whether a solicitor could 'accept instructions to act' – in other words the mischief at which the principle is aimed is a situation in which it is *already* clear that the solicitor is or is likely to be a material witness. One can well see that if the solicitor had, for example, been a witness to a road accident and one of the drivers or passengers subsequently instructed that solicitor's firm, professional issues would be likely to arise.

The rule has far less logical application when the solicitor acts for the client perfectly properly, and then something arises as a result of the solicitor/client relationship which makes it appropriate or necessary for the solicitor to give supportive evidence. It is commonplace for solicitors to give evidence for their clients about matters arising in the course of the retainer, for example, on procedural matters and as to dealings with opposing solicitors in civil proceedings, and in criminal proceedings where evidence may be needed that the defendant exercised his right of silence on advice. The idea that, in this situation, the solicitor would be obliged to cease to act, simply because the rule appeared to suggest it, would make little sense.

In our view the primary historical concern was the situation where a solicitor who is a material witness to matters unrelated to the solicitor/client relationship is subsequently instructed. In the guidance notes to the former rule 11.06 it was said that it would be 'extremely rare' for it to be proper to act in litigation where you are also a witness. This could not make sense unless the rule is interpreted as we suggest.

The 2011 Code in this specific outcome does permit this interpretation more easily than its predecessor in the form of rule 11.06, by shifting the focus from the giving of evidence, *per se*, to whether giving evidence would offend any of the principles requiring independence, the interests of the client and the interests of justice to be considered. No such concerns tend to arise in the everyday situations in which most solicitors find themselves giving evidence.

Chapter 6: Your client and introductions to third parties

4.48

There may be circumstances in which you wish to refer your *clients* to third parties, perhaps to another *lawyer* or a financial services provider. This chapter describes the conduct duties which arise in respect of such introductions. It is important that you retain your independence when recommending third parties to your *client* and that you act in the *client's* best interests.

The outcomes in this chapter show how the *Principles* apply in the context of your *client* and introductions to third parties.

Outcomes

You must achieve these outcomes:

O(6.1) whenever you recommend that a *client* uses a particular *person* or business, your recommendation is in the best interests of the *client* and does not compromise your independence;

O(6.2) *clients* are fully informed of any financial or other interest which you have in referring the *client* to another *person* or business;

O(6.3) *clients* are in a position to make informed decisions about how to pursue their matter.

O(6.4) you are not *paid* a *prohibited referral fee*.

Indicative behaviours

Acting in the following way(s) may tend to show that you have achieved these outcomes and therefore complied with the *Principles*:

IB(6.1) any *arrangement*[1] you enter into in respect of *regulated mortgage contracts*,[2] *general insurance contracts*[3] (including after the event insurance) or *pure protection contracts*,[4] provides that referrals will only be made where this is in the best interests of the particular *client* and the contract is suitable for the needs of that *client*;

IB(6.2) any referral to a third party that can only offer products from one source, is made only after the *client* has been informed of this limitation.

IB(6.3) having effective systems in place for assessing whether any *arrangement* complies with the statutory and regulatory requirements;

IB(6.4) retaining records and management information to enable you to demonstrate that any *payments* you receive are not *prohibited referral fees*.

Acting in the following way(s) may tend to show that you have not achieved these outcomes and therefore not complied with the *Principles*:

IB(6.5) entering into any *arrangement* which restricts your freedom to recommend any particular business, except in respect of *regulated mortgage contracts*, *general insurance contracts* or *pure protection contracts*;

IB(6.6) being an *appointed representative*.[5]

1 Defined in relation to financial services, fee sharing and referrals, in Chapters 1, 6 and 9, as 'any express or tacit agreement' between a solicitor and another person, 'whether contractually binding or not'.
2 Has the meaning given by the Financial Services and Markets Act 2000 (Regulated Activities) Order 2001 (SI 2001/544) (RAO 2001).
3 Defined as any contract of insurance within Part I of Schedule 1 to RAO 2001.
4 In the SRA Handbook Glossary 2012 a pure protection contract is defined as either '(i) a long-term insurance contract: (A) under which the benefits are payable only in respect of death or of incapacity due to injury, sickness or infirmity; (B) which has no surrender value or the consideration consists of a single premium and the surrender value does not exceed that premium; and (C) which makes no provision for its conversion or extension in a manner which would result in its ceasing to comply with (A), or (B)'; or '(ii) a reinsurance contract covering all or part of a risk to which a person is exposed under a long-term insurance contract'.
5 Has the meaning given in the Financial Services and Markets Act 2000.

4.49

Chapter 6 derives from rule 9.03 and rule 19.01(1)(a) of the 2007 Code. An important change made in 2011 is that the referral provisions in Chapter 6 apply to referrals between lawyers. Solicitors have to be fully transparent as to any referral fee paid by them to other lawyers from whom they obtain work.

Version 6 of the 2011 Code, effective from 1 January 2013, incorporated amendments to the rules in relation to referrals and recommendations to financial intermediaries. This relaxed the former requirement that if solicitors referred or recommended clients to third parties for advice on investments they could only be referred to an independent intermediary (outcome 6.3). An 'independent intermediary' meant 'whole of market' advisers: those who are not restricted in any way in the choice of products they can offer.

The revised form of outcome 6.3 requires that clients are in a position to make informed decisions about referrals for investment advice. The firm has to ensure that the client is involved in the decision-making process and can make a fully informed choice. This means that a 'whole of market' adviser would *not* need to be chosen, but solicitors need to ensure that clients understand any potential restrictions in the choice of product.

The SRA's position is that removing a restrictive rule is more in keeping with outcomes-focused regulation, but the change appears to have been driven primarily by the result of the Retail Distribution Review by the then Financial Services Authority (FSA), which changed the way in which financial advisers were regulated from 1 January 2013, and which in particular changed what is meant by 'independent' in terms of FSA, now Financial Conduct Authority (FCA), regulation.

The changes will mean more responsibility and greater risk. Solicitors run the risk that, if a referral is made to a restricted financial adviser, however 'fully informed' that choice may be, if things go wrong the solicitor may well be blamed. The SRA vision of the solicitor and client sitting together to discuss the choice imposes greater burdens, in circumstances where the client may neither want such a discussion nor expect to pay for it. Many solicitors would make no claim to the expertise required to have this kind of discussion.

4.50

Reflections of the pre-existing rules in respect of regulated mortgage contracts, general insurance contracts or pure protection contracts (by which solicitors could tie themselves to particular providers) are found in the non-mandatory indicative behaviours 6.1 and 6.2. Solicitors must be satisfied that referrals to the preferred provider are in the best interests of clients, that the contract is suitable for the needs of the client (arguably a matter outside the expertise of the solicitor), and the clients must be made aware of the solicitor's lack of freedom in making the referral before the referral is made. In the light of the terms of outcome 6.1 it is doubtful if indicative behaviours 6.1 and 6.2 were actually necessary.

Indicative behaviour 6.6, which states that being an appointed representative may tend to show that a solicitor has not achieved the outcomes of Chapter 6 and therefore not complied with the Principles, again has all the appearance of a mandatory rule; a prohibition against being an appointed representative was formerly found in rule 19.01(1)(a) of the 2007 Code.

4.51

It is no longer formally necessary for solicitors to provide written notification where the client is referred to a business that can only offer products from one source. However, it is difficult to see how a solicitor could be acting in the best interests of the client if he or she were to opt not to provide such important information to the client.

4.52

Although outcome 6.2, by which solicitors must fully inform clients of any financial or other interest which they have in referring the client to another person or business, was introduced in 2011, it is doubtful whether this ought to make any practical difference, save in the context of referrals between lawyers. Solicitors have always been prevented by the general law from making a secret profit, although the Law Society created a *de minimis* exception in respect of commissions of £20 or less. This topic is dealt with in detail at **4.16** to **4.18**.

All in all, it is doubtful whether Chapter 6 has significantly altered or liberalised the rules which preceded it. The language is more liberal, but the obligations appear to remain much the same. By extending those obligations to referrals between lawyers, the regulatory burden on solicitors has actually been increased. Additionally, there is the April 2013 provision in outcome 6.4 that solicitors must not be paid a prohibited referral fee.

Chapter 7: Management of your business

4.53

> This chapter is about the management and supervision of your *firm* or *in-house practice*.

Everyone has a role to play in the efficient running of a business, although of course that role will depend on the individual's position within the organisation. However, overarching responsibility for the management of the business in the broadest sense rests with the *manager(s)*. The *manager(s)* should determine what arrangements are appropriate to meet the outcomes. Factors to be taken into account will include the size and complexity of the business; the number, experience and qualifications of the *employees*; the number of offices; and the nature of the work undertaken.

Where you are using a third party to provide services that you could provide, (often described as "outsourcing"), this chapter sets out the outcomes you need to achieve.

The outcomes in this chapter show how the *Principles* apply in the context of the management of your business.

Outcomes

You must achieve these outcomes:

O(7.1) you have a clear and effective governance structure and reporting lines;

O(7.2) you have effective systems and controls in place to achieve and comply with all the *Principles*, rules and outcomes and other requirements of the Handbook, where applicable;

O(7.3) you identify, monitor and manage risks to compliance with all the *Principles*, rules and outcomes and other requirements of the Handbook, if applicable to you, and take steps to address issues identified;

O(7.4) you maintain systems and controls for monitoring the financial stability of your *firm* and risks to money and *assets* entrusted to you by *clients* and others, and you take steps to address issues identified;

O(7.5) you comply with legislation applicable to your business, including anti-money laundering and data protection legislation;

O(7.6) you train individuals working in the *firm* to maintain a level of competence appropriate to their work and level of responsibility;

O(7.7) you comply with the statutory requirements for the direction and supervision of *reserved legal activities* and *immigration work*;

O(7.8) you have a system for supervising *clients'* matters, to include the regular checking of the quality of work by suitably competent and experienced people;

O(7.9) you do not outsource *reserved legal activities* to a *person* who is not authorised to conduct such activities;

O(7.10) subject to Outcome 7.9, where you outsource *legal activities* or any operational functions that are critical to the delivery of any *legal activities*, you ensure such outsourcing:

(a) does not adversely affect your ability to comply with, or the *SRA's* ability to monitor your compliance with, your obligations in the Handbook;

(b) is subject to contractual arrangements that enable the *SRA* or its agent to obtain information from, inspect the records (including electronic records) of, or enter the premises of, the third party, in relation to the outsourced activities or functions;

(c) does not alter your obligations towards your *clients*; and

(d) does not cause you to breach the conditions with which you must comply in order to be authorised and to remain so.

O(7.11) you identify, monitor and manage the compliance of your *overseas practices* with the SRA Overseas Rules;

O(7.12) you identify, monitor and manage all risks to your business which may arise from your *connected practices*.

Indicative behaviours

Acting in the following way(s) may tend to show that you have achieved these outcomes and therefore complied with the *Principles*:

IB(7.1) safekeeping of documents and *assets* entrusted to the *firm*;

IB(7.2) controlling budgets, expenditure and cash flow;

IB(7.3) identifying and monitoring financial, operational and business continuity risks including *complaints*, credit risks and exposure, claims under legislation relating to matters such as data protection, IT failures and abuses, and damage to offices;

IB(7.4) making arrangements for the continuation of your *firm* in the event of absences and emergencies, for example holiday or sick leave, with the minimum interruption to *clients'* business.

IB(7.5) you maintain systems and controls for managing the risks posed by any financial inter-dependence which exists with your *connected practices*;

IB(7.6) you take appropriate action to control the use of your brand by any body or individual outside of England and Wales which is not an *overseas practice*.

4.54

This chapter is the successor to rule 5 of the 2007 Code, but with important changes; it emphasises that everyone has a role to play in the efficient running of a business, although of course that role will depend on the individual's position within the organisation. The responsibility for the management of the business in the broadest sense rests with the managers. The managers should determine what arrangements are appropriate to meet the outcomes, having regard to the size and complexity of the business; the number, experience and qualifications of the employees; the number of offices; and the nature of the work undertaken.

Chapter 7 marks a significant move towards a more aggressive regulation of business management. Although many of the words are familiar, whereas rule 5 was mainly concerned with ensuring that firms had 'systems', including, for example, systems concerned with financial control, there was no regulatory obligation to ensure that the business was financially sound, with the consequence that if it was not, it would become a matter of interest to and potential action by the regulator.

4.55

It is in this area of regulation that the greatest impact of outcomes-focused regulation is being felt, because of its focus on risk and risk avoidance. For example, a firm in which no partner or employee has ever been guilty of misconduct in the traditional sense, which has complied meticulously with the Accounts Rules and to whom any breach of the rules of conduct would be anathema, may nevertheless feel the full force of regulatory interest and supervision if it constantly struggles to stay within its overdraft limit, and to pay the VAT, PAYE and rent on time. For these are indications that the firm may not be viable, or that the partners are imprudent in terms of the level of drawings.

Not long ago, if the question were to be asked: 'Is it professional misconduct to fail to pay the office rent?' the answer would have been that the regulator was not a debt collection agency and business debts did not raise issues of conduct, although depending on the facts they might trigger a precautionary inspection of the firm's accounts because of the enhanced risk that money might be 'borrowed' from the client account in such circumstances.

The current view would be that the same facts could amount to a breach of outcome 7.4 – which requires a firm to monitor financial stability and take steps to address identified issues. A firm might be required to demonstrate the steps that are being taken to deal with the situation, including redundancy programmes, a freeze on drawings, capital injection, or an acceptance that the business has become unviable and that a plan for the orderly closure of the practice is required, under the SRA's supervision.

The recession which followed the financial crash in 2008 had a substantial impact upon the legal profession. The financial stability of many firms was called into question, and there were a number of high-profile failures of law firms. Much of the SRA's focus and resources during 2012–13 was devoted to this issue, demonstrating the central importance that Chapter 7 of the 2011 Code now has in the regulation of the profession.

4.56

The requirements for supervision are now split between two concepts: supervision of client matters; and ensuring that reserved legal activities and immigration work (in other words, work that is reserved to those statutorily entitled to carry it out, either under the Legal Services Act (LSA) 2007 or the Immigration and Asylum Act 1999) are carried out within a regulated environment.

The requirements for supervision of client matters emphasise the need for regular checking of the quality of work by those of suitable competence and experience.

Both of these changes are to be expected in a regime in which businesses, through an ABS structure, may be supplying regulated and unregulated services; outcome 7.7 is designed to ensure that there is no slippage of regulated services into the unregulated part of the business. An emphasis on checking by suitable people is appropriate when it can no longer be assumed that qualified lawyers will be involved in the day-to-day supply of commoditised legal services, other than in a supervisory role.

4.57

Whereas outcome 7.2 requires systems that are designed to ensure compliance, outcome 7.3 requires firms to identify, monitor and manage 'risks to compliance' and to take steps to address issues identified. This is enhanced by outcome 7.4 requiring firms to monitor risks to financial stability.

A standard question post-2011 might be: 'What are the major risks to compliance and the financial viability of your firm that you have identified, and what steps have you taken to address them?'.

This question could cover the relatively traditional matters – the risk of misappropriation of funds by accounts staff, and the checks and balances established to minimise those risks, but will also relate to larger concepts, such as an over-dependence on work of a particular kind, which could dry up or be lost to competition, or an over-dependence on one or a small number of sources of work the withdrawal of which would threaten the viability of the business.

4.58

There is no reference in this chapter of the 2011 Code to the concept of the person 'qualified to supervise' – a material part of rule 5 of the 2007 Code. At first blush this could have appeared to be a deregulatory move entirely consistent with outcomes-focused regulation, but Chapter 7 of the 2011 Code does not contain a complete list of all the 'outcomes' required for compliant management of the business. Firms must also comply with the SRA Practice Framework Rules, and rule 12 of those rules maintains this aspect of the former rule 5 of the 2007 Code.[1]

SRA Practice Framework Rules 2011

Rule 12: Persons who must be "qualified to supervise"

12.1 The following persons must be "*qualified to supervise*":

(a) a *recognised sole practitioner*;

(b) one of the *lawyer managers* of an *authorised body* or of a *body corporate* which is a *legally qualified body* and which is a *manager* of the *authorised body*;

(c) one of the *solicitors* or *RELs* employed by a law centre in England and Wales, unless the law centre is licensed under Part 5 of the *LSA* in which case the provisions in Rule 12.1(b) will apply; or

(d) one *in-house solicitor* or *in-house REL* in any department in England and Wales where *solicitors* and/or *RELs*, as part of their employment:

(i) do publicly funded work; or

(ii) do or supervise advocacy or the conduct of proceedings for members of the public before a *court* or immigration tribunal.

12.2 To be "*qualified to supervise*" for the purpose of 12.1 a person must:

(a) have completed the training specified from time to time by the *SRA* for this purpose; and

> (b) be a practising *lawyer*, and have been entitled to practise as a *lawyer* for at least 36 months within the last ten years; and
>
> must be able to demonstrate this if asked by the *SRA*.

1 This is expressed in its post-transitional form, effective in part from 31 March 2012 and in part from a later date relating to abolition of the concept of recognised sole practitioners.

4.59

The indicative behaviour as to the safekeeping of documents and client assets entrusted to the firm (indicative behaviour 7.1) is somewhat otiose, and that as to controlling budgets, expenditure and cashflow (7.2) is a reflection of rule 5 of the 2007 Code. Indicative behaviour 7.3 provides a convenient but non-exhaustive list of business risks. Indicative behaviour 7.4, dealing with business continuity, appears to downgrade this obligation from a rule (rule 5.01(1)(k) of the 2007 Code) to a non-binding recommendation, but a better way of considering the matter is that continuity is a business risk, and a risk to the management of client matters, and thus something to be addressed for compliance with outcomes 7.3 and 7.4.

Outsourcing

4.60

The 2011 Code contained for the first time provisions specifically dealing with outsourcing, though the provisions are somewhat unformed and indicative of a recognition on the part of the SRA that regulation is needed in this area, but without as yet much in the way of practical detail. There are some indications that this whole subject was a late entrant to the 2011 Code. Outsourcing is one of the few material words that are not defined in the SRA Handbook Glossary 2012, possibly the only one (there are over 400 words and phrases specifically defined).

On its website the SRA explains that the outsourcing provisions are aimed at firms or in-house solicitors 'who use a third party to undertake work that the firm or in-house solicitor would normally do themselves and for which the firm or in-house solicitor remains responsible'. However, it is also said that 'The outsourcing provisions in the Code … do not apply when you use a specialist service to assist with the provision of legal services to a client, for example instructing counsel, medical experts, tax experts or accountancy services'.

This is neither satisfactory nor consistent. Firms may very frequently instruct counsel in circumstances where it would be 'normal' for the firm to have done the work itself, but where such instruction is an efficient use of time and resources, and no more. The firm would nevertheless remain 'responsible' for the service overall, including the choice of counsel and would (perhaps jointly) be liable for any mistakes in the sense that counsel's advice or drafts could not be uncritically passed on.[1]

1 See *Davy-Chiesman v Davy-Chiesman* [1984] 2 WLR 291, CA per May LJ at 303: 'a solicitor is in general entitled to rely on the advice of counsel properly instructed. However, this does not operate so as to give a solicitor an immunity in every such case. A solicitor is highly trained and rightly expected to be experienced in his particular legal fields. He is under a duty at all times to exercise that degree of care, to both client and the court, that can be expected of a reasonably prudent solicitor. He is not entitled to rely blindly and with no mind of his own on counsel's views'.

4.61

Outcome 7.9 prohibits the outsourcing of reserved legal activities to a person who is not authorised to conduct such activities (since to conduct unauthorised reserved legal activities is unlawful).[1]

Applying the words of the 2011 Code, instructing counsel, at least in cases where this is done for reasons of efficiency or expedience and not, for example, to obtain specialist assistance unavailable within the firm, is subject to outcome 7.10. The SRA website guidance cannot change the interpretation of the Code; that is a matter of statutory construction. It can be a reliable indication as to how the SRA is intending to interpret the rules it has made (always bearing in mind the ephemeral nature of websites and that guidance can change without notice).

What we appear to have here is something of a half-way house where the rules are being supplemented with guidance, while what is needed is a better drafted rule and in particular a better definition of what is really meant by outsourcing.

1 Section 14 of LSA 2007.

4.62

The SRA appears to have two main aims, again as apparent from its website rather than the Code: 'It is important that when firms outsource work this does not affect our ability to regulate the firm's activities and that clients remain fully protected'. So in part this element of regulation is intended to ensure that outsourcing does not take matters outside the ability of the SRA to regulate, as well as stating what might be described as the basic requirement that any practitioner would appreciate.

Outcome 7.10 refers to the outsourcing of 'legal activities or any operational functions that are critical to the delivery of any legal activities'. A legal activity is defined in section 12 of LSA 2007 and includes reserved legal activities[1] and also includes the provision of legal advice or assistance, or representation, in connection with the application of the law or with any form of resolution of legal disputes.

1 The exercise of a right of audience, the conduct of litigation, reserved instrument activities (key elements of conveyancing), probate activities (limited to the application and grant), notarial activities and administration of oaths.

4.63

The SRA has offered a non-exhaustive list of examples of activities which, if outsourced, would be caught by outcome 7.10:

- activities which would normally be conducted by a paralegal;
- initial drafting of contracts;
- legal secretarial services – digital dictation to an outsourced secretarial service for word processing or typing;
- proofreading;
- research;
- document review;
- Companies House filing;

- due diligence, for example, in connection with the purchase of a company;
- IT functions which support the delivery of legal activities;
- business process outsourcing.

None of these activities could be expected to be within the definition of legal activities in relation to either legal advice or representation (as distinct from 'assistance'). In reality it seems that the SRA's view of what constitutes outsourcing is in itself uncontroversial: that it relates to the delivery of services which support the delivery of legal services, without themselves amounting to legal activities, still less reserved legal activities. The problem is in the form of the 2011 Code as currently drafted.

4.64

Outcome 7.10(a) is not controversial and may be said to be stating the obvious. Outcome 7.10(b), on the other hand, could become a substantial problem in requiring contractual arrangements with the outsourcing company that 'enable the SRA or its agent to obtain information from, inspect the records (including electronic records) of, or enter the premises of, the third party, in relation to the outsourced activities or functions'. It is to be hoped that the profession will not have to fund SRA investigation teams jetting off to India, South Africa or the Philippines.

Further, the existence of a clause in a contract between firm and outsourcing company enabling access by the SRA to the company's premises and records will comply with the solicitors' obligations, but it may not be straightforward to enforce that against an unco-operative company in a foreign jurisdiction. It seems likely that the SRA's remedy will be directed to the regulated firm, requiring the determination of the relationship with an unco-operative company.

4.65

Outcome 7.10(c) and (d) are unexceptionable. Those involved or contemplating involvement in outsourcing arrangements are not doing so to prejudice clients; quite the reverse – this is likely to be a client-led initiative in the interests of economy and improved service, particularly where clients are sophisticated users of legal services.

4.66

Matters which firms should focus upon will include quality control and supervision, security (including data protection issues), confidentiality and informed client consent, in addition to a consideration of the proper limits on what may be outsourced (unlikely to be a significant problem) and the new contractual obligations on SRA accessibility.

The first issue is the repute of the outsourcing company. This is a growth field and new entrants to the market are to be expected. It is necessary to investigate the background of the company and to establish reputation by suitable enquiry, including the taking of references if necessary, to review the company's systems for security of data, the control of conflicts, and the protection of client confidentiality. Assurances are required as to the qualifications and competence of those who will be undertaking the work and their supervision, and also as to their ethical standards which can vary by reference to local *mores*. There need to be systems for review of the quality of the work undertaken; how problems are rectified and disputes resolved; what records the outsourcing company is required to keep.

4.67

Although as mentioned outsourcing is likely to be driven by clients, particularly sophisticated clients who may themselves be outsourcing business processes and may demand reduced legal costs on the basis of similar efficiencies, inevitably there are enhanced risks because control of such things as access to premises is not in the hands of the firm. It is important to obtain the informed consent of clients, and for there to be openness in charging. There is no reason why a firm cannot take a profit from outsourcing, just as it takes a profit from the product of its own employees.[1] There is no obligation to charge clients for the outsourced services at cost, any more than there is an obligation to charge for the work of employed staff at no more than their overhead cost to the firm, but equally clients will expect savings to be made and that charging policies are clear.

Finally, it is stating the obvious that outsourcing is not abdication of responsibility; the firm remains entirely responsible.

1 See e.g. *Crane v Canons Leisure Centre* [2008] 1 WLR 2549, CA.

The importance of Chapter 7

4.68

There is a real and substantial new emphasis on the need to identify and assess risks to the business, and risks to compliance in the widest sense, including in particular financial viability. Firms must think about their specific business model, its sustainability and threats to its stability, and must be able to demonstrate an understanding of those risks and what steps have been taken in the light of them.

Further, Chapter 7 cannot be considered in isolation, in terms of the responsibilities associated with running a business authorised by the SRA. A fundamental change is the obligation on all firms including sole practitioners to have a compliance officer for legal practice (COLP) and a compliance officer for finance and administration (COFA) who must be expressly approved in these roles by the SRA. In small firms the same individual may perform both roles, and a sole practitioner may be his or her own COLP and COFA, provided approval is obtained.

For a full review of the relevant rules and the responsibilities of the COLP and COFA see **CHAPTER 6**.

Chapter 8: Publicity

4.69

This chapter is about the manner in which you publicise your *firm* or *in-house practice* or any other businesses. The overriding concern is that *publicity* is not misleading and is sufficiently informative to ensure that *clients* and others can make informed choices.

In your *publicity*, you must comply with statutory requirements and have regard to voluntary codes.

The outcomes in this chapter show how the *Principles* apply in the context of *publicity*.

Outcomes

You must achieve these outcomes:

O(8.1) your *publicity* in relation to your *firm* or *in-house practice* or for any other business is accurate and not misleading, and is not likely to diminish the trust the public places in you and in the provision of legal services;

O(8.2) your *publicity* relating to charges is clearly expressed and identifies whether VAT and *disbursements* are included;

O(8.3) you do not make unsolicited approaches in person or by telephone to *members of the public* in order to publicise your *firm* or *in-house practice* or another business;

O(8.4) *clients* and the public have appropriate information about you, your *firm* and how you are regulated;

O(8.5) your letterhead, website and e-mails show the words "authorised and regulated by the Solicitors Regulation Authority" and either the *firm's* registered name and number if it is an *LLP* or *company* or, if the *firm* is a *partnership* or *sole practitioner*, the name under which it is licensed/authorised by the *SRA* and the number allocated to it by the *SRA*.

Indicative behaviours

Acting in the following way(s) may tend to show that you have achieved these outcomes and therefore complied with the *Principles*:

IB(8.1) where you conduct other regulated activities your *publicity* discloses the manner in which you are regulated in relation to those activities;

IB(8.2) where your *firm* is an *MDP*, any *publicity* in relation to that *practice* makes clear which services are regulated legal services and which are not;

IB(8.3) any *publicity* intended for a jurisdiction outside England and Wales complies with the *Principles*, voluntary codes and the rules in force in that jurisdiction concerning *publicity*;

IB(8.4) where you and another business jointly market services, the nature of the services provided by each business is clear.

Acting in the following way(s) may tend to show that you have not achieved these outcomes and therefore not complied with the *Principles*:

IB(8.5) approaching people in the street, at ports of entry, in hospital or at the scene of an accident; including approaching people to conduct a survey which involves collecting contact details of potential *clients*, or otherwise promotes your *firm* or *in-house practice*;

IB(8.6) allowing any other *person* to conduct *publicity* for your *firm* or *in-house practice* in a way that would breach the *Principles*;

IB(8.7) advertising an estimated fee which is pitched at an unrealistically low level;

IB(8.8) describing overheads of your *firm* (such as normal postage, telephone calls and charges arising in respect of *client* due diligence under the Money Laundering Regulations 2007) as *disbursements* in your advertisements;

IB(8.9) advertising an estimated or fixed fee without making it clear that additional charges may be payable, if that is the case;

IB(8.10) using a name or description of your *firm* or *in-house practice* that includes the word "solicitor(s)" if none of the *managers* are *solicitors*;

IB(8.11) advertising your *firm* or *in-house practice* in a way that suggests that services provided by another business are provided by your *firm* or *in-house practice*;

IB(8.12) producing misleading information concerning the professional status of any *manager* or *employee* of your *firm* or *in-house practice*.

4.70

This chapter is the successor to rule 7 of the 2007 Code and its provisions are not materially different. Publicity is however now comprehensively defined as including:

> 'all promotional material and activity, including the name or description of your firm, stationery, advertisements, brochures, websites, directory entries, media appearances, promotional press releases, and direct approaches to potential clients and other persons, whether conducted in person, in writing, or in electronic form, but does not include press releases prepared on behalf of a client.'

4.71

There are predictable requirements suitable for the ABS era: outcome 8.4 and indicative behaviours 8.1 and 8.2, to ensure that clients are aware of the scope of regulation in a practice supplying regulated and unregulated services.

Indicative behaviour 8.10 reminds us that the title 'Solicitors' can only be used for a firm in which there is at least one solicitor manager.

Indicative behaviour 8.8 is somewhat contentious in stipulating (theoretically by way of non-binding guidance) that the client-specific cost of electronic money laundering due diligence checks may not be described as disbursements. There does not appear, however, to be any reason why the cost could not be re-charged to the client and designated as costs, with VAT, provided that this is part of a transparent charging policy.

Chapter 9: Fee sharing and referrals

4.72

This chapter is about protecting *clients'* interests where you have *arrangements*[1] with third parties who introduce business to you and/or with whom you share your fees. The relationship between *clients* and *firms* should be built on trust, and any such *arrangement* should not jeopardise that trust by, for example, compromising your independence or professional judgement.

The outcomes in this chapter show how the *Principles* apply in the context of fee sharing and *referrals*.

Outcomes

You must achieve these outcomes:

O(9.1) your independence and your professional judgement are not prejudiced by virtue of any *arrangement* with another *person*;

O(9.2) your *clients'* interests are protected regardless of the interests of an *introducer*[2] or *fee sharer* or your interest in receiving *referrals*;

O(9.3) *clients* are in a position to make informed decisions about how to pursue their matter;

O(9.4) *clients* are informed of any financial or other interest which an *introducer* has in referring the *client* to you;

O(9.5) *clients* are informed of any fee sharing *arrangement* that is relevant to their matter;

O(9.6) you do not make payments to an *introducer* in respect of *clients* who are the subject of criminal proceedings or who have the benefit of public funding;

O(9.7) where you enter into a financial *arrangement* with an *introducer* you ensure that the agreement is in writing;

O(9.8) you do not *pay* a *prohibited referral fee*.

Indicative behaviours

Acting in the following way(s) may tend to show that you have achieved these outcomes and therefore complied with the *Principles*:

IB(9.1) only entering into *arrangements* with reputable third parties and monitoring the outcome of those *arrangements* to ensure that *clients* are treated fairly;

IB(9.2) in any case where a *client* has entered into, or is proposing to enter into, an *arrangement* with an *introducer* in connection with their matter, which is not in their best interests, advising the *client* that this is the case;

IB(9.3) terminating any *arrangement* with an *introducer* or *fee sharer* which is causing you to breach the *Principles* or any requirements of the Code;

CHAPTER 4
SRA CODE OF CONDUCT
2011

IB(9.4) being satisfied that any *client* referred by an *introducer* has not been acquired as a result of marketing or other activities which, if done by a *person* regulated by the *SRA*, would be contrary to the *Principles* or any requirements of the Code;

IB(9.5) drawing the *client's* attention to any payments you make, or other consideration you provide, in connection with any *referral*;

IB(9.6) where information needs to be given to a *client*, ensuring the information is clear and in writing or in a form appropriate to the *client's* needs.

IB(9.7) having effective systems in place for assessing whether any *arrangement* complies with statutory and regulatory requirements;

IB(9.8) ensuring that any *payments* you make for services, such as marketing, do not amount to the *payment* of *prohibited referral fees*;

IB(9.9) retaining records and management information to enable you to demonstrate that any *payments* you make are not *prohibited referral fees*.

Acting in the following way(s) may tend to show that you have not achieved these outcomes and therefore not complied with the *Principles*:

IB(9.10) entering into any type of business relationship with a third party, such as an unauthorised *partnership*, which places you in breach of the *SRA Authorisation Rules* or any other regulatory requirements in the Handbook;

IB(9.11) allowing an *introducer* or *fee sharer* to influence the advice you give to *clients*;

IB(9.12) accepting *referrals* where you have reason to believe that *clients* have been pressurised or misled into instructing you.

1 'Arrangement' in relation to financial services, fee sharing and referrals, in Chapters 1, 6 and 9, means any express or tacit agreement between the solicitor and another person, whether contractually binding or not.

2 Any person, business or organisation who or that introduces or refers potential clients to the solicitor's business, or recommends that business to clients or otherwise puts solicitors and clients in touch with each other.

4.73

The somewhat bland words of the introduction to Chapter 9 mask what were in fact fundamental changes to the regulation of referral arrangements and fee sharing in the 2011 Code. Old prohibitions and conditions were swept away, and the result is a less complex system than existed under the 2007 Code. We shall examine referral fees in personal injury cases; the provisions of the 2011 Code in non-personal injury cases; and the abolition of the rule against fee sharing.

Referral fees: introduction

4.74

No subject has been more controversial for solicitors than the payment of referral fees by solicitors to introducers. The profession itself has been sharply divided over the issue. One part regards the whole idea of buying work, and thereby increasing the basic overhead cost of conducting a client's case, to be distasteful, and damaging in tending to increase costs. The other maintains that solicitors' practices are businesses, that the payment of commissions for the introduction of work is a common and inevitable feature of business life, and that a return to more restrictive practices would defy the marketplace, which never really works, and in any event it would probably be unlawful as being anti-competitive. From 2004 until the passing of the Legal Aid, Sentencing and Punishment of Offenders Act (LASPOA) 2012, this liberal attitude prevailed. However, LASPOA 2012 has turned the clock back and, with effect from 1 April 2013, the profession has again had to come to terms with the fact that in personal injury cases, solicitors cannot pay referral fees.

In his *Review of Civil Litigation Costs: Final Report* (published in 2010), Lord Justice Jackson recommended the abolition of referral fees, alternatively their capping at £200. The Government issued a Green Paper late in 2010, and consultation upon it closed at the end of February 2011. The Green Paper did not make any recommendation as to the future of referral fees: the Government was apparently awaiting the Report of the Legal Services Board (LSB) before making its decision. That Report emerged in May 2011 and concluded that the purely regulatory case for a general ban in the legal services market had not been made out. This was because sufficient evidence of consumer detriment, which would have been needed to merit a ban, had not been found.

During the summer of 2011, a number of politicians called publicly for the banning of referral fees. They had become concerned both by the so-called 'compensation culture' that had grown over the previous decade leading to some spurious or exaggerated claims, and by the aggressive, often unscrupulous, and on occasions fraudulent activities of those who sought, for commercial gain, to incite personal injury victims to make legal claims in respect of the injuries they had sustained. This political campaign proved to be very successful, and the necessary provisions were somewhat hastily inserted into the Bill that was making its way through Parliament.

4.75

Other than arrangements caught by sections 56 to 60 of LASPOA 2012, there is no inhibition against the payment by solicitors of referral fees in the general law.

As for agreements between introducers and their clients entered into before the client is introduced to the solicitor, solicitors may need to consider the doctrine of unconscionable bargain. In *Strydom v Vendside Limited*,[1] in which an attempt was made to set aside an agreement with a claims handling company associated with the Union of Democratic Mineworkers. Blair J, on appeal from the county court judge's decision, summarised the law on unconscionable bargains as follows (at [36]):

> 'before the court will consider setting a contract aside as an unconscionable bargain, one party has to have been disadvantaged in some relevant way as regards the other party, that other party must have exploited that disadvantage in some morally culpable manner, and the resulting transaction must be overreaching and oppressive. No single one of these factors is sufficient – all three elements must be proved, otherwise the enforceability of contracts is undermined (see the reasoning in Goff & Jones, *The Law of Restitution*, 7th edition, para 12–006). Where all these requirements are met, the burden

then passes to the other party to satisfy the court that the transaction was fair, just and reasonable (*Snell's Equity*, 31st edition, para 8–47).'

1 [2009] EWHC 2130 (QB).

The referral fee ban in personal injury cases: sections 56 to 60 of LASPOA 2012

4.76

LASPOA 2012[1] received Royal Assent on 1 May 2012, and sections 56 to 60, which contain the referral fee ban, came into force in April 2013. In March 2013, the SRA published guidance to enable practitioners to plan for the forthcoming changes with a reasonably clear view of what the regulator regarded as acceptable and unacceptable arrangements. This was particularly helpful in explaining the SRA's interpretation of the statute, what was prohibited and, constructively, what in the SRA's interpretation was not prohibited.

In October 2013, just six months after the referral fee ban came into force, the SRA issued a warning notice to practitioners who have arrangements with introducers in connection with personal injury work. The full text of the warning notice is at **APPENDIX 6**. The reason for issuing the warning notice was explained thus:

> 'We know that the ban on referral fees has raised difficult issues in relation to its application and interpretation. We are also aware that, because of the wording of LASPO [alternative abbreviation of LASPOA 2012], it is possible for firms to have arrangements that involve the introduction of personal injury work without being in breach of LASPO. We are concerned, however, that in setting up arrangements in a way that does not breach LASPO, firms are failing to consider their wider duties to their clients and others, and in doing so may be breaching the Principles or failing to achieve the Outcomes. Examples include:
>
> - agreeing with an introducer to deduct money from clients' damages;
> - inappropriate outsourcing of work to introducers;
> - referrals to other service providers which are not in the best interests of clients;
> - failure to properly advise clients about the costs and how their claim should be funded; and lack of transparency about the arrangement.'

This guidance was rather less helpful and in many respects caused some confusion. For example, because LASPOA 2012 removed the principal source of income of many introducers including claims management companies, it would be expected that where a genuine service was provided such companies would charge for it. Further, Parliament had expressly sanctioned this because the Damages-Based Agreements Regulations 2013, SI 2013/609, provided for permissible DBAs with claims management companies. By regulation 1(2) of those regulations a representative with whom a DBA could be entered into is defined as: 'the person providing the advocacy services, litigation services or claims management services to which the damages-based agreement relates'.

It was therefore illogical for the SRA to object, in principle, to any deduction from damages arising from such authorised and regulated activity, and no solicitor could realistically be expected to fail to obtain any necessary client consent.

The overall impression given by this guidance was that it reflected certain extremes of behaviour which the SRA encountered, the details of which were not disclosed, and that it was likely to be unhelpful and confusing to those who were trying to get it right (the kind of people who would read warnings from the SRA).

1 LASPOA 2012 currently only affects the relationship between introducers and law firms in relation to claims for personal injury or death.

Mechanism of the ban

4.77

By section 56(1) and (2), a regulated person is in breach of the section if he refers prescribed legal business to another and is paid for the referral; or if the regulated person pays or has paid for the referral of prescribed legal business. Regulated persons are defined in section 59, and in simple terms are persons regulated by the Financial Conduct Authority, the Ministry of Justice, the Law Society and the Bar Council, in other words barristers, solicitors, claims management companies and insurers. The definition of prescribed legal business is complex and requires consideration of section 56(4) and (6) of LASPOA 2012, and section 12(3) of LSA 2007. Initially, the ban will be restricted to legal services relating to claims for personal injury and death: other areas of legal work where referral fees are commonplace, such as conveyancing and non-personal injury claims, e.g. damage-only accidents, and claims arising out of allegedly missold payment protection insurance, are untouched. However, the Lord Chancellor has power to make regulations to widen the definition of prescribed legal business.[1]

1 See section 56(4)(c) of LASPOA 2012.

4.78

A referral is defined in section 56(5): there is a referral if a person (not the client) provides information to another person and it is information that a solicitor would need to make an offer to act for a client. Thus in the typical scenario of a claims management company and a solicitor, the introducer will pass on the details of the prospective client: the solicitor will then make contact with the client. Such a situation is clearly caught by the legislation if a payment is made. Where, however, the flow of information is in a different direction, e.g. where the introducer gives information about the solicitor to the prospective client, and the client is then left to contact the solicitor if he or she so chooses, this would not be a referral within the meaning of the Act.

The following extract from the March 2013 guidance published by the SRA confirms the correctness of this analysis:

> **14.** We consider that the communication of a client's name and contact details to or by a regulated person would amount to a referral, as this information would enable the recipient to make an offer to the client to provide relevant services.

15. Example: An insurance company has an agreement with a firm of solicitors for the referral of clients. The insurance company is contacted by the claimant who notifies the insurer of a claim involving personal injury. The client's details are provided to the firm, who write to the claimant/client offering their services. The firm pays a fee for each email sent from the website. We would regard this as a referral because the insurer has passed to the firm information which will enable the firm to offer to act for the claimant.

16. Example: A website offers to find a suitable firm of solicitors for members of the public. The potential client is required to input their postcode and the area of law in which they need help. They then receive an email providing contact details of a suitable firm in their area.

17. We do not consider that this amounts to a referral within the terms of LASPO as the potential client's details are not being provided to the firm. (However, the transparency requirements set out in Chapter 9 of the SRA Code of Conduct 2011 would still apply.)'

4.79

By section 56(8), payment includes any form of consideration (whether the benefit is received by the solicitor or a third party) but excludes the provision of reasonable hospitality.

Enforcing the ban

4.80

Parliament has thrown the responsibility for monitoring and enforcing the referral fee ban upon the regulators, who must ensure that they have appropriate arrangements in place and may make rules for this purpose.[1] As a result, the SRA amended the 2011 Code to add outcomes 6.4 and 9.8 and indicative behaviour 9.8 with effect from 1 April 2013.

1 See section 57(1)–(3) of LASPOA 2012.

4.81

LASPOA 2012 provides that a breach of section 56 does not make the perpetrator guilty of a criminal offence, nor does it give rise to an action for breach of statutory duty.[1] A breach of section 56 does not make anything void or unenforceable, but a contract to make or pay for a referral or arrangement in breach of that section is unenforceable.[2]

1 See section 57(5) of LASPOA 2012.
2 See section 57(6).

Anti-avoidance provisions

4.82

The pre-2004 ban was widely circumvented by solicitors. Instead of paying referral fees *per se*, solicitors paid 'administration fees' or 'marketing fees' for services allegedly provided by the latter. The SRA was doubtless anxious to prevent a return to those days, and as a result section 57 of LASPOA 2012 includes within it some important anti-avoidance provisions.

4.83

Section 57(7) provides in substance from a solicitor's perspective that where a referral is made to a solicitor and it appears to the SRA that payment by the solicitor may be a referral fee, subsection (8) will apply. That subsection provides that rules under section 57(2) may provide for the payment to be treated as a referral fee unless the solicitor shows that the payment was made (a) as consideration for the provision of services, or (b) for another reason, and not as a referral fee. The sting is in section 57(9), which provides that a payment which would otherwise be regarded as consideration for the provision of services of any description may be treated as a referral fee if it exceeds the amount specified in relation to services of that description in regulations made by the Lord Chancellor.

4.84

Some commentators have expressed the view that these subsections permit a kind of pre-2004 device, i.e. payments being made for 'services' to avoid the ban, but it is submitted that this is plainly not so. Regulations made under section 57(2) could not have the effect of changing the definition of what is prohibited by virtue of section 56. Rather, a statutory mechanism has been created in deliberately vague terms (to cater for business ingenuity) to enable regulators to identify arrangements which on the surface would not offend section 56, but avoid the legislative intent. In reality, section 56 may be so effective in its terms that these anti-avoidance provisions may prove to be unnecessary. If it becomes necessary to deploy them it is unclear precisely how the Lord Chancellor will decide upon an approved fee or cost for a particular kind of service.

The referral fee ban and ABSs

4.85

Although the creation of ABSs under LSA 2007 was unconnected with the new referral fee ban, on the face of it introducers and solicitors should be able to surmount the difficulties caused by the ban by joining forces in an ABS. As soon as solicitor and introducer are under the same legal roof as part of the same legal entity there can no longer be a 'referral', which requires information flowing from one legal person to another. In its discussion paper, the SRA recognised this:

> 'Concern has been expressed that businesses may become ABSs in order to circumvent the ban. For example, a claims management company might join forces with a firm of solicitors to form an ABS, which would do all of the work previously carried out by the two different businesses within one entity. There would be no need for referrals, and therefore no referral fees would be paid. We believe that provided that all of the requirements for authorisation are met and the ABS complies with all of its regulatory obligations, we cannot seek to prevent such arrangements simply because they are set up to avoid being caught by the ban. An ABS is a legitimate form of business, supported by a strong statutory and regulatory framework.'

The referral fee ban and collective advertising by solicitors

4.86

There have been a number of successful schemes under which solicitors have pooled resources and created a third party organisation such as Injury Lawyers 4U, and National Accident Helpline, to carry out advertising and marketing on behalf of the firms, and then to refer claims generated by such activities to the solicitors on their panels. On the face of it, these collective schemes have the potential to be caught by the referral fee ban. However, where enforcement of the ban has been delegated by Parliament to the regulators, the view of the latter will be of decisive importance. The SRA's March 2013 guidance contained the following:

> **21.** Our view is that where there is a referral of a matter to or by a regulated person, or an arrangement for another person to provide services, a payment will be prohibited to the extent that it is being paid for the referral or arrangement. Where a payment is for the provision of other services of for another reason, the payment would not be in breach of LASPO.
>
> **22.** This may cause difficulties where a third party refers clients to a firm of solicitors in addition to or in the course of providing other services such as marketing.
>
> **23.** Example: a company carries out marketing for a group of firms. Enquiries are made to a call centre, details of potential clients are passed to member firms on a rota basis and each firm pays an equal share of the costs of advertising and operating the scheme. There has been a referral within the terms of LASPO because the details of potential clients have been passed to firms by the company carrying out the marketing. The firms involved will need to be satisfied that any payments they make to the marketing company are for the marketing and not for the referral of clients. If a payment is made for each "lead" or the payment varies according to the number of referrals made, this is likely to suggest that the payment is for the referrals rather than for the marketing. Even if there is no specific number of leads guaranteed the solicitor would need to be satisfied that the payment they are making is reasonable in view of the services being provided.
>
> **24.** If it appears to us that a payment may have been made for a referral or for making an arrangement, we will treat that as a prohibited referral fee for the purposes of LASPO, unless the regulated person can show that the payment was made for services or for another reason and not as a referral fee. Where you advertise jointly and pay only for that service, you are unlikely to breach the provisions of LASPO – however, you will need to be satisfied that the arrangement does not contain a referral fee element.
>
> **25.** Example: A CMC advertises in local newspapers in its own name and has a panel of firms to which they refer cases. When a potential client contacts the CMC, the CMC takes brief details and asks a standard set of questions to ensure the claim is not time barred. The client is told that a solicitor will contact them within the next 24 hours. Firms pay a fixed fee in respect of each client referred. The CMC says that the payments are for advertising, operating the call centre and vetting potential claims.

26. A firm in this situation would need to show that the payments were genuinely for the services described. In this case the vetting would appear to be minimal and it is difficult to see how the payment for advertising could be genuine as it is being paid "per client" rather than reflecting the actual cost of advertising. It is therefore likely that the payment would include a referral fee element.

27. When determining whether referral fees are being paid, we will take into account all of the circumstances but the following factors may indicate a prohibited referral fee:

- payment for services appear to be excessive;
- an arrangement where receipt of referrals is conditional upon payment;
- payments that are made per referral or which are otherwise linked to the number of referrals;
- no evidence that a genuine service is being provided.

28. Where it appears to us that a referral fee may have been paid, the onus will be on the regulated person to demonstrate that the payment was not for the referral (reference section 57(7) of LASPO). Firms should therefore fully investigate all relevant matters before making or receiving referrals of prescribed legal business.'

The SRA amended the 2011 Code to add indicative behaviour 9.8, 'ensuring that any payments you make for services, such as marketing, do not amount to the payment of prohibited referral fees'. In the light of the SRA guidance, genuine collective marketing schemes based upon a 'cost plus' model, ought to be seen as compliant by the regulator.

Referral arrangements in the 2011 Code

4.87

It should be stressed that the referral fee ban currently applies only to personal injury cases. In most other areas of practice, solicitors may pay referral fees to introducers, and the solicitor's conduct is governed by the provisions of the 2011 Code.

The outcomes required by Chapter 9 of the 2011 Code centre upon maintaining the solicitor's independence, protecting the best interests of clients and ensuring transparency. The Chapter 1 outcomes are also relevant in this context: the client must be treated fairly. Although outcome 9.4 requires that clients are informed of any financial interest which an introducer has in referring the client to the solicitor, the provision does not mandate when this has to be done. Indicative behaviour 1.4 to Chapter 1 suggests that solicitors should explain any arrangements such as fee sharing or referral arrangements which are relevant to the client's instructions. Outcome 9.7 requires financial arrangements between solicitors and introducers to be in writing, and outcome 9.6 outlaws referral fees in respect of clients who are the subject of criminal proceedings or who have the benefit of public funding.

4.88

The nearest that the SRA has come to giving guidance to the interpretation of relevant outcomes is a series of 'Q and As' on its website. The answer to the question 'When do I have to give this information to clients?' is:

> 'The outcomes do not specify when the information should be provided. However, in order to achieve outcome 9.3, you will need to consider whether you need to give the information before the client has committed themselves to instructing your firm i.e. at the outset of the matter. The nature of the referral arrangement may affect the client's decision to instruct your firm.'

It would however be equally logical, and much easier in pragmatic terms, if solicitors used the medium of routine client care documents to provide this information, provided there is no detriment or prejudice to clients or potential clients if they were to decide to terminate the retainer in the light of the disclosure of a referral arrangement.

Solicitors must also have in mind indicative behaviour 9.6, which requires information to be clear and in writing, or in a form appropriate to the client's needs, where, for instance, the client may have difficulty in reading English.

4.89

On the other hand, in the absence of any specific rule to that effect solicitors can now safely abandon any attempt to require the introducer to provide information to clients. Claims management companies and other introducers are regulated by the Ministry of Justice under the Compensation Act 2006, and are subject to their own suite of regulatory rules. In the absence of any specific requirement in the 2011 Code upon solicitors to police the activities of introducers, the old provisions in rules 9.01(2), 9.02(a), (b) (e) and (f) of the 2007 Code can no longer apply. They will not be missed.

4.90

The provision in rule 9.02(c) of the 2007 Code that solicitors must be satisfied that the introducers had not referred clients acquired as a result of marketing, etc. activities which would breach SRA rules if done by a solicitor (the most obvious example being cold calling) is specifically retained in indicative behaviour 9.4.

4.91

A further important change is that the referral provisions in Chapter 9 now apply to referrals between lawyers. Rule 9 of the 2007 Code did not apply to such referrals, by virtue of a specific exception in rule 9.01(3). Such referrals now have to be disclosed to clients and, if a referral fee is paid, that too must be disclosed in writing (outcome 9.4 and indicative behaviours 9.5 and 9.6).

Pre-retainer arrangements between clients and introducers: indicative behaviour 9.2

4.92

Indicative behaviour 9.2 requires special mention: it provides that where a client *has entered into* or proposes to enter into an arrangement with an introducer in connection with their matter, which is not in the client's best interests, solicitors should advise the client that this is the case.

Until recent years, it has not been suggested that solicitors are under any duty to advise their clients as to the wisdom or otherwise of contractual arrangements that they (the clients) may have made before instructing the solicitor. Indeed the imposition of such a duty in the general law is fraught with danger, and the courts have consistently pointed out the limits of a solicitor's retainer. In the words of Lord Jauncey in *Clark Boyce v Mouat* [1994] 1 AC 428, at 437D:

> 'When a client in full command of his faculties and apparently aware of what he is doing seeks the assistance of a solicitor in the carrying out of a particular transaction, that solicitor is under no duty whether before or after accepting instructions to go beyond those instructions by proffering unsought advice on the wisdom of the transaction. To hold otherwise could impose intolerable burdens on solicitors.'

However, in some of the disciplinary prosecutions arising out of the miners' compensation cases, and later in disciplinary prosecutions arising out of the activities of an organisation known as Justice Direct, the Tribunal held that solicitors should have advised clients about agreements with introducers entered into before instruction of the solicitors, by which the client agreed to yield up a proportion of their compensation to the introducer.

4.93

The wording of indicative behaviour 9.2 is very wide. For instance, what is the solicitor to do where the client is introduced by an estate agent who charges significantly more than its competitors, with no apparent added value for the client? Is the solicitor to advise the new client that he or she is paying far too much to the estate agency which has introduced the client to the solicitor? In the judgment in the *Beresford* appeal[1] the Divisional Court discussed this issue at some length ([61]–[80] inclusive) but declined to decide it; observing that:

> 'It would for instance be a distraction to set about determining whether the Vendside agreements were indeed unenforceable in law. They were certainly questionable, as Beresfords knew or ought to have known. Vendside were not providing the services for which the fee was stated to be payable.'

The court appeared to take the view that there was an obligation to advise that the agreement was 'questionable' (at [75]). There remains uncertainty. In the *Beresford* case itself, the Tribunal provided some guidance as to what was expected of solicitors acting for claimants in the miners' compensation cases:

> 'The Tribunal had no doubt it was part of Beresfords' retainer for them to read the agreement and comment on it to ensure the miners fully

> understood what they had agreed to and to indicate to them that there was some uncertainty about the agreement and therefore about their deductions from their compensation.'[2]

1 *Beresford and Smith v SRA* [2009] EWHC 3155 (Admin).
2 SDT 9666–2007 at para 156.

4.94

After its success in the *Beresford* case, the SRA prosecuted four separate sole practitioner solicitors who had accepted work from Justice Direct, an organisation that charged a hefty slice of a client's damages for doing little more than finding a solicitor for the client. All four admitted the allegations, and the Tribunal followed its approach in *Beresford* by agreeing that the failure to alert the clients to the disadvantageous nature of the Justice Direct contract amounted to professional misconduct. In the first such case, *Tilbury*,[1] the Tribunal stated:

> 'The Tribunal was satisfied that by entering into the agreement with Justice Direct, the Respondent effectively disabled himself from advising his clients as to the desirability of the client becoming liable to pay 25% of any recoverable damages to Justice Direct in return for an introduction to the solicitor. The benefits to the client of entering into the Purchase Order were claimed to be some initial screening of the claim and introduction of a suitably qualified solicitor. Neither in the Tribunal's view could justify the payment to Justice Direct of so disproportionate a share of the damages awarded to the client and the Tribunal considered that no competent solicitor rendering advice in the best interests of the client could recommend the client to enter into such an agreement.'

Both the Justice Direct cases and *Beresford* are therefore consistent with a duty to advise in relation to a pre-existing contract, if on the facts there is something obviously inaccurate or uncertain, or a fee that is apparently wholly unreasonable and disproportionate. The question remains open as to what, in the case of a lawful contract, which is unreasonable and unfair, but not unconscionable and liable to be set aside, solicitors are expected to advise. They may find themselves in an unenviable position, in breach of regulatory duty if they stay silent, and at risk of committing the tort of inducing a breach of contract if they advise in accordance with indicative behaviour 9.2. It may not be very constructive, but it would be compliant, for solicitors to 'advise' that the client would have been better not to have entered into the agreement, but that nothing can now be done about it.

1 SDT 9880–2008.

Involvement of the introducer after the case has been referred to the solicitor

4.95

One of the legitimate concerns of the SRA in policing referral fee arrangements is that solicitors may develop an unhealthy dependence upon a flow of work from a particular introducer, and then permit the introducer an inappropriate degree of control over how the solicitor carries out the work. An introducer has a legitimate interest in ensuring that the chosen solicitor carries out the work to a reasonable standard, as the introducer has entrusted the client to the solicitor. It is commonplace to see agreements between solicitors and introducers by which the introducer has the right to audit the work of the solicitor. However, unless dealt with in the agreement between introducer and client and/or the retainer letter between solicitor and client, such a right of audit may cut across the confidentiality that is owed by the solicitor to the client. Appropriate contractual provisions can reduce or eliminate any regulatory concern on that front, but solicitors should be aware that the SRA remains very concerned at the ability of introducers to weaken the independence of solicitors' advice to their clients. Indicative behaviour 9.11 warns specifically against allowing an introducer or fee sharer to influence the advice given by a solicitor to his or her client. Likewise, indicative behaviour 9.12 warns against accepting referrals where the solicitor has reason to believe that clients have been pressurised or misled into instructing them.

Fee sharing

4.96

The rule against solicitors fee sharing with non-solicitors was traditionally based upon the risk of a non-solicitor having an inappropriate amount of influence over a solicitor in the handling of a claim for a client. It was steadily eroded over the years. Historically, there was an absolute prohibition, but that was relaxed in March 2004 to permit fee sharing with those who introduced capital or services into a firm. Rule 8.02 of the 2007 Code maintained this exception. Because the former Practice Rules (and therefore the Solicitors' Code of Conduct 2007) had the effect of subordinate legislation enacted for the protection of the public,[1] the rule against fee sharing with non-solicitors rendered an agreement to share fees in breach of the rule illegal and unenforceable.[2]

The advent of alternative business structures means that the old objection to fee sharing between solicitors and non-solicitors has fallen away. The whole purpose of the reforms is to permit non-lawyers to share profits with solicitors. Fee sharing will be inevitable where, for instance, a company merges with a firm of solicitors to create an ABS, or sets up an SRA-regulated subsidiary to provide legal services to existing clients. If fee sharing will be permissible *within* one overall corporate structure from October 2011, there is no logical reason why fee sharing *between* two independent corporate structures should be outlawed. In order to make such an important distinction, clear rules would have to be made so that solicitors could know where they stood.

1 *Swain v Law Society* [1983] 1 AC 598, HL.
2 *Mohamed v Alaga & Co (a firm)* [1999] 3 All ER 699, CA; *Westlaw Services Limited and anor v Boddy* [2010] EWCA Civ 929.

4.97

The only specific references to fee sharing in the 2011 Code are in Chapter 1 – indicative behaviour 1.4 – 'explaining any arrangements, such as fee sharing or referral arrangements, which are relevant to the client's instructions' and Chapter 9 – particularly outcome 9.2 and indicative behaviours 9.3 and 9.11. These make it clear that fee sharing is no longer outlawed. In a nutshell, solicitors simply have to (a) be transparent to clients about arrangements with fee sharers; (b) ensure that there is no sacrifice of their independence (i.e. permitting the fee sharer inappropriate influence); and (c) ensure that the best interests of clients remain paramount.

Chapter 10: You and your regulator

4.98

This chapter is about co-operation with your regulators and ombudsmen, primarily the *SRA* and the *Legal Ombudsman*.

The information which we request from you will help us understand any risks to *clients*, and the public interest more generally.

The outcomes in this chapter show how the *Principles* apply in the context of you and your regulator.

Outcomes

You must achieve these outcomes:

O(10.1) you ensure that you comply with all the reporting and notification requirements in the Handbook that apply to you;

O(10.2) you provide the *SRA* with information to enable the *SRA* to decide upon any application you make, such as for a practising certificate, registration, recognition or a licence and whether any conditions should apply;

O(10.3) you notify the *SRA* promptly of any material changes to relevant information about you including serious financial difficulty, action taken against you by another regulator and serious failure to comply with or achieve the *Principles*, rules, outcomes and other requirements of the Handbook;

O(10.4) you report to the *SRA* promptly, serious misconduct by any person or *firm* authorised by the *SRA*, or any *employee*, *manager* or *owner* of any such *firm* (taking into account, where necessary, your duty of confidentiality to your *client*);

O(10.5) you ensure that the *SRA* is in a position to assess whether any persons requiring prior approval are fit and proper at the point of approval and remain so;

O(10.6) you co-operate fully with the *SRA* and the *Legal Ombudsman* at all times including in relation to any investigation about a *claim for redress* against you;

O(10.7) you do not attempt to prevent anyone from providing information to the *SRA* or the *Legal Ombudsman*;

O(10.8) you comply promptly with any written notice from the *SRA*;

O(10.9) pursuant to a notice under Outcome 10.8, you:

- (a) produce for inspection by the *SRA* *documents*[1] held by you, or held under your control;
- (b) provide all information and explanations requested; and
- (c) comply with all requests from the *SRA* as to the form in which you produce any *documents* you hold electronically, and for photocopies of any *documents* to take away;

in connection with your *practice* or in connection with any trust of which you are, or formerly were, a trustee;

O(10.10) you provide any necessary permissions for information to be given, so as to enable the *SRA* to:

(a) prepare a report on any *documents* produced; and

(b) seek verification from *clients*, staff and the banks, building societies or other financial institutions used by you;

O(10.11) when required by the *SRA* in relation to a matter specified by the *SRA*, you:

(a) act promptly to investigate whether any *person* may have a *claim for redress*[2] against you;

(b) provide the *SRA* with a report on the outcome of such an investigation, identifying *persons* who may have such a claim;

(c) notify *persons* that they may have a right of redress against you, providing them with information as to the nature of the possible claim, about the *firm's complaints* procedure and about the *Legal Ombudsman*; and

(d) ensure, where you have identified a *person* who may have a *claim for redress*, that the matter is dealt with under the *firm's complaints* procedure as if that *person* had made a *complaint*;

O(10.12) you do not attempt to abrogate to any third party your regulatory responsibilities in the Handbook, including the role of Compliance Officer for Legal Practice (*COLP*) or Compliance Officer for Finance and Administration (*COFA*);

O(10.13) once you are aware that your *firm* will cease to *practise*, you effect the orderly and transparent wind-down of activities, including informing the *SRA* before the *firm* closes.

Indicative behaviours

Acting in the following way(s) may tend to show that you have achieved these outcomes and therefore complied with the *Principles*:

IB(10.1) actively monitoring your achievement of the outcomes in order to improve standards and identify non-achievement of the outcomes;

IB(10.2) actively monitoring your financial stability and viability in order to identify and mitigate any risks to the public;

IB(10.3) notifying the *SRA* promptly of any indicators of serious financial difficulty, such as inability to pay your professional indemnity insurance premium, or rent or salaries, or breach of bank covenants;

IB(10.4) notifying the *SRA* promptly when you become aware that your business may not be financially viable to continue trading as a going concern, for example because of difficult trading conditions, poor cash flow, increasing overheads, loss of *managers*[3] or *employees* and/or loss of sources of revenue;

IB(10.5) notifying the *SRA* of any serious issues identified as a result of monitoring referred to in IB10.1 and IB10.2 above, and producing a plan for remedying issues that have been identified;

IB(10.6) responding appropriately to any serious issues identified concerning competence and fitness and propriety of your *employees*, *managers* and *owners*;

IB(10.7) reporting disciplinary action taken against you by another regulator;

IB(10.8) informing the *SRA* promptly when you become aware of a significant change to your *firm*, for example:

(a) key personnel, such as a *manager*, *COLP* or *COFA*, joining or leaving the *firm*;

(b) a merger with, or an acquisition by or of, another *firm*;

IB(10.9) having appropriate arrangements for the orderly transfer of *clients*' property to another *authorised body* if your *firm* closes;

IB(10.10) having a "whistle-blowing" policy.

Acting in the following way(s) may tend to show that you have not achieved these outcomes and therefore not complied with the *Principles*:

IB(10.11) entering into an agreement which would attempt to preclude the *SRA* or the *Legal Ombudsman* from investigating any actual or potential *complaint* or allegation of professional misconduct;

IB(10.12) unless you can properly allege malice, issuing defamation proceedings in respect of a *complaint* to the *SRA*.

1 This includes documents, whether written or electronic, relating to the firm's client accounts and office accounts.

2 As defined in the SRA Handbook Glossary 2012, this has the same meaning as in section 158 of LSA 2007, which does not contain any definition, but provides: 'Section 157 does not prohibit the regulatory arrangements of an approved regulator from making provision requiring, or authorising the approved regulator to require, a relevant authorised person (a) to investigate whether there are any persons who may have a claim against the relevant authorised person in relation to a matter specified by the approved regulator'.

3 Meaning a partner in a partnership, a member of an LLP, a director of a company, or a member of the governing body of any other body.

4.99

Chapter 10 appears to represent a return to the type of prescriptive rule-making which has been abandoned in the remainder of the 2011 Code. Consisting of 13 outcomes and 12 indicative behaviours, it is second only to Chapter 1 in the amount of regulation that it contains. The clear message for solicitors is that all of those regulated by the SRA must co-operate in all respects with their regulator.

For the most part, the contents of Chapter 10 speak for themselves. The following alterations to what has gone before are particularly worthy of note.

Self-reporting

4.100

The 2011 Code introduces for the first time, by outcome 10.3, an unequivocal duty upon a solicitor to report his or her own professional misconduct: solicitors must report 'serious failure to comply with or achieve the Principles, rules, outcomes and other requirements of the Handbook' by themselves (outcome 10.3) and 'serious misconduct by any person or firm authorised by the SRA, or any employee, manager or owner of any such firm' (outcome 10.4). There is now therefore clearly an obligation upon solicitors to self-report, and report any serious misconduct within their own organisation.

Continuing obligations

4.101

The terms of outcome 10.5 are very wide – the SRA must be put in the picture about those who require prior approval, not only at the point of the application for such approval, but at all times thereafter.

Non-delegation of regulatory duties

4.102

Outcome 10.12 is new, and is designed to prevent solicitors from delegating performance of their regulatory duties to third parties, particularly the COLP or the COFA.

Financial difficulty

4.103

There is a new emphasis upon informing the SRA when financial difficulties arise in a regulated entity (see outcomes 10.3 and 10.13, indicative behaviours 10.2, 10.3, 10.4, 10.9). This is a direct result of the recession and the difficult trading conditions faced by solicitors since 2008. It can also be seen as a corollary of the obligations in Chapter 7 concerning the management of the business, and the identification and management of the risks to financial stability. The SRA is anxious to ensure the orderly wind-down of law firms where the business is failing, so as to avoid the costs and distress of an intervention. The sooner that the SRA is informed about an entity's financial problems, the greater will be the opportunity to avoid an intervention. Costs of interventions tend to be very high, and to fall for the most part upon the profession rather than the intervened-upon solicitor, who rarely has the funds to discharge the obligation to pay those costs.[1]

1 The costs of an intervention are recoverable from the intervened-upon solicitor as a debt by virtue of para 13 of Schedule 1 to the Solicitors Act 1974.

Schemes of redress

4.104

Outcome 10.11 effectively permits the SRA to require solicitors to *investigate* whether a person may have a claim for redress; to *report* the outcome of the investigation; to *notify* persons that they may have a right of redrees, together with providing information about the solicitors' complaints procedures; and to deal with the matter under the firm's complaint s procedure if a complaint is made.

However, solicitors should have in mind section 157(1) of LSA 2007 which provides:

> 'The regulatory arrangements of an approved regulator must not include any provision relating to redress.'

Section 158 provides, so far as relevant:

> '(1) Section 157 does not prohibit the regulatory arrangements of an approved regulator from making provision requiring, or authorising the approved regulator to require, a relevant authorised person –
>
> (a) to investigate whether there are any persons who may have a claim against the relevant authorised person in relation to a matter specified by the approved regulator;
>
> (b) to provide the approved regulator with a report on the outcome of the investigation;
>
> (c) to identify persons ("affected persons") who may have such a claim;
>
> (d) to notify affected persons that they may have such a claim;'

4.105

LSA 2007 does not authorise the SRA to require solicitors to write letters in a particular form drafted by the SRA, or to require solicitors to provide redress. The clear legislative intention is that regulators should *not* be involved in the provision of redress. The role of the regulator, as circumscribed by Parliament, is simply to require solicitors to carry out investigations, identify potential claimants, and then to notify potential claimants that they may have a claim. It is no longer part of the regulator's function effectively to organise a widespread compensation scheme for a solicitor's former clients. That is the function, if appropriate, of the Legal Ombudsman.

Chapter 11: Relations with third parties

4.106

This chapter is about ensuring you do not take unfair advantage of those you deal with and that you act in a manner which promotes the proper operation of the legal system.

This includes your conduct in relation to *undertakings*; there is no obligation to give or receive an *undertaking* on behalf of a *client* but, if you do, you must ensure that you achieve the outcomes listed in this chapter.

The conduct requirements in this area extend beyond professional and business matters. They apply in any circumstances in which you may use your professional title to advance your personal interests.

The outcomes in this chapter show how the *Principles* apply in the context of your relations with third parties.

Outcomes

You must achieve these outcomes:

O(11.1) you do not take unfair advantage of third parties in either your professional or personal capacity;

O(11.2) you perform all *undertakings* given by you within an agreed timescale or within a reasonable amount of time;

O(11.3) where you act for a seller of land, you inform all buyers immediately of the seller's intention to deal with more than one buyer;

O(11.4) you properly administer oaths, affirmations or declarations where you are authorised to do so.

Indicative behaviours

Acting in the following way(s) may tend to show that you have achieved these outcomes and therefore complied with the *Principles*:

IB(11.1) providing sufficient time and information to enable the costs in any matter to be agreed;

IB(11.2) returning documents or money sent subject to an express condition if you are unable to comply with that condition;

IB(11.3) returning documents or money on demand if they are sent on condition that they are held to the sender's order;

IB(11.4) ensuring that you do not communicate with another party when you are aware that the other party has retained a *lawyer* in a matter, except:

(a) to request the name and address of the other party's *lawyer*; or

(b) the other party's *lawyer* consents to you communicating with the *client*; or

(c) where there are exceptional circumstances;

IB(11.5) maintaining an effective system which records when *undertakings* have been given and when they have been discharged;

IB(11.6) where an *undertaking* is given which is dependent upon the happening of a future event and it becomes apparent the future event will not occur, notifying the recipient of this.

Acting in the following way(s) may tend to show that you have not achieved these outcomes and therefore not complied with the *Principles*:

IB(11.7) taking unfair advantage of an opposing party's lack of legal knowledge where they have not instructed a *lawyer*;

IB(11.8) demanding anything for yourself or on behalf of your *client*, that is not legally recoverable, such as when you are instructed to collect a simple debt, demanding from the debtor the cost of the letter of claim since it cannot be said at that stage that such a cost is legally recoverable;

IB(11.9) using your professional status or qualification to take unfair advantage of another *person* in order to advance your personal interests;

IB(11.10) taking unfair advantage of a public office held by you, or a member of your family, or a member of your *firm* or their family.

4.107

The last two sentences of the introduction to Chapter 11 contain an important reminder and warning to solicitors. If they choose to use their status as solicitors, or their firm's notepaper, to conduct essentially private business, they are as much at risk of regulatory action as when they are acting in their ordinary professional capacity.

Taking unfair advantage

4.108

Outcome 11.1 reflects a long-standing rule of professional conduct, previously contained in rule 10.01 of the 2007 Code, that solicitors must not take unfair advantage of anyone. However, the wording of outcome 11.1 is significantly wider than rule 10.01 which provided 'You must not use your position to take unfair advantage of anyone either for your own benefit or for another person's benefit'. The important addition in the 2011 Code is that the outcome specifically includes actions taken in the solicitor's personal capacity. A solicitor will be taking unfair advantage when acting in his or her personal capacity if his or her status as a solicitor, or the trappings of the profession, such as the firm's headed notepaper or professional e-mail address, is used to gain advantage over a third party. The golden rule is that when transacting in a private capacity, solicitors should not state that they are solicitors, and should not use their firm's notepaper (or professional e-mail address unless this is unavoidable).

Practitioners will need to consider virtually all of the indicative behaviours set out above when considering the issue of taking unfair advantage of third parties.

Undertakings

4.109

Outcome 11.2 is concerned with undertakings. An undertaking is defined in the SRA Handbook Glossary 2012 to mean:

> 'a statement, given orally or in writing, whether or not it includes the word "undertake" or "undertaking", made by or on behalf of you or your firm, in the course of practice, or by you outside the course of practice but as a solicitor or REL, to someone who reasonably places reliance on it, that you or your firm will do something or cause something to be done, or refrain from doing something.'

This definition is similar in meaning, though different in sentence construction, to the definition in the 2007 Code, which for the first time placed a solicitor's duty to perform undertakings on a statutory footing.

Outcome 11.2 is a great deal simpler than the equivalent provision in rule 10.05 of the 2007 Code. Two specific provisions that have been *dropped* are:

> '(3) If you give an undertaking which is dependent upon the happening of a future event, you must notify the recipient immediately if it becomes clear that the event will not occur.
>
> (4) When you give an undertaking to pay another's costs, the undertaking will be discharged if the matter does not proceed unless there is an express agreement that the costs are payable in any event.'

Multiple buyers

4.110

Similarly, outcome 11.3 greatly simplifies rule 10.06 of the 2007 Code and is reduced to a single obligation, i.e. to inform all buyers of the seller's intention to deal with more than one buyer. Rule 10.06 had required the solicitor to stop acting where the seller refused to agree to such disclosure, and had provided that the solicitor should not act for both the seller and any of the prospective buyers, or for more than one of the prospective buyers. These prohibitions were not carried forward into the 2011 Code, although a combination of outcome 11.3 and Chapter 3 on conflicts of interest may be thought to achieve the same result. For the position in relation to acting for seller and buyer, see **4.31**.

Administration of oaths, etc.

4.111

The equivalent provision in the 2007 Code (rule 10.03) prevented solicitors from administering oaths or affirmations or taking declarations if their firm was acting for any party in the matter or was otherwise 'interested' in the subject matter. This prohibition has apparently been removed, in the sense that there is simply no reference to it at all, but that is not actually so. Outcome 11.4 requires solicitors to administer oaths properly when 'authorised to do so' leaving the practitioner to apply the law. The former rule simply reflected the prohibition to the same effect in section 81(1) of the Solicitors Act 1974. Section 81 has been repealed by LSA 2007. However, LSA 2007 specifies who may properly carry out the reserved legal activity of administering oaths, and defines this activity by reference (primarily) to the Commissioners for Oaths Act 1889. Section 1(3) of the 1889 Act contains exactly the same provision:

> 'Provided that a commissioner for oaths shall not exercise any of the powers given by this section in any proceeding in which he is interested.'

Chapter 12: Separate businesses

4.112

The purpose of this chapter is to ensure *clients* are protected when they obtain mainstream legal services from a *firm* regulated by the *SRA*. This is accomplished by restricting the services that can be provided through a *separate business* that is not authorised by the *SRA* or another *approved regulator.*

This chapter addresses two kinds of services:

1. those which you cannot offer through a *separate business* ("*prohibited separate business activities*"). These are "mainstream" legal services which members of the public would expect you to offer as a *lawyer* regulated by the *SRA* or another *approved regulator*, and
2. those which you can offer either through a *separate business* ("*a permitted separate business*"), or through an *authorised body*. These are the kind of services a member of the public would not necessarily expect to be provided only by a *lawyer* regulated by the *SRA* or another *approved regulator,* but which are "solicitor-like" services.

Clients of a *permitted separate business* will not have the same statutory protections as *clients* of an *authorised body* and it is important that this is clear to *clients* of the *separate business,* particularly where they are being referred from one business to the other.

The outcomes in this chapter show how the *Principles* apply in the context of *separate businesses.*

Outcomes

You must achieve these outcomes:

O(12.1) you do not:

(a) *own*;[1] or

(b) *actively participate in*,[2]

a *separate business* which conducts *prohibited separate business activities*;

O(12.2) if you are a *firm*:

(a) you are not *owned by*; or

(b) *connected with*,

a *separate business* which conducts *prohibited separate business activities*;

O(12.3) where you:

(a) *actively participate in*;

(b) *own*; or

(c) are a *firm* and *owned by* or *connected with*,[3]

a *permitted separate business*, you have safeguards in place to ensure that *clients* are not misled about the extent to which the services that you and the *separate business* offer are regulated;

O(12.4) you do not represent any *permitted separate business* as being regulated by the *SRA* or any of its activities as being provided by an individual who is regulated by the *SRA*;

O(12.5) you are only *connected with* reputable *separate businesses*;

O(12.6) you are only *connected with* a *permitted separate business* which is an *appointed representative*[4] if it is an *appointed representative* of an independent financial adviser.

Indicative behaviours

Acting in the following way(s) may tend to show that you have achieved these outcomes and therefore complied with the *Principles*:

IB(12.1) ensuring that *client* information and records are not disclosed to the *permitted separate business*, without the express consent of the *client*;

IB(12.2) complying with the *SRA Accounts Rules* and not allowing the *client account* to be used to hold money for the *permitted separate business*;

IB(12.3) where you are referring a *client* to a *permitted separate business*, informing the *client* of your interest in the *separate business*;

IB(12.4) terminating any connection with a *permitted separate business* where you have reason to doubt the integrity or competence of that *separate business*.

1 An 'owner' is defined as a person who holds a material interest in the body and 'own' and 'owned by' are to be construed accordingly.

2 Defined, in relation to a separate business, as having any active involvement in the separate business, and includes: (a) any direct control over the business, and any indirect control through another person such as a spouse; and (b) any active participation in the business or the provision of its services to customers.

3 Defined, in relation to a separate business for the purpose of Chapter 12, as: (a) having one or more partner(s), owner(s), director(s) or member(s) in common with the separate business; (b) being a subsidiary company of the same holding company as the separate business; or (c) being a subsidiary company of the separate business.

4 Has the meaning given in the Financial Services and Markets Act 2000.

4.113

Chapter 12 not only replaces rule 21 of the 2007 Code, but also sweeps up some of rule 19, which was devoted to financial services. The philosophy behind rule 21 of the 2007 Code was that clients should not be confused into believing that they are dealing with a firm regulated by the SRA (which is highly controlled and provides them with the benefit of minimum levels of insurance and the Compensation Fund) when they are not. The rule was also designed to ensure that core legal services are only provided through a properly regulated firm and by properly regulated individuals, and to prevent part of a case or matter being severed so as to remove statutory protections available to the client. In a regulatory world which permits alternative business structures, the rule needed to be relaxed, although much has been retained.

By version 3 of the SRA Handbook, dated 23 April 2012, outcomes 12.1(b) and 12.3(a) were amended to remove the reference to 'significant interest' in a separate business.

4.114

In the SRA Handbook Glossary 2012 definitions, there are prescriptive lists of *permitted* separate businesses (the kind of services a member of the public would not necessarily expect to be provided only by a regulated lawyer but are 'solicitor-like' services), and *prohibited* separate business activities (mainstream legal services which members of the public would expect to be offered by a regulated lawyer).

permitted separate business means for the purpose of Chapter 12 of the *SRA Code of Conduct*, a *separate business* offering any of the following services:

(i) alternative dispute resolution;

(ii) financial services;

(iii) estate agency;

(iv) management consultancy;

(v) company secretarial services;

(vi) acting as a parliamentary agent;

(vii) practising as a lawyer of another jurisdiction;

(viii) acting as a bailiff;

(ix) acting as nominee, *trustee* or executor outside England and Wales;

(x) the services of a wholly owned nominee *company* in England and Wales, which is operated as a subsidiary but necessary part of the work of a *separate business* providing financial services;

(xi) providing legal advice or drafting legal documents not included in (i) to (x) above, where such activity is provided as a subsidiary but necessary part of some other service which is one of the main services of the *separate business*; and

(xii) providing any other business, advisory or agency service which could be provided through a *firm* or *in-house practice* but is not a *prohibited separate business activity*.

prohibited separate business activities means, for the purpose of Chapter 12 of the *SRA Code of Conduct*:

(i) the conduct of any matter which could come before a *court*, whether or not proceedings are started;

(ii) advocacy before a *court*;

(iii) instructing counsel in any part of the *UK*;

(iv) *immigration work*;

(v) any activity in relation to conveyancing, applications for probate or letters of administration, or drawing *trust* deeds or *court* documents, which is reserved to *solicitors* and others under the *LSA*;

(vi) drafting wills;

(vii) acting as a nominee, *trustee* or executor in England and Wales, except for the services of a wholly owned nominee *company* where such services are provided as a subsidiary but necessary part of the work of a *separate business* providing financial services; and

(viii) providing legal advice or drafting legal documents not included in (i) to (vii) above where such activity is not provided as a subsidiary but necessary part of some other service which is one of the main services of the *separate business.*

4.115

The Chapter 12 outcomes are a good example of outcomes-focused regulation in action. In the notes to the chapter, solicitors are warned that particular care needs to be taken over the name and branding of the separate business, misleading publicity, and geographical proximity of the two businesses, particularly where premises are shared. Otherwise, the long list of safeguards in rule 21.05(2) of the 2007 Code has not been reproduced in the 2011 Code, as solicitors are free to decide for themselves how to ensure compliance. The safeguards in the 2007 Code are nevertheless reproduced here as they are a useful checklist for solicitors who operate separate businesses.

'You must ensure that the following safeguards are in place in relation to a separate business which offers or provides any of the services listed in 21.04(1):

(a) the separate business must not be held out or described in such a way as to suggest that the separate business is carrying on a practice regulated by the Solicitors Regulation Authority or another approved regulator, or that any lawyer connected with your firm is providing services through the separate business as a practising lawyer regulated by the Solicitors Regulation Authority or another approved regulator;

(b) all paperwork, documents, records or files relating to the separate business and its customers must be kept separate from those of any firm or in-house practice, even where a customer of the separate business is also a client of the firm or in-house practice;

(c) the client account or other account used to hold money for the clients of any firm or in-house practice must not be used to hold money for the separate business, or for customers of the separate business in their capacity as such;

(d) if the separate business shares premises, office accommodation or reception staff with any firm or in-house practice:

  (i) the areas used by the firm or in-house practice must be clearly differentiated from the areas used by the separate business; and

  (ii) all customers of the separate business must be informed that it is not regulated by the Solicitors Regulation Authority and that the statutory protections attaching to clients of a lawyer regulated by the Authority are not available to them as customers of that business;

(e) if you or your firm refer a client to the separate business, the client must first be informed of your interest in the separate business, that the separate business is not regulated by the Solicitors Regulation Authority, and that the statutory protections attaching to clients of a lawyer regulated by the Authority are not available to them as customers of the separate business; and

(f) if the separate business is an estate agency, then without prejudice to the provisions of these rules regarding conflicts of interests, neither you nor any firm through which you practise may act in the conveyance for the buyer of any property sold through the estate agency unless:

(i) the firm shares ownership of the estate agency with at least one other business in which neither you nor the firm have any financial interest;

(ii) neither you nor anyone else in the firm is dealing with or has dealt with the sale of the seller's property for the separate business; and

(iii) the buyer has given written consent to you or the firm acting, after your financial interest in the sale going through has been explained to the buyer.'

Needless to say, solicitors must constantly have in mind the Principles: to act in the best interests of each client (principle 4) and not to allow their independence to be compromised (principle 3). In particular, it will remain best practice for the solicitor to give the client the information set out in safeguard (e) above, and this is reflected in indicative behaviour 12.3.

Financial services

4.116

Solicitors who provide 'mainstream' financial services must be regulated by the Financial Conduct Authority (FCA), but if the financial services offered are incidental to other legal work and are within the limits set by the SRA Financial Services (Scope) Rules 2001,[1] solicitors will be engaged in 'exempt regulated activities' and can be regulated by the SRA. Solicitors regulated by the SRA (as opposed to the FCA) must comply with the SRA Financial Services (Conduct of Business) Rules 2001.[2]

Under the 2007 Code, services which could be provided through a separate business included financial services, except for those that could not form part of a solicitors' practice such as banking, stockbroking and insurance underwriting – see rule 21.04 of the 2007 Code and guidance note 17 thereto. This exception has not been retained in the 2011 Code.

Rule 19 of the 2007 Code was devoted to financial services. Rule 19.01(1) provided:

'You must not, in connection with any regulated activity:

(a) be an appointed representative; or

(b) have any arrangement with other persons under which you could be constrained to recommend to clients or effect for them (or refrain from doing so) transactions:

(i) in some investments but not others;

(ii) with some persons but not others; or

(iii) through the agency of some persons but not others; or

(c) have any arrangement with other persons under which you could be constrained to introduce or refer clients or other persons with whom you deal to some persons but not others.'

The rule against solicitors becoming appointed representatives is now found in the theoretically non-mandatory indicative behaviour 6.6; see **4.50**, but solicitors can now (at least in theory) have arrangements which constrain them to recommending a limited number of investments, investment management companies, etc. The practical difficulty in the way of that is that the recommendation must be in the best interests of the client, and the solicitor cannot compromise his or her independence.

1 As the successors to the Solicitors' Financial Services (Scope) Rules 2001.
2 Likewise as successors to the Solicitors' Financial Services (Conduct of Business) Rules 2001.

Chapters 13 to 15 (Application, waivers and interpretation)

4.117

Chapter 13 sets out the wide reach of the 2011 Code, in terms of those to whom it applies. The bulk of the Code applies to those covered below.

13.1 Subject to paragraphs 2 to 10 below and any other provisions in this Code, this Code applies to you, in relation to your activities carried out from an office in England and Wales, if you are:

(a) a *solicitor*, *REL* or *RFL*, and you are *practising* as such, whether or not the entity through which you *practise* is subject to this Code;

(b) a *solicitor*, *REL* or *RFL* who is:

(i) a *manager*, *employee* or *owner* of a body which should be a *recognised body*, but has not been recognised by the *SRA*;

(ii) a *manager*, *employee* or *owner* of a body that is a *manager* or *owner* of a body that should be a *recognised body*, but has not been recognised by the *SRA*;

(iii) an *employee* of a *sole practitioner* who should be a *recognised sole practitioner*, but has not been recognised by the *SRA*;

(iv) an *owner* of an *authorised body* or a body which should be a *recognised body* but has not been recognised by the *SRA*, even if you undertake no work for the body's *clients*; or

(v) a *manager* or *employee* of an *authorised non-SRA firm*, or a *manager* of a body which is a *manager* of an *authorised non-SRA firm*, when doing work of a sort authorised by the *SRA*, for that firm;

(c) an *authorised body*, or a body which should be a *recognised body* but has not been recognised by the *SRA*;

(d) any other person who is a *manager* or *employee* of an *authorised body*, or of a body which should be a *recognised body* but has not been recognised by the *SRA*;

> (e) any other person who is an *employee* of a *recognised sole practitioner*, or of a *sole practitioner* who should be a *recognised sole practitioner* but has not been recognised by the *SRA*;
>
> and "you" includes "your" as appropriate.

It follows that solicitors practising as such in non-SRA regulated entities, such as ABSs regulated by a different regulator, remain subject to the SRA's regulatory control. So too do non-solicitor employees in SRA-regulated entities. Paragraph 13.8 provides:

> 'The extent to which you are expected to implement the requirements of the Code will depend on your role in the firm, or your way of practising. For example, those who are managing the business will be expected to have more influence on how the firm or business is run than those practising in-house but not managing a legal department, or those practising as employees of a firm.'

4.118

Chapter 13 also contains the power for the SRA to grant waivers in appropriate cases:

> 'In any particular case or cases the SRA Board shall have the power, in exceptional circumstances, to waive in writing the provisions of these outcomes for a particular purpose or purposes expressed in such waiver, to place conditions on and to revoke such a waiver.'

This is in similar terms to rule 22 of the 2007 Code, but the reference to exceptional circumstances is new. In version 3 of the 2011 Code, dated 18 April 2012, Chapter 13.6 was amended to clarify that if, in relation to an overseas practice, compliance with the Code would result in a breach of local law or regulation, the outcomes can be disregarded to the extent necessary to comply with the local law or regulation.

4.119

Chapter 14 was the interpretation section of the 2011 Code, and has been replaced by the SRA Handbook Glossary 2012. Chapter 14 now contains only a cross-reference to the Glossary.

4.120

Chapter 15 contains transitional provisions, most of which cover the period before the SRA became a licensing authority for ABSs and have ceased to be relevant. The remaining significant point is that conduct prior to 6 October 2011 will be considered by reference to the rules in force at the time, even if the rule in question has been repealed.

Application of the 2011 Code to in-house practice

4.121

Most of the 2011 Code applies to in-house practice. The modifications are set out here, but first we have to fight our way through the definitions as to what constitutes in-house and overseas practice.

In-house practice defined

4.122

Rather obscurely, 'in-house practice' is defined in the SRA Handbook Glossary 2012 in a manner which involves a great deal of page-turning. The definition is:

> 'practice as a solicitor, REL or RFL (as appropriate) in accordance with Rules 1.1(c)(ii), 1.1(d)(ii), 1.1(e), 1.2(f), 2.1(c)(ii), 2.1(d)(ii), 2.1(e), 2.2(f), 3.1(b)(ii) or 3.1(c)(ii) of the SRA Practice Framework Rules'

In translation, this means practice in all the ways that a solicitor (or REL or RFL) may practise, subject to the one set of limitations which distinguish in-house practice from ordinary practice – requiring all work to be undertaken for the body of which the individual is a manager, employee, member or interest holder, and for other persons (including members of the public) only as specified in the exceptional circumstances set out in rule 4 of the Practice Framework Rules.

The reason for the multiple references is that the rules cover: bodies authorised by the SRA; regulated providers of legal services not authorised by the SRA, but by another regulator; other organisations which do not provide regulated legal services; and overseas practice; category by category.

Rule 4 is in two parts, in-house practice within England and Wales, and in-house practice overseas.

4.123

The normal rule (rule 4.1) is that if you are an in-house lawyer you must not act for clients other than your employer. Rules 4.4 to 4.11 of the Practice Framework Rules provide exceptions which relate to (expressed informally):

- work done for work colleagues; past or present fellow employees and similar persons, and when employed by a media organisation includes work on behalf of a contributor to a broadcast or publication in defamation claims;
- work for companies and the like associated with the employer;
- pro bono work subject to specified limitations and exceptions.

4.124

Further exceptions, rules 4.12 to 4.18, cover practitioners who are employed not by law firms (entities regulated either by the SRA or other approved regulators) but by other organisations, to which the whole of rule 4 applies, not just rules 4.4 to 4.11. These are in short:

- acting for members of an association which employs the practitioner, subject to express restrictions (4.12);
- acting on behalf of an insured when employed by an insurer, in certain circumstances (4.13);
- working for commercial legal advice services, principally telephone legal advice helplines (4.14);
- when employed in local government working for other persons or bodies in specified limited circumstances (4.15);
- acting for members of the public through law centres, charities and other non-commercial providers of advice and other legal services, subject to express conditions (4.16);
- when employed in central government or by other public bodies, including the Legal Aid Agency, acting for other persons if doing so in pursuance of the lawful functions of the employer (4.18);
- the provision of legal services to clients of a foreign law firm (lawyers qualified in foreign jurisdictions practising as such, but within England and Wales), subject to specified controls and restrictions (4.19 to 4.21);
- when employed by a regulatory body, giving advice to other persons and acting for them if carrying out the employer's statutory functions (4.26).

4.125

Rules 4.22 to 4.25 of the Practice Framework Rules cover in-house practice overseas.

Rule 4.22 enables the exception permitting pro bono work to be done for clients other than the employer (4.10 and 4.11) to apply to in-house practice overseas. Rule 4.23 disapplies the remainder of rule 4 and substitutes an obligation to comply only with the overseas-specific rules 4.24 and 4.25.

By rule 4.25 a solicitor registered with the professional body for a local legal profession in another EU state under the Establishment Directive (98/5/EC) may practise in-house to the extent that a member of that legal profession is permitted to do so.

Otherwise an in-house solicitor in overseas practice may only act for his or her employer, a company substantially controlled by the employer, or another group company or parent company, or for fellow employees subject to specified limitations (rule 4.24).

Application of the 2011 Code to in-house practice, by chapter

4.126

All the Chapter 1 outcomes (client care) apply directly or indirectly, apart from outcome 1.8 – compulsory professional indemnity insurance, which is replaced by an outcome specific to in-house practice.

Outcomes 1.1 to 1.5, 1.7, 1.15 and 1.16 apply to in-house practice without any variation.

Outcomes 1.6 and 1.9 to 1.14 apply to in-house practice where the practitioner acts for someone other than his or her employer unless it is clear that the outcome is not relevant to the particular circumstances.

An in-house-specific outcome is substituted for outcome 1.8 – in-house practice outcome 1.1. That requires compliance with the SRA Practice Framework Rules in relation to professional indemnity insurance.

This means that if a practitioner is acting for a client other than the employer by taking advantage of the exceptions in the SRA Practice Framework Rules for pro bono work (rule 4.10), commercial advice services (rule 4.14), law centres, charities, etc. (rule 4.16), or foreign law firms (rule 4.19) professional indemnity cover must be in place. In all other cases the practitioner must consider whether the employer has appropriate indemnity insurance, and if it does not, the client must be informed in writing.

All the Chapter 2 outcomes apply depending on the status of the employed lawyer.

Outcomes 2.1 and 2.2 (avoiding discrimination and respecting diversity) apply to all in-house practice.

Outcomes 2.3 to 2.5 envisage a management responsibility (practical arrangements to accommodate disability, recruitment policies and complaints handling). In place of those provisions an in-house solicitor who has management responsibilities must take all reasonable steps to encourage equality of opportunity and respect for diversity in the workplace (in-house practice outcome 2.1).

All the Chapter 3 outcomes apply depending on the status of the employed lawyer.

Outcomes 3.1 to 3.3 (systems and controls relating to conflicts of interest) apply if the employed solicitor has management responsibilities.

All other outcomes (3.4 to 3.7) apply without variation.

All the outcomes in Chapter 4 (confidentiality and disclosure); Chapter 5 (duties to the court); and Chapter 6 (clients introduced to third parties) apply to in-house practice without variation.

Chapter 7 is concerned with business management. All save two outcomes only apply to in-house solicitors if they have management responsibilities. The exceptions are outcomes 7.5 and 7.7 which apply to employed solicitors – compliance with legislation, including anti-money laundering and data protection provisions, and compliance with the statutory requirements for the carrying on of reserved legal activities and immigration work.

The first four outcomes of Chapter 8 (publicity) apply to in-house practice unless it is clear from the context that the outcome is not relevant in the particular circumstances. These are the requirements as to publicity being accurate and not misleading, clarity of charges, the prohibition on cold calling, and clarity as to the extent of regulation.

Outcome 8.5 is concerned with the proper content of a law firm's letterhead, etc. and has no application.

Chapter 9 (fee sharing and referrals) applies to in-house practice with practical modifications.

Outcomes 9.1 to 9.3 apply without variation, and are concerned with independence, the protection of clients' interests and the ability of clients to make informed decisions.

Outcomes 9.4 to 9.8 apply unless it is clear from the context that the outcome is not relevant in the particular circumstances (disclosure of financial arrangements with introducers, disclosure of any fee sharing arrangement relevant to the client, exclusion of criminal matters and publicly funded matters from any referral fee arrangement, and the requirement that an agreement with an introducer must be in writing).

The outcomes of Chapter 10 (duties to the regulator) and Chapter 11 (relations with third parties – the duty not to take advantage, undertakings, contract races, the proper administration of oaths and affirmations) apply to in-house practice without variation.

Chapter 12 (separate businesses) applies to in-house practice with one exception: outcome 12.2, which only applies to a regulated firm and prohibits ownership of the firm by a separate business which provides core legal services, or a connection with such an entity (connection meaning something like common ownership or closely associated companies).[1]

1 'Connected with' is defined as (a) having one or more partner(s), owner(s), director(s) or member(s) in common with the separate business; (b) being a subsidiary company of the same holding company as the separate business; or (c) being a subsidiary company of the separate business.

Application of the 2011 Code to overseas practice

4.127

Until 2013, the regulatory scheme for overseas practice was similar to that for in-house practice, in that each chapter of the 2011 Code would set out which of its provisions apply to overseas practice. However in October 2013, the Code, so far as it relates to overseas practice, was significantly amended. The outcomes which referred to overseas practice were removed, and a new Chapter 13A, with a new set of outcomes, added in order to cover the conduct requirements when a regulated individual or entity is practising temporarily overseas. This ensures, amongst other things, that the European Cross-border Rules, and any other rules that apply in the jurisdiction in which the legal service is being supplied, also apply to temporary practice. The new definition of 'established' in the Glossary explains the distinction between temporary and permanent practice overseas.

Chapter 13A provides as follows:

13A.1 If you are an individual or body *practising overseas*, the Code does not apply to you, but you must comply with the SRA Overseas Rules.

13A.2 Subject to rule 13A.1 above, the Code is applicable to you as set out in 13A.3 to 13.A.6 below if you are:

(a) a body practising from an office outside England and Wales, only if you are required to be an *authorised body* as a result of the nature of your practice and you have been authorised by the *SRA* accordingly;

(b) a *manager* of such a body; or

(c) an individual engaged in *temporary practice overseas*.

13A.3 The following provisions of the Code apply:

(a) chapter 3 (conflicts of interests);

(b) chapter 4 (confidentiality and disclosure);

(c) chapter 5 (your client and the court), to the extent that your practice relates to litigation or advocacy conducted before a court, tribunal or enquiry in England and Wales or a British court martial;

(d) outcomes 6.1 to 6.3 (your client and introductions to third parties);

(e) chapter 7 (management of your business);

(f) outcomes 8.1 and 8.4 (publicity);

(g) outcomes 9.1 to 9.7 (fee sharing and referrals),except where they conflict with the *SRA European Cross-Border Practice*, in which case the latter will prevail;

(h) chapter 10 (you and your regulator);

(i) chapter 11 (relations with third parties), except that Outcome 11.3 only applies if the land in question is situated in England and Wales; and

(j) outcomes 12.3 to 12.6 (separate businesses).

13A.4 In addition, you must meet the following outcomes:

O(13A.1) you properly account to your *clients* for any *financial benefit* you receive as a result of your instructions unless it is the prevailing custom of your local jurisdiction to deal with *financial benefits* in a different way;

O(13A.2) *clients* have the benefit of insurance or other indemnity in relation to professional liabilities which takes account of:

(a) the nature and extent of the risks you incur in your practice overseas;

(b) the local conditions in the jurisdiction in which you are *practising*; and

(c) the terms upon which insurance is available;

and you have not attempted to exclude liability below the minimum level required for practice in the local jurisdiction;

O(13A.3) you do not enter into unlawful contingency fee arrangements;

CHAPTER 4
SRA CODE OF CONDUCT 2011

O(13A.4) you do not discriminate unlawfully according to the jurisdiction in which you are practising; and

O(13A.5) *publicity* intended for a jurisdiction outside England and Wales must comply with any applicable law or rules regarding 'lawyers' *publicity* in the jurisdiction in which your office is based and the jurisdiction for which the *publicity* is intended.

13A.5 you must be aware of the local laws and regulations governing your practice in an overseas jurisdiction;

13A.6 if compliance with any outcome in the Code would result in your breaching local laws or regulations you may disregard that 'outcome to the extent necessary to comply with that local law or regulation.

PART 3

Other rules

CHAPTER 5

The SRA Accounts Rules 2011

5.1

The SRA Accounts Rules 2011 form part of the SRA Handbook and replace the Solicitors' Accounts Rules 1998, which were in force from 2000.

The introduction to the new rules includes a reference to desired outcomes:

'• client money is safe;
- clients and the public have confidence that client money held by firms will be safe;
- firms are managed in such a way, and with appropriate systems and procedures in place, so as to safeguard client money;
- client accounts are used for appropriate purposes only; and
- the SRA is aware of issues in a firm relevant to the protection of client money.'

Because, following the introduction of alternative business structures (ABSs), businesses may be supplying both regulated and unregulated services (through multi-disciplinary practices (MDPs)), in relation to MDPs the rules apply only in respect of those activities for which the practice is regulated by the Solicitors Regulation Authority (SRA), and are concerned only with money handled by the practice which relates to those regulated activities.

This results in there being a third category of money handled by the firm. As well as client money and office money there will be 'out-of-scope money' – funds held by an MDP which relate to activities that are not regulated by the SRA.

The SRA Accounts Rules 2011 are in eight parts. Although they largely follow the pattern of the 1998 Rules, repeals of three of the earlier rules mean that most rule numbers have changed. The eight parts are as follows:

- Part 1, comprising rules 1 to 12, is concerned with general matters, persons governed by and exempt from the Accounts Rules and, importantly, an explanation of the categories of money handled by solicitors (rule 12) – all money held or received in the course of practice (except 'out-of-scope' money as mentioned above) is 'client money' or 'office money'. Further comment will be made about this subject, which is of crucial importance;
- Part 2, rules 13 to 21, concerns the proper handling of client money and the correct operation of client account;
- Part 3, rules 22 to 25, sets out the requirements as to accounting for interest;
- Part 4, rules 26 to 30, is concerned with the proper maintenance of accounting systems and records;

- Part 5, rule 31, provides the monitoring and investigation powers of the SRA;
- Part 6, rules 32 to 46, regulates the provision of accountants' reports;[1]
- Part 7, rules 47 to 52, covers overseas practice;
- Part 8, rule 53, contained transitional provisions and was deleted in April 2012.

1 Section 34 of the Solicitors Act 1974.

5.2

The SRA Accounts Rules 2011 are accompanied by guidance notes. In contrast to the position under the 1998 Rules, the guidance notes do not form part of the 2011 Rules.[1]

Failure to comply with any of the SRA Accounts Rules may be the subject of a complaint to the Solicitors Disciplinary Tribunal ('the Tribunal' or SDT).[2] Compliance with the Rules is an absolute requirement, and a breach of the Rules is one of absolute liability. Indeed it is commonplace for solicitors to be unaware that breaches have occurred until well after the event (because the accounts function is usually delegated to non-solicitors), but still to be liable for the breaches and to disciplinary sanctions. The lack of knowledge or complicity does not mean that a breach has not occurred on the part of the ignorant individual: he or she had an obligation to ensure it did not happen. That is why robust systems and hands-on involvement and oversight at partnership or management level are essential (more of which later).

1 Rule 2.1.
2 Section 32(3) of the Solicitors Act 1974.

5.3

Although the SRA Accounts Rules are lengthy, and in some respects complex, the underlying principles are straightforward, and are well known to all practitioners – even if they may not claim to be familiar with all the detail.

The principles underlying the SRA Accounts Rules are set out in rule 1. Effective compliance with the SRA Accounts Rules involves an understanding of relatively few principles:

(1) have a proper accounts system and keep it up to date;
(2) keep your own money separate from other people's money;
(3) use only each client's or trust's money for that client's or trust's matters;
(4) pay interest in accordance with the rules;
(5) deliver your annual accountant's reports on time; and
(6) co-operate with regulatory checks and inspections by the SRA.

Proper accounting systems

5.4

The obligation to have and to maintain proper accounting systems generally needs no explanation. However, rule 1.2 requires that: 'You must comply with the

Principles set out in the Handbook, and the outcomes in Chapter 7 of the SRA Code of Conduct in relation to the effective financial management of the firm …'. Chapter 7 includes the obligation to 'maintain systems and controls for monitoring the financial stability of your firm and risks to money and assets entrusted to you by clients and others, and … take steps to address issues identified' (outcome 7.4). Thus the Accounts Rules expressly incorporate further obligations relating to the firm's management, a matter relevant to the role of the COFA (see **CHAPTER 6**).

One issue, which is both a requirement of the Accounts Rules and a matter of business management, deserves special mention: it is accepted that errors will occur in the best ordered systems and one of the most effective controls in ensuring that mistakes are identified is a bank reconciliation that satisfies rule 29.12. This compares the total of all individual client ledger balances with the client cashbook and the amount shown on the bank statement or statements, shows any difference between any one of those three components and any other, and reconciles that difference. If this is done properly most significant errors will be identified – certainly any client account shortage should be immediately spotted. The bank reconciliation is important; it is not a tedious bureaucratic requirement, but an essential management tool designed to enable principals who are not concerned with the day-to-day minutiae of the accounts to be informed of any serious underlying problems.

All of the principals in a firm ('managers' in SRA terminology) have an obligation to ensure compliance with the SRA Accounts Rules: that is, compliance not only by the principals themselves but by everyone employed in the practice.[1] Any breach of the SRA Accounts Rules must be remedied promptly upon discovery. This includes the replacement of any money improperly withheld or withdrawn from client account[2] using a principal's own money if necessary. This duty falls on all principals in the practice, and not just on the individual causing the breach or who was, for example, the partner responsible for supervising the person at fault.[3]

For this reason all principals should know what is going on in their own accounts department; they will be personally responsible for putting right any problem, with their own money. While accounting functions are invariably delegated to non-solicitors in all but the tiniest practices, there must be effective oversight at management level, for example, in checking client balances; that the five-weekly (monthly in practice) reconciliation has been carried out, and is understood; and that any information given by it which prompts action is acted upon.

1 Rule 6.
2 Rule 7.1.
3 Rule 7.2.

Client money or office money?

5.5

Keeping your own money and that of other people separate should create no problems of interpretation, but solicitors still appear to have problems with this issue from time to time. All money held or received in the course of practice is 'client money' (held or received for a client or as trustee) or 'office money' (which belongs to the solicitor or the practice).[1]

The simplest approach is to ask the question: does this money belong, now, unconditionally and exclusively, to me or to my firm? If the answer is 'yes', the money must be paid into office account. If the answer is 'no', it must be paid into client account (or trust account, if relevant).

The word 'unconditionally' is used to emphasise the fact that if a condition has to be satisfied in order for the solicitor or firm to be entitled (such as the delivery of a bill), it is client money. The word 'exclusively' is used to emphasise that if someone else has an interest in the money, even the solicitor's wife, if she is not a partner in the firm, it is client money.

1 Rule 12.

Costs

5.6

Particular issues arise over costs. When a firm is paid on account of costs for work that has not yet been done, that money still belongs to the client and must be paid into client account. In contrast, where a firm agrees a fee which cannot be varied upwards or downwards, and which is not dependent on the transaction being completed, and receives funds in payment of that agreed fee, it is the solicitor's or firm's money and must be paid into office account.[1]

Firms may legitimately transfer money from client account to office account for the payment of their fees, *but only if a bill or other written notification of costs has been sent to the client.*[2] The Tribunal's records are packed with cases involving solicitors who transferred money to which they considered they were fully entitled, because they had done the work, but where they had 'not got around to sending a bill'. Similar numbers of cases have involved 'tidying up the accounts' by sweeping old and small balances from client to office account on the basis of 'dummy bills' or 'accounts only bills' (meaning pieces of paper that were never intended to be delivered to the clients whose money was being taken).

1 Rule 17.4 and 17.5.
2 Rule 17.2; an agreed fee must be evidenced in writing.

Teeming and lading

5.7

Using a client's money only for that client's purposes is a fundamental requirement. The Tribunal's caseload is materially increased by those solicitors who, when something goes wrong (either by miscalculation or through a transactional problem) and more money is needed for the client than is available, simply overdraw that client's individual ledger, using the substantial balance available in the general client bank account. This invariably means that the funds of one or more clients are being used, without their knowledge, for someone else's benefit. Transfers may be effected between the clients' ledgers in these circumstances to 'cover' the shortage. If the client whose money was wrongly used needs it, a third client's funds may need to be moved. This is teeming and lading – robbing Peter to pay Paul. It does not overcome the fundamental problem – that there is an overall shortage of client funds. Rule 30 of the 1998 Rules (now rule 27 of the 2011 Rules) was introduced in an attempt to inhibit this practice: it is not permissible to make a private (i.e. non-institutional) loan of one client's funds to another, even by means of a paper transfer between ledgers, except with the prior written authority of both clients.

Professional disbursements

5.8

Another problem area is the treatment of professional disbursements, which are defined as the fees of counsel or other lawyer or of a professional or other agent or expert instructed by the solicitor, and will include interpreters, translators, process servers, surveyors and the like.[1] It is common and proper to bill a client for costs and disbursements, including professional disbursements that are yet to be paid. It is permissible to pay the whole sum received in payment of such a bill into office account *provided* that the element relating to unpaid professional disbursements is paid either into client account or to the professionals entitled to the money *by the end of the second working day following receipt.*[2] Alternatively, the whole sum may be paid into client account and the part of the payment which is office money transferred to office account within 14 days.

It is a well-known but wholly improper practice in such circumstances to credit the whole sum to office account and to withhold payment of the unpaid disbursements so that the office overdraft is reduced by the amount owed to counsel and others, possibly many thousands or tens of thousands of pounds. A slightly more sophisticated version of this practice is to write cheques to those entitled, which when entered on the accounts appear to show a compliant picture, but the cheques are not sent and, rather, accumulate in the top left-hand drawer of the principal's or bookkeeper's desk, or comparable location. This would be regarded very seriously.

Special rules apply to the treatment of payments from the Legal Aid Agency.[3] Though complex the advantage is that they are contained within one rule to which legal aid practitioners can readily refer.

1 SRA Handbook Glossary 2012.
2 Rule 17.1(b).
3 Rule 19.

Withdrawals from client account

5.9

Money may only be withdrawn from client account in favour of the solicitor or firm by cheque or transfer, never in cash.[1]

Under the SRA Accounts Rules 2011, there is no longer a specific list of persons who may be authorised to withdraw money from client account (as there was under rule 23 of the 1998 Rules).

Instead, by rule 21 of the 2011 Rules:

> 21.1 A withdrawal from a *client account* may be made only after a specific authority in respect of that withdrawal has been signed by an appropriate

person or persons in accordance with the *firm's* procedures for signing on *client account*. An authority for withdrawals from *client account* may be signed electronically, subject to appropriate safeguards and controls.

21.2 *Firms* must put in place appropriate systems and procedures governing withdrawals from *client account*, including who should be permitted by the *firm* to sign on *client account*. A non-*manager* owner or a non-employee owner of a *licensed body* is not an appropriate person to be a signatory on *client account* and must not be permitted by the *firm* to act in this way.

...

Guidance notes

(i) A firm should select suitable people to authorise withdrawals from the client account. Firms will wish to consider whether any employee should be able to sign on client account, and whether signing rights should be given to all managers of the practice or limited to those managers directly involved in providing legal services. Someone who has no day-to-day involvement in the business of the practice is unlikely to be regarded as a suitable signatory because of the lack of proximity to client matters. An appropriate understanding of the requirements of the rules is essential.

So the onus is on the firm to determine a policy and put in place suitable systems. All responsible firms will already have addressed these issues in detail, so this is a truly deregulatory development, allowing firms to decide who is best suited and qualified to authorise withdrawals from client account, rather than being restricted to persons of particular professional qualifications.

1 Rule 21.4.

Interest

5.10

Under the SRA Accounts Rules 2011 (the relevant rules being 22–25), there is no longer any list or specific guidance as to when interest, or a sum in lieu of interest, must be paid. Instead, there is a general requirement to account for interest 'when it is fair and reasonable to do so in all the circumstances', but, importantly rule 22.3 provides:

> 'You must have a written policy on the payment of interest, which seeks to provide a fair outcome. The terms of the policy must be drawn to the attention of the client at the outset of a retainer, unless it is inappropriate to do so in the circumstances.'

So there is another item to be included in client care information, and the firm must first design the policy.

There is no reason, however, why firms should not adopt a policy which bears a close resemblance to rules 24 and 25 of the Solicitors' Accounts Rules 1998, including the £20 *de minimis* provision, if that is suitable having regard to the nature of the practice.

Compliance

5.11

When required to do so, all those regulated by the SRA must make available all relevant documents to any person appointed by the SRA and must be prepared to explain any departures from the SRA's published guidelines for accounting procedures and systems.[1]

The SRA is reviewing the need for accountant's reports and may abolish the requirement, replacing it with a form of certificate to be signed annually by the compliance officer for finance and administration (COFA), but retaining the option to require reports in specified circumstances, as a condition of a firm's recognition or licence. At the time of writing there remains uncertainty. As a result of responses to its consultation the SRA has deferred a final decision on this issue, but it is more likely than not that the accountant's report regime will not survive in its present form. What follows describes the current system. A solicitor who has held or received client money during an accounting period must deliver to the SRA an accountant's report for that accounting period within six months of the end of the period.[2] In addition, the SRA may require the delivery of an accountant's report in any other circumstances 'if the SRA has reason to believe that it is in the public interest to do so'.[3] Examples of such circumstances are:

- when no report has been delivered but the SRA has reason to believe that a report should have been delivered;
- when a report has been delivered but the SRA has reason to believe that it may be inaccurate;
- when the conduct of the solicitor gives the SRA reason to believe that it would be appropriate to require earlier delivery of a report (e.g. three months after the end of the accounting period);
- when the conduct of the solicitor gives the SRA reason to believe that it would be appropriate to require more frequent delivery of reports (e.g. every six months);
- when the SRA has reason to believe that the regulatory risk justifies the imposition on a category of solicitors of a requirement to deliver reports earlier or at more frequent intervals;
- when a condition on a solicitor's practising certificate requires earlier delivery of reports or the delivery of reports at more frequent intervals.[4]

The Accounts Rules restrict those who may prepare such reports to members of various accountants' professional bodies who are also registered auditors, or their employees.[5] Stringent provisions govern the terms upon which the accountant can be retained.[6] The accountant must request, and the firm must provide, details of all accounts held at banks, building societies and other financial institutions operated by the firm during the relevant accounting period,[7] and the accountant is duty-bound to carry out detailed and specified tests to ensure the compliance of the firm's accounting systems with the Accounts Rules.[8]

A waiver from the requirement to deliver an accountant's report may be obtained from the SRA if only a small number of transactions is undertaken or a small volume of client money is held in an accounting period.[9] This is the only form of waiver of the Accounts Rules that is permitted.

If there is a genuine difficulty in providing the required report by the specified date, an application can be made for an extension of time, but this must be done before the deadline in question. It is too late to apply for an extension when the six-month period has already expired, and every principal will in that event be in default. Regulation 3 of the SRA Practising Regulations 2011 will automatically apply to every partner/manager and there will be a requirement to give advance notice of application for a practising certificate, and to pay additional fees.[10]

1 Rule 31.
2 Rule 32.
3 Rule 32.2.
4 Note (i) to rule 32.
5 Rule 34.
6 Rule 35.
7 Rule 38.
8 Rule 39.
9 Rule 46 and note (xi) to rule 32.
10 Regulation 3.1(c). Currently the additional fee payable is £200 for each applicant.

Dormant balances

5.12

Rules have been in force since 14 July 2008 to deal with the substantial problem caused by dormant accounts or 'residual balances'. There is an obligation to return funds to the client or other person entitled promptly, as soon as there is no longer any proper reason to retain them. If money is received after the firm has accounted to the client, for example, a refund of some kind, it must be paid to the client promptly.[1] If money is retained after the end of a matter or the substantial conclusion of a matter, the firm must promptly inform the client (or other person entitled) in writing of the amount held and the reason for retaining it, and must provide a written report every 12 months, again as to the amount and the reason for retaining it, for so long as the fund is held.[2]

It is permissible to dispose of minor residual balances without obtaining the specific consent of the SRA[3] by paying such sums to charity if:

- the amount does not exceed £500[4] for any one client or trust;
- the firm establishes the identity of the owner of the money, or makes reasonable attempts to do so;
- the firm makes adequate attempts to ascertain the proper destination of the money and to return it to the rightful owner, unless the reasonable costs of doing so are likely to be excessive in relation to the amount held;
- the firm records the steps taken and retains the records, including all relevant documentation such as receipts from the charity (like most other accounting information, for six years); and

- the firm keeps a central register of all such withdrawals, detailing the name of the client, trust or other person entitled (if established), the amount, the name of the recipient charity and the date.

Applications may also be made to the SRA (through the Professional Ethics Guidance Team) for authorisation to withdraw funds from client account when it would not otherwise be permitted, either if the amount is greater than £500, or if it is not intended to pay the amount to charity (as could occur if the amount is genuinely owed to the firm but it is not possible to deliver a bill because the client is untraceable). Firms may also choose to apply for authorisation in all cases rather than use the procedure permitted by rule 20.1(j) and 20.2.[5]

1 Rule 14.3.
2 Rule 14.4.
3 Rule 20.1(j).
4 The figure was changed from £50 to £500 with effect from 31 October 2014.
5 Rule 20.1(k).

CHAPTER 6

Compliance officers (COLPs and COFAs)

6.1

Compliance officers for legal practice (COLPs) and compliance officers for finance and administration (COFAs) have their origins in the Legal Services Act (LSA) 2007 which requires alternative business structures licensed under Part 5 of that Act to have individuals to fulfil the roles and to perform the duties of Head of Legal Practice (HOLP) and Head of Finance and Administration (HOFA).[1]

It was perfectly logical to require that there should be a person who has to be a qualified lawyer, in a senior role with a responsibility for compliance matters, in an organisation providing legal services but which might be wholly owned by non-lawyers. The same logic dictated the need to have someone with appropriate knowledge and responsibility for the firm's accounts, and particularly the Solicitors' Accounts Rules or now the SRA Accounts Rules.

The logic does not altogether hold good when the concept is extended to all traditional law firms where all partners already have those responsibilities. There did not seem to be any very obvious reason why another person, or two other people, should also have those responsibilities, particularly as the responsibilities that fall on the compliance officers are not in any way in substitution for those of the partners/managers. The managers remain liable in any event.

The Solicitors Regulation Authority (SRA) elected to extend the concept to all firms, and to create the roles of COLP and COFA, and all practices, alternative business structures (ABSs), legal disciplinary practices, traditional partnerships and LLPs, and sole practitioners, must all have a COLP and COFA (who may be the same person, and a sole practitioner may fulfil both the roles him- or herself).

1 Sections 91 and 92 of LSA 2007.

6.2

Compliance officers must be expressly approved by the SRA in their role. Whereas non-lawyer managers of firms have likewise to be expressly approved, solicitors are deemed to be approved, as managers,[1] but not as compliance officers. This implies that some higher level of qualification will be required. There is no clear indication as yet what that higher standard might be but it has become plain that even partners in a firm might face a battle to be approved if there is a material regulatory history (for example, allegations found proved by the Solicitors Disciplinary Tribunal) even though no practising certificate conditions had been applied.

The roles of COLP and COFA are not interchangeable. Someone already approved as a COLP cannot step into the role of a COFA without going through a further process of approval.

1 Rule 13.2 of the SRA Authorisation Rules for Legal Services Bodies and Licensable Bodies 2011.

6.3

Rule 8.5 of the SRA Authorisation Rules for Legal Services Bodies and Licensable Bodies 2011 is given below.

8.5 Compliance officers

(a) An *authorised body* must have suitable arrangements in place to ensure that its *compliance officers* are able to discharge their duties in accordance with these rules.

(b) Subject to Rule 8.5(h), an *authorised body* must at all times have an individual:

- (i) who is a *manager* or an *employee* of the *authorised body*;
- (ii) who is designated as its *COLP*;
- (iii) who is of sufficient seniority and in a position of sufficient responsibility to fulfil the role; and
- (iv) whose designation is approved by the *SRA*.

(c) The *COLP* of an *authorised body* must:

- (i) take all reasonable steps to:
  - (A) ensure compliance with the terms and conditions of the *authorised body's authorisation* except any obligations imposed under the *SRA Accounts Rules*;
  - (B) ensure compliance with any statutory obligations of the body, its *managers*, *employees* or *interest holders* in relation to the body's carrying on of *authorised activities*; and
  - (C) record any failure so to comply and make such records available to the *SRA* on request; and
- (ii) in the case of a *licensed body*, as soon as reasonably practicable, report to the *SRA* any failure so to comply, provided that:
  - (A) in the case of non-material failures, these shall be taken to have been reported as soon as reasonably practicable if they are reported to the *SRA* together with such other information as the *SRA* may require in accordance with Rule 8.7(a); and
  - (B) a failure may be material either taken on its own or as part of a pattern of failures so to comply.
- (iii) in the case of a *recognised body*, as soon as reasonably practicable, report to the SRA any material failure so to comply (a failure may be material either taken on its own or as part of a pattern of failure so to comply).

(d) Subject to Rule 8.5(i), an *authorised body* must at all times have an individual:

(i) who is a *manager* or an *employee* of the *authorised body*;

(ii) who is designated as its *COFA*;

(iii) who is of sufficient seniority and in a position of sufficient responsibility to fulfil the role; and

(iv) whose designation is approved by the *SRA*.

(e) The *COFA* of an *authorised body* must:

(i) take all reasonable steps to

(A) ensure that the body and its *employees* and *managers* comply with any obligations imposed upon them under the *SRA Accounts Rules*;

(B) record any failure so to comply and make such records available to the *SRA* on request; and

(iii) as soon as reasonably practicable, report to the *SRA* any failure so to comply, provided that:

(A) in the case of non-material failures, these shall be taken to have been reported as soon as reasonably practicable if they are reported to the *SRA* together with such other information as the *SRA* may require in accordance with Rule 8.7(a);[1] and

(B) a failure may be material either taken on its own or as part of a pattern of failures so to comply.

(iii) in the case of a *recognised body*, as soon as reasonably practicable, report to the SRA any material failure so to comply (a failure may be material either taken on its own or as part of a pattern of failure so to comply).

(f) The *SRA* may approve an individual's designation as a *COLP* or *COFA* if it is satisfied, in accordance with Part 4, that the individual is a suitable person to carry out his or her duties.

(g) A designation of an individual as a *COLP* or *COFA* has effect only while the individual:

(i) consents to the designation;

(ii) in the case of a *COLP*:

(A) is not *disqualified* from acting as a *HOLP*;[2] and

(B) is:

(I) a *lawyer of England and Wales*;

(II) an *REL*; or

(III) registered with the *BSB* under Regulation 17 of the European Communities (Lawyer's Practice) Regulations 2000 (SI 2000/1119);

and is an *authorised person* in relation to one or more of the *reserved legal activities* which the body is authorised to carry on; and

CHAPTER 6
COLPS AND COFAS

(iii) in the case of a *COFA*, is not *disqualified* from acting as a *HOFA*.[3]

(h) An *authorised body* is not required to comply with Rule 8.5(b)(i) where the individual designated as its *COLP*:

(i) has been approved by the *SRA* as a *COLP* for a *related authorised body*; and

(ii) is a *manager* or *employee* of that *related authorised body*.

(i) An *authorised body* is not required to comply with Rule 8.5(d)(i) where the individual designated as its *COFA*:

(i) has been approved by the *SRA* as a *COFA* for a *related authorised body*; and

(ii) is a *manager* or *employee* of that *related authorised body*.

1 A reference to the annual report required to be delivered to the SRA.
2 Under section 99 of LSA 2007.
3 Under section 99 of LSA 2007.

6.4

As originally envisaged the role of the COFA was expected to be quite narrow. Despite the title and the references to 'finance' and 'administration' the origins of the role are found in section 92 of LSA 2007 in relation to ABSs:

> 'The Head of Finance and Administration of a licensed body must take all reasonable steps to ensure compliance with licensing rules made under paragraph 20 of Schedule 11 (accounts)'

and in the quoted paragraph of Schedule 11:

> 'The licensing rules must make provision as to the treatment of money … and the keeping of accounts in respect of such money.'

The 'money' in question is 'money (including money held on trust) which is received, held or dealt with by the licensed body, its managers and employees for clients or other persons'. Thus the role of the HOFA was to be very specific: responsibility for the correct treatment of client and trust money and the keeping of accounts. It did not entail, as drafted, any wider responsibility for running the business. However, there has been a considerable amount of 'regulatory creep'. The SRA Accounts Rules (see **Chapter 5**) include rule 1.2: 'You must comply with the Principles set out in the Handbook, and the outcomes in Chapter 7 of the SRA Code of Conduct in relation to the effective financial management of the firm …'. Chapter 7 includes the obligation to 'maintain systems and controls for monitoring the financial stability of your firm and risks to money and assets entrusted to you by clients and others, and … take steps to address issues identified' (outcome 7.4). By this means the SRA asserts that the COLP and COFA have overlapping roles in relation to financial stability, although it is highly questionable whether this was ever originally intended by LSA 2007. There has been an extension of the compliance officer system to all practices, when originally this was designed for ABSs and also an extension to the role of the COFA.

The role of the COLP is very wide indeed and even more onerous. The obligation is to 'take all reasonable steps' to 'ensure' compliance with the terms and conditions of the authorised body's authorisation (except any obligations imposed under the SRA Accounts Rules). This is basically an obligation to ensure compliance with the whole of the SRA Handbook, and to 'ensure' compliance with any statutory obligations of the body, its managers, employees or interest holders. Both COLPs and COFAs have obligations to record any breach (theoretically even if unaware of it); to assess any and every breach to determine whether it is material; and to reassess any such breach considered at the time to be immaterial, if a later incident should suggest that it might be part of a material pattern of failures, and to report as necessary.

6.5

Nevertheless it is important to appreciate the distinction between the responsibilities of compliance officers and managers. The COLPs and COFAs are responsible for *systems*, and for recording and reporting compliance failings. The obligation to 'ensure compliance' does not mean, in our view, that the compliance officer is personally liable if there is non-compliance. He or she can expect to face disciplinary consequences if there are no adequate systems in place to minimise risks or to monitor the effectiveness of controls, or if there is a failure to keep adequate records, or a failure to report to the SRA when it was appropriate to do so.

However, the managers remain responsible for the firm, and individuals remain responsible for their own conduct. If the compliance officer is not provided with adequate facilities and resources that will be the responsibility of the managers, but that in itself will be a failure of compliance which is likely to mean that the compliance officer cannot carry out his/her duties, which would trigger an obligation for the compliance officer to report.

There can be expected to be consequential tensions between COLPs and COFAs and managers.

Published guidance on the roles and duties of compliance officers

6.6

The guidance notes to rule 8.1 of the Authorisation Rules give additional insight and are reproduced below.

> (vi) The roles of COLP and COFA are a fundamental part of a firm's compliance and governance arrangements. COLPs' and COFAs' ability to take the steps they need to ensure compliance is dependent on the firm having suitable arrangements in place under Rule 8.2. The firm must therefore ensure that any person designated as its COLP or COFA is of sufficient seniority, in a position of sufficient power and responsibility and has clear reporting lines to enable them to have access to all management systems and arrangements and all other relevant information including client files and business information. The existence of compliance officers in a firm and the requirements on them to ensure that the firm, as well as its managers and employees, are complying with the regulatory arrangements (COLP) and the SRA Accounts Rules (COFA) is not a substitute for the

firm's and managers' responsibilities and their obligations to comply with Rule 8.1 (Regulatory compliance). Firms and managers need to take care not to obstruct, whether intentionally or unwittingly, a COLP or COFA in fulfilling their role.

(vii) COLPs and COFAs are responsible for ensuring that the firm has systems and controls in place to enable the firm, as well as its managers and employees and anyone who owns any interest in the firm, to comply with the requirements on them. The firm and its managers are not absolved from any of their own obligations and remain fully responsible for compliance (see Rule 8.1).

(viii) Those designated as COLP will need to be in a position to be able to discharge the role. They will need to consider whether they are in a position to, for example:

(a) take all reasonable steps to ensure compliance with the terms of the firm's authorisation; compliance with the SRA's regulatory arrangements by the firm, its employees and managers; and with relevant statutory obligations e.g.

(A) that non-authorised persons comply with the duty imposed by section 90 of the LSA (duty not to do anything which causes or substantially contributes to a breach of the SRA's regulatory arrangements by an authorised body or its employee or manager);

(B) that authorised persons and other managers and employees comply with the duty imposed by section 176 of the LSA (duty to comply with the SRA's regulatory arrangements);

(C) under the LSA, AJA and the SA in respect of practice matters;

(b) in the case of a licensed body, as soon as reasonably practicable, report to the SRA any failure to comply. Where such failure is material, either on its own or because it forms part of a pattern, the immediacy of the report will depend on the circumstances and seriousness of the breach. Where such failure is neither material of itself nor because it forms part of a pattern of non-compliance, the report need not be made until the annual information report under Rule 8.7.

(c) in the case of a recognised body, as soon as reasonably practicable, report to the SRA any material failure to comply, whether such failure is material either on its own or because it forms part of a pattern of non-compliance. The immediacy of the report will depend on the circumstances and seriousness of the breach.

(ix) Those designated as COFA will need to be in a position to be able to discharge the role. They will need to consider whether they are in a position to, for example:

(a) ensure that they have access to all accounting records;

(b) carry out regular checks on the accounting systems;

(c) carry out file and ledger reviews;

(d) ensure that the reporting accountant has prompt access to all the information needed to complete the accountant's report;

(e) take steps to ensure that breaches of the SRA Accounts Rules are remedied promptly;

(f) monitor, review and manage risks to compliance with the SRA Accounts Rules;

(g) in the case of a licensed body, as soon as reasonably practicable report to the SRA any failure to comply with the SRA Accounts Rules. Where such failure is material, either on its own or because it forms part of a pattern, the immediacy of the report will depend on the circumstances and seriousness of the breach. The report need not be made until the annual information report under Rule 8.7 where such failure is neither material of itself nor because it forms part of a pattern of non-compliance.

(h) in the case of a recognised body, as soon as reasonably practicable, report to the SRA any material failure to comply with the SRA Accounts Rules, whether such failure is material either on its own or because it forms part of a pattern of non-compliance. The immediacy of the report will depend on the circumstances and seriousness of the breach.

(x) In considering whether a failure is "material", the COLP or COFA, as appropriate, will need to take account of various factors, such as:

(a) the detriment, or risk of detriment, to clients;

(b) the extent of any risk of loss of confidence in the firm or in the provision of legal services;

(c) the scale of the issue;

(d) the overall impact on the firm, its clients and third parties.

In addition, the COLP/COFA will need to keep appropriate records of failures in compliance to:

(e) monitor overall compliance with obligations;

(f) assess the effectiveness of the firm's systems;

(g) be able to decide when the need has arisen to report breaches which are material because they form a pattern.

(xi) In developing their governance and administrative arrangements firms will need to consider how they approach unexpected risks such as the absence of key staff, including COLP and COFA, and whether the nature of the absence will trigger the need to notify the SRA (see Rule 8.7) and to obtain approval for a replacement.

(xii) The core statutory obligations of a recognised body are contained in the AJA and the SA and those for licensed bodies are contained in sections 90 and 176 of the LSA. An important aspect of the roles of COLP and COFA is the need to report breaches to the SRA. Although it will commonly be appropriate for the firm to take steps to remedy breaches immediately, this does not obviate the need for compliance officers to record the breach and make a report in compliance with Rule 8.5 where appropriate.

(xiii) Approval (see Rules 8.5 and 8.6) relates only to the role for which it is granted. Any change from one role that requires approval to another, will require a further approval. Firms need to ensure that they notify the SRA of any changes and, where necessary, apply for appropriate approval, for example where an employee develops into the role of manager, or an owner's participation amounts to being a manager.

Timing issues

6.7

The approval of compliance officers for ABSs is part of the authorisation process, and any application for authorisation as an ABS must therefore name the proposed compliance officers, whenever the application is first made. The same applies to all new non-ABS practices.

For existing non-ABS firms, compliance officers had to be nominated by 31 July 2012, with a view to completion of the approval process by 31 December 2012. COLPs and COFAs took up their duties from 1 January 2013.

Who should be appointed?

6.8

The requirement for a COFA is only that he or she should not be disqualified under section 99 of LSA 2007 and has consented, and is approved, but he or she must be a manager or an employee of the authorised body of sufficient seniority and in a position of sufficient responsibility to fulfil the role. The finance director or the head of the firm's accounting function could fulfil this role (if prepared to volunteer).

The COLP must fulfil those requirements and must also be either a solicitor, an REL or a European lawyer registered with the Bar Standards Board, and must be authorised, as a lawyer, to provide at least one of the regulated legal services being provided by the firm.

In small firms, and sole practice in particular, one person may fulfil all roles, and there is no requirement that it should be otherwise. Small firms, however, must bear in mind that it is compulsory to have compliance officers at all times and they must be expressly approved by the SRA. If there is no COLP or COFA the firm cannot maintain its authorisation, and would have to close.

Larger firms will face difficult questions: should the COLP be the managing partner, or would that create an unmanageable conflict for someone with the primary role of driving the business? Or should it be the general counsel, but would not that create a conflict with that person's role in being able to give advice in privileged circumstances?

If the compliance officer is not in the top echelon in the firm, what protections will it be necessary to provide to someone who may have the role of a whistle-blower, against the wishes of senior partners or managers?

What level of access to information, at board level for example, must a compliance officer have? The likely inference and position of the SRA is that he/she must have access to everything. Will that mean that a COLP will have to be a partner/manager, or is the situation capable of being regulated by contract?

None of these questions is easy to answer and we do not make the attempt. It is understandable at the simplest level that the SRA should want to have a stable contact with each firm and one or two people with the primary responsibility to deal with the regulator, but the SRA must, it seems to us, be sensitive to the problems inherent in requiring compliance officers to be the firm's internal policemen. The danger is that it may become increasingly difficult to recruit and retain managers prepared to fulfil the role.

Withdrawal of approval

6.9

Under rule 17 of the Authorisation Rules the SRA may withdraw approval of a compliance officer if it is not satisfied that he or she continues to meet the criteria for approval; or if it is satisfied that a condition imposed on the body's authorisation has not been or is not being complied with; or if the compliance officer has breached a duty or obligation imposed upon him or her under the SRA Handbook or any statute; or if information or documentation is not promptly supplied in response to a request made by the SRA.

Withdrawal of approval of a COLP or COFA could be terminal for a practice. If for any reason a firm ceases to have an approved COLP and COFA it must notify the SRA within seven days and designate a replacement or replacements within the same time; temporary approval may be granted for 28 days.

Larger firms may find it desirable to have more than one potential compliance officer of each class in a position to take over the role in the event of unforeseen circumstances, although as things stand there is no mechanism by which approval can be sought other than by the formal process of approval of the appointment (there is no process whereby one can obtain approval of someone with a view to later appointment).

The powers of the SRA to disqualify a HOLP or HOFA of an ABS are considered in **CHAPTER 25**.

Temporary emergency approvals for compliance officers

6.10

If a firm (traditional or ABS) ceases to have a compliance officer of either class it must immediately, and in any event within seven days:

- notify the SRA;
- designate another manager or employee to replace its previous COLP or COFA; and
- make an application for temporary approval of the new COLP or COFA.[1]

If the SRA is to grant a temporary approval it must be satisfied that the application could not reasonably have been commenced in advance, and on the face of the application and any other information immediately available, there is no evidence suggesting that the new compliance officer is not suitable.[2]

Any grant of temporary approval will normally be for 28 days, which may be extended in response to a reasonable request. It may be granted effective from the date when the firm ceased to have an approved compliance officer, so that the firm is not in default, but does not guarantee that a substantive application for approval will be granted, or granted without conditions. In exceptional circumstances and for reasonable cause the SRA may withdraw the temporary approval.[3]

A substantive application for approval of a permanent appointment must be submitted within the period of temporary approval or any extension of it.[4]

1 Rule 18.1 of the Authorisation Rules.
2 Rule 18.2.
3 Rule 18.3.
4 Rule 18.4.

Appeals

6.11

In the case of COLPs and COFAs of ABSs, the ABS and the individual affected have a right of appeal to the Solicitors Disciplinary Tribunal ('the Tribunal' or SDT) against the SRA's refusal of an application for approval, a decision to approve an appointment subject to conditions and a decision to withdraw approval, but must first invoke the SRA's appeal procedure; see **2.21**. For appeals to the Tribunal see **CHAPTER 22**.

However, where a COLP or COFA is appointed within a non-ABS authorised practice, exactly the same decisions are not subject to any right of appeal to an independent body; they are subject only to the SRA's internal appeal process.

This is the anomalous consequence of the SRA applying the concepts of Head of Legal Practice and Head of Finance and Administration, specifically designed for alternative business structures by LSA 2007 and accompanied by a complete statutory framework including rights of appeal, to all practices despite the absence of a comparable framework for other more traditional practices.

Because every practice must have an approved COLP and COFA, and the withdrawal of approval would mean that a practice has to close, it is not entirely satisfactory that one kind of authorised practice has a right of appeal to the Tribunal, with possible costs consequences if the SRA got it wrong, and another kind of authorised practice bound by exactly the same set of SRA rules has no external right of appeal, so that the only remedy is litigation, by judicial review. Judicial review does not generally entail a full review of the merits of the original decision and is consequently an unsatisfactory remedy.

Disqualification

6.12

Within the ABS regime, the licensing authority has the power under section 99 of LSA 2007 to disqualify a person from being a Head of Legal Practice, a Head of Finance and Administration, or a manager, or employee of any licensed body, so that a COLP or COFA of an ABS may face the near equivalent of being struck off by the SRA as licensing authority (someone disqualified in these circumstances is likely to be unemployable in the regulated legal community).

For these powers and associated rights of appeal see **CHAPTERS 25** and **22** respectively.

These are powers which are specific to ABSs and do not apply to COLPs and COFAs of other kinds of authorised practices.

CHAPTER 7

Financial services regulation

7.1

The statutory framework for financial services regulation is provided by the Financial Services and Markets Act (FSMA) 2000. Section 19(1) of FSMA 2000 provides that no person may carry on a regulated activity in the United Kingdom or purport to do so unless he is (a) an authorised person or (b) an exempt person. This is referred to as the general prohibition. A breach of this requirement is a criminal offence with a maximum penalty of two years' imprisonment.

Regulated activities are defined by the Financial Services and Markets Act 2000 (Regulated Activities) Order 2001 (RAO 2001).[1] Activities are regulated if an *activity* of a specified kind is carried on *by way of business* in relation to an *investment* of a specified kind. The Financial Services and Markets Act 2000 (Carrying on Regulated Activities by Way of Business) Order 2001[2] makes provision as to when a person is or is not to be regarded as carrying on a regulated activity by way of business. We are dealing with solicitors acting in the course of their professional practice and will assume that this requirement will be met.

1 SI 2001/544.
2 SI 2001/1177.

'Activities'

7.2

Until 31 March 2014 the specified *activities* were:

- accepting deposits;[1]
- issuing electronic money;
- effecting and carrying out contracts of insurance;
- dealing or arranging deals in investments;
- managing investments;
- assisting in the administration and performance of a contract of insurance;
- safeguarding and administering investments;
- sending dematerialised instructions;[2]
- specified involvement in collective investment schemes;
- the like involvement in pension schemes;
- providing basic advice on stakeholder products;
- advising on investments;
- various forms of activity at Lloyd's;

- providing funeral plan contracts; and
- specified involvement in regulated mortgage contracts, regulated home reversion plans, and regulated home purchase plans.

There are exclusions applicable to the various categories of activity.

With effect from 1 April 2014 consumer credit activity was added as a new category of regulated activity.[3] It was formerly regulated by being licensed by the Office of Fair Trading, and the solicitors' profession enjoyed the benefits of a group licence. The consequences are considered in further detail below.

1 A sum is not a deposit for these purposes if it is received by a practising solicitor acting in the course of his profession: article 7 of RAO 2001. A 'practising solicitor' includes recognised bodies, registered European lawyers and registered foreign lawyers.
2 See the Uncertificated Securities Regulations 2001 (SI 2001/3755) – essentially the process whereby shares and other investments can be held in electronic form on computer systems.
3 Financial Services and Markets Act 2000 (Regulated Activities) (Amendment) (No 2) Order 2013, SI 2013/1881.

'Investments'

7.3

The specified *investments* are:

- deposits;
- electronic money;
- rights under a contract of insurance;
- shares;
- debt instruments (debentures, loan stock, bonds, certificates of deposit);
- government and public securities (gilts);
- warrants and other instruments giving entitlement to investments;
- certificates representing certain securities (conferring contractual or property rights in shares, debentures, etc.);
- units in a collective investment scheme;
- rights under a pension scheme;
- options;
- futures;
- contracts for differences (for example, trading on the expected performance of a share or other index);
- Lloyd's syndicate capacity and syndicate membership; and
- rights under a funeral plan contract, regulated mortgage contract, regulated home reversion plan or regulated home purchase plan.

7.4

This book does not attempt to deal with the requirements imposed by the Financial Conduct Authority (FCA) on those authorised and regulated by that Authority.

Solicitors and their practices may become involved in mainstream investment business and be required to be authorised by the FCA, but the vast majority of the profession take advantage of Part XX of FSMA 2000 which allows persons who are regulated by designated professional bodies (of which the Law Society/Solicitors Regulation Authority (SRA) is one) to undertake regulated activities without being authorised by the FCA, provided that they comply with rules made by their own professional body. Solicitors and others regulated by the SRA complying with their own professional rules will be carrying on 'exempt regulated activities'.[1]

The rules applicable to solicitors and their practices; any form of 'authorised body', traditional firm, legal disciplinary partnership, alternative business structures or authorised sole practitioner, are the SRA Financial Services (Scope) Rules 2001 and the SRA Financial Services (Conduct of Business) Rules 2001, which in this chapter will be referred to as the 'Scope Rules' and the 'COB Rules'.

The Scope Rules specify the regulated activities which solicitors and others regulated by the SRA may and may not undertake if they are to take advantage of the Part XX exemption, and the conditions that must be satisfied. The COB Rules regulate the manner in which exempt regulated activities may be carried on by solicitors and their practices.

1 Section 327 of FSMA 2000.

The Scope Rules

7.5

The Scope Rules require that certain basic conditions be met. These are primarily:

(1) that the regulated activities arise out of, or are complementary to, the provision of a particular professional service to a particular client;

(2) that the provision of any service relating to regulated activities is incidental to the provision of professional services (this would, for example, therefore cover the arrangement of after the event insurance which is incidental to the main purpose of the retainer, i.e. the pursuit of a claim for damages);

(3) that the firm accounts to the client for any pecuniary reward or other advantage which the firm receives from a third party; and

(4) that the firm does not carry on or hold itself out as carrying on any regulated activity that is not permitted under the Scope Rules.[1]

As to whether the regulated activity is incidental, it is necessary to consider the scale of regulated activity in proportion to other professional services provided; whether and to what extent activities that are regulated activities are held out as separate services; and the impression given as to how the firm provides regulated activities, for example, through its advertising of its services.

As to accounting for commission and other financial benefits see outcome 1.15 and indicative behaviour 1.20 and the commentary in **CHAPTER 4**; see **4.16** to **4.18**. Notes to the Scope Rules also encourage practitioners at the outset, in advance of the arrangement or the provision of the financial service, to inform clients of their rights to any commission; to inform clients that the arrangement and/or provision of the service is not dependent on their agreement to waive their right to any commission; and to seek and to record client agreement as to whether any commission should be passed to the client, retained by the firm to offset fees, or retained by the firm with the client waiving their right to it.

This is consistent with the FCA guidance to the Council for Licensed Conveyancers on the same subject; see **12.8**.

1 Rule 4 of the Scope Rules.

Prohibited activities

7.6

Activities from which solicitors are prohibited under the Scope Rules are:

- market-making in investments;
- buying, selling, subscribing for or underwriting investments as principal where the firm holds itself out as engaging in the business of buying with a view to selling, or as engaging in the business of underwriting such investments or where the firm regularly solicits members of the public to enter into such transactions;
- buying or selling investments with a view to stabilising or maintaining the market price;
- acting as a stakeholder pension scheme manager;
- entering into a broker funds arrangement;
- effecting and carrying out contracts of insurance as principal;
- establishing, operating or winding up a collective investment scheme or a stakeholder pension scheme;
- managing the underwriting capacity of a syndicate as a managing agent at Lloyd's;
- advising a person to become a member of a particular Lloyd's syndicate;
- entering as provider into a funeral plan contract;
- entering into:
  - a regulated mortgage contract as lender or administering a regulated mortgage contract;
  - a regulated home purchase plan as a provider or administering a regulated home purchase plan;
  - a regulated home reversion plan as a provider or administering a regulated home reversion plan; and
  - a regulated sale and rent back agreement as an agreement provider or administering a regulated sale and rent back agreement,

  unless in the firm's capacity as a trustee or personal representative and the borrower, home purchaser, reversion seller or agreement seller is a beneficiary of the trust, will or intestacy.[1]

All relevant definitions are contained in the Scope Rules or RAO 2001.

1 Rule 3 of the Scope Rules.

7.7

There are other restrictions depending on the kind of investment.

- Firms must not recommend or make arrangements for a client to buy a retail investment product (typically a life policy with an investment element such as an endowment or pension policy, or units or shares in a unit trust or investment trust savings scheme) unless the proposed purchase is by way of assignment, or where the firm is managing assets in accordance with advice from someone authorised for that purpose by the FCA or who is exempt from the general prohibition, or where the firm only arranges the transaction on the basis that the client is not relying on the firm for advice.[1]
- Firms must not recommend that a client buys or disposes of rights or interests in a personal pension scheme.[2]
- Firms must not make arrangements for a client to buy any rights or interests in a personal pension scheme unless it is on the basis that the client is not relying on the firm for advice. However, the benefit of this exception is not available where the transaction involves a pension transfer or opt-out.[3]
- Firms must not recommend that a client buys or subscribes for investments that are not retail investment products where the transaction would be:
  - made with a person acting in the course of the business of buying, selling, subscribing or underwriting the investment (whether as principal or agent);
  - made on an investment exchange or market to which the investment is admitted for dealing; or
  - made in response to an invitation to subscribe for an investment which is or is to be admitted for dealing on an investment exchange or market.

  This prohibition does not apply if the client is not an individual, or is an individual who is the controller of a business or an individual acting in his or her capacity as trustee of an occupational pension scheme.[4]
- Firms must not engage in discretionary management of investments unless the firm (or a partner, officer or employee of the firm) is a trustee, personal representative, donee of a power of attorney or receiver appointed by the Court of Protection *and* all decisions are taken by, or in accordance with, the advice of a person authorised for that purpose by the FCA or who is exempt from the general prohibition.[5]
- Firms must not act as a sponsor to an issue of securities to be admitted for dealing on the London Stock Exchange or as nominated adviser to an issue of securities to be admitted for dealing on the Alternative Investment Market of the London Stock Exchange or as corporate adviser to an issue in respect of securities to be admitted for dealing on the PLUS Market.[6]

1 Rule 5.1 of the Scope Rules.
2 Rule 5.2(a).
3 Rule 5.2(b).
4 Rule 5.3.

5 Rule 5.4.
6 Rule 5.5.

Insurance mediation

7.8

Firms must not carry on any insurance mediation activities unless they are registered in the FCA Financial Services register and have appointed an insurance mediation officer who will be responsible for those activities.[1]

The phrase 'insurance mediation' has caused much confusion, not least because of the use of the word 'mediation'. This is a term of art used in the Scope Rules and involves dealing as an agent in contracts of insurance, making arrangements with a view to a person entering into a contract of insurance, assisting in the administration or performance of a contract of insurance, advising on the merits of buying or selling a contract of insurance, or agreeing to do any of the above.

Most insurance contracts are now regulated investments, including life and pension policies, defective title and missing beneficiary indemnity policies, household and building insurance, long-term care insurance and after the event legal expenses insurance.

In practice, therefore, most of the profession will be likely to become involved in insurance mediation activities, even if only by advising on or arranging a title indemnity policy or after the event insurance. The process of being registered with the FCA for these purposes is arranged through the SRA (usually by completing the question on the annual application for practising certificates or recognition renewal to confirm that the firm does carry out this activity) or by informing the SRA separately if this has not been done or if the circumstances have changed since certificates or recognitions were renewed.

It seems that many firms have made mistakes in this respect. All that is required is that the person filling in the firm's annual application forms does not appreciate that 'insurance mediation' has a special meaning and ticks the box for 'No' as to whether the firm engages in that activity. In consequence the firm will not be registered with the FCA and there will be criminal offences committed every time the firm arranges an after the event legal expenses policy or title indemnity insurance.

1 Rule 5.6 of the Scope Rules.

Regulated mortgages and other property plans

7.9

Firms must not recommend that a client enters into a regulated mortgage contract as a borrower, but can endorse a recommendation given by a person who is regulated by the FCA for this purpose or who is exempt from the general prohibition.[1]

A regulated mortgage contract is one where the borrower is an individual or trust, the lender takes a first legal charge over property in the United Kingdom and at least 40 per cent of the property is occupied or intended to be occupied by the borrower as a dwelling or, in the case of a trust, by a beneficiary, or (in either case) by that person's spouse (or someone, whether or not of the opposite sex, whose relationship with the borrower or beneficiary has the characteristics of the relationship between husband and wife) or that person's parent, brother, sister, child, grandparent or grandchild (article 61(3) of RAO 2001).

Firms must not recommend that a client, as a purchaser, enters into a regulated home purchase plan or a regulated home reversion plan or, as a seller, a regulated sale and rent back agreement with a particular person but can endorse a recommendation given by a person who is regulated by the FCA or who is exempt from the general prohibition.[2]

A regulated home purchase plan is an arrangement under which a 'home purchase provider' buys all or part of a freehold or leasehold interest which provides for a home purchaser to buy the provider's interest during the course of or at the end of a specified period and the purchaser or a related person is entitled to occupy at least 40 per cent of the land as a dwelling and intends to do so (article 63F(3) of RAO 2001).

A regulated home reversion plan is an arrangement whereby a person, the reversion provider, buys all or part of a freehold or leasehold interest from an individual or trustees (the reversion occupier), and the reversion occupier or a related person is entitled to occupy at least 40 per cent of the land as a dwelling and intends to do so, and the arrangement specifies that the entitlement to occupy will end in specified circumstances (article 63B(3) of RAO 2001).

A regulated sale and rent back agreement is an arrangement whereby a provider buys all or part of a freehold or leasehold interest on terms that the seller or a related person is entitled to occupy at least 40 per cent of the land as a dwelling and intends to do so, but which is not a home reversion plan (article 63J(3)(a) of RAO 2001).

1 Rule 5.7 of the Scope Rules.
2 Rules 5.8 to 5.10.

Consumer credit activity

7.10

On 1 April 2014 consumer credit activity became a mainstream financial services activity regulated by the FCA. From that date solicitors may only carry out consumer credit activities:

- if they are fully FCA-authorised, or had previously been granted interim permission to continue to do so, for which application had to be made by 31 March 2014 (and which will not therefore be considered);
- if they have the benefit of the Part XX exemption (see **7.4**) though this may be more problematic in its application than in relation to other regulated activities; or
- if they are acting in the course of contentious business as defined in section 87 of the Solicitors Act 1974 (which must involve proceedings before a court or arbitrator, excluding non-contentious probate business). It is important to note that this therefore only applies where proceedings have been commenced, and not to any activity carried out before proceedings have been issued.[1]

Regulated consumer credit activities include:

- credit broking;
- operating an electronic system in relation to lending;
- debt adjusting;
- debt-counselling;
- debt-collecting;
- debt administration;
- entering into a regulated credit agreement as lender;
- exercising or having the right to exercise lender's rights under a regulated consumer credit agreement;
- entering into a regulated consumer hire agreement as owner;
- exercising or having the right to exercise owner's rights under a regulated consumer hire agreement;
- providing credit information services;
- providing credit references;
- agreeing to carry on any of the above.

Each of the listed activities has exemptions specific to the relevant activity and those firms likely to be undertaking these activities as a mainstream activity (to which this book is not addressed) need to consider RAO 2001 in detail, as amended by the Financial Services and Markets Act 2000 (Regulated Activities) (Amendment) (No 2) Order 2013, SI 2013/1881.

Of greater relevance to most solicitors' firms will be the Part XX exemption, which is available where the activity arises out of, or is complementary to, the provision of a particular professional service to a particular client; the manner of the provision of any service in the course of carrying on the activities is incidental to the provision of professional services; the firm accounts to a client for any pecuniary reward or other advantage which the firm receives from a third party; and the firm does not carry on any activities regulated by the FCA other than those permitted under Part XX of FSMA 2000, or in relation to which the firm is an exempt person.

The 'incidental' test must be applied on a case-by-case basis and it is unlikely that firms specialising in debt collection to any substantial extent would be able to avoid being regulated by the FCA.

The new SRA requirement to reflect these changes is rule 5.11 of the Scope Rules:

> 'Where a firm carries on a credit-related regulated activity or a connected activity it must comply with the provisions and guidance set out in Rule 1.3R of the transitional provisions in the [Consumer Credit sourcebook] as they were in force immediately before 1 April 2014 in relation to that activity, with any appropriate modification to take into account the coming into force of HM Treasury Orders that give effect to the transfer of consumer credit regulation from the OFT to the FCA.'

Rule 1.3R of the FCA's Consumer Credit sourcebook can be found at http://fshandbook.info/FS/html/handbook/CONC/TP/1.

The SRA's accompanying guidance is:

> 'During the transitional period between 1 April 2014 and 1 April 2015, firms carrying on credit-related regulated activities will be required to comply with the guidance and other provisions listed in the transitional provisions in theFCA's CONC. These provisions should not impose any new obligations as firms should already be complying with them but firms will need to adopt a common sense approach in interpreting them, for example, references to the OFT in these provisions and guidance should be read as if they referred to the FCA and references to the relevant supervisory authority mean the SRA.'

1 For example articles 36F(1)(b) and 39K(1)(b) of RAO 2001 as amended.

The COB Rules

7.11

As explained above, the COB Rules govern the manner in which solicitors' firms may carry out regulated activities that they are permitted to carry out under the Scope Rules. The Rules apply to licensed bodies (alternative business structures, ABSs) only in respect of that part of their business which is regulated under the Legal Services Act 2007; in other words to the provision of legal services as opposed to any other services that the business may be providing (such as funeral services). They apply, with one exception, to firms that are not regulated by the FCA and to firms that are regulated by the FCA but only in relation to non-mainstream regulated activities.

Status disclosure

7.12

The exception is rule 3, which relates to status disclosure and which applies only to firms that are *not* regulated by the FCA. Before such a firm provides any service which includes a regulated activity it must give the client the following information in writing, in a manner that is clear, fair and not misleading:

- a statement that the firm is not regulated by the FCA;
- the name and address of the firm;
- the nature of the regulated activities carried on by the firm and the fact that they are limited in scope;
- a statement that the firm is regulated by the SRA; and
- a statement explaining that complaints and redress mechanisms are provided through the SRA and the Legal Ombudsman (LeO).[1]

The following words are not compulsory but are in an acceptable form when combined with the other specific requirements listed above:

> 'The Law Society is a designated professional body for the purposes of the Financial Services and Markets Act 2000 but responsibility for regulation and complaints handling has been separated from the Law Society's representative functions. The Solicitors Regulation Authority is the independent regulatory body of the Law Society.'

The following specific written disclosure, in these precise words, must be provided to the client before any service is provided that includes an insurance mediation activity:

> '[This firm is] [We are] not authorised by the Financial Conduct Authority. However, we are included on the register maintained by the Financial Conduct Authority so that we can carry on insurance mediation activity, which is broadly the advising on, selling and administration of insurance contracts. This part of our business, including arrangements for complaints or redress if something goes wrong, is regulated by the Solicitors Regulation Authority. The register can be accessed via the Financial Conduct Authority website at www.fca.org.uk/register.'

There is no reason why the required disclosures cannot be incorporated in the firm's standard client care material, but they can be provided separately. It is not necessary to tailor the disclosure to the needs of the specific client.[2] However, LeO's service is available not to all clients, but only to individuals and small businesses (see **CHAPTER 13**) and care should be used in making reference to the availability of a redress mechanism.

1 Rule 3.2 of the COB Rules.
2 Rule 3.3 of the COB Rules, and associated guidance notes.

Other requirements

7.13

Firms must ensure that when it has been decided or agreed to effect a transaction they must do so as soon as possible, unless it is reasonably believed that it is not in the best interests of the client to do so.[1]

The COB Rules contain provisions requiring specified records to be kept of transactions, commissions received, how the firm accounted for commission to the client, and as to the safekeeping of clients' investments.[2] As to the principles involved in accounting for commission, see **7.5**.

If a firm arranges any transaction for a client involving a retail investment product on an execution-only basis, the firm must send written confirmation to the client that, as the case may be, no advice had been sought from or given by the firm, or advice had been given but the client nevertheless persisted in requiring the transaction to be effected – and in either case that the transaction is effected on express instructions.[3]

There are additional detailed requirements where firms engage in insurance mediation activities. These are primarily concerned with the disclosure of information and the extent to which a comparative market analysis has been carried out, with the need to establish by reasonable steps that the recommended policy is suitable for the client's demands and needs, and with the obligation to provide a 'demands and needs statement' before the contract is finalised (among other things explaining any recommendation made).[4]

1 Rule 4 of the COB Rules.
2 Rules 5, 6, 7 and 10.
3 Rule 8.
4 Rule 9.1 and Appendix 1.

Financial promotions

7.14

There is a second separate strand of regulation under FSMA 2000 of which practitioners should be aware. Under section 21 of FSMA 2000, you are prohibited from, in the course of business, communicating an invitation or inducement to engage in investment activity unless this is done by an authorised person, or the content of the communication is approved by an authorised person. Solicitors' practices are not authorised persons but can take advantage of an exemption to undertake exempt regulated activities as explained above, for the purposes of RAO 2001. This regime does not, however, apply to financial promotions, which are covered by the Financial Services and Markets Act 2000 (Financial Promotion) Order 2005 (FPO 2005).[1] Regulated activities for the purposes of RAO 2001 are not precisely the same as (though are very similar to) controlled activities for the purposes of FPO 2005.

If a firm, therefore, does communicate invitations or inducements to engage in an investment activity, it must, if it is regulated by the SRA rather than the FCA, be able to rely on an exemption within FPO 2005. Fortunately, there are exemptions specifically in favour of members of professions. Under article 55 of FPO 2005, the financial promotion restriction does not apply to a real time communication (whether solicited or unsolicited) which is made by a person who carries on a regulated activity to which the general prohibition does not apply by virtue of section 327 of FSMA 2000 (in other words those carrying out exempt regulated activities and who are regulated by their own professional body); and which is made to a recipient who has, prior to the communication being made, engaged that person to provide professional services, and where the activity to which the communication relates is (in short) for the purposes of, and incidental to, the provision of professional services to or at the request of the recipient.

A real time communication is any communication made in the course of a personal visit, telephone conversation or other interactive dialogue.[2] Note that this exemption applies to communications with existing clients, but can be solicited or unsolicited.

The article 55 exemption does not apply to non-real time communications, including letters, e-mails and material in a publication such as a brochure. Article 55A provides an exemption for members of a profession in relation to non-real time communications if the stated conditions are satisfied. The financial promotion restriction does not apply to a non-real time communication which is made by a person who carries on Part XX activities (that is, again, those who are carrying out exempt regulated activities and who are regulated by their own professional body) and which is limited to a communication expressly provided for in article 55A: that is, one that promotes an activity that is within Part XX of FSMA

2000 (in other words, one that is not prohibited by the Scope Rules). The communication must contain the following:

> 'This [firm/company] is not authorised under the Financial Services and Markets Act 2000 but we are able in certain circumstances to offer a limited range of investment and consumer credit-related services to clients because we are members of [relevant designated professional body]. We can provide these investment and consumer credit-related services if they are an incidental part of the professional services we have been engaged to provide.'[3]

Note that this is similar to but not identical with the notice that is required by the COB Rules for insurance mediation activities (see **7.12**).

Firms can therefore communicate an invitation or inducement in writing provided the promoted activities fall within the scope of exempt regulated activities and the invitation or inducement is accompanied by the specified notice.

1 SI 2005/1529.
2 Article 7 of FPO 2005.
3 Article 55A(2) of FPO 2005.

CHAPTER 8

Property selling

8.1

The professional rules concerned with property selling were formerly part of the 2007 Code of Conduct, as rule 18. It was necessarily a fairly prescriptive form of regulation as it had to mirror the obligations of estate agents under the Estate Agents Act 1979.

The 2011 Code is not intended to be comprised of black letter rules, but is rather a set of outcomes within a scheme of outcomes-focused regulation. A set of black letter rules could not readily fit within the 2011 Code. The Solicitors Regulation Authority (SRA)'s solution has been to hive off the rules that had to remain in a statutory or near-statutory form into a separate part of the SRA Handbook under the generic title of 'specialist services'.

Financial services (see **CHAPTER 7**), property selling, and European cross-border practice (see **CHAPTER 9**) are in this category.

Rule 18 of the 2007 Code has been reborn as the SRA Property Selling Rules 2011.

The rules, as they necessarily imply, are only concerned with property selling, that is, estate agency services provided through a solicitor's firm. If the property-selling service is provided through a separate business, and not through the firm, Chapter 12 of the 2011 Code applies.

The rules impose standards of competency and service, require the prompt provision of clear information, in writing, as to the basis of the retainer and the fees to be charged, and provide for the avoidance of conflicts of interests.

8.2

Firms must ensure that they and any employees through whom the work is carried out are competent to do such work, and meet any standards of competence set by the Secretary of State under section 22 of the Estate Agents Act 1979.[1]

Firms must not seek from any buyer a pre-contract deposit in excess of any limit prescribed by the Secretary of State under section 19 of the Estate Agents Act 1979.[2]

If firms receive from any buyer a pre-contract deposit which exceeds the prescribed limit, so much of that deposit as exceeds the prescribed limit shall be either repaid to the buyer or paid to such other person as the buyer may direct.

These requirements[3] are in addition to the requirements in Chapter 1 of the 2011 Code in respect of client relations.

1 The standards of competence are to be set by regulations made by the Secretary of State, but the section is not yet in force and no regulations have been made, so that this remains at present a general requirement of competence to undertake the work in question.
2 The prescribed limit is to be set by regulations made by the Secretary of State, but the section is not yet in force and no regulations have been made.
3 Which comprise rule 3 of the SRA Property Selling Rules 2011.

8.3

Firms must, at the outset of communication with the client, or as soon as is reasonably practicable, and before the client is committed to any liability for fees or otherwise, give the client a written statement setting out whether or not there is to be a 'sole agency' or 'sole selling rights'. The statement must include a clear explanation of the intention and effect of those terms, or any similar terms used, which must be in the prescribed words:[1]

> 'Sole agency: You will be liable to pay a fee to us, in addition to any other costs or charges agreed, if unconditional contracts for the sale of the property are exchanged at any time: with a buyer introduced by us with whom we had negotiations about the property in the period during which we have sole agency; or with a buyer introduced by another agent during the period of our sole agency.'
>
> 'Sole selling rights: You will be liable to pay a fee to us, in addition to any other costs or charges agreed, in each of the following circumstances:
>
> (i) if unconditional contracts for the sale of the property are exchanged in the period during which we have sole selling rights, even if the buyer was not found by us but by another agent or by any other person, including yourself; or
>
> (ii) if unconditional contracts for the sale of the property are exchanged after the expiry of the period during which we have sole selling rights but to a buyer who was introduced to you during that period or with whom we had negotiations about the property during that period.'[2]

If the statement refers to a 'ready, willing and able' buyer (or similar term), a clear explanation of the term must be included in the prescribed words:[3]

> 'A buyer is a "ready, willing and able" buyer if he or she is prepared and is able to exchange unconditional contracts for the purchase of your property. You will be liable to pay a fee to us, in addition to any other costs or charges agreed, if such a buyer is introduced by us in accordance with your instructions and this must be paid even if you subsequently withdraw and unconditional contracts for sale are not exchanged, irrespective of your reasons.'[4]

The explanations must be reproduced prominently, clearly and legibly without any material alterations or additions. They should be given no less prominence than that given to any other information in the statement apart from the heading, firm names, names of the parties, numbers or lettering subsequently inserted.[5]

The requirements of rule 4 correspond to the Estate Agents (Provision of Information) Regulations 1991 (SI 1991/859) and are in addition to the requirements of Chapter 1 of the 2011 Code in respect of client relations.

1 Unless in context the prescribed explanation is itself misleading, in which case the words must be altered to describe the client's liability accurately – rule 4.3.
2 Rule 4.1 of the SRA Property Selling Rules 2011.
3 Unless in context the prescribed explanation is itself misleading, in which case the words must be altered to describe the client's liability accurately – rule 4.3.
4 Rule 4.2 of the SRA Property Selling Rules 2011.
5 Rule 4.3 of the SRA Property Selling Rules 2011.

8.4

The client must be promptly informed in writing if the firm, or any 'connected person' to the firm's knowledge[1] has, or is seeking to acquire, a beneficial interest in the property or in the proceeds of sale of any interest in the property.

Any person negotiating to acquire or dispose of any interest in the property must be promptly informed in writing if the firm or any connected person has a beneficial interest in a property or in the proceeds of sale of any interest in it. This must be done before entering into any negotiations with that person, whether or not the negotiations are on your own behalf or on behalf of a client.[2]

A 'connected person' is widely defined to include any associated firm;[3] anyone with whom you are related by blood, marriage or adoption, or with whom you are living together in a civil or domestic partnership; owners and employees of your firm or of an associated firm, and their relatives, etc., and various company arrangements, as well as any other 'associate' as defined in section 32 of the Estate Agents Act 1979 (which covers relationships, company and partnership arrangements in a similar way).[4]

The requirements in relation to avoidance of conflicts of interest are additional to those imposed by Chapter 3 of the 2011 Code. They are similar to those imposed on estate agents by the Estate Agents (Undesirable Practices) (No 2) Order 1991 (SI 1991/1032).

1 'Knowledge' includes circumstances in which you may reasonably be expected to have knowledge – SRA Handbook Glossary 2012.
2 Rule 5.1 of the SRA Property Selling Rules 2011.
3 An associated firm means: a partnership with whom you have one partner in common; an LLP or a company without shares with whom you have one member in common; or a company with shares with whom you have one owner in common – SRA Handbook Glossary 2012.
4 SRA Handbook Glossary 2012.

CHAPTER 9

European cross-border practice

9.1

In the same way that the rules on property selling have moved outside the 2011 Code and for the same reasons (see **8.1**), what was rule 16 of the 2007 Code has become the SRA European Cross-border Practice Rules 2011.

European cross-border practice involves professional activity regulated by the SRA in a CCBE state (see **9.2**) other than the United Kingdom, whether or not the practitioner or firm is physically present in that state, and any professional contact of a kind that is regulated by the SRA with a lawyer of a CCBE state other than the United Kingdom. Contacts and activities within a firm or in-house legal department are not within the definition.[1]

1 Rule 2.1 of the SRA European Cross-border Practice Rules 2011.

9.2

CCBE is the recognised abbreviation for the Council of the Bars and Law Societies of Europe and was originally the Commission Consultative des Barreaux d'Europe. Its correct current French title is 'Conseil des Barreaux Européens'. The Council's principal object is to study all questions affecting the legal profession in the Member States of the European Union and the European Economic Area and to formulate solutions designed to co-ordinate and harmonise professional practice. It has set up a Council for Advice and Arbitration to assist in resolving complaints between lawyers in different member states.

The CCBE has published a Code of Conduct for Lawyers in the European Community (in October 1988; most recently updated in May 2006) for the purposes of regulating the conduct of lawyers within the Community concerned in cross-border activities.

There are 32 full member states of the CCBE, three associated members and ten observer members. The CCBE Code of Conduct applies to all of them without distinction.

The full members are:

Austria Belgium Bulgaria Croatia Cyprus Czech Republic Denmark Estonia Finland France Germany	Greece Hungary Iceland Ireland Italy Latvia Liechtenstein Lithuania Luxembourg Malta Norway	Poland Portugal Romania Slovak Republic Slovenia Spain Sweden Switzerland The Netherlands United Kingdom

The associated members are:

Montenegro
Serbia
Turkey

The observer members are:

Albania Andorra Armenia Bosnia and Herzegovina Georgia	Former Yugoslav Republic of Macedonia Moldova Russia	San Marino Ukraine

9.3

The purpose of the SRA European Cross-border Practice Rules is to bring together in one place the requirements imposed by the CCBE Code of Conduct for Lawyers in the European Community to the extent that those requirements are not replicated in other rules within the SRA Code of Conduct 2011.

The consequence is that if solicitors comply with the 2011 Code generally in relation to their practices, and with the Cross-border Practice Rules in relation to any cross-border practice, they will comply in all respects with the CCBE Code of Conduct. The CCBE Code is nevertheless for completeness included at **APPENDIX 3**.

9.4

There are essentially seven elements to the Rules:

- occupations considered incompatible with legal practice, which is an issue to be determined by reference to the rules of the CCBE state in question (rule 3);
- fee sharing with non-lawyers (rule 4);
- co-operation between lawyers of different CCBE states (rule 5);

- considerations arising from correspondence between lawyers of different CCBE states, because 'confidential' and 'without prejudice' may be interpreted differently (rule 6);
- a prohibition on payment of referral fees to non-lawyers (rule 7);
- the proper procedure in the event of a dispute between lawyers (rule 8); and
- obligations in relation to fees when other lawyers are instructed (rule 9).

9.5

Rule 3 provides that if you act in legal proceedings or proceedings before public authorities in a CCBE state other than the United Kingdom, you must, in that state, comply with any rules regarding occupations incompatible with the practice of law, as if you were a lawyer of that state, whether or not you are based at an office in that state; and if you are a solicitor based at an office in a CCBE state other than the United Kingdom, you must respect any rules regarding participation in commercial or other activities not connected with the practice of law, as they are applied to lawyers of that state.

Rule 4 provides that whether you are practising in a CCBE state other than the United Kingdom, or in the United Kingdom, you must not share your fees with a non-lawyer in a CCBE state (other than the United Kingdom) except within the firm as permitted by the SRA Practice Framework Rules 2011, or with retired partners, members, etc. or their dependants.

Rule 5 imposes an obligation to provide reasonable co-operation to other lawyers. It requires that if you are approached by a lawyer of a CCBE state other than the United Kingdom to undertake work which you are not competent to undertake, you must assist that lawyer to obtain the information necessary to find and instruct a lawyer capable of providing the service requested. When co-operating with a lawyer of a CCBE state other than the United Kingdom you must take into account the differences which may exist between the respective legal systems and the professional organisations, competencies and obligations of lawyers in their respective states.

9.6

Rule 6 seeks to avoid misunderstandings in professional correspondence when communications are intended to be 'confidential' or 'without prejudice'. Before sending the communication you must clearly express your intention in order to avoid misunderstanding, and ask if the lawyer is able to accept the communication on the intended basis. When you send the communication you must express your intention clearly at the head of the communication or in a covering letter. If you are the intended recipient of a communication from a lawyer in another CCBE state which is stated to be 'confidential' or 'without prejudice', but which you are unable to accept on the basis intended by that lawyer, you must inform the sender accordingly without delay. If the communication has already been sent you must return it unread without revealing the contents to others. If you have already read the communication and you are under a professional duty to reveal it to your client you must inform the sender immediately.

9.7

Under rule 7 the payment of referral fees to non-lawyers is prohibited if the non-lawyer is situated in a CCBE state other than the United Kingdom or if you are practising from an office in a CCBE state other than the United Kingdom, whether or not you are physically present at that office. The rule applies to any fee, commission or any other compensation as a consideration for referring a client.

By virtue of rule 8, if you consider that a lawyer in a CCBE state other than the United Kingdom has acted in breach of a rule of professional conduct you must draw the breach to the other lawyer's attention and, before commencing any form of proceedings against the other lawyer, you must inform the Law Society and the other lawyer's bar or law society in order to allow them an opportunity to assist in resolving the matter.

Under rule 9, you are under a professional obligation to pay the fees of a lawyer or legal business in another CCBE state instructed by you, subject to specified exceptions including an express disclaimer.

CHAPTER 10

Professional indemnity insurance

10.1

The compulsory requirement that solicitors should be insured against professional risks dates from 1976, when the Law Society made indemnity rules under the powers provided by section 37 of the Solicitors Act 1974. From then until 1987 the Law Society negotiated the terms of a master policy with the insurance industry year by year. In 1987 the Solicitors Indemnity Fund (SIF) was established to replace the master policy scheme.

In 2000 the requirement that all solicitors be insured through the SIF was abolished and solicitors became free to negotiate their professional indemnity insurance on the open market.

The Solicitors Regulation Authority (SRA) is consulting on proposals to change the arrangements for professional indemnity insurance to reduce the minimum level of cover of £2 million to £500,000 and to impose a new regulatory obligation on firms to assess the adequacy of the level of cover they need. These plans are currently on hold awaiting consideration by the Legal Services Board as a result of widespread opposition, but have not been abandoned.

From 2000 and continuing there remain two stipulations, within what is otherwise a free market:

(1) the insurer must be a participating insurer, that is an authorised insurer (essentially any insurer authorised to carry out that class of business under the Financial Services and Markets Act 2000)[1] which has entered into a Participating Insurer's Agreement with the Law Society which remains in force for the purposes of underwriting new business at the date of the insurance contract; and

(2) the terms of the insurance cover must meet the 'Minimum Terms and Conditions' set by the current indemnity insurance rules.[2]

Qualifying insurance may be underwritten by more than one insurer provided that, collectively, the minimum terms and conditions are satisfied and that one insurer is identified as the lead insurer.[3] A list of participating insurers can be found on the SRA website.

Until 30 September 2013 all insurance policies ran for one year from 1 October in each year. From 1 October 2013 insurers are free to issue policies with variable renewal dates. Policies may be for periods of any length.

1 See the Participating Insurer's Agreement 2014.
2 Appendix 1 to the SRA Indemnity Insurance Rules 2013.
3 Appendix 1, clause 2.6.

10.2

The SIF remains relevant to current regulatory requirements in that it will provide run-off cover for new claims against principals who retired before 1 September 2000 in circumstances where there is no successor practice, and will also provide run-off cover for claims where the run-off cover provided by qualifying insurers has expired. Qualifying insurers provide run-off cover for a period of six years under the minimum terms and conditions. The SIF will provide cover between 1 September 2007 and 1 September 2020 for claims notified within that period after the six-year period of commercial run-off cover has expired (and has arranged reinsurance in respect of those risks).

Solicitors are currently subject to two sets of indemnity rules – the SRA Indemnity Rules 2012, which regulate the relationship between the profession and the SIF, and the SRA Indemnity Insurance Rules 2013 (SIIR 2013), which set out the requirements for qualifying insurance obtained on the open market.

The SIF is in surplus, in spite of the fact that contributions made to the Fund for the indemnity periods 2001/02 and 2002/03 have been repaid to those who made them or their estates. It is therefore expected that the SRA Indemnity Rules 2012 will only be relevant in practice to the mechanisms for dealing with an increasingly small number of potential claims capable of being indemnified under the run-off arrangements. These issues are likely to be of minimal significance and will therefore not be considered.

The SRA Indemnity Insurance Rules 2013 – the basic requirements

10.3

Solicitors are not entitled to practise without having qualifying insurance in force. It is necessary to produce evidence of qualifying insurance when an application is made for a practising certificate. The SRA must refuse an application for a practising certificate if it is not satisfied that the solicitor is complying with current indemnity rules.[1] SIIR 2013 enable the SRA to require the production of information and evidence that qualifying insurance is in place.[2]

Every practice regulated by the SRA must arrange insurance with one or more qualifying insurers that must comply with the minimum terms and conditions set out in Appendix 1 to SIIR 2013; the obligation is imposed both on the firm and on every principal.[3] Licensed bodies (alternative business structures, ABSs) must have qualifying insurance in relation to their regulated activities, where they undertake both regulated and unregulated activities, and SIIR 2013 apply to licensed bodies generally only in relation to their regulated activities.

SIIR 2013 do not apply to overseas practice. For overseas practice see **4.127** and outcome 13A.2.

The minimum level of cover is £2 million, or £3 million if the firm is a recognised body or licensed body (ABS), with narrow exceptions.[4] Firms are free to arrange cover in excess of the minimum levels and may do so with insurers which are not participating insurers, and are also free to negotiate the level of any excess which the firm may elect to meet in respect of claims. The minimum terms and conditions require that if the excess is not paid by the insured the insurer must meet the full amount of the claim and recover the amount due from the firm.

A minimum of six years' run-off cover is required if the firm ceases to practise during an indemnity period. Run-off cover is not required if there is a successor practice. In that event the qualifying insurance will be that of the successor practice.

1 Regulation 2.2 of the SRA Practising Regulations 2011. But see *Hidveghy v Law Society (No 9 of 2003)* (unreported), where the solicitor was a former partner in a firm which had been dissolved, but which remained in default of the requirements to pay insurance contributions. Neither he nor the other partner was in a position to meet these liabilities. The petitioning solicitor was insolvent and had become employed by an unconnected firm which was not in default. Lord Phillips MR held that section 10 had to be given a purposive construction and that the solicitor was no longer a member of a firm which was in default, and the Society was obliged to issue a practising certificate.

2 Rule 7 of SIIR 2013.

3 Rules 4 and 5.

4 The exceptions are unlimited companies, companies acting in a purely nominee capacity and 'ordinary' partnerships where no partner is an LLP or corporate body with limited liability, or a sole practitioner who is a recognised body; see the definitions of 'relevant recognised body' and 'relevant licensed body' in the SRA Handbook Glossary 2012.

The extended indemnity period and the cessation period

10.4

Until 30 September 2013 there was an expensive safety net for firms which were unable to acquire insurance in the open market; the Assigned Risks Pool (ARP). For an analysis of this system see Chapter 10 of the *Solicitor's Handbook 2013*. From 1 October 2013 the ARP was abolished save in respect of run-off cover. From that date, if a firm is unable to renew its existing policy or to obtain insurance from another participating insurer on or by the renewal date it has 30 days within which to obtain cover, during which its existing insurer will continue to insure (the 'extended indemnity period'). If no qualifying insurance is found in that period the firm must cease practice promptly, and in any event no later than a further 60 days (the 'cessation period'), unless qualifying insurance can be found within the cessation period which will be effective from the renewal date. The existing insurer will also provide cover during the cessation period.[1]

During the cessation period (after the extended indemnity period has expired) the firm and every principal must ensure that the firm, every principal and every employee undertakes no work in relation to private legal practice and accepts no instructions, save to the extent that the work or the instructions are necessary to discharge obligations within the scope of the firm's existing instructions or are otherwise necessary to fulfil those obligations.[2]

In short, from the date of renewal, the firm has 30 days to find cover during which it may continue to work normally, but from that point on, although it may still try to find insurance for a further 60 days, it is obliged to work towards an orderly close down, accepting no new work.

The insurer providing cover for the previous insurance period must extend cover for the whole of the 90 days, unless another participating insurer steps in.

The minimum terms and conditions permit insurers to require reimbursement, to the extent that it is just or equitable having regard to the prejudice caused to the insurer's interests, where the firm undertakes work in the cessation period contrary to rule 5.2 of SIIR 2013.[3]

The circumstances in which firms were able to continue in practice without being able to obtain insurance on the open market and without (in many cases) paying the ARP premium has been brought to an end.

1 Rule 4.2 of SIIR 2013.
2 Rule 5.2.
3 Clause 7.2(b) of Appendix 1 to SIIR 2013.

The minimum terms and conditions

10.5

The minimum terms and conditions are set out in Appendix 1 to SIIR 2013. Some aspects have already been mentioned, namely the minimum level of cover at £2 million or £3 million for relevant recognised bodies or licensed bodies for each claim.[1] The insurance must indemnify against civil liability to the extent that it arises from private legal practice in connection with the insured firm's practice, on a 'claims made' basis; that is, claims are covered if made within the period of insurance, or after it in respect of an occurrence notified during the period of insurance.

The insurance must indemnify against any amount paid or payable in accordance with the recommendation of the Legal Services Ombudsman (no longer likely to be relevant), the Legal Ombudsman or any other regulatory authority to the same extent as it indemnifies the insured against civil liability, but not in respect of any determination requiring the firm to refund fees.[2]

Defence costs must also be covered without limit.[3] Where a claim exceeds the sum insured, the insurer may limit its liability for costs to the proportion that the sum insured bears to the total amount paid or payable to dispose of the claim.[4]

The insurance may make provision as to the meaning of 'one claim' for the purposes of determining the limit of indemnity and, in particular, may provide that all claims against any one or more insured will be regarded as one claim when arising from:

(1) one act or omission;

(2) one series of related acts or omissions;

(3) the same act or omission in a series of related matters or transactions; or

(4) similar acts or omissions in a series of related matters or transactions; and

(5) all claims against one or more insured arising from one matter or transaction.[5]

As already mentioned, firms are free to negotiate the level of excess to be applied – meaning firms can elect to self-insure to a substantial extent without regard to the minimum terms.[6] Protection for the public is maintained as, if the insured fails to pay the amount of any excess to the claimant, the insurer must make good the sum, reclaiming it from the insured as necessary.[7] Any excess may not reduce the total limit of liability.[8] The excess must not apply to defence costs.[9] The insurance may provide for multiple claims to be treated as one claim for the purpose of calculating any excess, on terms that may be agreed between insurer and insured.[10]

The most important element of the minimum terms and conditions consists of the restrictions they impose on insurers for the purpose of ensuring that members of the public are not deprived of the benefits of compulsory professional indemnity insurance as a result of matters which, in other circumstances, might enable an insurer to disclaim or avoid liability. These are referred to in Appendix 1 to SIIR 2013 as 'special conditions'.[11]

1 Appendix 1, clause 2.1 to SIIR 2013.
2 Appendix 1, clause 1.8.
3 Appendix 1, clause 2.2.
4 Appendix 1, clause 2.3.
5 Appendix 1, clause 2.5. See also *Lloyds TSB General Insurance Holdings Ltd v Lloyds Bank Group Insurance Co Ltd* [2003] UKHL 48, [2003] 4 All ER 43. Clause 2.5 has been drafted to overcome the difficulties in aggregating claims caused by the manner in which policies were drafted prior to that decision.
6 Appendix 1, clause 3.1.
7 Appendix 1, clause 3.4.
8 Appendix 1, clause 3.2.
9 Appendix 1, clause 3.3.
10 Appendix 1, clause 3.5.
11 Appendix 1, clause 4.

Restrictions on insurers – the 'special conditions'

10.6

Insurers are not entitled to avoid or repudiate insurance on any grounds whatsoever, including non-disclosure or misrepresentation (fraudulent or otherwise). They are not entitled to reduce or deny their liability on any grounds whatsoever, including any breach of any term or condition of the insurance, other than if one of the specified exclusions applies (see further below). They are not entitled to cancel the insurance unless alternative qualifying insurance is in place (for example, in the event of a merger of firms), and cancellation must not affect rights and obligations that accrued prior to the cancellation. Insurers cannot set off any amounts due from the insured, such as any premium or reimbursement that may be due, against any amount payable to a claimant; they cannot reduce or exclude liability by reason of the existence or availability of other insurance (except other qualifying insurance in respect of an earlier period or cover by the SIF), although insurers are not prevented from seeking an appropriate contribution from that other insurer; and they cannot exclude or limit liability because relevant matters occurred before a specified date.

Insurers must meet defence costs as and when they are incurred unless and until the insured admits that he or she has committed or condoned dishonesty or a fraudulent act or omission, or a court or other judicial body finds that the insured was guilty of such dishonesty or fraudulent act or omission.[1]

The parties are required to take all reasonable steps to resolve disputes about coverage as between potentially liable insurers and there is a provision entitling the Law Society to give directions as to how the claim should be conducted and, if necessary, compromised and paid in the meantime.[2]

The insurance must provide that it is to be construed or rectified so as to comply with the requirements of the minimum terms and conditions, and that any inconsistent provision must be severed or rectified to be compliant.[3]

1 Appendix 1, clauses 4.1 to 4.8 to SIIR 2013.
2 Appendix 1, clauses 4.9 and 4.10.
3 Appendix 1, clause 4.11.

Run-off and successor practices

10.7

Clause 5 of Appendix 1 to SIIR 2013 deals with the extended indemnity period, the cessation period (see **10.4**), and run-off cover, which must be for a minimum period of six years from the end of the indemnity period, if the practice ceases during the indemnity period *without* a successor practice. As explained above claims may be made on the SIF if they are made later than six years after the end of the primary indemnity period.

What is or is not a successor practice is a very material consideration, and not just in this respect, because the insurers of a successor practice will become liable for any claims against the former practice that have not already been discovered and notified. This term has its own definition in the SRA Handbook Glossary 2012 and is reproduced here for convenience.

successor practice

(i) means a *practice* identified in this definition as 'B', where:

(A) 'A' is the *practice* to which B succeeds; and

(B) 'A's owner' is the owner of A immediately prior to transition; and

(C) 'B's owner' is the owner of B immediately following transition; and

(D) 'transition' means merger, acquisition, absorption or other transition which results in A no longer being carried on as a discrete legal *practice*.

(ii) B is a successor practice to A where:

(A) B is or was held out, expressly or by implication, by B's owner as being the successor of A or as incorporating A, whether such holding out is contained in notepaper, business cards, form of electronic communications, publications, promotional material or otherwise, or is contained in any statement or declaration by B's owner to any regulatory or taxation authority; and/or

(B) (where A's owner was a *sole practitioner* and the transition occurred on or before 31 August 2000) – the *sole practitioner* is a *principal* of B's owner; and/or

(C) (where A's owner was a *sole practitioner* and the transition occurred on or after 1 September 2000) – the *sole practitioner* is a *principal* or *employee* of B's owner; and/or

(D) (where A's owner was a *recognised body* or a *licensed body* (in respect of its *regulated activities*)) – that body is a *principal* of B's owner; and/or

(E) (where A's owner was a *partnership*) – the majority of the *principals* of A's owner have become *principals* of B's owner; and/or

(F) (where A's owner was a *partnership* and the majority of *principals* of A's owner did not become *principals* of the owner of another legal *practice* as a result of the transition) – one or more of the *principals* of A's owner have become *principals* of B's owner and:

(I) B is carried on under the same name as A or a name which substantially incorporates the name of A (or a substantial part of the name of A); and/or

(II) B is carried on from the same premises as A; and/or

(III) the owner of B acquired the goodwill and/or assets of A; and/or

(IV) the owner of B assumed the liabilities of A; and/or

(V) the majority of staff employed by A's owner became *employees* of B's owner.

(iii) Notwithstanding the foregoing, B is not a successor practice to A under paragraph (ii)(B), (C), (D), (E) or (F) if another *practice* is or was held out by the owner of that other *practice* as the successor of A or as incorporating A, provided that there is insurance complying with the *MTC* in relation to that other *practice*.

In brief, most circumstances involving the partners or other owners of a practice (or a majority of them) being absorbed into another firm – or even a minority in certain circumstances, or anything done or said which holds out expressly or impliedly that the second firm is succeeding to or incorporating the first firm – will result in the second firm being a successor practice. The definition focuses on people and ownership, rather than on cases and clients, so that if a firm does not hold itself out as a successor practice and acquires the clients and files of a firm that closes (for example) but does not take on its owners, either as principals or employees, it will not be a successor practice.

However, a firm which is about to close and to which there would be a successor practice for the purpose of SIIR 2013 has an option. It may allow that situation to occur, or it may, before the cessation of its business, elect to trigger its own run-off cover and pay the premium. Notice must be given to the SRA by the insurer within seven days of receipt of notice of the election, to which the firm must irrevocably agree. In that event, there is no successor practice. If the election is not made, or if the run-off premium is not paid, the option is lost and the normal rules on succession will apply.[1]

1 Clause 5.6 of Appendix 1 to SIIR 2013.

Permitted exclusions

10.8

The minimum terms and conditions specify the permitted exclusions from liability in clause 6 of Appendix 1 to SIIR 2013. They are:

- claims where cover is provided by the SIF or under insurance for a prior period;
- claims for death or bodily injury, except psychological injury and emotional distress arising from an insured breach of duty (that is, in the performance of or failure to perform legal work);
- claims for damage or loss to, or destruction of, property – unless it is property in the care of the insured or where the damage or loss arises from an insured breach of duty;
- claims arising from partnership disputes within the firm or the like;
- claims in the nature of employment disputes about dismissal, harassment or discrimination and the like;
- personal debts and trading liabilities (excluding Land Registry fees);
- claims in relation to guarantees, indemnities or undertakings in connection with the provision of financial or other benefits for the personal advantage of the insured;
- any fine or penalty or order for costs in relation to a professional conduct complaint; and
- punitive or exemplary damages awarded under US or Canadian law, other than in defamation.

Insurers may also exclude liability (and always do) for dishonesty or a fraudulent act or omission committed or condoned by an individual insured, but insurance must nonetheless cover each other insured and no dishonesty can be imputed to a body corporate unless it was committed or condoned by all directors of a company or members of a limited liability partnership.

Cover may also be excluded for company directors' or officers' liability, in that capacity (unless it arises from an insured breach of duty) and for claims arising from terrorism, war and other hostilities, and asbestos-related injury or damage (unless arising from an insured breach of duty).

Defence costs

10.9

Defence costs include costs and disbursements reasonably and necessarily incurred with the consent of the insurer in:

- defending any proceedings relating to a claim;
- conducting any proceedings for indemnity, contribution or recovery relating to a claim;

- investigating, reducing, avoiding or compromising any actual or potential claim; and
- acting for any insured in connection with any investigation or inquiry (save in respect of any disciplinary proceeding under the authority of the Law Society (including, without limitation, the SRA and the Solicitors Disciplinary Tribunal)).[1]

The costs of disciplinary proceedings were formerly covered, with some limitations, but this aspect of cover was removed from 1 October 2010.

A claim includes any civil claim for damages or compensation or an intimation of the same, and also includes an obligation on the insured to remedy any breach of the Solicitors' Accounts Rules 1998 or SRA Accounts Rules 2011 – even if no individual has made any claim or given any intimation of a claim in relation to such breach.[2]

1 Defence costs are defined in the SRA Handbook Glossary 2012.
2 See the definition of a claim in the Glossary.

Other regulatory obligations

10.10

Any breach of the SIIR 2013 is a disciplinary matter.[1]

Any participating insurer must bring to the attention of the SRA:

- any failure on the part of a firm to pay any sum by the date specified in SIIR 2013;
- any failure to reimburse any payment made by the insurer which is within a policy excess;
- any material inaccuracy in a proposal form;
- the fact that a firm is in run-off or believed to be;
- any matter or circumstances which would entitle the insurer to avoid or repudiate the insurance were it not for the provisions of clause 4.1 of Appendix 1 to SIIR 2013 (including non-disclosure and misrepresentation);
- any suspected dishonesty or fraud on the part of an insured; or
- any claim of inadequate professional services against the firm,[2]

at any time and without notice to the firm concerned.[3]

A firm must notify the SRA and its insurer as soon as reasonably practicable, and in any event within five business days, after entering the extended indemnity period, and after entering the cessation period, and must also notify both parties if qualifying insurance is obtained within either period, with the details of the participating insurer and policy.[4]

A firm, and any principal, is required to provide details of its qualifying insurance to any person who asserts a claim apparently covered by the policy, and to anyone who is insured under the policy, upon request.[5]

CHAPTER 10
PROFESSIONAL INDEMNITY
INSURANCE

Any accountant's report provided under section 34 of the Solicitors Act 1974 must contain a statement certifying whether the firm has qualifying insurance for the whole of the period covered by the report.[6]

1 Rule 16 of SIIR 2013.
2 This may also be notified to the Legal Ombudsman.
3 Rule 17.1 of SIIR 2013.
4 Rule 17.3.
5 Rule 18.
6 Rule 20.

CHAPTER 11

Registered European lawyers and registered foreign lawyers

11.1

A registered European lawyer (REL) is an individual registered with the Solicitors Regulation Authority (SRA) under regulation 17 of the European Communities (Lawyer's Practice) Regulations 2000[1] ('the 2000 Regulations'): see **APPENDIX 5**.

A registered foreign lawyer (RFL) is an individual registered with the SRA under section 89 of the Courts and Legal Services Act (CLSA) 1990: see **APPENDIX 17**.

By virtue of their registration, both RELs and RFLs become subject to regulation by the SRA and are subject to the same rules of professional conduct and the whole regulatory and disciplinary regime that is in place for solicitors, with very little modification or exception. Further, as a result of the move to entity-based regulation, RELs and RFLs are liable for compliance with all relevant professional rules, including the SRA Code of Conduct 2011, as managers or employees of regulated practices (see **CHAPTER 2**).

1 SI 2000/1119.

11.2

RELs may practise, for all practical purposes, as if they are solicitors, and subject to the same restrictions, in that they can practise on their own account (but only if they are authorised to be sole practitioners as solicitors are required to be under the SRA Authorisation Rules for Legal Services Bodies and Licensable Bodies 2011), or jointly with other RELs, with non-registered European lawyers, and with RFLs, as well as with solicitors and recognised bodies and in any combination.[1]

RELs may carry out under their home professional titles any professional activity that may be carried out by solicitors,[2] with only three exceptions:

(1) In any proceedings before a court, tribunal or public authority where the professional activities in question may only be carried out by a solicitor, barrister or other qualified person an REL must act in conjunction with a solicitor or barrister who is entitled to practise in that forum and who could lawfully provide those professional activities, and the solicitor or barrister in question is answerable to the court or tribunal as the case may be.[3]

(2) In property transactions RELs are not entitled to prepare for remuneration any instrument creating or transferring an interest in land unless their home professional titles were obtained in Denmark, Republic of Ireland, Finland, Sweden, Iceland, Liechtenstein, Norway, Czech Republic, Cyprus, Hungary or Slovakia.[4]

(3) In relation to probate matters RELs are not entitled to prepare for remuneration any instrument for obtaining title to administer the estate of a deceased person unless their home professional titles were obtained in Denmark, Germany, Republic of Ireland, Austria, Finland, Sweden, Iceland, Liechtenstein, Norway, Cyprus or Slovakia.[5]

1 Rule 2 of the SRA Practice Framework Rules 2011.
2 Regulation 6 of the 2000 Regulations.
3 Regulation 11.
4 Regulation 12.
5 Regulation 13.

11.3

RFLs, in contrast, are more restricted in the way they can practise. The main purpose of being registered as an RFL is to enable the individual to practise in a recognised body with a solicitor or solicitors, or an REL or RELs or a combination of the two – that is, as a manager, member or owner of a recognised body.[1] There is no requirement on a foreign lawyer to become an RFL for the purposes of being employed by a recognised body or a sole practitioner, or to be an owner, manager or employee of a licensed body. Registration does not permit an RFL to practise as a sole practitioner or an in-house RFL.

A foreign lawyer practising as a sole principal, or as a manager, member or owner of any business or organisation other than a recognised body or an authorised non-SRA firm (or with a comparable interest in a body which is a manager, member or owner of such a firm), or as an employee of such a firm, is not practising as an RFL and must not be held out or described as an RFL or as registered with or regulated by the Law Society or the SRA.[2] If an RFL is involved in this kind of business as well as one which may properly include an RFL, the former will be a separate business for the purpose of Chapter 12 of the SRA Code of Conduct 2011.[3]

Further, an RFL may not be held out in any way which suggests that he or she is, or is entitled to practise as, a lawyer of England and Wales, and is prohibited from undertaking certain reserved activities, such as advocacy, the conduct of litigation, the administration of oaths and declarations, the preparation of documents relating to court proceedings, transfer or charging of land and probate papers, subject to certain exceptions.[4] There are also restrictions on the provision of immigration advice and immigration services.[5]

1 Rule 3.1 of the SRA Practice Framework Rules 2011 and guidance notes.
2 Rule 3.2.
3 Rule 3.3.
4 Broadly, advocacy in chambers and the preparation of documents is permitted under direction and supervision as necessary: rule 3.4(a) to (d).
5 Rule 3.4(e).

11.4

Under Schedule 4 to the 2000 Regulations most of the statutory regime applying to solicitors through the Solicitors Act (SA) 1974 is extended to RELs, including provisions relating to:

- regulation through practising certificates (section 28 of SA 1974);

- all the rule making powers in relation to professional conduct, accounts and insurance (sections 31, 32, 33A, 34 and 37 of SA 1974);
- the SRA's investigative and disciplinary powers (sections 44B, 44BA, 44BC, 44C and 44D of SA 1974);
- the control of the employment of disqualified persons, equally applicable to RELs as employers and employees (sections 41 to 44 of SA 1974);
- the powers of the Solicitors Disciplinary Tribunal and the High Court (sections 46 to 53 of SA 1974); and
- the powers of intervention (section 35 of and Schedule 1 to SA 1974).

This is not intended to be an exhaustive list.

The statutory regime governing RFLs is to be found in Schedule 14 to CLSA 1990 (see **APPENDIX 17**). This makes provision for applications for registration, registration subject to conditions, the renewal of registration, and for appeals to the High Court against a refusal to register, refusal to renew registration, and the imposition of conditions.

The Schedule also provides for contributions to the Compensation Fund (and this also is extended to RELs by the 2000 Regulations), imposes a requirement to provide accountants' reports, provides for the effect of bankruptcy and for the effect of disciplinary action leading to the RFL being dealt with in his or her home jurisdiction in a way that is equivalent to being struck off or suspended, and extends the jurisdiction of the Solicitors Disciplinary Tribunal to RFLs.

CHAPTER 12

Regulation by other approved regulators

12.1

As pointed out in **CHAPTER 2**, in any analysis of the regulation of solicitors it is no longer possible to consider only the rules and regulations promulgated by the Solicitors Regulation Authority (SRA). From 31 March 2009, a solicitor could be individually regulated by the SRA, but employed by or a manager of a business entity supplying legal services that is regulated by another approved regulator. In that situation, the solicitor, in his professional dealings, must comply with the rules of the business's regulator, because the Legal Services Act (LSA) 2007 specifies that if there is a conflict between the regulation of the entity and the regulation of the individual, the regulation of the entity takes precedence.[1]

Currently, the only other approved regulator likely to be relevant in this context is the Council for Licensed Conveyancers (CLC) (though others may enter the market in the future). Other current regulators have shown less interest in regulating business entities, as opposed to their own members. The Bar Standards Board permits barristers to be managers or employees of alternative business structures but has not made an application to become a licensing authority. The CLC was the first regulator to be approved as a licensing authority by the Legal Services Board and became able to license alternative business structures some months ahead of the SRA. However, at present it may only regulate the supply of conveyancing and probate services, whether the services are provided through a traditional practice or alternative business structure (ABS), but it intends to widen its remit to regulate other reserved legal activities. In the meantime, the number of solicitors likely to find themselves employed by a CLC-regulated business can be expected to be a very small minority. Therefore, while a consideration of the CLC rules is justified, this is not intended to be exhaustive.

1 Section 52(4) of LSA 2007.

Conduct rules

12.2

The Council for Licensed Conveyancers has its own 'Handbook' comprising principles, a Code of Conduct, and a series of supplementary codes dealing with accounts, anti-money laundering and combating terrorist financing, complaints handling, conflicts of interest, continuing professional development, dealing with non-authorised persons, disclosure of profits and advantages, equality, estimates and terms of engagement, management and supervision, notification requirements, professional indemnity insurance, undertakings, acting as insurance intermediaries, mortgage fraud, management of transaction (client matter) files, and litigation and advocacy (in anticipation of the CLC being permitted to regulate in this area). There are also codes relating to the governance and operation of recognised bodies and licensed bodies.

The CLC has, like the SRA, embraced outcomes-focused regulation. It has its own six 'overriding principles' (compared with the SRA's ten):

'1. Act with independence and integrity;

2. Maintain high standards of work;

3. Act in the best interests of your Clients;

4. Comply with your duty to the court;

5. Deal with regulators and ombudsmen in an open and co-operative way;

6. Promote equality of access and service.'

12.3

The whole of the CLC Code of Conduct is contained within some seven pages at **APPENDIX 7**.

Whereas the SRA Principles are a series of threads running through the SRA Code of Conduct 2011, with the chapters of the 2011 Code addressing different elements of practice, the CLC Code of Conduct is in six parts, each developing and expanding one of the six overriding principles by stating required outcomes, principles underlying the outcomes and specific requirements associated with the overriding principle. Stylistically, they are readily interpreted as rules, with little that is vague or uncertain.

Conflicts of interest – acting for buyer and seller

12.4

Perhaps the most stark variation between the approach of the CLC and the SRA is in this aspect of the regulation of conveyancing practice. It is notable that the attitude of the CLC to conflicts of interest in conveyancing is in vivid contrast to that of the SRA – in acting for buyer and seller the SRA considers that a conflict of interests is almost inevitable, and that solicitors should not generally act for both parties (see **4.31** to **4.33**). The CLC's requirement is: 'Where the entity represents parties with different interests in any transaction each party is at all times represented by different Authorised Persons conducting themselves in the matter as though they were members of different entities'.[1]

Further guidance is given in the CLC's Conflicts of Interest Code:

'7. Before or when accepting instructions to act for a second Client you inform each Client in writing that the body has been asked to act for another Client in the same matter and you explain the relevant issues and risks to them.

8. You only act for both Clients if each Client has provided informed written consent that you may act for another Client in the matter.

9. You do not act, or do not continue to act, for a Client where your ability to give independent advice is in any way restricted. This may arise if:

   (a) you owe separate duties to act in the best interests of two or more clients in relation to the same or related matters, and those duties conflict, or there is a significant risk that those duties may conflict; or

   (b) your duty to act in the best interests of any client in relation to a matter conflicts, or there is a significant risk that it may conflict, with your own interests in relation to that or a related matter.

10. If a conflict arises which was or should have been foreseen, you do not charge either Client a fee for the work undertaken (other than for disbursements properly incurred).'[2]

1 CLC Code of Conduct, overriding principle 3 (client's best interests), specific requirement (n).
2 CLC Conflicts of Interest Code, specific requirements 7 to 10.

12.5

The CLC also expressly permits sole practitioners (or businesses where there is only one authorised person) to act for buyer and lender in the same transaction, if the lender is providing mortgages in the normal course of its business activities, without additional obligations.[1]

The guidance to the Conflicts of Interest Code includes references that solicitor conveyancers will find familiar, which are now missing from the SRA Code of Conduct 2011, as to the nature and significance of transactions that are not at arm's length, and as to the need for additional caution when the selling client is a developer or builder, or a lessor granting a lease.[2]

1 CLC Conflicts of Interest Code, specific requirement 11.
2 CLC Conflicts of Interest Guidance.

Referrals and commission

12.6

The CLC's regulatory requirements in these areas are succinct and straightforward. Referral arrangements and fees are dealt with primarily within overriding principle 3 (the requirement to act in the client's best interests): that clients have the information they need to make informed decisions; clients are aware of any referral arrangements and that they are consistent with the practitioner's responsibilities both to them and to the CLC; and clients are informed promptly in writing of the existence and amount of any sum payable directly or indirectly as a result of receipt of the client's instructions.[1]

All referral arrangements between the CLC practice and a third party including any fee sharing arrangement must be in writing, and referral arrangements must be periodically reviewed to ensure that they deliver the appropriate outcomes to clients. Practitioners must provide clients with information about the existence of the arrangement no later than when receiving instructions (or when referring the client to another person). Clients should be advised that they have a choice of provider, and informed of the nature of the arrangement (including any payment made), with whom it is made, and any impact (including any legal costs they are charged).[2]

The CLC requirement in relation to payments received by the practitioner or business when the client is introduced to another party is found in principle 3 of the Code of Conduct, specific requirement (s): 'You promptly inform the Client in writing of the existence and amount of any sum payable (whether directly or indirectly) as a result of receipt of that Client's instructions.'

It may be noted that the requirement is to inform, not to account. However, as discussed at **4.16** the obligation to account arises from the fiduciary relationship between the professional person and the client and is a matter of law independent of any professional rule. The CLC Code of Conduct, overriding principle 1: acting with independence and integrity, includes a compulsory outcome that clients receive an honest and lawful service,[3] and compliance with the law would require the client's informed consent if the sum is to be retained. However, it can be said that the CLC regulations follow the law, with no further complications, and the issue could be dealt with by standard terms and conditions of business if there is sufficient clarity.

Moreover, in relation to financial services, the CLC position also follows the law precisely. If commission is earned in relation to services regulated under the Financial Services and Markets Act 2000, there is an obligation to account to the client for any pecuniary award or other advantage received other than from the client.[4] See further at **12.8**.

1 CLC Code of Conduct, overriding principle 3, outcomes 3.3 and 3.4 and specific requirement (s).
2 CLC Disclosure of Profits and Advantages Code, specific requirements 12 to 16.
3 CLC Code of Conduct, overriding principle 1, outcome 1.2.
4 Section 327(3) of FSMA 2000 and specific requirement 36 of the CLC Acting as Insurance Intermediaries Code.

Accounts and financial services

12.7

Solicitors familiar (historically) with the Solicitors' Accounts Rules 1998 or the current SRA Accounts Rules 2011 will not encounter any difficulties in complying with the CLC's Accounts Code & Guidance. The latter are a rather less complex set of rules but directed to the same ends.

The Accounts Code is in five parts, comprising basic rules on the treatment of client money, the obligation to maintain proper accounts, including the completion of bank reconciliations, provisions as to deposit interest, arrangements for monitoring by the CLC, and accountant's reports. There is separate guidance on aged balances.

All individuals and bodies regulated by the CLC must:

- comply with the Accounts Code, and not permit anyone else to act or fail to act in breach of the Code;
- ensure that partners, employees and directors (including partners, employees and directors who are not authorised persons) comply with the Code;

- use each client's money only for that client's matters;
- only pay money into, and withdraw money from the client account and office account for purposes related to the provision of services regulated by the CLC;
- establish and maintain proper accounting systems, procedures, processes and internal controls, to ensure compliance with the Code;
- ensure there is no debit balance on the client side of a client ledger account nor a credit balance on the office side of a client ledger account;
- remedy any breach of these requirements without delay (which means normally the same day or the next working day); and
- account to the client as soon as possible after completion of any transaction or after a retainer has been terminated.[1]

Money held on account of costs and disbursements must be withdrawn from client account within 28 days of the date on which a bill of costs is sent to a client, provided it is made clear to the client or the paying party either before or at the time the bill of costs is sent that such money will be applied towards or in payment of that bill of costs.[2] Undrawn costs or disbursements must not remain in client account, either in anticipation of future errors which could result in a shortage on that account or to make good any current shortage on that account, and are not available as a set-off against any general shortage on client account.[3] The CLC must be notified without delay (in normal circumstances, the same day or the next working day) upon discovery of any misappropriation of client money.[4]

When money is held for a client in a client account or if money should have been held in a client account but was not so held, the firm must account to the client for any interest earned or which should have been earned on that money. A client may apply to the CLC for a direction for the payment of interest, which must be paid within 15 days. If appropriate the CLC may require an interest calculation from the relevant bank or building society. There is no *de minimis* provision. There is a provision enabling contracting out which requires that clients are fully informed in writing, give informed consent and are treated fairly and reasonably, having regard to the amounts involved.[5]

The guidance on aged balances is in two parts; the first part concentrates on mechanisms and systems designed to avoid the problem occurring. The CLC arrangements for withdrawing aged balances are in three bands depending on the amount: less than £20; £20 or more but less than £100, or £100 and over. In the first category the CLC may authorise payment to the office account subject to the provision of basic information about each balance and an undertaking from the firm to pay the amount due to a rightful recipient within 14 days of any request. The CLC may give permission for larger sums to be paid to the CLC's Compensation Fund, subject to being satisfied that all reasonable steps have been taken to trace the recipient. The difference in the 'banding' relates to the information the CLC needs before authority will be given.[6]

1 Preamble to and requirement 9 of the CLC Accounts Code.
2 Requirement 12.1.4.
3 Requirement 12.6.
4 Requirement 13.16.
5 Requirement 15.1 to 15.3.
6 CLC Accounts Code, Aged Balances Guidance.

12.8

The CLC has issued the Acting as Insurance Intermediaries Code & Guidance to regulate the supply of services under Part XX of the Financial Services and Markets Act 2000 by bodies regulated by the CLC enabling firms to provide specified financial services that are incidental to conveyancing or other services regulated by the CLC.

The obligation to account for commission related to the supply of services regulated under FSMA 2000 has been mentioned above; see **12.6**. The CLC clarified the position with the Financial Services Authority (as it then was) and has offered further guidance, updated to reflect the replacement of the Financial Services Authority by the Financial Conduct Authority:

> 'The FCA considers that, in order for a Client to be accounted to for the purposes of s.327(3) FSMA, you must treat any commission or other pecuniary benefit received from third parties and which results from Regulated Activities carried on by the body, as held to the order of the Client. You will not be accounting to the Client simply by telling them that you receive commission. Unless the client agrees to you keeping it, the commission belongs to them and must be paid to them. There is no de minimis below which you may retain the sum. In the FCA's opinion, the condition would be satisfied if you pay over to the Client any third party payment received. Otherwise, it would be satisfied by informing the Client of the payment received and advising the Client that they have the right to require the body to pay them the sum concerned. This could then be used to offset fees due from the Client in respect of Professional Services provided or in recognition of other services provided. However, it does not permit retention of third party payments by seeking the Client's agreement through standard terms and conditions. Similarly, a mere notification to the Client that a particular sum has been received coupled with your request to retain it does not satisfy the condition.'[1]

1 Paragraph 9 of the CLC's Acting as Insurance Intermediaries Code & Guidance.

PART 4

The regulatory system in practice

CHAPTER 13

The Legal Ombudsman

13.1

The date 6 October 2010 was another major milestone on the road to the transformation of the regulation of legal services brought about by the Legal Services Act (LSA) 2007: the Legal Ombudsman opened for business. The Legal Ombudsman (LeO), is the brand adopted by the Office for Legal Complaints, a body corporate established by section 114 of LSA 2007.

All consumer complaints about the quality of service provided by any regulated legal professional (or 'authorised person' to use the terminology of LSA 2007), are now made to LeO. The previous fragmented system, whereby complaints about barristers went to the Bar Standards Board, those about solicitors went to the Legal Complaints Service (LCS) of the Law Society, and those about licensed conveyancers went to the Council for Licensed Conveyancers, has been replaced with a single complaints body. A typical consequence will be that a litigation client who knows or believes that something has gone wrong, but does not know whether it is the fault of his solicitor or barrister, no longer has to guess to whom he or she should complain, in the expectation of choosing the wrong one first. LeO has the task of establishing whether anything did go wrong and, if so, who should provide redress.

LeO started with a clean slate; it did not take over any complaints which were already in the hands of the former organisations.

The new approach

13.2

In no sense should LeO be seen as a seamless successor to the LCS, as has been amply demonstrated in practice. LeO has been keen to distance itself as far as possible from the approach of the LCS. Aspects of the latter which are now happily consigned to history were: a determination to identify anything the client might have complained about but did not; an adversarial approach which encouraged a ping-pong of rebuttals and rejoinders; over-lengthy and often bewilderingly complex analyses unlikely to assist the average complainant; and an over-emphasis on the presence or absence of any breach of a rule.

LSA 2007 does not contain any words which are the equivalent of 'inadequate professional service' as used in Schedule 1A to the Solicitors Act 1974. LeO has jurisdiction in relation to complaints made by clients (and limited other categories) about acts or omissions of authorised persons; the only threshold or test to be satisfied for an award or direction to be made is that it is fair and reasonable in all the circumstances of the case.[1]

LeO concentrates on what the client is actually complaining about, and in particular what would put it right (not, for example, what the client would like to happen to the solicitor). This may be as simple as an acknowledgement that something had gone wrong, and an apology or a modest amount of money to recognise non-economic or non-quantifiable loss for inconvenience, annoyance and distress; but may also be the equivalent of common law damages (in amount) for real financial loss.

The investigative approach is inquisitorial, not adversarial; a fact-gathering exercise. LeO examines what happened, and what if anything went wrong; to establish this it requests information and documents from the parties. The flow of information follows targeted requests, and the ping-pong of charge and counter-charge is now avoided so far as possible. With that in mind there is no automatic exchange of documents containing complaints and explanations; instead the investigator summarises the points to which answers are required. Documents are only disclosed when the investigation is complete and a recommendation report is provided to the parties. This has led to regulated lawyers complaining that they do not fully know the case they have to meet and to a lack of natural justice. It is understood that the policy is under review following *Bar Standards Board v Julian Smith*, PC 2013/0193, a Bar disciplinary hearing, in which the barrister was acquitted of professional misconduct for failing to co-operate with LeO. The disciplinary tribunal held that although the barrister was in breach of the rules requiring him to co-operate, the breach did not amount to professional misconduct because he 'could be forgiven, if not justified in taking the stance that he did' in declining to co-operate when LeO refused to release material supplied by the complainant on which the LeO investigator intended to rely, until after she had reached her conclusion, albeit that her conclusion would not at that stage be binding. The tribunal added: 'A barrister could not reasonably or necessarily be expected to co-operate with the Ombudsman in that situation'. The consequence of the non-co-operation, however, was that the complaint to LeO by the client was inevitably upheld.

The existence or otherwise of rule breaches is no longer a central consideration; after all, a clear, helpful and comprehensive client care letter may be followed by appalling service, and an excellent service might be provided despite muddled initial correspondence. Rule breaches are primarily matters for the regulator, not LeO.

Nor is the degree of fault the measure of compensation – a very bad error could have negligible consequences, and a small mistake could be very costly; redress will relate to the consequence of the failing, and is designed to put the complainant so far as possible in the position he or she should have been in; but it is not a penalty imposed on the professional for a more or less serious mistake.

Sometimes, in what they see as 'nuisance' complaints, solicitors are prepared to offer a small sum on an *ex gratia* and without prejudice basis to the disaffected client in order to retain goodwill and save the time and effort involved in dealing with complaints. We understand that LeO has no objection in principle to such proposals, and that if the offer is rejected, this will not be held against the solicitor who made it, or regarded as an admission. Any subsequent complaint would be dealt with on its merits. If such an offer were to be accepted, but the client nevertheless makes a complaint to LeO, the acceptance of the offer would be seen as an important factor in LeO's consideration of the case.

1 Section 137(1) of LSA 2007.

Structure and process in outline

13.3

When it was set up, LeO expected to receive about 100,000 contacts a year, in the sense of enquiries and expressions of interest, of which about 20,000 would become legitimate complaints within LeO's jurisdiction. Experience of other ombudsman schemes suggests that only 10 per cent of that figure reaches the point of formal adjudication, the remainder being resolved by agreement or abandonment. LeO's latest available annual report, to 31 March 2013, reveals that 71,000 people contacted the organisation over the full year, a decline of 5,000 from the previous year, of which 8,430 required investigation and resolution.

13.4

LeO caseworkers first determine exactly what the complaint is about and what is sought by way of redress. Assuming that the complaint is not premature because the complainant has not used the solicitors' own complaints procedures, is not out of time and is not obviously without merit (more of which below), the caseworker investigates in the inquisitorial manner described above and, having given both parties the opportunity to make representations, comes to a provisional decision. However, LeO is committed to resolving complaints at the earliest possible stage, so that the process of investigation should not prevent an agreed resolution at any time.

Because LeO expects to look at complaints, in the ordinary course, only after the client has exhausted the firm's own complaints handling process, one of the first requests is likely to be for the firm's complaint file – its record of the handling of the complaint. Some firms are taken by surprise by this request, as opposed to a request for the client matter file or core extracts. But a key element of a LeO inquiry is to determine how the firm itself handled the matter. Firms have had to adjust to this, and to realise that it may be imprudent to exchange memoranda and e-mails with forthright expressions of opinion not originally intended for external consumption, but which are a part of the firm's investigation of the complaint, and thus discloseable to LeO.

If both parties accept the caseworker's provisional decision, the matter is resolved on that basis; if either party demurs, the matter is referred to an ombudsman for final determination. Only information and documentation to be considered by the ombudsman will be disclosed to the parties, not necessarily everything gathered by the caseworker in the course of the investigation. The ombudsman may require further information and, for example, may conduct an oral hearing. However, it has always been envisaged that these will be exceedingly rare and only justified by compelling and exceptional circumstances (particularly in the case of solicitors whose actions are generally heavily documented).

If the ombudsman comes to a conclusion which is materially different from that of the caseworker's provisional decision, the ombudsman will provide an opportunity to both parties to make further representations.

It is open to the complainant (only) to accept or reject an ombudsman's determination. If it is accepted by the complainant, it is binding on all parties and final.[1] If it is rejected, the role of LeO is concluded and the complainant is free to pursue other remedies.

There is no appeal from an ombudsman's determination, so that judicial review is the only available mechanism for challenge. However, if it is clear that an obvious mistake has been made, an ombudsman might well be prepared voluntarily to reconsider the matter.

Despite LeO being threatened with judicial review on a fairly regular basis only four cases have yet reached a hearing. All have been decided on a fact-sensitive basis (two in favour of LeO[2] and two against)[3] without developing any new body of law or changes in public law principles. The one clear point is the consistent acceptance that LeO has a wide discretion within a statutory framework which is itself drawn in very broad terms – what is fair and reasonable in all the circumstances of the case.[4] It can be expected that successful challenges will be rare. The successful challenges so far have involved an obvious misinterpretation of the facts,[5] and a result influenced by the failure of LeO to file evidence which might have caused a different conclusion;[6] something that is unlikely to be repeated.

Provisional decisions and ombudsman determinations are narrative in form and seek to avoid the black and white concepts which involve 'upholding' the complaint or the opposite. It may be difficult or inappropriate to say whether a multiple complaint, of which one element was found to justify criticism, was 'upheld'. Rather, the decision recites what the caseworker or ombudsman has considered to have gone wrong and what the redress should be.

Compensation for non-financial loss is in modest amounts: the low hundreds of pounds.

1 Section 140(4) of LSA 2007.
2 *Layard Horsfall Ltd v Legal Ombudsman* [2013] EWHC 4137 (Admin) and *R (Rosemarine) v Office for Legal Complaints* [2014] EWHC 601 (Admin).
3 *R (Crawford) v Legal Ombudsman and anor* [2014] EWHC 182 (Admin) and *R (Hafiz & Haque Solicitors) v Legal Ombudsman* [2014] EWHC 1539 (Admin).
4 Section 137(1) of LSA 2007.
5 *Crawford* supra.
6 *Hafiz & Haque* supra.

The overlap with negligence

13.5

The limit of compensation available through LeO is £50,000 (considered in more detail below), plus a reduction in costs in a theoretically unlimited amount, capped only by the amount of the costs that has been charged. This is sufficiently large to attract many cases which might otherwise have been pursued as negligence claims. A complaint to LeO involves no expense and no adverse costs risk for a complainant.

LeO does not reject complaints simply because they could be pursued as negligence claims. However, neither are they considered as if they were negligence claims. As in all matters, the question is whether it is fair and reasonable for redress to be provided in all the circumstances, in consequence of an act or omission by an authorised person. Awards may be made by LeO whether or not the complainant may have a cause of action against the authorised person in negligence.[1]

It must follow that there can be circumstances in which complainants might achieve a higher award of damages by court action than could be directed by LeO, and in accepting an award capped at £50,000, might lose what might have been available in another jurisdiction. If a LeO award is accepted and becomes binding, it is full satisfaction; no further proceedings may be taken in relation to the subject matter (see **13.17**) and the potential for a higher award of damages will be lost. On the other hand, litigation is risky and expensive. It is essentially a choice for the consumer. In appropriate cases LeO may consider it prudent to remind the complainant of the options available where obviously high levels of loss are claimed to have been sustained, but the complaint will not be rejected; nor can it be expected that the complainant will, for example, be required to take advice before pursuing a complaint or accepting a determination.

1 Section 137(5) of LSA 2007.

Fee structure

13.6

No fee is payable by the complainant to LeO. No fee is payable by the authorised person who is the subject of complaint if the complaint is abandoned or withdrawn. If the complaint is resolved by any other means, the authorised person is normally liable to pay a fee, called a case fee, but will not be liable if both of two conditions are satisfied: first, that the complaint is settled, resolved or determined in favour of the authorised person; and, second, that LeO is satisfied that the authorised person took all reasonable steps to try to resolve the complaint under his or her own complaints handling system.

In all other cases, the authorised person is liable to pay the case fee, currently £400 for each complaint.[1]

1 Rules 6.1 to 6.3 of the LeO Scheme Rules 2013.

Publicity

13.7

The extent to which decisions of LeO are published in a manner which will identify the lawyers involved has proved to be a vexed question. LeO conducted two full consultations on the subject. The Legal Services Board's Legal Services Consumer Panel, and others broadly representing consumer interests, favoured naming and shaming by the publication of awards and directions. Others are more cautious as to whether this is ultimately in the interests of consumers, if it discourages solicitors from taking on work associated with high levels of sometimes ill-informed complaint, such as immigration, or encourages the settlement of undeserving and unmeritorious complaints because of the perceived commercial consequences of publicity. Ultimately LeO is there to provide redress, not to impose penalties on lawyers, and publicity has a direct and effectively penal consequence. If there are 'season ticket holders' in terms of complaint generation, it may be a matter for the regulator, rather than the LeO.

Anonymised case studies are published to give assistance in identifying trends and to offer guidance as to how typical cases are resolved. From the summer of 2011 anonymised summaries of all formal decisions by ombudsmen have been published.

Following the completion of the consultation process and the tracking of data the decision was finally made to publish the names of lawyers in two circumstances; first, discretionary publication of cases where a pattern of complaints raises sufficient concerns that the public interest requires publication as a warning to consumers and potential consumers; it is expected that this will arise in a very small number of cases in any year. It is quite probable that by the time such a pattern emerges there will have been regulatory action or the firm may have failed.

Second, on a quarterly basis all decisions made by ombudsmen will be published, even where the decision is favourable to the lawyer and no action by LeO was necessary. The first list was published on 17 September 2012. More than half of the decisions in that list did not involve any remedy being directed.

This is something of a compromise; cases which are resolved at an early stage, or where the parties accept a caseworker's recommendation, will not require an ombudsman's decision and so will not be published. On the other hand, if an aggrieved client insists on an ombudsman's decision, as is his or her right, the firm's name will appear on the list even though no fault may be found. So far, the information lacks a certain amount of context. Because LeO does not know how many clients a firm may have it cannot say whether the number of complaints is comparatively large or a tiny percentage of the firm's cases. This is a point made in the FAQs part of LeO's website.

The scheme rules in more detail

Who can complain[1]

13.8

A complainant must be an individual, or any of the following:

- a small business: a micro-enterprise as defined in European Recommendation 2003/361/EC of 6 May 2003 (broadly, an enterprise with fewer than ten staff and a turnover or balance sheet value not exceeding €2 million);
- a charity with an annual income less than £1 million;
- a club, association or society with an annual income less than £1 million;
- a trustee of a trust with a net asset value less than £1 million;
- a personal representative or the residuary beneficiaries of an estate where a person with a complaint died before referring it to the ombudsman scheme.

If a complainant who has referred a complaint to LeO dies or is otherwise unable to act, the complaint may be continued by anyone authorised by law (for example, the executor of a complainant who has died or someone with a lasting power of attorney from a complainant who is incapable or the residuary beneficiaries of the estate of a complainant who has died).

A complainant must not have been, at the time of the act or omission to which the complaint relates, a public body (or acting for a public body) in relation to the services complained about, or an authorised person who procured the services complained about on behalf of someone else. For example, where the complaint is about a barrister who was instructed by a solicitor on behalf of a consumer, the consumer may complain but the solicitor may not.

A complainant may authorise someone else in writing (including an authorised person) to act on behalf of the complainant in pursuing a complaint, but LeO remains free to contact the complainant direct where it considers that to be appropriate.

1 See rules 2.1 to 2.5 of the LeO Scheme Rules 2013.

What can be complained about[1]

13.9

There are no categories of complaint that are excluded. The complaint must relate to an act or omission by someone who was an authorised person at the relevant time. An act or omission by an employee is usually treated as an act or omission by the employer, whether or not the employer knew or approved. An act or omission by a partner is usually treated as an act or omission by the partnership, unless the complainant knew (at the time of the act or omission) that the partner had no authority to act for the partnership.[2]

The act or omission does not have to relate to a reserved legal activity, nor to have occurred after LSA 2007 came into force. The complaint must normally relate to services which the authorised person provided to the complainant or to another authorised person who procured them on behalf of the complainant, or to – or as – a personal representative or trustee where the complainant is a beneficiary of the estate or trust. However, a complaint may also be made about services which an authorised person offered or refused to provide to the complainant. This jurisdiction is not likely to be employed frequently. It would cover circumstances in which, for example, a lawyer refused to accept instructions for an unlawfully discriminatory reason, and would also be appropriate where a lawyer agrees to look at papers with a view to representing the complainant at a forthcoming court hearing, for example, but later decides not to accept instructions, leaving the complainant unrepresented with no adequate notice.

A complaint is not affected by any change in the composition of a partnership or other unincorporated body. Where a firm or business closes and another business succeeds to the whole of it, or substantially the whole of it, the successor body becomes responsible for the acts and omissions of and complaints against the original firm[3] unless an ombudsman decides that this is not fair and reasonable in all the circumstances.[4]

1 Rules 2.6 to 2.10 of the LeO Scheme Rules 2013.
2 Section 131 of LSA 2007.
3 Section 132.
4 Rule 2.10 of the LeO Scheme Rules 2013.

Jurisdiction and time limits

13.10

Ordinarily, a complainant cannot complain to LeO unless the complainant has first used the authorised person's complaints procedure.[1] However, this does not apply if the complaint has not been resolved to the complainant's satisfaction within eight weeks of being made to the authorised person, or if an ombudsman considers that there are exceptional reasons to consider the complaint sooner, or without it having been made first to the authorised person, or where in-house resolution is not possible due to irretrievable breakdown in the relationship between the lawyer and the person making the complaint. For example, an ombudsman may decide that the ombudsman service should consider the complaint where the authorised person has refused to consider it, or where delay would harm the complainant.[2]

Ordinarily, a complainant must refer a complaint to LeO within six months of the date of the authorised person's written response (within the firm's complaints handling system), but only if that written response prominently included an explanation that the LeO service was available if the complainant remained dissatisfied and full contact details for LeO were given, together with a warning that the complaint must be referred to LeO within six months.[3]

A complainant must also generally refer a complaint to LeO no later than six years from the act or omission complained of, or three years from the point at which the complainant should reasonably have known that there was cause for complaint.[4] Ordinarily the act or omission must also have occurred after 5 October 2010. In the case of a complaint made by a personal representative of the estate of a person who had not complained before he or she died, the period runs from the point at which the deceased should reasonably have known that there was cause for complaint.

If an ombudsman considers that there are exceptional circumstances (for example, a delay caused by illness), he or she may extend any of these time limits to the extent that he or she considers fair.[5] An ombudsman is likely to extend a time limit where the time limit had not expired when the complainant raised the complaint with the authorised person.[6]

1 Section 126 of LSA 2007.
2 Rules 4.1 to 4.3 and 5.3 of the LeO Scheme Rules 2013.
3 Rule 4.4.
4 Rule 4.5.
5 Rules 4.7 and 4.8.
6 Rule 4.8(b).

Preliminary consideration and summary dismissal

13.11

If an ombudsman considers that all or part of the complaint is not within LeO's jurisdiction, or is out of time, or may be one that should be dismissed without considering its merits, the ombudsman will give the complainant an opportunity to make representations before deciding. If an authorised person challenges the complaint on the same grounds, the ombudsman will give all parties an opportunity to make representations. In either case, the ombudsman will then make a decision and give reasons.[1]

An ombudsman may (but does not have to) dismiss all or part of a complaint without considering its merits if, in his or her opinion:

- the complaint does not have any reasonable prospect of success, or is frivolous or vexatious;

- the complainant has not suffered (and is unlikely to suffer) financial loss, distress, inconvenience or other detriment;
- the authorised person has already offered fair and reasonable redress in relation to the circumstances alleged by the complainant and the offer is still open for acceptance;
- the complainant has previously complained about the same issue to LeO or a predecessor complaints scheme (unless the ombudsman considers that material new evidence, likely to affect the outcome, only became available to the complainant afterwards);
- a comparable independent complaints (or costs-assessment) scheme or a court has already dealt with the same issue;
- a comparable independent complaints (or costs-assessment) scheme or a court is dealing with the same issue, unless those proceedings are first stayed, by the agreement of all parties or by a court order, so that LeO can deal with the issue;
- it would be more suitable for the issue to be dealt with by a court, by arbitration or by another complaints (or costs-assessment) scheme;
- the issue concerns an authorised person's decision when exercising a discretion under a will or trust;
- the issue concerns an authorised person's failure to consult a beneficiary before exercising a discretion under a will or trust, where there is no legal obligation to consult;
- the issue involves someone else who has not complained and the ombudsman considers that it would not be appropriate to deal with the issue without that person's consent;
- it is not practicable to investigate the issue fairly because of the time which has elapsed since the act or omission;
- the issue concerns an act or omission outside England and Wales and the circumstances do not have a sufficient connection with England and Wales;
- the complaint is about an authorised person's refusal to provide a service and the complainant has not produced evidence that the refusal was for other than legitimate or reasonable reasons;
- there are other compelling reasons why it is inappropriate for the issue to be dealt with under the ombudsman scheme.[2]

Exceptionally, an ombudsman may refer a discrete legal question to a court if the resolution of the question is necessary to resolve the matter, but it is not more suitable for the court to deal with the whole dispute. The authorised person may request that a matter be considered as a test case by a court and an ombudsman may accommodate that request by dismissing the complaint to enable proceedings to be taken, but only on an undertaking that the authorised person will pay the complainant's costs and on such other terms as the ombudsman considers appropriate.[3]

An ombudsman may also refer the complaint to another complaints scheme in appropriate circumstances.[4]

1 Rules 5.4 to 5.6 of the LeO Scheme Rules 2013.
2 Rule 5.7.
3 Rules 5.8 to 5.11.
4 Rule 5.12.

Procedure, evidence and hearings

13.12

LeO may request the assistance of others, including approved regulators, in the investigation and consideration of complaints.[1] LeO is not restricted by the terms of the complaint as to who is to be investigated. If appropriate LeO will investigate another authorised person as a joint respondent.[2]

Efforts will be made to resolve all complaints at the earliest possible stage by any appropriate means, including informal resolution.[3] If an investigation is necessary, a caseworker will send the parties what is referred to in the Scheme Rules as a recommendation report but which is described in practice as a provisional decision, after both parties have been given an opportunity to make representations, and will set a time limit for response. If no party disagrees within the specified time limit, the complaint may be treated as resolved by the provisional decision. If any party disagrees, the matter is referred to an ombudsman for final determination.[4]

1 Rule 5.14 of the LeO Scheme Rules 2013.
2 Rules 5.15 and 5.16.
3 Rule 5.17.
4 Rules 5.19 and 5.20.

13.13

An apology will not of itself be treated as an admission of liability. An ombudsman cannot require anyone to produce any information or document which that person could not be compelled to produce in High Court civil proceedings. An ombudsman may:

- give directions as to the issues on which evidence is required and the way in which evidence should be given; may take into account evidence from approved regulators or the Legal Services Board (LSB) or from other third parties;
- treat any finding of fact in disciplinary proceedings against the authorised person as conclusive;
- include or exclude evidence that would be inadmissible or admissible in court;
- accept information in confidence where he or she considers that this is both necessary and fair;
- make a determination on the basis of what has been supplied;
- draw inferences from any party's failure to provide information requested; and
- dismiss a complaint if the complainant fails to provide information that has been requested.[1]

An ombudsman may require a party to attend to give evidence and produce documents at a specified time and place. An ombudsman may require a party to produce any information or document that the ombudsman considers necessary for the determination of a complaint; may specify the time within which this must be done; may specify the manner or form in which the information is to be provided; and may require the person producing the document to explain it. If the document is not produced, an ombudsman may require the relevant party to say, to the best of his or her knowledge and belief, where the document is.

If an authorised person fails to comply with a requirement to produce information or a document, the ombudsman will tell the relevant approved regulator and may require that approved regulator to tell the ombudsman what action it will take (and may report any failure by the approved regulator to the LSB). If any party fails to comply with a requirement to produce information or a document, the ombudsman may also enforce the requirement through the High Court.[2]

An ombudsman may fix (and may extend) a time limit for any stage of the investigation, consideration and determination of a complaint. If any party fails to comply with such a time limit, the ombudsman may proceed with the investigation, consideration and determination; and draw inferences from the failure. Where the failure is by the complainant, the ombudsman may dismiss the complaint; or where the failure is by the authorised person, the ombudsman may include compensation for any inconvenience caused to the complainant in any award.[3]

1 Rules 5.21 to 5.24 of the LeO Scheme Rules 2013.
2 Sections 147 to 149 of LSA 2007; rules 5.25 to 5.30 of the LeO Scheme Rules 2013.
3 Rules 5.31 and 5.32 of the LeO Scheme Rules 2013.

13.14

An ombudsman will only hold an oral hearing where he or she considers that the complaint cannot be fairly determined without one. In deciding whether (and how) to hold a hearing, the ombudsman will take account of Article 6 of the European Convention on Human Rights. A party who wishes to request a hearing must do so in writing setting out the issues he or she wishes to raise and (if appropriate) any reasons why the hearing should be in private. The ombudsman will consider whether the issues are material, whether a hearing should take place and whether any hearing should be in public or private. A hearing may be held by any means the ombudsman considers appropriate in the circumstances, including (for example) by telephone.[1]

1 Rules 5.33 to 5.35 of the LeO Scheme Rules 2013.

Determinations and awards

13.15

An ombudsman will determine a complaint by reference to what is, in his or her opinion, fair and reasonable in all the circumstances of the case. In determining what is fair and reasonable, the ombudsman will take into account (but is not bound by) what a court might decide, the relevant approved regulator's rules of conduct at the time of the act or omission, and what the ombudsman considers to have been good practice at the time.[1]

Awards and determinations may include any one or more of the following directions to the authorised person in favour of the complainant:

- to apologise;
- to pay compensation of a specified amount for loss suffered;
- to pay interest on that compensation from a specified time;
- to pay compensation of a specified amount for inconvenience or distress caused;
- to ensure (and pay for) putting right any specified error, omission or other deficiency;
- to take (and pay for) any specified action in the interests of the complainant;
- to pay a specified amount for costs incurred by the complainant in pursuing the complaint (however, as a complainant does not usually need assistance to pursue a complaint with LeO, awards of costs are likely to be rare);
- to limit the authorised person's fees to a specified amount.[2]

If the determination contains a direction to limit fees to a specified amount, it may also require the authorised person to ensure that: all or part of any amount paid is refunded; interest is paid on that refund from a specified time; all or part of the fees are remitted; the right to recover the fees is waived, wholly or to a specified extent; or any combination of these.[3]

An ombudsman may set a time limit for the authorised person to comply with a determination, and may set different time limits for different parts of a determination. Any interest payable under the determination will be at the rate specified in the determination or, if not specified, at the rate payable on High Court judgment debts.[4]

1 Section 137 of LSA 2007; rules 5.36 and 5.37 of the LeO Scheme Rules 2013.
2 Rules 5.38 and 5.39 of the LeO Scheme Rules 2013.
3 Rule 5.40.
4 Rules 5.41 and 5.42.

13.16

There is a limit of £50,000 on the total value that can be awarded on the determination of a complaint in respect of the total of: compensation for loss suffered; compensation for inconvenience or distress caused; the reasonable cost of putting right any error, omission or other deficiency; and the reasonable cost of any specified action in the interests of the complainant. If (before or after the determination is issued) it appears that the total value will exceed £50,000, an ombudsman may direct which part or parts of the award are to take preference.[1]

The £50,000 limit does not apply to: an apology; interest on specified compensation for loss suffered; any specified amount for costs the complainant incurred in pursuing the complaint; the financial consequences of limiting fees to a specified amount; or interest on fees to be refunded.[2]

1 Section 138 of LSA 2007; rules 5.43 and 5.44 of the LeO Scheme Rules 2013.
2 Rule 5.45 of the LeO Scheme Rules 2013.

13.17

The determination is in writing, signed by the ombudsman. It must give reasons and require the complainant to notify the ombudsman, before a specified time, whether the complainant accepts or rejects the determination. The ombudsman may require any acceptance or rejection to be in writing, but will have regard to any reason why the complainant may be unable to communicate in writing. The ombudsman will send copies of the determination to the parties and the relevant approved regulator. If the complainant tells the ombudsman that he or she accepts the determination it is binding on the parties and final.[1]

Once a determination becomes binding and final, neither party may start or continue legal proceedings in respect of the subject matter of the complaint.[2]

If the complainant does not tell the ombudsman, before the specified time, that he or she accepts the determination, it is treated as rejected. But if the complainant later tells the ombudsman that he or she accepts the determination, and the complainant has not previously told the ombudsman that he or she rejects the determination, and if the ombudsman is satisfied that there are sufficient reasons why the complainant did not respond in time, the determination will be treated as accepted, final and binding. If the complainant does not respond before the specified time, the ombudsman will notify the parties and the relevant approved regulator of the outcome, describing the provisions concerning late acceptance. Whether the complainant accepts or rejects the determination, the ombudsman will notify the parties and the relevant approved regulator of the outcome.[3]

If a determination is rejected (or treated as rejected) by the complainant, it has no effect on the legal rights of any party.[4]

1 Section 140(1) to (4) of LSA 2007; rules 5.46 to 5.49 of the LeO Scheme Rules 2013.
2 Section 140(11) of LSA 2007; rule 5.50 of the LeO Scheme Rules 2013.
3 Rules 5.51 to 5.53 of the LeO Scheme Rules 2013.
4 Rule 5.54.

Enforcement and misconduct

13.18

A binding and final determination can be enforced through the High Court or a county court by the complainant: in August 2011 the legal press reported that LeO had commenced proceedings in the Birmingham County Court against two firms in order to enforce awards. LeO may also enforce a determination through the courts if the complainant agrees and LeO considers it appropriate in all the circumstances. A court which makes an enforcement order must inform LeO and LeO will then inform the relevant approved regulator, may require the approved regulator to tell LeO what action it will take, and may report any failure by the approved regulator to the LSB.[1]

At any stage after LeO receives a complaint, if LeO considers that the complaint discloses any alleged misconduct about which the relevant approved regulator should consider action against the authorised person, or if LeO considers that an authorised person has failed to co-operate with LeO, LeO will tell the relevant approved regulator, may require the approved regulator to tell LeO what action it will take, and may report any failure by the approved regulator to the LSB. If an approved regulator is informed about a matter involving potential misconduct, LeO will tell the complainant that this has been done.[2] The duty to report potential misconduct is not affected by any withdrawal or abandonment of the complaint.

LeO will disclose to an approved regulator any information that the regulator requests to enable it to investigate alleged misconduct or to fulfil its regulatory functions, if LeO considers that the information is reasonably required, and the approved regulator has regard to any right of privacy of any complainant involved.[3]

1 Sections 141 and 142 of LSA 2007; rules 5.56 to 5.58 of the LeO Scheme Rules 2013.
2 Sections 143 and 146 of LSA 2007; rules 5.59 and 5.60 of the LeO Scheme Rules 2013.
3 Rule 5.61 of the LeO Scheme Rules 2010.

CHAPTER 14

SRA investigations

14.1

Until relatively recently, from the perception of the solicitor, an investigation by the Solicitors Regulation Authority (SRA) was likely to commence in one of three ways:

(1) as a result of a complaint by a client or other party (for example, a client's complaint dealt with by the Legal Ombudsman (LeO), which includes a conduct element such as delay or conflict of interest, or a complaint by other solicitors of a failure to comply with an undertaking, or misconduct in litigation);[1]

(2) as a consequence of a visit by the Practice Standards Unit (PSU); or

(3) by notice of a forensic investigation by the SRA.

Only the first of these options involved a third party; in the other two situations only the SRA as the regulator was involved.

The PSU has been disbanded; historically, it carried out 'monitoring visits' to firms which were targeted on the basis of risk assessment. These visits could be made as a result of the firm's profile or complaints history, but could also be genuinely random. They were, broadly speaking, pastoral in nature as the practice standards adviser engaged in a dialogue with the firm to encourage good practice and the improvement of office systems as well as, more directly, regulatory compliance. The purpose of the visit was not expressly to investigate the firm, in a hostile sense, but to maintain standards and give advice. Nevertheless, if any issues of professional conduct arose that were considered to merit a more formal investigation, that would inevitably follow. This was very much a 'tick the boxes' approach in relation to the firm's systems; for example, in relation to arrangements with introducers, client care issues and accounts and business management. A 'tick-box' approach is alien to the concept of outcomes-focused regulation and a risk-based approach to regulation, adopted in 2011, thus the unit's demise.

Now, the 'visit process' falls within the SRA's new function of supervision. A range of supervisory tools is employed. They include desk-based supervision, written or telephone contact, risk-based visits and relationship management. The intention is that the SRA will be able to respond to potential risk before its impact is felt upon clients or the wider public.

1 Such complaints are sometimes made by judges who have tried cases in which a solicitor has apparently misconducted him- or herself.

14.2

In the case of third party complaints the current practice is to treat the source of the complaint as an informant, rather than a complainant. It is a matter for the supervisor to decide whether and to what extent the informant is kept advised and informed on the progress of the investigation. This will usually be done only where the informant can continue to contribute to the investigation by providing further information (for example) or where the informant has a legitimate personal interest in the outcome, as where the informant is complaining about non-compliance with an undertaking which is causing him prejudice.

In the overwhelming majority of cases complainants are advised that the SRA welcomes the information and will use it as an aid in assessing risks as a risk-based regulator, and that such action as is thought necessary will be taken, but the complainant will not be kept informed.

Forensic investigations

14.3

A forensic investigation is not pastoral in character: whereas monitoring visits by the PSU typically took a few days, and the supervision visits that have so far been reported appear to last one or two days, a forensic investigation can take weeks or months, with investigators staying for many days at a time. A forensic investigation is never random; the investigators will have specific concerns or specific reasons for their visit. Until quite recently (2009/10) reasons were never given (although they could usually be deduced). Now some reason for the inquiry will usually be given, unless it is believed that this would amount to a breach of any duty of confidentiality; or would risk disclosure of a confidential source of information; or significantly increase the risk that someone under investigation might destroy evidence, influence a witness, default or abscond; or it would otherwise prejudice the investigation or other regulatory action.[1]

Solicitors are under an obligation to co-operate fully with the SRA at all times.[2] They must also promptly comply with any written notice from the SRA for the production of documents and for 'all information and explanations requested', as well as providing consents and permissions necessary for investigators to seek verification from clients, staff, banks, building societies or other financial institutions, and comply with requests for the supply of copies of documents or documents in electronic form.[3]

Refusal to co-operate either generally or in relation to specific requests is most unwise, at least in the absence of strong expert advice that the investigators are exceeding their powers or otherwise acting unlawfully. The SRA has the ultimate deterrent: if there is a failure to comply with any part of the Code of Conduct (or rule 31 of the SRA Accounts Rules 2011 which contains comparable powers to require documents and information in relation to accounting matters) the powers of intervention will have arisen. No solicitor could prudently take that risk.

However, an obligation to provide information promptly is not an obligation to do so instantly, or without proper consideration or advice (if appropriate); nor is it unreasonable in a situation of complexity or apparent seriousness to obtain clarification of requests by seeking them in writing. Investigators are fully aware of this and should not object. In an exceptional case, however, where the facts appear clear and the investigators consider that such requests amount to evasion and prevarication, rather than proper caution, the invitation may be declined and the investigation concluded without further response from the person investigated.

1 Guidance notes to rule 31 of the SRA Accounts Rules 2011.
2 Outcome 10.6 of the SRA Code of Conduct 2011.
3 Outcomes 10.8, 10.9 and 10.10.

14.4

Many forensic investigations result in no action but, at the other extreme, when the public interest requires, they can result in an intervention into the solicitor's practice without notice (as where apparent dishonesty is revealed).

Other than in the most extreme case of obvious dishonesty, when an urgent intervention will occur after a very brief inspection, forensic investigations will begin with an initial fact-finding exercise concerned with basic details about the practice and partners/managers (questionnaires are provided for completion in advance). Then will come investigations into accounts, office systems and business arrangements (such as agreements with introducers) and client files over a period of time, requests being made for further information and explanation as matters arise. Investigations have become increasingly focused on business viability; the financial stability of firms, including such things as banking arrangements and levels of partner drawings, even if this is not the main focus of the inquiry. The investigation concludes with a final interview at which the investigators summarise all matters identified as causing apparent concern, and on which they require a more formal response.

That interview is not under caution; there is no obligation to give a caution, as this is not a criminal investigation. However, it has some of the characteristics of a police interview in that it can be expected to be searching, challenging and potentially hostile in terms of the style of questioning. Admissions that rules have been broken may be expressly required or invited. The preferred option is to record the whole interview on a digital medium, although this can result in large and potentially unwieldy transcripts. While the historical position has been that individuals have not been compelled to have the interview recorded, it is now likely that investigators will insist, if this is what they want (it is not always necessary), which it will not be possible to resist as a consequence of the solicitor's obligation to 'co-operate fully'. Further, there are additional powers under which the SRA can clearly compel such a process; see **14.9**.

The investigators are unlikely to be drawn on the question that virtually every solicitor will ask: 'What is going to happen?'. They will ordinarily say that they will submit a report that will be disclosed to you and you will be given an opportunity to comment, but are unlikely to be persuaded to go further. In the case of an urgent intervention the report will not be disclosed until after the intervention has occurred.

Subsequent investigation

14.5

Following the conclusion of the on-site investigation the investigatory process may take any one of three routes. One has already been mentioned – if the situation is obviously serious enough to justify intervention, that may be the next event.

Otherwise there are two options; the investigator may continue the investigation him- or herself, in correspondence, or the matter may be passed from 'Investigation' to 'Supervision' for a supervisor to follow up in the same way. The basis of the choice between the two methods is not clear on any published guidance, but the implication is that if the investigators choose themselves to produce a final report incorporating all the explanations and representations the solicitor may have provided, it is likely to be because a decision is expected to be made within the legal department of the SRA to authorise proceedings before the Solicitors Disciplinary Tribunal ('the Tribunal' or SDT) (see **14.12**).

If it is anticipated that a different result is more likely, such as a rebuke or fine imposed by the SRA, or if more than one regulated person or body is affected, with different levels of involvement and responsibility, it is more likely to be passed to a supervisor for a 'normal' correspondence-based investigation and a process of adjudication. This is because although the legal department can authorise a referral to the Tribunal, it does not have the power to impose rebukes or fines.

This two-strand process may not continue. There are increasing signs that all investigative work will be managed and overseen by the firm's supervisor or relationship manager.

A supervisor's investigation

14.6

Whether a matter arrives in a supervisor's hands as a direct complaint, as a referral from elsewhere within the SRA or as a result of a Forensic Investigations Report (an FI Report), the procedure that follows is the same. The process, which has largely been unchanged for a number of years, is now regulated by rules 4 to 6 of the SRA Disciplinary Procedure Rules 2011.

The supervisor, who may or may not be legally qualified, writes to the individual solicitor, or to the senior partner or an equivalent person if a number of individuals are affected (in which case the request will be made that it be confirmed whether the response is on behalf of all, or whether separate responses will be made), requesting a formal explanation of the matters which the supervisor has identified as requiring an explanation. The letter may seek an explanation from the regulated entity itself, independently of any being sought from individuals. The letter will contain warnings that any reply may be used in disciplinary proceedings, and that a failure to provide a sufficient and satisfactory explanation may result in regulation 3 of the SRA Practising Regulations 2011 and the regime relating to conditional practising certificates coming into force (see **15.3**).

The letter will usually require a reply within 14 days. Some leeway is likely to be available, but it is wise to make progress as best you can, and then to explain that there are specific reasons why more time is needed, rather than to complain that the deadline is impossible and that you need (for example) a minimum of three months.

14.7

There is no doubt that regulatory investigations can be exceptionally demanding and stressful, and may well interfere materially with your ability to carry on your practice. Specialist advice and assistance can assist, both in ensuring that efforts are appropriately targeted, and in ensuring balance and objectivity.

The process of interrogation by correspondence may continue with further requests for clarification or supplementary questions. The supervisor may consult with the forensic investigators or seek further information from the informant.

It is currently unclear whether this method of investigation by correspondence will remain the norm, or will be replaced by less formal contact in person or by telephone in the supervision process. It seems overwhelmingly likely, if the SRA (at any level) has in contemplation any form of enforcement action (the imposition of sanctions, as opposed to more pastoral encouragement to improve), that correspondence will be necessary as responses in writing will be required for evidential reasons.

It is to be hoped, however, that 'enforcement' will take a back seat to 'supervision' and that the former will only be employed when encouragement through the latter is plainly insufficient in the public interest.

Firm or individual?

14.8

The shift to entity-based regulation (see **CHAPTER 2**) has resulted in the firm being the main focus of any enquiry, with individuals targeted concurrently where appropriate. The SRA has published guidance as to how it intends to approach this.

The opening words of the 2009 guidance were 'The primary responsibility for ensuring compliance with a firm's regulatory obligations rests with the firm itself'.

This was capable of being misconstrued. The firm's obligations are those of the business to comply with the SRA Handbook. If a rogue employee or partner fails to act with integrity, it does not mean that the firm as a whole has done so. Entity regulation is not a means of imposing vicarious liability on the firm or the principals for everything that happens in it. Rather it is the responsibility of the firm to manage, in order to avoid regulatory risks as far as possible. The firm can be held to account for deficient management and systems, but there is no vicarious liability in conduct.[1]

In September 2011 the SRA reviewed this guidance. The opening is subtly different: 'Firms are responsible for delivering outcomes and for all aspects of compliance within the firm. Action may be taken against the firm only, individuals or both'.

The supporting paper to the SRA's Compliance Committee (before the 2011 Code came into force) contains this:

> 'A reminder which arises mainly in response to the position taken by some respondents is that firms are directly liable for misconduct which arises within them.
>
> In particular, it is important to be clear that this is not some form of "vicarious liability" but is a direct regulatory responsibility. On the basis of the current Solicitors' Code of Conduct 2007 and indeed in the draft handbook, firms are clearly caught and required to achieve outcomes (see Annex 3: Chapter 13 makes it clear that the Code in the Handbook applies to individuals and firms, referred to as "authorised bodies").

Firms are therefore directly liable. Subject to legal challenge, that should put to rest the argument by defence lawyers that responsibility of a firm is somehow vicarious.

Staff may have sometimes slipped back into a previous practice by which responsibility on the part of firms tended to be addressed by a specific allegation of failure to supervise or failure to operate proper management systems. Although in an appropriate case such allegations might still be made in addition to an allegation of substantive failure, they are not necessary to establish responsibility on the part of the firm for the original breach or failure to achieve an outcome – firms are responsible for the conduct itself. Even though an individual may also be responsible, the firm's direct liability remains.'

So – where a partner or trusted employee abuses the firm's expenses policy and clients are overcharged (although the abuse was extremely difficult if not impossible to detect, and was discovered by accident, or only on voluntary disclosure); or a member of staff is indiscreet and confidential information is overheard in a public place; or an employee behaves in an abusive, harassing or discriminatory way to a colleague, although the firm's policies and record are unimpeachable; or an employee creates a false file record to hide a mistake or inactivity – the firm has thus, in all these cases, failed to achieve a compulsory outcome and/or comply with a principle.

On the basis of SRA policy, in all these examples the firm is in breach and liable to sanction.

Firms are 'directly liable' for the breach; 'firms are responsible for the conduct itself'.

Firms are therefore, in terms of the 2011 Code as interpreted by the SRA, responsible as a matter of professional conduct and discipline for everything that goes wrong in the firm.

Any solicitor who commits serious professional misconduct will inevitably be in breach of one or more of the principles, most notably principle 6 (public trust). Conversely, many less serious breaches of a principle or an outcome could not properly be described as professional misconduct or conduct unbefitting a solicitor which historically was, in effect, the test as to whether disciplinary action, particularly an application to the Tribunal, was justified.

This may still have some relevance when consideration is given to the conduct, or misconduct, of individuals. The SRA's policy as to when it may take enforcement action against individuals, as opposed to the firm, is in broad terms that this will be when the individual's conduct occurred outside practice or if it raises separate and different risks from those of the entity. The thought process in relation to individuals will be to consider first whether there is a breach of an outcome, and then to consider whether the actions of the individual raise risks that require enforcement action being taken against the individual. This process will involve some assessment of that individual's personal responsibility or culpability but that assessment will be based on risk, rather than whether it amounts to unbefitting conduct (although these may be two sides of the same coin).

The SRA Handbook is a combination of high level principles, more detailed outcomes and very detailed rules. Despite the focus on 'outcomes' there are still many rules capable of being broken.

Because the SRA has adopted firm-based regulation, and the policies referred to above, its primary focus will be on the organisation and what it did and did not do. Professional misconduct as a concept does not fit easily into such a framework. Misconduct, moral culpability and unbefitting conduct are very personal concepts. The SRA is moving away from personal or professional regulation to simply regulation.

In future, the process in respect of entities will be to ask first whether they have achieved the outcomes; if not, what risks are represented by that failure and what is the correct regulatory response to it in the light of the identified risks? In many cases the response will be to ensure that the firm improves its processes, which will be addressed within the SRA's 'supervision' function, and enforcement action will not need to be taken. However, enforcement or disciplinary action against the entity, whether it be a multi-national LLP or a three- or four-partner traditional partnership, will remain an important part of the regulatory framework.

This new approach will raise novel issues. It is not yet clear whether any direction, advice or sanction 'follows' the entity or individuals. If there is action against the firm but not the individual, is the partner or manager who was involved in any breach then free of any relevant history when he joins another firm? Enforcement action taken against the firm may well affect the firm's reputation as a whole, including the reputation of those persons who were not directly involved in any breach. In this respect, firm-based regulation in solicitors' firms may well have a very different impact from that of the similar approach adopted by the Financial Conduct Authority, where reputational issues are very much less personal and more manageable.

This is all new territory for both firms and the SRA. Many firms are still partnerships, albeit within LLPs. Partners, teams and their work can transfer from one firm to another with relative ease. There is a risk that if a public record hangs over the firm as a whole as a result of the enforcement action, the break-up of firms could follow, as partners or practice groups leave to avoid having to declare an entity sanction in their continuing client acquisition (tendering for example), or in relation to professional indemnity insurance. If the SRA's focus in these circumstances is on supervision and advice rather than enforcement, sanction and publicity, there may be no problem, but any entity-based sanction and/or publicity could be disastrous to firms and wholly disproportionate.

There is no doubt that the new regime is intended to drive firms into ensuring that they have systems in place to manage risk and achieve the required outcomes, and that there is a will to impose financial penalties on firms who do not do so.

A further issue is that a financial penalty could fall on a firm and all its partners despite a change in composition and the departure of the person or persons who caused the problem.

It is understood to be the official position of the SRA in terms of policy, despite indications in the policy paper quoted above that firms could be guilty and liable to sanction for practically anything, that entity regulation should primarily involve 'supervision', with 'enforcement' being deployed only in two circumstances: (a) where there has been a serious failure of management – something fundamentally attributable to the way that the firm is being run; or (b) where on a problem being identified the firm is unwilling or unable to work with the SRA to put things right.

Despite all the above current experience is that there has been little change in the way that the SRA communicates with the profession when something is perceived to have gone wrong. The supervisor's letter may start by emphasising that the responsibility for compliance is that of the firm, but questions generally focus on individuals, which is very much as it has always been.

1 *Akodu v SRA* [2009] EWHC 3588 (Admin).

Further investigatory powers

14.9

The SRA may require production of the full file or files, and other information from any person or body it regulates.[1] If this is not volunteered, it can use statutory powers to compel the production of files and use the powers of intervention to enforce that requirement.[2]

If there is a forensic investigation it is normal for investigators to come armed with notices under section 44B of the Solicitors Act (SA) 1974 to reinforce their requests for documents and information.

If a notice has been given under section 44B, the SRA may by notice under section 44BA require the person notified to attend at a specified time and place to provide an explanation of any information provided or document produced pursuant to the original notice. Because this also involves the use of intervention powers, non-compliance is a criminal offence and the costs of the process are a debt due from the individual to the SRA, unless the court orders otherwise.[3] It is a criminal offence deliberately to interfere in this investigation process, or deliberately or recklessly to give false or misleading information.[4]

This is a powerful and potentially oppressive weapon. A solicitor may be required to attend the SRA's offices at his own expense, to be subjected to interrogation while under an obligation to answer questions, with criminal sanctions for failing to co-operate or for providing inaccurate answers. The investigators are likely to be accompanied by their own legal adviser. While a solicitor (or other regulated person) is entitled to be accompanied by, for example, a specialist adviser, the latter may be excluded at the discretion of the SRA investigators if they conclude that the adviser's presence is obstructing the inquiry. And the solicitor may be required to pay the costs of the SRA (including its legal costs) incurred in the section 44BA investigation.

It is devoutly to be hoped that this process will be used sparingly and only in exceptional circumstances, which is understood to be the position to date.

Sections 44B and 44BA apply to solicitors, employees of solicitors, recognised bodies, employees and managers or a person having an interest in a recognised body. They do not apply to alternative business structures (ABSs), or to non-solicitor managers and employees of ABSs. For the parallel powers in relation to ABSs see **25.4**.

The SRA may apply to the High Court for an order directing the provision of information and documents material to a regulatory investigation held by a person or body that is not regulated by the SRA.[5]

1 See outcomes 10.6 and 10.8 to 10.10 of the SRA Code of Conduct 2011.
2 Section 44B of SA 1974. See also 'limited intervention' at **16.26**. See also **APPENDIX 15** for the statutory provisions.
3 Section 44BA(3) and paras 9(3) and 13 of Schedule 1 to SA 1974.
4 Section 44BC.
5 Section 44BB.

14.10

The SRA may also in effect require solicitors and law firms to investigate themselves. By virtue of outcome 10.11 of the SRA Code of Conduct 2011, if the SRA gives notice requiring such action to be taken in relation to a matter specified in the notice, you must:

- act promptly to investigate whether any person may have a claim for redress against you;
- provide the SRA with a report on the outcome of such an investigation, identifying persons who may have such a claim;
- notify persons that they may have a right of redress against you, providing them with information as to the nature of the possible claim, about the firm's complaints procedures and about the Legal Ombudsman; and
- ensure, where you have identified a person who may have a claim for redress, that the matter is dealt with under the firm's complaints procedures as if that person had made a complaint.

This somewhat remarkable provision was designed, during the course of the Legal Services Bill through Parliament, to give the SRA additional powers to deal with firms caught up in the miners' compensation scheme in a manner thought to justify criticism. It enables the SRA to direct firms to act in a way which may result in an identified class of client being compensated *en masse*, although it would not be the SRA which imposes the obligation to provide the compensation. The SRA can only compel the firm to treat that class of client as if they had made a complaint. It cannot compel, even indirectly, the payment of compensation or redress, because of an express statutory provision.

Section 157 of LSA 2007 provides that 'The regulatory arrangements of an approved regulator must not include any provision relating to redress' – the clear legislative intent being that this is now exclusively a matter for the Legal Ombudsman. The powers of the SRA set out in outcome 10.11 reflect a saving provision in section 158 of LSA 2007 in virtually identical words.

The report stage

14.11

At the conclusion of the investigation process the supervisor has several options. He or she may decide that there are no grounds for action, which will result in the file being closed, or may decide that although there have been errors or rule breaches they are not such as to justify a referral to an adjudicator. In this event a 'letter of advice' will be sent, which identifies the fault found and advises against repetition, but confirms that there is no sanction. Such a result will, however, remain on the 'record' of the individuals affected in case it should ever be relevant in the future.

Items on a solicitor's record are never 'spent'; they remain forever, but can of course become irrelevant in practice due to lapse of time.

If the matter is to go forward to adjudication the supervisor prepares a report which is disclosed to the affected solicitor(s)[1] and (optionally) to the informant, if any, at the supervisor's discretion. This will set out the facts in summary, identify the relevant issues, state the supervisor's conclusions and make recommendations to the adjudicator. This does not bind the adjudicator but gives a clear indication to the solicitor as to what he or she faces so that focused representations can be made on the report. The solicitor might of course agree with the recommendations. Despite the fact that adjudicators can and do disagree with the recommendations and come to different conclusions there is a rather unfortunate practice of providing with the disclosed adjudication papers a 'draft decision' in the form of the recommended outcome, which gives the (misleading) impression that it awaits only the descent of the rubber stamp.

The supervisor may recommend that some issues should be resolved in favour of the solicitor or firm. In respect of investigations into matters occurring before 1 June 2010, the option remains of an in-house sanction consisting of a reprimand or severe reprimand, if fault is found but the matter does not warrant proceedings in the Tribunal. Reprimands of this kind are informal in character in that they are not in pursuance of any statutory power and amount to no more than an expression of opinion by the regulator. With effect from 1 June 2010, in respect of regulatory breaches occurring or continuing on or after that date, the SRA has powers to impose a statutory rebuke, to require the payment of a fine not exceeding £2,000 to be forfeit to the Crown, and to publicise such decisions (see **CHAPTER 19**). For the much more extensive disciplinary powers of the SRA in relation to ABSs see **CHAPTER 25**.

Yet more seriously for the solicitor, the recommendation may be that he or she should be referred to the Tribunal, and/or that practising certificate conditions and/or intervention should be considered.

The individual and/or firm will have 14 days to respond, with some leeway unless intervention is in contemplation.

1 See rule 6 of the SRA Disciplinary Procedure Rules 2011.

14.12

Just as the forensic investigators can report direct to the SRA's legal department if it is considered appropriate to refer the matter to the Tribunal without further formality, so can the supervisor. The formal process of adjudication, involving disclosure of a report with recommendations, can be bypassed, with the result that a decision to refer the solicitor's conduct to the Tribunal can be made after a solicitor's explanation is received, but otherwise without notice and without any right of appeal.[1]

The decision may be taken by the SRA's in-house advocates or their managers if they are satisfied that the evidential and public interest tests are satisfied. There is no published guidance as to when this 'fast track' system may be employed or as to the criteria to be applied in making that choice, beyond the bare terms of rule 10 of the SRA Disciplinary Procedure Rules 2011 which specify an evidential test, a public interest test, and a conclusion that the likely result would be beyond the powers of the SRA itself. Moreover, it appears likely that the SRA will seek to streamline the process of decision-making and that in any case in which it is felt by the investigators or supervisors that these tests are likely to be met, this system, involving a dialogue between the supervisor and/or investigator and the legal department, will become the norm. It is of course open to the legal department to advise either that the decision is premature and that further questions need to be asked, or that the case is more suitable for consideration by an adjudicator.

Bearing in mind the absence of notice, the absence of any right of appeal, and the absence of any but the broadest guidance as to when this system could be expected to be used (based on the opinions of individuals), it is to be hoped that it would only be used in the clearest cases where, for example, there is nothing more that the solicitor could say that could possibly affect the outcome: that is, where a referral to the Tribunal is absolutely inevitable. Many cases historically involved a fine judgement as to whether the matter requires referral to the Tribunal or can proportionately be dealt with by a severe reprimand, and the same will apply with greater force to the new regime of in-house rebukes and fines. It would be most unfortunate if in any such case a solicitor was deprived of the opportunity to make submissions on that issue, on an informed basis that a referral to the Tribunal was clearly in prospect, if that was indeed the case.

At present, the dialogue between supervisor and the legal department involves an exchange of internal memoranda without disclosure to the regulated person or body. There is accordingly scope for human error, for example, in misunderstanding the facts or misinterpreting the explanations provided, without the solicitor having an opportunity to correct any such fault. On the assumption that this system is an SRA-preferred option in the interests of efficiency, it is to be hoped that solicitors will at least be given an opportunity to comment on the investigator's or supervisor's provisional conclusions so as to avoid the possibility of errors influencing the decision.

Less sensitively, this fast track system may also be employed to add further matters to a case to be considered by the Tribunal, after the conduct of a solicitor has already been the subject of a referral on other matters.

1 Rule 10 of the SRA Disciplinary Procedure Rules 2011.

Publicity during investigations – acts and omissions prior to 1 June 2010

14.13

Generally, no publicity is given to investigations and matters remain confidential as between the solicitor and the SRA, but the SRA has a discretion to publish information if it considers that it is in the public interest to do so, for example, where there is an investigation giving rise to significant public concern. The SRA may disclose how the investigation is progressing or that it has been concluded without an adverse finding against the solicitor. This policy applies to investigations which commenced on or after 1 January 2008. For the post-June 2010 regime for publication of SRA-imposed fines and rebukes see **CHAPTER 19**.

Although matters of this nature were treated as confidential as between the SRA and the solicitor, nothing prevented the complainant, if informed, from disclosing the result.[1]

1 *Napier and anor v Pressdram Ltd* [2009] EWCA Civ 443; [2010] 1 WLR 934.

The supervision function

14.14

To achieve what it wants to achieve, the SRA needs far more information from firms than it has previously required. New firms will go through a rigorous authorisation process, with the possibility of conditions being applied (perhaps restricting the nature of the work that can be undertaken if adequate expertise cannot be demonstrated). All firms must provide an annual report from January 2013 (when the COLP and COFA regime came into force) and have to notify the SRA of serious misconduct, serious financial difficulty and material breaches of the SRA Handbook. 'Self-reporting' is now a requirement – for the first time in the profession's history, from October 2011.[1]

From and since the 2011/12 renewal process a breakdown has been required of all complaints received by the firm in the previous 12 months, allocated between 15 categories (including 'other'), the number resolved (meaning resolved to the client's satisfaction), and the number referred to the Legal Ombudsman. In addition, from 2012 the SRA has required firms to report on diversity in the workplace.

The SRA now risk-rates firms in order to apply its finite resources to firms who pose serious risks or to those who are unable or unwilling to identify and manage risk.

The focal point will be likely in future to be on firms' internal governance, and the ability of managers to develop workable monitoring systems. These will need to be capable of identifying serious breaches of the Principles and outcomes, and other business risks, and firms will need to demonstrate how they will respond appropriately. The SRA supervision process, including visits to firms, will need to be able to review and assess these systems.

The SRA's risk assessment focus will change from a consideration of compliance or non-compliance with detailed rules, to an assessment of the risks to the Principles and outcomes, and to the risks associated with firms failing to have adequate processes and systems in place.

1 Outcomes 10.3 and 10.4 of the SRA Code of Conduct 2011.

14.15

Supervision will entail 'desk-based supervision' – presumably an analysis of available information and intelligence, and contact with compliance officers, where the level of risk is perceived as low. There will also be 'relationship management', a much closer working relationship between regulator and regulated in the form of more frequent contact – large firms, and global and City firms will have a nominated contact point at the SRA as their 'relationship manager' on a permanent basis. Firms perceived to have a potentially short-term issue requiring a closer degree of oversight may have imposed temporary relationship management, which will entail regular reporting as to the firm's solution to the problem.

Firms perceived to be high risk may receive a risk-based visit.

Risk-based visits

14.16

In the 2013 edition of this book we attempted some speculation (with the able assistance of Vanessa Shenton of The Compliance Partner) as to how risk-based visits would develop. What has emerged is that, effectively throughout the intervening period, the SRA has been concentrating on themed exercises focusing on the consequences of the Legal Aid, Sentencing and Punishment of Offenders Act (LASPOA) 2012 and the financial stability of law firms. LASPOA 2012 had three material consequences: removing swathes of work from the ambit of legal aid, removing the ability to recover success fees and after the event insurance premiums from defendants, and prohibiting the payment of referral fees; these gave it the capacity to make serious inroads into the profitability of law firms. Themed investigations have taken place into legal aid practices and personal injury claimant firms, as to their viability and compliance with the referral fee prohibition. This morphed into a wider investigation into all practices which the SRA perceived to be in financial difficulties, or at risk of financial difficulties. In fact many firms, large and small, have failed, only some being rescued by merger or other means. An enormous amount of the SRA's resources has been taken up in these exercises and in managing the fallout, effecting some interventions and overseeing a considerable number of close downs under varying degrees of SRA oversight; and over the past year (as we write) there has been very little evidence of activity other than in these areas. The number of applications to the SDT for example has dramatically dropped. There has not been a stable basis on which to judge how the supervision function would operate in the absence of resources being diverted in this way.

14.17

As and when some stability is reached there is some insight into how the SRA might go about its visit process within various consultation papers and other documents it has issued. The November 2010 SRA policy statement 'Delivering outcomes-focused regulation' indicated that a visit to a firm under 'close and continuous supervision' might entail an assessment of:

'• The environmental risks affecting the firm, for example, the economic environment for conveyancing firms;

- The firm's business model, for example the spread of the firm's business, how is it financed, and what services it offers;
- The firm's business processes, for example:
  - the firm's structure and ownership
  - the extent of any risks posed by staff, including owners or managers

  - controls over its financial position
  - IT systems
  - exposure to legal/litigation risk
  - conflict and client care procedures
  - quality control and management of client matters;
- The firm's control functions, for example the work done by the COLP and COFA, together with internal audit (if the firm has an internal audit function – many smaller firms will not need one). We will consider the firm's governance arrangements, the strength of the relationship with the SRA (and its other regulators, if any), together with the strength of its management and its internal culture.'

CHAPTER 15

Practising certificate controls

15.1

Every solicitor must at all times hold a valid practising certificate in order to practise as such.[1] Very few solicitors outside government service can escape the requirement to hold a practising certificate.[2] Accordingly, the power to impose conditions on a solicitor's practising certificate represents a very powerful regulatory control in the hands of the Solicitors Regulation Authority (SRA).

An additional control, with effect from 1 July 2009, was the requirement on sole practitioners to have a sole solicitor endorsement on their practising certificates to enable them to practise as such. Existing sole practitioners were 'passported' into compliance with the new regulations provided they were currently lawfully practising in that capacity. From November 2009, however, a sole practitioner had to satisfy the SRA, as part of the process for renewing the practising certificate and sole solicitor endorsement, that he or she may properly practise as a sole practitioner by showing, among other things, that he or she has sufficient skills or knowledge in relation to the running and management of a business which provides regulated legal services. This short-lived regime is intended to be replaced in the near future with the requirement that sole practitioners be authorised in the same way that all other practices, recognised bodies or licensed bodies (alternative business structures, ABSs), are authorised, under the SRA Authorisation Rules for Legal Services Bodies and Licensable Bodies 2011 (see **CHAPTER 2**), but no doubt the same principles that were applied to sole practitioner recognition will continue to apply.

1 Section 1 of the Solicitors Act (SA) 1974.
2 See rule 9 of the SRA Practice Framework Rules 2011 and commentary at **2.25**.

15.2

The whole regulatory system in relation to practising certificates changed on 1 July 2009, when section 12 of SA 1974 and associated provisions were repealed and replaced by a rule-based system, now comprised principally in the SRA Practising Regulations 2011. Although the statutory basis of regulation has changed, there are only modest changes of substance (the list of circumstances in which conditions can be applied is somewhat longer). There are unlikely to be any material changes in the processes of investigation and adjudication, or in the principles to apply. Past decisions by the Master of the Rolls will therefore remain relevant.

15.3

The equivalent of section 12 of SA 1974 is now regulation 3.1 of the SRA Practising Regulations 2011. On an initial application for a practising certificate or on an application for its renewal, the SRA has a discretion to impose conditions on the certificate, or to refuse the application 'following certain events' which are listed.

3.1 Regulation 3 applies … in any of the following circumstances …

(a) The applicant has been:

(i) reprimanded, made the subject of disciplinary sanction or made the subject of an order under section 43 of the *SA*, ordered to pay costs or made the subject of a recommendation to the *Society* or the *SRA* to consider imposing a condition, by the *Tribunal*, or struck off or suspended by the *court*;

(ii) made the subject of an order under section 43 of the *SA* by the *Society* or the *SRA* or rebuked or fined under section 44D of that Act by the *SRA*;

(iii) made the subject of an intervention by the *Society*, the *SRA* or by any other *approved regulator*, or been:

(A) a *manager, interest holder* or *compliance* officer, of a *recognised body*;

(B) a *compliance officer* of a *sole practitioner firm*;

(C) a *manager, owner* or *compliance officer* of a *licensed body*;

(D) a *manager* or *interest holder* of an *authorised non-SRA firm* which is not licensed under Part 5 of the *LSA*; or

(E) a *manager, material interest* holder, *HOLP* or *HOFA* of an *authorised non-SRA firm* licensed under Part 5 of the *LSA*;

which has been the subject of, an intervention by the *Society*, the *SRA* or by any other *approved regulator*;

(iv) made the subject of a disciplinary sanction by, or refused registration with or authorisation by, another *approved regulator*, professional or regulatory tribunal, or regulatory authority, whether in England and Wales or elsewhere;

(v) *disqualified* from acting as a *HOLP* or a *HOFA* or from being a *manager* of, or being employed by, a *licensed body* or an *authorised non-SRA firm*;

(vi) refused authorisation as a *recognised sole practitioner* or approval as a *compliance officer* of such a *firm* or had such authorisation revoked under regulation 10.2(b)(i), (iii), (iv) or (vi);[1]

(vii) refused approval to be a *manager, owner* or *compliance officer* of an *authorised body* or had such approval withdrawn;

(viii) refused approval to be a *manager, material interest* holder, *HOLP* or *HOFA* of an *authorised non-SRA firm* or had such approval withdrawn;

(ix) a *manager, owner* or *compliance officer* of an *authorised body* the authorisation of which has been suspended or revoked by the *SRA* under Rule 22 of the *SRA Authorisation Rules*, except under 22.1(a)(vii);[2]

(x) a *manager, material interest* holder, *HOLP* or *HOFA* of an *authorised non-SRA firm* the authorisation of which has been suspended or revoked by another *approved regulator*; or

(xi) made subject to a *revocation* of his or her practising certificate or registration under regulation 10.2(a)(i) or (v) or of his or her authorisation as a *recognised sole practitioner* under regulation 10.2(b)(i), (iv) or (vi).[3]

(b) The *SRA* (or previously the *Society*) has requested an explanation from the applicant in respect of a matter relating to the applicant's conduct and has notified the applicant in writing that it does not regard the applicant's response, or lack of response, as satisfactory.

(c) The applicant has failed to deliver within the period allowed an accountant's report required by rules made under section 34 of the *SA*.

(d) The applicant's practising certificate or registration has been suspended and the suspension:

(i) has come to an end;

(ii) was continuing when the applicant's last practising certificate or previous registration expired or was revoked; or

(iii) is continuing.

(e) The applicant has been suspended from *practice* (or suspended from the register, if the applicant is a European *lawyer*), and the suspension has come to an end.

(f) The applicant's last practising certificate or previous registration expired or was revoked whilst subject to a condition.

(g) The applicant's practising certificate or registration is currently subject to a condition.

(h) The applicant's right to practise as a *lawyer* of another jurisdiction or as a *lawyer of England and Wales* (other than as a *solicitor*) is subject to a condition or restriction.

(i) The applicant has been restored to the roll or register, having previously been struck off.

(j) The applicant is an undischarged bankrupt.

(k) The applicant:

(i) has been adjudged bankrupt and discharged;

(ii) has entered into an individual voluntary arrangement or a partnership voluntary arrangement under the Insolvency Act 1986;

(iii) has at any time during the last 36 months of trading of a *recognised body*, a *licensed body* or an *authorised non-SRA firm* which has entered into a voluntary arrangement under the Insolvency Act 1986, been a *manager* of that *recognised body*, *licensed body* or *authorised non-SRA firm*;

(iv) has at any any time during the last 36 months of trading of a *company* or of an *LLP* which has been the subject of a winding up order, an administration order or administrative receivership; or has entered into a voluntary arrangement under the Insolvency Act 1986; or has been voluntarily wound up in circumstances of insolvency, been a *director* of that company or a *member* of that LLP.

(l) The applicant lacks capacity (within the meaning of the Mental Capacity Act 2005) and powers under sections 15 to 20 or section 48 of that Act are exercisable in relation to the applicant.

(m) The applicant has been committed to prison in civil or criminal proceedings and:

(i) has been released; or

(ii) has not been released.

(n) The applicant has been made subject to a judgment which involves the payment of money, other than one:

(i) which is limited to the payment of costs; or

(ii) in respect of which the applicant is entitled to indemnity or relief from another person as to the whole sum; or

(iii) which the applicant has paid, and supplied evidence of payment to the *SRA* (or previously to the *Society*).

(o) The applicant is currently charged with an indictable offence.

(p) The applicant has been convicted of an indictable offence or any offence under the *SA*, the Financial Services and Markets Act 2000, the Immigration and Asylum Act 1999 or the Compensation Act 2006.

(q) The applicant has been disqualified from being a *company director*.

(r) The applicant has been removed from the office of charity trustee or trustee for a charity by an order within the terms of section 72(1)(d) of the Charities Act 1993.

(s) The applicant has been the subject in another jurisdiction of any circumstance equivalent to those listed in (j) to (r).

If regulation 3 applies by reason of paragraphs (j) (bankruptcy), (m) (committal to prison), (n) (money judgment) or (p) (conviction of a relevant criminal offence) and the judgment or order is subject to appeal, the application for a practising certificate must not be refused before the determination of the appeal, unless in the opinion of the SRA the appeal proceedings have been unduly protracted by the appellant or (again in the opinion of the SRA) they are unlikely to be successful, but the SRA may in the meantime postpone a decision on the application and may impose a condition on the applicant's practising certificate.[4]

If regulation 3 applies by reason of paragraph (o) (the applicant is currently charged with an indictable offence), the application may not be refused unless the applicant is convicted, but the SRA may postpone a decision on the application and may impose a condition on the applicant's practising certificate in the meantime.[5]

If the SRA has decided to impose a condition, it may postpone the issue of the certificate pending determination or discontinuance of any appeal against the decision; but the postponement may be rescinded if in its opinion proceedings on appeal have been unduly protracted by an appellant or (again in the SRA's opinion) are unlikely to be successful.[6]

1 Where the authorisation was granted as a result of error or fraud; where the individual no longer meets the criteria for authorisation; where there is a failure to comply with regulatory duties including failing to pay any fine imposed by the SRA, the Solicitors Disciplinary Tribunal or the court; or where a decision has been made not to renew authorisation.
2 Rule 22.1(a)(vii) of the SRA Authorisation Rules for Legal Services Bodies and Licensable Bodies 2011 involves revocation on the application of the authorised body itself.
3 Regulation 10.2(a)(i) and (v) of the SRA Practising Regulations 2011: where the application was granted as a result of error or fraud or revocation followed a refusal to replace a practising certificate or renew a registration.
4 Regulation 3.3(b).
5 Regulation 3.3(c).
6 Regulation 7.3.

Immediate imposition of conditions

15.4

The SRA may impose one or more conditions on a practising certificate at any time during the practising year.[1] The SRA Practising Regulations 2011 do not specify that the power to do so is only exercisable if one or more of the circumstances set out in regulation 3.1 applies. Section 13A of SA 1974 (as amended by LSA 2007) provides that conditions may be imposed on a current practising certificate if it appears to the SRA that the case is of a 'prescribed description' and 'prescribed' means prescribed by the relevant regulations.[2] It is possible that the SRA Practising Regulations 2011 are intended to be read so as to mean that the prescribed circumstances for the imposition of immediate conditions are those set out in regulation 3.1, but an alternative reading is that the 'prescribed description' is a reference to those circumstances in which there is a need for regulatory action on the basis of the stated purposes for which conditions may be imposed (see **15.5**).

If a condition is to be imposed on a current certificate, the SRA must give 28 days' written notice, with reasons, to the individual concerned, but may shorten or dispense with the 28-day period if it is satisfied on reasonable grounds that it is in the public interest to do so.[3]

1 Regulation 7.1 of the SRA Practising Regulations 2011.
2 Sections 13A and 28 of SA 1974.
3 Regulation 7.4 of the SRA Practising Regulations 2011.

The specified purposes

15.5

The purposes for which the SRA may impose conditions, either on renewal or on a current certificate, are spelled out in regulation 7.1 of the SRA Practising Regulations 2011:

> 7.1 The *SRA* may impose one or more conditions on a practising certificate or

on the registration of a European *lawyer* when granting an application under regulation 3 to 6, or at any time during the practising year, for the following purposes.

(a) The *SRA* considers the individual concerned unsuitable to undertake certain activities in relation to a legal *practice*, either at all or save as specified in the condition, and that imposing the condition will, in the public interest, limit, restrict, halt or prevent the involvement of the individual concerned in those activities.

(b) The *SRA* considers that the individual concerned is putting or is likely to put at risk the interests of *clients*, third parties or the public by taking certain steps in relation to a legal *practice*, and that imposing the condition will, in the public interest, limit, restrict, halt or prevent the taking of such steps by the individual concerned.

(c) The *SRA* considers the individual concerned unsuitable to engage in certain business agreements, business associations or *practising* arrangements and that imposing a condition requiring the applicant to obtain the *SRA's* written approval before taking certain steps will, in the public interest, limit, halt or prevent a risk to *clients*, third parties or the public.

(d) The *SRA* considers that imposing the condition will, in the public interest, require the individual concerned to take specified steps conducive to the carrying on of efficient *practice* by the individual concerned.

(e) The *SRA* considers that imposing the condition will, in the public interest, facilitate closer monitoring by the *SRA* of compliance by the individual concerned with rules and regulations.

(f) The *SRA* considers that it would be in the public interest to impose the condition in any other case during the currency of a practising certificate or registration.

Paragraph (f) would seem to be sufficiently broad that the other stated purposes are scarcely required to be listed, but it remains, as affirmed by the Master of the Rolls (see **15.12**) a question as to what is necessarily and proportionately required for the protection of the public. The other paragraphs, however, do give some indication as to the nature of the conditions that will be considered.

Revocation of practising certificates and sole solicitor endorsements

15.6

The SRA may revoke a practising certificate at any time, if it is satisfied that it was granted as a result of error or fraud; if the replacement or renewal date has passed and the SRA has not received an application for renewal of the certificate; or as a result of a decision to refuse to renew a practising certificate.[1]

From a date expected to be some time in 2015 the concept of the recognised sole practitioner will disappear; sole practitioners will be subject to the SRA Authorisation Rules for Legal Services Bodies and Licensable Bodies 2011 and the revocation provisions in those rules (see rule 22 of the Authorisation Rules and **2.16**). The current provisions in the SRA Practising Regulations 2011 are therefore of limited significance. But for completeness, the SRA may revoke authorisation as a recognised sole practitioner at any time:[2]

- if the authorisation was granted as a result of error or fraud;
- if the solicitor is not practising from an office in England and Wales;
- if the SRA is not satisfied that the recognised sole practitioner continues to meet the criteria for authorisation as a recognised sole practitioner;
- if the recognised sole practitioner or any employee of the firm fails to comply with the duties imposed under the SRA's regulatory arrangements or any statutory obligations, including failure to pay any fine or other financial penalty imposed by the SRA, the Solicitors Disciplinary Tribunal ('the Tribunal' or SDT) or the High Court;[3]
- if the recognised sole practitioner has a temporary emergency recognition but has not within the initial 28-day period or any extension of that period commenced a substantive application for recognition;[4] or
- if the SRA has decided not to renew authorisation as a recognised sole practitioner.

The SRA may revoke a practising certificate or authorisation as a recognised sole practitioner on the application of the person concerned but there is no discretion to refund any part of the fee paid for that practising year, and the SRA may refuse the application if there is an outstanding complaint against the applicant, or for any other reason relating to the public interest.[5]

If the SRA decides to revoke a practising certificate or authorisation as a recognised sole practitioner, it must give the person concerned 28 days' notice, with reasons. The notice may be given together with notification of refusal of an application to replace a practising certificate or renew an authorisation. Revocation takes effect on expiry of the notice or on such later date as may be stated in the notice, except that if an appeal is made during the period of notice the revocation does not take effect until determination or discontinuance of any appeal, whether under the SRA's own procedure, or to the High Court.[6]

1 Regulation 10.2(a) of the SRA Practising Regulations 2011.
2 Regulation 10.2(b).
3 This is a new provision introduced in 2011 which appears in similar terms in the Authorisation Rules, as rule 22.1(a)(ix). It can be seen to provide another substantial regulatory weapon, both to enforce the payment of fines imposed by the SRA and as an additional threat in respect of any regulatory failure.
4 For 'temporary emergency recognition' or 'authorisation' as it will become, see **2.18** and **2.19**.
5 Regulation 10.2(c) of the SRA Practising Regulations 2011.
6 Regulation 10.3.

Suspension of practising certificate

15.7

A practising certificate may also be suspended with immediate effect in the following circumstances:

- where the solicitor has been convicted of an offence involving dishonesty or deception, or an indictable offence, *and* the SRA has referred his conduct to the Tribunal, the SRA may suspend his practising certificate for up to six months, and may renew that suspension once for a maximum of a further six months;[1]
- where an order has been made for the suspension of a solicitor from practice by a court or the Tribunal, or on a solicitor's bankruptcy. These operate as an automatic suspension of the practising certificate[2] – from any date specified by the court or Tribunal in the case of a suspension from practice, and immediately on an adjudication of bankruptcy;
- where there is an intervention on the grounds of suspected dishonesty, or breaches of the SRA Accounts Rules 2011, or breaches of any rules made under section 31 of SA 1974 (which include the SRA Code of Conduct 2011), or because the solicitor has been committed to prison in criminal or civil proceedings. This also automatically suspends the solicitor's practising certificate, unless the adjudicator or adjudication panel which resolves to intervene directs otherwise.[3] The additional provision relating to rules made under section 31 (the successive Practice Rules and Codes of Conduct, in addition to the Accounts Rules, made under section 32), which was effected by amendment of SA 1974 by LSA 2007, means that in practical terms the practising certificate can be expected to be suspended on every intervention unless the decision-maker directs otherwise.

1 Section 13B of SA 1974.
2 Section 15(1).
3 Section 15(1A) and (1B).

15.8

When a practising certificate is suspended on intervention or by reason of bankruptcy the solicitor may apply to the SRA to terminate the suspension.[1]

It is a common and erroneous belief that bankruptcy is the equivalent of being struck off. It is not; indeed, when a solicitor knows that he or she will be made bankrupt, or is very likely to be, it used to be possible to apply to the SRA in advance of the date on which the adjudication is expected for the inevitable and automatic suspension to be terminated on acceptable conditions. In the case of bankruptcy the usual conditions will require the solicitor to practise only in employment that has been expressly approved by the SRA and that the solicitor has no access to client funds.

If an insolvent solicitor is already in employment or has a willing potential employer it is possible to apply for the suspension to be terminated and for the employment to be approved in advance in one adjudication process. It used to be possible to arrange all this so that the adjudicator's decision became effective immediately the bankruptcy order was made, so that the solicitor could continue to practise seamlessly. The present practice, however, is that the bankruptcy has actually to occur before the decision can be made, but the duration of any hiatus in practice should be limited to a short number of days, if as much as possible is arranged in advance.

For the situation that arises following interventions, see **16.10**.

1 Section 16(3) and (4) of SA 1974.

Common conditions on practising certificates – the test to apply

15.9

Practising certificate conditions are imposed solely to protect the public, primarily the solicitor's clients, by managing risk. The 'certain events' listed in regulation 3.1 of the SRA Practising Regulations 2011 are situations in which a solicitor may be regarded as representing an increased risk. Conditions are not imposed for the purposes of punishing solicitors, although conditions may be expensive for the solicitor, or even drive him or her out of business (for example, a condition of approved employment upon a sole practitioner who cannot or does not wish to find such employment).

The correct approach to the imposition of conditions is:

(1) to identify the risk;

(2) to identify a mechanism to manage and control the risk to minimise its consequences; and

(3) to determine whether the proposed mechanism is necessary and proportionate to the risk. As conditions are not intended to be penal, the control mechanism should be no more than is necessary to manage the risk.

Thus in cases of accounts that have been badly kept, resulting in substantial accounting errors and breaches of the Accounts Rules, the imposition of a condition requiring more frequent accountants' reports (usually half-yearly rather than annually) would be the obvious course. Where serious errors of judgement have occurred, and there is a risk of repetition, or where there have been serious administrative failings, a condition requiring a solicitor to practise only in approved partnership or, in extreme cases, approved employment, could be appropriate.

In *Razeen (No 15 of 2008)*[1] the Master of the Rolls stated:

> 'Mr Goodwin [for the SRA] submits that regulatory conditions are imposed either to protect the public interest or the reputation of the profession or both. It appears to me that the essential point is whether conditions are necessary and proportionate to protect the public interest. Reference to reputation of the profession is really an incident of the protection of the public interest … I am also unable, however, to accept what I think may be Mr Goodwin's submission, that the SRA does not have to identify a specific risk. Absent identification of the risk, it appears to me that the SRA cannot properly assess the reasonableness or proportionality of any conditions that it seeks to impose.'

1 *Razeen (No 15 of 2008)* [2008] EWCA Civ 1220 at [12] and [13]. See also *Lebow (No 13 of 2007)* [2008] EWCA Civ 411 at [23]: 'Conditions, however, if they are to be imposed, must be both necessary and proportionate'.

15.10

The precise content of conditions will depend upon the regulatory concerns of the SRA, and as to how the public can best be protected. For instance, the solicitor may be excluded from carrying out specified work of a particular kind, such as probate, or may be required to attend a particular type of training course on solicitors' accounting procedures or practice management. The SRA may take into account, when imposing conditions, that an application has been made against the solicitor to the Solicitors Disciplinary Tribunal if the allegations are sufficiently serious, even though those allegations have not yet been adjudicated upon.[1]

Conditions, once imposed, are likely to be re-imposed from year to year, although it is open to the solicitor upon renewal to apply for a certificate free from conditions. If the condition was imposed by reason of a set of circumstances which by their nature continue (for example, the existence of judgment debts), the solicitor can expect the condition to continue until the underlying cause is removed (for example, by the discharge of those debts).[2]

If the cause of the condition was a particular event, such as the imposition of a penalty by the Tribunal, or a return to practice after suspension, conditions are likely to be imposed for at least three or four years. There is, however, no hard rule to this effect and it may well be possible for the solicitor to secure an unconditional certificate if it can clearly be demonstrated that the problem period is over, and there is no continuing cause for concern or the need for any additional safeguard.

If an unconditional certificate is granted to a solicitor upon whom conditions were previously imposed by reason of regulation 3.1(a), (b), (c), (d)(i), (e), (j), (k), (m)(i), (n), (o), (p), (q), (r) or (s) of the SRA Practising Regulations 2011, then conditions cannot be re-imposed by reason of the same facts. In effect, the cause of the problem becomes 'spent' for regulatory purposes. However, this does not apply where the decision to grant an unconditional certificate was made by the SRA in ignorance of the relevant circumstances.[3]

1 *Burdett (No 8 of 2002)* [2002] EWCA Civ 1194; *Awan v Law Society* [2003] EWCA Civ 1969; *Walker (No 13 of 2001)* [2001] EWCA Civ 1596.
2 Comments by Lord Donaldson MR in *No 6 of 1990* (unreported).
3 Regulation 3.3(a) of the SRA Practising Regulations 2011.

Procedure

15.11

The procedure followed is similar to that used for adjudication on matters of conduct (see **14.11**), by the production of a supervisor's report which contains recommendations on which the solicitor has the opportunity to comment, usually within 14 days. If the solicitor does not oppose the recommended course or does not respond, the provisional decision becomes final (subject to appeal). To that extent the power to make decisions rests with the individual supervisor.

If the proposed course is not accepted and representations are made, the matter is adjudicated upon, but the level and seniority of the decision-maker can vary. The matter may be referred to an adjudicator, but increasingly decisions at first instance are being taken by supervisors or their managers.

Similar procedures are followed where, for example, there is an existing practising certificate condition requiring approval of any proposed partnership or employment, and application is made for approval.

Appeals

15.12

All the decisions of the SRA set out above can be contested by way of appeal to the High Court (rather than to the Master of the Rolls as was the case prior to Legal Services Act (LSA) 2007).[1] Previous decisions of successive Masters of the Rolls will continue to be highly persuasive, as the High Court comes to grips with this, still relatively new, jurisdiction. In *Akodu v SRA*,[2] Moses LJ candidly accepted the inexperience of the High Court in dealing with such issues, and remitted the issue of practising certificate conditions to the adjudicator, stating:[3]

> 'I would, for my part, underline that which Mr Barton [for the SRA] urged, namely, that in the normal case, this court should deal with these questions rather than remitting them. No doubt, as the body of experience expands, confined as it will be to a number of nominated judges as we were told, it will not be necessary to adopt the course I have reluctantly decided should be adopted.'

Although the High Court has an unfettered discretion in hearing such appeals, appropriate weight will be accorded to the professional expertise of the SRA decision-makers who imposed the conditions.[4] When such appeals were heard by the Master of the Rolls, costs were in the discretion of the Master of the Rolls by virtue of his inherent power when exercising his quasi-visitorial jurisdiction over solicitors.[5] The High Court can be expected to apply traditional costs principles to practising certificate appeals, so that costs will ordinarily follow the event.

The SRA also operates an in-house appeals system, which it encourages solicitors to utilise before exercising their statutory rights of appeal (historically the Master of the Rolls took the same view).[6] If the first instance decision is by a decision-maker other than an adjudicator, the appeal lies to an adjudicator; if it was by an adjudicator, appeal lies to an adjudication panel.

Appeals under the SRA's own appeals procedure must be commenced within 28 days of notification of the relevant decision.[7]

If and when the SRA makes rules to this effect, appeals may lie to the Tribunal rather than the High Court.[8] There is no sign that the SRA has any current intention of making such rules.

The Tribunal has no power itself to impose conditions on a practising certificate when imposing a penalty upon a solicitor, but it can make recommendations to the SRA and, because it can make 'such order as it may think fit',[9] it can also make orders requiring solicitors not to practise in particular ways (such as a sole practitioner) either for a finite period or indefinitely with liberty to apply. The Divisional Court has encouraged the Tribunal to use such a power, where it considers it to be in the public interest to do so, rather than to leave such future considerations to the SRA.[10] In *Olufeku (No 7 of 2007)* and *Brandon (No 12 of 2008)*,[11] the Master of the Rolls considered the overlapping jurisdictions of the SRA and Tribunal in such matters. The decisions of the Tribunal are punitive and disciplinary; those of the SRA are regulatory and not punitive.

Inevitably, if the Tribunal were to make such orders, the SRA would impose matching or more restrictive practising certificate conditions.

1 Sections 13, 13A(6), 13B(7) and 16(5) of SA 1974.
2 [2009] EWHC 3588 (Admin).
3 At [14].
4 See *Lebow (No 13 of 2007)* [2008] EWCA Civ 411 at [23]: 'This appeal is by way of re-hearing, although one of the factors which successive Masters of the Rolls and I myself have taken into account in the past is the importance of the judgment of the adjudicator and the appeal panel'. It may be noted, however, that the policy of the SRA is to have decisions made at the lowest practicable level of staff within the organisation and it remains to be seen whether this degree of confidence will continue to be held when all decisions are, for all practical purposes, made by individuals employed by the SRA, with no consideration by independent practitioners. It was the case that adjudication panels comprised representatives of the profession and the public, rather than employed adjudicators as is now mostly the case.
5 Sir Thomas Bingham MR gave this as his opinion when requested for a ruling on 20 September 1993.
6 Regulation 8 of the SRA Practising Regulations 2011.
7 Regulation 8.6(a).
8 Section 49A of SA 1974.
9 Section 47(2).
10 *Camacho v Law Society* [2004] 33 LS Gaz R 37; *Taylor v Law Society* [2005] EWCA Civ 1473.
11 [2007] EWCA Civ 840 and [2008] EWCA Civ 967, respectively.

Publicity

15.13

The SRA publishes regulatory decisions on its website unless there are exceptional reasons not to do so. It appears that all or virtually all decisions to impose practising certificate conditions, where the investigation that led to the decision commenced on or after 1 January 2008, are being published when conditions are first imposed or materially varied. This is so even when the conditions have little relevance to members of the public (such as a condition requiring a solicitor to attend a course on the new Code of Conduct). Decisions will not generally be published when they are the subject of an appeal (either internally or to the High Court). Published information will usually be limited to a short statement as to the decision and the reasons for it. The current practice when a solicitor succeeds in obtaining a certificate free from conditions, having previously been subject to conditions, is not as one might expect to remove the reference to the former conditions from the SRA's website, but to publish the decision removing the conditions as well, and to retain the public record of the former conditions for three years.

The Master of the Rolls has emphasised the importance of appeals to him being held in public save in exceptional circumstances.[1]

1 *L v Law Society (No 13 of 2008)* [2008] EWCA Civ 811. This appeal concerned the revocation of a student's membership on the grounds of fitness for admission to the roll, but considered the principles of public and private hearings generally.

Agreements

15.14

The SRA may be prepared to enter into a regulatory settlement as an alternative to the imposition of practising certificate conditions (for regulatory settlements generally, see **19.14**). Such agreements may enable undertakings to be given, for example:

- not to engage in a particular form of work, such as conveyancing, acting for lenders or litigation;
- to practise only as an employee after a specified date, pending the outcome of an investigation; or
- to provide independent evidence that accounts are in compliance, or of a return to medical or psychiatric good health.

The roll

15.15

A solicitor may keep his or her name on the roll without holding a practising certificate on payment of an annual fee of £20 (which is waived if a solicitor has been on the roll for 50 years or more),[1] but as explained above the circumstances in which a solicitor may practise or be held out as a solicitor without a practising certificate are now very few. A solicitor without a practising certificate may nevertheless be described as a 'solicitor – not practising'.

Until 2011, the SRA wrote every year during March or April to every solicitor whose name was on the roll but who did not have a practising certificate enquiring whether he or she wanted to remain on the roll. The process was changed and letters were written to all in this category in August 2011 with a requirement to register online, though the substance of the rules is unchanged at present.[2] Anyone who either replies asking to be removed from the roll, or who fails to reply or to pay the required fee, may have his or her name removed from the roll. A solicitor may also apply to have his or her name removed from the roll at any time.[3]

A person whose name has been removed from the roll in this way may apply to the SRA for it to be restored.[4] The SRA may refuse to restore the name of a solicitor to the roll if there are outstanding complaints, and may refuse to remove the solicitor from the roll in the same circumstances.[5]

The SRA will not remove a solicitor's name from the roll when there are proceedings pending before the Tribunal.[6] There is provision for appeal to the High Court for persons aggrieved by decisions of the SRA to remove a name from the roll, or refuse to restore a name to the roll, after first exhausting the SRA internal appeal process.[7]

Arrangements for the change of name of a solicitor on the roll are covered by the same Regulations.

1 Regulation 15 of the Solicitors (Keeping of the Roll) Regulations 2011.
2 Regulation 6.
3 Regulation 7.
4 Regulation 8. This does not, of course, apply if the solicitor has been struck off or the Tribunal has ordered that the solicitor may not be restored to the roll other than by order of the Tribunal.
5 Regulation 10.
6 Regulation 11.
7 Regulation 16. Appeals must be made within four weeks of the relevant decision. Regulation 16.5 specifies 28 days, unless otherwise provided in rules of court. The Practice Direction to CPR Part 52 also specifies 28 days (para 17.3).

Removal from the roll by consent

15.16

The SRA can, where it is in the interests of the public to do so, agree to the removal from the roll of a solicitor where that would not otherwise be done under the Solicitors (Keeping of the Roll) Regulations 2011 because proceedings are pending in the Solicitors Disciplinary Tribunal or there are outstanding complaints (for the circumstances in which regulatory settlements may or may not be contemplated, see **19.14**).

Such an agreement will be associated with a witness statement from the solicitor containing a statement of truth and which makes relevant admissions as to the facts, the allegations of misconduct and any previous relevant disciplinary history. It will record that a serious sanction from the Tribunal could be expected in the light of the admissions and will request removal from the roll to avoid costs, distress and further risk to the public. The statement will acknowledge that the statement itself and the agreement will be publicised by the SRA. Undertakings will be required not to apply to be restored to the roll, not to work in a solicitors' practice without the written permission of the SRA, and to make full and frank disclosure to any prospective employer of the agreement that had been reached.

CHAPTER 16

Intervention and orderly closure

16.1

The intervention regime was introduced in the Solicitors Act 1941 as a necessary adjunct to the creation in the same statute of the Law Society Compensation Fund: if a solicitor's conduct might give rise to a claim on the Compensation Fund (which would then have to be met by the profession as a whole), it was felt that a power to intervene could operate to prevent or minimise such a claim. The Law Society has been described as the guardian not only of the profession, but also of the public in their dealings with the profession. The power to intervene provides the Solicitors Regulation Authority (SRA) with the opportunity to nip dishonesty in the bud, to preserve public confidence in the profession and to reduce claims on the Compensation Fund.[1]

Intervention represents the most powerful regulatory weapon available to the SRA, as it involves the effective destruction of a solicitor's practice (see **16.11** to **16.14**). In the many decades since the introduction of the intervention regime, there have been only three successful statutory challenges to interventions,[2] and in those cases the Law Society did not oppose the withdrawal of the intervention. The claimant in *Sheikh v Law Society* succeeded in a contested challenge at first instance,[3] but the decision was reversed by the Court of Appeal.[4]

The statutory provisions are draconian. They have been described as such, and as potentially striking a mortal blow to the solicitor's practice.[5]

1 See *Buckley v Law Society (No 2)* [1984] 1 WLR 1101, ChD at 1105–6, per Sir Robert Megarry VC; *Sritharan v Law Society* [2005] EWCA Civ 476 at [17] and [18], [2005] 1 WLR 2708 at 2714A–D; and *Sheikh v Law Society* [2006] EWCA Civ 1577, [2007] 3 All ER 183.
2 See *Yogarajah v Law Society* (1982) 126 Sol Jo 430, *Patel v Law Society* [2008] EWHC 3564 (Ch) and *Khan v SRA* (18 May 2012, unreported). In each of these cases, the Law Society/SRA either consented to, or did not oppose, the setting aside of the intervention.
3 [2005] EWHC 1409 (Ch), [2005] 4 All ER 717.
4 [2006] EWCA Civ 1577, [2007] 3 All ER 183.
5 See *Buckley v Law Society (No 2)* [1984] 3 All ER 313, ChD; *Giles v Law Society* (1996) 8 Admin LR 105 at 116D–E, CA, per Ward LJ.

Grounds for action

16.2

The grounds upon which the SRA is entitled to intervene in a solicitor's practice are contained in Schedule 1 to the Solicitors Act (SA) 1974 as amended by the Legal Services Act (LSA) 2007. Essentially, these are designed to permit intervention when a solicitor cannot run (through ill health, imprisonment, bankruptcy and the like), or alternatively cannot be trusted to run, a solicitor's practice so as to ensure that clients' moneys are secure. The statutory grounds are the following:[1]

- The SRA has reason to suspect dishonesty on the part of the solicitor, an employee of the solicitor or the personal representatives of a deceased solicitor, in connection with that solicitor's practice or former practice, or in connection with any trust of which that solicitor is or formerly was a trustee or that employee is or was a trustee in his capacity as such an employee (para 1(1)(a) of Schedule 1).

- The SRA has reason to suspect dishonesty on the part of a solicitor in connection with (i) the business of any body of which the solicitor is or was a manager or (ii) any business carried on by the solicitor as a sole trader (para 1(1)(aa) of Schedule 1).
- The SRA considers that there has been undue delay on the part of the personal representatives of a deceased solicitor who immediately before his death was practising as a sole solicitor, in connection with that solicitor's practice or in connection with any trust (para 1(1)(b) of Schedule 1).
- The SRA is satisfied that the solicitor has failed to comply with rules made by virtue of sections 31, 32 or 37(2)(c) of SA 1974. Section 31 refers to rules of professional conduct, section 32 to accounts rules and section 37 to rules in relation to professional indemnity insurance. In essence any breach of any part of the SRA Handbook or its statutory predecessors will suffice.
- The solicitor has been adjudged bankrupt or has made a composition or arrangement with his creditors (para 1(1)(d) of Schedule 1).
- The solicitor has been committed to prison in any civil or criminal proceedings (para 1(1)(e) of Schedule 1).
- The SRA is satisfied that a sole solicitor is incapacitated by illness, injury or accident to such an extent as to be unable to attend to his practice (para 1(1)(ee) of Schedule 1).
- The solicitor lacks capacity within the meaning of the Mental Capacity Act 2005 to act as a solicitor and powers under sections 15 to 20 or section 48 of that Act are exercisable in relation to him (para 1(1)(f)) of Schedule 1).
- The name of a solicitor has been removed from or struck off the roll or a solicitor has been suspended from practice (para 1(1)(g) of Schedule 1).
- The SRA is satisfied that a sole solicitor has abandoned his practice (para 1(1)(h) of Schedule 1).
- The SRA is satisfied that a sole solicitor is incapacitated by age to such an extent as to be unable to attend to his practice (para 1(1)(i) of Schedule 1).
- Any power conferred by Schedule 1 to SA 1974 has been exercised in relation to a sole solicitor by virtue of sub-paragraph (1)(a) (reason to suspect dishonesty) and he has acted as a sole solicitor within the period of 18 months beginning with the date on which it was so exercised (para 1(1)(j) of Schedule 1).[2]
- The SRA is satisfied that a person has acted as a solicitor at a time when he did not have a practising certificate which was in force (para 1(1)(k) of Schedule 1).
- The SRA is satisfied that the solicitor has failed to comply with any condition, subject to which his practising certificate was granted or otherwise has effect, to the effect that he may act as a solicitor only in employment which is approved by the SRA in connection with the imposition of that condition, or as a member of a partnership which is so approved, or as a manager of a body

recognised by the SRA under section 9 of the Administration of Justice Act 1985 and so approved – or in any specified combination of those ways (para 1(1)(l) of Schedule 1). The word 'manager' has the same meaning as in LSA 2007 (see section 207 of LSA 2007).[3]

- The SRA is satisfied that it is necessary to exercise the powers of intervention, or any of them, to protect the interests of clients, or former or potential clients, of the solicitor or his firm, or the interests of the beneficiaries of any trust of which the solicitor is or was a trustee (para 1(1)(m) of Schedule 1).

1 The statute refers to 'the Society' but in practice the powers are exercised by the SRA.
2 This is an anachronism – it has been superseded by the provision for the automatic suspension of the solicitor's practising certificate when an intervention occurs by reason of a suspicion of dishonesty. Before this power was acquired (by section 15(1A) of SA 1974, inserted by the Courts and Legal Services Act 1990) a solicitor who was the subject of an intervention could theoretically immediately set himself up in practice again and encourage all his clients to reinstruct him.
3 Paragraph 1(1A) of Schedule 1 to SA 1974.

16.3

It is arguable that the ground for intervention, paragraph 1(1)(m) of Schedule 1, introduced by LSA 2007, is so widely drawn that all other grounds are obsolete, but it is anticipated that reliance will continue to be placed on the traditional grounds, if only because there will be an obligation to explain why the SRA considered it 'necessary' to intervene.

Another ground added by LSA 2007 is paragraph 1(1)(aa) of Schedule 1, which envisages intervention when there is suspected dishonesty on the part of a solicitor in connection with a business that is not a solicitor's practice; that is, a business (not being a solicitor's practice or trust) of which the solicitor is the sole proprietor, or of which he or she is an employee or manager. This is intended to deal with the situation in which a solicitor has a legal practice but is also involved in another business, for example, one that provides financial services, where there is reason to suspect dishonesty in relation to that separate business. One could see that if the Financial Conduct Authority (using the same example) took action against such a business in circumstances where a suspicion of dishonesty arose, there could be a need to intervene in the solicitor's practice, as the same person could be seen to pose a risk to clients.

It was the case that the powers of intervention could only be exercised after specific notice had been given to the solicitor if they were to be exercised under sub-paragraph 1(c) – breaches of specified rules including the Solicitors' Code of Conduct 2007.[1] The solicitor had to be given notice in writing that he had failed to comply with the rules specified in the notice and also (at the same or any later time) notice that the powers of intervention were accordingly exercisable, but this provision was repealed by LSA 2007.

Intervention can therefore occur with no notice at all, and the solicitor may have no opportunity to make any representations on his or her own behalf before the decision to intervene is made.

1 Paragraph 1(2) of Schedule 1 to SA 1974 was repealed by para 77(2)(k) of Schedule 16 to LSA 2007.

The adjudication process

16.4

The resolution to intervene may be made by two adjudicators, including members of the adjudication panel and employed adjudicators, save that one adjudicator may so resolve in cases of urgency. Accordingly, an intervention into a solicitor's practice can be authorised by a single employee of the SRA. Typically the adjudicators will consider a Forensic Investigation Report, any representations the solicitor may have made in answer to that report, and the recommendations of a supervisor contained in his or her own report which will summarise the facts and issues. The recommendation of a supervisor is in no sense binding upon the panel; in *Sheikh v Law Society*,[1] the supervisor had recommended against intervention but the adjudication panel nevertheless resolved to intervene.

In cases of clear suspected dishonesty or where it is intended that the intervention should occur without notice, the supervisor's report will not be disclosed to the solicitor. Indeed, in the most serious cases, usually involving an obvious and substantial client account shortfall in circumstances amounting to theft, the procedure may involve a brief visit from an investigating officer, a report by way of a one-page memorandum and an intervention as soon as the necessary practical arrangements have been made.

1 [2006] EWCA Civ 1577, [2007] 3 All ER 183.

Natural justice and Human Rights Act 1998 implications

16.5

Solicitors who are the subject of interventions have challenged the exercise of this powerful and terminally damaging regulatory weapon without any requirement for notice, on the grounds that it is in breach of the principles of natural justice and that it is incompatible with the rights protected by the Human Rights Act (HRA) 1998. All such challenges have failed. The natural justice arguments were rejected in *Giles v Law Society*,[1] and the HRA 1998 arguments failed in *Holder v Law Society*.[2] In the latter case, the Court of Appeal held that the statutory regime as a whole did not offend HRA 1998, although it remained open to a solicitor to assert that an intervention in a particular case breached the rights protected by the European Convention.

1 (1996) 8 Admin LR 105, CA. See also *Yogarajah v Law Society* (1982) 126 Sol Jo 430; and *Buckley v Law Society* (9 October 1985, unreported).
2 [2003] EWCA Civ 39, [2003] 3 All ER 62, [2003] 1 WLR 1059.

The extent of the powers

16.6

The mechanism selected by Parliament to permit the Law Society to achieve intervention in a solicitor's practice is, in essence, to vest the solicitor's practice moneys in the Society, and to require the solicitor to yield up the practice documents. These powers have been delegated to and are exercised by the SRA.

Money

16.7

The intervention resolution vests all sums of money held by or on behalf of a solicitor or his firm in connection with his practice, and the right to recover or receive those sums, in the SRA.[1] In short, the SRA takes control of office and client accounts. Where the intervention is solely by reason of the death of a sole practitioner, only client account is affected.[2]

The SRA holds the money on trust for the purposes of the intervention and 'subject thereto … upon trust for the persons beneficially entitled to them'.[3] What this means in practice is that the SRA holds client money on trust for the clients, and office money (if any) in circumstances where the solicitor is likely to be in substantial debt (a) to his clients in the event of any client account shortfall and (b) to the SRA in respect of the intervention costs (more of which below: see **16.13**). The SRA deals with the money in accordance with the SRA Intervention Powers (Statutory Trust) Rules 2011, which form part of the SRA Handbook. While the solicitor is 'beneficially entitled' to anything that might be left, it is unlikely that there will be anything. Sums recovered by the solicitor after the intervention in connection with his practice, such as payment of outstanding bills of costs, also vest in the SRA.[4]

Schedule 1 to SA 1974 provides the court with specific powers to assist the SRA in gaining control of the practice moneys. The court may order that no payment shall be made without the leave of the court by any person (whether or not named in the order) of any money held by him (in whatever manner and whether it was received before or after the making of the order) on behalf of the solicitor or his firm.[5] The court may require a person suspected of holding money on behalf of the solicitor or his firm to provide information to the SRA as to such money and the accounts in which it is held.[6]

The SRA may also resolve to vest in itself the right to recover or receive debts due to the solicitor or his firm in connection with his practice or former practice.[7]

1 Paragraph 6 of Schedule 1 to SA 1974.
2 Paragraphs 2 and 6(2)(b) of Schedule 1.
3 Paragraph 6(1) of Schedule 1.
4 *Dooley v Law Society (No 2)* [2001] All ER (D) 362, *Times*, 16 January 2002, ChD.
5 Paragraph 5(1) of Schedule 1 to SA 1974.
6 Paragraph 8 of Schedule 1.
7 Paragraph 6A of Schedule 1. This was added by LSA 2007 and puts on an express statutory footing that which had been held in *Dooley* (above) to be the case as a matter of proper interpretation of the statute prior to its amendment.

Practice documents

16.8

The intervention resolution results in a notice to the solicitor or his firm requiring the production or delivery to any person appointed by the SRA of all documents in the possession of the solicitor or his firm in connection with his practice.[1] Failure or refusal to comply with the notice is a criminal offence.[2] The High Court has power to order the production or delivery of documents by the solicitor and/or by any person suspected of being in possession of relevant documents.[3] Once possession has been taken of the documents, the SRA must serve on the solicitor a notice that possession has been taken by the person appointed on its behalf.[4]

1 Paragraph 9 of Schedule 1 to SA 1974.
2 Paragraph 9(3) of Schedule 1.
3 Paragraph 9(4) and (5) of Schedule 1.
4 Paragraph 9(7) of Schedule 1.

Other powers

16.9

The SRA's intervention costs, which can easily amount to £100,000 or more, are a debt due from the solicitor or his estate, unless the High Court orders otherwise.[1] The High Court may also make orders permitting forcible entry to premises to search for and seize documents,[2] for the redirection of mail, telephone and electronic communications[3] and for the appointment of a new trustee in substitution for the solicitor as trustee of any trust.[4]

The High Court may, on the application of the SRA, order a former partner of the solicitor to pay a specified proportion of the intervention costs otherwise payable by the solicitor if it is satisfied that the conduct of the solicitor that led to the intervention was carried on with the consent or connivance of, or attributable to any neglect on the part of, the former partner.[5]

The SRA's statutory powers in relation to money and documents take precedence over any lien or other right to possession in any other person.[6] These powers continue to be exercisable after a solicitor's death, or after his name has been removed from or struck off the roll.

1 Paragraph 13 of Schedule 1 to SA 1974.
2 Paragraph 9(6) of Schedule 1.
3 Paragraph 10 of Schedule 1.
4 Paragraph 11 of Schedule 1.
5 Paragraph 13A of Schedule 1.
6 Paragraph 12 of Schedule 1.

Practising certificate

16.10

Where an intervention is authorised because of a suspicion of dishonesty on the part of the solicitor, breaches of the SRA Accounts Rules 2011, breaches of any other rule or provision made under section 31 of SA 1974, including the SRA Code of Conduct 2011, or the solicitor's committal to prison, any practising certificate of the solicitor then in force is immediately suspended[1] – unless the adjudicator or adjudication panel authorising the intervention directs otherwise.[2]

The solicitor may (at any time before the certificate expires) apply to the SRA to terminate the suspension and the SRA may terminate the suspension conditionally or unconditionally or refuse the application.[3] If the SRA refuses the application, or the solicitor is aggrieved at the conditions imposed he or she may appeal to the High Court.[4]

In practice, the SRA is usually prepared to restore a solicitor's practising certificate subject to stringent conditions, commonly a requirement that the solicitor may only practise in employment approved by the SRA, and on condition that he or she has no access to clients' money.

1 Section 15(1A) of SA 1974, inserted by section 91(2) of the Courts and Legal Services Act 1990.
2 Section 15(1B) of SA 1974.
3 Section 16(3) and (4).
4 Section 16(5).

The practical reality

16.11

The legal department of the SRA, which manages interventions, appoints an intervening agent, a solicitor who is a member of the SRA's Intervention Panel practising in the relevant area, who will take direct responsibility for (in particular) client files. Provisional arrangements may be made in advance of the intervention resolution when it can reasonably be expected to occur. Notice of the intervention will not be given to the solicitor (even if the Panel has resolved on the intervention some days before) until the agents are ready to act and the solicitor's bank has received notice. The solicitor will therefore not know of the intervention until after his or her bank accounts are frozen. The first that a solicitor will typically hear of the decision will be by a cryptic telephone call from the SRA requesting him to stand by his fax machine to receive an important communication. This is likely to be in the late afternoon when the agents and representative of the SRA are due to arrive at the firm's offices the following morning.

The intervening agents attend at the solicitor's address and take possession of the practice documents which in most cases are removed without delay. Matters which are urgent and require prompt action are identified and (hopefully, assuming the solicitor's co-operation) discussed. Practice moneys are transferred to a bank account under the control of the intervening agents. The intervening agents attempt to bring the practice's accounting records into proper order.

Clients will receive a standard letter informing them that the SRA has been obliged to exercise its statutory powers and inviting them to nominate successor solicitors or, if appropriate, to accept delivery of the papers themselves.

If claims in professional negligence or breach of fiduciary duty are made against the solicitor, the solicitor's professional indemnity insurers may wish to see the files seized by the SRA to seek to discover grounds for declining indemnity cover. However, the SRA refuses to provide insurers with the files in those circumstances unless the lay client has provided consent, and this refusal was upheld by the Court of Appeal in *Quinn Direct Insurance Ltd v Law Society*[1] on the ground that privilege and confidentiality in the documents remains after intervention, and there is no room for implying into the statutory scheme any entitlement in insurers to see the documents.[2]

1 [2010] EWCA Civ 805.
2 At [29].

16.12

The intervening agents do not in any sense take over or run the practice. They seek to ensure that all clients are informed of the intervention and find alternative solicitors, and that the practice moneys are distributed properly; they may have to seek directions from the court to achieve this. They are likely to have to take urgent and protective steps in circumstances where it is necessary to guard the interests of clients, but it is not their function to take over client matters in any other sense or for any other purpose.

The description of intervention as striking a mortal blow to the practice[1] is, if anything, an understatement. Quite apart from the automatic suspension of the practising certificate, the solicitor loses control of the practice's bank accounts and the practice's documentation. It instantly becomes impossible to service any bank overdraft. Unless the intervention is rapidly reversed by the court, the solicitor's practice is lost without any compensation, and the solicitor faces almost inevitable financial ruin.

1 *Giles v Law Society* (1996) 8 Admin LR 105, CA.

16.13

Many practices have little in the way of measurable assets – offices are rented, equipment and cars leased, and the office account is likely to be in substantial overdraft. Assets represented by goodwill and work in progress suddenly become worthless. In addition, as has been said, the solicitor is liable for the costs of intervention, recoverable as a debt due to the SRA.[1] As already indicated, these costs can be very substantial. Unless the solicitor has private wealth there will be nothing left. Intervention and subsequent bankruptcy commonly go hand in hand.

Although, in theory, a solicitor subject to an intervention is entitled to payment for work in progress at the time of the intervention, this entitlement is more apparent than real. The successor solicitor taking over an individual file will have to extract such payment from the client, and will often doubtless be met by an argument from the lay client that he or she should not be liable for two sets of fees in respect of the same legal work. The intervened solicitor has no means of compelling anyone to recover outstanding costs. The SRA is under no obligation to do so.[2] Any payments recovered in respect of work in progress will first be set off against the solicitor's liability for the intervention costs.[3] Further, the SRA may have vested in itself the right to recover debts due to the practice, including outstanding bills and the value of work in progress.

Ownership of the solicitor's other assets, such as office furniture, computer equipment and the like is not affected by the intervention. Only practice moneys and documents are affected (save that the SRA may require possession of computer equipment necessary to access documents held only in electronic form).[4] Similarly, the solicitor's contractual obligations are unaffected – the intervention does not have the effect of dismissing employees or in itself making them redundant.[5]

1 Paragraph 13 of Schedule 1 to SA 1974. The solicitor may require the detailed assessment of the costs: *Pine v Law Society (No 2)* [2002] EWCA Civ 175, [2002] 2 All ER 658.
2 *Dooley v Law Society (No 2)* [2001] All ER (D) 362, *Times*, 16 January 2002. Under LSA 2007, the SRA will acquire the right to recover sums due to the solicitor and may therefore elect to pursue outstanding costs and work in progress to meet client liabilities or intervention costs.
3 *Dooley v Law Society (No 2)* [2001] All ER (D) 362, *Times*, 16 January 2002.

4 Paragraphs 9(5A) and (6)(b) of Schedule 1 to SA 1974.
5 *Rose v Dodd* [2005] EWCA Civ 957, [2006] 1 All ER 464.

16.14

Essentially, therefore, an intervention means the total destruction of a solicitor's practice. The solicitor is unable to sell that practice to a willing purchaser. The practice's clients have to find new solicitors. The practice's employees have to find new jobs. And the solicitor has to apply for the suspension of the practising certificate to be lifted if he or she is to resume any sort of practice as a solicitor. The solicitor will only be able to practise at all by finding a willing employer.

Ordinarily, at the time of making the resolution to intervene, the adjudication panel will also refer the solicitor's conduct to the Solicitors Disciplinary Tribunal.

Because all the statutory provisions refer to a solicitor, and a solicitor's practice, it is possible (and it does occur) that interventions are authorised into the practice of a solicitor who may be a partner in a firm, rather than a sole practitioner. In that event only the client funds, client documents and any practice funds and papers personal to that solicitor are subject to the intervention. Inevitably this has the potential to be highly disruptive for the remaining partners, but they are not directly affected by the exercise of the statutory powers.

Challenging an intervention[1]

16.15

The SRA must serve on the solicitor or his or her firm, and on any other person having possession of sums of money caught by the intervention, a certified copy of the intervention resolution and a notice prohibiting the payment out of any such sums of money.[2] Within eight days of the service of that notice, the solicitor, on giving not less than 48 hours' notice in writing to the SRA, may apply to the High Court for an order directing the SRA to withdraw the notice.[3]

Likewise, where the SRA has taken possession of practice documents, the solicitor may apply to the High Court (again, within eight days of the service of the notice) for an order directing the SRA to deliver the documents to such person as the solicitor claimant may require.[4]

If the court makes an order in favour of the solicitor, it shall have power also to make such other order as it may think fit.[5]

The eight-day time limit is mandatory, and cannot be extended by the court or by the consent of the parties.[6] The proceedings are assigned to the Chancery Division and are governed by CPR Part 8 and rule 67.4. If the proceedings are not litigated expeditiously by the solicitor, so that they eventually become academic as a result of the destruction of his practice, they may be struck out as an abuse of process.[7]

There is no power for the SRA to withdraw an intervention once it has been put in place. If it is rapidly concluded that the decision was lawful but not justified or was ill advised, the solution is a consent order of the High Court.[8]

1 This term is used as there is no 'appeal' against an intervention – the remedy is an application to the High Court for an order directing the withdrawal of the intervention.

2 Paragraph 6(3) of Schedule 1 to SA 1974.
3 Paragraph 6(4) of Schedule 1. The eight-day limitation period should be seen as a strict requirement: as to whether the courts may be able to apply any flexibility, see *Gadd v SRA* [2013] EWCA Civ 837.
4 Paragraph 9(8) and (9) of Schedule 1.
5 Paragraphs 6(5) and 9(11) of Schedule 1.
6 *Re a Solicitor* [1994] Ch 1994 B 4973.
7 *Virdi v Law Society* [1999] 29 LS Gaz R 29. Mr Virdi's appeal to the Court of Appeal was dismissed, but this is unreported.
8 *Patel v Law Society* [2008] EWHC 3564 (Ch). Norris J commented in approving a consent order that the parties were right to seek such an order as there was no power provided to the SRA by the statute to reverse its own decision.

16.16

As has been seen, it has proved to be almost impossible to challenge an intervention successfully. This is at least in part because of the financial consequences of an intervention described above. The solicitor is in a quandary – does he or she recognise the likely reality that the only way in which family and personal financial commitments can be met is if he or she finds a job with a willing employer? If so, the solicitor must recognise also that the original practice will not survive; the conditions on his or her practising certificate will prevent recovery of the remnants of that practice, even if the challenge is successful. There is the additional risk that the proceedings will be struck out as an abuse as they will no longer have any practical purpose.

Alternatively, does the solicitor fight on, without employment or other income, with mounting and unserviceable debts, probably without funds to pay for the needed specialist assistance, and with no prospect of obtaining public funding, against an opponent with unlimited resources?

If a solicitor believes that he or she is at risk of intervention, it is wise to take precautions (such as putting another solicitor in funds) to ensure that a rapid statutory challenge can be mounted if so advised. Once the intervention has commenced, it will be impossible to draw upon office account. Any attempt to put funds beyond the reach of the SRA after the intervention has commenced may well be taken into account against the solicitor at the High Court hearing.[1]

It is highly doubtful whether the courts have jurisdiction to provide interim relief by 'unscrambling' the intervention and/or reversing the suspension of the solicitor's practising certificate pending the full hearing. Where the solicitor challenges the intervention, the SRA will ordinarily be prepared to co-operate in slowing down the practical effect of the intervention (i.e. by not informing clients of the intervention unless the particular matter is urgent).

However, the problem will remain as to what is to be done for those clients whose matters are not particularly pressing but who cannot be ignored. The solicitor who is the subject of the intervention cannot continue to act; he or she has no practising certificate. It is possible, if there is a suitable and willing person and the solicitor can afford to remunerate him or her (allowing for the fact that money coming in to the practice will vest in the SRA), for the solicitor to appoint another solicitor with an unconditional practising certificate as practice manager; this might be an existing employee or someone brought in for the purpose. Such arrangements will in practice require the co-operation of the SRA but will provide a mechanism for maintaining the status quo where a challenge is credibly made and expeditiously pursued.

1 See *Sheikh v Law Society* [2006] EWCA Civ 1577, [2007] 3 All ER 183.

16.17

The solicitor mounting a statutory challenge will be well advised to make an early application for directions to ensure that the case is brought on speedily for trial, and that the essential issues are identified at the outset.

The statutory challenge provided for by paras 6 and 9 of Schedule 1 to SA 1974 is the only manner in which an intervention can be challenged.[1] Any issues under HRA 1998 can be considered within the statutory proceedings.

1 *Hedworth v Law Society* (1994, unreported); *Miller v Law Society* [2002] EWHC 1453 (Ch), [2002] 4 All ER 312.

The proceedings and the test to be applied

16.18

In providing an extremely short mandatory limitation period (see **16.15**), Parliament clearly envisaged a swift summary procedure. One reason for the lack of successful challenges to interventions may be that this laudable aim has become lost in the complexities of High Court litigation. The tortuous course of the proceedings in *Sheikh v Law Society*[1] indicated that the statutory remedy was not working efficiently. The claimant's application to set aside the intervention did not come on for hearing for four months, and occupied eight days of court time. The judgments at first instance and of the Court of Appeal each ran to 70 pages of single-spaced typescript.

In most cases, the reasons for intervention will be obvious to all. However, this is not invariably so, and unless the reasons are properly identified at an early stage, there is a danger that the solicitor will be denied the effective summary remedy that Parliament intended to provide.

The burden of proof to justify the continuation of the intervention rests on the SRA – the solicitor, though nominally the claimant, is in reality the defendant.[2] Accordingly, unless the parties agree otherwise, the SRA will present its case first.

The traditional approach to the statutory challenge was the 'two-stage test' propounded by Neuberger J in *Dooley v Law Society*[3] approved by the Court of Appeal in *Holder v Law Society*:[4]

> 'The court's decision is a two-stage process. First it must decide whether the grounds under paragraph 1 are made out; in this case, primarily, whether there are grounds for suspecting dishonesty. Secondly, if the court is so satisfied, then it must consider whether in the light of all the evidence before it the intervention should continue. In deciding the second question, the court must carry out a balancing exercise between the need in the public interest to protect the public from dishonest solicitors and the inevitably very serious consequences to the solicitor if the intervention continues.'

1 [2006] EWCA Civ 1577, [2007] 3 All ER 183.
2 See *Giles v Law Society* (1996) 8 Admin LR 105 at 114F–G, CA, per Nourse LJ.
3 (2000) HC Transcript 0002868.
4 [2003] EWCA Civ 39, [2003] 3 All ER 62.

16.19

That must now be considered in the light of the more subtle approach suggested by the Court of Appeal in *Sheikh v Law Society*.[1] The court may need to decide whether, at the time of the resolution to intervene, the statutory ground relied upon by the SRA actually existed – for example, whether there was, at that time, reason to suspect dishonesty on the basis of the information available to the SRA. It has not been conclusively decided whether, if no such ground existed, the solicitor is entitled to have the notices of intervention withdrawn for that reason alone, but it seems likely that in that event the resolution will have been fundamentally flawed and liable to be set aside. On the other hand, such a circumstance is likely to be very rare.

If there is no challenge to the validity of the resolution or to the service of the intervention notices, the single issue for the court is whether the notices should be withdrawn. In considering this, the court is exercising its own judgement and is entitled to take into account material that was not available to the SRA when resolving to intervene, but which is available to the court. Moreover, the court will also take into account the views of the SRA as a relevant evidential factor, although it is unclear how these views are ascertained in practice – save through the mouths of the advocates representing the SRA at the hearing of the application to withdraw the intervention notices. This is an unsatisfactory 'evidential' basis upon which to ask a court to make decisions.

As noted above, the intervention regime is in principle compliant with the requirements of natural justice and HRA 1998, but is capable of being operated unfairly in an individual case.

1 [2006] EWCA Civ 1577, [2007] 3 All ER 183.

16.20

If the challenge is successful the statute envisages an order requiring the withdrawal of the paragraph 6(3) notice[1] so as to return control of practice moneys to the solicitor, and an order directing the SRA to deliver the practice documents to such person as the solicitor claimant may require. In addition, the court probably has jurisdiction to restore the suspended practising certificate to the solicitor,[2] and in *Sheikh v Law Society*,[3] the judge at first instance imposed a condition on the successful claimant's practising certificate.

The statutory scheme set out in Schedule 1 to SA 1974 cannot be replaced by a judge-made scheme. There is no 'half-way house': the court must either direct or decline to direct withdrawal of the intervention[4] (although the court's power to make consequential orders should enable it to ensure that the SRA is able to exercise proper regulatory control over the solicitor in the light of the facts found by the court).

There is no statutory entitlement to damages at the suit of the successful solicitor if the challenge succeeds. Whether damages may be awarded at common law, under the statute or under the Human Rights Act 1998, has not been decided and may well depend upon the court's view as to whether the decision to intervene was justified at the time it was made.

1 *Holder v Law Society* [2003] EWCA Civ 39, [2003] 3 All ER 62; *Sritharan v Law Society* [2005] EWCA Civ 476, [2005] 4 All ER 1105.
2 *Sritharan v Law Society* [2005] EWCA Civ 476, [2005] 4 All ER 1105.
3 [2006] EWCA Civ 1577, [2007] 3 All ER 183.
4 *Sritharan v Law Society* [2005] EWCA Civ 476, [2005] 4 All ER 1105.

Alternatives to intervention

16.21

In recent years the Law Society increasingly sought to find alternatives to intervention, principally because the cost of intervention is high and recovery of this from the solicitor is uncertain. The SRA is more willing than hitherto to achieve tight regulatory control over a solicitor who would otherwise have been subject to an intervention by means of the imposition of stringent conditions on his practising certificate. Alternatively, the SRA may permit the orderly disposal of the practice. The SRA may be prepared to enter into a regulatory settlement whereby the solicitor agrees to close his firm within a set period, or to correct errors in the firm's accounts and provide independent evidence of the accounts being compliant, or to seek medical treatment and provide independent evidence, for example, as to an addiction being overcome (see **19.14** as to regulatory settlements generally).

Orderly closure

16.22

There are a number of instances when a practice may be required to close, for example:

- retirement;
- ill health or death of a sole practitioner (where there is no special executorship clause in a will);
- financial restructure;
- compulsory professional indemnity insurance cannot be obtained; or
- to avoid an intervention by the SRA because:
  - the practice is not financially viable; or
  - the practice is no longer authorised by the SRA, for example as a result of a decision to revoke authorisation or following restrictive practising certificate conditions.

It is prudent to consider the possibility of selling the practice rather than closing. It is often cheaper to do so, not least as a result of the impact of liability for run-off indemnity insurance; and it is less disruptive for staff and clients. However, the very same insurance factor will inhibit potential purchasers; if they become a successor practice (see **10.7**) the acquiring firm's insurers are liable for any possible negligence claims.

When closing a practice, the principals will normally wish to wind up the entity in an orderly manner (although there is nothing in practice to prevent the entity deregistering with the SRA and continuing in existence, without undertaking regulated legal activities). The procedure to be followed upon closure varies from practice to practice, reflecting factors such as the regulated entity's legal status (limited liability company, LLP or traditional partnership), the complexity of the structure of the practice, the practice's relationships with third parties and its obligations to clients. No two practices are the same and each closure will have its challenges.

Compliance plans

16.23

The SRA is now very likely to impose obligations on a closing firm in the form of a 'compliance plan', and can insist on its terms with a threat of intervention as an alternative. Although the circumstances in which this will occur will inevitably be fraught and pressured, it is extremely important that the terms of the required plan are considered with care. The terms are likely to incorporate undertakings, express or implied, as to the achievement of targets, for example to reduce the client account to a nil balance. A failure to achieve a target has been treated by the SRA as a breach of undertaking and potentially a disciplinary matter. It is important only to accept obligations which are achievable. If necessary it may be desirable to seek specialist advice. Indeed anyone facing pressure to close a solicitors' practice is likely to benefit from specialist advice.

The closure process

16.24

For regulatory and insurance purposes closure takes place when a regulated entity ceases to conduct work for clients. This is not the same as the winding up of the regulated entity. There is likely to be a lapse of time between the practice ceasing to engage in fee earning work and the winding up of the entity.

From the point of closure the practice cannot engage in fee earning work and its activities are restricted to recovery of fees and effecting a closure programme. Failure to adhere to the restriction on undertaking client work will revoke the practice's run-off insurance provision and imposes an obligation to obtain a new professional indemnity insurance policy. Therefore it is important to plan ahead for closure.

When a practice has set a date for closure it must inform the SRA. It is best practice to set out a closure programme, addressing procedures for dealing with current client matters, the client bank account, accounting requirements, relationships with third parties and the storage of archived files. The SRA may accept this but may also seek to impose its own terms, as above. If the programme is accepted (with or without amendments) the SRA will expect to receive regular reports on progress.

Clients must be contacted with information as to the proposed closure, and to make arrangements concerning the collection of their files and client funds or their transfer to another practice. Inevitably this is likely to be stressful for clients and the firm will have to determine how this is best done bearing in mind the nature of its clients, their degree of vulnerability and their chosen method of communication. A letter 'out of the blue' may not always be the best option. Clients must be advised that they are free to choose a solicitor of their choice although it is permissible to indicate that a client would be welcome to join principals or fee earners in any new practices they may have joined.

Client account balances need to be returned or transferred as instructed. If the practice has historical dormant balances any gradual process being followed to deal with such matters will have to be accelerated. Every effort should be made to reduce the client account to a nil balance, and this should receive priority as soon as a decision is made to close (as to dealing with dormant balances see **5.12**).

Archived files can be returned to clients, stored or, where permitted, destroyed. If files are stored then the SRA must be advised of their whereabouts. There have been situations where intervention has taken place in respect of archived files alone, which remain client property pending their destruction.

16.25

Upon closure the practice must accurately indicate its new status. The practice's letterhead, website, e-mails and all other material will need to be adapted. Incoming telephone calls should be greeted with a message indicating the closure and who can be contacted for guidance. A notice of closure should be advertised in the *London Gazette* and a local newspaper. All regulated persons should make necessary amendments to their 'MySRA' account.

When planning ahead for closure the practice will need to consider how best it can service its creditors at a time when the only income will be payment for work undertaken prior to closure. The advice of an insolvency practitioner may be required. It will necessary to control overheads and manage redundancies, amongst other things. If the firm is a legal aid practice the Legal Aid Agency should become involved at an early stage, to manage both the transfer of cases and payments on account.

The practice must inform its professional indemnity insurer of the intended closure as closure triggers the run-off provisions in its contract of insurance. The practice must pay the contractual run-off premium as set out in the schedule of insurance. A failure to make such payment is a regulatory offence and the practice's insurer is required to report default to the SRA. The practice's insurer is often the largest creditor in a solvent closure. If the practice is not in a financial position to make the payment, it is sometimes possible to negotiate a reduced premium. This is an area in which specialist advice can be sought.

The process of closure and the examination of all files in the practice not infrequently gives rise to the discovery of problems not previously identified which will need to be reported to insurers and possibly to the SRA by either the compliance officer for legal practice (COLP) or compliance officer for finance and administration (COFA), who will retain their responsibilities throughout (see **CHAPTER 6**). Some level of complaint from clients, including opportunistic complaints, should be anticipated. Principals may continue to be liable in respect of awards by the Legal Ombudsman despite closure of the practice (see **13.9**).

We are indebted to Andrew Blatt and Robert Forman of Murdochs Solicitors for their contribution to this section.

Limited intervention

16.26

This form of intervention is of a very different character and for very different purposes and is almost entirely unrelated to the matters discussed above.

It is designed solely to recover from a solicitor a file or files relating to specific matters, either for the purposes of the file(s) being handed to clients or for the purposes of inspection by the SRA to assist in the investigation of complaints or regulatory concerns, respectively.

It may occur in two circumstances. The first is concerned exclusively with delay, and is somewhat convoluted. If the SRA is satisfied that there has been undue delay in connection with any matter in which the solicitor or his firm is or was acting on behalf of a client or with any trust, or by any employee of a solicitor in connection with a trust of which the employee is or was a trustee in his capacity as such an employee, and the solicitor has been invited to give an explanation in answer to the complaint within a specified period[1] and:

- the solicitor fails within that period to give an explanation which is regarded as satisfactory;
- notice has been given to the solicitor of the fact that he has failed to give a satisfactory explanation; and
- either then or later a notice is given that the powers of intervention are exercisable for those reasons,

the SRA may 'intervene' in the solicitor's practice for the limited purpose of recovering the file or files in question, and for that purpose only.[2] In this event the file(s) will be obtained and handed to the client or to successor solicitors appointed by the client, so that the problems encountered as a result of the unexplained delays are overcome.

The second circumstance arises if a decision is made to require the solicitor to produce a file or files for inspection by the SRA for the purposes of an investigation;[3] the powers of intervention can be employed to compel the delivery up of such file(s).[4] The documents required in these circumstances will be all the documents in the possession of the solicitor or his firm relevant to the matter under investigation.

In either event the procedure is the same: an agent of the SRA is appointed, usually a solicitor on the SRA's Intervention Panel or a member of the staff of the SRA. The solicitor is given notice of the time and date on which the agent will attend at his offices for the purposes of collecting the file or files, and the agent is instructed to collect the file or files accordingly. Such limited interventions generally occur only after an unsuccessful attempt has been made to persuade the solicitor to deliver up the file(s) voluntarily.

Because these powers are part of the intervention regime the statutory powers of the High Court are available and in the event of non-co-operation on the part of the solicitor an application could be made by the SRA for an order to compel delivery. One would naturally expect this to be an extremely rare occurrence, and it is understood only to have been necessary once.[5]

1 Paragraph 3 of Schedule 1 to SA 1974 requires not less than eight days' notice. In practice invariably 14 days' notice is given.
2 Paragraph 3 of Schedule 1 to SA 1974.
3 Section 44B(1) of SA 1974.
4 Section 44B(6).
5 *Stevenson*, 7814–1999, SDT.

CHAPTER 17

Control of solicitors' employees

17.1

Originally through the Solicitors Act (SA) 1974 and its predecessors, Parliament provided regulatory powers to the Law Society and the Solicitors Disciplinary Tribunal ('the Tribunal' or SDT) to enable the control of non-solicitors who work in solicitors' firms, and who may abuse their position. The rationale for the existence of these powers is the need to protect those who deal with solicitors, and to safeguard the reputation of the profession. The Legal Services Act (LSA) 2007 promotes the concept of firm- or business entity-based regulation so that all managers and employees of regulated practices are now subject to personal regulation by virtue of their employment, whether or not they are legally qualified. In consequence, regulation of solicitors' employees now takes three forms: (1) statutory restrictions on the employment of certain disqualified persons, for example, former solicitors who have been struck off (see **17.2** and **17.3**); (2) the making of orders that control the employment of non-solicitors guilty of material misconduct (see **17.4** to **17.7**); and (3) direct disciplinary control of employees of regulated practices (see **17.8** and **17.9**).

Restriction on employment of persons struck off or suspended

17.2

A solicitor may not, in connection with his practice as a solicitor, employ or remunerate persons who to his knowledge have been disqualified from acting as solicitors through being struck off or suspended from practice, save with the written permission of the Solicitors Regulation Authority (SRA). The SRA may grant permission for such period and subject to such conditions as it thinks fit.[1]

Until 31 March 2009, section 41(4) of SA 1974 provided a mandatory penalty of suspension or striking off for any solicitor found to have acted in breach of this prohibition. There were originally two offences attracting a mandatory penalty: acting as an agent for an unqualified person in court proceedings (section 39 of SA 1974 which was repealed in full in 1991, so removing the statutory offence as well as the mandatory penalty); and employing or remunerating a struck off or suspended solicitor without written permission. LSA 2007 retained the statutory offence but removed the mandatory penalty. In *Re a Solicitor (Rosen)*,[2] the Divisional Court requested and was provided with a schedule of penalties imposed upon solicitors for breaches of section 41. There was a wide range, some suspensions being for a few days only, sometimes being timed to coincide with holidays already arranged by the solicitor concerned or (in the case of a number of partners all requiring to be sentenced) being staggered so as to minimise disruption to the practice concerned.[3] In these instances, the Tribunal had plainly felt that little or no moral blame attached to the solicitors in question, and would not have suspended them in the absence of the mandatory provision. At the other end of the spectrum were solicitors who had been struck off for deliberately flouting the statutory provisions. The removal of the mandatory penalty enables the Tribunal more effectively to tailor the penalty to the breach.

It is important to appreciate that a breach of section 41 is a strict liability offence. All that is required is (1) that the solicitor knows the true status of the employee, namely that he or she has been struck off or suspended; and (2) that, as a matter of fact, the written permission of the Law Society/SRA has not been obtained (or that conditions imposed on the grant of permission have not been met). It does not provide a defence, for example, to show that one partner had responsibility for making the employment arrangements and reassured all other partners that there was no compliance issue, and they reasonably relied on that reassurance.[4] It has even happened that a struck off solicitor has forged the permission; the employing solicitor was still guilty of the offence.[5] Indeed, this serves to reinforce the point that the employer, and not the proposed employee, must obtain the necessary SRA permission.

1 Section 41 of SA 1974.
2 [2004] EWHC 907 (Admin).
3 Cases in which this sort of leniency was shown include *McMillan,* 5740–1989, SDT; *Cunnew,* 6134–1992, SDT; and *Coxall,* 8401–2001, SDT.
4 *Coxall,* 8401–2001, SDT.
5 *Awoloye-Kio,* 8940–2003, SDT.

17.3

The Tribunal has also emphasised that wilful ignorance of the true status of the employee could lead to a breach of this provision:

> 'The Tribunal take the view that a solicitor can only claim not to have knowledge of a striking off order if he has first made appropriate enquiries. Total ignorance as a result of a total failure to make the enquiries which a prudent solicitor employer would make is not a state of knowledge but a state of deliberate ignorance.'[1]

As this is a statutory offence to be construed by reference to the precise words of the section this conclusion must be open to some doubt. Nevertheless, it is apparent that the Tribunal will strive to give a purposive construction to the section to meet the perceived mischief:

> 'The Tribunal accept that the mischief which section 41 seeks to avert is the handling of clients' affairs in a solicitors office by a struck off solicitor except in circumstances where he is subject to strict controls. It is clear that the constraints are imposed to protect the interests of the public and maintain the good name of the solicitors' profession.'[2]

The words 'employ or remunerate' have been construed widely, to include even the payment of expenses:

> 'The Tribunal consider that "employment" should be construed in the wider sense of "keeping busy" or "keeping occupied". It follows from that that payment of a wage is not essential to establish employment. The intention of section 41 is that struck off solicitors be kept out of solicitors offices save in exceptional and closely regulated cases. Although not argued

before them, the Tribunal believe it is useful to add that in its view the word "remunerate" should also be interpreted in its widest sense so that it not only means "to reward" or "to pay for services" but also "to provide recompense for". The payment of out of pocket expenses by the respondent was therefore remuneration.'[3]

1 *Cunnew,* 6134–1992, SDT.
2 *Cunnew,* 6134–1992, SDT.
3 *Cunnew,* 6134–1992, SDT.

Control of solicitors' employees and consultants

17.4

The SRA may act to prevent or control the employment in legal practice of those individuals whom it considers to be undesirable.[1] Both the SRA and the Tribunal have the power to make the relevant order preventing all solicitors from employing or remunerating, in connection with their practice as solicitors, the individual in question (except in accordance with permission in writing granted by the SRA for such period and subject to such conditions as the SRA may think fit). The order can also prevent any employee of a solicitor from employing or remunerating the individual in relation to legal practice, and can prevent an individual being a manager of or having an interest in a legal practice. It seems that the SRA will consider it appropriate to make the order itself at the adjudication stage if there has been a conviction or there is no dispute as to the facts, and will make an application to the Tribunal for an order when there is likely to be a dispute of fact or other factor justifying an oral hearing, or when the employing solicitor also faces Tribunal proceedings arising from the same facts.

The Tribunal has held that the standard of proof in either event should be the criminal standard.[2] It can be assumed that the SRA would be resistant to this in relation in cases where it chooses to make an order itself under section 43, as it employs the civil standard in making other disciplinary decisions,[3] but it can also be assumed that should the person affected seek a review from the Tribunal (see **17.7**), the latter would continue to apply the criminal standard – a good reason for cases involving a factual dispute to be referred to the Tribunal in any event.

There are two statutory grounds for making this order: (a) criminal convictions, and (b) certain acts or defaults while working in a legal practice.

1 Section 43 of SA 1974.
2 *Ahmed*, 8645–2002, SDT.
3 Rule 7.7 of the SRA Disciplinary Procedure Rules 2011.

Criminal convictions

17.5

The order may be made when the person concerned has been convicted of a criminal offence which is such that, in the opinion of the SRA, it would be undesirable for him to be involved in legal practice.[1]

1 Section 43(1)(a) of SA 1974.

Acts or defaults while working in a legal practice

17.6

The order may also be made when the person concerned has 'occasioned or been a party to, with or without the connivance of a solicitor, an act or default in relation to a legal practice which involved conduct on his part of such a nature that, in the opinion of the [SRA], it would be undesirable for him to be involved in a legal practice'.[1]

This somewhat convoluted subsection requires the SRA or the Tribunal to answer two essential questions:

(1) Has the person concerned occasioned an act or default which involved conduct on his part of such a nature that it would be undesirable for him to be involved in a legal practice?

(2) If so, was that act or default occasioned in relation to a legal practice?

The two subsections must be construed independently of each other. Section 43(1)(a) requires there to have been a criminal conviction, but subsection (b) does not require similar or equivalent conduct. An order under section 43(1)(b) can be founded upon foolishness, recklessness or errors of judgement if the consequence is that it is undesirable for the individual concerned to work in a legal practice.[2]

The statutory jurisdiction did not (as originally enacted) extend to or cover a situation in which the party alleged to be at fault remunerated himself, purporting to be an employee of a solicitor but in fact being his own employer in a sham arrangement;[3] however, the section as amended by LSA 2007 is probably sufficiently wide to overcome this difficulty.

The SRA and the Tribunal have, respectively, the power to make orders for costs when exercising this jurisdiction.[4]

1 Section 43(1)(b) of SA 1974.
2 See *Ojelade v Law Society* [2006] EWHC 2210 (Admin); and, particularly, *Gregory v Law Society* [2007] EWHC 1724 (Admin).
3 *Izegbu and Okoronkwo v Law Society* [2008] EWHC 1043 (Admin).
4 Section 43(2A) and (4) of SA 1974.

Appeals and reviews

17.7

Both the SRA and the Tribunal can revoke section 43 orders. If the SRA makes the order an application can be made to it to revoke it, for example, because it is no longer required as the individual has been employed in the profession without further fault for a period of years. If the order was made by the Tribunal any application for revocation is made to the Tribunal.[1] A person aggrieved by an order made by the SRA can apply to the Tribunal for a review of that order and the Tribunal can quash it, vary it or confirm it.[2] An order made by the Tribunal can be appealed to the High Court.[3] The High Court has power to make such order on an appeal as it thinks fit. Any decision of the High Court is final and there is no further appeal.[4]

If an application is made to revoke a section 43 order, the central issue will be whether the order remains necessary to protect the public interest and/or the reputation of the profession. In *R (SRA) v Solicitors Disciplinary Tribunal*[5] a decision by the SDT to revoke an order was overturned because the Tribunal had wrongly focused its attention upon the individual's unsuccessful efforts to rehabilitate himself, rather than upon the issue identified above.

1 Section 43(3) of SA 1974.
2 Section 43(3A).
3 Section 49(1).
4 Section 49(6).
5 [2013] EWHC 2584 (Admin).

Disciplinary control of employees

17.8

LSA 2007 amended SA 1974 by adding sections 34A and subsection 47(2E). Section 34A enables the SRA to provide that the rules of professional conduct: 'have effect in relation to employees of solicitors with such additions, omissions or other modifications as appear to the [SRA] to be necessary or expedient'. With effect from 31 March 2009 the SRA amended the Solicitors' Code of Conduct 2007 and other professional rules (including the Solicitors' Accounts Rules 1998) to make clear that it regulates not only solicitors but also the employees of solicitors, registered European lawyers and their employees, registered foreign lawyers, recognised bodies (including authorised sole practitioners) and their managers and employees. The 2011 SRA Handbook maintains this position. Section 47(2E) of SA 1974 extends the Tribunal's jurisdiction to the employees of solicitors. LSA 2007 also amended Schedule 2 to the Administration of Justice Act (AJA) 1985 (which relates to incorporated practices or 'recognised bodies') to give the same powers to the Tribunal in relation to managers and employees of recognised bodies.

17.9

In relation to managers and employees, the Tribunal may:

- impose a fine, unlimited in amount, payable to the Treasury;[1]
- require the SRA to take such steps in relation to the relevant person as the Tribunal may specify;[2] and/or
- order the SRA to refer the conduct of the relevant person to an appropriate regulator,[3] as well as being able to make an order controlling the employment of the relevant person under section 43 of SA 1974.[4] An 'appropriate regulator' would be the relevant approved regulator authorised under LSA 2007 if the manager or employee is an authorised person in relation to a reserved legal activity (e.g. a barrister or licensed conveyancer) or any body which regulates the activities actually undertaken by the person concerned, if he or she was not an authorised person for LSA 2007 purposes.[5]

1 Section 47(2E)(a) of SA 1974; para 18A(2)(a) of Schedule 2 to AJA 1985.
2 Section 47(2E)(b) of SA 1974; para 18A(2)(b) of Schedule 2 to AJA 1985.
3 Section 47(2E)(d) of SA 1974; para 18A(2)(d) of Schedule 2 to AJA 1985.
4 Section 47(2E)(c) of SA 1974; para 18A(2)(c) of Schedule 2 to AJA 1985.
5 Section 47(2H) of SA 1974; para 18A(7) of Schedule 2 to AJA 1985.

17.10

There are mechanisms for the control of compliance officers for legal practice and compliance officers for finance and administration (COLPs and COFAs) including the power to disqualify, which could have the effect of rendering the individual unemployable in the legal services market. While COLPs and COFAs may be principals in the firm, partners, members or directors, they may also be employees. These powers are considered in detail in **CHAPTER 6**.

PART 5
The disciplinary system in practice

CHAPTER 18

Professional misconduct

18.1

Historically, there have been two types of professional misconduct by solicitors:

(1) statutory misconduct, consisting of breaches of provisions of the Solicitors Act 1974 (for example, in relation to the obligation to deliver accountants' reports) or of rules made by virtue of that Act (such as the Solicitors' Accounts Rules 1998); and

(2) non-statutory misconduct – what could be called the common law of conduct, which covered anything and everything that could bring the individual or the profession into sufficient disrepute so as to engage the risk of disciplinary sanction, but which was not covered by any specific rule.

In the Solicitors Disciplinary Tribunal ('the Tribunal' or SDT), any action, failing or course of conduct that offended the common law of conduct was alleged to be 'professional misconduct', until the late 1950s when the phrase 'conduct unbefitting a solicitor' was substituted. The latter formulation enabled the point to be made as necessary that misconduct outside a solicitor's professional practice, in his or her private life, could have disciplinary consequences.

On 1 July 2007 the Solicitors' Code of Conduct 2007 came into force. The 2007 Code was designed to be an all-embracing and codified system of professional regulation. Accordingly, it seemed as though the concept of non-statutory misconduct would fade away, and prosecutors in the Tribunal started to allege a breach of a rule *simpliciter* (rather than conduct unbefitting) against solicitors whose conduct had been referred to the Tribunal. This presupposed that any breach of any rule could amount to a disciplinary offence – a controversial proposition which was rejected by the Tribunal in *Pabla and Pabla*.[1]

This debate has now become largely academic, as the 2007 Code has been abolished and replaced by far less prescriptive rules under the 2011 Code. The modern tendency is for prosecutors to allege breaches of either the Principles or the mandatory outcomes (or both), and allegations of conduct unbefitting a solicitor have largely fallen into disuse. Where prescriptive rules, such as the SRA Accounts Rules, are alleged to have been breached, the relevant allegation should make that clear.

1 10376–2009.

18.2

'Professional misconduct' and 'conduct unbefitting a solicitor' are not defined; there is no reference to either phrase in the Solicitors Act (SA) 1974: 'misconduct' is that which the Tribunal and the judges from time to time consider it to be. Thus, 'conduct which would be regarded as improper according to the consensus of professional, including judicial, opinion could be fairly stigmatised as such whether it violated the letter of a professional code or not'.[1] On the other hand, it has always been the case that solicitors were not penalised for making mistakes – 'generally the honest and genuine decision of a solicitor on a question of professional judgment does not give rise to a disciplinary offence'.[2] Negligence may, however, amount to misconduct if it is sufficiently reprehensible or 'inexcusable and such as to be regarded as deplorable by his fellows in the profession'.[3]

1 *Ridehalgh v Horsefield* [1994] Ch 205, [1994] 3 All ER 848, CA.
2 *Connolly v Law Society* [2007] EWHC 1175 (Admin).
3 *Re a Solicitor* [1972] 2 All ER 811, CA at 815.

18.3

It is in fact undesirable to attempt a comprehensive definition:

> 'The suggestion was that the phrase "moral turpitude" is analogous to conduct unbefitting. My response to that is that it may be in some circumstances, but not in all. Allegations against professional men vary infinitely in gravity. What constitutes conduct unbefitting a solicitor is best judged, in my view, by his professional colleagues, applying their undoubted experience of what is to be properly expected of a solicitor in his practice, when they are sitting formally as part of a disciplinary tribunal in judgment of one of them. I should be most reluctant to attempt to provide any kind of definition of a term which is used, the words being slightly different here and there, in many professions, including the armed forces.'[1]

It has been argued that only conduct specifically referred to and prohibited in *The Guide to the Professional Conduct of Solicitors* current at that time or specific rules is capable of being treated as conduct which is conduct unbefitting a solicitor. This was, unsurprisingly, rejected:

> 'The purpose of Professional Conduct Rules ... is to identify in particular those areas of conduct in respect of which there should be specific prohibitions or requirements because they are likely to represent the most prevalent situations and the most prevalent conduct then in the profession. The fact that such a particular area of conduct is specifically dealt with does not mean that all other conduct is permissible or within the standards of the profession. It is thus ordinarily open to professional disciplinary tribunals to apply sanctions for professional misconduct generally, regardless of whether it is conduct singled out for mention in the rules. Were it otherwise, professional people might be permitted to conduct themselves in plainly deplorable ways without any disciplinary control.'[2]

1 *Re a Solicitor* (1991, unreported), per Watkins LJ; cited with approval in *Re a Solicitor* (1995, unreported), per Lord Taylor CJ.
2 *Henneberry v Law Society* (2000, unreported).

CHAPTER 19

SRA-imposed sanctions

The statutory provisions

19.1

Until the summer of 2010 the only regulatory 'sanction' that the Solicitors Regulation Authority (SRA) could impose upon a solicitor was a reprimand or severe reprimand. This was generally kept confidential as between the solicitor and the SRA though if there was a third party complainant or informant involved that party would be informed, and was free to disclose it.[1] The Legal Services Act (LSA) 2007 introduced a new section 44D into the Solicitors Act (SA) 1974. This provided a statutory power for the SRA to impose fines of up to £2,000, or a written rebuke, upon solicitors. A parallel power in relation to recognised bodies, their managers and employees, was inserted in the Administration of Justice Act 1985 as paragraph 14B of Schedule 2. Parliament's intention was to remove the less serious cases from the Solicitors Disciplinary Tribunal ('the Tribunal' or SDT), and to allow the SRA to deal with them more speedily and cheaply instead. The worrying feature for solicitors is that the confidentiality of the process has been swept away. The SRA may itself publish details of any action it has taken under section 44D if it considers this to be in the public interest.

The new statutory powers could not be exercised until the SRA had made rules in accordance with the terms of section 44D, which also required consultation with the Tribunal about the content of the rules. There was considerable delay in the promulgation of the rules, caused largely by disagreement over the standard of proof to be adopted by the SRA in making disciplinary decisions. Eventually the SRA (which wanted to use the civil standard against the wishes of the Tribunal and the Master of the Rolls) prevailed, and the Legal Services Board (LSB) approved the SRA (Disciplinary Procedure) Rules 2010 (2010 Rules), which commenced on 1 June 2010. The 2010 Rules did not apply to any matters where the relevant act or omission occurred before that commencement date.[2] Those Rules have now been replaced by the SRA Disciplinary Procedure Rules 2011, which form part of the SRA Handbook. Like their predecessors, the 2011 Rules do not apply to any acts or omissions occurring wholly before 1 June 2010.[3]

1 *Napier and another v Pressdram Ltd* [2009] EWCA Civ 443, [2010] 1 WLR 934.
2 Rule 12 of the SRA (Disciplinary Procedure) Rules 2010.
3 Rule 16.1 of the SRA (Disciplinary Procedure) Rules 2011.

19.2

By section 44D(10), the Lord Chancellor may by order increase the £2,000 limit to such other amount as may be specified in the order. The SRA is anxious to secure an increase, in part at least to reduce the disparity between its powers in relation to tradional law firms and those who work in them, and its powers in relation to ABSs and those who work in them: the SRA has a power to impose huge fines upon ABSs. For the more extensive powers of the SRA to take disciplinary action against ABSs see **CHAPTER 25**.

19.3

The issue of publicity is a vexed one. On the one hand, as a statutory regulator, regulating in the public interest, the SRA wishes to operate in an open and transparent manner. On the other, the effect of publicity for the individual solicitor may be wholly disproportionate to the regulatory breach that occurred. In the internet age, such information is easily obtained by a prospective client, and is bound to have a deterrent effect upon the prospective client's intention to instruct the solicitor in question.

19.4

Section 44E of SA 1974 confers a right of appeal upon a solicitor who is fined or rebuked under section 44D if, in the case of a rebuke, a decision has been made to publish the rebuke. The appeal lies to the Tribunal. For a consideration of this and other appellate jurisdictions of the Tribunal see **CHAPTER 22**.

The powers of the adjudicator and adjudication panels

19.5

By rule 3 of the SRA Disciplinary Procedure Rules 2011, three conditions must be met before a rebuke or fine can be imposed:

- The first condition is that the SRA must be satisfied that the relevant act or omission by the solicitor fulfils one or more of the following:
  - it was deliberate or reckless;
  - it caused or had the potential to cause loss or significant inconvenience to another;
  - it was or was related to a failure or refusal to ascertain, recognise or comply with the regulated person's professional or regulatory obligations such as, but not limited to, compliance with requirements imposed by legislation or rules made pursuant to legislation, the SRA, the Law Society, LeO, the Tribunal or the court;
  - it continued for an unreasonable period taking into account its seriousness;
  - it persisted after the regulated person realised or should have realised that it was improper;
  - it misled or had the potential to mislead clients, the court or other persons, whether or not that was appreciated by the regulated person;
  - it affected or had the potential to affect a vulnerable person or child;
  - it affected or had the potential to affect a substantial, high-value or high-profile matter;

- it formed or forms part of a pattern of misconduct or other regulatory failure by the regulated person.

- The second condition is that a fine or rebuke represents a proportionate outcome.
- The third condition is that the relevant act or omission was neither trivial nor justifiably inadvertent.

The third element of the first condition is nonsensical. All other elements of the first condition have the character of exacerbating features; in other words, a factor which makes a 'bare' breach of a rule more serious. However, the third element simply requires there to have been a rule breach. As sanctions could only ever be imposed in circumstances where there had been a rule breach of some kind, that particular provision adds nothing and makes no sense. The entire thrust of rule 3 conveys the impression that something beyond a bare breach of a rule is required before a sanction would be considered appropriate. If the third element of the first condition is to be taken at face value, this impression is wholly misleading, and no exacerbating feature is required.

As yet there has been insufficient opportunity to observe how the rule is used in practice and how this anomaly is resolved.

19.6

The decision may be made by an adjudicator or an adjudication panel consisting of at least two members. The strict rules of evidence do not apply. By rule 7.7 the standard of proof adopted is the civil standard, in contrast to the Tribunal which operates on the criminal standard (see **21.2**). Any fine is payable to the Treasury, but is not payable until the time for appealing has expired.

Any decision may also be taken by agreement with the regulated person.

Setting the level of fine

19.7

If a financial penalty is in contemplation the SRA may require a statement as to the financial means of the person or body, verified by a statement of truth, within a specified time.[1] In fixing a penalty regard can be had to any failure to provide such information.[2] Appendix 1 to the SRA Disciplinary Procedure Rules 2011 contains the criteria to be considered in imposing a financial penalty. These require the fine to be proportionate to the fault, the harm done and the means of the person or body, to take account of any mitigating or aggravating circumstances (examples of which are given), and to take account of any indicative guidance published by the SRA (of which there is none at present).

Two criteria are likely to be more relevant to the high levels of fines for ABSs (a maximum of £250 million for a licensed body and £50 million for a manager or employee; see **CHAPTER 25**) – that fines should be of an amount that is likely to deter repetition by the fined person or body and to deter misconduct by others; and to eliminate any financial gain or other benefit obtained as a direct or indirect consequence of the misconduct.

The SRA may suspend a fine, which may have the result of making it payable only if there is a further adverse finding within the period of the suspension.[3]

1 Rule 8.1 of the SRA Disciplinary Procedure Rules 2011.
2 Paragraph 6 of Appendix 1.
3 Rules 8.2. and 8.3.

Publication of decisions

19.8

The criteria for publication are included as Appendix 2 to the SRA Disciplinary Procedure Rules 2011. This lists a series of factors supporting a decision to publish and a (smaller) series of factors supporting a decision not to publish. The most important of the latter is '(e) in all the circumstances the impact of publication on the individual or the firm would be disproportionate'. In paragraph 7 of the Appendix, the SRA states that it will from time to time publish indicative guidance about the application of these criteria but none has yet emerged.

Oral hearings

19.9

It is theoretically open to a solicitor to request an oral hearing, but such hearings have rarely if ever been granted, and attempts to obtain such hearings via judicial review in the past in relation to comparable Law Society systems have invariably foundered.[1] In order to have any prospect of persuading the adjudicator to grant an oral hearing, the solicitor will have to explain why such a hearing is necessary, and why the matter cannot be adequately considered on paper. In order to have any prospect of success in judicial review proceedings based upon the failure to have an oral hearing, it will be essential for the solicitor to have requested such a hearing; failure to have done so will be fatal to the application.[2]

The rarity of oral hearings is likely to continue under the new regime, at least in relation to traditional (non-ABS) practices, although now that the SRA has powers to impose sanctions that have a material consequence in financial and reputational terms it is probable that pressure for oral hearings will increase. Indeed, there are signs that the SRA recognises that the pressure will become irresistible when, for example, licensing and disciplinary decisions in relation to ABSs are likely to have serious financial consequences.

1 *R v Law Society, ex p Curtin, Times*, 3 December 1993, CA.
2 *R (Thompson) v Law Society* [2004] 1 WLR 2522. See also *R (Smith) v Parole Board (No 2)* [2004] 1 WLR 421.

Costs of the investigation

19.10

Where the SRA investigates possible professional misconduct by a solicitor, or a failure or apprehended failure by a solicitor to comply with any regulatory requirement, the solicitor may be directed to pay an amount which is calculated to be the cost of investigating and dealing with the matter – or a reasonable contribution towards that cost.[1] The current practice is to charge on a time basis in bands. If an investigation takes less than two hours' work (which would be unusual), the costs are a fixed figure of £300. If the time spent is more than two but under eight hours, the charge is £600. Between eight and 16 hours' work results in a charge of £1,350 and longer investigations are charged at £1,350 plus £75 for each hour and £37.50 for every half hour over the sixteenth hour, rounded up or down to the nearest half hour. There is a further fixed charge of £250 for an unsuccessful internal appeal.[2]

1 Section 44C of SA 1974.
2 Appendix 1 to the SRA (Cost of Investigations) Regulations 2011.

Internal appeals

19.11

The powers to rebuke, fine and publicise the sanction are subject to a right of appeal.[1] The appeal must be launched within 14 days and is dealt with on paper, and it is important for the appellant to provide properly reasoned arguments in support of the appeal. A failure to do so may result in summary dismissal.

There is no right of appeal in relation to a decision to refer a person or body to the Tribunal.[2]

Importantly, the SRA itself can 'appeal' a decision by requiring it to be reconsidered if it appears to be fundamentally wrong, whether or not the decision has been disclosed to any person. This may be done if it appears to someone with the necessary authority that the decision-maker was not provided with material evidence that was available to the SRA; was materially misled by anyone; failed to take proper account of material facts or evidence; took into account immaterial facts or evidence; made a material error of law; made a decision which was otherwise irrational or procedurally unfair; made a decision which was otherwise ultra vires; or failed to give sufficient reasons. This is a matter for the absolute discretion of the decision-maker, without any right of appeal.[3] Therefore, despite the apparent independence of the adjudication process there is a theoretical possibility that senior staff of the SRA could keep putting a matter back to an adjudicator or successive adjudicators until a 'satisfactory' decision was reached. The rules do not make any particular provision as to the extent to which affected solicitors are to be kept informed of such steps when they are taken.

1 Rule 11 of the SRA Disciplinary Procedure Rules 2011.
2 Rule 10.4.
3 Rule 13.2.

Appeals to the Tribunal

19.12

In respect of regulatory breaches occurring after 1 June 2010, there is a free-standing right of appeal to the Tribunal against a fine, against any direction for publicity, and against a rebuke only if there is a direction to publicise.[1]

1 Section 44E of SA 1974. See **CHAPTER 22**.

Judicial review

19.13

Judicial review continues to be theoretically available in respect of decisions by an adjudicator or an adjudication panel to impose a reprimand or rebuke without publication, as there is no statutory right of appeal to the Tribunal against such decisions. Ordinary public law principles would apply to such applications. Judicial review is often seen as a disproportionate response in circumstances where the decision, even if challengeable, makes little difference to the solicitor in practice, and permission can be refused on that basis alone.

As for decisions in respect of which a statutory right of appeal to the Tribunal exists, these cannot be challenged in judicial review proceedings owing to the existence of this alternative remedy.

Regulatory settlements

19.14

The SRA is now prepared to enter into agreements to settle regulatory and disciplinary cases. The agreement may take two forms: a settlement agreement, which will resolve the whole matter, or an issue agreement, which will resolve a particular issue within an investigation without concluding the investigation.

There is no requirement or compulsion on the SRA to consider a regulatory settlement of either kind or to enter into negotiations. If negotiations are conducted they will be on a without prejudice basis, and will not be referred to in any investigations or proceedings unless the court or the Tribunal orders otherwise. Agreements may be rescinded if there proves to have been material misrepresentation.

It is understood that agreements will only be contemplated if the solicitor's integrity is not in issue and if compliance with the agreement by the solicitor can be assured.

Agreements will be in writing, state the relevant facts, identify any failings admitted by the solicitor, identify the action the solicitor has taken or intends to take, identify any sanction imposed (such as a reprimand) and will be published by the SRA unless expressly agreed otherwise.

Any agreed course of action will be supported by professional undertakings and a breach of the agreement will be considered to be misconduct.

The investigation will be reopened if the solicitor fails to comply with the agreement or acts inconsistently with it (for example, by denying misconduct that has been admitted for the purposes of the agreement).

Examples of regulatory settlements are:

- agreed public statements, whereby a solicitor publicly acknowledges a failure and states what has been and will be done to avoid repetition, where the publicity, in conjunction with any other sanction, is considered to be a proportionate result; and

- schemes for correction, improvement and restitution (for example, where failings have impacted on clients), whereby relevant faults can be properly and proportionately addressed by identifying and contacting all affected clients, refunding money to them, reporting periodically to the SRA and submitting to the scheme being monitored.

CHAPTER 20

Proceedings before the SDT: (1) pre-trial

Membership and constitution of the Tribunal

20.1

Members of the Solicitors Disciplinary Tribunal ('the Tribunal' or SDT) are appointed by the Master of the Rolls. The Tribunal consists of solicitor members who are practising solicitors of not less than ten years' standing, and lay members, who are neither solicitors nor barristers. Lay members are paid a daily stipend by the Ministry of Justice; until 2009 solicitor members were unpaid but can now be paid from the Tribunal's annual budget met by the Law Society. The President of the Tribunal is elected to the post, and must be a solicitor member.[1] The members also appoint one solicitor member and one lay member to be vice-presidents. The Tribunal has been held to be an independent and impartial tribunal for the purposes of Article 6 of the European Convention on Human Rights.[2]

1 Rule 3 of the Solicitors (Disciplinary Proceedings) Rules 2007 (SI 2007/3588).
2 *Pine v Law Society* (2000) DC Transcript CO 1385/2000.

The Tribunal's statutory powers

20.2

On the hearing of an application, the Tribunal has the power, in relation to solicitors, to make such order as it thinks fit, and any such order may in particular include provision for any of the following matters:[1]

'(a) the striking off the roll of the name of the solicitor to whom the application or complaint relates;

(b) the suspension of that solicitor from practice indefinitely or for a specified period;

(ba) the revocation of that solicitor's sole solicitor's endorsement (if any);

(bb) the suspension of that solicitor from practice as a sole solicitor indefinitely or for a specified period;

(c) the payment by that solicitor or former solicitor of a penalty, which shall be forfeit to Her Majesty;[2]

(d) in the circumstances referred to in subsection (2A), the exclusion of that solicitor from criminal legal aid work (either permanently or for a specified period);

(e) the termination of that solicitor's unspecified period of suspension from practice;

(ea) the termination of that solicitor's unspecified period of suspension from practice as a sole solicitor;

(f) the restoration to the roll of the name of a former solicitor whose name has been struck off the roll and to whom the application relates;

(g) in the case of a former solicitor whose name has been removed from the roll, a direction prohibiting the restoration of his name to the roll except by order of the Tribunal;

(h) in the case of an application under subsection (1)(f) [of the Solicitors Act 1974], the restoration of the applicant's name to the roll; and

(i) the payment by any party of costs or a contribution towards costs of such amount as the Tribunal may consider reasonable.'

1 Section 47(2) of Solicitors Act (SA) 1974.
2 The former limit of £5,000 for each offence was removed by the Legal Services Act (LSA) 2007 with effect from 31 March 2009. It can be expected that much higher fines may be levied on recognised bodies in the context of firm-based regulation (see **CHAPTER 2**) if the offence has led to material financial gain, although there is, as yet, little evidence that this is happening.

Other powers and jurisdictions

20.3

The Tribunal has jurisdiction over recognised bodies (incorporated practices registered with the Solicitors Regulation Authority (SRA)),[1] registered European lawyers,[2] registered foreign lawyers[3] and in respect of non-solicitors involved in legal practice.[4] The Tribunal also has jurisdiction to disqualify solicitors from undertaking legal aid work,[5] but so far as can be established the power has never been used.

The Tribunal has jurisdiction to consider the conduct of and to impose sanctions on an individual who was not a solicitor at the time of the actions complained of but who had since been admitted as a solicitor.[6]

The Tribunal has jurisdiction over former solicitors in respect of conduct while they were solicitors.[7]

Appeal lies to the Tribunal from the imposition of fines by the SRA under section 44D of SA 1974 and/or under paragraph 14B of Schedule 2 to the Administration of Justice Act (AJA) 1985 and in respect of written rebukes by the SRA (under the same provisions) if a decision is made that the rebuke should be published, and also against any decision to publish the details of any action taken by the SRA under section 44D of SA 1974.[8] On such an appeal the Tribunal may affirm or revoke the SRA's decision, vary the amount of any fine, and also may exercise its normal jurisdiction over the appellant (to strike off, suspend, revoke a sole solicitor endorsement, fine, and so forth) as if an application had been made against that person.[9] Appeal also lies to the Tribunal from licensing decisions of the SRA concerning alternative business structures (ABSs). For the appellate jurisdiction of the Tribunal see **CHAPTER 22**.

Section 47(3B) of SA 1974, inserted by LSA 2007, provides that the Tribunal is not permitted to make any order requiring redress to be made in respect of any act or omission of any person. An order, for example, that a solicitor compensate a client would therefore not be permitted. The parliamentary intention is clear: that redress is not a matter for either the SRA or the Tribunal, rather it is an issue for the Legal Ombudsman (see **CHAPTER 13**). This section came into force on 1 October 2011.

The SRA may also make rules, with the approval of the Tribunal, providing for appeals to the Tribunal from certain decisions of the SRA where appeal would otherwise lie to the High Court. These relate primarily to practising certificate conditions, and no such rules have yet been made.[10] It is understood that these are not in immediate contemplation.

1 Paragraphs 16 to 18A of Schedule 2 to AJA 1985.
2 Regulation 26 of the European Communities (Lawyer's Practice) Regulations 2000 (SI 2000/1119).
3 Paragraphs 15 to 17 of Schedule 14 to the Courts and Legal Services Act (CLSA) 1990.
4 Sections 43 and 47(2E) of SA 1974: see **17.4** to **17.10**.
5 Section 47(2A), (2B), (2C) and (2D) of SA 1974. These subsections were introduced by AJA 1985, granting the Tribunal the powers formerly vested in the Legal Aid (Complaints) Tribunal (established by the Legal Aid Act 1974, and which had dealt with two cases in its lifetime) and the Legal Aid in Criminal Cases (Complaints) Tribunal (established under the Criminal Justice Act 1967, which had dealt with one).
6 *Re a Solicitor (Ofosuhene)* (21 February 1997, unreported).
7 Section 47(1)(c) of SA 1974.
8 Section 44E(1) of SA 1974; para 14C of Schedule 2 to AJA 1985.
9 Section 44E(4) of SA 1974; para 14C of Schedule 2 to AJA 1985.
10 Section 49A of SA 1974. The matters which, subject to the rules if and when they are made, may be appealed to the Tribunal are: decisions under the Solicitors Keeping of the Roll Regulations 2011 as to restoring the name of a solicitor removed from the roll under those Regulations (section 8(4) of SA 1974); the imposition of conditions on practising certificates or refusal to issue practising certificates or sole solicitor endorsements (sections 13A(6) and 28(3D)); decisions relating to the termination of the suspension of practising certificates (section 16(5)); decisions relating to the grant of permission to employ a struck off or suspended solicitor (section 41(3)); and decisions under the parallel jurisdiction in relation to conditions on the registration of foreign lawyers (para 14 of Schedule 14 to CLSA 1990).

The Solicitors (Disciplinary Proceedings) Rules 2007

20.4

The Tribunal's procedures are currently governed by the Solicitors (Disciplinary Proceedings) Rules 2007 ('the 2007 Rules'),[1] which came into force on 14 January 2008. They replaced the 1994 Rules of the same name. The 2007 Rules are set out in full in **APPENDIX 12**.

1 SI 2007/3588.

Commencing the proceedings

20.5

When an adjudicator or adjudication panel or other authorised person of the SRA resolves to refer the conduct of a solicitor to the Tribunal, the case is allocated by the Legal Directorate of the SRA either to an in-house advocate in that department or to a solicitor member of the panel of solicitors instructed by the SRA to prosecute cases. That individual, referred to in the proceedings as the applicant, is responsible for drafting the originating process, which is known as the rule 5 statement (so named from rule 5 of the 2007 Rules),[1] although occasionally counsel is instructed to draft the document. The rule 5 statement sets out the allegations and facts relied upon against the solicitor, who is termed the respondent.

1 Under the 1994 Rules regime it was the rule 4 statement.

The rule 5 statement

20.6

Great care is required in drafting the rule 5 statement. It is the entire basis of the prosecution case, containing not only the allegations which the respondent solicitor will have to face, but also the narrative supporting those allegations. If the narrative is unclear, or does not properly reflect the allegations, the Tribunal, or the High Court on appeal, is likely to be critical. One such instance was the recent case of *Thaker v SRA,*[1] in which the court was highly critical of the drafting of the relevant statement (at [17]):

> 'I regret to say that both the RAS [the re-amended statement of the SRA's case] and the schedule are chaotic documents. Although these documents are formidable at first sight, when one settles down to study them it is quite impossible to understand the case which Mr Thaker was being called upon to answer. The order in which matters are set out in the RAS is neither chronological nor logical. There are many cross references which are impossible to follow up, as the reader seeks to navigate a path through the hundreds of pages which form attachments to the RAS.'

Three further passages from reported cases should be borne in mind by any prosecutor. In his judgment in *Constantinides v Law Society,*[2] Lord Justice Moses said (at [35]):

> 'We should stress that we do not consider that the allegations of dishonesty were clearly and properly made in the Rule 4 statement. The Rule 4 statement, after alleging conduct unbefitting a solicitor, should have identified that conduct and stated with precision in relation to each aspect of the allegedly guilty conduct the respects in which it was said to be dishonest. It should have alleged that when the appellant acted, despite the conflict of interest, that that conduct was dishonest by the ordinary standards of honest behaviour and that he knew that he was transgressing the ordinary standards of honest behaviour.'

Likewise in *Thaker v SRA*, Jackson LJ observed:

> '[64] In order to have an effective re-trial, the SRA must serve a properly drafted Rule 4 statement in respect of any of the twelve allegations which it wishes to pursue. For the avoidance of doubt a properly drafted Rule 4 statement will set out a summary of the facts relied upon. It would be helpful if those facts are set out concisely and in chronological order … It is the duty of the draftsman (not the reader) of a pleading or a Rule 4 statement to analyse the supporting evidence and to distil the relevant facts, discarding all irrelevancies.
>
> [65] If the Rule 4 statement alleges that Mr Thaker knew or ought to have known certain matters, the facts giving rise to that actual or constructive

knowledge should also be set out. Once the Rule 4 statement has set out the primary facts asserted, it should then set out the allegations which are made on the basis of those primary facts. The person who drafts the Rule 4 statement should heed the guidance given by this court in *Constantinides* in relation to pleading dishonesty. In a complex case such as this the Solicitors' Disciplinary Tribunal needs to have a coherent and intelligible Rule 4 statement, in order to do justice between the parties.'

In *Connolly v Law Society*[3] Stanley Burnton J (with whom Laws LJ agreed) held (at [104]):

'the Law Society should avoid where possible formulating charges which include "and/or" allegations, such as charge (xl) in the present case, which comprised numerous alternatives. Where such a charge is laid, the Tribunal should make specific findings as to which allegation has been proved.'

These criticisms have to some extent fallen on deaf ears. 'And/or' allegations remain commonplace. In *SRA v Andersons and others*,[4] Treacy LJ observed, at [3]:

'During the course of the hearing we commented on the highly complicated structure of the charges, involving multiple allegations of breaches of rules, either cumulatively or in the alternative. Mr Dutton QC, for the SRA, acknowledged the force of this criticism. We would hope that in the future consideration would be given to a significantly clearer method of framing charges.'

1 [2011] EWHC 660 (Admin).
2 [2006] EWHC 725 (Admin).
3 [2007] EWHC 1175 (Admin).
4 [2013] EWHC 4021 (Admin).

Alleging dishonesty

20.7

If dishonesty is to be alleged against a solicitor, this must be made clear – ideally in the rule 5 statement. Failure expressly to allege or particularise dishonesty in a document in advance of the Tribunal hearing is likely to amount to a serious procedural flaw, which may well result in any finding of dishonesty by the Tribunal being overturned.[1]

The test for dishonesty is that set out in *Twinsectra Ltd v Yardley*.[2] This requires both objective and subjective elements. It was expressed thus by Lord Hutton (at [27]):

'before there can be a finding of dishonesty it must be established that the defendant's conduct was dishonest by the standards of reasonable and honest people *and* that he himself realised that by those standards his conduct was dishonest.' (emphasis added)

The words before the highlighted 'and' can be referred to as the objective test and those after it as the subjective element of the combined test.

Lord Hutton went on (at [36]):

> 'dishonesty requires knowledge by the defendant that what he was doing would be regarded as dishonest by honest people, although he should not escape a finding of dishonesty because he set his own standards of honesty and does not regard as dishonest what he knows would offend the normally accepted standard of honest conduct.'

In *Twinsectra*, Lord Millett delivered a powerful dissenting speech, advocating a purely objective test in respect of dishonesty in the context of accessory liability for breach of trust. Two subsequent cases suggested that the courts were moving away from the twin subjective/objective test enunciated by Lord Hutton in *Twinsectra*, towards a predominantly objective test.[3] In the context of disciplinary proceedings, however, the Divisional Court emphatically held in *Bryant and Bench v Law Society*[4] that the *Twinsectra* test, as previously understood, should continue to determine whether a solicitor has been dishonest:

> 'In our judgment, the decision of the Court of Appeal in *Bultitude* stands as binding authority that the test to be applied in the context of solicitors' disciplinary proceedings is the *Twinsectra* test as it was widely understood before *Barlow Clowes*, that is a test that includes the separate subjective element. The fact that the Privy Council in *Barlow Clowes* has subsequently placed a different interpretation on *Twinsectra* for the purposes of the accessory liability principle does not alter the substance of the test accepted in *Bultitude* and does not call for any departure from that test.
>
> In any event there are strong reasons for adopting such a test in the disciplinary context and for declining to follow in that context the approach in *Barlow Clowes*. As we have observed earlier, the test corresponds closely to that laid down in the criminal context by *R v Ghosh*; and in our view it is more appropriate that the test for dishonesty in the context of solicitors' disciplinary proceedings should be aligned with the criminal test than with the test for determining civil liability for assisting in a breach of a trust. It is true, as Mr Williams [leading counsel for the Law Society] submitted, that disciplinary proceedings are not themselves criminal in character and that they may involve issues of dishonesty that could not give rise to any criminal liability (e.g. lying to a client as to whether a step had been taken on his behalf). But the tribunal's finding of dishonesty against a solicitor is likely to have extremely serious consequences for him both professionally (it will normally lead to an order striking him off) and personally. It is just as appropriate to require a finding that the defendant had a subjectively dishonest state of mind in this context as the court in *R v Ghosh* considered it to be in the criminal context.'

The Tribunal is regularly called upon to consider whether the failings of a solicitor amount to dishonesty, with an understanding that if that is found to be the correct description, the solicitor will almost inevitably be struck off (see **21.16** and **21.17**).

1 *Singleton v Law Society* [2005] EWHC 2915 (Admin); *Constantinides v Law Society* [2006] EWHC 725 (Admin); *Onibudo v Law Society* [2002] EWHC 2030 (Admin). In contrast, it is not necessary that recklessness should be specifically pleaded: see *Keazor v Law Society* [2009] EWHC 267 (Admin).
2 [2002] UKHL 12, [2002] 2 All ER 377.
3 See *Barlow Clowes International Ltd (in liquidation) v Eurotrust International Ltd* [2005] UKPC 37, [2006] 1 WLR 1476, [2006] 1 All ER 333; *Abou-Rahmah v Abacha* [2006] EWCA Civ 1492, [2007] 1 Lloyd's

Rep 115. This trend continued with the Court of Appeal decision in *Starglade Properties Ltd v Nash* [2010] EWCA Civ 1314, [2011] 1 Lloyd's Rep. FC 102.
4 [2007] EWHC 3043 (Admin) at [153]–[154].

Conduct unbefitting a solicitor and rule breaches

20.8

As explained in **CHAPTER 18** allegations have traditionally been of two kinds – either of specific breaches of rules, such as the Solicitors' Accounts Rules 1998, or of conduct unbefitting a solicitor in specified circumstances (which can vary infinitely). There is no all-embracing definition of conduct unbefitting a solicitor. In essence, conduct unbefitting is conduct which is regarded as professional misconduct by the Tribunal as supervised by the courts. There is no need to prove intention or recklessness; conduct may be conduct unbefitting even though the solicitor attempted to conform to the highest professional standards. Negligent conduct may amount to conduct unbefitting a solicitor.[1] Since the advent of outcomes-focused regulation and the 2011 Code, prosecutors have tended to allege breaches of the Principles or outcomes in the Code, rather than conduct unbefitting a solicitor.

A breach of the SRA Accounts Rules 2011 is effectively a disciplinary offence of absolute liability owing to the terms of rule 6 of those Rules, which requires all the principals ('managers' in the terminology of the SRA Handbook) in a practice to ensure compliance with the Rules by themselves and by everyone else working in the practice; this also applies to the firm's compliance officer for finance and administration (COFA) whether or not that individual is a manager.

1 *Re a Solicitor* [1972] 2 All ER 811, CA and *Connolly v Law Society* [2007] EWHC 1175 (Admin) at [62]. See also **CHAPTER 18**, where this subject is discussed in greater detail.

Prosecuting 'innocent' partners

20.9

In recent years there has been some confusion as to whether partners who have not known of or directly participated in a decision that breached a regulatory rule should face disciplinary action as a result. It was felt by the SRA that if, for instance, an equity partner benefited financially from a breach of the prohibition against referral fees, that partner should face disciplinary proceedings. It is submitted that the better view is that unless a disciplinary offence is one of strict liability (such as an Accounts Rule breach), a solicitor should only face disciplinary consequences if he or she is in some way culpable.

This had been the general approach of the Tribunal.[1] The concept of conduct unbefitting a solicitor carries with it some degree of moral culpability: the Tribunal had held that partners should not be required to supervise or monitor the work of other partners, and that a partner is not guilty of professional misconduct merely because he is the partner of a solicitor who is guilty of professional misconduct.[2]

This general approach has been approved by the Divisional Court in *Akodu v SRA* [2009] EWHC 3588 (Admin) per Moses LJ:

> 'there is no other reasonable conclusion that can be reached other than that the basis upon which he had been found guilty was merely on the basis that

he was a partner of the firm. If that was the only basis, then there has been no argument advanced on behalf of the Law Society to suggest that that was a lawful basis upon which any solicitor can be found guilty of conduct unbefitting his profession. If authority is needed for the proposition, it can be found in *Cordery on Solicitors* at J 2225. Some degree of personal fault is required.'

1 See *Pabla and Pabla*, 10376–2009, in which the Tribunal held that admitted breaches of the 2007 Code of Conduct were too trivial to merit prosecution in the Tribunal, and dismissed the allegations.
2 *Ali and Shabir*, 9339–2005, SDT; *Aziz and Saunders*, 9032–2004, SDT; *Ross and others*, 10002–2008, SDT; and *Bagri and others*, 10229–2009, SDT.

20.10

For the same reason, it will not be enough to establish professional misconduct against a solicitor or an entity that something has gone seriously wrong in a regulated entity. It is not unknown for a rogue employee, or sometimes even a rogue partner, to engage in fraudulent activity under the noses of his or her colleagues, but without their knowledge. In order for individual solicitors in the firm (or the entity itself – see below) to be liable in conduct, there must be some culpable failure by them, most typically a failure of supervision. However, in order to succeed with such a prosecution, the SRA must be able to point to something concrete that the respondent solicitor (or the entity) did that ought not to have been done, or failed to do that ought to have been done. If this cannot be proved to the criminal standard, the prosecution will fail.[1] Sadly, no system of oversight or supervision will always be proof against a determined and resourceful fraudster.

1 See *Bass and Ward v SRA* [2012] EWHC 2012 (Admin), especially at [24], and *Wilson and Carroll*, 10767–2011, SDT.

Prosecuting entities

20.11

From the point at which it became possible to practise through a corporate structure as a recognised body in 1986,[1] the Law Society as regulator has been able to exercise direct control over the business entity. Disciplinary action could be taken against the recognised body by the revocation of recognition and applications could be made to the Tribunal for disciplinary sanctions, but in practice these powers were not used. Between 1986 and 31 March 2009, only two applications were made to the Tribunal against such a body as a respondent.[2] In both cases the company was a respondent to proceedings which were primarily directed at individuals, and in one of those two cases the Tribunal accepted a submission that any sanction on the company would simply be a second sanction against the individual who owned it, for the same offence, and declined to impose any separate sanction.[3]

The growth of entity regulation since 2009 means that there will be a dramatic increase in the number of entities (as opposed to individual solicitors) prosecuted before the Tribunal, and this has already started to happen. There is as yet no published policy by the SRA as to when it will consider it appropriate to prosecute an entity as well as, or instead of, individual solicitors, but it is understood to be the 'official position' of the SRA in terms of policy that entity regulation should primarily involve 'supervision', with 'enforcement' being deployed only in two circumstances: (a) where there has been a serious failure of management – something fundamentally attributable to the way that the firm is being run; or (b) where on a problem being identified the firm is unwilling or unable to work with the SRA to put things right. It is submitted that such an approach is sensible, and that the Tribunal is most unlikely to welcome any approach which simply substitutes the entity for the individual solicitor, save where there is true strict liability. A professional, whether human or corporate, should only be found guilty of professional misconduct where there has been genuine culpability by that person or body.

1 Section 9 of and Schedule 2 to AJA 1985.
2 *Atikpakpa and others*, 8913–2004, SDT and *Le Moine and others*, 9048–2004, SDT.
3 *Le Moine and others*, 9048–2004, SDT.

The Tribunal's pre-trial procedures

Certification of a case to answer

20.12

When the rule 5 statement and supporting documents are filed with the Tribunal, the papers are considered by a solicitor member of the Tribunal, who certifies whether a 'case to answer' is made out against the respondent.[1] If no such case is revealed, the papers are considered by another solicitor member and a lay member, and, if all agree, the case will be dismissed without hearing any party. Under the 1994 Rules, the Tribunal could invite representations from the parties at this stage, but if they were received uninvited they were unlikely to be entertained. The 2007 Rules contain no comparable provision.

The removal of the 1994 provision has deprived the Tribunal of an opportunity in an appropriate case to obtain assistance which could be valuable in clarifying the case and narrowing issues. The respondent solicitor is not invited to make any representations as to why the Tribunal should not certify a prima facie case – indeed the solicitor will not even know that this process is taking place. No reasons are given for the Tribunal's decision to certify, and indeed the affected solicitor is not even informed when and by whom this certification has been provided.

1 See generally rule 6 of the 2007 Rules.

Standard Directions

20.13

Before October 2013, pre-trial procedures were governed by the 2007 Rules, and ad hoc arrangements made between the legal representatives for the parties. There were serious drawbacks in these procedures. In particular, there was no provision in the Rules for the defence case to be properly pleaded or set out for the benefit of the Tribunal unless the respondent chose to serve a defence case statement or detailed witness statement in answer to the allegations in the rule 5 statement. There is no specific obligation in the 2007 Rules upon the respondent to provide a defence case statement, and respondents often failed to serve a witness statement until the last moment or even at all. A second major problem was that as time has gone by, the financial means of the respondent have become steadily more relevant to the amount of any fine or costs ordered, yet there was no provision in the Rules which required the respondent to provide proper particulars of his or her means in sufficiently good time to enable the SRA to investigate the assertions made by or on behalf of the respondent.

These and other deficiencies were addressed in a Practice Direction (No. 6) issued by the Tribunal in October 2013 entitled 'Practice Direction on Case Management for First Instance Proceedings'. This document is set out in full at **APPENDIX 12**, and the following important provisions should be noted:

- Where there is a time estimate of two days or more, the SDT will convene a case management hearing.
- The respondent must file an answer to the application stating which allegations are admitted and which denied – the result, hopefully, will be that the Tribunal will have a properly pleaded defence case statement when it comes to hear the case, with the result that the real issues between the parties will be clearer.
- The respondent must file and serve all documents upon which he or she intends to rely at the substantive hearing.
- The Tribunal can draw appropriate inferences from a party's failure to comply with the Standard Directions and can make appropriate costs orders in respect of such failures.
- The parties are directed to serve certificates of readiness not less than 28 days before the substantive hearing.
- If the respondent wishes his or her means to be taken into consideration by the Tribunal in relation to possible sanction and/or costs, that respondent must file and serve a statement of means not less than 28 days before the substantive hearing. Failure to do so may result in the Tribunal drawing adverse inferences.
- There is also a timetable (not less than five days) for the service of schedules of costs by those parties who are seeking an award of costs against the other at a particular hearing.

Four copies will be required of any document filed with the Tribunal – one for each of the members and one for the clerk.

Witness statements and defence material

20.14

No witness may be called to give evidence unless a witness statement or proof of evidence is provided to the Tribunal and the other parties at least ten days in advance of the hearing.[1] In the case of the respondent him- or herself it has usually been accepted that the representations made to the SRA at the investigation stage can stand as his or her evidence.

The respondent has the option whether or not to give evidence, although it is unusual for him or her to elect not to do so in a contested case, particularly now in the light of the SDT's Practice Direction No. 5, 'Inference To Be Drawn Where Respondent Does Not Give Evidence' – see **APPENDIX 12**.

It is common to produce, without undue formality, bundles of testimonials as to the respondent's good character. This can be by way of pure mitigation but can also be directly relevant to issues of honesty and integrity. Such evidence is relevant and admissible where the disciplinary allegations brought against the solicitor impugn his or her honesty.[2]

1 Rule 11(1), (2) and (4) of the 2007 Rules.
2 *Donkin v Law Society* [2007] EWHC 414 (Admin) and *Bryant and Bench v Law Society* [2007] EWHC 3043 (Admin).

Public hearings

20.15

The 2007 Rules provide that hearings should be held in public but that a party, or any person affected by the application, may seek an order from the Tribunal that all or part of the hearing be conducted in private on the grounds of exceptional hardship or exceptional prejudice.[1] Applications have been granted for the purposes of protecting members of the public (such as former clients of the respondent) but not for the protection of the respondent from the consequences of publicity.[2] In any event, the usual practice in the Tribunal is to refer to clients only by their initials.

In *L v Law Society* (a case concerned with an appeal against a decision of the SRA to revoke student membership, but which canvassed wider issues concerning public and private hearings), the Master of the Rolls emphasised the importance of public hearings in the Tribunal in maintaining the confidence of the public in the disciplinary process.[3]

1 Rules 11(5) and 12(4) to (6) of the 2007 Rules.
2 Though in one case, which did not in fact proceed to a final hearing for the same reason, a hearing in private was contemplated where medical and psychiatric evidence showed that there was a serious and credible risk of the respondent self-harming to the extent that his life might have been threatened if the hearing took place in public.
3 [2008] EWCA Civ 811 at [41].

Adjournments

20.16

The Tribunal has published a practice note on the subject of adjournments (see **Appendix 12**). It is generally not prepared to adjourn the disciplinary proceedings pending completion of a criminal investigation or prosecution.[1] The same applies in relation to civil proceedings.[2] The only exception is where there is a risk of 'muddying the waters of justice' but in practice this is usually either an illusory or a manageable risk.

1 *R v Solicitors Disciplinary Tribunal, ex p Gallagher* (1991, unreported).
2 *Lipman Bray v Hillhouse and Jacob* [1987] NLJR 171, CA.

Disputed facts and hearsay evidence

20.17

Not less than 28 days before the date of the hearing, the applicant may require the respondent to indicate within 14 days which of the facts set out in the rule 5 statement are in dispute. This is invariably done in a standard form letter at an early stage. There is no sanction for any failure to co-operate in this way (other than in costs).

The absence of co-operation will usually mean that the applicant will serve notices to admit documents under the Civil Evidence Act 1995, and witness statements if required, so that in the absence of a constructive response the case can be proved on documents without the attendance of witnesses.

It is likely that these provisions will need to be used less often than hitherto, in the light of the Standard Directions described above.

The nature of legal practice means that normally the case against the solicitor is wholly documented. The primary evidence against the respondent in most cases is likely to be the content of his or her own files. Serious disputes of fact as to the prosecution case are comparatively rare, and often it is unnecessary for the applicant to call any oral evidence. The outcome of the case will usually depend upon the respondent's evidence.

As for hearsay evidence, rule 13 of the 2007 Rules imports the hearsay provisions in the Civil Evidence Act 1995 into disciplinary proceedings before the Tribunal.[1]

1 See also *R (Bonhoeffer) v General Medical Council* [2011] EWHC 1585 (Admin).

Witness summonses

20.18

Either party may compel the attendance of witnesses and the production by witnesses of documents by means of witness summonses.[1] Although a form of subpoena is contained in the Rules, witness summonses are issued not by the Tribunal itself but by the Administrative Court under CPR rule 34.4 and the form must be compliant with the Civil Procedure Rules 1998.

The 2007 Rules as drafted also implied that an application may be made to the Tribunal to set aside any witness summons. The reference in the form to the Tribunal should be a reference to the court. This has now been corrected.[2]

1 Section 46(11) of SA 1974.
2 Form 5 in the Schedule to the 2007 Rules.

Absence of the respondent

20.19

The Tribunal may proceed in the absence of the respondent upon proof of service of the notice of hearing.[1] This regularly occurs. Where a respondent was neither present nor represented, and the Tribunal decided the case in his absence, he may apply for a re-hearing within 14 days of the filing of the order (in practice therefore within 14 days of the hearing) – which the Tribunal may grant upon such terms as it thinks fit.[2] A solicitor who voluntarily absents himself from the hearing will ordinarily, however, receive little sympathy from the Tribunal, and is unlikely to obtain a re-hearing. In *R (Elliott) v Solicitors Disciplinary Tribunal*,[3] the applicant applied for an adjournment of the substantive hearing, and then walked out when the adjournment was refused. The Tribunal heard the remainder of the case in his absence, and subsequently refused an application for a re-hearing. It was held in judicial review proceedings that the rule (then rule 25 of the 1994 Rules) did not apply to such a situation.

1 Rule 16(2) of the 2007 Rules.
2 Rule 19(1) of the 2007 Rules.
3 [2004] EWHC 1176 (Admin). See also *Gurpinar v SRA* [2012] EWHC 192 (Admin).

Findings of another court or tribunal

20.20

Findings of fact by another court or tribunal are admissible as prima facie proof of those facts. Accordingly, civil judgments relevant to issues before the Tribunal can be admitted into evidence but may be rebutted. The Tribunal is free to depart from findings in civil proceedings and has done so in several cases,[1] although it will be slow to do so.[2] The situation in relation to criminal convictions is otherwise: it has been held that the Tribunal was right to refuse to hear evidence intended to show a wrongful conviction, as public policy required that, save in exceptional circumstances, a challenge to a criminal conviction should not be entertained by a disciplinary tribunal.[3] Rule 15 of the 2007 Rules makes more explicit provision as to these matters than did rule 30 of the 1994 Rules: findings of fact upon which a criminal conviction was based are admissible as conclusive proof of those facts save in exceptional circumstances, whereas a civil court judgment is admissible as proof but not conclusive proof of the findings of fact upon which the judgment was based.

As for views formed by a judge in earlier proceedings, in *Constantinides v Law Society*,[4] Moses LJ stated at [28]–[33]:

> '[28] … The judgment was admissible to prove background facts in the context of which the appellant's misconduct had to be considered. But that was the limit of its function, in the particular circumstances of this case. The judge's views as to the appellant's dishonesty and lack of integrity were not admissible to prove the Law Society's case against this appellant in these disciplinary proceedings …
>
> [33] We ought, however, to record that we do not see why it was necessary to refer to the judgment at all. The background facts were not in dispute. Provided they were clearly set out within the Rule 4 statement there was no need to rely upon it save in so far as it emerged that the appellant disputed those primary facts. However, the Rule 4 statement was itself a mixture of assertion of fact and argument. We would suggest that had a simple account of the facts been set out with a reference to relevant paragraphs in the judgment there would have been no further need to refer to it.'

1 See *Gold*, 6050–1991, SDT; *Brebner*, 8805–2003, SDT; *Slater*, 9619–2006, SDT; and, for the general approach, *Choudry v Law Society* [2001] EWHC Admin 633.
2 See *General Medical Council v Spackman* [1943] AC 627, HL.
3 *Re a Solicitor, Times*, 18 March 1996.
4 [2006] EWHC 725 (Admin).

Power to regulate its own procedure

20.21

Rule 21(1) and (2) of the 2007 Rules confer the all-important powers on the Tribunal to regulate its own procedure subject to the Rules, and to dispense with any requirements of the Rules in respect of notices, statements, witnesses, service or time in any case where it appears to be just to do so. At the discretion of the Tribunal, the strict rules of evidence do not apply.[1]

1 Rule 13(10) of the 2007 Rules.

Interlocutory orders

20.22

Because it can regulate its own procedure, although there is no specific provision in the Rules for interlocutory processes the Tribunal will entertain applications for interlocutory relief, such as disclosure or further particularisation, and will direct the exchange of skeleton arguments in appropriate circumstances. There is a practice direction on the position of the Tribunal on disclosure of documents: see **APPENDIX 12**.

There is no statutory appeal against an interlocutory order of the Tribunal, and the only avenue of challenge is therefore an application for judicial review. In *Stokes v Law Society*,[1] Kennedy LJ observed that relief would be given only in exceptional circumstances 'and never where, as here, the error relied upon has been rectified'.

1 [2001] EWHC Admin 1101.

Abuse of process

20.23

The Tribunal may strike out proceedings if it considers that the prosecution amounts to an abuse of process. In the criminal courts, it has long been held that applications to stay proceedings for abuse of process should only rarely be granted, and that the threshold to be surmounted by the applicant is a high one.[1] The Tribunal takes a similar approach, and successful abuse of process applications are rare.

One particular area in which such applications have succeeded is where there has been inordinate delay in bringing the case before the Tribunal.[2] This may amount to an abuse of process on a traditional common law analysis, or it may breach the 'reasonable time' requirement in Article 6(1) of the European Convention on Human Rights. The Tribunal has held that time starts for this purpose when the decision to refer the solicitor to the Tribunal is made, and has struck out cases which have been inordinately delayed thereafter.[3]

The Tribunal has ruled that proceedings should generally be issued within three months of the decision to refer a respondent to the Tribunal, and that if necessary an application for further time (if needed before the matter was listed for hearing) could be considered by the Tribunal.[4]

1 The leading cases are *Connelly v DPP* [1964] AC 1254, HL; *DPP v Humphrys* [1977] AC 1, HL; *R v Horseferry Road Magistrates' Court, ex p Bennett* [1994] 1 AC 42, HL; and *R v Maxwell* [2011] 1 WLR 1837.

2 For the general approach of the courts, see *Attorney-General's Reference (No 2 of 2001)* [2004] 2 AC 72; *Porter v Magill* [2002] 2 AC 357; and *Dyer v Watson* [2004] 1 AC 379.

3 See generally *Loomba and Loomba*, 9022–2004, SDT; *Davis*, 9017–2004, SDT; *Judge and Stanger*, 9028–2004, SDT; *Rutherford*, 9074–2004, SDT; *Fallon*, 9154–2004, SDT and *Sancheti and others*, 7976–2007, SDT.

4 *Nulty and Trotter*, 9871–2008, SDT – memorandum of preliminary hearing, 1 July 2008.

Summary disposal

20.24

If the respondent considers that there is a fatal flaw in the applicant's case against him, the Tribunal may be willing to consider that as a preliminary issue with a view to saving time and expense. Accordingly, cases can be disposed of summarily at the start of the substantive hearing, and there would seem to be no reason in principle in an appropriate case why the respondent should not seek an early listing of the case to ascertain whether it can be summarily disposed of in this way.[1] It must be accepted that these situations are likely to be rare.

1 *Law Society v Adcock and Mocroft* [2006] EWHC 3212 (Admin) at [30].

Withdrawal of allegations

20.25

By rule 11(4)(a) of the 2007 Rules, the Tribunal must give its consent to the withdrawal of an allegation where it has certified a case to answer under rule 6. The Tribunal will often be resistant to giving that consent, because it has earlier certified a prima facie case on the papers, and it has often enquired of the SRA advocate what has changed to justify withdrawal. Such an approach contrasts not only with the role of the court in criminal proceedings, but also with that of other courts or tribunals in proceedings that are similar to disciplinary proceedings: ordinarily, such courts and tribunals are discouraged from insisting that particular charges, allegations or issues be tried where the parties have agreed that they need not be tried: see e.g. *Secretary of State for Trade and Industry v Rogers*[1] in the context of directors' disqualification proceedings.

1 [1996] 1 WLR 1569, CA.

Pre-trial procedure – what happens in practice

20.26

Following a decision to refer a solicitor to the Tribunal the solicitor will receive, after an interval, confirmation that the papers have been referred to an external panel solicitor or to an in-house advocate. On the assumption that the Tribunal determines that there is a case to answer, the next development will be service of the papers. It is not unusual for there to be a delay of several months before proceedings are issued.

Service is arranged by the Tribunal by special delivery mail. It is possible to inform the applicant in advance that papers can be served on a nominated representative. The documents served will include the rule 5 statement and any documents annexed or exhibited to it, a full set of the current Solicitors (Disciplinary Proceedings) Rules, copies of the Tribunal's published practice directions, a list of those most regularly appearing in the Tribunal as advocates, and details of the Solicitors' Assistance Scheme.

20.27

The Tribunal generally sits between two and three days a week, in addition to any court time needed for multi-day cases, and has four courtrooms so that long cases can be accommodated in one court while routine matters occupy the other courts in greater numbers. A typical list of routine matters will have three to five applications listed for hearing. Because the Tribunal members pre-read the papers and most cases are well documented (see above), even quite substantial contests can be disposed of in less than a day.

The Tribunal expects the parties to have a sensible dialogue to refine issues and avoid unnecessary contention. The overwhelming majority of cases proceed on the basis of admissions and mitigation, or on the basis of admitted facts with argument limited to the proper interpretation of those facts and the inferences that it is proper to draw. In cases which are likely to last two days or more, there will be a case management hearing. Only infrequently, in very substantial or complex cases, is there any need to consider other interlocutory applications. For example, even if there is a perceived need for the applicant to clarify the case the respondent has to meet, one would expect that clarification to be volunteered without the need for any formal intervention by the Tribunal.

Pre-trial publication of disciplinary allegations

20.28

After the Tribunal has certified a prima facie case, the SRA may publish on its website details of the allegations against the affected solicitor. The SRA's written publication policy is reproduced in **APPENDIX 9**. In paragraph 5 of the policy document, the following passage appears:

> 'bringing a case before the SDT, once a case has been certified, will lead to a public hearing, and controls, such as practising certificate conditions are already publicly available to telephone enquirers. Accordingly, whilst each decision in these circumstances will be taken on its own merits, it is expected that decisions will be published unless we consider that one or more of the factors at paragraph 9 below would make such publication inappropriate.'

The legality of the SRA's publication policy was challenged unsuccessfully in *Andersons v SRA*.[1]

1 [2012] EWHC 3659 (Admin).

CHAPTER 21

Proceedings before the SDT: (2) trial, sanctions, costs and appeals

The hearing

21.1

The Solicitors Disciplinary Tribunal ('the Tribunal' or SDT) sits in Gate House, at the south (Ludgate Circus) end of Farringdon Street, London EC4M 7LG. Hearings in the Tribunal are a mixture of the formal and informal; evidence is taken on oath but, as has been seen, the strict rules of evidence do not apply. The parties conduct their advocacy seated. No pleas to the allegations are formally taken. The applicant is expected to have established the position in this respect and will inform the Tribunal which allegations are admitted and which require to be resolved by the Tribunal. The respondent is required to do no more at this stage, hopefully, than give a monosyllabic confirmation.

The applicant will then open the case and call his or her evidence. As has been said, only rarely is it necessary for the applicant to rely on oral evidence, and usually the applicant's case can be presented entirely by reference to documents, including the written explanations and submissions of the respondent at the investigation stage. The one witness most frequently called by applicants will be the investigating officer of the Solicitors Regulation Authority (SRA)'s Forensic Investigation Unit who undertook the original investigation of, for example, the respondent's accounts.

Examination, cross-examination and re-examination of witnesses proceed as normal, following the pattern of the civil courts as to the use of any witness statement as primary evidence-in-chief.

Following the conclusion of the applicant's case the respondent may make a submission of no case to answer,[1] and then will open his or her case, give evidence and call witnesses, and may make a closing submission. In contested cases it tends to be assumed that the respondent will give evidence; in cases where the respondent is accused of and denies dishonesty it would be an exceptional course to fail to do so, and the Tribunal may draw an adverse inference from such a failure.[2] It is not usual for the applicant to make a closing speech, but he or she may do so in a lengthy or complex case where evidence can helpfully be summarised and commented upon. The applicant does not have a right of reply save in relation to points of law or to correct mistakes.[3]

1 The Tribunal has frequently demonstrated a reluctance to accede to such a submission. There is at this stage in a contested application an understandable interest in hearing what the respondent has to say. For an exceptional case in which the Tribunal acceded to such a submission see *Cohen and Others*, 9942–2008, SDT.

2 See *Iqbal v SRA* [2012] EWHC 3251 (Admin) and SDT Practice Direction (No. 5) at **APPENDIX 12**.

3 This should be taken to reflect current practice; there is no formal rule as to this.

Standard of proof

21.2

It has been held by the Privy Council that the standard of proof in deciding facts against a respondent solicitor in disciplinary proceedings should be the criminal standard, irrespective of whether dishonesty is alleged.[1] The SRA is resistant to application of the criminal standard, and in *Richards v Law Society*[2] sought to argue for the civil standard: the Divisional Court held that on the particular facts of the case, the issue was academic, but strongly implied that the Tribunal was bound to apply the criminal standard unless and until the Supreme Court ruled otherwise.[3]

1 *Campbell v Hamlet* [2005] UKPC 19, [2005] 3 All ER 1116, interpreting *Re a Solicitor* [1993] QB 69. The adoption of the criminal standard is of long standing, is supported by high authority, and mirrors the practice in disciplinary proceedings against barristers. The Tribunal has regularly asserted that it will consistently employ the criminal standard, see e.g. *Beresford and Smith*, 9666–2007, SDT (a case in which the SRA sought to argue the contrary), and has ruled that this should also be applied in cases involving orders against employees of solicitors; see *Ahmed*, 8645–2002, SDT.

2 [2009] EWHC 2087 (Admin). The case was remarkable, in that the two component parts of the Law Society (SRA and representative body) argued on opposite sides for opposite conclusions.

3 [2009] EWHC 2087 (Admin) at [22]. See also *Law Society v Waddingham and others* [2012] EWHC 1519 (Admin), in which the SRA appealed against a finding by the Tribunal that it was not satisfied that dishonesty had been proved against two of the respondents: the High Court dismissed the appeal specifically on the basis that dishonesty had not been established to the criminal standard (at [60]).

Decision, mitigation and penalty

21.3

The Tribunal invariably announces its findings, together with brief reasons, at the conclusion of the hearing. If it finds any of the allegations against the respondent substantiated, the Chairman asks the Tribunal clerk whether there have been previous findings against the respondent. The respondent is permitted to make a plea in mitigation (possibly at this stage adducing testimonials as to character) and the Tribunal then determines penalty.[1] If the Tribunal decides to suspend a solicitor, it may be prepared to delay the start of that suspension to enable the solicitor to make appropriate arrangements for running his practice during the period of suspension. The Tribunal is noticeably more reluctant to delay the effect of a striking-off order although this does occasionally happen.[2] Respondents seeking a stay pending appeal must, if the Tribunal does not grant a stay, appeal and apply to the Administrative Court for a stay pending a hearing of the substantive appeal. The appeal does not operate as a stay. For further guidance on appeals, see **21.32** to **21.37**.

The written judgment of the Tribunal is ordinarily delivered some weeks after the hearing. In *Virdi v Law Society*[3] a full-scale attack was made on the Tribunal's process for production of the findings, on the basis that the clerk had a role in producing a first draft of the document based, inter alia, on the oral findings and reasons given by the Chairman at the conclusion of the hearing. Although the (exceptional) delay in producing the findings in that case was the subject of criticism, the process was held to be entirely proper by both the Divisional Court and the Court of Appeal.

1 This summary of the current practice is now enshrined in rule 16 of the Solicitors (Disciplinary Proceedings) Rules 2007 ('the 2007 Rules').

2 *Aaronson*, 10099–2008, SDT.

3 [2009] EWHC 918 (Admin) (Divisional Court); [2010] EWCA Civ 100 (Court of Appeal).

The range of penalties available to the Tribunal and Tribunal guidance

21.4

From the 'bottom' upwards, the Tribunal may:

- make no order – this course is followed when the Tribunal considers that it would be unfair or disproportionate to impose a sanction. It may nevertheless decide to make an order for costs against the respondent solicitor;
- impose a reprimand;
- impose restrictions upon practice;
- impose an unlimited fine;
- suspend, either for a fixed period or indefinitely;
- strike off.

21.5

Until the summer of 2012, the Tribunal provided no published guidance to the profession or the public as to how it exercised its disciplinary powers. This was the subject of criticism by Nicola Davies J in *Hazelhurst v SRA*[1] in which she said (at [38]):

> 'It is of note that the SDT has not published Indicative Sanctions Guidance. Such guidance identifies the purpose, parameters and range of sanctions. It permits those who appear before it to better understand the proceedings and the thinking of the SDT. It assists the transparency of the proceedings. Such guidance has been used by other regulatory bodies for some years and is a valuable reference point both for the tribunal and for those who appear in front of it, as practitioners or advocates.'

Following this criticism, a Guidance Note was issued by the Tribunal in late August 2012 and amended in September 2013. It is set out in full in **APPENDIX 14**. For the first time, it brought together in one document the Tribunal's principles, procedure and policies in imposing sanctions.

1 [2011] EWHC 462 (Admin).

The general approach – Bolton v Law Society

21.6

In *Bolton v Law Society*,[1] the Master of the Rolls, Sir Thomas Bingham, made a general and oft-cited statement of the rationale for and purpose of punishment by the Tribunal. It merits citation here, as it provides the logical cornerstone for much of what both the Tribunal and appellate courts decide:

> 'It is required of lawyers practising in this country that they should discharge their professional duties with integrity, probity and complete trustworthiness …

> Any solicitor who is shown to have discharged his professional duties with anything less than complete integrity, probity and trustworthiness must expect severe sanctions to be imposed upon him by the Solicitors Disciplinary Tribunal. Lapses from the required high standard may, of course, take different forms and be of varying degrees. The most serious involves proven dishonesty, whether or not leading to criminal proceedings and criminal penalties. In such cases the tribunal has almost invariably, no matter how strong the mitigation advanced for the solicitor, ordered that he be struck off the Roll of Solicitors ... If a solicitor is not shown to have acted dishonestly, but is shown to have fallen below the required standards of integrity, probity and trustworthiness, his lapse is less serious but it remains very serious indeed in a member of a profession whose reputation depends upon trust. A striking off order will not necessarily follow in such a case, but it may well. The decision whether to strike off or to suspend will often involve a fine and difficult exercise of judgment, to be made by the tribunal as an informed and expert body on all the facts of the case. Only in a very unusual and venial case of this kind would the tribunal be likely to regard as appropriate any order less severe than one of suspension.'

The Master of the Rolls explained in addition to the need to punish in appropriate cases, there was an additional purpose in imposing sanctions, and that this was:

> 'the most fundamental of all: to maintain the reputation of the solicitors' profession as one in which every member, of whatever standing, may be trusted to the ends of the earth. To maintain this reputation and sustain public confidence in the integrity of the profession it is often necessary that those guilty of serious lapses are not only expelled but denied re-admission. If a member of the public sells his house, very often his largest asset, and entrusts the proceeds to his solicitor, pending re-investment in another house, he is ordinarily entitled to expect that the solicitor will be a person whose trustworthiness is not, and never has been, seriously in question. Otherwise, the whole profession, and the public as a whole, is injured. A profession's most valuable asset is its collective reputation and the confidence which that inspires.'

1 [1994] 1 WLR 512, CA.

Reprimands

21.7

Although it has no express statutory power to do so, the Tribunal frequently issues a reprimand to a solicitor. It has also censured a solicitor, stating that this was a more serious order than a reprimand and has directed a solicitor to pay counsels' fees (thereby making an unenforceable obligation enforceable as a High Court order).[1]

1 *Prince*, 6578–1994, SDT, unsuccessfully appealed as *Re a Solicitor*, CO 1324–1995. See also section 48(4) of Solicitors Act (SA) 1974.

Practising restrictions

21.8

The Tribunal has no power itself to impose conditions on a practising certificate when imposing a penalty upon a solicitor, but can make recommendations to the SRA and, because it can make 'such order as it may think fit', it can also make orders requiring a solicitor not to practise in particular ways, for example as a sole practitioner.

In *Camacho v Law Society*,[1] the Tribunal had ordered the indefinite suspension of a solicitor. On the solicitor's appeal, the Divisional Court substituted a finite period of suspension but identified five conditions which it considered should be imposed in relation to the way in which the solicitor might practise. The court held that the terms of section 47(2) of SA 1974 were sufficiently wide to give the Tribunal itself power to impose restrictions on the manner in which a solicitor might practise, and that if the Tribunal considered that a period of complete suspension followed by a period of restricted practice was the appropriate sanction to protect the public, that was part of the decision it had made and – unless there were exceptional reasons – it should be for the Tribunal to make that order, rather than to make recommendations to the SRA as had been the former practice.

Where the Tribunal makes such an order for an indefinite period it should grant liberty to apply, as there is otherwise no mechanism for a solicitor subject to such an order to apply for it to be varied or reviewed.[2]

The Tribunal has on one occasion refined this approach by imposing a suspension from practice for one year, but suspending that order for so long as the solicitor practised only (in substance) in employment expressly approved by the SRA without access to clients' money. The Tribunal gave guidance as to the circumstances in which an application might be made to the Tribunal to vary or revoke the terms of the restriction.[3]

Restriction orders are only made when considered necessary to protect the public or the reputation of the profession – they have no punitive function.[4] Inevitably, when the Tribunal makes such orders the SRA can be expected to impose matching or more restrictive practising certificate conditions.

1 [2004] EWHC 1675 (Admin), [2004] 1 WLR 3037. See too *Ebhogiaye v SRA* [2013] EWHC 2445 (Admin).
2 *Taylor v Law Society* [2005] EWCA Civ 1473. The formula substituted on appeal to the Master of the Rolls in *Taylor* was: 'In the future the petitioner may not practise as a sole practitioner but only in employment or partnership. When employed he must not operate a client account. The petitioner to have liberty to apply to the Tribunal to vary these conditions'.
3 *Bajela and Fonkwo*, 9543–2006, SDT.
4 See SDT Guidance Note, para 27.

Fines

21.9

Since March 2009, there is no statutory limit on the amount of the fine (until then it was £5,000 per allegation). Fines are payable to the Treasury, which is responsible for enforcing payment.

The level of fines imposed by the Tribunal is fairly modest. It is unusual for a fine to exceed £20,000: the vast majority fall below that level. The highest individual fine yet imposed is the £50,000 ordered in the case of *Fuglers v SRA*[1] upon the firm with the two respondent partners being fined £20,000 and £5,000.

This general approach of the Tribunal to the level of fines was supported by the High Court in *SRA v Andersons and others*.[2] For the first time the SRA launched an appeal simply to obtain an increase in the fines imposed by the Tribunal. Although the High Court did order an increase in the fines (from £1,000 upon each of the human respondents to £15,000 in one case and £5,000 in the others), these increases fell far below the figures contended for by the SRA. It would seem therefore, that the general approach of the Tribunal is unlikely to change, unless, for instance, the Tribunal was satisfied that a solicitor had deliberately breached the rules in order to make a substantial profit. In such a case, it would be open to the Tribunal to impose a very substantial fine.

As in the criminal courts, the financial circumstances of the respondent are highly relevant to the decision whether or not to impose a fine. This was made clear in *D'Souza v Law Society*,[3] in which apparent account had been taken of the admittedly parlous circumstances of Mr D'Souza, who had been ordered to pay a fine of £1,500 and costs in the order of £8,000. The total was reduced on appeal from £9,500 to £2,000; £500 by way of fine and £1,500 for costs.[4]

The Standard Directions issued by the Tribunal in October 2013 provide a mechanism by which the respondent's means can be disclosed to the SRA and the Tribunal, so that proper enquiries can be made in advance of the hearing.

In imposing a financial penalty, the Tribunal should consider the respondent's overall financial liability for the fine and costs. In *Matthews v SRA*,[5] Collins J reduced a fine of £5,000 and costs of £16,000 to an overall liability of £5,000 on account of the appellant's limited means. The costs, which made up £4,500 of this sum, were not to be enforced without leave of the Tribunal.

1 [2014] EWHC 179 (Admin).
2 [2013] EWHC 4021 (Admin).
3 [2009] EWHC 2193 (Admin).
4 See also *Tinkler and others v SRA* [2012] EWHC 3645 (Admin) and the Guidance Note on Sanctions under the heading 'Level of Fine' at **APPENDIX 14**. The respondent's means may also be highly relevant to the correct costs order and this is discussed below at **21.29**.
5 [2013] EWHC 1525 (Admin).

Suspensions

21.10

Suspensions may be for a fixed term or for an indefinite period. The effect of a suspension for a solicitor will vary according to the size of the practice. For a middle-aged sole practitioner, suspension may in reality be equivalent to a striking off, as it may prove impossible for the solicitor to arrange cover during the period of the suspension, and/or the solicitor may face insurmountable practising certificate conditions when he or she returns to practice. For a solicitor working in a large firm, whose partners/employers have not dismissed him or her, the effect of a short suspension may be little more than an inconvenience.

Indefinite suspensions are usually imposed where there is a medical explanation for the solicitor's misconduct, or where there is truly exceptional personal mitigation. Such suspensions come within a whisker of a striking off, but the Tribunal may consider that there is a real prospect of successful rehabilitation, thus meriting an order which will not make it impossible for the solicitor to resume practice.[1]

Suspensions are normally imposed for one year or more. Where they are for a period of months (or less) it is important to note that the expiry of the suspension does not enable an automatic return to practice. The solicitor's practising certificate is not automatically restored; rather it remains suspended until the SRA terminates the suspension on the application of the solicitor (although an application may be made before the suspension expires, so minimising the consequences).[2] The termination of the suspension may be accompanied by the imposition of conditions on the practising certificate[3] and almost certainly will.

Suspensions may themselves be suspended, when accompanied by a Restriction Order.[4]

1 See para 36 of the SDT Guidance Note.
2 Section 16(3) of SA 1974.
3 Section 16(4).
4 See para 33 of the SDT Guidance Note.

Striking off and restoration to the roll

21.11

A struck off solicitor can no longer describe him- or herself as a solicitor, and to do so may be a criminal offence under section 20 and/or section 21 of SA 1974. An unqualified person, as the struck off solicitor becomes, may not perform those activities which only a qualified solicitor may perform, in particular the reserved legal activities set out in the Legal Services Act (LSA) 2007. A struck off solicitor may not be employed by a solicitor without the prior consent of the SRA.[1]

1 See section 41 of SA 1974.

21.12

The Tribunal has a statutory power under section 47(1)(e) of SA 1974 to restore struck off solicitors to the roll. However, the guidance provided by the Court of Appeal in *Bolton v Law Society*[1] as to the purposes of imposing disciplinary sanctions and summarised at **21.6** above, applies to applications to restore to the roll:

> 'the most fundamental [purpose] of all: to maintain the reputation of the solicitors' profession as one in which every member, of whatever standing, may be trusted to the ends of the earth. To maintain this reputation and sustain public confidence in the integrity of the profession it is often necessary that those guilty of serious lapses are not only expelled but denied re-admission.'

1 [1994] 1 WLR 512, CA at 518.

21.13

As a result, it has hitherto proved all but impossible for former solicitors who have been struck off for disciplinary offences involving dishonesty, to persuade the Tribunal to permit restoration to the roll. The former Master of the Rolls, Lord Donaldson of Lymington said in one case:[1]

> 'however sympathetic one may be towards an individual member of either branch of the legal profession, if you fall very seriously below the standards of that profession and are expelled from it, there is a public interest in the profession itself in hardening its heart if any question arises of your rejoining it. Neither branch of the profession is short of people who have never fallen from grace. There is considerable public interest in the public as a whole being able to deal with members of those professions knowing that, save in the most exceptional circumstances, they can be sure that none of them have ever been guilty of any dishonesty at all.'

In his final decision as Master of the Rolls, Lord Donaldson went further, and wondered whether Parliament had ever contemplated that a solicitor who had been guilty of fraud could be restored to the roll, although he continued:[2]

> 'It may be that in a very exceptional case it did – something which really could be described as a momentary aberration under quite exceptional strain, the sort of strain which not everybody meets but some people do meet in the course of their everyday lives.'

To date in the modern era (that is for some three decades at least), only one solicitor who has been struck off for dishonesty has successfully applied for restoration to the roll.[3]

1 No 5 of 1987, unreported.
2 No 11 of 1990, unreported.
3 *Vane*, 8607–2002, SDT. For an example of a case in which the SRA appealed successfully against the SDT's decision to restore to the roll a solicitor who had been convicted of offences involving dishonesty, see *SRA v Kaberry* [2012] EWHC 3883 (Admin).

21.14

A former solicitor who has been struck off for less serious disciplinary offences, not involving dishonesty, may be more fortunate. In order to contemplate making an order of restoration, the Tribunal will need to be satisfied first that the former solicitor has demonstrated his or her complete rehabilitation, and secondly that restoration to the roll would not involve any damage to the reputation of the profession. Lord Donaldson encouraged the Tribunal to ask:[1]

> 'If this was the sort of case where, even if the back history was known (that is whatever explanation and mitigation was available to explain why the solicitor committed the original offence), and without the explanation as to what has happened subsequently, the members of the public would say "that does not shake my faith in solicitors as a whole".'

These hurdles, particularly the second, remain very difficult to surmount. Even if they are overcome, it is unlikely that the Tribunal, or the SRA, would contemplate permitting the solicitor, once restored to the roll, to practise without any form of restriction upon his or her practising certificate. Moreover, save in the most exceptional circumstances, an application for restoration to the roll within six years of the original striking off is likely to be regarded by the Tribunal as premature.[2]

1 No 11 of 1990, unreported.
2 See para 52 of the SDT Guidance Note.

Penalties – the approach in practice

21.15

Cases before the Tribunal vary infinitely and no analytical consideration of particular facts, individual cases or individual penalties is of material assistance. There are, however, some general principles and typical classes of case that can usefully be considered.

The Tribunal adopts the procedure used in the criminal courts when the solicitor makes admissions but there is a dispute between the parties as to the facts upon which the admissions are based. In such cases, the Tribunal will hold a *Newton* hearing.[1] Often, the Tribunal does not differentiate between individual allegations when imposing a sanction. This is particularly the case with fines – the Tribunal may impose an overall fine without distinguishing between the allegations as to how the fine is calculated.[2] This may cause difficulties for the High Court on appeal where an appeal is partially successful and the court cannot know how much of the overall fine related to the allegations that have been quashed.

The SDT Guidance Note sets out details of how the Tribunal assesses seriousness, and what may be seen as aggravating and mitigating factors.

1 See *R v Newton* [1983] Crim LR 198, and paras 7 to 10 of the SDT Guidance Note. For an example of the events during a *Newton* hearing being considered on appeal, see *Slater v SRA* [2012] EWHC 3256 (Admin).
2 See paras 11 to 12 of the SDT Guidance Note.

Dishonesty in connection with client account

21.16

Such is the importance of the principle that clients' money must be held separately from a solicitor's own funds, that any dishonest misappropriation of clients' moneys will lead inevitably to a striking-off order, whether or not the misappropriation also amounts to theft. This is now seen as all but automatic.[1] In *Bultitude v Law Society*,[2] the Law Society appealed against the reduction of a striking-off order to a suspension by the Divisional Court. The appeal was allowed by the Court of Appeal, and the court was informed that there was only one known instance of dishonesty in connection with client account that had not resulted in a striking off.

1 See *Bolton v Law Society* [1994] 1 WLR 512, CA; *Weston v Law Society*, *Times*, 15 July 1998.
2 [2004] EWCA Civ 1853.

Other forms of dishonesty

21.17

Historically, a solicitor found guilty of any form of dishonesty could be expected to be struck off, and as a general proposition this undoubtedly remains the position.[1]

Indeed, any solicitor who is dishonestly involved in a mortgage fraud, investment fraud or money laundering will inevitably be struck off. Even without dishonesty, solicitors who become caught up in the criminal activity or dubious commercial practices of others are likely to be struck off or suspended for a considerable period.[2]

Very occasionally, the Tribunal permits a solicitor found guilty of dishonesty to remain on the roll. This may be because in recent times, the SRA has alleged dishonesty in circumstances where the solicitor has not personally profited (other than by way of fee income charged at a reasonable rate) from improper acts which are alleged to have been carried out dishonestly.[3] In such cases, the Tribunal may consider that even if dishonesty or conscious impropriety has been established, the public interest can be served by a period of suspension, and thereafter by regulatory controls such as practising certificate conditions being imposed upon the solicitor. Moreover, in some cases which could reasonably have attracted the label of dishonesty, but where the failing is isolated and plainly out of character, the Tribunal and/or the Divisional Court has on occasion taken a merciful approach,[4] recognising that honest people can do very strange and irrational things in circumstances of acute stress. It should be emphasised, however, that these are exceptional cases, and in *SRA v Sharma*[5] the Divisional Court allowed an appeal by the SRA against a three-year suspension imposed upon a solicitor who had forged documents, and sent them as 'duly signed' under cover of a letter written on his firm's notepaper. The court imposed a striking-off order in place of the suspension, and Coulson J stated (at [13]):

> '(a) Save in exceptional circumstances, a finding of dishonesty will lead to the solicitor being struck off the roll, see *Bolton*[6] and *Salsbury*.[7] That is the normal and necessary penalty in cases of dishonesty: see *Bultitude*.[8]
>
> (b) There will be a small residual category where striking off will be a disproportionate sentence in all the circumstances: see *Salsbury*.
>
> (c) In deciding whether or not a particular case falls into that category, relevant factors will include the nature, scope and extent of the dishonesty itself; whether it was momentary, such as *Burrowes*,[9] or over a lengthy period of time, such as *Bultitude*; whether it was a benefit to the solicitor (*Burrowes*), and whether it had an adverse effect on others.'

And also (at [26]):

> 'The question for this court is whether in the light of the principles outlined above, the Tribunal's decision can be described as excessively lenient. If it can, then this court should substitute for the Tribunal's sentence, the sentence that it considers to be commensurate with these offences. If the sentence cannot be regarded as excessively lenient, even if it is not necessarily the sentence which this court would itself have imposed, the sentence should remain unchanged.'

Similar approaches were taken by the Divisional Court in *SRA v Tilsiter*,[10] in which an indefinite suspension was increased on appeal to a striking-off order, and in *SRA v Dennison*,[11] in which a fine was similarly increased to a striking-off order. In the latter case, the solicitor's appeal to the Court of Appeal failed.[12]

1 *Law Society v Salsbury* [2008] EWCA Civ 1285.
2 See *Bryant and Bench v Law Society* [2007] EWHC 3043 (Admin).
3 *Pitts-Tucker*, 9722–2007, SDT.

4 See *Burrowes v Law Society* and the cases referred to in the judgment: [2002] EWHC 2900 (QB) at [6], [10]–[13], [17] and [20].
5 [2010] EWHC 2022 (Admin).
6 *Bolton v Law Society* [1994] 1 WLR 512, CA.
7 *Law Society v Salsbury* [2008] EWCA Civ 1285.
8 *Bultitude v Law Society* [2004] EWCA Civ 1853.
9 *Burrowes v Law Society* [2002] EWHC 2900 (QB).
10 [2009] EWHC 3787 (Admin).
11 [2011] EWHC 291 (Admin).
12 [2012] EWCA Civ 421. For further examples of successful appeals by the SRA to achieve strikings off, see *SRA v Rahman* [2012] EWHC 1037 (Admin) and *SRA v Spence* [2012] EWHC 2977 (Admin).

Non-dishonest serious misconduct

21.18

It should be stressed that the absence of a finding of dishonesty does not protect a solicitor from a striking-off order. Many solicitors have been struck off in such circumstances, and an appeal mounted on the principal basis that no finding of dishonesty has been made by the Tribunal is unlikely to attract much judicial sympathy. In *Moseley v SRA*,[1] Lewis J stated at [19]:

> 'In my judgment there is no requirement or presumption that, if the conduct is independent of the discharge of professional duties, then it must involve either dishonesty or a serious criminal offence, or that there be exceptional circumstances before striking off is appropriate. Rather, where the conduct complained of is found to involve a lack of integrity and diminishes public trust in the profession it may still, depending on the particular facts, be appropriate to impose the sanction of striking off the roll. Where conduct is dishonest or criminal, it is very likely that that would be the result. But even where conduct is not dishonest or criminal and even if it is unconnected the discharge of professional duties, it may justify striking off where it involves a lack of integrity or results in a diminution in the public trust in the profession.'

1 [2013] EWHC 2108 (Admin); see too *Afolabi v SRA* [2012] EWHC 3502 (Admin) and *Law Society (SRA) v Emeana and others* [2013] EWHC 2130 (Admin).

Breaches of the Solicitors' or SRA Accounts Rules

21.19

Breaches of the Accounts Rules can range from the serious to the trivial. Improper transfers from client accounts to office accounts falling short of dishonesty may merit a striking-off order or suspension, as may a chaotic accounting system which creates risk to clients and to the public. The importance of regular reconciliations and submission of accountants' reports cannot be overestimated, as these are the mechanisms by which problems can be detected at a relatively early stage. Other administrative failings and errors, including failure to carry out reconciliations timeously or to submit accountants' reports at the correct time, if standing alone, are likely to be visited with a fine.

Solicitors providing banking facilities

21.20

Rule 14.5 of the SRA Accounts Rules provides:

> 'You must not provide banking facilities through a client account. Payments into, and transfers or withdrawals from, a client account must be in respect of instructions relating to an underlying transaction (and the funds arising therefrom) or to a service forming part of your normal regulated activities.'

The precise extent of this rule has still to be worked out, but there have been a number of cases in which solicitors who have provided banking facilities to clients have been fined by the Tribunal.[1] In *Patel v SRA*, Moore Bick LJ stated at [42–43]:

> '[Counsel for the Appellant] submitted that the word "or" is to be read disjunctively and that the existence of an underlying transaction of any kind which a solicitor can lawfully undertake, including one that does not form part of a solicitor's normal professional activities, is capable of supporting the use of a client account. The tribunal, he submitted, had erred in conflating the two limbs of rule 14.5 which had led it to hold that there must be an underlying transaction of a legal nature.
>
> In my view that argument states the position too broadly. The primary purpose of maintaining a client account is to segregate funds held for the client from the solicitor's own funds in order to provide the client with a measure of protection. One would therefore expect it to be used to hold funds which have come into the solicitor's hands in relation to services carried out for the client, to be paid out in due course to the client or in accordance with his instructions. Rule 14.5 of the SRA Accounts Rules refers to instructions relating to an underlying transaction or a service forming part of the solicitor's normal regulated activities.'

1 See *Wood and Burdett* 8669–2002; *Patel v SRA* [2012] EWHC 3373 (Admin); and *Fuglers v SRA* [2014] EWHC 179 (Admin).

Culpable or dishonest overcharging

21.21

There is potentially a wide spectrum of 'overcharging' by a solicitor. The reduction of a solicitor/own client bill at a detailed assessment is an everyday experience for solicitors and implies no professional misconduct of any sort. Where such a reduction is very substantial, however, the solicitor may be open to a charge of 'culpable overcharging'. As a rule of thumb, if a bill is reduced by more than 50 per cent on assessment, this may give cause for regulatory concern, and may lead to further investigation (and possible disciplinary proceedings).[1] The concept of culpable overcharging does not incorporate within it any allegation of dishonesty.

At the most serious end of the spectrum is dishonest overcharging, where the solicitor has no honest belief that the sum charged is a reasonable sum for the work done. As with any form of dishonesty, a solicitor found guilty of dishonest overcharging can expect to be struck off.

Unsurprisingly, therefore, penalties imposed by the Tribunal on this subject vary considerably. Particular care may be required in probate cases, where a solicitor may be the sole executor of the estate and there may be no independent scrutiny of his or her charges.[2] In *Sheikh v Law Society*, Chadwick LJ observed that evidence from a costs draftsman with suitable experience as to what he would expect to see in such cases provides a useful starting point in evaluating the issue as to whether there has been not merely culpable but possibly dishonest overcharging, in the sense that significant deviation from the norm may require explanation.[3]

1 This is consistent with article 5(1) of the Solicitors' (Non-Contentious Business) Remuneration Order 1994 (SI 1994/2616), since repealed, which required any costs judge who reduces a solicitor/client non-contentious bill by more than half on detailed assessment to report the matter to the Law Society.
2 See e.g. *Sheikh v Law Society* [2006] EWCA Civ 1577, [2007] 3 All ER 183 at [45].
3 *Sheikh v Law Society* [2006] EWCA Civ 1577, [2007] 3 All ER 183 at [64].

Conflicts of interest

21.22

Actual or potential conflicts of interests may arise in a variety of ways and those of a relatively innocent nature, such as those due to an error of judgement, will merit no more than a fine.[1] Some conflicts are infinitely more serious and involve solicitors deliberately or recklessly preferring their own interests to those of their clients, for example, by obtaining unsecured loans from clients without ensuring that the clients receive independent advice. These are likely to be regarded very seriously and to result in the solicitor being struck off.[2]

1 For example *O'Brien*, 9574–2006, SDT (the 'Freshfields Two' case).
2 Unhappily, there have been very many cases in this category – over 100 in the last ten years. Examples are *Predko*, 7099–1996, SDT and *Austin-Olsen*, 9361–2005, SDT. A recent example is *Beller v Law Society* [2009] EWHC 2200 (Admin).

Payment of referral fees

21.23

As described above (at **4.74**), until 2004, there was an outright ban on the payment of referral fees by solicitors to introducers of work. This proved difficult to enforce, and there were concerns that it might offend competition law. In 2004 the ban was abolished. Instead, the Law Society required that solicitors be transparent about the fact and amount of referral fees in a new section 2A of the Solicitors' Introduction and Referral Code. This has been substantially replicated, successively, by rule 9 of the Solicitors' Code of Conduct 2007 and Chapter 9 of the SRA Code of Conduct 2011. The Tribunal recognised that regulation in this area had proved to be problematic and in the past dealt with such cases by way of a fine, save where there had been a deliberate and wholesale breach of the ban.[1]

It is likely that both the SRA and the Tribunal will take a less emollient view towards breaches of the referral fee ban in the Legal Aid, Sentencing and Punishment of Offenders Act (LASPOA) 2012 than in the past. The ban is imposed by an Act of Parliament rather than a somewhat controversial professional rule. The Government will expect the ban to be enforced by the regulators, and part of that enforcement is likely to involve significant penalties being imposed upon those who transgress.

1 For example, *Mendelson*, 9212–2005, SDT. In *Barber and others*, 9698–2007, SDT, two solicitors were suspended for deliberate and wholesale breach of the ban, in the context of the miners' compensation cases.

Solicitor involvement in SDLT avoidance schemes

21.24

This subject assumed considerable importance in 2011, as political opposition to tax avoidance schemes, particularly schemes which seek to avoid stamp duty land tax (SDLT), became increasingly vocal. Many solicitors have acted in transactions by which purchasers sought legitimately to avoid paying SDLT on the purchase of a property. In February 2012, the SRA issued a warning notice, which is included at **APPENDIX 6**, and it goes without saying that solicitors must tread very cautiously, and enter into carefully circumscribed retainers, if they are to become involved in facilitating such schemes.

At the time of writing, three cases have been decided by the Tribunal, and more are in the pipeline. In *Buckeridge and Heath*, 10476–2010, heard in September 2010, and *Harjit Dlay*, 10855–2011, heard 9 December 2011, the professional misconduct identified lay principally in inadequate disclosure to the mortgagee clients of the firms, and in *Dlay*, a failure adequately to explain matters to the firm's purchaser clients. The result was a reprimand for the two respondents in *Buckeridge and Heath* and a £15,000 fine in *Dlay*. The case of *Dlay* is referred to, without being named, in the SRA warning notice. In the summer of 2013, the Tribunal decided the case of *Grindrod and others,* 11030–2012, which resulted in acquittals for two of the three respondents. The third was fined.

Failure to reply to correspondence from clients and/or the SRA and the Legal Ombudsman

21.25

Failures to reply to correspondence are regarded seriously by the Tribunal, as they damage the reputation of the profession. Standing alone, such failures will merit a fine – even if the original complaint, to which the respondent failed to respond, was in fact without merit.

Tribunal's reasons for imposing sanctions

21.26

Whereas cases in which a solicitor has to be struck off or suspended will usually be fairly easy to identify, as will the misconduct that justifies such a sanction, the Tribunal nevertheless must reveal proper reasoning and explanation for selecting the sanction imposed. This was made clear by Nicola Davies J in *Hazelhurst v SRA*[1] in which she said (at [36]–[37]):

> '[36] … it is difficult to understand how the SDT decided that a monetary penalty was appropriate. No mention of other sanctions is made, no reason is given for the sum imposed nor how such sum is apportioned as between

the three breaches so as to permit the respondents or indeed members of the public to understand what degree of seriousness should be attached to any given breach of the professional rules.

[37] The absence of any or any adequate reasoning by the SDT as to why the sanction of the financial penalty was appropriate, the amount of that penalty and specifically in respect of any breach, how much of that penalty applied, renders it impossible for this court to determine whether the considerations of the SDT which led to the financial penalty were fair and/or reasonable.'

1 [2011] EWHC 462 (Admin) especially at [30] to [31]; see also *English v Emery Reinbold & Strick Ltd* [2002] 1 WLR 2409.

Regulatory settlements[1]

21.27

The Tribunal is prepared in an appropriate case to adopt a process akin to a *Carecraft* procedure,[2] whereby the matter can be dealt with on agreed facts and with an agreed result, subject always to the Tribunal's permission and discretion.[3] Legal costs claimed by the SRA against unsuccessful respondents can be very high, as the regulator has frequently instructed large London firms of solicitors and/or barristers from commercial London Chambers. As for this, a word of warning was sounded by Lord Thomas CJ in *Brett v SRA*[4] in which he stated at [114]:

'It is now well established that the cost of proceedings which a person may be ordered to pay must be proportionate. It may well be that in a particular case, the regulatory authority bringing proceedings will wish to instruct a person or firm who in the current state of the legal market can command high fees which the regulatory authority may be prepared to pay. However the fact that the market enables such persons or firms to command such high fees does not mean that it is proportionate to make an order for costs by reference to the rates which the legal services market enables such persons or firms to command from the regulatory authority. A tribunal must assess what is proportionate, taking into account all the material circumstances.'

It regularly occurs that the SRA succeeds in large part against the respondent solicitor, but that some of the allegations are nevertheless dismissed by the Tribunal. In such circumstances, it may be appropriate for the Tribunal to take that into account when determining costs issues, and perhaps apply a discount to reflect the fact that the SRA failed in part.[5]

1 See also **19.14**.
2 *Re Carecraft Construction Co Ltd* [1994] 1 WLR 172, ChD.
3 *Wilson-Smith*, 8772–2003, SDT.
4 [2014] EWHC 2974 (Admin).
5 The authorities are not consistent. No discount was applied in *Baxendale-Walker v Law Society* [2007] EWCA Civ 233, [2007] 3 All ER 330, *Beresford v SRA* [2009] EWHC 3155 (Admin) and *Levy v SRA* [2011] EWHC 740 (Admin). See now though *Broomhead v SRA* [2014] EWHC 2772 (Admin), in which the High Court applied a discount and doubted *Levy*.

Costs

Costs against the unsuccessful respondent

21.28

A very high percentage of applications against solicitors are successful in whole or in part and the respondent in those cases will ordinarily be ordered to pay the costs of the SRA.[1] Even if not all allegations are found proved it is the Tribunal's practice to award all the costs against the respondent if, on the facts, it was reasonable to make those allegations.[2] If there has been a substantial contest over part of the case in which the respondent has been successful, the order may be to pay a reduced percentage of the SRA's costs.

The normal order for costs in a case where there has been a forensic investigation is an order for the payment of costs 'of and incidental to the application and enquiry' to include the costs of the forensic investigation. These are usually considerable – several thousands of pounds – and can exceed the applicant's legal costs. Regrettably, there is little published material as to how these costs are calculated, and it is usually difficult or impossible for the respondent solicitor to make a meaningful challenge as to the quantum of those costs at a summary assessment by the Tribunal.

The Tribunal can endorse an agreement between the parties and make an order for fixed costs, can summarily assess the costs in appropriate circumstances, or can order that the costs be subject to detailed assessment if not agreed – with or without an interim payment of costs being directed. As orders made by the Tribunal are enforceable as orders of the High Court,[3] detailed assessment is dealt with by the Supreme Court Costs Office and the Civil Procedure Rules 1998 apply to that assessment in the usual way.

1 There is a section on costs in the SDT Guidance Note at paras 53–62.
2 See generally para 59 of the SDT Guidance Note.
3 Section 48(4) of SA 1974.

The relevance of the respondent's means

21.29

In imposing fines and making costs orders the Tribunal should take into account the means of the respondent. In particular, where a solicitor is suspended or struck off, enquiry as to the solicitor's means must be made before any decision is made.[1] These propositions were unsuccessfully attacked by the SRA in *SRA v Davis and McGlinchey*.[2] The SRA asserted that the respondent's means should be irrelevant to the making of an order for costs. This was rejected by Mitting J, who provided valuable guidance as to how the issue should be tackled in future (at [22]–[24]):

> '[22]… where a solicitor admits the disciplinary charges brought against him, and who therefore anticipates the imposition of a sanction upon him, it should be incumbent upon him before the hearing to give advance notice to the SRA and to the Tribunal that he will contend either that no order for costs should be made against him, or that it should be limited in amount by reason of his own lack of means. He should also supply to the SRA and

to the Tribunal, in advance of the hearing, the evidence upon which he relies to support that contention. In a case in which the solicitor disputes the charges brought against him, it would be burdensome to impose an advance obligation upon him of providing information about his means.

[23]… [But] once the Tribunal has found that the charges are proved, then the same obligations … will be imposed upon a solicitor arguing that he cannot meet an order for costs, or that one should be limited in amount.

[24] In either of the two sets of circumstances the SRA must be afforded a reasonable opportunity to test the evidence relied upon by the solicitor, and in an appropriate case to call evidence itself on the question of the solicitor's means and of course to make submissions about the matter to the Tribunal.'

The judge's recommendations in paragraph 22 of the judgment were acted upon by the SDT in promulgating the Standard Directions, which require proper disclosure of a respondent's means when the respondent wishes the Tribunal to take those means into account.

Where the respondent is shown to be impecunious, if the Tribunal is satisfied that there is a reasonable prospect that at some time in the future his or her ability to pay a costs order will improve, it may order the respondent to pay costs, but direct that such order is not to be enforced without further leave of the Tribunal.[3] However, a respondent must think carefully whether he or she wishes to plead poverty. While to do so may well reduce the amount of the fine or costs payable, there may be other regulatory repecussions for solicitors shown to be impecunious. As a result of the post-2008 recession, the SRA has devoted considerable resources to the issue of the financial stability of solicitors and entities, because of the potential damage to the reputation of the profession caused by the uncontrolled failures of law firms.

1 See *Merrick v Law Society* [2007] EWHC 2997 (Admin) at [60]–[66], in which an order for costs in the sum of £45,000 against a suspended solicitor, who did not have the means or ability to pay, was quashed on appeal. See also *Agyeman v SRA* [2012] EWHC 3472 (Admin) and *Sharma v SRA* [2012] EWHC 3176 (Admin) – in the latter case the Divisional Court observed that the solicitor must adduce evidence of inability to pay a costs order, including independent valuations of properties. In *Matthews v SRA* [2013] EWHC 1525 (Admin), Collins J held that In imposing a financial penalty, the Tribunal should consider the respondent's overall financial liability for the fine and costs, and reduced a fine of £5,000 and costs of £16,000 to an overall liability of £5,000 on account of the appellant's limited means.

2 [2011] EWHC 232 (Admin).

3 See para 57 of the SDT Guidance Note and e.g. *Ijomantu v SRA* [2013] EWHC 3905 (Admin).

Costs against a successful respondent solicitor

21.30

Rule 22 of the 1994 Rules specifically provided that an order for costs may be made by the Tribunal against the respondent without finding any allegation proved – and even if no other order is made if, having regard to his or her conduct or to all the circumstances (or both), the Tribunal thinks it fit.[1] In *Rowe v Lindsay*, the Divisional Court indicated that this rule did not justify an order for costs against a successful respondent who had been acquitted of misconduct and whose conduct in relation to the questions before the Tribunal, and since the commencement of proceedings against him, had not in the event been criticised.[2]

If intending to impose a costs sanction (either an order under rule 22 or an order depriving a successful respondent solicitor of his costs) by reason of any fault found against the solicitor, the Tribunal is bound to consider what impact the conduct of the solicitor, of which it is critical, has had on the costs incurred. The calculation need not be exact, but there must be a reasonable and just balance between the order made and what has occurred in the proceedings. There must be a causal connection between the fault found by the Tribunal and the incurring of costs.[3]

1 This provision is not replicated in the 2007 Rules, rule 18 of which gives the Tribunal a wide discretion as to costs orders.
2 (2001) DC Transcript CO/4737/2000.
3 *Hayes v Law Society* [2004] EWHC 1165 (QB). In referring to depriving the successful respondent of his costs (as distinct from the possibility of an order under rule 22) this decision should now be considered to have been overruled by *Baxendale-Walker v Law Society* [2007] EWCA Civ 233, [2007] 3 All ER 330.

Costs orders against the Law Society/SRA

21.31

Until relatively recently, those appearing in the Tribunal could expect, and advise their clients to expect, that costs would probably follow the event. If a respondent were to be acquitted of all charges in the Tribunal, the successful solicitor could generally expect an order that his or her costs should be paid by the Law Society.

This state of affairs altered with the decision of the Divisional Court in *Baxendale-Walker v Law Society*,[1] which was upheld by the Court of Appeal.[2] The rationale is that the Law Society is a statutory regulator, exercising its powers in the public interest; when the Law Society/SRA is addressing the question whether there is sufficient evidence to justify an application to the Tribunal, the ambit of its responsibility is far greater than it would be for a litigant deciding whether to bring civil proceedings.

The normal approach to costs decisions in ordinary civil litigation, that costs should follow the event, accordingly has no direct application to disciplinary proceedings against solicitors. What will be considered just and reasonable will depend on all the relevant facts and circumstances. The Tribunal may consider it just that costs should follow the event, but need not think so in all cases. Where the regulatory authority has acted reasonably, properly and on grounds that reasonably appear to be sound in the exercise of its public duty, the Tribunal should consider – in addition to any other relevant fact or circumstance – the financial prejudice to the particular respondent if an order for costs is not made in his or her favour and the need to encourage public authorities to make and stand by honest, reasonable and apparently sound decisions made in the public interest without fear of exposure to undue financial prejudice if the decision is successfully challenged.

Success by a respondent is a factor in his or her favour, but is not decisive; it is not the starting point but simply one factor for consideration.

However, where for example disciplinary proceedings are held to amount to an abuse of process, have been inefficiently prosecuted or have been mounted upon inadequate evidence, the respondent solicitor will ordinarily have a powerful argument that costs should follow the event.

The principles set out in *Baxendale-Walker* do not apply to appeals from the Solicitors Disciplinary Tribunal to the High Court. On such appeals, the costs provisions of the Civil Procedure Rules are applied. An appellant who successfully challenges findings against him or her can ordinarily expect to be awarded the costs of the appeal.[3]

1 [2006] EWHC 643 (Admin), [2006] 3 All ER 675.
2 [2007] EWCA Civ 233, [2007] 3 All ER 330. See too *Murtagh v SRA* [2013] EWHC 2024 (Admin).
3 See *Bryant and Bench v Law Society* [2007] EWHC 3043 (Admin) at [251] and *Bass and Ward v SRA* (judgment on costs) [2012] EWHC 2457 (Admin).

Appeals from the Tribunal

Statutory provisions

21.32

Either party may appeal to the High Court without permission and such appeals are governed by CPR Part 52.[1]

The time for appealing is now 21 days from the receipt by the appellant of the judgment.[2]

The court has power to make such order on an appeal as it may think fit.[3] Appeals to the High Court are heard in the Administrative Court, usually by a single judge or on occasion by a two-judge Divisional Court.

1 Section 49 of SA 1974. The one exception, which will only be relevant when rules are made to permit appeals to the Tribunal from decisions of the SRA in relation to practising certificate and comparable issues, is that the decision of the Tribunal on such appeals will be final; see section 49A(3) of SA 1974. See footnote 10 to **20.3**.
2 CPR Part 52.4 modified by PD52D para 3.3A.
3 Section 49(4) of SA 1974.

Stay pending appeal

21.33

As has been said (see **21.3**), the Tribunal does not readily grant a stay pending appeal, or any other period of grace, in cases where an order for striking off is made, still less when there has been a finding of dishonesty, and an appeal does not in itself operate as a stay.[1] It is necessary to lodge an appeal and to apply within that appeal for interlocutory relief. The test that will be applied is set out in *Re a Solicitor*:[2]

> 'For such a submission to succeed, it would be necessary to establish not only that the applicant's appeal against striking off would have a reasonable prospect of success, but, further, that this Court would be likely to impose in substitution for the order of the Tribunal a penalty no greater than suspension from practice for some three or four months [being the period within which the substantive appeal could be expected to be heard].'

In that case, in which the application was heard in November 1998, the appeal was expected to be heard in February 1999.

It will be seen that an application for a stay pending appeal would be more likely to succeed in a case of a suspension from practice where the suspension would substantially have been served by the time the appeal came to be heard. Successful applications for a stay pending appeal where the solicitor has been struck off can be expected to be rare.

Where the Tribunal has directed that inadequate professional services (IPS) awards are enforceable as orders of the High Court, and there is an appeal, it would similarly be necessary to seek a stay pending appeal if the enforcement of the awards is intended to be avoided or postponed in the meantime.

1 CPR rule 52.7.
2 16 November 1998, unreported, transcript CO/4359/98, per Rose LJ.

Approach of the courts

21.34

Until the advent of the Human Rights Act 1998, the courts were reluctant to interfere with the decisions of the Tribunal as an expert professional disciplinary tribunal. It was stated that it would require a very strong case to interfere with sentence, because the Tribunal was best placed to weigh the seriousness of professional misconduct.[1] The modern approach of the courts in the light of the Human Rights Act 1998 has altered in this respect, and was first determined in *Langford v Law Society*.[2] The following extracts from Lord Millett's speech in *Ghosh v General Medical Council*[3] were cited by Rose LJ in *Langford*:

> 'their Lordships wish to emphasise that their powers are not as limited as may be suggested by some of the observations which have been made in the past …
>
> … the Board will accord an appropriate measure of respect to the judgment of the committee whether the practitioner's failings amount to serious professional misconduct and on the measures necessary to maintain professional standards and provide adequate protection to the public. But the Board will not defer to the committee's judgment more than is warranted by the circumstances. The council conceded, and their Lordships accept, that it is open to them to … decide whether the sanction of erasure was appropriate and necessary in the public interest or was excessive and disproportionate; and in the latter event either to substitute some other penalty or to remit the case to the committee for reconsideration.'

The correct approach of the courts to appeals from the Tribunal was comprehensively reviewed in *Law Society v Salsbury*:[4]

> 'The correct analysis is that the Solicitors Disciplinary Tribunal comprises an expert and informed tribunal, which is particularly well placed in any case to assess what measures are required to deal with defaulting solicitors and to protect the public interest. Absent any error of law, the High Court must pay considerable respect to the sentencing decisions of the tribunal. Nevertheless if the High Court, despite paying such respect, is satisfied that the sentencing decision was clearly inappropriate, then the court will

interfere. It should also be noted that an appeal from the Solicitors Disciplinary Tribunal to the High Court normally proceeds by way of review; see CPR rule 52.11(1).'

1 See *McCoan v General Medical Council* [1964] 1 WLR 1107; and *Bolton v Law Society* [1994] 1 WLR 512, CA.
2 [2002] EWHC 2802 (Admin); see particularly at [14] and [15].
3 [2001] 1 WLR 1915.
4 [2008] EWCA Civ 1285 at [30]. For a somewhat different approach, see the judgment of Mostyn J in *Obi v SRA* [2013] EWHC 3578 (Admin).

Miscellaneous matters

21.35

Solicitors may wish to adduce fresh evidence on appeal, often of the medical or financial variety. The *Ladd v Marshall* principles (which in any event do not hold sway to the extent that they did before the Woolf reforms) are not always applied with their full rigour in statutory appeals of this type, where the likelihood of prejudice to the regulator is minimal, and it is in the interests of both parties that the correct sanction is applied to the regulated individual.[1] Although the court may adopt a more flexible approach than in conventional civil litigation, this cannot be taken for granted.[2]

1 See *R (Adelakun) v SRA* [2014] EWHC 198 (Admin) and *R (Khan) v GMC* [2014] EWHC 404 (Admin).
2 See *Sohal v SRA* [2014] EWHC 1613 (Admin).

21.36

It has already been noted (**21.31** above) that costs in the High Court will ordinarily follow the event in accordance with CPR 44.2(2), and that *Baxendale-Walker* has no application to appeals from the SDT. In the case of an impecunious unsuccessful appellant, the court may be prepared to order that its own costs order should not be enforced by the SRA without leave.[1]

1 See *Webb v SRA* [2013] EWHC 2225 (Admin) and *R (Adelakun) v SRA* [2014] EWHC 198 (Admin).

Further appeal to the Court of Appeal

21.37

Further appeals require the permission of the Court of Appeal, as a second appeal governed by CPR rule 52.13, and are rarely mounted. The Law Society has appealed to the Court of Appeal on only three occasions, in each case to establish important points of principle.[1]

1 *Bolton v Law Society* [1994] 1 WLR 512, CA; *Bultitude v Law Society* [2004] EWCA Civ 1853, *Times*, 14 January 2005; and *Law Society v Salsbury* [2008] EWCA Civ 1285.

Miscellaneous matters

Further appeals to the Court of Appeal

CHAPTER 22

Proceedings before the SDT: (3) appeals to the Tribunal

22.1

CHAPTER 19 dealt, among other things, with the Solicitors Regulation Authority (SRA)'s powers to impose fines of £2,000 on practices and practitioners, to impose rebukes, and to publish its decisions; see **19.1**. Those decisions are made, so far as they relate to individual solicitors and employees, under section 44D of the Solicitors Act (SA) 1974 (see **APPENDIX 15**); and so far as they relate to recognised bodies, their managers and employees, under paragraph 14B of Schedule 2 of the Administration of Justice Act (AJA) 1985 (see **APPENDIX 16**).

CHAPTER 2 considers the powers of the SRA in relation to the authorisation of alternative business structures (ABSs) or 'licensable bodies', including the power to refuse an application, to impose conditions and to revoke or suspend an authorisation, and the power to withhold approval of individuals as managers or compliance officers and to withdraw approval; see **2.9** to **2.15**. **CHAPTER 24** explains the process whereby ownership of ABSs is regulated. **CHAPTER 25** deals with the disciplinary powers of the SRA to fine ABSs and disqualify individuals. All of those decisions are made as a licensing authority under Part 5 of the Legal Services Act (LSA) 2007 (see **APPENDIX 18**) or licensing rules. For relevant purposes the 'licensing rules' comprise the SRA Handbook and most relevantly the SRA Authorisation Rules for Legal Services Bodies and Licensable Bodies 2011.

Appeals lie to the Solicitors Disciplinary Tribunal ('the Tribunal' or SDT) against decisions of the SRA:

- to impose fines up to £2,000 on individuals or recognised bodies;[1]
- to impose a rebuke on individuals or recognised bodies, if the SRA decides to publish the rebuke, but not otherwise;[2]
- to disqualify a person from acting as Head of Legal Practice or Head of Finance and Administration or from being a manager or employee of a licensed body;
- to refuse to bring a disqualification to an end following a review;
- to impose fines on licensed bodies or managers or employees of licensed bodies;
- to refuse an application for authorisation as a licensed body;
- to impose a condition on the authorisation of a licensed body;
- to revoke or suspend a licensed body's authorisation;
- to modify, or to refuse to modify on an application for modification of the terms and conditions of authorisation of a licensed body;

- not to approve a person to be a manager or compliance officer of a licensed body;
- to approve a person to be a manager or compliance officer of a licensed body subject to conditions on the body's authorisation;
- to withdraw approval of a manager or compliance officer of a licensed body;
- not to approve a person being an owner of a licensed body;
- to impose conditions on the authorisation of a licensed body in connection with the approval of an owner;
- to withdraw approval of a person as an owner of a licensed body;

and against a failure of the SRA to make a decision on an application for authorisation within the required period.[3]

1 Section 44E of SA 1974 and para 14C of Schedule 2 to AJA 1985.
2 Section 44E of SA 1974 and para 14C of Schedule 2 to AJA 1985.
3 Legal Services Act 2007 (Appeals from Licensing Authority Decisions) (No 2) Order 2011 (SI 2011/2863).

22.2

In this chapter we consider only the procedural aspects of such appeals. The Tribunal has not adapted its existing rules, the Solicitors (Disciplinary Proceedings) Rules 2007 ('the 2007 Rules', see **APPENDIX 12**) for its appellate jurisdiction but has made completely new rules specifically for this purpose. In fact it has made two sets of rules. There was an immediate need to have rules in relation to appeals under SA 1974 and AJA 1985, as the SRA has had the power to rebuke and fine since 1 June 2010, although because the powers could only be exercised in respect of acts and failings occurring or continuing on or after that date, and the investigatory process takes a finite time, there has not been a pressing need until relatively recently.

In contrast, the first decisions in relation to the licensing of ABSs could not be made until the first months of 2012, and it is not expected that there will be an early rash of appeals. Further, no rules could be made in relation to the Tribunal as an appellate body in respect of decisions made by the SRA until the Law Society had been designated as a licensing authority.

Accordingly the Tribunal has made, with the approval of the Legal Services Board, the Solicitors Disciplinary Tribunal (Appeals and Amendment) Rules 2011[1] ('the Appeal Rules') which deal with appeals under SA 1974 and AJA 1985 and are effective from 1 October 2011, and also the Solicitors Disciplinary Tribunal (Appeals) (Amendment) Rules 2011[2] which amend the Appeal Rules to include provision for ABS appeals, from the date on which the Law Society was designated as a licensing authority.

The 'amendment' in the Appeal Rules is a tiny one to amend the 2007 Rules, to correct an anomaly in one the Tribunal's standard forms concerned with written evidence.

Somewhat surprisingly, at the time of writing, the SDT has not yet adjudicated upon a single appeal. It is not known whether any are pending.

In **APPENDIX 13** we have included the Appeal Rules, including the ABS-specific provisions.

1 SI 2011/2346. See also **APPENDIX 13**.
2 SI 2011/3070.

Constitution of appeal panels, delegation and general powers

22.3

The one certainty in relation to alternative business structures is that, however much informed opinion there may be, no one can predict reliably exactly how the market will develop, what forms the new businesses will take and what degree of complexity will be involved in licensing decisions, and therefore in appeals from licensing decisions. The Tribunal has sensibly created for itself a degree of flexibility. The 2007 Rules dealing with the historical and original jurisdiction of the Tribunal are rigid as to the constitution of the adjudicating panel; it consists of three and only three: a lay member and two solicitors.[1]

The Appeal Rules state that for the hearing of any appeal a panel will be 'at least three members of the Tribunal', and that 'Unless the President otherwise directs, the majority of Panel members shall be solicitor members'.[2]

The lay members of the Tribunal have a wealth of expertise in a wide variety of subjects outside the law, including, for example, business management, and it could be foreseen that in appropriate cases an expanded appeal panel could draw on that experience.

1 Rule 4 of the 2007 Rules.
2 Rule 3 of the Appeal Rules.

22.4

A single solicitor member may make case management decisions and give directions under rule 9 of the Appeal Rules;[1] may waive or require a procedural failure to be remedied under rule 11; may make a direction adding, substituting or removing a party under rule 13; may deal with the prohibition of disclosure of documents under rule 14; may make orders about lead cases, rule 15, consent to the withdrawal of an appeal under rule 16, and give directions as to disclosure, evidence and submissions under rule 19(1).[2]

The Tribunal clerks have delegated authority to give case management directions under rules 9, 13 and 19(1), subject to the right of a party to apply, within 14 days, for the decision to be considered afresh by a panel or single solicitor member.[3]

The Tribunal (or a panel of Tribunal members consisting of no fewer than five members, of whom no fewer than two shall be lay members) may make general practice directions: notices or directions concerning the practices or procedures of the Tribunal, consistent with the Appeal Rules, which are to be promulgated under the authority of the President.[4]

Subject to the Appeal Rules themselves, the Tribunal may regulate its own procedure, and may dispense with any requirements of the Rules in respect of notices, statements or other documents, witnesses, service or time in any case where it appears to the Tribunal to be just so to do.[5] This does not extend, however, to the time limit for appeals from decisions of the SRA as a licensing authority relating to the ownership of ABSs; see **22.5**.

The Tribunal may consent to a witness giving, or require any witness to give, evidence on oath, and may administer an oath for that purpose.[6]

1 The detailed rules referred to in this paragraph are considered below at **22.8** and **22.9**.
2 Rule 5(4) of the Appeal Rules.
3 Rule 5(1) and (3).
4 Rule 10.
5 Rule 18.
6 Rule 19(3).

Preliminary steps

22.5

The time for appeal is in all cases 28 days from notification of the decision. In relation to some ABS appeals this is a statutory time limit fixed by rules made by the Legal Services Board under its powers in paragraph 8 of Schedule 13 to LSA 2007,[1] and may not be exceeded. Neither the Tribunal nor any other party has power to waive the limit or consent to its extension.

This statutory time limit only applies to appeals concerning licensing decisions as to ownership of a licensed body – SRA decisions:

- to approve an investor's notified interest subject to conditions, on granting a licence;
- to object to an investor's notified interest;
- to approve an investor's notifiable interest subject to conditions, after a licence has been granted;
- to object to an investor's notifiable interest;
- to impose conditions or further conditions on an existing restricted interest;
- to object to an existing restricted interest; and
- to notify the Legal Services Board that an owner has exceeded a share or voting limit.[2]

1 Rule 5 of the LSB Rules on the Prescribed Period for the Making of Appeals against Decisions of a Licensing Authority Regarding Ownership of Licensed Bodies 2011.
2 Respectively paras 17(1), 19(1), 28(1), 31(1), 33(1), 36(1) and 49(2) of Schedule 13 to LSA 2007.

22.6

There is no form for a notice of appeal, but under rule 6(4) of the Appeal Rules the notice of appeal must set out:

- the name and address of the appellant;
- the name and address of the appellant's representative (if any);
- an address where documents for the appellant may be sent or delivered;

- the basis on which the appellant has standing to start proceedings before the Tribunal;
- the name and address of the respondent;
- details of the decision or act to which the proceedings relate;
- the result the appellant is seeking;
- the grounds on which the appellant relies;
- any application for a stay, if the appellant is allowed to make such an application under the licensing rules;
- a statement as to whether the appellant would be content for the case to be dealt with without a hearing if the Tribunal considers it appropriate; and
- any further information or documents required by a practice direction.

A copy of any record of the decision which is the subject of the appeal, and any statement of reasons that the appellant has or can reasonably obtain, must be supplied. Three additional copies of the notice and all accompanying documents must be filed with the Tribunal. A copy of the notice of appeal and all accompanying documents must be served on the respondent at the same time that the appellant sends or delivers the notice of appeal to the Tribunal.[1]

1 Rule 6(5), (6) and (7) of the Appeal Rules.

22.7

The respondent's response to the notice of appeal must be sent or delivered to the Tribunal and the appellant within 28 days of receipt by the respondent of the notice of appeal. There is no set form but the response must include:

- the name and address of the respondent;
- the name and address of the respondent's representative (if any);
- an address where documents for the respondent may be sent or delivered;
- any further information or documents required by a practice direction or direction;
- a statement as to whether the respondent would be content for the case to be dealt with without a hearing if the Tribunal considers it appropriate; and
- a statement as to whether the respondent opposes the appellant's case and, if so, any grounds for such opposition which are not contained in another document sent or delivered with the response.

Documents relied on by the respondent in making the decision and any documents considered by the respondent to be relevant to the appeal should accompany the response, including any record of the decision under appeal or reasons if not provided by the appellant.[1]

The onus is thus placed initially on the respondent to produce all documents that are 'relevant' to the extent that they have not already been placed before the Tribunal by the appellant. This requires an exercise of judgement as the documents required are not limited simply to those upon which the respondent may wish to rely. The

Tribunal's practice direction as to disclosure and discovery made under the 2007 Rules may be relevant by analogy; see **APPENDIX 12**.

Three copies of the respondent's material must be provided to the Tribunal and service must be effected contemporaneously. If the response is out of time a request for an extension of time and the reason for it must be included.

An appellant may file and serve a reply within 14 days from receipt of the respondent's response, and any additional documents intended to be relied upon. At the same time the appellant may elect to supply a list of documents intended to be relied upon that were not appended to the notice of appeal, and if requested by the respondent or the Tribunal must provide copies or make those documents available for inspection and/or copying within seven days.[2]

1 Rule 7 of the Appeal Rules.
2 Rule 8.

Case management

22.8

On the direction of the Tribunal parties may be added, substituted or removed as an appellant or a respondent.[1]

The Tribunal may give directions to:

- extend or shorten the time for complying with any rule, practice direction or direction, unless such extension or shortening would conflict with a provision of another enactment (or of any rule made under another enactment) containing a time limit;
- consolidate or hear together two or more sets of proceedings or parts of proceedings raising common issues, or treat a case as a lead case;
- hear any application for a stay;
- permit or require a party to amend a document;
- permit or require a party or another person to provide documents, information or submissions which are relevant to the proceedings to the Tribunal or a party;
- deal with an issue in the proceedings as a preliminary issue;
- hold a hearing to consider any matter, including a case management issue;
- decide the form of any hearing;
- adjourn or postpone a hearing;
- require a party to produce a bundle for a hearing;
- require a party to provide a skeleton argument;
- decide the place and time of any hearing;
- make requirements about documentation and inspection:
- stay proceedings;

- suspend the effect of its own decision pending the determination by the High Court of an application for permission to appeal against, and any appeal of, that decision.[2]

A clerk may appoint a time and place for the review of the progress of the matter and notify the parties.[3]

1 Rule 13 of the Appeal Rules.
2 Rule 9(1) and (2).
3 Rule 9(3).

22.9

Directions may also be given by the Tribunal as to:

- the exchange between parties of lists of documents which are relevant to the appeal, or relevant to particular issues, and the inspection of such documents;
- the provision by parties of statements of agreed matters;
- issues on which it requires evidence or submissions;
- the nature of the evidence or submissions it requires;
- whether the parties are permitted or required to provide expert evidence, and if so whether the parties must jointly appoint a single expert to provide such evidence;
- any limit on the number of witnesses whose evidence a party may put forward, whether in relation to a particular issue or generally;
- the manner in which any evidence or submissions are to be provided, which may include a direction for them to be given orally at a hearing or by written submissions or witness statement; and
- the time at which any evidence or submissions are to be sent or delivered.[1]

The Tribunal may admit evidence whether or not the evidence would be admissible in a civil trial in the United Kingdom; or the evidence was available to a previous decision-maker. It may also exclude evidence that would otherwise be admissible where the evidence was not provided within the time allowed by a direction or a practice direction; or where the evidence was otherwise provided in a manner that did not comply with a direction or a practice direction; or it would otherwise be unfair, disproportionate or unnecessary in the interests of justice to admit it.[2]

The Tribunal may in its discretion proceed on the basis of written evidence subject to provisions as to service, notice, and the entitlement of the other party to object. If a witness is to be called to give oral evidence a witness statement with a statement of truth must be filed and served at least ten days before the hearing date. Five copies must be provided to the Tribunal.

By rule 11 of the Appeal Rules a failure to comply with any provision of the Rules, a practice direction or a direction does not render void either the appeal or any step taken in the appeal. The Tribunal may waive the requirement; require the failure to be remedied; exercise its power to strike the whole or part of the appeal (see further below); bar or restrict a party's participation in the appeal, but an order barring or restricting a party's participation in the appeal may not be made without giving the party an opportunity to make representations.

Where two or more appeals give rise to common or related issues one or more lead cases may be selected and other affected appeals may be stayed.[3]

1 Rule 19(1) of the Appeal Rules.
2 Rule 19(2).
3 Rule 15.

Private and public hearings

22.10

All hearings, including interlocutory hearings, are heard in public unless the Tribunal is satisfied that exceptional hardship or exceptional prejudice will be caused to a party, a witness or any other person affected by the appeal, or if a hearing would prejudice the interests of justice.[1]

The Tribunal has the power to direct that someone be excluded from any hearing if he or she is likely to prove disruptive, or for comparable reasons.[2]

It may also, as it regularly does at present without an express power under the 2007 Rules, exclude a witness until he or she has given evidence.[3]

Under rule 14 of the Appeal Rules there is a power to prohibit the disclosure or publication of documents or other material likely to identify someone the Tribunal considers should not be identified (which is regularly if not invariably done to protect the identity of clients, by identifying them by initials alone).

Under the same rule there are more complex provisions enabling documents to be withheld from a party altogether if there is a likelihood of serious harm to someone and in the interests of justice, with appropriate safeguards. The use of such powers is likely to be highly exceptional.

1 Rule 23(1) to (4) of the Appeal Rules.
2 Rule 23(5).
3 Rule 23(6).

Listing, hearings and other methods of disposal

22.11

Appeals may be disposed of without a hearing if both parties consent and the Tribunal considers it can properly determine the issues in this way.[1] Otherwise, hearings are listed on the basis that at least 28 days' notice is given, unless all the parties agree and the Tribunal has ordered a shorter period.[2] Any party may appoint a representative, who need not be a legal representative.[3]

Appeals can be disposed of by consent if the Tribunal considers the agreement appropriate, and in this event there need not be a hearing.

Either party may withdraw – the appeal or opposition to it – but the withdrawal does not take effect until the Tribunal consents to it, which it may do on terms as to costs. A party may also apply to reinstate an appeal or opposition to an appeal. The application must be made in writing within 28 days of the withdrawal (whether that was on written notice or orally at a hearing).[4]

Under rule 12 the Tribunal may strike out the whole or part of an appeal if the appellant has failed to comply with a direction which stated that a failure to comply could lead to that result (if the appeal or part of it is struck out on this basis the appellant may apply to reinstate it, within 28 days). An appeal or part of it may also be struck out if the appellant has failed to co-operate to such an extent that the appeal cannot be dealt with fairly and justly, or if the Tribunal considers that there is no reasonable prospect of the appellant's case, or that part of it, succeeding.

The same provisions apply in relation to striking out a respondent's opposition to an appeal *mutatis mutandis*.[5]

If an appeal has been finally disposed of at a hearing at which a party neither attended in person nor was represented, that party may apply for a re-hearing. The application must be made within 14 days of receipt of the Tribunal's order. It can be expected that such applications will be dealt with in no different a manner from applications made in the same circumstances under the 2007 Rules; see **20.19**.

1 Rule 21 of the Appeal Rules.
2 Rule 22.
3 Rule 28
4 Rule 16.
5 Rule 12(6).

Costs

22.12

By rule 29 of the Appeal Rules the Tribunal may make such order for costs as it thinks fit, at any stage of an appeal, including an order disallowing costs incurred unnecessarily; and may order that costs be paid by any party judged to be responsible for wasted or unnecessary costs.

The Tribunal may order that any party bear the whole or a part or a proportion of the costs, and the amount of costs may either be fixed by the Tribunal or be subject to detailed assessment by a costs judge. The Tribunal may also make an order for costs where an appeal is withdrawn or amended.

The costs regime in relation to the normal (original as opposed to appellate) jurisdiction of the Tribunal is very burdensome on successful respondents – see **21.28**, **21.30** and **21.31**. However, this would not seem to be relevant to an appellate jurisdiction. The same public interest considerations do not apply. Certainly, one can expect that those who appeal unsuccessfully to the Tribunal against a decision of the SRA will be ordered to pay the SRA's costs in the normal course of events, but if appellants are successful, unless there is some unusual circumstance, it will be on the basis that the SRA's decision will have been wrong.

One would expect successful appellants to be awarded their costs. There are two analogies, situations where the SRA has historically made decisions which are open to challenge by appeal: the first relates to the imposition of practising certificate conditions and similar decisions; the second involves matters of character and fitness, and appeals by those seeking enrolment as students with the SRA or admission to the roll as solicitors. In both cases appeal lies to the High Court (to the Master of the Rolls before 2008). In both situations the normal considerations under the Civil Procedure Rules apply and the general position is that costs follow the event. If the SRA is held to be wrong to have imposed the practising certificate conditions or wrong to have refused enrolment or admission the starting point is that the appellant is entitled to his or her costs against the SRA. The same principles have been applied in relation to appeals from the Tribunal to the High Court, despite an attempt by the SRA to suggest that the principles of *Baxendale-Walker v Law Society*[1] applied not only to the original prosecution in the Tribunal but also to appeals from the Tribunal; see *Bryant and Bench v Law Society*.[2]

1 [2007] EWCA Civ 233, [2007] 3 All ER 330; for the principles see **21.31**.
2 [2007] EWHC 3043 (Admin) at [251].

The burden and standard of proof

22.13

The appellate jurisdiction of the Tribunal covers three areas: appeals against SRA in-house sanctions of rebukes and fines, imposed in relation to individual solicitors and traditional (non-ABS) practices; appeals against decisions of a disciplinary character involving ABSs to impose fines, revoke authorisations and and disqualify individuals; and appeals against licensing decisions, such as to refuse to grant an ABS licence, to refuse to approve individual applicants in regulated positions, or to impose conditions. The bulk of appeals can be expected to occur in one or other of the first two classes of appeal where the SRA has exercised a disciplinary jurisdiction – to fine or rebuke solicitors and/or their firms, to fine ABSs, to disqualify managers and compliance officers of ABSs, to impose conditions on authorisation or approval and to withdraw approval or revoke authorisations (the last four being strictly regulatory decisions, but with potentially serious or terminal business consequences).

The third class of appeal will involve challenges to licensing decisions of the SRA – to refuse applications for authorisation of ABSs or approval of managers or compliance officers. The two classes of appeal involve wholly different considerations.

In what might be termed disciplinary matters the appeals can be expected to be by way of re-hearing, in which the SRA will present its case and the appellant will effectively be the defendant, seeking to reargue a case where, at first instance, the matter was dealt with by written submissions and there was (probably) no opportunity to appear at an oral hearing or, in appropriate cases, to challenge witnesses.

It is well known that the Tribunal considers itself bound to apply the criminal standard of proof (see **21.2**), whereas the SRA will have applied the civil standard of proof in its own decision-making.[1] This may not become a major issue, however, bearing in mind that in the overwhelming majority of cases the evidence will be heavily documented and there may be little or no dispute of fact, as opposed to the proper interpretation of the facts.

1 Rule 7.7 of the SRA Disciplinary Procedure Rules 2011.

22.14

In licensing appeals the reverse will apply; the burden will be on the appellant. The closest analogy is that of those seeking to join the solicitors' profession, and about whom there is a question over character and fitness. The SRA Suitability Test applies equally to all seeking to join the profession or, as a non-lawyer, to be part of the regulated community providing legal services through an SRA-regulated entity.

Cases have been decided by the Master of the Rolls identifying the correct approach where individuals seek to join the profession and their fitness to do so is in question. The important points are that no one has the right to become a solicitor, and the burden is on the applicant to demonstrate his or her fitness.

In July 2007 Sir Anthony Clarke MR considered three appeals, listed together as raising the same question of principle: *Jideofo v Law Society*, *Evans v SRA* and *Begum v SRA*.[1] The appeals were under the Training Regulations 1990. The appellants were all students; one (Jideofo) had been refused admission as a solicitor; the second (Evans) had been refused enrolment with the SRA as a student, and the third (Begum) had had her student membership cancelled and been refused admission as a solicitor. All had been convicted of criminal offences in the past and the question was whether they were of the necessary character and suitability to be admitted as student members or to the roll of solicitors. There was formerly no direct authority as to the test to apply. The Master of the Rolls noted (at [8]):

> 'The Law Society is thus under a statutory duty to assess at a number of stages whether an unadmitted person has the requisite "character and suitability" to become a solicitor. While there is no authoritative guidance as to the correct approach to be taken when carrying out these assessments, there is a well-established analogous jurisdiction, which arises where the question is whether a solicitor ought to be struck off the roll and what are the circumstances relevant to any application to be restored to the roll following a strike-off made on the grounds of the solicitor's dishonesty. It is this jurisdiction which it is submitted ought to also govern the position pre-admission.'

Sir Anthony Clarke MR accepted this submission and held that the correct test was set out in the well-known leading authority of *Bolton v Law Society*.[2] *Re a Solicitor (Ofusehene)*[3] was also cited. That was a case of a solicitor who had been found to have misconducted himself at a time before he was admitted, and the facts were discovered after admission. The Divisional Court (Rose LJ, Nelson and Hooper JJ) applied the *Bolton* principles.

That part of the '*Bolton* test' relevant to the correct approach to the imposition of penalties by the Tribunal is set out at **21.6**. The whole of the passage is (518A to 519E):

> 'It is required of lawyers practising in this country that they should discharge their professional duties with integrity, probity and complete trustworthiness. That requirement applies as much to barristers as it does to solicitors. If I make no further reference to barristers it is because this appeal concerns a solicitor, and where a client's moneys have been misappropriated the complaint is inevitably made against a solicitor, since solicitors receive and handle clients' moneys and barristers do not.

Any solicitor who is shown to have discharged his professional duties with anything less than complete integrity, probity and trustworthiness must expect severe sanctions to be imposed upon him by the Solicitors Disciplinary Tribunal. Lapses from the required high standard may, of course, take different forms and be of varying degrees. The most serious involves proven dishonesty, whether or not leading to criminal proceedings and criminal penalties. In such cases the tribunal has almost invariably, no matter how strong the mitigation advanced for the solicitor, ordered that he be struck off the Roll of Solicitors. Only infrequently, particularly in recent years, has it been willing to order the restoration to the Roll of a solicitor against whom serious dishonesty had been established, even after a passage of years, and even where the solicitor had made every effort to re-establish himself and redeem his reputation. If a solicitor is not shown to have acted dishonestly, but is shown to have fallen below the required standards of integrity, probity and trustworthiness, his lapse is less serious but it remains very serious indeed in a member of a profession whose reputation depends upon trust. A striking off order will not necessarily follow in such a case, but it may well. The decision whether to strike off or to suspend will often involve a fine and difficult exercise of judgment, to be made by the tribunal as an informed and expert body on all the facts of the case. Only in a very unusual and venial case of this kind would the tribunal be likely to regard as appropriate any order less severe than one of suspension.

It is important that there should be full understanding of the reasons why the tribunal makes orders which might otherwise seem harsh. There is, in some of these orders, a punitive element: a penalty may be visited on a solicitor who has fallen below the standards required of his profession in order to punish him for what he has done and to deter any other solicitor tempted to behave in the same way. Those are traditional objects of punishment. But often the order is not punitive in intention. Particularly is this so where a criminal penalty has been imposed and satisfied. The solicitor has paid his debt to society. There is no need, and it would be unjust, to punish him again. In most cases the order of the tribunal will be primarily directed to one or other or both of two other purposes. One is to be sure that the offender does not have the opportunity to repeat the offence. This purpose is achieved for a limited period by an order of suspension; plainly it is hoped that experience of suspension will make the offender meticulous in his future compliance with the required standards. The purpose is achieved for a longer period, and quite possibly indefinitely, by an order of striking off. The second purpose is the most fundamental of all: to maintain the reputation of the solicitors' profession as one in which every member, of whatever standing, may be trusted to the ends of the earth. To maintain this reputation and sustain public confidence in the integrity of the profession it is often necessary that those guilty of serious lapses are not only expelled but denied re-admission. If a member of the public sells his house, very often his largest asset, and entrusts the proceeds to his solicitor, pending re-investment in another house, he is ordinarily entitled to expect that the solicitor will be a person whose trustworthiness is not, and never has been, seriously in question. Otherwise, the whole profession, and the public as a whole, is injured. A profession's most valuable asset is its collective reputation and the confidence which that inspires.

> Because orders made by the tribunal are not primarily punitive, it follows that considerations which would ordinarily weigh in mitigation of punishment have less effect on the exercise of this jurisdiction than on the ordinary run of sentences imposed in criminal cases. It often happens that a solicitor appearing before the tribunal can adduce a wealth of glowing tributes from his professional brethren. He can often show that for him and his family the consequences of striking off or suspension would be little short of tragic. Often he will say, convincingly, that he has learned his lesson and will not offend again. On applying for restoration after striking off, all these points may be made, and the former solicitor may also be able to point to real efforts made to re-establish himself and redeem his reputation. All these matters are relevant and should be considered. But none of them touches the essential issue, which is the need to maintain among members of the public a well-founded confidence that any solicitor whom they instruct will be a person of unquestionable integrity, probity and trustworthiness. Thus it can never be an objection to an order of suspension in an appropriate case that the solicitor may be unable to re-establish his practice when the period of suspension is past. If that proves, or appears likely, to be so the consequence for the individual and his family may be deeply unfortunate and unintended. But it does not make suspension the wrong order if it is otherwise right. The reputation of the profession is more important than the fortunes of any individual member. Membership of a profession brings many benefits, but that is a part of the price.'

The Master of the Rolls held, secondly, that the test of character and suitability is a necessarily high test; that the character and suitability test is not concerned with 'punishment', 'reward' or 'redemption', but with whether there is a risk to the public or a risk that there may be damage to the reputation of the profession; that no one has the right to be admitted as a solicitor and it is for the applicant to discharge the burden of satisfying the test of character and suitability. It will be rare for a person with convictions of dishonesty to be found to have the requisite character.

These principles are equally relevant to applicants seeking approval of the SRA as non-lawyer managers and compliance officers, and will likewise be relevant to company governance issues and history. It is to be expected that they will therefore be directly material in licensing appeals.

1 Respectively No 6 of 2006, No 1 of 2007 and No 11 of 2007, unreported.
2 [1994] 1 WLR 512, CA, citing the general principles at 518A to 519E.
3 21 February 2007, Divisional Court, unreported.

Further appeals

22.15

As in the case of the Tribunal's original (non-appellate) jurisdiction, appeal from the Tribunal lies to the High Court without permission,[1] save in relation to ABS appeals. All appeals from decisions of the SRA as a licensing authority for ABSs, whether under Part 5 of LSA 2007 or the SRA's rules (and not only those made under Schedule 13 to LSA 2007 listed in **22.5**) are governed by the Legal Services Act (Appeals from Licensing Authority Decisions) (No 2) Order 2011.

In those cases appeal lies to the High Court only on a point of law arising from the decision of the Tribunal, and only with the permission of the High Court.[2] The time limit for appeals in that category is also a statutory limit set by the Legal Services Board and is 28 days from the date the party is given notice of the decision of the Tribunal.[3] If the Tribunal follows its normal practice of making an immediate decision but providing full written reasons on a later date it may therefore be necessary to lodge an appeal before the reasons are available.

1 Section 49 of SA 1974 and see **21.32**.
2 Article 5(3) of the Legal Services Act (Appeals from Licensing Authority Decisions) (No 2) Order 2011 (SI 2011/2863).
3 Rule 6 of the LSB Rules on the Prescribed Period for the Making of Appeals against Decisions of a Licensing Authority Regarding Ownership of Licensed Bodies 2011.

CHAPTER 23

Disciplinary jurisdiction of the High Court

23.1

Solicitors are officers of the Senior Courts: the court itself can discipline solicitors, and may order that a solicitor's name be struck off the roll of solicitors, rather than referring the matter to the Solicitors Regulation Authority (SRA). This power is available to the High Court, the Crown Court and the Court of Appeal, or any division or judge of those courts.[1] This jurisdiction is only rarely exercised, and the relevant principles as to its exercise were summarised by Hickinbottom J in *Coll v Floreat MB*[2] in the following terms at paragraph [45]:

> '(i) The court's jurisdiction over solicitors is conceptually very wide, being curtailed only to the extent that legislation limits it.
>
> (ii) However, although now maintained by section 50 of the Solicitors Act, the jurisdiction is one which the High Court has taken to itself as part of its inherent powers in pursuit of its duty to supervise the conduct of solicitors as officers of the court. The court has, in practice, imposed boundaries on the exercise of its own jurisdiction.
>
> (iii) The jurisdiction has both punitive and compensatory elements. However, given that solicitors are now the subject of a comprehensive and sophisticated regulatory regime through the SRA, the jurisdiction will only usually be exercised where someone has lost out as a result of the solicitor's conduct and the court is the appropriate forum to require that loss to be put right on a summary basis. The jurisdiction is therefore primarily compensatory, although in a disciplinary context. However, whilst misconduct is necessary, simply because there has been misconduct is not sufficient for the jurisdiction to be exercised. Whether the court intervenes in a particular case is always a matter for the court's discretion.
>
> (iv) Where another forum is more appropriate than the court for the investigation of misconduct by a solicitor and the subsequent imposition of a sanction, then the court will not exercise its discretion to act against that solicitor. The SRA is appointed by Parliament to investigate and deal with allegations of misconduct by solicitors: the court will not exercise its disciplinary function over solicitors if the alleged misconduct conduct can be as, or more, appropriately dealt with by the SRA.'

A claimant applying to the High Court to exercise this jurisdiction, rather than making an application to the Tribunal, would need to show that it was reasonable to follow this exceptional course. This has been done only once successfully in modern times.[3] The power has also been used in the course of other litigation, on the application of the Law Society.[4]

Applications of this kind made by litigants in person will not be entertained because the Solicitors Act (SA) 1974 preserves the court's inherent jurisdiction as it had been prior to the Supreme Court of Judicature Act 1873, and both before and after that Act it was settled law that the jurisdiction was limited in practice, in that an application could only be made if supported by counsel.[5]

Ordinarily, if a judge is concerned that a solicitor may have been guilty of professional misconduct, he will order that the matter be referred to the SRA, and a transcript made of the relevant part of the proceedings. Alternatively the judge may write to the SRA, setting out his or her concerns about the professional conduct of the solicitor in question.

1 Section 50 of the Solicitors Act 1974; the procedure is set out in section 51.

2 [2014] EWHC 1741 (QB) – see the discussion at paragraphs [36]–[45].

3 *Parsons v Davies* (1983, CA, unreported).

4 *Penna v Law Society (No 3)* (1999, unreported); and *Law Society v Young* [2002] EWHC 2962 (Admin). In each case the solicitor had been the subject of an intervention on the grounds of a suspicion of dishonesty. In *Penna*, in the subsequent proceedings by which he sought to challenge the intervention the solicitor so misconducted himself in defiance of court orders that the court on the Law Society's application used its inherent powers to strike him off, taking the facts that led to the intervention and his subsequent conduct into account. In *Young* the solicitor continued to practise as a solicitor and to hold himself out as a solicitor in court proceedings, so that there was contempt as well as continuing misconduct.

5 *Re Solicitors, ex p Peasegood* [1994] 1 All ER 298, DC.

PART 6
The regulation of ABSs

CHAPTER 24

Alternative business structures: getting started

24.1

CHAPTER 2 deals with the authorisation of legal services bodies (traditional practices or recognised bodies – a recognised body is a legal services body that has become recognised and authorised by the Solicitors Regulation Authority (SRA)) and licensable bodies (alternative business structures (ABSs) or licensed bodies – in the same way, a licensed body is a licensable body that has become authorised).

The SRA approach to regulation is to apply the same authorisation system to all, regardless of size, label or structure. However, there are some ABS-specific considerations, principally concerned with ownership.

It is relevant to bear in mind that ABSs may vary enormously. The popular concept remains that of 'Tesco law' (despite the retail giant being among those who have, so far, shown no interest at all in providing legal services) – in other words a large, possibly national or international, company taking control of one or more law firms or choosing to invest in them.

The main focus of the regulatory provisions of the Legal Services Act (LSA) 2007 in Part 5 and Schedules 11 to 14 is to ensure that the wrong kind of people do not end up controlling law firms, and to incorporate necessary checks and balances, including the requirement to have a lawyer as Head of Legal Practice.

But at the other end of the spectrum, any law firm which is currently a traditional practice of, say, four partners, which has chosen to appoint its non-lawyer financial director as one of the four, and is therefore designated as a legal disciplinary practice with a non-lawyer manager, is an ABS, and will have to have become authorised as such at some point (the end of the transitional period, when existing recognised bodies of that kind will have to convert to ABSs, is to be set by the Legal Services Board and has not yet been set).

An ABS, or in LSA 2007 terminology a licensable body, is a body that carries on (or wishes to carry on) reserved legal activities, and a non-authorised person[1] is a manager[2] of the body or has an interest[3] in it.[4] Alternatively, a body (B) is a licensable body if another body (A) is a manager of the body or has an interest in it and non-authorised persons are entitled to exercise, or control the exercise of, at least 10 per cent of the voting rights in A.[5] Accordingly, if a holding or parent company of a firm providing reserved legal activities is partly owned by a non-authorised person who holds less than 10 per cent of its voting rights then the firm would not need to be authorised as an ABS, but would still need to be regulated by an approved regulator in the provision of reserved legal activities.

Many firms who would not apply the 'Tesco law' label to themselves may have no option but to be regulated as ABSs.

1 The term 'person' includes a body of persons corporate or unincorporated (section 207 of LSA 2007). A non-authorised person is not defined in LSA 2007 but 'authorised person' is, and refers to a person who is authorised to provide reserved legal activities; see section 18.
2 The term 'manager' is defined in section 207. In summary, a manager will be a member of a limited liability partnership or similar organisation, director of a company, partner in a partnership or the member of a governing body of an unincorporated association.
3 'Interest' is defined as either holding shares or being entitled to exercise, or control the exercise of, voting rights in the body – section 72(4).
4 Section 72(1) of LSA 2007.
5 Section 72(2).

24.2

There is a choice of regulator. Both the SRA and the Council for Licensed Conveyancers (CLC) are licensing authorities approved by the Legal Services Board (LSB). Currently the SRA regulates the supply of all reserved legal activities apart from notarial activities, and the CLC may only regulate those supplying conveyancing and probate services, but the CLC has applied to the LSB to extend its remit to include litigation and advocacy, and has made rules in anticipation of this application being granted (see **CHAPTER 12**). It is foreseeable that there will be two regulators in direct competition.

Regulation of ownership

24.3

LSA 2007 regulates ownership of an ABS by a non-authorised person where that person controls a material interest in an ABS. Broadly, a material interest is one where the non-authorised person holds at least 10 per cent of the shares of the ABS (or equivalent) or at least 10 per cent of the shares of the parent of the ABS, or is able to exercise significant influence in the management of the ABS or its parent by virtue of the shareholding.[1] The licensing authority has to be satisfied that the non-authorised person holding a material interest in the ABS does not compromise the regulatory objectives set out in section 1 of LSA 2007 (see **1.4**). It must also not compromise the duty of regulated persons employed by the ABS to fulfil their duty to comply with regulatory requirements; and the person must be fit and proper to hold the interest.[2] In determining whether the licensing authority is satisfied as to the above matters, it must have regard to the non-authorised person's probity and financial position, whether he or she is disqualified from being a Head of Legal Practice, Head of Finance and Administration or as a manager or employee of a licensed body, under section 99 of LSA 2007, or included on the LSB's list of persons subject to objections and conditions (that is objections and conditions relating to ownership notified to the LSB by licensing authorities), and must also have regard to the person's associates.[3]

Where the ABS is owned by one or more non-authorised persons who have a less than 10 per cent interest in the ABS, these persons will not be subject to the same controls.

Where it is applicable, the SRA Suitability Test will be applied to interest holders as it is to non-lawyer managers, which is essentially the same as that which applies in relation to admission to the solicitors' profession. It is entirely logical that the character and suitability requirements for non-lawyers having a material interest in a regulated business should be identical to those applied to the lawyers. In some respects the test may need to be more onerous as LSA 2007 clearly contemplates consideration of the associates of the non-authorised owners and managers as part of the assessment process. These are widely defined to include family and other businesses related directly or indirectly to the non-authorised person.[4] There is no equivalent process for admission to one of the legal professions. However, part 2 of the SRA Suitability Test, which applies only to those holding roles within ABSs, including interest holders, includes a reference to the relevance of evidence reflecting on the honesty and integrity of associates where there is reason to believe that those others have influence over the way in which the intended authorised role will be fulfilled.

1 Paragraph 3 of Schedule 13 to LSA 2007.
2 Paragraph 6(1) of Schedule 13.
3 Paragraph 6(3) of Schedule 13.
4 Paragraph 5 of Schedule 13.

24.4

There is a requirement to identify any non-authorised person who has or is expected to have a material interest in the ABS in the application for a licence.[1] There is also an obligation to inform the licensing authority when a non-authorised person acquires a material interest in an ABS.[2] It is a criminal offence to fail to do so.[3] The licensing authority may impose conditions on the approval of the non-authorised person, either in the context of an application (a notified interest) or when notification is made of a new interest in an existing licensed body (a notifiable interest).[4] If it proposes to do so it must give a warning notice as to the proposed conditions and the reasons for imposing them, and permit representations to be made before a final decision is made. The licensing authority may also object altogether to the non-authorised person's interest in the ABS, with the same limitations.[5] Where a licence has already been granted and the objection or conditions relate to a new notifiable interest, notice and the opportunity for representations may be dispensed with if it is necessary or desirable to do so for the purpose of protecting any of the regulatory objectives.[6]

It is also possible to impose conditions or further conditions on an existing interest holder, or to raise an objection to an existing interest holder, with the same limitations and exceptions.[7]

There is a right of appeal to the Solicitors Disciplinary Tribunal (if the licensing authority is the SRA) against such decisions. See **CHAPTER 22** for appeals to the Tribunal.

There is, of course, no indication at present as to what conditions could sensibly be applied to an interest holder if in all respects he or she is suitable to hold the interest.

1 Paragraph 10 of Schedule 13 to LSA 2007.
2 Paragraph 21 of Schedule 13.
3 Paragraphs 11 and 22 of Schedule 13.
4 Paragraphs 17 and 28 of Schedule 13.
5 Paragraphs 17(3) to (5), 19(2) to (4), 28(3) to (5) and 31(2) to (5) of Schedule 13.
6 Paragraphs 28(4) and 31(3) of Schedule 13.
7 Paragraphs 33 and 36 of Schedule 13.

24.5

Paragraph 38 of Schedule 13 to LSA 2007 enables licensing rules to make general provision for the limitation of the level of the shareholding, control or voting rights of non-authorised persons. The SRA's rules do not expressly provide for this, but the same effect can be achieved by imposing conditions on a case-by-case basis. There is no restriction in LSA 2007 as to the number of ABSs in which a non-authorised person can take an interest.

24.6

If a non-authorised person continues to hold an interest in an ABS in breach of conditions or despite objection the licensing authority may apply to the High Court for an order that the person be divested of the interest; see **25.8**.

Other controls

24.7

All non-lawyer managers of ABSs must also be expressly approved, as must the Heads of Legal Practice and of Finance and Administration who, within the SRA Authorisation Rules for Legal Services Bodies and Licensable Bodies 2011, become compliance officers for legal practice (COLPs) or for finance and administration (COFAs). No distinction is drawn by the SRA between the mechanisms for approval of COLPs and COFAs or non-lawyer managers by reference to whether the body is an ABS or a traditional law practice. As to authorisation generally see **CHAPTER 2**. As to COLPs and COFAs, see **CHAPTER 6**.

CHAPTER 25

Alternative business structures: discipline and enforcement

Disciplinary powers

25.1

For law firms in their traditional form the relationship between their practices and their regulatory and disciplinary bodies had been unchanged for decades; indeed for a century. Discipline, in the sense of penalty, including the ultimate deterrent of being struck off the roll, was the province of the court (initially exclusively, but in modern times only through a surviving inherent jurisdiction rarely used – see **CHAPTER 23**), and the Solicitors Disciplinary Committee (from the nineteenth century until 1975), and the Solicitors Disciplinary Tribunal ('the Tribunal' or SDT) from 1975.

The Law Society, and latterly the Solicitors Regulation Authority (SRA), had no disciplinary powers at all; it could exercise control through the training and admission process, and by means of practising certificate conditions, and by intervention, and it could elect to prosecute solicitors before the Tribunal, but in that respect it was not a decision-maker, it was a party in adversarial proceedings.

The practice which grew up of imposing what were first called rebukes, severe rebukes and chairman's rebukes (which involved the solicitor attending at the Law Society to be told off by the chairman of the relevant committee, warned that he (or much more rarely she) had come within a whisker of being referred to the Tribunal, and cautioned not to do it again),[1] and which later changed their name to reprimands and severe reprimands (for no discernible reason) had never had any statutory origin. They were developed as a mechanism by which a solicitor could be told that something had gone wrong in circumstances in which no further action was necessary.

1 These fell into disuse in the 1990s when solicitors became more argumentative.

25.2

It all changed as a result of the Legal Services Act (LSA) 2007 and another raft of changes to the much amended Solicitors Act (SA) 1974. After some wrangling over the required procedural rules the Law Society, in the guise of the SRA, became a disciplinary body in relation to solicitors in relation to acts and omissions occurring or continuing on or after 1 June 2010 (see **CHAPTER 19**).

Those powers however, in relation to solicitors in traditional law firms, remain modest. Formal statutory and potentially public rebukes have replaced informal non-statutory and largely private reprimands, and there is a power to impose a fine not exceeding £2,000. Importantly, this was only designed to reduce the caseload of the Tribunal and remove low level cases from its jurisdiction. The Tribunal remains the primary disciplinary body, although the SRA has, from a time shortly after it acquired the power, been seeking to increase the level of fines it can impose.

25.3

It may come as a shock to those solicitors who, instead of being partners or managers or employees of a traditional firm or recognised body, are partners or managers or employees of an ABS, to learn that their primary disciplinary body has become the SRA.

The structure of LSA 2007 is that the licensing authority is responsible for disciplinary as well as licensing decisions, with the Tribunal reverting to being an appeal body (see **CHAPTER 22**).

It is the SRA which has the power to fine the business, its managers and employees (not the Tribunal),[1] and the fine is not limited to £2,000, but extends to a maximum of £250 million, for the business, and £50 million, for an individual.[2]

Further the SRA has the power of disqualification – to disqualify any individual from being a Head of Legal Practice (HOLP) or Head of Finance and Administration (HOFA) (compliance officer for legal practice (COLP) or compliance officer for finance and administration (COFA) in SRA terminology) and from being a manager of an ABS, and from being even an employee of an ABS.[3]

A disqualification from being employed in one or more of those capacities could be as devastating in its consequences as being struck off as a solicitor.

However, although the consequences of an adverse result are infinitely more serious, the disciplinary powers in relation to ABSs and all individuals within ABSs are dealt with under the same rules and the same procedures as are applied to traditional practices (see **CHAPTERS 14** and **19**).

The SRA has not made clear whether and to what extent it will move from its present position of rarely if ever conducting oral hearings, bearing in mind that the procedural rules and the policies followed in this respect have been substantially unchanged for a period of years, but that the consequences of the decisions it can now make are so different. It is likely to be argued that an opportunity to appeal to the Tribunal and to obtain a discretionary stay would not be sufficient to provide a fair disciplinary system. It is understood that the SRA may well accept that oral hearings and a more formal and transparent approach to decision-making will be necessary for serious or contentious matters affecting ABSs.

For appeals to the Tribunal against the exercise of the SRA's disciplinary powers and licensing decisions see **CHAPTER 22**.

1 Section 95 of LSA 2007.
2 Legal Services Act 2007 (Licensing Authorities) (Maximum Penalty) Rules 2011 (SI 2011/1659).
3 Section 99 of LSA 2007.

Investigatory powers

25.4

The SRA's investigatory powers under sections 44B and 44BA of SA 1974 are considered in **CHAPTER 14** (see **14.9**). These apply to solicitors subject to the regulation of the SRA whether they are employed in ABSs or traditional firms. They do not otherwise apply to ABSs. The parallel provisions in relation to non-solicitor managers or employees of ABSs are in sections 93 and 94 of LSA 2007.

The terms of section 93 are similar to sections 44B and 44BA combined, and extend the powers of the SRA, to require information to be provided and documents to be produced, to former managers and employees of the licensed body and any non-authorised person who has an interest or an indirect interest, or holds a material interest, in the licensed body. However, the powers are not backed by criminal sanctions and the remedy for non-compliance, provided by section 94, is an application by the licensing authority to the High Court for an order to comply with the notice.

The duty to co-operate fully with the SRA in relation to any investigation (outcome 10.6 and Chapter 10 of the SRA Code of Conduct 2011 generally) continues to apply to every person and body regulated by the SRA, as does rule 31 of the SRA Accounts Rules 2011, imposing an obligation to co-operate and supply information and documents related to the practice accounts.

Other quasi-disciplinary powers

25.5

The licence of an ABS may be suspended or revoked[1] in circumstances which are regulated by paragraph 24 of Schedule 11 to LSA 2007. These are replicated in rule 22 of the SRA Authorisation Rules.[2] The SRA may revoke or suspend an authorised body's authorisation (that is, any practice that the SRA has authorised, ABS or non-ABS) where:

- authorisation was granted as a result of error, misleading or inaccurate information, or fraud;
- the body is or becomes ineligible to be authorised in accordance with the criteria set out in the Authorisation Rules;
- the SRA is satisfied that the body has no intention of carrying on the legal activities for which it has been authorised;
- the body has failed to provide any information required by the SRA under the Authorisation Rules;
- the body has failed to pay any fee payable to the SRA under the Authorisation Rules;
- a relevant insolvency event[3] has occurred in relation to the body;
- the body makes an application to the SRA for its authorisation to be revoked or suspended;
- the SRA has decided to exercise its intervention powers;

- the body, or an owner, interest holder, manager or employee of the body fails to comply with the duties imposed by or under the Authorisation Rules or under any statutory obligations in relation to the body's business of carrying on authorised activities, including payment of any fine or other financial penalty imposed on the body by the SRA, the Tribunal or the High Court;
- in the case of a licensed body (applicable to ABSs alone) the body fails to comply with the prohibition on appointing disqualified managers; or in the case of any authorised body, the body fails to comply with the prohibition on employing disqualified persons (struck off solicitors and the like) if the manager or employee concerned was disqualified as a result of breach of the duties imposed upon the manager or employee by sections 176 or 90 of LSA 2007 (the general duties imposed to comply with all regulatory arrangements for ABSs);
- the body does not comply with the requirements in relation to compliance officers;
- the body fails to comply with the management and control requirements (to ensure that those requiring approval are approved and that no disqualified person is employed without permission); or
- for any other reason it is in the public interest.

In the case of a *licensed* body (applicable to ABSs alone), it may revoke or suspend a body's authorisation, where a non-authorised person holds an interest in the licensed body:

- as a result of the person taking a step in circumstances where that constitutes an offence under paragraph 24(1) of Schedule 13 to LSA 2007 (whether or not the person is charged with or convicted of an offence under that paragraph) – this is failing to give notice as to the proposed or actual acquisition of a material interest in an ABS;
- in breach of conditions imposed on the owners of material interests in the ABS; or
- the person's holding of which is subject to an objection by the licensing authority.

1 Section 101 of LSA 2007.
2 This subject is also dealt with in **CHAPTER 2** but is repeated here for convenience.
3 See the footnote to **2.8**.

25.6

Before the SRA can revoke or suspend an authorisation it must first give the authorised body an opportunity to make representations to it on the issues that have led the SRA to consider this course, and it must also give at least 28 days' notice of its intention to make the decision to revoke or suspend.[1]

Guidance notes to rule 22 emphasise that the SRA is unlikely to revoke or suspend authorisation if to do so would present any risk to clients, the public, the protection of public money or to any SRA investigation.

1 Rule 22.2 of the Authorisation Rules.

25.7

Where an interest holder holds a material interest in an ABS in breach of conditions imposed by a licensing authority the authority may apply to the High Court for an order to secure compliance with the conditions. The licensing authority may not make an application to the court unless it has given notice of its intention to do so and, at the end of the notice period, the interest holder is still in breach of the conditions. In other words, an opportunity must be given to the interest holder to regularise the position. The notice period is to be prescribed by the Legal Services Board (LSB) and has not yet been set.

No order may be made by the court until the end of any period for appeal against the imposition of conditions and, if there is an appeal, until the appeal is disposed of.[1]

1 Paragraph 46(5) of Schedule 13 to LSA 2007.

Divestiture

25.8

Part 5 of Schedule 13 to LSA 2007 contains provisions enabling the licensing authority to apply to the High Court for an order divesting an interest holder of an interest in an ABS where the interest consists of a shareholding in a company with a share capital, if the non-authorised person holds a material interest in the licensed body either in circumstances where notice has not been given of the acquisition or intended acquisition of the interest so that an offence has been committed under paragraph 24(1) of Schedule 13, or the interest is held in breach of conditions imposed by the licensing authority or in contravention of an objection by the authority.

The licensing authority may serve a 'restriction notice' which may provide that a transfer of shares or similar arrangement is void, that no voting rights may be exercised, that no further shares be issued to the holder and that no payment may be made by the company in relation to the shares (other than in a liquidation).[1]

On an application to the High Court the court may order the sale of the shares. The licensing authority may not make an application to the court for a divestiture order unless it has given notice of its intention to do so and, at the end of the notice period, the conditions for divestiture still apply. In other words, an opportunity must be given to the interest holder to regularise the position. The notice period is to be prescribed by the LSB and has not yet been set.

No order may be made by the court until the end of any period for appeal against the imposition of conditions or the objection and, if there is an appeal, until the appeal is disposed of.[2]

1 Paragraph 44 of Schedule 13 to LSA 2007.
2 Paragraph 45(5).

Intervention

25.9

Powers of intervention are available to the licensing authority which are broadly comparable to those applying to solicitors' practices under Schedule 1 to SA 1974. They are set out in Schedule 14 to LSA 2007.

An intervention may be authorised where a licence granted to a body has expired, and has not been renewed or replaced by the relevant licensing authority, or where one or more of the intervention conditions is satisfied.

The intervention conditions are:

'(a) that the licensing authority is satisfied that one or more of the terms of the licensed body's licence have not been complied with;

(b) that a person has been appointed receiver or manager of property of the licensed body;

(c) that a relevant insolvency event has occurred in relation to the licensed body;

(d) that the licensing authority has reason to suspect dishonesty on the part of any manager or employee of the licensed body in connection with—

  (i) that body's business,

  (ii) any trust of which that body is or was a trustee,

  (iii) any trust of which the manager or employee of the body is or was a trustee in that person's capacity as such a manager or employee, or

  (iv) the business of another body in which the manager or employee is or was a manager or employee, or the practice (or former practice) of the manager or employee;

(e) that the licensing authority is satisfied that there has been undue delay—

  (i) on the part of the licensed body in connection with any matter in which it is or was acting for a client or with any trust of which it is or was a trustee, or

  (ii) on the part of a person who is or was a manager or employee of the licensed body in connection with any trust of which that person is or was a trustee in that person's capacity as such a manager or employee,

and the notice conditions are satisfied;[1]

(f) that the licensing authority is satisfied that it is necessary to exercise the powers conferred by this Schedule (or any of them) in relation to a licensed body to protect:

  (i) the interests of clients (or former or potential clients) of the licensed body,

(ii) the interests of the beneficiaries of any trust of which the licensed body is or was a trustee, or

(iii) the interests of the beneficiaries of any trust of which a person who is or was a manager or employee of the licensed body is or was a trustee in that person's capacity as such a manager or employee.'

1 This only applies if the licensing authority has requested an explanation, that at least eight days have been given for a reply, and if notice has then been given that the licensing authority does not regard the response to be satisfactory and that the powers of intervention have arisen.

25.10

Essentially the same relief is available to challenge the intervention by application to the High Court as is available to solicitors' practices; see **CHAPTER 16**.

PART 7
Fraud and money laundering

CHAPTER 26

The risks of fraud

26.1

In this section it is intended to highlight certain danger areas which have resulted in guidance being given to the profession but which are not reflected in any specific rule.

Mortgage fraud

26.2

The Law Society has issued successive warnings on mortgage fraud (the 'Green Cards'). The Solicitors Regulation Authority (SRA) has withdrawn its own warning notice on property fraud and it is understood that a revised notice is being drafted to reflect the requirements of the SRA Handbook. Also at the time of writing, having visited more than 100 firms, the SRA is developing a supervision and enforcement strategy for conveyancing with a view to issuing a more practical conveyancing fraud policy bridging the gap between the old prescriptive rules and the new outcomes-focused regulation.

The involvement, innocent or otherwise, of solicitors or licensed conveyancers is essential to all mortgage fraud, in the sense that they are required to enable the transaction to occur.

There have historically been four basic types of 'traditional' mortgage fraud, with a potentially endless selection of variations on the basic theme:

(1) exaggeration of the borrower's income to obtain a mortgage that would otherwise be declined;

(2) multiple purchases, where a fraudster uses false names or nominees to build up a portfolio of property through residential rather than commercial borrowing;

(3) identity theft, where money is borrowed in the name of the proprietor on a remortgage, and diverted to the fraudsters; and

(4) exaggeration of price or value, to obtain a higher mortgage than would properly be justified.

Of course, sometimes more than one element can feature in a fraudulent scheme.

Identity theft as a mortgage fraud device has been extended to situations in which property is sold from under the genuine proprietor by a fraudster using the proprietor's name or situations where the fraudster sets up a bogus law firm or a bogus branch office of a legitimate firm.[1]

Solicitors will not generally expect to encounter false employers' references, for example, although there could well arise circumstances to put any reasonable solicitor on notice that the borrower client's means do not appear to match the lender's requirements for the amount being loaned. Furthermore, the obligations under the Money Laundering Regulations 2007[2] of due diligence and enhanced due diligence, and the obligation to monitor business relationships and transactions as they develop (considered in detail in **CHAPTER 27**) now have a direct relevance to these issues and should result in such patterns being detected. Regrettably, there have been solicitors who have been prepared to provide false references for their own employees or even to indulge in this kind of fraud for their own benefit.[3]

Solicitors are well placed to detect and prevent frauds of the second and third kinds and in some cases their active complicity, or determinedly deliberate Nelsonian blindness, is essential to the success of the frauds.

1 See the SRA's warning notice on bogus law firms and identity theft.
2 SI 2007/2157.
3 *Re a Solicitor (Maharaj)* (1999, unreported).

26.3

In a rising market fraud can frequently remain undetected as, if questions are asked or arrears develop, the property can be sold at a profit and the lender's concerns assuaged. It is when a sudden drop in prices occurs and there is no escape route that frauds become particularly apparent. It is for that reason that following the recession that started in about 1989 and continued into the 1990s the profession was caught up in one of its greatest scandals as the extent of widespread mortgage fraud became known, and the extent to which the negligence of solicitors, or worse, had contributed to it.

The recent recession is having the same effect in disclosing mortgage fraud and, as expected, extensive fraudulent activities have been and are being uncovered. The adverse effects on the buy-to-let market caused by the economic downturn have provided opportunities for fraudsters in relation to the bulk refinancing/remortgaging of such borrowing. Lenders and the SRA, as well as other regulators, are becoming ever more proactive in policing and detecting trends and risks.

Multiple purchases

26.4

When it was the norm to meet your client in routine domestic conveyancing it was easier to spot warning signs. Now, despite the requirement for identity checks imposed by money laundering legislation, because of the development of commoditised conveyancing and online dealings, the conveyancing environment remains relatively friendly to frauds of this kind.

Individual buyers may be real people, but nominees. A common feature of this kind of fraud is a central figure through whom communications are required to be channelled. This could be a broker or a senior family member. All or most instructions are given by the key individual; solicitors may be encouraged to correspond with clients through that individual, and to send money and documents to that individual. Documents are sent to him or her to be signed by others and come back signed and witnessed. It all seems very efficient.

26.5

Solicitors should be alive to the fact that commercial pressures exist, and that fraudsters are highly attuned to the business community. They may be attracted to your practice, not because it has the best local reputation for efficient conveyancing, but because it is new or not apparently very wealthy, so that offers of substantial work might encourage the turning of a blind eye. Fraudsters will have their own intelligence network and will seek out those perceived to be vulnerable or susceptible to financial pressures, flattery, or occasionally coercion and blackmail. Coercion and blackmail sound like extreme scenarios, but you need to bear in mind that if a solicitor bends or breaks a rule as a 'favour' he also gives any person with knowledge of his wrongdoing power over him, including the person to whom he gave the favour ('We are now in this together …').

A more sophisticated version of this fraud involves the fraudster instructing a panel of solicitors, without disclosing to any firm that he is using more than one. Multiple transactions become more difficult to detect. If you become aware that an individual has more than one firm acting for him in such circumstances or for unexplained reasons, be suspicious.

Mules

26.6

Experienced conveyancers are very familiar with the patterns of behaviour of purchaser clients. To most, buying a new home is a very substantial, serious and potentially stressful transaction; they will ask questions, be concerned about matters of detail, be anxious about dates and progress. If clients introduced by Mr X show a pattern of near indifference, and contact is limited and amounts to virtually no more than an exchange of documents, there are likely to be grounds for suspicion. If the attitude of Mr X appears to be that of a businessman asking questions that are consistent with a businessman's outlook, rather than the questions clients could be expected to ask, it is more likely that it is he who has the true interest in the transaction, rather than those he purports to represent.

Mules – nominees or people with false identification used as buyers of property to facilitate fraud – have none of the normal interest that buyers of property will display. They may sometimes be exposed by even casual questioning.

Identity theft

26.7

Fraudsters can steal the identity of property owners, either to remortgage the property or to sell it to a genuine buyer or a co-conspirator. Ensure you know with whom you are dealing. Be concerned if it is said that there are reasons why the seller cannot be contacted. Common features are:

- a central figure, usually a broker introducing multiple transactions to the practice. He will be the only point of contact and will deal with clients on your behalf. He will reassure you that all regulatory and professional obligations have already been attended to. You may rarely if ever meet or have direct dealings with the client;

- rushed transactions; there will be an explanation such as a family crisis or other reason for urgency;
- the only money changing hands being the mortgage advance;
- instructions to remit funds to the client account of a named firm of solicitors (possibly the funds are urgently needed for mother's nursing home fees). The destination account may involve a bogus firm of solicitors or a ghost branch office of a genuine firm.

Exaggerated price or value

26.8

At its most basic this involves a friendly valuer putting too high a figure on the property and some private arrangement between buyer and seller, but in this type of fraud it is more often than not the case that the manipulation of the price is apparent to a watchful solicitor.

A solicitor should be alive to anything which could artificially inflate the price to be paid so that the amount of money that changes hands is less than the stated purchase price. Historically, this has been done by such things as mythical 'deposits paid direct' or an 'allowance on completion' operating as a substantial discount on the stated price.

Another mechanism is to introduce a third party into the chain so that the transaction proceeds as a sale and sub-sale, or a 'back-to-back' sale and resale – the first half of the transaction being at the correct price agreed to be paid to the seller and the second half involving a sale to the real buyer at the inflated price declared to the mortgagee.

The purpose is to achieve a situation in which the mortgagee lends more than 100 per cent of the true value or price so that the fraudulent buyer acquires the property and a cash bonus.

Another warning sign is a client instructing a solicitor geographically distant from the property for no good apparent reason; this limits the opportunities for personal dealing and avoids local knowledge of the housing market.

A flat property market offers limited opportunities for price leverage but sale and leaseback can be used for this purpose, for example where there is a distressed vendor (facing repossession), genuine or impersonated. A firm may be approached by a broker and offered a package of such transactions, all pre-agreed and pre-arranged.

26.9

Solicitors can become complicit by failing to identify the relevant features of the transaction for what they are, or occasionally by more active assistance. One solicitor, when faced with solicitors acting for the seller who refused to co-operate by agreeing, as requested, to an inflated contract price and an 'allowance on completion' amounting to more than 25 per cent of the true price, solved his fraudulent client's problem by acquiring an off the shelf Isle of Man company and arranging the sale to the company at the true price and immediate sale on by the company to his client at the inflated price declared to the mortgagee. He charged for both conveyancing transactions, and the services involved in arranging the company and its involvement.[1]

Solicitors will face not only civil claims from mortgagees if fraud has occurred, but also disciplinary proceedings with serious consequences – even if it is ultimately established that the solicitor was not actively complicit as a co-conspirator, but only insufficiently alert to the danger signs.

1 *Levinson,* 6942–1995, SDT. Mr Levinson explained to the Tribunal that this was not his own idea; he had copied it from his former partner, a Mr Nathan, who had in the meantime been struck off and sent to prison. Mr Levinson was struck off.

Fraud factories

26.10

Another relatively recent development involves the acquisition of law practices by fraudsters. Genuine firms facing difficulties or under financial pressure may be offered the opportunity of being taken over by a team which offers to introduce a portfolio of transactions, and conveyancing clerks to manage it. The purchaser may purport to be a solicitor, impersonating a genuine solicitor. Alternatively it may be a non-solicitor who makes the same offer, on the basis that he will become a financial controller or office manager. All such new arrivals, and their support teams, will be heavily resistant to supervision.

These arrangements are not designed to last for long, and the new owners have no interest in the success of the business; they are simply designed to obtain mortgage advances which are stolen. These 'fraud factories' may have a life of only three months, but those who control them can steal millions in that time.

Solicitors as victims

26.11

Criminals, particularly international criminals, appear to have concluded that solicitors can be a soft touch by being too trusting. The Serious Organised Crime Agency (now the National Crime Agency) has issued a warning to solicitors, particularly litigation practices which, because they may undertake little or no transactional work and may not even be subject to the Money Laundering Regulations, may be less alive to the risks. Fraudsters are approaching British firms for assistance in relation to personal injury, debt and other claims. The firms shortly receive large cheques representing purported settlements. If the solicitors are incautious enough, under pressure, to release funds without waiting for the received cheques to clear, they find that the cheques are fraudulent or stolen, leaving the firm to bear the loss.

The Law Society has issued an update (22 October 2012) which provides guidance on recognising what it terms 'Advance fee fraud'.

Investment fraud

26.12

Investment fraud is another serious issue for the profession because, in relation to the kinds of fraud that are discussed here, solicitors are essential to their success.

The broad nature of these frauds is that they offer to be highly profitable – to the point of absurdity – while being at the same time wholly secure. The justification for this investment paradox, which defies all normal rules, is that they are reserved to the few insiders who know about them. They are also targeted at those who can afford, or at least can find, large sums to invest – commonly US$1 million or more (the medium is usually US dollars) – so that the victim may think that it is his wealth that enables him to engage in business ventures unavailable to others.

The trap

26.13

These frauds are more successful than would otherwise be expected because of the involvement of solicitors. The necessity for the involvement of solicitors is explained by an understanding of the different attitudes of the three participants – fraudster, victim and solicitor – which the fraudster exploits.

The victim will think, 'This is new to me; I have not heard of this form of investment before, but I am sure that if it was not genuine no solicitor would permit himself to be involved'.

The solicitor's attitude is, 'I do not truly understand what is going on here, but I do not have to. All I am being asked to do is to confirm that this copy document is a true copy of an original, or that I have received a particular document or a document of a particular description, or that I have received a specific sum of money. I do not have to go beyond that and I am not required to'.

The fraudster's position is, 'If I can get a solicitor involved the victim will be reassured, and the scheme given a credibility that it would not otherwise have. I am prepared to pay substantial sums for that involvement; it will be money well spent'.

The solicitor may be offered generous fees for doing very little, or the opportunity to earn interest on very large sums of money that pass through his or her client account.

The test

26.14

It is not considered to be particularly helpful to attempt to describe the range of possible kinds of fraud or the (usually highly complex and turgid) details of those that have been attempted in the past. They change and become more sophisticated as time passes. The one thing they have in common is that if they are carefully considered they do not make sense. They were often referred to as 'Prime Bank Instrument' frauds, by reference to the kind of document that was used to perpetrate them; they have also been termed 'High Yield Investment Programmes'. They were described by Neuberger J in *Dooley v Law Society*[1] in these words:

'Bank instrument frauds are based on documents which are full of impressive phrases, which on analysis make little sense, and which promise returns which are fantastic in both senses in which that word is used, namely fictitious and enormous. They are used by unscrupulous rogues to encourage the badly advised, the ignorant, the gullible and the greedy to part with their money, tempted by promises of the fantastically high returns. Once these investors part with their money, they are lucky if they see any of it again. Generally speaking, a man may as well burn his money for all the good it would do him. At least it would remove the false hopes and subsequent agony that such so-called investments involve.'

1 2000, unreported.

26.15

The Tribunal has dealt with many such cases. The following comments made by the Tribunal help to identify the pattern, and particularly the kind of mistake, that solicitors make:

'Members of the solicitors' profession had been warned about the dangers of becoming involved in prime bank instrument fraud or money laundering. The matter in which the Respondent had become involved demonstrated many of the notified hallmarks of fraud; it was entirely clear that the Respondent himself had no understanding of the investment scheme and had simply done what he was told and allowed his client account to be a repository for a huge sum of money.

The Tribunal has had cause in the past to make the observation which it again makes. A solicitor is not a bank. A solicitor can have no business simply in receiving and paying out money with no purpose attached to it. If a solicitor is not more knowledgeable about the subject matter of the cases of which he has conduct than his clients then he should not be handling such cases. A solicitor's stock-in-trade is his knowledge and expertise. If his clients are not utilising such knowledge and expertise it is likely that the solicitor is being involved in order that a spurious scheme be given a cloak of respectability.'[1]

'It is not for a client to explain the nature of a transaction to a solicitor but rather the solicitor's role is to explain the nature of a transaction to the client. It can be described as nothing other than crass stupidity to accept a role as, for example, an "escrow agent" when the solicitor cannot know what that means as, indeed, that expression has no meaning in English law. It is, in any event, serious professional misconduct for a solicitor to accept instructions to undertake work in connection with which he has no knowledge, expertise or experience and where the only reason for his involvement is to add a "cloak of respectability" and thereby induce the victims of fraud to take part. The Respondent himself accepts that he should have known or suspected that the transactions in which he became involved were not viable commercial transactions.'[2]

'The Respondent had ensured that scurrilous transactions were given a cloak of respectability by allowing his firm's name to be used in connection with what was on its face a transaction of the type against which the Law

Society had issued warnings. It is in the Tribunal's opinion perhaps the most important aspect of this case that the Respondent was prepared to write letters regarding a matter in which he played no part as a solicitor. He had no knowledge of the type of transactions involved, he had no relevant experience and he did not, and indeed could not, give anybody any advice as to the legal aspects. A solicitor becomes involved in acting for a client when the client needs the solicitor's advice and expertise in the relevant area of law. The Tribunal accepts that there are rogues and fraudsters who are extremely plausible. A solicitor is unlikely to be taken in by such a person if he asks himself the question "why am I invited to become involved in this matter?" If the answer is not "because the client seeks to rely upon my legal expertise, knowledge and experience", he should not be playing any part in the matter.'[3]

'The Respondent at the relevant time had been an experienced practitioner. He had stated that he had not seen the yellow warning card issued by the Law Society. The warning card had however not changed the then existing duties on solicitors but had provided clarificatory guidance. The Respondent had clearly been asked to become involved in something which was out of his ordinary line of business involving overseas countries and huge sums of money. The Respondent had put his name to unintelligible documents and to documents drafted by his client which he had not questioned. He had distributed funds received from third parties at the direction of his client and had produced no evidence of proper authority to do so. He had written letters of comfort to banks and solicitors. He had involved himself in the transactions over a period of time. The transactions had never completed. The Respondent had expected significant personal gain from his involvement.'[4]

'The Respondent himself had come to recognise that he should not have been involved in the dubious HYI [High Yield Investment] transactions details of which had been placed before the Tribunal. The attention of members of the profession had been drawn to the proliferation of fraudulent investment schemes purporting to produce extraordinarily high returns on investments. It was recognised that a number of fraudsters sought to deprive potential investors of large sums of money by the production of bizarre schemes, spurious documentation and promises of very high returns indeed, often with the added incentive to invest provided by an assurance that monies would be used for charitable causes or humanitarian projects. It ill behoves a solicitor to use phrases and expressions that have no meaning in English law. It beggars belief that a solicitor should employ such phrases in letters that he himself has written. The question has to be asked, "how can a solicitor offer advice to any client or third party upon a scheme which is so nonsensical that he himself cannot have any useful knowledge of it?" It is well recognised that the fraudsters customarily seek to involve a member of the solicitors' profession in order that a cloak of respectability may be achieved and those defrauded are encouraged to part with large sums of money because of the comfort they derive from the fact that a solicitor is involved in the transaction. In becoming involved in the fraudulent schemes, as the Respondent did, he falsely allowed his own status and the good reputation of the solicitors' profession to be used improperly to persuade potential "investors" to make substantial investment of money. The only proper way for a solicitor to behave when invited to participate in one of these schemes, in whatever capacity, is to refuse to do so and report the approach made to him to the appropriate authorities. For a solicitor to become involved in dubious and/or fraudulent transactions of this type was not compatible with his continued membership of the profession.'[5]

1 *Wayne*, 8189–2000, SDT.
2 *Wilson-Smith*, 8772–2003, SDT.
3 *Rose*, 9067–2004, SDT.
4 *Rosling*, 9242–2005, SDT.
5 *Heath*, 9502–2006, SDT.

26.16

It will have been noted that the single strand of logical concern that permeates these cases is that the client knows more about the subject matter than the solicitor: he is not seeking legal advice and assistance; he is directing the solicitor in what he is required to do and explaining matters to the solicitor, not seeking guidance. In fact, many such schemes are constructed purely for the purposes of money laundering between individuals with a common interest, serving only to move large amounts of money into and out of a solicitor's client account. Compliance with the Money Laundering Regulations 2007 considered in **CHAPTER 27** is vital, and would be effective to prevent involvement in such schemes if faithfully followed.

Further, if solicitors ask themselves the questions identified by the Tribunal in *Rose* and *Heath* the precise nature of the fraudulent scheme will not matter. However much fraudsters change the language and apparent structure, and even if the consequence of such changes is that every 'common characteristic' or 'typical phrase' appearing in the Law Society's/SRA's warning card/notice[1] is avoided, it will be a straightforward matter for solicitors to identify dubious transactions and avoid involvement.

In *Bryant and Bench v Law Society*,[2] solicitors who had acted for clients in a series of 'dubious' transactions, even though not themselves dishonest, were both suspended. 'Dubious' in this context meant that the transactions bore the indicia of fraud or possible fraud, and that it was professional misconduct for the appellants to act or to continue to act in relation to them without carrying out sufficient enquiries to satisfy themselves that the transactions were not, in fact, fraudulent. The Divisional Court stated (at [199] and [239]):

> '[199] In our view the appellants should have concluded that these transactions involving NIC and Mr Alonso were "dubious" in the sense described above at the very latest by the end of August 2003. But they never did so. They appeared to be naïve, uncommercial and unwilling to question matters; whereas we would have expected solicitors who had considerable experience of international clients and transactions to have developed a healthy scepticism.
>
> [239] … In the case of Mr Bryant, the incompetence displayed was considerable and continued for approximately a year. In the case of Mr Bench, his culpability was far less, but, on our findings, remains significant. We accept the submission on behalf of the Law Society that such incompetence threatens the reputation of the profession for prudence as well as competence and that it puts the public at risk.'

1 See **APPENDIX 6**.
2 [2007] EWHC 3043 (Admin). See also *Yildiz* 10997–2012 and the litigation which followed on the same facts: *Global Marine Drillships Ltd v La Bella and others* [2014] EWHC 2242 (Ch).

Land banking schemes

26.17

A further species of investment fraud, which also contains features of mortgage fraud, relates to so-called land banking schemes. These typically occur where agricultural, brownfield or other blighted land is acquired at low cost and divided into plots for sale to investors. Investors are informed that the land will soar in value once planning permission is obtained. However, as the land will usually be on a green belt or protected site, the land is unlikely to obtain planning permission or achieve the value intimated by the operator, resulting in the investor paying an inflated price for the land. Such schemes are often promoted on the basis that planning permission is imminent or that a well-known company is about to buy the land. Forged Land Registry letters and Land Registry estate plan approval letters have been used as evidence that planning permission is available when this is not the case. Also the obtaining of planning permission may be in the control of a management company which may have no intention of applying for planning permission. Operators of land banking schemes are often based overseas, making it difficult for an investor to recover funds invested in a scheme or for enforcement action to be taken against the operator. Operators may also attempt to conceal the original value of the land by inter-company transactions which inflate the original purchase price. In September 2012, the SRA issued a warning notice in respect of land banking schemes, and this is included in **APPENDIX 6**. The notice includes the following warning for solicitors acting for investors in these schemes:

> 'Please take extra care if it is envisaged that your retainer is to be limited in nature, for example it excludes providing advice to clients or is solely restricted to the registration of the properties. Before agreeing to act in these circumstances you should consider whether it is necessary to carry out due diligence in relation to the scheme in order to avoid unwittingly becoming involved in a fraudulent scheme.'

CHAPTER 27

Money laundering

27.1

This chapter provides a brief introduction to this important and complex subject, specific guidance on the Money Laundering Regulations 2007,[1] and some commentary on the principal elements of the criminal law that are engaged. It does not provide an all-encompassing guide to the subject, which derives from the criminal law and is beyond the scope of this book. The focus in this chapter is on the regulation of practitioners and the warning signs.

1 SI 2007/2157.

What is money laundering?

27.2

To quote the Financial Action Task Force of the Organisation for Economic Co-operation and Development:

> 'The goal of a large number of criminal acts is to generate a profit for the individual or group that carries out the act. Money laundering is the processing of these criminal proceeds to disguise their illegal origin. This process is of critical importance, as it enables the criminal to enjoy these profits without jeopardising their source.'

Money laundering is the process by which assets illegally obtained are 'cleaned' to give them apparent legitimacy to enable their subsequent use. It involves the purported legitimisation of *any asset* that is illegitimately obtained. An accumulation of small amounts obtained or retained by tax evasion would be criminal property for these purposes. Money laundering is designed to disguise the true origin of criminal proceeds. The process typically involves three stages – placement, layering and integration – but these are not clear cut distinctions and money laundering may become a seamless blend of all three.

Placement

27.3

The placement stage involves the placing in the financial/banking system of the proceeds of crime. The intention is to change the identity of the illegitimate asset. A solicitor's client account will serve this purpose.

Layering

27.4

The layering stage involves moving the asset through the financial system. The intention is to hide the origins of the illegitimate asset, making it difficult to trace and recover. Complex transactions may be used to disguise the source of funds. Sometimes the transactions may have no legitimate economic purpose, but simply result in money moving around (see the commentary on investment frauds at **26.12**).

Integration

27.5

The integration stage involves the translation of the laundered funds into a legitimate asset, such as the purchase of property through a conveyancing solicitor.

Solicitors as 'gatekeepers'

27.6

According to the Serious Organised Crime Agency (now the National Crime Agency):

> 'Serious organised criminals have a number of options when looking to realise the proceeds of their criminal activities. These include smuggling cash or assets out of the UK; laundering the money themselves; employing "gatekeepers", such as solicitors and accountants, with access to financial facilities; corrupting or coercing bank employees; or using professional launderers.'[1]

Professionals, including solicitors, may have a lack of awareness or lack of curiosity, so allowing themselves to be used by criminals to access the banking system and to enable the conversion of criminal funds into legitimate assets.

Solicitors may assist by becoming involved in normal transactions, such as a property purchase, but in circumstances where the client's true identity or status as nominee are disguised, and/or where the source of funds cannot be ascertained or is suspicious. Solicitors may also become involved in unusual transactions with no obvious logic where large amounts of money move about without any apparent aim. Investment frauds of the kind considered in **CHAPTER 26** invariably 'fail' in the sense that nothing comes of the 'investment' but it can be that all parties to the scheme are colluding and that the only real purpose is to move money in and out of a solicitor's client account.

A derivative of investment frauds is sham litigation. Here the fraudsters collude to litigate over an original scheme which, on close analysis, may make little sense. Signs to watch for will include clients with an unusual lack of interest in the risks of litigation, and who seem reluctant to engage in the detail. Another indicator is that one party to the litigation will suddenly capitulate, submitting to judgment for the full amount, without material effort to achieve a compromise solution.

1 The Serious Organised Crime Agency, *United Kingdom Threat Assessment of Serious Organised Crime 2006/07*.

Six key questions for solicitors

27.7

There is no substitute for understanding and following the Money Laundering Regulations 2007 (see **27.9**), but solicitors should always ask themselves:

- Am I confident I know who this person is and that I understand with whom I am really dealing?
- Am I confident that I know and understand the source of funds?
- Am I confident that I know and understand the transaction?
- Is there anything about the transaction which is unusual or financially illogical?
- Is the client showing an appropriate degree of interest in the transaction?
- Do I understand why this client has chosen to instruct me?

These are issues of which solicitors should be aware at the beginning of a business relationship or transaction, *and* which they should also continue to have in mind and to monitor as relationships and transactions develop.

Law Society guidance and assistance

27.8

The Law Society has published an Anti-Money Laundering Practice Note, updated in October 2013, aimed at assisting solicitors to understand the current anti-money laundering legislation. Treasury approval has been given to this guidance. Therefore, in assessing whether any solicitor has committed an offence, took all reasonable steps or exercised all due diligence to avoid committing an offence, the prosecution will consider whether there has been compliance with the Law Society's guidance when making a decision whether to charge.

The SRA will also take the Practice Note into account when exercising its regulatory and supervisory functions.

The full guidance, which runs to more than 100 pages, can be found at www.lawsociety.org.uk/productsandservices/practicenotes/aml.page. In addition the Society's Practice Advice Service will assist in understanding the Practice Note and by talking through any problems (Tel: 020 7320 5675). There is also a list[1] of solicitors with relevant expertise willing to give other solicitors 30 minutes' free advice on legal issues relating to money laundering.

The Law Society also produces a bi-monthly AML e-newsletter which provides useful information on developments in money laundering, including a section titled 'Launderers in the News', which summarises recent prosecutions.

1 See www.lawsociety.org.uk/Advice/Anti-money-laundering/AML-directory/.

Money Laundering Regulations 2007

27.9

The Money Laundering Regulations 2007 ('the 2007 Regulations')[1] were implemented to ensure compliance with the Third Money Laundering Directive.[2] They came into force on 15 December 2007, and have been amended with effect from 1 October 2012 by the Money Laundering (Amendment) Regulations 2012 (SI 2012/2298). The amendments mainly focus on enhancing the supervisory powers of the default regulators and do not generally require law firms to make changes to their policies and procedures. The 2007 Regulations in their amended form are at **Appendix 8**.

There is a Fourth Money Laundering Directive currently in consultation. Latest estimates suggest that this will come into force in late 2015 or early 2016. It will introduce some key changes including:

- the requirement for written risk assessments;
- additional requirements of policies and procedures;
- changes to the customer due diligence requirements;
- official ownership of registers.

1 SI 2007/2157.
2 Directive 2005/60/EC of the European Parliament and of the Council on the prevention of the use of the financial system for the purposes of money laundering and terrorist financing.

Relevant persons

27.10

The 2007 Regulations set administrative requirements for the anti-money laundering regime within the regulated sector and 'outline the scope of customer due diligence'.[1]

The 2007 Regulations aim to limit the use of professional services for money laundering by requiring professionals to know their clients and monitor the use of their services by clients.

Regulation 3 states that the 2007 Regulations apply to persons acting in the course of business carried on in the United Kingdom including independent legal professionals, which do not include solicitors employed by a public authority or working in-house.

The 2007 Regulations only apply to certain solicitors' activities where there is a high risk of money laundering occurring, as follows:

'(a) the buying and selling of real property or business entities;

(b) the managing of client money, securities or other assets;

(c) the opening or management of bank, savings or securities accounts;

(d) the organisation of contributions necessary for the creation, operation or management of companies; or

(e) the creation, operation or management of trusts, companies or similar structures,

and, for this purpose, a person participates in a transaction by assisting in the planning or execution of the transaction or otherwise acting for or on behalf of a client in the transaction.'[2]

The Treasury has confirmed that the following would not generally be viewed as participation in financial transactions, and therefore are not covered by the 2007 Regulations:

- payment on account of costs to a solicitor or payment of a solicitor's bill;
- provision of legal advice;
- participation in litigation or a form of alternative dispute resolution;
- will-writing, although you should consider whether any accompanying taxation advice is covered;
- work funded by the Legal Aid Agency.

It is important therefore to identify whether a solicitor's work comes within the regulated sector; a firm conducting exclusively claimant litigation would not come within the regulated sector for example. The Practice Note goes on to state:

> 'If you are uncertain whether the regulations apply to your work, seek legal advice on the individual circumstances of your practice or simply take the broadest of the possible approaches to compliance with the regulations.'

1 Law Society Anti-Money Laundering Practice Note October 2013, paragraph 1.4.5.
2 Regulation 3(9).

Customer due diligence and ongoing monitoring

27.11

A solicitor must conduct customer due diligence (CDD) on clients who retain the solicitor services regulated under the 2007 Regulations. Regulation 7 requires that CDD be conducted when:

- establishing a business relationship;[1]
- carrying out an occasional transaction;[2] or
- the solicitor suspects money laundering or terrorist financing; or
- the solicitor doubts the veracity or adequacy of documents, data or information previously obtained for the purposes of CDD.[3]

A relevant person 'must also apply customer due diligence measures at other appropriate times to existing customers on a risk-sensitive basis'.[4]

Customer due diligence measures are defined by regulation 5 of the 2007 Regulations and are:

'(a) identifying the customer and verifying the customer's identity on the basis of documents, data or information obtained from a reliable and independent source;

CHAPTER 27
MONEY LAUNDERING

(b) identifying, where there is a beneficial owner who is not the customer, the beneficial owner and taking adequate measures, on a risk-sensitive basis, to verify his identity so that the relevant person is satisfied that he knows who the beneficial owner is, including, in the case of a legal person, trust or similar legal arrangement, measures to understand the ownership and control structure of the person, trust or arrangement; and

(c) obtaining information on the purpose and intended nature of the business relationship.'

A relevant person must 'determine the extent of customer due diligence measures on a risk-sensitive basis depending on the type of customer, business relationship, product or transaction', and 'be able to demonstrate to his supervisory authority that the extent of the measures is appropriate in view of the risks of money laundering and terrorist financing'.[5] This is required as part of both customer due diligence measures, and ongoing monitoring. Where a relevant person has to apply customer due diligence in the case of a trust or similar arrangement and the beneficial owner consists of a class of persons, it is not necessary to identify all members of the class.[6]

A relevant person must keep under review every business relationship and conduct 'ongoing monitoring'. This means:

'(a) scrutiny of transactions undertaken throughout the course of the relationship (including, where necessary, the source of funds) to ensure that the transactions are consistent with the relevant person's knowledge of the customer, his business and risk profile; and

(b) keeping the documents, data or information obtained for the purpose of applying customer due diligence measures up-to-date.'[7]

1 A 'business relationship' means a business, professional or commercial relationship between a relevant person and a customer, which is expected by the relevant person, at the time when contact is established, to have an element of duration: regulation 2 of the 2007 Regulations.
2 An 'occasional transaction' means a transaction (carried out other than as part of a business relationship) amounting to 15,000 Euro or more, whether the transaction is carried out in a single operation or several operations which appear to be linked: regulation 2 of the 2007 Regulations.
3 Regulation 7(1)(a) to (d).
4 Regulation 7(2).
5 Regulation 7(3)(a) and (b).
6 Regulation 7(4).
7 Regulation 8(2)(a) and (b).

27.12

It is important to note that, by requiring a risk-based assessment of the needs of due diligence and a full and proper understanding of transactions, the 2007 Regulations impose obligations actively to monitor the way that business relationships and transactions develop, with an understanding of the aims of money laundering. This is not a box-ticking exercise so that, having obtained a copy passport and a utility bill (for example), a solicitor can consider the money laundering requirements to have been satisfied. There is an ongoing obligation for relevant persons in relation to all clients and all transactions. Many will involve minimal risk and commensurate monitoring, but the Regulations require relevant persons to be watchful and thoughtful.

A client's identity must be verified before a business relationship is established or an occasional transaction is carried out[1] but the verification process may be completed during the establishment of a business relationship, if it is 'necessary not to interrupt the normal conduct of business' and 'there is little risk of money laundering or terrorist financing occurring' provided that the verification is completed as soon as practicable after contact is first established.[2]

A solicitor unable to establish a client's identity must not carry out any transaction with or for the client through a bank account; must not establish a business relationship or carry out an occasional transaction with the client; must terminate any existing business relationship with the client and must consider whether he or she is required to make a disclosure (under Part 7 of the Proceeds of Crime Act 2002 or Part 3 of the Terrorism Act 2000).[3]

There is an important exception in favour of a solicitor where he is 'in the course of establishing the legal position for his client or performing his task of defending or representing that client in, or concerning, legal proceedings, including advice on the institution or avoidance of proceedings'.[4]

This exception does not apply to transactional work so solicitors should be careful to distinguish between advice and litigation work, and transactional work.

1 Regulation 9(2) of the 2007 Regulations.
2 Regulation 9(3).
3 Regulation 11(1)(a) to (d). For matters concerning disclosure under the Terrorism Act 2000 and Proceeds of Crime Act 2002, see **27.24**.
4 Regulation 11(2) of the 2007 Regulations.

Enhanced customer due diligence

27.13

There are requirements for 'enhanced customer due diligence and ongoing monitoring' where the customer has not been physically present for identification purposes,[1] where the client is a 'politically exposed person'[2] or in any other situation which by its nature can present a higher risk of money laundering or terrorist financing.[3] A politically exposed person is an individual who is or has at any time in the preceding year been entrusted with a prominent public function by a state other than the United Kingdom, by a EU institution or by an international body, or who is an immediate family member or known close associate of such a person.[4]

Enhanced due diligence in the case of clients who are not physically present for identification purposes requires additional specific and adequate measures to compensate for the higher risk, for example by obtaining additional documents, data or information verifying identity; by taking supplementary measures to verify documents supplied; by obtaining confirmation by a bank or other financial institution; or by ensuring that the first payment is carried out through a bank or other financial institution.

Enhanced due diligence in the case of politically exposed persons requires: senior management approval of the business relationship; measures to be taken to establish the source of wealth and source of funds involved in the proposed business relationship or occasional transaction; and enhanced ongoing monitoring.

1 Regulation 14(2) of the 2007 Regulations.
2 Regulation 14(4).
3 Regulation 14(1)(b).
4 Regulation 14(5). The phrases 'immediate family member' and 'known close associate' are defined in Schedule 2 to the 2007 Regulations.

Law Society guidance on customer due diligence

27.14

Chapter 4 of the Law Society Practice Note contains comprehensive guidance on CDD. It provides detailed advice as to how to deal with the verification of UK residents; persons not resident in the United Kingdom; clients unable to produce standard documentation; other professionals; partnerships and LLPs; public companies listed in the United Kingdom; private and unlisted companies in the United Kingdom; public overseas companies; and private and unlisted overseas companies. It also explains how to approach money laundering issues concerning other legal or quasi-legal entities such as trusts, foundations, charities, deceased persons' estates, churches, schools, clubs and pension funds.

As for ongoing monitoring, the Note states:

> 'Regulation 8 requires that you conduct ongoing monitoring of a business relationship on a risk-sensitive and appropriate basis. Ongoing monitoring is defined as:
>
> - scrutiny of transactions undertaken throughout the course of the relationship (including where necessary, the source of funds), to ensure that the transactions are consistent with your knowledge of the client, their business and the risk profile;
> - keeping the documents, data or information obtained for the purpose of applying CDD up to date. You must also be aware of obligations to keep clients' personal data updated under the Data Protection Act.
>
> You are not required to:
>
> - conduct the whole CDD process again every few years;
> - conduct random audits of files;
> - suspend or terminate a business relationship until you have updated data, information or documents, as long as you are still satisfied you know who your client is, and keep under review any request for further verification material or processes to get that material;
> - use sophisticated computer analysis packages to review each new retainer for anomalies.
>
> Ongoing monitoring will normally be conducted by fee earners handling the retainer, and involves staying alert to suspicious circumstances which may suggest money laundering, terrorist financing, or the provision of false CDD material.'

Sanctions and counter-measures

27.15

Customer due diligence systems should be able to enable identification of persons subject to counter-measures by the Financial Action Taskforce or the UK Treasury, where the Treasury has imposed financial restrictions.[1]

These restrictions can be accessed at www.gov.uk/government/publications/financial-sanctions-consolidated-list-of-targets/consolidated-list-of-targets.

Customer due diligence systems should also be able to enable identification of persons subject to financial sanctions following designation by the United Nations or the European Commission. The full list can be accessed at www.gov.uk/government/publications/financial-sanctions-consolidated-list-of-targets.

1 Regulation 18 of the 2007 Regulations contained powers allowing HM Treasury to issue directions to the financial sector, for example, to require a relevant person not to enter into, or to cease, business with certain persons connected to a country of money laundering, terrorist financing or proliferation concern. These powers were superseded by arrangements in Schedule 7 to the Counter-Terrorism Act 2008, and regulation 18 was revoked with effect from 1 October 2012.

Reliance on third parties and outsourcing

27.16

Solicitors may rely on a third party to conduct customer due diligence on their behalf, provided the third party consents to be relied upon[1] and the third party is a bank or other financial institution, a professionally regulated auditor, insolvency practitioner, external accountant, tax adviser or independent legal professional.[2] However, the solicitor remains liable for any default by the person they relied upon.[3]

The reliance provisions are not required:

- for use of e-verification information to verify identity;
- for passporting clients between offices of the same legal practice;
- for receiving actual identity documents (including certified copied) to assist you with verification; or
- by financial institutions when applying the simplification provisions in regulation 13 to a solicitor's client account.

1 Regulation 17(1)(a) of the 2007 Regulations.
2 Regulation 17(2).
3 Regulation 17(1)(b) and (4).

Record-keeping

27.17

Relevant persons must keep records to demonstrate compliance with the 2007 Regulations. In substance this requires you to keep evidence of identity and other file records of a relationship or transaction for five years from the completion of the transaction or the end of the relationship.[1]

1 Regulation 19 of the 2007 Regulations.

Systems and training

27.18

Relevant persons must establish and maintain appropriate risk-sensitive policies and procedures to prevent activities relating to money laundering or terrorist financing. These must address:

- customer due diligence measures and ongoing monitoring;
- reporting;
- record-keeping;
- internal control;
- risk assessment and management; and
- the monitoring and management of compliance with, and the internal communication of, such policies and procedures.[1]

Solicitors' firms must have a money laundering reporting officer (MLRO) – a 'nominated officer' for the purpose of the 2007 Regulations to receive and to make disclosures.[2]

Policies and procedures must include those which provide for the identification and scrutiny of:

- complex or unusually large transactions;
- unusual patterns of transactions which have no apparent economic or visible lawful purpose; and
- any other activity which the relevant person regards as particularly likely by its nature to be related to money laundering or terrorist financing.[3]

As mentioned above, the requirement to have a full and proper understanding of transactions is reinforced, and it will be seen that a responsible application of regulation 20 will avoid the involvement of solicitors in the kind of investment frauds considered in **CHAPTER 26**.

Relevant persons must take appropriate measures to ensure that 'all relevant employees' are 'made aware of the law relating to money laundering and terrorist financing', and are 'regularly given training in how to recognise and deal with transactions and other activities which may be related to money laundering and terrorist financing'.[4]

For the Law Society's guidance on training see paragraphs 3.9.1 to 3.9.4 of the Practice Note. Paragraph 3.9.2 contains the following advice:

> 'When setting up a training and communication system you should consider:

- which staff require training;
- what form the training will take;
- how often training should take place;
- how staff will be kept up to date with emerging risk factors for the firm.

Assessments of who should receive training should include who deals with clients in areas of practice within the regulated sector, handles funds or otherwise assists with compliance. Consider fee earners, reception staff, administration staff and finance staff, because they will each be differently involved in compliance and so have different training requirements.

Training can take many forms and may include:

- face-to-face training seminars;
- completion of online training sessions;
- attendance at AML/CTF conferences;
- participation in dedicated AML/CTF forums;
- review of publications on current AML/CTF issues;
- firm or practice group meetings for discussion of AML/CTF issues and risk factors.

Providing an AML/CTF policy manual is useful to raise staff awareness and can be a continual reference source between training sessions.'

1 Regulation 20(1)(a) to (f) of the 2007 Regulations.
2 Regulation 20(2)(d)(i).
3 Regulation 20(2)(a)(i) to (iii).
4 Regulation 21(a) and (b).

Compliance

27.19

The Law Society, through the SRA, is a supervisory authority with responsibility to monitor those it regulates and to take necessary measures for the purposes of securing compliance with the 2007 Regulations.[1] A failure to comply with any of the requirements of the 2007 Regulations listed above is a criminal offence punishable by a term of imprisonment of up to two years.[2] No offence is committed if all reasonable steps were taken and all due diligence was exercised to avoid committing the offence.[3]

1 Regulation 23(1)(c), Schedule 3 to, and regulation 24 of the 2007 Regulations.
2 Regulation 45.
3 Regulation 45(4).

Communications with clients

27.20

Although not required by the 2007 Regulations, it may be regarded as good practice and good client relations to explain the statutory obligations to which solicitors are subject, in terms of customer due diligence and reporting, in client care material and/or terms of business.

The criminal law – primary offences

27.21

The primary money laundering offences are currently found in Part 7 of the Proceeds of Crime Act (POCA) 2002. There are also separate offences aimed at preventing the laundering of and dealing with terrorist property in Part 3 of the Terrorism Act (TA) 2000.

The three primary money laundering offences are those contained in sections 327, 328 and 329 of POCA 2002. These are:

- transferring, converting, concealing, disguising or removing criminal property from the United Kingdom (section 327);
- arrangements involving criminal property (section 328); and
- acquiring, using or possessing criminal property (section 329).

A prohibited arrangement involving criminal property exists if a person 'enters into or becomes concerned in an arrangement which he knows or suspects facilitates (by whatever means) the acquisition, retention, use or control of criminal property by or on behalf of another person'.[1]

Knowledge or suspicion that the property is criminal property is required for an offence to be committed. The Crown must show that the offender knew or suspected that the arrangement was an arrangement which facilitated the acquisition, retention or control of criminal property. For property to be 'criminal property' the offender must be proved to have known or suspected that the property constituted a person's benefit from criminal conduct, or that it represented such a benefit (in whole or in part, directly or indirectly).[2]

There is no statutory definition of an arrangement; the courts have only been called upon to rule as to what 'arrangements' do *not* include. In *Bowman v Fels*,[3] the Court of Appeal held that an arrangement does not include action undertaken in the context of litigation:

> 'the issue or pursuit of ordinary legal proceedings with a view to obtaining the court's adjudication upon the parties' rights and duties is not to be regarded as an arrangement or a prohibited act within ss 327–9.'[4]

The Law Society's views as to whether and in what circumstances solicitors are involved in an 'arrangement' in the light of *Bowman v Fels* are set out in the Practice Note at paragraph 5.4.3 in the following terms:

'*Bowman v Fels* [2005] EWCA Civ 226 held that s.328 does not cover or affect the ordinary conduct of litigation by legal professionals, including any step taken in litigation from the issue of proceedings and the securing of injunctive relief or a freezing order up to its final disposal by judgment.

Our view, supported by Counsel's opinion, is that dividing assets in accordance with the judgment, including the handling of the assets which are criminal property, is not an arrangement. Further, settlements, negotiations, out of court settlements, alternative dispute resolution and tribunal representation are not arrangements. However, the property will generally still remain criminal property and you may need to consider referring your client for specialist advice regarding possible offences they may commit once they come into possession of the property after completion of the settlement.

The recovery of property by a victim of an acquisitive offence will not be committing an offence under either s.328 or s.329 of the Act.'

1 Section 328(1) of POCA 2002.
2 Section 340.
3 [2005] EWCA Civ 226, [2005] 1 WLR 3083, [2005] 4 All ER 609.
4 [2005] EWCA Civ 226, [2005] 1 WLR 3083, [2005] 4 All ER 609 at [95].

27.22

There are broadly comparable offences under TA 2000. Those most likely to be of concern to solicitors are contained in sections 17 and 18 of TA 2000. A person commits an offence if he 'enters into or becomes concerned in an arrangement as a result of which money or other property is made available or is to be made available to another', and he 'knows or has reasonable cause to suspect that it will or may be used for the purposes of terrorism';[1] and a person commits an offence if he 'enters into or becomes concerned in an arrangement which facilitates the retention or control by or on behalf of another person of terrorist property' by concealment, removal from the jurisdiction, transfer to nominees or in any other way.

It is a defence to prove that the person accused did not know and had no reasonable cause to suspect that the arrangement related to terrorist property.[2]

Although, as has been seen, the Money Laundering Regulations 2007 encourage and require a proportionate risk-based approach, this is not the test applied to the primary and secondary criminal offences, where the obligations not to engage in prohibited activities and to make disclosure when required are mandatory.

1 Section 17 of TA 2000.
2 Section 18.

Disclosure

27.23

The concept of 'disclosure' in relation to this area of the law is relevant in two respects.

The offence of non-disclosure

27.24

Section 330 of POCA 2002 applies to information received in the course of business in the regulated sector, and therefore applies to solicitors who are relevant persons for the purposes of the Money Laundering Regulations 2007. The corresponding non-disclosure offence in respect of terrorist funding is found in section 21A of TA 2000. It is a criminal offence for a person to fail to disclose information received in those circumstances where that person knows or suspects or has reasonable grounds to know or suspect that another person is involved in money laundering or terrorist funding, and is either able to identify the person concerned, or the whereabouts of any of the laundered property, or believes (or can reasonably be expected to believe) that the information will or may assist in identifying the person or the whereabouts of laundered property.

The information required to be disclosed is the identity of the person concerned if known, the whereabouts of the laundered property, so far as known, and any information leading to the identification of the person or location of the property.

Non-disclosure, tipping-off or otherwise prejudicing the course of an investigation (see further at **27.33** to **27.35**) are referred to as secondary offences.

It will have been noted that by introducing the concept of having 'reasonable grounds for knowing or suspecting', an objective test is applied. In the regulated sector you may be guilty of the offence under section 330 or 331 if you should have known or suspected money laundering was taking place.

Where a solicitor has the relevant knowledge, suspicion or reasonable grounds to suspect, he or she should make a disclosure to their legal practice's nominated officer (often known as a MLRO) to avoid committing this offence.

Once the nominated officer receives such a disclosure, if he or she has the relevant knowledge, suspicion or reasonable grounds to suspect, the officer must make a disclosure to the National Crime Agency (NCA), in order to avoid committing an offence under section 331 of POCA 2002. This obligation is subject to considerations regarding privilege, see **27.29**.

If a nominated officer acting outside the regulated sector similarly has the relevant knowledge or suspicion, he or she too must make a disclosure to NCA, in order to avoid committing an offence under section 332 of POCA 2002. Again, this obligation is subject to considerations regarding privilege, see **27.29**.

Authorised disclosure – a defence

27.25

If a person is involved in an arrangement such as would be caught by section 328 of POCA 2002 (or would otherwise be dealing with criminal property contrary to section 327 or 329), it is a defence to make an authorised disclosure, and a solicitor in this position does not commit an offence of money laundering despite carrying through the transaction to completion if, having made proper disclosure, he or she is given 'appropriate consent' to continue to act. It is essential that all the statutory requirements are met. Such appropriate consent will not be a defence to any complicity in the underlying offence, such as fraud.

Timing

27.26

To constitute an authorised disclosure sufficient to amount to a defence for someone who has become involved in an activity prohibited by sections 327 to 329 of POCA 2002, disclosure must be made as soon as practicable after the information or other matter on which his or her knowledge or suspicion (or reasonable grounds for such knowledge or suspicion) was acquired.

Disclosure should be made *before* a prohibited act takes place.[1]

If disclosure is made *during* the prohibited act the solicitor must have had no relevant knowledge or suspicion when the act was started; the disclosure must be made as soon as practicable after relevant knowledge or suspicion was acquired; and the disclosure must be made on the solicitor's own initiative (that is, not for example prompted by the realisation of imminent discovery or the encouragement of another). The burden of proof will be on the accused to satisfy the court that these conditions are met, otherwise the disclosure is not an authorised disclosure and no defence is available.[2]

If disclosure is made *after* the prohibited act has taken place there must have been good reason why a disclosure was not made before the prohibited act was carried out; the disclosure must have been made as soon as practicable after the prohibited act has taken place; and the disclosure must have been made on the solicitor's own initiative. Again, the burden of proof will be on the accused to satisfy the court that these conditions are met, otherwise the disclosure is not an authorised disclosure and no defence is available.[3]

1 Section 338(2) of POCA 2002.
2 Section 338(2A).
3 Section 338(3).

Making the report

27.27

For individual solicitors an internal report may be made in any form and manner designed by the firm (there is no statutory requirement as to this) to the firm's nominated officer. Once such a report is made the reporting solicitor has no further responsibility and the onus is on the nominated officer to consider the information and, if required, to make disclosure to NCA. Because of the complicated considerations around privilege, the potential civil and criminal liability for continuing with a retainer even where consent has been given, and the need to manage different stakeholder expectations if consent is refused, it is best practice for the nominated officer or a designated deputy to make the report to NCA.

NCA has now removed the need to complete and post or fax paper-based forms or other existing certification processes and all reports are now made online to the NCA website which is self-explanatory and very user friendly.

Otherwise, the more onerous responsibilities falling on nominated officers are beyond the scope of this chapter.

'Appropriate consent' to further action

27.28

In general terms, once a disclosure has been made, the disclosing party can take no further action until consent is obtained. A nominated officer may give consent, but only if he or she has obtained consent from NCA or certain time limits have expired. In reality, in a firm of solicitors, further action is determined exclusively by the reaction of NCA.[1]

There are three possibilities:

(1) NCA may give consent to the transaction continuing.
(2) If NCA does not reply refusing consent within seven working days starting with the first working day after disclosure is made, this is treated as appropriate consent.
(3) NCA may reply within the same period refusing consent. This imposes a moratorium on further action which lasts for 31 days starting with the day on which notice of refusal of consent is given. If the moratorium expires without any further action being taken by NCA this is treated as appropriate consent.

The delay could of course cause prejudice to clients, and although compliance with the statutory obligation would be a defence to any claim, solicitors may be required ultimately to justify the suspicion that prompted the report and caused the delay.[2]

1 Sections 335 and 336 of POCA 2002.
2 *Shah v HSBC Private Bank (UK) Ltd* [2010] EWCA Civ 31.

Disclosure, confidentiality and privilege

27.29

The disclosure offences under sections 330 to 332 of POCA 2002 and section 21A of TA 2000 specifically exclude any obligation to disclose information received in privileged circumstances.[1] The phrase 'privileged circumstances' is a term of art defined in section 330(10) of POCA 2002 and section 21A(8) of TA 2000 and is not identical with legal professional privilege. However, the two are closely linked concepts.

As noted above, the Court of Appeal held in *Bowman v Fels* that litigation did not involve an arrangement for the purposes of sections 327 to 329 of POCA 2002. It was also held that the giving of legal advice (other than where the crime/fraud exception applies) did not constitute an arrangement and did not itself give rise to any duty of disclosure.[2]

1 Section 330(6), (7B), (10) of POCA 2002; section 21A(5) of TA 2000.
2 *Bowman v Fels* [2005] EWCA Civ 226, [2005] 1 WLR 3083, [2005] 4 All ER 609 at [63].

27.30

Solicitors must keep the affairs of clients and former clients confidential except where disclosure is required or permitted by law,[1] but confidentiality and privilege are not synonymous, and confidentiality is overridden by the statutory duties of disclosure here being considered. The duties of disclosure are express duties imposed by statute and an authorised disclosure 'is not to be taken to breach any restriction on the disclosure of information (however imposed)'.[2]

Not all confidential information is covered by legal professional privilege, the ambit of which is quite narrow. Legal advice privilege covers all communications made in confidence between solicitors and their clients for the purpose of giving or obtaining legal advice. It does not matter whether the communication is directly between the client and his legal adviser or is made through an intermediate agent of either.[3]

Litigation privilege covers oral or written communications between a person or his lawyer (on the one hand) and third parties (on the other) or other documents created by or on behalf of the client or his lawyer, which came into existence once litigation is in contemplation or has commenced, and which came into existence for the dominant purpose of obtaining information or advice in connection with, or of conducting or aiding in the conduct of, such litigation (for example, obtaining evidence to be used in litigation or information which might lead to such evidence).[4]

A characteristic of litigation privilege is that it involves dealings between a lawyer and a third party (such as a potential witness). The characteristic of legal advice privilege is that it always relates to dealings between solicitor and client.

As has already been seen, litigation will not be likely to engage any of the primary offences.

Legal advice privilege is, expressly, limited to communications 'for the purposes of giving or obtaining legal advice'. Privilege does not attach to documents which are the products of legal advice. If one considers a typical property purchase (something that could readily engage money laundering concerns), the conveyancing documents and records of the financing of the transaction are not the subject of legal professional privilege, whereas correspondence between solicitor and client is privileged if directly related to the performance of the solicitor's professional duties as legal adviser.[5]

1 Outcome 4.1 of the SRA Code of Conduct 2011: see **4.36**.
2 Sections 337(4A) and 338(4) of POCA 2002; see also section 21B(1) of TA 2000.
3 *Three Rivers District Council and others v Governor and Company of the Bank of England (No 6)* [2005] 1 AC 610 at [50].
4 *Three Rivers District Council and others v Governor and Company of the Bank of England (No 6)* [2005] 1 AC 610 at [102].
5 *R v Inner London Crown Court, ex p Baines* [1988] 1 QB 579, [1988] 2 WLR 549, [1987] 3 All ER 1025; and see *Three Rivers District Council and others v Governor and Company of the Bank of England (No 6)* [2005] 1 AC 610 at [111].

Law Society guidance on disclosure

27.31

In short, legal professional privilege in both its limbs – litigation privilege and legal advice privilege – overrides the duty to disclose. The Law Society Practice Note offers valuable further guidance at paragraph 6.4 in the following terms:

'6.4.2 Advice privilege

Principle

Communications between a lawyer, acting in his capacity as a lawyer, and a client, are privileged if they are both:

- confidential;
- for the purpose of seeking legal advice from a solicitor or providing it to a client.

Scope

Communications are not privileged merely because a client is speaking or writing to you. The protection applies only to those communications which directly seek or provide advice or which are given in a legal context, that involve the lawyer using his legal skills and which are directly related to the performance of the lawyer's professional duties (*Passmore on Privilege* 2nd edition 2006).

Case law helps define what advice privilege covers.

Communications subject to advice privilege:

- a solicitor's bill of costs and statement of account (*Chant v Brown* (1852) 9 Hare 790);
- information imparted by prospective clients in advance of a retainer will attract LPP if the communications were made for the purpose of indicating the advice required (*Minster v Priest* [1930] AC 558 per Lord Atkin at 584).

Communications not subject to advice privilege:

- notes of open court proceedings (*Parry v News Group Newspapers* (1990) 140 New Law Journal 1719) are not privileged, as the content of the communication is not confidential;
- conversations, correspondence or meetings with opposing lawyers (*Parry v News Group Newspapers* (1990) 140 New Law Journal 1719) are not privileged, as the content of the communication is not confidential;
- a client account ledger maintained in relation to the client's money (*Nationwide Building Society v Various Solicitors* [1999] PNLR 53);
- an appointments diary or time record on an attendance note, time sheet or fee record relating to a client (*R v Manchester Crown Court, ex p. Rogers* [1999] 1 WLR 832);

- conveyancing documents are not communication so not subject to advice privilege (*R v Inner London Crown Court, ex p. Baines & Baines* [1988] QB 579).

Advice within a transaction

All communications between a lawyer and his client relating to a transaction in which the lawyer has been instructed for the purpose of obtaining legal advice are covered by advice privilege, notwithstanding that they do not contain advice on matters of law and construction, provided that they are directly related to the performance by the solicitor of his professional duty as legal adviser of his client (*Three Rivers District Council and Others v Bank of England* [2004] UKHL 48 at 111).

This will mean that where you are providing legal advice in a transactional matter (such as a conveyance) the advice privilege will cover all:

- communications with;
- instructions from; and
- advice given to

the client, including any working papers and drafts prepared, as long as they are directly related to your performance of your professional duties as a legal adviser.

6.4.3 Litigation privilege

Principle

This privilege, which is wider than advice privilege, protects confidential communications made after litigation has started, or is reasonably in prospect, between either:

- a lawyer and a client;
- a lawyer and an agent, whether or not that agent is a lawyer;
- a lawyer and a third party.

These communications must be for the sole or dominant purpose of litigation, either:

- for seeking or giving advice in relation to it;
- for obtaining evidence to be used in it;
- for obtaining information leading to obtaining such evidence.

6.4.4 Important points to consider

An original document not brought into existence for these privileged purposes and so not already privileged, does not become privileged merely by being given to a lawyer for advice or other privileged purpose.

Further, where you have a corporate client, communication between you and the employees of a corporate client may not be protected by LPP if the employee cannot be considered to be "the client" for the purposes of the retainer. As such some employees will be clients, while others will not (*Three Rivers District Council v The Governor and Company of the Bank of England (No.5)* [2003] QB 1556).

It is not a breach of LPP to discuss a matter with your nominated officer for the purposes of receiving advice on whether to make a disclosure.

6.4.5 Crime/fraud exception

LPP protects advice you give to a client on avoiding committing a crime (*Bullivant v Att-Gen of Victoria* [1901] AC 196) or warning them that proposed actions could attract prosecution (*Butler v Board of Trade* [1971] Ch 680). LPP does not extend to documents which themselves form part of a criminal or fraudulent act, or communications which take place in order to obtain advice with the intention of carrying out an offence (*R v Cox & Railton* (1884) 14 QBD 153). It is irrelevant whether or not you are aware that you are being used for that purpose (*Banque Keyser Ullman v Skandia* [1986] 1 Lloyd's Rep 336).

Intention of furthering a criminal purpose

It is not just your client's intention which is relevant for the purpose of ascertaining whether information was communicated for the furtherance of a criminal purpose. It is also sufficient that a third party intends the lawyer/client communication to be made with that purpose (e.g. where the innocent client is being used by a third party) (*R v Central Criminal Court, ex p. Francis & Francis* [1989] 1 AC 346).

Knowing a transaction constitutes an offence

If you **know** the transaction you're working on is a principal offence, you risk committing an offence yourself. In these circumstances, communications relating to such a transaction are not privileged and should be disclosed.

Suspecting a transaction constitutes an offence

If you merely suspect a transaction might constitute a money laundering offence, the position is more complex. If the suspicions are correct, communications with the client are not privileged. If the suspicions are unfounded, the communications should remain privileged and are therefore non-disclosable.

Prima facie evidence

If you suspect you are unwittingly being involved by your client in a fraud, the courts require prima facie evidence before LPP can be displaced (*O'Rourke v Darbishire* [1920] AC 581). The sufficiency of that evidence depends on the circumstances: it is easier to infer a prima facie case where there is substantial material available to support an inference of fraud. While you may decide yourself if prima facie evidence exists, you may also ask the court for directions (*Finers v Miro* [1991] 1 WLR 35).

> The Crown Prosecution Service guidance for prosecutors indicates that if a solicitor forms a genuine, but mistaken, belief that the privileged circumstances exemption (…) applies (for example, the client misleads the solicitor and uses the advice received for a criminal purpose) the solicitor will be able to rely on the reasonable excuse defence. It is likely that a similar approach would be taken with respect to a genuine, but mistaken, belief that LPP applies.
>
> We believe you should not make a disclosure unless you know of prima facie evidence that you are being used in the furtherance of a crime.'

Further, information obtained on disclosure of documents in litigation which gives rise to a relevant suspicion about the opposing party, but which is subject to the implied undertaking that the documents may not be used for any purpose other than the conduct of the litigation, is not subject to any duty of disclosure.[1]

But as privileged material is excluded from the duty of disclosure it is important to understand what is, and what is not, covered by legal professional privilege.

1 *Bowman v Fels* [2005] 4 All ER 609, [2005] EWCA Civ 226 at [89].

Other offences

27.32

Other secondary offences relevant to solicitors involve tipping-off or otherwise prejudicing the course of an investigation.

Tipping-off

27.33

It is an offence if a person discloses (other than in strictly limited circumstances) that a disclosure has made under section 337 or 338 if it is likely to prejudice any investigation that might be conducted following the disclosure, and if the information came to the person in the course of business in the regulated sector.[1]

It is an offence if a person discloses that an investigation into allegations that an offence has been committed under Part 7 of POCA 2002 is being contemplated or carried out, if the disclosure is likely to prejudice that investigation and the information came to the person in the course of business in the regulated sector.[2]

It is *not* an offence if a professional legal adviser makes the disclosure to a client and it is made for the purposes of dissuading the client from committing an offence.[3] It is a defence if the person making the disclosure does not know or suspect that disclosure is likely to prejudice any investigation.[4]

1 Section 333A(1) and (2) of POCA 2002. The circumstances in which disclosure may be made are set out in sections 333B, 333C and 333D of POCA 2002 and relate, in summary, to disclosures within the same organisation; between financial organisations and legal professionals in relation to a client or transaction common to both parties, if the purpose is only to prevent an offence being committed; and to disclosures to the authorities with a view to the detection, investigation or prosecution of offences.

2 Section 333A(3) of POCA 2002.
3 Section 333D(2).
4 Section 333D(3) and (4).

Prejudicing an investigation

27.34

It is an offence if a person outside the regulated sector who knows or suspects that a relevant investigation[1] is being conducted or is about to be conducted makes a disclosure that is likely to prejudice an investigation, or if that person falsifies, conceals, destroys or otherwise disposes of documents that are relevant to any investigation, or causes any of the above to take place. An investigation for these purposes is a confiscation investigation, a civil recovery investigation or a money laundering investigation.[2]

It is a defence if a disclosure is made by a legal adviser to a client, or a client's representative, in connection with the giving of legal advice or to any person in connection with legal proceedings or contemplated legal proceedings. However, this defence will not apply if the disclosure is made with the intention of furthering a criminal purpose.

1 Section 342(1) of POCA 2002. The various kinds of investigations are defined in section 341.
2 Section 342(2)(a) and (b).

Law Society guidance on tipping-off and prejudicing an investigation

27.35

The Law Society's Practice Note contains helpful guidance at paragraphs 5.8.1 and 5.8.2:

> **'5.8.1 Offences**
>
> *Tipping off – in the regulated sector*
>
> There are two tipping off offences in s.333A of POCA. They apply only to business in the regulated sector.
>
> **s.333A(1)** – disclosing a suspicious activity report (SAR). It is an offence to disclose to a third person that a SAR has been made by any person to the police, HM Revenue and Customs, the NCA or a nominated officer, if that disclosure might prejudice any investigation that might be carried out as a result of the SAR. This offence can only be committed:
>
> - **after** a disclosure to the NCA or a nominated officer
> - if you know or suspect that by disclosing this information, you are likely to prejudice any investigation related to that SAR
> - the information upon which the disclosure is based came to you in the course of business in the regulated sector.
>
> **s.333A(3)** – disclosing an investigation. It is an offence to disclose that an investigation into a money laundering offence is being contemplated or

carried out if that disclosure is likely to prejudice that investigation. The offence can only be committed if the information on which the disclosure is based came to the person in the course of business in the regulated sector. The key point is that you can commit this offence, even where you are unaware that a SAR was submitted.

Prejudicing an investigation – outside the regulated sector

Section 342(1) contains an offence of prejudicing a confiscation, civil recovery or money laundering investigation, if the person making the disclosure knows or suspects that an investigation is being, or is about to be conducted. Section 342(1) was amended by paragraph 8 of the TACT and POCA Regulations 2007. The offence in s.342 (2) (a) only applies to those outside the regulated sector. The offence in s.342 (2) (b) applies to everyone.

You only commit the offence in s.342 (2) (a) if you knew or suspected that the disclosure would, or would be likely to prejudice any investigation.

5.8.2 Defences

Tipping off

The following disclosures are permitted:

s.333B – disclosures within an undertaking or group, including disclosures to a professional legal adviser or relevant professional adviser

s.333C – disclosures between institutions, including disclosures from a professional legal adviser to another professional legal adviser

s.333D – disclosures to your supervisory authority

s.333D(2) – disclosures made by professional legal advisers to their clients for the purpose of dissuading them from engaging in criminal conduct.

A person does not commit the main tipping off offence if he does not know or suspect that a disclosure is likely to prejudice an investigation.

s.333B – Disclosures within an undertaking or group etc. It is not an offence if an employee, officer or partner of a firm discloses that a SAR has been made if it is to an employee, officer or partner of the same undertaking.

A solicitor will not commit a tipping off offence if a disclosure is made to another lawyer either:

- within a different undertaking, if both parties carry on business in an EEA state
- in a country or territory that imposes money laundering requirements equivalent to the EU and both parties share common ownership, management or control.

s.333C – disclosures between institutions etc. A solicitor will not commit a tipping off offence if **all** the following criteria are met:

- The disclosure is made to another lawyer in an EEA state, or one with an equivalent AML regime.
- The disclosure relates to a client or former client of both parties, or a transaction involving them both, or the provision of a service involving them both.
- The disclosure is made for the purpose of preventing a money laundering offence.
- Both parties have equivalent professional duties of confidentiality and protection of personal data.

s.333D(2) – limited exception for professional legal advisers. A solicitor will not commit a tipping off offence if the disclosure is to a client and it is made for the purpose of dissuading the client from engaging in conduct amounting to an offence. This exception and the tipping off offence in s.333A apply to those carrying on activities in the regulated sector.

Prejudicing an investigation

s.342(4) – professional legal adviser exemption. It is a defence to a s.342(1) offence that a disclosure is made by a legal adviser to a client, or a client's representative, in connection with the giving of legal advice or to any person in connection with legal proceedings or contemplated legal proceedings.

Such a disclosure will not be exempt if it is made with the intention of furthering a criminal purpose (s.342(5)).'

PART 8
Appendices

APPENDIX 1

SRA Principles 2011

[6 October 2011]

SRA Principles 2011

Contents

Preamble

The SRA Principles dated 17 June 2011 commencing 6 October 2011 made by the Solicitors Regulation Authority Board under sections 31, 79 and 80 of the Solicitors Act 1974, sections 9 and 9A of the Administration of Justice Act 1985 and section 83 of the Legal Services Act 2007, with the approval of the Legal Services Board under paragraph 19 of Schedule 4 to the Legal Services Act 2007, regulating the conduct of solicitors and their employees, registered European lawyers, recognised bodies and their managers and employees, and licensed bodies and their managers and employees.

Part 1: SRA Principles

1: SRA Principles

These are mandatory *Principles* which apply to all.

You must:

1. uphold the rule of law and the proper administration of justice;
2. act with integrity;
3. not allow your independence to be compromised;
4. act in the best interests of each *client*;
5. provide a proper standard of service to your *clients*;
6. behave in a way that maintains the trust the public places in you and in the provision of legal services;
7. comply with your legal and regulatory obligations and deal with your regulators and ombudsmen in an open, timely and co-operative manner;
8. run your business or carry out your role in the business effectively and in accordance with proper governance and sound financial and risk management principles;
9. run your business or carry out your role in the business in a way that encourages equality of opportunity and respect for diversity; and
10. protect *client* money and *assets*.

2: SRA Principles – notes

2.1 The Principles embody the key ethical requirements on firms and individuals who are involved in the provision of legal services. You should always have regard to the Principles and use them as your starting point when faced with an ethical dilemma.

2.2 Where two or more Principles come into conflict, the Principle which takes precedence is the one which best serves the public interest in the particular circumstances, especially the public interest in the proper administration of justice.

2.3 These Principles:

(a) apply to individuals and firms we regulate, whether traditional firms of solicitors or ABSs, in private practice or in-house. Where a firm or individual is *practising overseas*, the Overseas Principles apply;

(b) will be breached by you if you permit another person to do anything on your behalf which if done by you would breach the Principles; and

(c) apply to you to the fullest extent if a sole practitioner or manager in a firm, but still apply to you if you work within a firm or in-house and have no management responsibility (for example, even if you are not a manager you may have an opportunity to influence, adopt and implement measures to comply with Principles 8 and 9).

2.4 Compliance with the Principles is also subject to any overriding legal obligations.

Principle 1: You must uphold the rule of law and the proper administration of justice.

2.5 You have obligations not only to clients but also to the court and to third parties with whom you have dealings on your clients' behalf – see, e.g., Chapter 5 (Your client and the court) and Chapter 11 (Relations with third parties) of the Code.

Principle 2: You must act with integrity.

2.6 Personal integrity is central to your role as the client's trusted adviser and should characterise all your professional dealings with clients, the court, other lawyers and the public.

Principle 3: You must not allow your independence to be compromised.

2.7 "Independence" means your own and your firm's independence, and not merely your ability to give independent advice to a client. You should avoid situations which might put your independence at risk – e.g. giving control of your practice to a third party which is beyond the regulatory reach of the SRA or other approved regulator.

Principle 4: You must act in the best interests of each client.

2.8 You should always act in good faith and do your best for each of your clients. Most importantly, you should observe:

(a) your duty of confidentiality to the client – see Chapter 4 (Confidentiality and disclosure) of the Code; and

(b) your obligations with regard to conflicts of interests – see Chapter 3 (Conflicts of interests) of the Code.

Principle 5: You must provide a proper standard of service to your clients.

2.9 You should, e.g., provide a proper standard of client care and of work. This would include exercising competence, skill and diligence, and taking into account the individual needs and circumstances of each client.

Principle 6: You must behave in a way that maintains the trust the public places in you and in the provision of legal services.

2.10 Members of the public should be able to place their trust in you. Any behaviour either within or outside your professional practice which undermines this trust damages not only you, but also the ability of the legal profession as a whole to serve society.

Principle 7: You must comply with your legal and regulatory obligations and deal with your regulators and ombudsmen in an open, timely and co-operative manner.

2.11 You should, e.g., ensure that you comply with all the reporting and notification requirements – see Chapter 10 (You and your regulator) of the Code – and respond promptly and substantively to communications.

Principle 8: You must run your business or carry out your role in the business effectively and in accordance with proper governance and sound financial and risk management principles.

2.12 Whether you are a manager or an employee, you have a part to play in helping to ensure that your business is well run for the benefit of your clients and, e.g. in meeting the outcomes in Chapter 7 (Management of your business) of the Code.

Principle 9: You must run your business or carry out your role in the business in a way that encourages equality of opportunity and respect for diversity.

2.13 Whether you are a manager or an employee, you have a role to play in achieving the outcomes in Chapter 2 (Equality and diversity) of the Code. Note that a finding of unlawful discrimination outside practice could also amount to a breach of Principles 1 and 6.

Principle 10: You must protect client money and assets.

2.14 This Principle goes to the heart of the duty to act in the best interests of your clients. You should play your part in e.g. protecting money, documents or other property belonging to your clients which has been entrusted to you or your firm.

Breach of the Principles

2.15 Our approach to enforcement is proportionate, outcomes-focused and risk-based. Therefore, how we deal with failure to comply with the Principles will depend on all the particular circumstances of each case. Our primary aim is to achieve the right outcomes for clients.

Part 2: SRA Principles – application provisions

The *Principles* apply to you in the following circumstances (and "you" must be construed accordingly).

3: Application of the SRA Principles in England and Wales

3.1 Subject to paragraphs 3.2 to 6.1 below and any other provisions in the *SRA Code of Conduct*, the *Principles* apply to you, in relation to your activities carried out from an office in England and Wales, if you are:

(a) a *solicitor*, *REL* or *RFL* who is *practising* as such, whether or not the entity through which you *practise* is subject to these *Principles*;

(b) a *solicitor*, *REL* or *RFL* who is:

(i) a *manager*, *employee* or *owner* of a body which should be a *recognised body*, but has not been recognised by the *SRA*;

(ii) a *manager*, *employee* or *owner* of a body that is a *manager* or *owner* of a body that should be a *recognised body*, but has not been recognised by the *SRA*;

(iii) an *employee* of a *sole practitioner* which should be a *recognised sole practitioner*, but has not been recognised by the *SRA*;

(iv) an *owner* of an *authorised body* or of a body which should be a *recognised body* but has not been recognised by the *SRA*, even if you undertake no work for the body's *clients*;

(v) a *manager* or *employee* of an *authorised non-SRA firm*, or a *manager* of a body which is a *manager* of an *authorised non-SRA firm*, when doing work of a sort authorised by the *SRA*, for that firm;

(c) an *authorised body*, or a body which should be a *recognised body* but has not been recognised by the *SRA*;

(d) any other person who is a *manager*, or *employee* of an *authorised body*, or of a body which should be a *recognised body* but has not been recognised by the *SRA*;

(e) any other person who is an *employee* of a *recognised sole practitioner*, or of a *sole practitioner* who should be a *recognised sole practitioner* but has not been recognised by the *SRA*;

and "you" includes "your" as appropriate.

3.2 The *Principles* apply to you if you are a *solicitor*, *REL* or *RFL*, and you are:

(a) *practising* as a *manager* or *employee* of an *authorised non-SRA firm* when doing work of a sort authorised by the *authorised non-SRA firm's approved regulator*, or

(b) an *owner* of an *authorised non-SRA firm* even if you undertake no work for the body's *clients*.

4: Application of the SRA Principles in relation to practice from an office outside England and Wales

4.1 The *Principles* apply to you if you are:

(a) a body practising from an office outside England and Wales only if you are required to be an *authorised body* as a result of the nature of your practice and you have been authorised by the *SRA* accordingly; or

(b) a *manager* of such a body.

GUIDANCE NOTE

(i) In most circumstances, overseas offices of authorised bodies based in England and Wales will not require authorisation with the SRA and will be governed by the SRA Overseas Rules. However, in some circumstances, because of the work that is being carried out from the overseas office, it will need to be authorised (see Rule 2.1(e) and have regard to Rule 2.1(g) of the SRA Overseas Rules). In those circumstances, the SRA Principles and Code of Conduct apply.

4.2 The *Principles* apply to you if you are an individual engaged in *temporary practice overseas*.

5: Application of the SRA Principles outside practice

5.1 In relation to activities which fall outside *practice*, whether undertaken as a *lawyer* or in some other business or private capacity, *Principles* 1, 2 and 6 apply to you if you are a *solicitor*, *REL* or *RFL*.

6: General provisions

6.1 You must comply with the *Principles* at all times, but the extent to which you are expected to implement the requirements of the *Principles* will depend on your role in the *firm*, or your way of *practising*. For example, those who are managing a business will be expected to have more influence on how the *firm* or business is run than those *practising* in-house but not managing a legal department, or those *practising* as *employees* of a *firm*.

Part 3: Transitional provisions

7: Transitional provisions

7.1 For the avoidance of doubt, where a breach of any provision of the Solicitors' Code of

Conduct 2007 comes to the attention of the *SRA* after 6 October 2011, this shall be subject to action by the *SRA* notwithstanding any repeal of the relevant provision.

7.2 From 31 March 2012 or the date on which an order made pursuant to section 69 of the *LSA* relating to the status of *sole practitioners* comes into force, whichever is the later, paragraph 3.1 shall have effect subject to the following amendments:

(a) paragraph 3.1(b)(iii), and

(b) paragraph 3.1(e)

shall be omitted.

7.3 The *Principles* shall not apply to *licensed bodies* until such time as the *Society* is designated as a *licensing authority* under Part 1 of Schedule 10 to the *LSA* and all definitions shall be construed accordingly.

7.4 References in the preamble to:

(a) the *Principles* being made under section 83 of the Legal Services Act 2007, and

(b) *licensed bodies* and their *managers* and *employees*,

shall have no effect until such time as the *Society* is designated as a *licensing authority* under Part 1 of Schedule 10 to the *LSA*.

Part 4: Interpretation

8: Interpretation

8.1 The SRA Handbook Glossary 2012 shall apply to these rules and, unless the context otherwise requires

(a) all italicised terms within these rules shall be defined; and

(b) terms within these rules shall be interpreted,

in accordance with the *Glossary*.

APPENDIX 2

SRA Code of Conduct 2011

SRA Code of Conduct 2011

[6 October 2011]

Introduction to the SRA Code of Conduct

Overview

Outcomes-focused regulation concentrates on providing positive outcomes which when achieved will benefit and protect *clients* and the public. The SRA Code of Conduct (the Code) sets out our outcomes-focused conduct requirements so that you can consider how best to achieve the right outcomes for your *clients* taking into account the way that your *firm* works and its *client* base. The Code is underpinned by effective, risk-based supervision and enforcement.

Those involved in providing legal advice and representation have long held the role of trusted adviser. There are fiduciary duties arising from this role and obligations owed to others, especially the *court*. No code can foresee or address every issue or ethical dilemma which may arise. You must strive to uphold the intention of the Code as well as its letter.

The Principles

The Code forms part of the Handbook, in which the 10 mandatory *Principles* are all-pervasive. They apply to all those we regulate and underpin all aspects of *practice*. They define the fundamental ethical and professional standards that we expect of all *firms* and individuals (including owners who may not be *lawyers*) when providing legal services. You should always have regard to the *Principles* and use them as your starting point when faced with an ethical dilemma.

Where two or more *Principles* come into conflict the one which takes precedence is the one which best serves the public interest in the particular circumstances, especially the public interest in the proper administration of justice. Compliance with the *Principles* is also subject to any overriding legal obligations.

You must:

1. uphold the rule of law and the proper administration of justice;

2. act with integrity;

3. not allow your independence to be compromised;

4. act in the best interests of each *client*;

5. provide a proper standard of service to your *clients*;
6. behave in a way that maintains the trust the public places in you and in the provision of legal services;
7. comply with your legal and regulatory obligations and deal with your regulators and ombudsmen in an open, timely and co-operative manner;
8. run your business or carry out your role in the business effectively and in accordance with proper governance and sound financial and risk management principles;
9. run your business or carry out your role in the business in a way that encourages equality of opportunity and respect for diversity; and
10. protect *client* money and *assets*.

Structure of the Code

The Code is divided into 5 sections:

- You and your client
- You and your business
- You and your regulator
- You and others
- Application, waivers and interpretation

Each section is divided into chapters dealing with particular regulatory issues, for example, client care, *conflicts of interests*, and *publicity*.

These chapters show how the *Principles* apply in certain contexts through mandatory and non-mandatory provisions.

Mandatory provisions

The following provisions are mandatory:

- the outcomes;
- the application and waivers provisions in Chapters 13 and 13A;
- the interpretations; and
- the transitional provisions in Chapter 15.

The outcomes describe what *firms* and individuals are expected to achieve in order to comply with the relevant *Principles* in the context of the relevant chapter. In the case of *in-house practice*, we have set out at the end of each chapter which outcomes apply and in some cases have specified different outcomes.

In respect of *in-house practice*, different outcomes may apply depending on whether you are acting for your employer or for a *client* other than your employer as permitted by rules 4.1 to 4.10 of the *SRA Practice Framework Rules*.

The outcomes contained in each chapter are not an exhaustive list of the application of all the *Principles*. We have tried to make them as helpful as possible.

Non-mandatory provisions

The following provisions are non-mandatory:

- indicative behaviours;
- notes.

The outcomes are supplemented by indicative behaviours. The indicative behaviours specify, but do not constitute an exhaustive list of, the kind of behaviour which may establish compliance with, or contravention of the *Principles*. These are not mandatory but they may help us to decide whether an outcome has been achieved in compliance with the *Principles*.

We recognise that there may be other ways of achieving the outcomes. Where you have chosen a different method from those we have described as indicative behaviours, we might require you to demonstrate how you have nevertheless achieved the outcome. We encourage *firms* to consider how they can best achieve the outcomes, taking into account the nature of the *firm*, the particular circumstances of the matter and, crucially, the needs of their particular *clients*.

Waivers

Due to the flexibility of approach this structure allows, we do not anticipate receiving many applications for waivers from the mandatory outcomes. The *SRA*, nonetheless, reserves power to waive a provision in exceptional circumstances.

Interpretation

Words shown in italics are defined in the *Glossary*.

Sources of help

You can access the Code and other elements of the Handbook and find information on particular issues on the *SRA* website. You can also seek guidance on professional conduct from our Professional Ethics Guidance Team.

List of contents of the Code

1st section: You and your client

Chapter 1 Client care
Chapter 2 Equality and diversity
Chapter 3 Conflicts of interests
Chapter 4 Confidentiality and disclosure
Chapter 5 Your client and the court
Chapter 6 Your client and introductions to third parties

2nd section: You and your business

Chapter 7 Management of your business
Chapter 8 Publicity
Chapter 9 Fee sharing and referrals

3rd section: You and your regulator

Chapter 10 You and your regulator

4th section: You and others

Chapter 11 Relations with third parties
Chapter 12 Separate businesses

5th section: Application, waivers and interpretation

Chapter 13 Application and waivers provisions

Chapter 13A Practice overseas
Chapter 14 Interpretation
Chapter 15 Transitional provisions

Preamble

The SRA Code of Conduct dated 17 June 2011 commencing 6 October 2011 made by the Solicitors Regulation Authority Board under sections 31, 79 and 80 of the Solicitors Act 1974, sections 9 and 9A of the Administration of Justice Act 1985 and section 83 of the Legal Services Act 2007, with the approval of the Legal Services Board under paragraph 19 of Schedule 4 to the Legal Services Act 2007, regulating the conduct of solicitors and their employees, registered European lawyers and their employees, registered foreign lawyers, recognised bodies and their managers and employees and licensed bodies and their managers and employees.

1st Section: You and your client

Chapter 1: Client care

This chapter is about providing a proper standard of service, which takes into account the individual needs and circumstances of each *client*. This includes providing *clients* with the information they need to make informed decisions about the services they need, how these will be delivered and how much they will cost. This will enable you and your *client* to understand each other's expectations and responsibilities. This chapter is also about ensuring that if *clients* are not happy with the service they have received they know how to make a *complaint* and that all *complaints* are dealt with promptly and fairly.

Your relationship with your *client* is a contractual one which carries with it legal, as well as conduct, obligations. This chapter focuses on your obligations in conduct.

You are generally free to decide whether or not to accept instructions in any matter, provided you do not discriminate unlawfully (see Chapter 2).

The outcomes in this chapter show how the *Principles* apply in the context of client care.

Outcomes

You must achieve these outcomes:

O(1.1) you treat your *clients* fairly;

O(1.2) you provide services to your *clients* in a manner which protects their interests in their matter, subject to the proper administration of justice;

O(1.3) when deciding whether to act, or terminate your instructions, you comply with the law and the Code;

O(1.4) you have the resources, skills and procedures to carry out your *clients'* instructions;

O(1.5) the service you provide to *clients* is competent, delivered in a timely manner and takes account of your *clients'* needs and circumstances;

O(1.6) you only enter into fee agreements with your *clients* that are legal, and which you consider are suitable for the *client's* needs and take account of the *client's* best interests;

O(1.7) you inform *clients* whether and how the services you provide are regulated and how this affects the protections available to the *client*;

O(1.8) *clients* have the benefit of your *compulsory professional indemnity insurance* and you do not exclude or attempt to exclude liability below the minimum level of cover required by the *SRA Indemnity Insurance Rules*;

O(1.9) *clients* are informed in writing at the outset of their matter of their right to complain and how *complaints* can be made;

O(1.10) *clients* are informed in writing, both at the time of engagement and at the conclusion of your *complaints* procedure, of their right to complain to the *Legal Ombudsman*, the time frame for doing so and full details of how to contact the *Legal Ombudsman*;

O(1.11) *clients' complaints* are dealt with promptly, fairly, openly and effectively;

O(1.12) *clients* are in a position to make informed decisions about the services they need, how their matter will be handled and the options available to them;

O(1.13) *clients* receive the best possible information, both at the time of engagement and when appropriate as their matter progresses, about the likely overall cost of their matter;

O(1.14) *clients* are informed of their right to challenge or complain about your bill and the circumstances in which they may be liable to pay interest on an unpaid bill;

O(1.15) you properly account to *clients* for any *financial benefit* you receive as a result of your instructions;

O(1.16) you inform current *clients* if you discover any act or omission which could give rise to a claim by them against you.

Indicative behaviours

Acting in the following way(s) may tend to show that you have achieved these outcomes and therefore complied with the *Principles*:

Dealing with the client's matter

IB(1.1) agreeing an appropriate level of service with your *client*, for example the type and frequency of communications;

IB(1.2) explaining your responsibilities and those of the *client*;

IB(1.3) ensuring that the *client* is told, in writing, the name and status of the person(s) dealing with the matter and the name and status of the person responsible for its overall supervision;

IB(1.4) explaining any arrangements, such as fee sharing or *referral arrangements*, which are relevant to the *client's* instructions;

IB(1.5) explaining any limitations or conditions on what you can do for the *client*, for example, because of the way the *client's* matter is funded;

IB(1.6) in taking instructions and during the course of the retainer, having proper regard to your *client's* mental capacity or other vulnerability, such as incapacity or duress;

IB(**1.7**) considering whether you should decline to act or cease to act because you cannot act in the *client's* best interests;

IB(**1.8**) if you seek to limit your liability to your *client* to a level above the minimum required by the *SRA Indemnity Insurance Rules*, ensuring that this limitation is in writing and is brought to the *client's* attention;

IB(**1.9**) refusing to act where your *client* proposes to make a gift of significant value to you or a member of your family, or a member of your *firm* or their family, unless the *client* takes independent legal advice;

IB(**1.10**) if you have to cease acting for a *client*, explaining to the *client* their possible options for pursuing their matter;

IB(**1.11**) you inform *clients* if they are not entitled to the protections of the SRA Compensation Fund;

IB(**1.12**) considering whether a *conflict of interests* has arisen or whether the *client* should be advised to obtain independent advice where the *client* notifies you of their intention to make a claim or if you discover an act or omission which might give rise to a claim;

Fee arrangements with your client

IB(**1.13**) discussing whether the potential outcomes of the *client's* matter are likely to justify the expense or risk involved, including any risk of having to pay someone else's legal fees;

IB(**1.14**) clearly explaining your fees and if and when they are likely to change;

IB(**1.15**) warning about any other payments for which the *client* may be responsible;

IB(**1.16**) discussing how the *client* will pay, including whether public funding may be available, whether the *client* has insurance that might cover the fees, and whether the fees may be paid by someone else such as a trade union;

IB(**1.17**) where you are acting for a *client* under a fee arrangement governed by statute, such as a conditional fee agreement, giving the *client* all relevant information relating to that arrangement;

IB(**1.18**) where you are acting for a publicly funded *client*, explaining how their publicly funded status affects the costs;

IB(**1.19**) providing the information in a clear and accessible form which is appropriate to the needs and circumstances of the *client*;

IB(**1.20**) where you receive a *financial benefit* as a result of acting for a *client*, either:

(a) paying it to the *client*;

(b) offsetting it against your fees; or

(c) keeping it only where you can justify keeping it, you have told the *client* the amount of the benefit (or an approximation if you do not know the exact amount) and the *client* has agreed that you can keep it;

IB(**1.21**) ensuring that *disbursements* included in your bill reflect the actual amount spent or to be spent on behalf of the *client*;

Complaints handling

IB(**1.22**) having a written *complaints* procedure which:

(a) is brought to *clients'* attention at the outset of the matter;

(b) is easy for *clients* to use and understand, allowing for *complaints* to be made by any reasonable means;

(c) is responsive to the needs of individual *clients*, especially those who are vulnerable;

(d) enables *complaints* to be dealt with promptly and fairly, with decisions based on a sufficient investigation of the circumstances;

(e) provides for appropriate remedies; and

(f) does not involve any charges to *clients* for handling their *complaints*;

IB(1.23) providing the *client* with a copy of the *firm's complaints* procedure on request;

IB(1.24) in the event that a *client* makes a *complaint*, providing them with all necessary information concerning the handling of the *complaint*.

Acting in the following way(s) may tend to show that you have not achieved these outcomes and therefore not complied with the *Principles*:

Accepting and refusing instructions

IB(1.25) acting for a *client* when instructions are given by someone else, or by only one *client* when you act jointly for others unless you are satisfied that the *person* providing the instructions has the authority to do so on behalf of all of the *clients*;

IB(1.26) ceasing to act for a *client* without good reason and without providing reasonable notice;

IB(1.27) entering into unlawful fee arrangements such as an unlawful contingency fee;

IB(1.28) acting for a *client* when there are reasonable grounds for believing that the instructions are affected by duress or undue influence without satisfying yourself that they represent the *client's* wishes.

In-house practice

Outcomes 1.1 to 1.5, 1.7, 1.15 and 1.16 apply to your *in-house practice*.

Outcomes 1.6 and 1.9 to 1.14 apply to your *in-house practice* where you act for someone other than your employer unless it is clear that the outcome is not relevant to your particular circumstances.

IHP(1.1) Instead of Outcome 1.8 you comply with the *SRA Practice Framework Rules* in relation to professional indemnity insurance.

NOTES

(i) The information you give to *clients* will vary according to the needs and circumstances of the individual *client* and the type of work you are doing for them, for example an individual instructing you on a conveyancing matter is unlikely to need the same information as a sophisticated commercial *client* who instructs you on a regular basis.

(ii) Information about the *Legal Ombudsman*, including the scheme rules, contact details and time limits, can be found at www.legalombudsman.org.uk.

Chapter 2: Equality and diversity

This chapter is about encouraging equality of opportunity and respect for diversity, and preventing unlawful discrimination, in your relationship with your *clients* and others. The requirements apply in relation to age, disability, gender reassignment, marriage and civil partnership, pregnancy and maternity, race, religion or belief, sex and sexual orientation.

Everyone needs to contribute to compliance with these requirements, for example by treating each other, and *clients*, fairly and with respect, by embedding such values in the workplace and by challenging inappropriate behaviour and processes. Your role in embedding these values will vary depending on your role.

As a matter of general law you must comply with requirements set out in legislation – including the Equality Act 2010 – as well as the conduct duties contained in this chapter.

The outcomes in this chapter show how the *Principles* apply in the context of equality and diversity.

Outcomes

You must achieve these outcomes:

O(2.1) you do not discriminate unlawfully, or victimise or harass anyone, in the course of your professional dealings;

O(2.2) you provide services to *clients* in a way that respects diversity;

O(2.3) you make reasonable adjustments to ensure that disabled *clients*, *employees* or *managers* are not placed at a substantial disadvantage compared to those who are not disabled, and you do not pass on the costs of these adjustments to these disabled *clients*, *employees* or *managers*;

O(2.4) your approach to recruitment and employment encourages equality of opportunity and respect for diversity;

O(2.5) *complaints* of discrimination are dealt with promptly, fairly, openly, and effectively.

Indicative behaviours

Acting in the following way(s) may tend to show that you have achieved these outcomes and therefore complied with the *Principles*:

IB(2.1) having a written equality and diversity policy which is appropriate to the size and nature of the *firm* and includes the following features:

(a) a commitment to the principles of equality and diversity and legislative requirements;

(b) a requirement that all *employees* and *managers* comply with the outcomes;

(c) provisions to encompass your recruitment and interview processes;

(d) details of how the *firm* will implement, monitor, evaluate and update the policy;

(e) details of how the *firm* will ensure equality in relation to the treatment of *employees*, *managers*, *clients* and third parties instructed in connection with *client* matters;

(f) details of how *complaints* and disciplinary issues are to be dealt with;

(g) details of the *firm's* arrangements for workforce diversity monitoring; and

(h) details of how the *firm* will communicate the policy to *employees*, *managers* and *clients*;

IB(2.2) providing *employees* and *managers* with training and information about complying with equality and diversity requirements;

IB(2.3) monitoring and responding to issues identified by your policy and reviewing and updating your policy.

Acting in the following way(s) may tend to show that you have not achieved these outcomes and therefore not complied with the *Principles*:

IB(2.4) being subject to any decision of a court or tribunal of the *UK*, that you have committed, or are to be treated as having committed, an unlawful act of discrimination;

IB(2.5) discriminating unlawfully when accepting or refusing instructions to act for a *client.*

In-house practice

Outcomes 2.1 and 2.2 apply to all *in-house practice.*

Instead of outcomes 2.3 to 2.5 you must achieve the following outcome:

IHP(2.1) if you have management responsibilities you take all reasonable steps to encourage equality of opportunity and respect for diversity in your workplace.

NOTES

(i) The obligations in this chapter closely mirror your legal obligations. You can obtain further information from the Equality and Human Rights Commission, www.equalityhumanrights.com.

(ii) See also Chapter 1 (Client care) for the handling of *client complaints.*

(iii) See also Chapter 7 (Management of your business) for your obligation to have in place appropriate systems and controls for complying with the outcomes in this chapter.

Chapter 3: Conflicts of interests

This chapter deals with the proper handling of *conflicts of interests*, which is a critical public protection. It is important to have in place systems that enable you to identify and deal with potential conflicts.

Conflicts of interests can arise between:

1. you and current *clients* ("*own interest conflict*"); and
2. two or more current *clients* ("*client conflict*").

You can never act where there is a conflict, or a significant risk of conflict, between you and your *client.*

If there is a conflict, or a significant risk of a conflict, between two or more current *clients*, you must not act for all or both of them unless the matter falls within the scope of the limited exceptions set out at Outcomes 3.6 or 3.7. In deciding whether to act in these limited circumstances, the overriding consideration will be the best interests of each of the *clients* concerned and, in particular, whether the benefits to the *clients* of you acting for all or both of the *clients* outweigh the risks.

You should also bear in mind that *conflicts of interests* may affect your duties of confidentiality and disclosure which are dealt with in Chapter 4.

The outcomes in this chapter show how the *Principles* apply in the context of *conflicts of interests.*

Outcomes

You must achieve these outcomes:

Systems

O(3.1) you have effective systems and controls in place to enable you to identify and assess potential *conflicts of interests*;

O(3.2) your systems and controls for identifying *own interest conflicts* are appropriate to the size and complexity of the *firm* and the nature of the work undertaken, and enable you to assess all the relevant circumstances, including whether your ability as an individual, or that of anyone within your *firm*, to act in the best interests of the *client(s)*, is impaired by:

(a) any financial interest;

(b) a personal relationship;

(c) the appointment of you, or a member of your *firm* or family, to public office;

(d) commercial relationships; or

(e) your employment;

O(3.3) your systems and controls for identifying *client conflicts* are appropriate to the size and complexity of the *firm* and the nature of the work undertaken, and enable you to assess all relevant circumstances, including whether:

(a) the *clients'* interests are different;

(b) your ability to give independent advice to the *clients* may be fettered;

(c) there is a need to negotiate between the *clients*;

(d) there is an imbalance in bargaining power between the *clients*; or

(e) any *client* is vulnerable;

Prohibition on acting in conflict situations

O(3.4) you do not act if there is an *own interest conflict* or a significant risk of an *own interest conflict*;

O(3.5) you do not act if there is a *client conflict*, or a significant risk of a *client conflict*, unless the circumstances set out in Outcomes 3.6 or 3.7 apply;

Exceptions where you may act, with appropriate safeguards, where there is a client conflict

O(3.6) where there is a *client conflict* and the *clients* have a *substantially common interest* in relation to a matter or a particular aspect of it, you only act if:

(a) you have explained the relevant issues and risks to the *clients* and you have a reasonable belief that they understand those issues and risks;

(b) all the *clients* have given informed consent in writing to you acting;

(c) you are satisfied that it is reasonable for you to act for all the *clients* and that it is in their best interests; and

(d) you are satisfied that the benefits to the *clients* of you doing so outweigh the risks;

O(3.7) where there is a *client conflict* and the *clients* are *competing for the same objective*, you only act if:

(a) you have explained the relevant issues and risks to the *clients* and you have a reasonable belief that they understand those issues and risks;

(b) the *clients* have confirmed in writing that they want you to act, in the knowledge that you act, or may act, for one or more other *clients* who are *competing for the same objective*;

(c) there is no other *client conflict* in relation to that matter;

(d) unless the *clients* specifically agree, no individual acts for, or is responsible for the supervision of work done for, more than one of the *clients* in that matter; and

(e) you are satisfied that it is reasonable for you to act for all the *clients* and that the benefits to the *clients* of you doing so outweigh the risks.

Indicative behaviours

Acting in the following way(s) may tend to show that you have achieved these outcomes and therefore complied with the *Principles*:

IB(3.1) training *employees* and *managers* to identify and assess potential *conflicts of interests*;

IB(3.2) declining to act for *clients* whose interests are in direct conflict, for example claimant and defendant in litigation;

IB(3.3) declining to act for *clients* where you may need to negotiate on matters of substance on their behalf, for example negotiating on price between a buyer and seller of a property;

IB(3.4) declining to act where there is unequal bargaining power between the *clients*, for example acting for a seller and buyer where a builder is selling to a non-commercial *client*;

IB(3.5) declining to act for *clients* under Outcome 3.6 (*substantially common interest*) or Outcome 3.7 (*competing for the same objective*) where the *clients* cannot be represented even-handedly, or will be prejudiced by lack of separate representation;

IB(3.6) acting for *clients* under Outcome 3.7 (*competing for the same objective*) only where the *clients* are sophisticated users of legal services;

IB(3.7) acting for *clients* who are the lender and borrower on the grant of a mortgage of land only where:

(a) the mortgage is a standard mortgage (i.e. one provided in the normal course of the lender's activities, where a significant part of the lender's activities consists of lending and the mortgage is on standard terms) of property to be used as the borrower's private residence;

(b) you are satisfied that it is reasonable and in the *clients'* best interests for you to act; and

(c) the certificate of title required by the lender is in the form approved by the *Society* and the Council of Mortgage Lenders.

Acting in the following way(s) may tend to show that you have not achieved these outcomes and therefore not complied with the *Principles*:

IB(3.8) in a personal capacity, selling to or buying from, lending to or borrowing from a *client*, unless the *client* has obtained independent legal advice;

IB(3.9) advising a *client* to invest in a business, in which you have an interest which affects your ability to provide impartial advice;

IB(3.10) where you hold a power of attorney for a *client*, using that power to gain a benefit for yourself which in your professional capacity you would not have been prepared to allow to a third party;

IB(3.11) acting for two or more *clients* in a *conflict of interests* under Outcome 3.6 (*substantially common interest*) where the *clients'* interests in the end result are not the same, for example one partner buying out the interest of the other partner in their joint business or a seller transferring a property to a buyer;

IB(3.12) acting for two or more *clients* in a *conflict of interests* under Outcome 3.6 (*substantially common interest*) where it is unreasonable to act because there is unequal bargaining power;

IB(3.13) acting for two buyers where there is a *conflict of interests* under Outcome 3.7 (*competing for the same objective*), for example where two buyers are competing for a residential property;

IB(3.14) acting for a buyer (including a lessee) and seller (including a lessor) in a transaction relating to the transfer of land for value, the grant or assignment of a lease or some other interest in land for value.

In-house practice

Outcomes 3.4 to 3.7 apply to your *in-house practice.*

Outcomes 3.1 to 3.3 apply if you have management responsibilities.

Chapter 4: Confidentiality and disclosure

This chapter is about the protection of *clients'* confidential information and the disclosure of material information to *clients.*

Protection of confidential information is a fundamental feature of your relationship with *clients.* It exists as a concept both as a matter of law and as a matter of conduct. This duty continues despite the end of the retainer and even after the death of the *client.*

It is important to distinguish the conduct duties from the concept of law known as legal professional privilege.

Bear in mind that all members of the *firm* or *in-house practice,* including support staff, consultants and locums, owe a duty of confidentiality to your *clients.*

The duty of confidentiality to all *clients* must be reconciled with the duty of disclosure to *clients.* This duty of disclosure is limited to information of which you are aware which is material to your *client's* matter. Where you cannot reconcile these two duties, then the protection of confidential information is paramount. You should not continue to act for a *client* for whom you cannot disclose material information, except in very limited circumstances, where safeguards are in place. Such situations often also give rise to a *conflict of interests* which is discussed in Chapter 3.

The outcomes in this chapter show how the *Principles* apply in the context of confidentiality and disclosure.

Outcomes

You must achieve these outcomes:

O(4.1) you keep the affairs of *clients* confidential unless disclosure is required or permitted by law or the *client* consents;

O(4.2) any individual who is advising a *client* makes that *client* aware of all information material to that retainer of which the individual has personal knowledge;

O(4.3) you ensure that where your duty of confidentiality to one *client* comes into conflict with your duty of disclosure to another *client,* your duty of confidentiality takes precedence;

O(4.4) you do not act for A in a matter where A has an interest adverse to B, and B is a *client* for whom you hold confidential information which is material to A in that matter, unless the confidential information can be protected by the use of safeguards, and:

(a) you reasonably believe that A is aware of, and understands, the relevant issues and gives informed consent;

(b) either:

(i) B gives informed consent and you agree with B the safeguards to protect B's information; or

(ii) where this is not possible, you put in place effective safeguards including information barriers which comply with the common law; and

(c) it is reasonable in all the circumstances to act for A with such safeguards in place;

O(4.5) you have effective systems and controls in place to enable you to identify risks to *client* confidentiality and to mitigate those risks.

Indicative behaviours

Acting in the following way(s) may tend to show that you have achieved these outcomes and therefore complied with the *Principles*:

IB(4.1) your systems and controls for identifying risks to *client* confidentiality are appropriate to the size and complexity of the *firm* or *in-house practice* and the nature of the work undertaken, and enable you to assess all the relevant circumstances;

IB(4.2) you comply with the law in respect of your fiduciary duties in relation to confidentiality and disclosure;

IB(4.3) you only outsource services when you are satisfied that the provider has taken all appropriate steps to ensure that your *clients'* confidential information will be protected;

IB(4.4) where you are an individual who has responsibility for acting for a *client* or supervising a *client's* matter, you disclose to the *client* all information material to the *client's* matter of which you are personally aware, except when:

(a) the *client* gives specific informed consent to non-disclosure or a different standard of disclosure arises;

(b) there is evidence that serious physical or mental injury will be caused to a person(s) if the information is disclosed to the *client*;

(c) legal restrictions effectively prohibit you from passing the information to the *client*, such as the provisions in the money-laundering and anti-terrorism legislation;

(d) it is obvious that privileged documents have been mistakenly disclosed to you;

(e) you come into possession of information relating to state security or intelligence matters to which the Official Secrets Act 1989 applies;

IB(4.5) not acting for A where B is a *client* for whom you hold confidential information which is material to A unless the confidential information can be protected.

Acting in the following way(s) may tend to show that you have not achieved these outcomes and therefore not complied with the *Principles*:

IB(4.6) disclosing the content of a will on the death of a *client* unless consent has been provided by the personal representatives for the content to be released;

IB(4.7) disclosing details of bills sent to *clients* to third parties, such as debt factoring companies in relation to the collection of book debts, unless the *client* has consented.

In-house practice

The outcomes listed above apply to your *in-house practice*.

NOTES

(i) The protection of confidential information may be at particular risk where:

(a) two or more *firms* merge;

(b) when you leave one *firm* and join another, such as if you join a *firm* acting against one of your former *clients*.

(ii) The following circumstances may make it difficult to implement effective safeguards and information barriers:

(a) you are a small *firm*;

(b) the physical structure or layout of the *firm* means that it will be difficult to preserve confidentiality; or

(c) the *clients* are not sophisticated users of legal services.

Chapter 5: Your client and the court

This chapter is about your duties to your *client* and to the *court* if you are exercising a right to conduct litigation or acting as an advocate. The outcomes apply to both litigation and advocacy but there are some indicative behaviours which may be relevant only when you are acting as an advocate.

The outcomes in this chapter show how the *Principles* apply in the context of your *client* and the *court*.

Outcomes

You must achieve these outcomes:

O(5.1) you do not attempt to deceive or knowingly or recklessly mislead the *court*;

O(5.2) you are not complicit in another *person* deceiving or misleading the *court*;

O(5.3) you comply with *court* orders which place obligations on you;

O(5.4) you do not place yourself in contempt of *court*;

O(5.5) where relevant, *clients* are informed of the circumstances in which your duties to the *court* outweigh your obligations to your *client*;

O(5.6) you comply with your duties to the *court*;

O(5.7) you ensure that evidence relating to sensitive issues is not misused;

O(5.8) you do not make or offer to make payments to witnesses dependent upon their evidence or the outcome of the case.

Indicative behaviours

Acting in the following way(s) may tend to show that you have achieved these outcomes and therefore complied with the *Principles*:

IB(5.1) advising your *clients* to comply with *court* orders made against them, and advising them of the consequences of failing to comply;

IB(5.2) drawing the *court's* attention to relevant cases and statutory provisions, and any material procedural irregularity;

IB(5.3) ensuring child witness evidence is kept securely and not released to *clients* or third parties;

IB(5.4) immediately informing the *court*, with your *client's* consent, if during the course of proceedings you become aware that you have inadvertently misled the *court*, or ceasing to act if the *client* does not consent to you informing the *court*;

IB(5.5) refusing to continue acting for a *client* if you become aware they have committed perjury or misled the *court*, or attempted to mislead the *court*, in any material matter unless the *client* agrees to disclose the truth to the *court*;

IB(5.6) not appearing as an advocate, or acting in litigation, if it is clear that you, or anyone within your *firm*, will be called as a witness in the matter unless you are satisfied that this will not prejudice your independence as an advocate, or litigator, or the interests of your *clients* or the interests of justice.

Acting in the following way(s) may tend to show that you have not achieved these outcomes and therefore not complied with the *Principles*:

IB(5.7) constructing facts supporting your *client's* case or drafting any documents relating to any proceedings containing:

(a) any contention which you do not consider to be properly arguable; or

(b) any allegation of fraud, unless you are instructed to do so and you have material which you reasonably believe shows, on the face of it, a case of fraud;

IB(5.8) suggesting that any *person* is guilty of a crime, fraud or misconduct unless such allegations:

(a) go to a matter in issue which is material to your own *client's* case; and

(b) appear to you to be supported by reasonable grounds;

IB(5.9) calling a witness whose evidence you know is untrue;

IB(5.10) attempting to influence a witness, when taking a statement from that witness, with regard to the contents of their statement;

IB(5.11) tampering with evidence or seeking to persuade a witness to change their evidence;

IB(5.12) when acting as an advocate, naming in open *court* any third party whose character would thereby be called into question, unless it is necessary for the proper conduct of the case;

IB(5.13) when acting as an advocate, calling into question the character of a witness you have cross-examined unless the witness has had the opportunity to answer the allegations during cross-examination.

In-house practice

The outcomes in this chapter apply to your *in-house practice*.

NOTES

(i) If you are a litigator or an advocate there may be occasions when your obligation to act in the best interests of a *client* may conflict with your duty to the *court*. In such situations you may need to consider whether the public interest is best served by the proper administration of justice and should take precedence over the interests of your *client*.

Chapter 6: Your client and introductions to third parties

There may be circumstances in which you wish to refer your *clients* to third parties, perhaps to another *lawyer* or a financial services provider. This chapter describes the conduct duties which arise in respect of such introductions. It is important that you retain your independence when recommending third parties to your *client* and that you act in the *client's* best interests.

The outcomes in this chapter show how the *Principles* apply in the context of your *client* and introductions to third parties.

Outcomes

You must achieve these outcomes:

O(6.1) whenever you recommend that a *client* uses a particular *person* or business, your recommendation is in the best interests of the *client* and does not compromise your independence;

O(6.2) *clients* are fully informed of any financial or other interest which you have in referring the *client* to another *person* or business;

O(6.3) *clients* are in a position to make informed decisions about how to pursue their matter;

O(6.4) you are not paid a prohibited referral fee.

Indicative behaviours

Acting in the following way(s) may tend to show that you have achieved these outcomes and therefore complied with the *Principles*:

IB(6.1) any *arrangement* you enter into in respect of *regulated mortgage contracts*, *general insurance contracts* (including after the event insurance) or *pure protection contracts*, provides that referrals will only be made where this is in the best interests of the particular *client* and the contract is suitable for the needs of that *client*;

IB(6.2) any referral to a third party that can only offer products from one source, is made only after the *client* has been informed of this limitation.

IB(6.3) having effective systems in place for assessing whether any *arrangement* complies with the statutory and regulatory requirements;

IB(6.4) retaining records and management information to enable you to demonstrate that any payments you receive are not *prohibited referral fees*.

Acting in the following way(s) may tend to show that you have not achieved these outcomes and therefore not complied with the *Principles*:

IB(6.5) entering into any *arrangement* which restricts your freedom to recommend any particular business, except in respect of *regulated mortgage contracts*, *general insurance contracts* or *pure protection contracts*;

IB(6.6) being an *appointed representative*.

In-house practice

The outcomes in this chapter apply to your *in-house practice*.

NOTES

(i) See Outcome 1.15, in relation to *financial benefits* that you may receive in respect of introductions to third parties.

(ii) If the introduction is in connection with the provision of financial services, and your *firm* is not authorised by the Financial Conduct Authority, you will need to comply with the SRA Financial Services (Scope) Rules 2001 and the SRA Financial Services

(Conduct of Business) Rules 2001. Where an introduction is not a *regulated activity* because you can rely on an exclusion in the *Regulated Activities Order*, you will need nevertheless to consider Outcome 1.15.

(iii) This chapter should be read in conjunction with Chapter 12 (Separate businesses).

2nd Section: You and your business

Chapter 7: Management of your business

This chapter is about the management and supervision of your *firm* or *in-house practice*.

Everyone has a role to play in the efficient running of a business, although of course that role will depend on the individual's position within the organisation. However, overarching responsibility for the management of the business in the broadest sense rests with the *manager(s)*. The *manager(s)* should determine what arrangements are appropriate to meet the outcomes. Factors to be taken into account will include the size and complexity of the business; the number, experience and qualifications of the *employees*; the number of offices; and the nature of the work undertaken.

Where you are using a third party to provide services that you could provide, (often described as "outsourcing"), this chapter sets out the outcomes you need to achieve.

The outcomes in this chapter show how the *Principles* apply in the context of the management of your business.

Outcomes

You must achieve these outcomes:

O(7.1) you have a clear and effective governance structure and reporting lines;

O(7.2) you have effective systems and controls in place to achieve and comply with all the *Principles*, rules and outcomes and other requirements of the Handbook, where applicable;

O(7.3) you identify, monitor and manage risks to compliance with all the *Principles*, rules and outcomes and other requirements of the Handbook, if applicable to you, and take steps to address issues identified;

O(7.4) you maintain systems and controls for monitoring the financial stability of your *firm* and risks to money and *assets* entrusted to you by *clients* and others, and you take steps to address issues identified;

O(7.5) you comply with legislation applicable to your business, including anti-money laundering and data protection legislation;

O(7.6) you train individuals working in the *firm* to maintain a level of competence appropriate to their work and level of responsibility;

O(7.7) you comply with the statutory requirements for the direction and supervision of *reserved legal activities* and *immigration work*;

O(7.8) you have a system for supervising *clients'* matters, to include the regular checking of the quality of work by suitably competent and experienced people;

O(7.9) you do not outsource *reserved legal activities* to a *person* who is not authorised to conduct such activities;

O(7.10) subject to Outcome 7.9, where you outsource *legal activities* or any operational functions that are critical to the delivery of any *legal activities*, you ensure such outsourcing:

(a) does not adversely affect your ability to comply with, or the *SRA's* ability to monitor your compliance with, your obligations in the Handbook;

(b) is subject to contractual arrangements that enable the *SRA* or its agent to obtain information from, inspect the records (including electronic records) of, or enter the premises of, the third party, in relation to the outsourced activities or functions;

(c) does not alter your obligations towards your *clients*; and

(d) does not cause you to breach the conditions with which you must comply in order to be authorised and to remain so.

O(7.11) you identify, monitor and manage the compliance of your *overseas practices* with the SRA Overseas Rules;

O(7.12) you identify, monitor and manage all risks to your business which may arise from your *connected practices*.

Indicative behaviours

Acting in the following way(s) may tend to show that you have achieved these outcomes and therefore complied with the *Principles*:

IB(7.1) safekeeping of documents and *assets* entrusted to the *firm*;

IB(7.2) controlling budgets, expenditure and cash flow;

IB(7.3) identifying and monitoring financial, operational and business continuity risks including *complaints*, credit risks and exposure, claims under legislation relating to matters such as data protection, IT failures and abuses, and damage to offices;

IB(7.4) making arrangements for the continuation of your *firm* in the event of absences and emergencies, for example holiday or sick leave, with the minimum interruption to *clients'* business.

IB(7.5) you maintain systems and controls for managing the risks posed by any financial inter-dependence which exists with your *connected practices*;

IB(7.6) you take appropriate action to control the use of your brand by any body or individual outside of England and Wales which is not an *overseas practice*.

In-house practice

Outcomes 7.5 and 7.7 apply to your *in-house practice*.

Outcomes 7.1 to 7.3, and 7.6 and 7.8 to 7.10 apply to you if you have management responsibilities.

NOTES

(i) All of the chapters in the Code will be relevant to the management of your business, in particular those which require you to have systems and controls in place.

(ii) This chapter should also be read with the *SRA Authorisation Rules*, the SRA Financial Services (Conduct of Business) Rules 2001 and the *SRA Indemnity Insurance Rules*.

Chapter 8: Publicity

This chapter is about the manner in which you publicise your *firm* or *in-house practice* or any other businesses. The overriding concern is that *publicity* is not misleading and is sufficiently informative to ensure that *clients* and others can make informed choices.

In your *publicity*, you must comply with statutory requirements and have regard to voluntary codes.

The outcomes in this chapter show how the *Principles* apply in the context of *publicity*.

Outcomes

You must achieve these outcomes:

O(8.1) your *publicity* in relation to your *firm* or *in-house practice* or for any other business is accurate and not misleading, and is not likely to diminish the trust the public places in you and in the provision of legal services;

O(8.2) your *publicity* relating to charges is clearly expressed and identifies whether VAT and *disbursements* are included;

O(8.3) you do not make unsolicited approaches in person or by telephone to *members of the public* in order to publicise your *firm* or *in-house practice* or another business;

O(8.4) *clients* and the public have appropriate information about you, your *firm* and how you are regulated;

O(8.5) your letterhead, website and e-mails show the words "authorised and regulated by the Solicitors Regulation Authority" and either the *firm's* registered name and number if it is an *LLP* or *company* or, if the *firm* is a *partnership* or *sole practitioner*, the name under which it is licensed/authorised by the *SRA* and the number allocated to it by the *SRA*.

Indicative behaviours

Acting in the following way(s) may tend to show that you have achieved these outcomes and therefore complied with the *Principles*:

IB(8.1) where you conduct other regulated activities your *publicity* discloses the manner in which you are regulated in relation to those activities;

IB(8.2) where your *firm* is an *MDP*, any *publicity* in relation to that *practice* makes clear which services are regulated legal services and which are not;

IB(8.3) any *publicity* intended for a jurisdiction outside England and Wales complies with the *Principles*, voluntary codes and the rules in force in that jurisdiction concerning *publicity*;

IB(8.4) where you and another business jointly market services, the nature of the services provided by each business is clear.

Acting in the following way(s) may tend to show that you have not achieved these outcomes and therefore not complied with the *Principles*:

IB(8.5) approaching people in the street, at ports of entry, in hospital or at the scene of an accident; including approaching people to conduct a survey which involves collecting contact details of potential *clients*, or otherwise promotes your *firm* or *in-house practice*;

IB(8.6) allowing any other *person* to conduct *publicity* for your *firm* or *in-house practice* in a way that would breach the *Principles*;

IB(8.7) advertising an estimated fee which is pitched at an unrealistically low level;

IB(8.8) describing overheads of your *firm* (such a normal postage, telephone calls and charges arising in respect of *client* due diligence under the Money Laundering Regulations 2007) as *disbursements* in your advertisements;

IB(8.9) advertising an estimated or fixed fee without making it clear that additional charges may be payable, if that is the case;

IB(8.10) using a name or description of your *firm* or *in-house practice* that includes the word "solicitor(s)" if none of the *managers* are *solicitors*;

IB(8.11) advertising your *firm* or *in-house practice* in a way that suggests that services provided by another business are provided by your *firm* or *in-house practice*;

IB(8.12) producing misleading information concerning the professional status of any *manager* or *employee* of your *firm* or *in-house practice*.

In-house practice

Outcomes 8.1 to 8.4 apply to your *in-house practice* unless it is clear from the context that the outcome is not relevant in your particular circumstances.

NOTES

(i) This chapter should be read in conjunction with Chapters 1 and 9.

Chapter 9: Fee sharing and referrals

This chapter is about protecting *clients'* interests where you have *arrangements* with third parties who introduce business to you and/or with whom you share your fees. The relationship between *clients* and *firms* should be built on trust, and any such *arrangement* should not jeopardise that trust by, for example, compromising your independence or professional judgement.

The outcomes in this chapter show how the *Principles* apply in the context of fee sharing and *referrals*.

Outcomes

You must achieve these outcomes:

O(9.1) your independence and your professional judgement are not prejudiced by virtue of any *arrangement* with another *person*;

O(9.2) your *clients'* interests are protected regardless of the interests of an *introducer* or *fee sharer* or your interest in receiving *referrals*;

O(9.3) *clients* are in a position to make informed decisions about how to pursue their matter;

O(9.4) *clients* are informed of any financial or other interest which an *introducer* has in referring the *client* to you;

O(9.5) *clients* are informed of any fee sharing *arrangement* that is relevant to their matter;

O(9.6) you do not make payments to an *introducer* in respect of *clients* who are the subject of criminal proceedings or who have the benefit of public funding;

O(9.7) where you enter into a financial *arrangement* with an *introducer* you ensure that the agreement is in writing;

O(9.8) you do not pay a prohibited referral fee.

Indicative behaviours

Acting in the following way(s) may tend to show that you have achieved these outcomes and therefore complied with the *Principles*:

IB(9.1) only entering into *arrangements* with reputable third parties and monitoring the outcome of those *arrangements* to ensure that *clients* are treated fairly;

IB(9.2) in any case where a *client* has entered into, or is proposing to enter into, an *arrangement* with an *introducer* in connection with their matter, which is not in their best interests, advising the *client* that this is the case;

IB(9.3) terminating any *arrangement* with an *introducer* or *fee sharer* which is causing you to breach the *Principles* or any requirements of the Code;

IB(9.4) being satisfied that any *client* referred by an *introducer* has not been acquired as a result of marketing or other activities which, if done by a *person* regulated by the *SRA*, would be contrary to the *Principles* or any requirements of the Code;

IB(9.5) drawing the *client's* attention to any payments you make, or other consideration you provide, in connection with any *referral*;

IB(9.6) where information needs to be given to a *client*, ensuring the information is clear and in writing or in a form appropriate to the *client's* needs;

IB(9.7) having effective systems in place for assessing whether any arrangement complies with statutory and regulatory requirements;

IB(9.8) ensuring that any *payments* you make for services, such as marketing, do not amount to the *payment* of *prohibited referral fees*;

IB(9.9) retaining records and management information to enable you to demonstrate that any *payments* you make are not *prohibited referral fees*.

Acting in the following way(s) may tend to show that you have not achieved these outcomes and therefore not complied with the *Principles*:

IB(9.10) entering into any type of business relationship with a third party, such as an unauthorised *partnership*, which places you in breach of the *SRA Authorisation Rules* or any other regulatory requirements in the Handbook;

IB(9.11) allowing an *introducer* or *fee sharer* to influence the advice you give to *clients*;

IB(9.12) accepting *referrals* where you have reason to believe that *clients* have been pressurised or misled into instructing you.

In-house practice

Outcomes 9.1 to 9.3 apply to your *in-house practice*.

Outcomes 9.4 to 9.8 apply unless it is clear from the context that the outcome is not relevant to your particular circumstances.

NOTES

(i) This chapter should be read in conjunction with:

(a) Chapter 1 (Client care)

(b) Chapter 4 (Confidentiality and disclosure)

(c) Chapter 8 (Publicity)

(d) The *SRA Authorisation Rules*

(e) The *SRA European Cross-Border Practice Rules*

3rd Section: You and your regulator

Chapter 10: You and your regulator

This chapter is about co-operation with your regulators and ombudsmen, primarily the *SRA* and the *Legal Ombudsman*.

The information which we request from you will help us understand any risks to *clients*, and the public interest more generally.

The outcomes in this chapter show how the *Principles* apply in the context of you and your regulator.

Outcomes

You must achieve these outcomes:

O(10.1) you ensure that you comply with all the reporting and notification requirements in the Handbook that apply to you;

O(10.2) you provide the *SRA* with information to enable the *SRA* to decide upon any application you make, such as for a practising certificate, registration, recognition or a licence and whether any conditions should apply;

O(10.3) you notify the *SRA* promptly of any material changes to relevant information about you including serious financial difficulty, action taken against you by another regulator and serious failure to comply with or achieve the *Principles*, rules, outcomes and other requirements of the Handbook;

O(10.4) you report to the *SRA* promptly, serious misconduct by any person or *firm* authorised by the *SRA*, or any *employee*, *manager* or *owner* of any such *firm* (taking into account, where necessary, your duty of confidentiality to your *client*);

O(10.5) you ensure that the *SRA* is in a position to assess whether any persons requiring prior approval are fit and proper at the point of approval and remain so;

O(10.6) you co-operate fully with the *SRA* and the *Legal Ombudsman* at all times including in relation to any investigation about a *claim for redress* against you;

O(10.7) you do not attempt to prevent anyone from providing information to the *SRA* or the *Legal Ombudsman*;

O(10.8) you comply promptly with any written notice from the *SRA*;

O(10.9) pursuant to a notice under Outcome 10.8, you:

(a) produce for inspection by the *SRA documents* held by you, or held under your control;

(b) provide all information and explanations requested; and

(c) comply with all requests from the *SRA* as to the form in which you produce any *documents* you hold electronically, and for photocopies of any *documents* to take away;

in connection with your *practice* or in connection with any trust of which you are, or formerly were, a trustee;

O(10.10) you provide any necessary permissions for information to be given, so as to enable the *SRA* to:

(a) prepare a report on any *documents* produced; and

(b) seek verification from *clients*, staff and the banks, building societies or other financial institutions used by you;

O(10.11) when required by the *SRA* in relation to a matter specified by the *SRA*, you:

(a) act promptly to investigate whether any *person* may have a *claim for redress* against you;

(b) provide the *SRA* with a report on the outcome of such an investigation, identifying *persons* who may have such a claim;

(c) notify *persons* that they may have a right of redress against you, providing them with information as to the nature of the possible claim, about the *firm's complaints* procedure and about the *Legal Ombudsman*; and

(d) ensure, where you have identified a *person* who may have a *claim for redress*, that the matter is dealt with under the *firm's complaints* procedure as if that *person* had made a *complaint*;

O(10.12) you do not attempt to abrogate to any third party your regulatory responsibilities in the Handbook, including the role of Compliance Officer for Legal Practice (*COLP*) or Compliance Officer for Finance and Administration (*COFA*);

O(10.13) once you are aware that your *firm* will cease to *practise*, you effect the orderly and transparent wind-down of activities, including informing the *SRA* before the *firm* closes.

Indicative behaviours

Acting in the following way(s) may tend to show that you have achieved these outcomes and therefore complied with the *Principles*:

IB(10.1) actively monitoring your achievement of the outcomes in order to improve standards and identify non-achievement of the outcomes;

IB(10.2) actively monitoring your financial stability and viability in order to identify and mitigate any risks to the public;

IB(10.3) notifying the *SRA* promptly of any indicators of serious financial difficulty, such as inability to pay your professional indemnity insurance premium, or rent or salaries, or breach of bank covenants;

IB(10.4) notifying the *SRA* promptly when you become aware that your business may not be financially viable to continue trading as a going concern, for example because of difficult trading conditions, poor cash flow, increasing overheads, loss of *managers* or *employees* and/or loss of sources of revenue;

IB(10.5) notifying the *SRA* of any serious issues identified as a result of monitoring referred to in IB10.1 and IB10.2 above, and producing a plan for remedying issues that have been identified;

IB(10.6) responding appropriately to any serious issues identified concerning competence and fitness and propriety of your *employees*, *managers* and *owners*;

IB(10.7) reporting disciplinary action taken against you by another regulator;

IB(10.8) informing the *SRA* promptly when you become aware of a significant change to your *firm*, for example:

(a) key personnel, such as a *manager*, *COLP* or *COFA*, joining or leaving the *firm*;

(b) a merger with, or an acquisition by or of, another *firm*;

IB(10.9) having appropriate arrangements for the orderly transfer of *clients*' property to another *authorised body* if your *firm* closes;

IB(10.10) having a "whistle-blowing" policy.

Acting in the following way(s) may tend to show that you have not achieved these outcomes and therefore not complied with the *Principles*:

IB(10.11) entering into an agreement which would attempt to preclude the *SRA* or the *Legal Ombudsman* from investigating any actual or potential *complaint* or allegation of professional misconduct;

IB(10.12) unless you can properly allege malice, issuing defamation proceedings in respect of a *complaint* to the *SRA*.

In-house practice

The outcomes in this chapter apply to your *in-house practice*.

NOTES

(i) A notice under this chapter is deemed to be duly served:

 (a) on the date on which it is delivered to or left at your last notified *practising* address;

 (b) on the date on which it is sent electronically to your e-mail or fax address; or

 (c) seven days after it has been sent by post or document exchange to your last notified *practising* address.

(ii) The outcomes in this chapter should be considered in conjunction with the following:

 (a) Chapter 7 (Management of your business) – requirements for risk management procedures; and

 (b) note (xv) to Rule 8 of the *SRA Authorisation Rules*.

4th Section: You and others

Chapter 11: Relations with third parties

This chapter is about ensuring you do not take unfair advantage of those you deal with and that you act in a manner which promotes the proper operation of the legal system.

This includes your conduct in relation to *undertakings*; there is no obligation to give or receive an *undertaking* on behalf of a *client* but, if you do, you must ensure that you achieve the outcomes listed in this chapter.

The conduct requirements in this area extend beyond professional and business matters. They apply in any circumstances in which you may use your professional title to advance your personal interests.

The outcomes in this chapter show how the *Principles* apply in the context of your relations with third parties.

Outcomes

You must achieve these outcomes:

O(11.1) you do not take unfair advantage of third parties in either your professional or personal capacity;

O(11.2) you perform all *undertakings* given by you within an agreed timescale or within a reasonable amount of time;

O(11.3) where you act for a seller of land, you inform all buyers immediately of the seller's intention to deal with more than one buyer;

O(11.4) you properly administer oaths, affirmations or declarations where you are authorised to do so.

Indicative behaviours

Acting in the following way(s) may tend to show that you have achieved these outcomes and therefore complied with the *Principles*:

IB(11.1) providing sufficient time and information to enable the costs in any matter to be agreed;

IB(11.2) returning documents or money sent subject to an express condition if you are unable to comply with that condition;

IB(11.3) returning documents or money on demand if they are sent on condition that they are held to the sender's order;

IB(11.4) ensuring that you do not communicate with another party when you are aware that the other party has retained a *lawyer* in a matter, except:

- (a) to request the name and address of the other party's *lawyer*; or
- (b) the other party's *lawyer* consents to you communicating with the *client*; or
- (c) where there are exceptional circumstances;

IB(11.5) maintaining an effective system which records when *undertakings* have been given and when they have been discharged;

IB(11.6) where an *undertaking* is given which is dependent upon the happening of a future event and it becomes apparent the future event will not occur, notifying the recipient of this.

Acting in the following way(s) may tend to show that you have not achieved these outcomes and therefore not complied with the *Principles*:

IB(11.7) taking unfair advantage of an opposing party's lack of legal knowledge where they have not instructed a *lawyer*;

IB(11.8) demanding anything for yourself or on behalf of your *client*, that is not legally recoverable, such as when you are instructed to collect a simple debt, demanding from the debtor the cost of the letter of claim since it cannot be said at that stage that such a cost is legally recoverable;

IB(11.9) using your professional status or qualification to take unfair advantage of another *person* in order to advance your personal interests;

IB(11.10) taking unfair advantage of a public office held by you, or a member of your family, or a member of your *firm* or their family.

In-house practice

The outcomes in this chapter apply to your *in-house practice*.

NOTES

(i) This chapter should be read in conjunction with Chapter 7 (Management of your business) in relation to the system you will need to have in place to control *undertakings*.

Chapter 12: Separate businesses

The purpose of this chapter is to ensure *clients* are protected when they obtain mainstream legal services from a *firm* regulated by the *SRA*. This is accomplished by restricting the services that can be provided through a *separate business* that is not authorised by the *SRA* or another *approved regulator*.

This chapter addresses two kinds of services:

1. those which you cannot offer through a *separate business* ("*prohibited separate business activities*"). These are "mainstream" legal services which members of the public would expect you to offer as a *lawyer* regulated by the *SRA* or another *approved regulator*; and
2. those which you can offer either through a *separate business* ("*a permitted separate business*"), or through an *authorised body*. These are the kind of services a member of the public would not necessarily expect to be provided only by a *lawyer* regulated by the *SRA* or another *approved regulator*, but which are "solicitor-like" services.

Clients of a *permitted separate business* will not have the same statutory protections as *clients* of an *authorised body* and it is important that this is clear to *clients* of the *separate business*, particularly where they are being referred from one business to the other.

The outcomes in this chapter show how the *Principles* apply in the context of *separate businesses*.

Outcomes

You must achieve these outcomes:

O(12.1) you do not:

(a) *own*; or

(b) *actively participate in*,

a *separate business* which conducts *prohibited separate business activities*;

O(12.2) if you are a *firm* you are not:

(a) *owned by*; or

(b) *connected with*,

a *separate business* which conducts *prohibited separate business activities*;

O(12.3) where you:

(a) *actively participate in*;

(b) *own*; or

(c) are a *firm* and *owned by* or *connected with*,

a *permitted separate business*, you have safeguards in place to ensure that *clients* are not misled about the extent to which the services that you and the *separate business* offer are regulated;

O(12.4) you do not represent any *permitted separate business* as being regulated by the *SRA* or any of its activities as being provided by an individual who is regulated by the *SRA*;

O(12.5) you are only *connected with* reputable *separate businesses*;

O(12.6) you are only *connected with* a *permitted separate business* which is an *appointed representative* if it is an *appointed representative* of an independent financial adviser.

Indicative behaviours

Acting in the following way(s) may tend to show that you have achieved these outcomes and therefore complied with the *Principles*:

IB(12.1) ensuring that *client* information and records are not disclosed to the *permitted separate business*, without the express consent of the *client*;

IB(12.2) complying with the *SRA Accounts Rules* and not allowing the *client account* to be used to hold money for the *permitted separate business*;

IB(12.3) where you are referring a *client* to a *permitted separate business*, informing the *client* of your interest in the *separate business*;

IB(12.4) terminating any connection with a *permitted separate business* where you have reason to doubt the integrity or competence of that *separate business*.

In-house practice

Outcomes 12.1 and 12.3 to 12.6 in this chapter apply to your *in-house practice*.

NOTES

(i) It is important that *clients* are not misled or confused about the regulatory status of a *permitted separate business*, the services it provides and the people working within it. Particular care needs to be taken regarding:

(a) the name or branding of the *separate business*;

(b) misleading *publicity*; and

(c) the proximity of the *permitted separate business* to your *firm*, particularly if you share premises.

(ii) This chapter should be read in conjunction with:

(a) Chapter 3 (Conflicts of interests)

(b) Chapter 6 (Your client and introductions to third parties); and

(c) Chapter 8 (Publicity).

5th Section: Application, waivers and interpretation

Chapter 13: Application and waivers provisions

The SRA Code of Conduct applies to you in the following circumstances (and "you" must be construed accordingly):

Application of the SRA Code of Conduct in England and Wales

13.1 Subject to paragraphs 2 to 10 below and any other provisions in this Code, this Code applies to you, in relation to your activities carried out from an office in England and Wales, if you are:

(a) a *solicitor*, *REL* or *RFL*, and you are *practising* as such, whether or not the entity through which you *practise* is subject to this Code;

(b) a *solicitor*, *REL* or *RFL* who is:

(i) a *manager*, *employee* or *owner* of a body which should be a *recognised body*, but has not been recognised by the *SRA*;

(ii) a *manager*, *employee* or *owner* of a body that is a *manager* or owner of a body that should be a *recognised body*, but has not been recognised by the *SRA*;

(iii) an *employee* of a *sole practitioner* who should be a *recognised sole practitioner*, but has not been recognised by the *SRA*;

(iv) an *owner* of an *authorised body* or a body which should be a *recognised body* but has not been recognised by the *SRA*, even if you undertake no work for the body's *clients*; or

(v) a *manager* or *employee* of an *authorised non-SRA firm*, or a *manager* of a body which is a *manager* of an *authorised non-SRA firm*, when doing work of a sort authorised by the *SRA*, for that firm;

(c) an *authorised body*, or a body which should be a *recognised body* but has not been recognised by the *SRA*;

(d) any other person who is a *manager* or *employee* of an *authorised body*, or of a body which should be a *recognised body* but has not been recognised by the *SRA*;

(e) any other person who is an *employee* of a *recognised sole practitioner*, or of a *sole practitioner* who should be a *recognised sole practitioner* but has not been recognised by the *SRA*;

and "you" includes "your" as appropriate.

13.2 Chapters 10, 12, 13, 14 and 15 of the Code apply to you if you are a *solicitor*, *REL* or *RFL* and you are:

(a) *practising* as a *manager* or *employee* of an *authorised non-SRA firm* when doing work of a sort authorised by the *authorised non-SRA firm's approved regulator*; or

(b) an *owner* of an *authorised non-SRA firm* even if you undertake no work for the body's *clients*.

Application of the SRA Code of Conduct in relation to practice from an office outside England and Wales

13.3 [deleted]

13.4 [deleted]

13.5 [deleted]

13.6 [deleted]

Application of the SRA Code of Conduct outside practice

13.7 In relation to activities which fall outside *practice*, whether undertaken as a *lawyer* or in some other business or private capacity, the following apply to you if you are a *solicitor*, or *REL*:

(a) Outcome 11.1; and

(b) Outcome 11.2.

General Provisions

13.8 The extent to which you are expected to implement the requirements of the Code will depend on your role in the *firm*, or your way of *practising*. For example, those who are managing the business will be expected to have more influence on how the *firm* or business is run than those *practising* in-house but not managing a legal department, or those *practising* as *employees* of a *firm*.

13.9 You must deliver all outcomes which are relevant to you and your situation.

13.10 Where in accordance with this chapter, the requirements of the Code apply to a *licensed body*, this extends to the *reserved legal activities*, and other activities regulated by the *SRA*, carried on by the body.

Waivers

In any particular case or cases the *SRA* Board shall have the power, in exceptional circumstances, to waive in writing the provisions of these outcomes for a particular purpose or purposes expressed in such waiver, to place conditions on and to revoke such a waiver.

Chapter 13A: Practice overseas

13A.1 If you are an individual or body *practising overseas*, the Code does not apply to you, but you must comply with the SRA Overseas Rules.

13A.2 Subject to rule 13A.1 above, the Code is applicable to you as set out in 13A.3 to 13.A.6 below if you are:

(a) a body practising from an office outside England and Wales, only if you are required to be an *authorised body* as a result of the nature of your practice and you have been authorised by the *SRA* accordingly;

(b) a *manager* of such a body; or

(c) an individual engaged in *temporary practice overseas*.

13A.3 The following provisions of the Code apply:

(a) chapter 3 (conflicts of interests);

(b) chapter 4 (confidentiality and disclosure);

(c) chapter 5 (your client and the court), to the extent that your practice relates to litigation or advocacy conducted before a court, tribunal or enquiry in England and Wales or a British court martial;

(d) outcomes 6.1 to 6.3 (your client and introductions to third parties);

(e) chapter 7 (management of your business);

(f) outcomes 8.1 and 8.4 (publicity);

(g) outcomes 9.1 to 9.7 (fee sharing and referrals),except where they conflict with the *SRA European Cross-Border Practice Rules*, in which case the latter will prevail;

(h) chapter 10 (you and your regulator);

(i) chapter 11 (relations with third parties), except that Outcome 11.3 only applies if the land in question is situated in England and Wales; and

(j) outcomes 12.3 to 12.6 (separate businesses).

13A.4 In addition, you must meet the following outcomes:

O(13A.1) you properly account to your *clients* for any *financial benefit* you receive as a result of your instructions unless it is the prevailing custom of your local jurisdiction to deal with *financial benefits* in a different way;

O(13A.2) *clients* have the benefit of insurance or other indemnity in relation to professional liabilities which takes account of:

(a) the nature and extent of the risks you incur in your practice overseas;

(b) the local conditions in the jurisdiction in which you are *practising*; and

(c) the terms upon which insurance is available;

and you have not attempted to exclude liability below the minimum level required for practice in the local jurisdiction;

O(13A.3) you do not enter into unlawful contingency fee arrangements;

O(13A.4) you do not discriminate unlawfully according to the jurisdiction in which you are practising; and

O(13A.5) publicity intended for a jurisdiction outside England and Wales must comply with any applicable law or rules regarding lawyers' publicity in the jurisdiction in which your office is based and the jurisdiction for which the publicity is intended.

13A.5 you must be aware of the local laws and regulations governing your practice in an overseas jurisdiction;

13A.6 if compliance with any outcome in the Code would result in your breaching local laws or regulations you may disregard that outcome to the extent necessary to comply with that local law or regulation.

Chapter 14: Interpretation

14.1 The SRA Handbook Glossary 2012 shall apply and, unless the context otherwise requires:

(a) all italicised terms shall be defined; and

(b) all terms shall be interpreted,

in accordance with the *Glossary*.

Chapter 15: Transitional provisions

15.1 For the avoidance of doubt, where a breach of any provision of the Solicitors' Code of Conduct 2007 comes to the attention of the *SRA* after 6 October 2011, this shall be subject to action by the *SRA* notwithstanding any repeal of the relevant provision.

15.2 The SRA Code of Conduct shall not apply to *licensed bodies* until such time as the *Society* is designated as a *licensing authority* under Part 1 of Schedule 10 to the *LSA* and all definitions shall be construed accordingly.

15.3 References:

(a) in the preamble, to:

(i) the Code being made under section 83 of the Legal Services Act 2007, and

(ii) licensed bodies and their managers and employees, and

(b) in Chapter 10, to:

(i) an application for a licence (O(10.2)), and

(ii) the role of *COLP* and *COFA* (O(10.12) and IB(10.8)),

shall have no effect until such time as the *Society* is designated as a *licensing authority* under Part 1 to Schedule 10 of the *LSA*.

15.4 In Chapter 8, the provision in IB(8.2) relating to multi-disciplinary practices, shall have no effect until such time as the *Society* is designated as a *licensing authority* under Part 1 of Schedule 10 to the *LSA*.

APPENDIX 3

CCBE Code of Conduct

[The Code is reproduced with the kind permission of the CCBE. For the latest updates to the material, please see www.ccbe.org.]

Code of Conduct for European Lawyers

This Code of Conduct for European Lawyers was originally adopted at the CCBE Plenary Session held on 28 October 1988, and subsequently amended during the CCBE Plenary Sessions on 28 November 1998, 6 December 2002 and 19 May 2006. The Code includes an Explanatory Memorandum which was updated during the CCBE Plenary Session on 19 May 2006. The Code also takes into account amendments to the CCBE statutes formally approved at an Extraordinary Plenary Session on 20 August 2007.

Editor: CCBE

Avenue de la Joyeuse Entrée, 1–5 – B-1040 Brussels
Tél. : +32 (0)2 234 65 10 – Fax : +32 (0)2 234 65 11/12
E-mail : ccbe@ccbe.org – http://www.ccbe.org

Contents

1. Preamble

1.1. The Function of the Lawyer in Society

In a society founded on respect for the rule of law the lawyer fulfils a special role. The lawyer's duties do not begin and end with the faithful performance of what he or she is instructed to do so far as the law permits. A lawyer must serve the interests of justice as well as those whose rights and liberties he or she is trusted to assert and defend and it is the lawyer's duty not only to plead the client's cause but to be the client's adviser. Respect for the lawyer's professional function is an essential condition for the rule of law and democracy in society.

A lawyer's function therefore lays on him or her a variety of legal and moral obligations (sometimes appearing to be in conflict with each other) towards:

- the client;
- the courts and other authorities before whom the lawyer pleads the client's cause or acts on the client's behalf;

- the legal profession in general and each fellow member of it in particular;
- the public for whom the existence of a free and independent profession, bound together by respect for rules made by the profession itself, is an essential means of safeguarding human rights in face of the power of the state and other interests in society.

1.2. The Nature of Rules of Professional Conduct

1.2.1. Rules of professional conduct are designed through their willing acceptance by those to whom they apply to ensure the proper performance by the lawyer of a function which is recognised as essential in all civilised societies. The failure of the lawyer to observe these rules may result in disciplinary sanctions.

1.2.2. The particular rules of each Bar or Law Society arise from its own traditions. They are adapted to the organisation and sphere of activity of the profession in the Member State concerned and to its judicial and administrative procedures and to its national legislation. It is neither possible nor desirable that they should be taken out of their context nor that an attempt should be made to give general application to rules which are inherently incapable of such application.

The particular rules of each Bar and Law Society nevertheless are based on the same values and in most cases demonstrate a common foundation.

1.3. The Purpose of the Code

1.3.1. The continued integration of the European Union and European Economic Area and the increasing frequency of the cross-border activities of lawyers within the European Economic Area have made necessary in the public interest the statement of common rules which apply to all lawyers from the European Economic Area whatever Bar or Law Society they belong to in relation to their cross-border practice. A particular purpose of the statement of those rules is to mitigate the difficulties which result from the application of "double deontology", notably as set out in Articles 4 and 7.2 of Directive 77/249/EEC and Articles 6 and 7 of Directive 98/5/EC.

1.3.2. The organisations representing the legal profession through the CCBE propose that the rules codified in the following articles:

- be recognised at the present time as the expression of a consensus of all the Bars and Law Societies of the European Union and European Economic Area;
- be adopted as enforceable rules as soon as possible in accordance with national or EEA procedures in relation to the cross-border activities of the lawyer in the European Union and European Economic Area;
- be taken into account in all revisions of national rules of deontology or professional practice with a view to their progressive harmonisation.

They further express the wish that the national rules of deontology or professional practice be interpreted and applied whenever possible in a way consistent with the rules in this Code.

After the rules in this Code have been adopted as enforceable rules in relation to a lawyer's cross-border activities the lawyer will remain bound to observe the rules of the Bar or Law Society to which he or she belongs to the extent that they are consistent with the rules in this Code.

1.4. Field of Application Ratione Personae

This Code shall apply to lawyers as they are defined by Directive 77/249/EEC and by Directive 98/5/EC and to lawyers of the Associate and Observer Members of the CCBE.

1.5. Field of Application Ratione Materiae

Without prejudice to the pursuit of a progressive harmonisation of rules of deontology or professional practice which apply only internally within a Member State, the following rules shall apply to the cross-border activities of the lawyer within the European Union and the European Economic Area. Cross-border activities shall mean:

(a) all professional contacts with lawyers of Member States other than the lawyer's own;

(b) the professional activities of the lawyer in a Member State other than his or her own, whether or not the lawyer is physically present in that Member State.

1.6. Definitions

In this Code:

"Member State" means a member state of the European Union or any other state whose legal profession is included in Article 1.4.

"Home Member State" means the Member State where the lawyer acquired the right to bear his or her professional title.

"Host Member State" means any other Member State where the lawyer carries on cross-border activities.

"Competent Authority" means the professional organisation(s) or authority(ies) of the Member State concerned responsible for the laying down of rules of professional conduct and the administration of discipline of lawyers.

"Directive 77/249/EEC" means Council Directive 77/249/EEC of 22 March 1977 to facilitate the effective exercise by lawyers of freedom to provide services.

"Directive 98/5/EC" means Directive 98/5/EC of the European Parliament and of the Council of 16 February 1998 to facilitate practice of the profession of lawyer on a permanent basis in a Member State other than that in which the qualification was obtained.

2. *General Principles*

2.1. Independence

2.1.1. The many duties to which a lawyer is subject require the lawyer's absolute independence, free from all other influence, especially such as may arise from his or her personal interests or external pressure. Such independence is as necessary to trust in the process of justice as the impartiality of the judge. A lawyer must therefore avoid any impairment of his or her independence and be careful not to compromise his or her professional standards in order to please the client, the court or third parties.

2.1.2. This independence is necessary in non-contentious matters as well as in litigation. Advice given by a lawyer to the client has no value if the lawyer gives it only to ingratiate him- or herself, to serve his or her personal interests or in response to outside pressure.

2.2. Trust and Personal Integrity

Relationships of trust can only exist if a lawyer's personal honour, honesty and integrity are beyond doubt. For the lawyer these traditional virtues are professional obligations.

2.3. Confidentiality

2.3.1. It is of the essence of a lawyer's function that the lawyer should be told by his or her client things which the client would not tell to others, and that the lawyer should be the recipient of other information on a basis of confidence. Without the certainty of confidentiality there cannot be trust. Confidentiality is therefore a primary and fundamental right and duty of the lawyer.

The lawyer's obligation of confidentiality serves the interest of the administration of justice as well as the interest of the client. It is therefore entitled to special protection by the State.

2.3.2. A lawyer shall respect the confidentiality of all information that becomes known to the lawyer in the course of his or her professional activity.

2.3.3. The obligation of confidentiality is not limited in time.

2.3.4. A lawyer shall require his or her associates and staff and anyone engaged by him or her in the course of providing professional services to observe the same obligation of confidentiality.

2.4. Respect for the Rules of Other Bars and Law Societies

When practising cross-border, a lawyer from another Member State may be bound to comply with the professional rules of the Host Member State. Lawyers have a duty to inform themselves as to the rules which will affect them in the performance of any particular activity.

Member organisations of the CCBE are obliged to deposit their codes of conduct at the Secretariat of the CCBE so that any lawyer can get hold of the copy of the current code from the Secretariat.

2.5. Incompatible Occupations

2.5.1. In order to perform his or her functions with due independence and in a manner which is consistent with his or her duty to participate in the administration of justice a lawyer may be prohibited from undertaking certain occupations.

2.5.2. A lawyer who acts in the representation or the defence of a client in legal proceedings or before any public authorities in a Host Member State shall there observe the rules regarding incompatible occupations as they are applied to lawyers of the Host Member State.

2.5.3. A lawyer established in a Host Member State in which he or she wishes to participate directly in commercial or other activities not connected with the practice of the law shall respect the rules regarding forbidden or incompatible occupations as they are applied to lawyers of that Member State.

2.6. Personal Publicity

2.6.1. A lawyer is entitled to inform the public about his or her services provided that the information is accurate and not misleading, and respectful of the obligation of confidentiality and other core values of the profession.

2.6.2. Personal publicity by a lawyer in any form of media such as by press, radio, television, by electronic commercial communications or otherwise is permitted to the extent it complies with the requirements of 2.6.1.

2.7. The Client's Interest

Subject to due observance of all rules of law and professional conduct, a lawyer must always act in the best interests of the client and must put those interests before the lawyer's own interests or those of fellow members of the legal profession.

2.8. Limitation of Lawyer's Liability towards the Client

To the extent permitted by the law of the Home Member State and the Host Member State, the lawyer may limit his or her liabilities towards the client in accordance with the professional rules to which the lawyer is subject.

3. Relations with Clients

3.1. Acceptance and Termination of Instructions

3.1.1. A lawyer shall not handle a case for a party except on that party's instructions. The lawyer may, however, act in a case in which he or she has been instructed by another lawyer acting for the party or where the case has been assigned to him or her by a competent body.

The lawyer should make reasonable efforts to ascertain the identity, competence and authority of the person or body who instructs him or her when the specific circumstances show that the identity, competence and authority are uncertain.

3.1.2. A lawyer shall advise and represent the client promptly, conscientiously and diligently. The lawyer shall undertake personal responsibility for the discharge of the client's instructions and shall keep the client informed as to the progress of the matter with which the lawyer has been entrusted.

A lawyer shall not handle a matter which the lawyer knows or ought to know he or she is not competent to handle, without co-operating with a lawyer who is competent to handle it.

3.1.3. A lawyer shall not accept instructions unless he or she can discharge those instructions promptly having regard to the pressure of other work.

3.1.4. A lawyer shall not be entitled to exercise his or her right to withdraw from a case in such a way or in such circumstances that the client may be unable to find other legal assistance in time to prevent prejudice being suffered by the client.

3.2. Conflict of Interest

3.2.1. A lawyer may not advise, represent or act on behalf of two or more clients in the same matter if there is a conflict, or a significant risk of a conflict, between the interests of those clients.

3.2.2. A lawyer must cease to act for both or all of the clients concerned when a conflict of interests arises between those clients and also whenever there is a risk of a breach of confidence or where the lawyer's independence may be impaired.

3.2.3. A lawyer must also refrain from acting for a new client if there is a risk of breach of a confidence entrusted to the lawyer by a former client or if the knowledge which the lawyer possesses of the affairs of the former client would give an undue advantage to the new client.

3.2.4. Where lawyers are practising in association, paragraphs 3.2.1 to 3.2.3 above shall apply to the association and all its members.

3.3. Pactum de Quota Litis

3.3.1. A lawyer shall not be entitled to make a *pactum de quota litis*.

3.3.2. By "*pactum de quota litis*" is meant an agreement between a lawyer and the client entered into prior to final conclusion of a matter to which the client is a party, by virtue of which the client undertakes to pay the lawyer a share of the result regardless of whether this is represented by a sum of money or by any other benefit achieved by the client upon the conclusion of the matter.

3.3.3. "*Pactum de quota litis*" does not include an agreement that fees be charged in proportion to the value of a matter handled by the lawyer if this is in accordance with an officially approved fee scale or under the control of the Competent Authority having jurisdiction over the lawyer.

3.4. Regulation of Fees

A fee charged by a lawyer shall be fully disclosed to the client, shall be fair and reasonable, and shall comply with the law and professional rules to which the lawyer is subject.

3.5. Payment on Account

If a lawyer requires a payment on account of his or her fees and/or disbursements such payment should not exceed a reasonable estimate of the fees and probable disbursements involved.

Failing such payment, a lawyer may withdraw from the case or refuse to handle it, but subject always to paragraph 3.1.4 above.

3.6. Fee Sharing with Non-Lawyers

3.6.1. A lawyer may not share his or her fees with a person who is not a lawyer except where an association between the lawyer and the other person is permitted by the laws and the professional rules to which the lawyer is subject.

3.6.2. The provisions of 3.6.1 above shall not preclude a lawyer from paying a fee, commission or other compensation to a deceased lawyer's heirs or to a retired lawyer in respect of taking over the deceased or retired lawyer's practice.

3.7. Cost of Litigation and Availability of Legal Aid

3.7.1. The lawyer should at all times strive to achieve the most cost effective resolution of the client's dispute and should advise the client at appropriate stages as to the desirability of attempting a settlement and/or a reference to alternative dispute resolution.

3.7.2. A lawyer shall inform the client of the availability of legal aid where applicable.

3.8. Client Funds

3.8.1. Lawyers who come into possession of funds on behalf of their clients or third parties (hereinafter called "client funds") have to deposit such money into an account of a bank or similar institution subject to supervision by a public authority (hereinafter called a "client account"). A client account shall be separate from any other account of the lawyer. All client funds received by a lawyer should be deposited into such an account unless the owner of such funds agrees that the funds should be dealt with otherwise.

3.8.2. The lawyer shall maintain full and accurate records showing all the lawyer's dealings with client funds and distinguishing client funds from other funds held by the lawyer. Records may have to be kept for a certain period of time according to national rules.

3.8.3. A client account cannot be in debit except in exceptional circumstances as expressly permitted in national rules or due to bank charges, which cannot be influenced by the lawyer. Such an account cannot be given as a guarantee or be used as a security for any reason. There shall not be any set-off or merger between a client account and any other bank account, nor shall the client funds in a client account be available to defray money owed by the lawyer to the bank.

3.8.4. Client funds shall be transferred to the owners of such funds in the shortest period of time or under such conditions as are authorised by them.

3.8.5. The lawyer cannot transfer funds from a client account into the lawyer's own account for payment of fees without informing the client in writing.

3.8.6. The Competent Authorities in Member States shall have the power to verify and examine any document regarding client funds, whilst respecting the confidentiality or legal professional privilege to which it may be subject.

3.9. Professional Indemnity Insurance

3.9.1. Lawyers shall be insured against civil legal liability arising out of their legal practice to an extent which is reasonable having regard to the nature and extent of the risks incurred by their professional activities.

3.9.2. Should this prove impossible, the lawyer must inform the client of this situation and its consequences.

4. Relations with the Courts

4.1. Rules of Conduct in Court

A lawyer who appears, or takes part in a case, before a court or tribunal must comply with the rules of conduct applied before that court or tribunal.

4.2. Fair Conduct of Proceedings

A lawyer must always have due regard for the fair conduct of proceedings.

4.3. Demeanour in Court

A lawyer shall while maintaining due respect and courtesy towards the court defend the interests of the client honourably and fearlessly without regard to the lawyer's own interests or to any consequences to him- or herself or to any other person.

4.4. False or Misleading Information

A lawyer shall never knowingly give false or misleading information to the court.

4.5. Extension to Arbitrators etc.

The rules governing a lawyer's relations with the courts apply also to the lawyer's relations with arbitrators and any other persons exercising judicial or quasi-judicial functions, even on an occasional basis.

5. Relations between Lawyers

5.1. Corporate Spirit of the Profession

5.1.1. The corporate spirit of the profession requires a relationship of trust and co-operation between lawyers for the benefit of their clients and in order to avoid unnecessary litigation and other behaviour harmful to the reputation of the profession. It can, however, never justify setting the interests of the profession against those of the client.

5.1.2. A lawyer should recognise all other lawyers of Member States as professional colleagues and act fairly and courteously towards them.

5.2. Co-operation among Lawyers of Different Member States

5.2.1. It is the duty of a lawyer who is approached by a colleague from another Member State not to accept instructions in a matter which the lawyer is not competent to undertake. The lawyer should in such case be prepared to help that colleague to obtain the information necessary to enable him or her to instruct a lawyer who is capable of providing the service asked for.

5.2.2. Where a lawyer of a Member State co-operates with a lawyer from another Member State, both have a general duty to take into account the differences which may exist between their respective legal systems and the professional organisations, competences and obligations of lawyers in the Member States concerned.

5.3. Correspondence between Lawyers

5.3.1. If a lawyer intends to send communications to a lawyer in another Member State, which the sender wishes to remain confidential or without prejudice he or she should clearly express this intention prior to communicating the first of the documents.

5.3.2. If the prospective recipient of the communications is unable to ensure their status as confidential or without prejudice he or she should inform the sender accordingly without delay.

5.4. Referral Fees

5.4.1. A lawyer may not demand or accept from another lawyer or any other person a fee, commission or any other compensation for referring or recommending the lawyer to a client.

5.4.2. A lawyer may not pay anyone a fee, commission or any other compensation as a consideration for referring a client to him- or herself.

5.5. Communication with Opposing Parties

A lawyer shall not communicate about a particular case or matter directly with any person whom he or she knows to be represented or advised in the case or matter by another lawyer, without the consent of that other lawyer (and shall keep the other lawyer informed of any such communications).

5.6.

(Deleted by decision of the Plenary Session in Dublin on 6 December 2002)

5.7. Responsibility for Fees

In professional relations between members of Bars of different Member States, where a lawyer does not confine him- or herself to recommending another lawyer or introducing that other lawyer to the client but instead him- or herself entrusts a correspondent with a particular matter or seeks the correspondent's advice, the instructing lawyer is personally bound, even if the client is insolvent, to pay the fees, costs and outlays which are due to the foreign correspondent. The lawyers concerned may, however, at the outset of the relationship between them make special arrangements on this matter. Further, the instructing lawyer may at any time limit his or her personal responsibility to the amount of the fees, costs and outlays incurred before intimation to the foreign lawyer of the instructing lawyer's disclaimer of responsibility for the future.

5.8. Continuing Professional Development

Lawyers should maintain and develop their professional knowledge and skills taking proper account of the European dimension of their profession.

5.9. Disputes amongst Lawyers in Different Member States

5.9.1. If a lawyer considers that a colleague in another Member State has acted in breach of a rule of professional conduct the lawyer shall draw the matter to the attention of that colleague.

5.9.2. If any personal dispute of a professional nature arises amongst lawyers in different Member States they should if possible first try to settle it in a friendly way.

5.9.3. A lawyer shall not commence any form of proceedings against a colleague in another Member State on matters referred to in 5.9.1 or 5.9.2 above without first informing the Bars or Law Societies to which they both belong for the purpose of allowing both Bars or Law Societies concerned an opportunity to assist in reaching a settlement.

Explanatory Memorandum

This Explanatory Memorandum was prepared at the request of the CCBE Standing Committee by the CCBE's deontology working party, who were responsible for drafting the first version of the Code of Conduct itself. It seeks to explain the origin of the provisions of the Code, to illustrate the problems which they are designed to resolve, particularly in relation to cross-border activities, and to provide assistance to the Competent Authorities in the Member States in the application of the Code. It is not intended to have any binding force in the interpretation of the Code. The Explanatory Memorandum was adopted on 28 October 1988 and updated on the occasion of the CCBE Plenary Session on 19 May 2006. The Explanatory Memorandum also takes into account amendments to the CCBE Statutes formally approved at an Extraordinary Plenary Session on 20 August 2007. The list of professions in the commentary on article 1.4 is subject to modification.

The original versions of the Code are in the French and English languages. Translations into other Community languages are prepared under the authority of the national delegations.

Commentary on Article 1.1 – The Function of the Lawyer in Society

The Declaration of Perugia, adopted by the CCBE in 1977, laid down the fundamental principles of professional conduct applicable to lawyers throughout the EC. The provisions of

Article 1.1 reaffirm the statement in the Declaration of Perugia of the function of the lawyer in society which forms the basis for the rules governing the performance of that function.

Commentary on Article 1.2 – The Nature of Rules of Professional Conduct

These provisions substantially restate the explanation in the Declaration of Perugia of the nature of rules of professional conduct and how particular rules depend on particular local circumstances but are nevertheless based on common values.

Commentary on Article 1.3 – The Purpose of the Code

These provisions introduce the development of the principles in the Declaration of Perugia into a specific Code of Conduct for lawyers throughout the EU the EEA and Swiss Confederation, and lawyers of the Associate and Observer Members of the CCBE, with particular reference to their cross-border activities (defined in Article 1.5). The provisions of Article 1.3.2 lay down the specific intentions of the CCBE with regard to the substantive provisions in the Code.

Commentary on Article 1.4 – Field of Application Ratione Personae

The rules are stated to apply to all lawyers as defined in the Lawyers Services Directive of 1977 and the Lawyers Establishment Directive of 1998, and lawyers of the Associate and Observer Members of the CCBE. This includes lawyers of the states which subsequently acceded to the Directives, whose names have been added by amendment to the Directives. The Code accordingly applies to all the lawyers represented on the CCBE, whether as full Members, Associate Members or as Observer Members, namely:

Albania	Avokat
Armenia	Pastaban
Austria	Rechtsanwalt
Belgium	Avocat / Advocaat / Rechtsanwalt;
Bosnia & Herzegovina	Advokat / Odvjetnik;
Bulgaria	Advokat
Croatia	Odvjetnik
Cyprus	Dikegóros
Czech Republic	Advokát
Denmark	Advokat
Estonia	Vandeadvokaat
Finland	Asianajaja / Advokat
FYROM	Advokat
France	Avocat
Georgia	Advokati / Advokatebi
Germany	Rechtsanwalt
Greece	Dikegóros
Hungary	Ügyvéd

Iceland	Lögmaður
Ireland	Barrister / Solicitor
Italy	Avvocato
Latvia	Zverinats advokats
Liechtenstein	Rechtsanwalt
Lithuania	Advokatas
Luxembourg	Avocat / Rechtsanwalt
Malta	Avukat / Prokuratur legali
Montenegro	Advokat
Moldova	Avocat
Netherlands	Advocaat
Norway	Advokat
Poland	Adwokat / Radca prawny
Portugal	Advogado
Romania	Avocat
Serbia	Advokat
Slovakia	Advokát / Advokátka
Slovenia	Odvetnik / Odvetnica
Spain	Abogado / Advocat / Abokatu / Avogado
Sweden	Advokat
Switzerland	Rechtsanwalt / Anwalt / Fürsprech / Fürsprecher / Advocat / avocat / avvocato /advocat
Turkey	Avukat
Ukraine	Advocate
United Kingdom	Advocate / Barrister / Solicitor

It is also hoped that the Code will be acceptable to the legal professions of other non-member states in Europe and elsewhere so that it could also be applied by appropriate conventions between them and the Member States.

Commentary on Article 1.5 – Field of Application Ratione Materiae

The rules are here given direct application only to "cross-border activities", as defined, of lawyers within the EU, the EEA and Swiss Confederation and lawyers of the Associate and Observer Members of the CCBE – see above on Article 1.4, and the definition of "Member State" in Article 1.6. (See also above as to possible extensions in the future to lawyers of other states.) The definition of cross-border activities would, for example, include contacts in state A even on a matter of law internal to state A between a lawyer of state A and a lawyer of state B; it would exclude contacts between lawyers of state A in state A of a matter arising in state B, provided that none of their professional activities takes place in state B; it would include any activities of lawyers of state A in state B, even if only in the form of communications sent from state A to state B.

Commentary on Article 1.6 – Definitions

This provision defines a number of terms used in the Code, "Member State", "Home Member State", "Host Member State", "Competent Authority", "Directive 77/249/EEC" and "Directive 98/5/EC".

The reference to "where the lawyer carries on cross-border activities" should be interpreted in the light of the definition of "cross-border activities" in Article 1.5.

Commentary on Article 2.1 – Independence

This provision substantially reaffirms the general statement of principle in the Declaration of Perugia.

Commentary on Article 2.2 – Trust and Personal Integrity

This provision also restates a general principle contained in the Declaration of Perugia.

Commentary on Article 2.3 – Confidentiality

This provision first restates, in Article 2.3.1, general principles laid down in the Declaration of Perugia and recognised by the ECJ in the *AM&S* case (157/79). It then, in Articles 2.3.2 to 4, develops them into a specific rule relating to the protection of confidentiality. Article 2.3.2 contains the basic rule requiring respect for confidentiality. Article 2.3.3 confirms that the obligation remains binding on the lawyer even if he or she ceases to act for the client in question. Article 2.3.4 confirms that the lawyer must not only respect the obligation of confidentiality him- or herself but must require all members and employees of his or her firm to do likewise.

Commentary on Article 2.4 – Respect for the Rules of Other Bars and Law Societies

Article 4 of the Lawyers Services Directive contains the provisions with regard to the rules to be observed by a lawyer from one Member State providing services on an occasional or temporary basis in another Member State by virtue of Article 49 of the consolidated EC treaty, as follows:

(a) activities relating to the representation of a client in legal proceedings or before public authorities shall be pursued in each Host Member State under the conditions laid down for lawyers established in that state, with the exception of any conditions requiring residence, or registration with a professional organisation, in that state;

(b) a lawyer pursuing these activities shall observe the rules of professional conduct of the Host Member State, without prejudice to the lawyer's obligations in the Member State from which he or she comes;

(c) when these activities are pursued in the UK, "rules of professional conduct of the Host Member State" means the rules of professional conduct applicable to solicitors, where such activities are not reserved for barristers and advocates. Otherwise the rules of professional conduct applicable to the latter shall apply. However, barristers from Ireland shall always be subject to the rules of professional conduct applicable in the UK to barristers and advocates. When these activities are pursued in Ireland "rules of professional conduct of the Host Member State" means, in so far as they govern the oral presentation of a case in court, the rules of professional conduct applicable to barristers. In all other cases the rules of professional conduct applicable to solicitors shall apply. However, barristers and advocates from the UK shall always be subject to the rules of professional conduct applicable in Ireland to barristers; and

(d) a lawyer pursuing activities other than those referred to in (a) above shall remain subject to the conditions and rules of professional conduct of the Member State from which he or she comes without prejudice to respect for the rules, whatever their source, which govern the profession in the Host Member State, especially those concerning the incompatibility of the exercise of the activities of a lawyer with the exercise of other activities in that state, professional secrecy, relations with other lawyers, the prohibition on the same lawyer acting for parties with mutually conflicting interests, and publicity. The latter rules are applicable only if they are capable of being observed by a lawyer who is not established in the Host Member State and to the extent to which their observance is objectively justified to ensure, in that state, the proper exercise of a lawyer's activities, the standing of the profession and respect for the rules concerning incompatibility.

The Lawyers Establishment Directive contains the provisions with regard to the rules to be observed by a lawyer from one Member State practising on a permanent basis in another Member State by virtue of Article 43 of the consolidated EC treaty, as follows:

(a) irrespective of the rules of professional conduct to which he or she is subject in his or her Home Member State, a lawyer practising under his home-country professional title shall be subject to the same rules of professional conduct as lawyers practising under the relevant professional title of the Host Member State in respect of all the activities the lawyer pursues in its territory (Article 6.1);

(b) the Host Member State may require a lawyer practising under his or her home-country professional title either to take out professional indemnity insurance or to become a member of a professional guarantee fund in accordance with the rules which that state lays down for professional activities pursued in its territory.

Nevertheless, a lawyer practising under his or her home-country professional title shall be exempted from that requirement if the lawyer can prove that he or she is covered by insurance taken out or a guarantee provided in accordance with the rules of the Home Member State, insofar as such insurance or guarantee is equivalent in terms of the conditions and extent of cover. Where the equivalence is only partial, the Competent Authority in the Host Member State may require that additional insurance or an additional guarantee be contracted to cover the elements which are not already covered by the insurance or guarantee contracted in accordance with the rules of the Home Member State (Article 6.3); and

(c) a lawyer registered in a Host Member State under his or her home-country professional title may practise as a salaried lawyer in the employ of another lawyer, an association or firm of lawyers, or a public or private enterprise to the extent that the Host Member State so permits for lawyers registered under the professional title used in that state (Article 8).

In cases not covered by either of these Directives, or over and above the requirements of these Directives, the obligations of a lawyer under Community law to observe the rules of other Bars and Law Societies are a matter of interpretation of any relevant provision, such as the Directive on Electronic Commerce (2000/31/EC). A major purpose of the Code is to minimise, and if possible eliminate altogether, the problems which may arise from "double deontology", that is the application of more than one set of potentially conflicting national rules to a particular situation (see Article 1.3.1).

Commentary on Article 2.5 – Incompatible Occupations

There are differences both between and within Member States on the extent to which lawyers are permitted to engage in other occupations, for example in commercial activities. The general purpose of rules excluding a lawyer from other occupations is to protect the lawyer from influences which might impair the lawyer's independence or his or her role in the administration of justice. The variations in these rules reflect different local conditions, different perceptions of the proper function of lawyers and different techniques of rule-making. For instance in some cases there is a complete prohibition of engagement in certain named occupations, whereas in other cases engagement in other occupations is generally permitted, subject to observance of specific safeguards for the lawyer's independence.

Articles 2.5.2 and 3 make provision for different circumstances in which a lawyer of one Member State is engaging in cross-border activities (as defined in Article 1.5) in a Host Member State when he or she is not a member of the Host State legal profession.

Article 2.5.2 imposes full observation of Host State rules regarding incompatible occupations on the lawyer acting in national legal proceedings or before national public authorities in the Host State. This applies whether the lawyer is established in the Host State or not.

Article 2.5.3, on the other hand, imposes "respect" for the rules of the Host State regarding forbidden or incompatible occupations in other cases, but only where the lawyer who is established in the Host Member State wishes to participate directly in commercial or other activities not connected with the practice of the law.

Commentary on Article 2.6 – Personal Publicity

The term "personal publicity" covers publicity by firms of lawyers, as well as individual lawyers, as opposed to corporate publicity organised by Bars and Law Societies for their members as a whole. The rules governing personal publicity by lawyers vary considerably in the Member States. Article 2.6 makes it clear that there is no overriding objection to personal publicity in cross-border practice. However, lawyers are nevertheless subject to prohibitions or restrictions laid down by their home professional rules, and a lawyer will still be subject to prohibitions or restrictions laid down by Host State rules when these are binding on the lawyer by virtue of the Lawyers Services Directive or the Lawyers Establishment Directive.

Commentary on Article 2.7 – The Client's Interest

This provision emphasises the general principle that the lawyer must always place the client's interests before the lawyer's own interests or those of fellow members of the legal profession.

Commentary on Article 2.8 – Limitation of Lawyer's Liability towards the Client

This provision makes clear that there is no overriding objection to limiting a lawyer's liability towards his or her client in cross-border practice, whether by contract or by use of a limited company, limited partnership or limited liability partnership. However it points out that this can only be contemplated where the relevant law and the relevant rules of conduct permit – and in a number of jurisdictions the law or the professional rules prohibit or restrict such limitation of liability.

Commentary on Article 3.1 – Acceptance and Termination of Instructions

The provisions of Article 3.1.1 are designed to ensure that a relationship is maintained between lawyer and client and that the lawyer in fact receives instructions from the client, even though these may be transmitted through a duly authorised intermediary. It is the responsibility of the lawyer to satisfy him- or herself as to the authority of the intermediary and the wishes of the client.

Article 3.1.2 deals with the manner in which the lawyer should carry out his or her duties. The provision that the lawyer shall undertake personal responsibility for the discharge of the instructions given to him or her means that the lawyer cannot avoid responsibility by delegation to others. It does not prevent the lawyer from seeking to limit his or her legal liability to the extent that this is permitted by the relevant law or professional rules – see Article 2.8.

Article 3.1.3 states a principle which is of particular relevance in cross-border activities, for example when a lawyer is asked to handle a matter on behalf of a lawyer or client from another state who may be unfamiliar with the relevant law and practice, or when a lawyer is asked to handle a matter relating to the law of another state with which he or she is unfamiliar.

A lawyer generally has the right to refuse to accept instructions in the first place, but Article 3.1.4 states that, having once accepted them, the lawyer has an obligation not to withdraw without ensuring that the client's interests are safeguarded.

Commentary on Article 3.2 – Conflict of Interest

The provisions of Article 3.2.1 do not prevent a lawyer acting for two or more clients in the same matter provided that their interests are not in fact in conflict and that there is no significant risk of such a conflict arising. Where a lawyer is already acting for two or more clients in this way and subsequently there arises a conflict of interests between those clients or a risk of a breach of confidence or other circumstances where the lawyer's independence may be impaired, then the lawyer must cease to act for both or all of them.

There may, however, be circumstances in which differences arise between two or more clients for whom the same lawyer is acting where it may be appropriate for the lawyer to attempt to act as a mediator. It is for the lawyer in such cases to use his or her own judgement on whether or not there is such a conflict of interest between them as to require the lawyer to cease to act. If not, the lawyer may consider whether it would be appropriate to explain the position to the clients, obtain their agreement and attempt to act as mediator to resolve the difference between them, and only if this attempt to mediate should fail, to cease to act for them.

Article 3.2.4 applies the foregoing provisions of Article 3 to lawyers practising in association. For example a firm of lawyers should cease to act when there is a conflict of interest between two clients of the firm, even if different lawyers in the firm are acting for each client. On the other hand, exceptionally, in the "chambers" form of association used by English barristers, where each lawyer acts for clients individually, it is possible for different lawyers in the association to act for clients with opposing interests.

Commentary on Article 3.3 – Pactum de Quota Litis

These provisions reflect the common position in all Member States that an unregulated agreement for contingency fees (*pactum de quota litis*) is contrary to the proper administration of justice because it encourages speculative litigation and is liable to be abused. The provisions are not, however, intended to prevent the maintenance or introduction of arrangements under which lawyers are paid according to results or only if the action or matter is successful, provided that these arrangements are under sufficient regulation and control for the protection of the client and the proper administration of justice.

Commentary on Article 3.4 – Regulation of Fees

Article 3.4 lays down three requirements: a general standard of disclosure of a lawyer's fees to the client, a requirement that they should be fair and reasonable in amount, and a requirement to comply with the applicable law and professional rules.

In many Member States machinery exists for regulating lawyers' fees under national law or rules of conduct, whether by reference to a power of adjudication by the Bar authorities or otherwise. In situations governed by the Lawyers Establishment Directive, where the lawyer is subject to Host State rules as well as the rules of the Home State, the basis of charging may have to comply with both sets of rules.

Commentary on Article 3.5 – Payment on Account

Article 3.5 assumes that a lawyer may require a payment on account of the lawyer's fees and/or disbursements, but sets a limit by reference to a reasonable estimate of them. See also on Article 3.1.4 regarding the right to withdraw.

Commentary on Article 3.6 – Fee Sharing with Non-Lawyers

In some Member States lawyers are permitted to practise in association with members of certain other approved professions, whether legal professions or not. The provisions of Article 3.6.1 are not designed to prevent fee sharing within such an approved form of association. Nor are the provisions designed to prevent fee sharing by the lawyers to whom the Code applies (see on Article 1.4 above) with other "lawyers", for example lawyers from non-Member States or members of other legal professions in the Member States such as notaries.

Commentary on Article 3.7 – Cost of Litigation and Availability of Legal Aid

Article 3.7.1 stresses the importance of attempting to resolve disputes in a way which is cost-effective for the client, including advising on whether to attempt to negotiate a settlement, and whether to propose referring the dispute to some form of alternative dispute resolution.

Article 3.7.2 requires a lawyer to inform the client of the availability of legal aid where applicable. There are widely differing provisions in the Member States on the availability of legal aid. In cross-border activities a lawyer should have in mind the possibility that the legal aid provisions of a national law with which the lawyer is unfamiliar may be applicable.

Commentary on Article 3.8 – Client Funds

The provisions of Article 3.8 reflect the recommendation adopted by the CCBE in Brussels in November 1985 on the need for minimum regulations to be made and enforced governing the proper control and disposal of clients' funds held by lawyers within the Community. Article 3.8 lays down minimum standards to be observed, while not interfering with the details of national systems which provide fuller or more stringent protection for clients' funds.

The lawyer who holds clients' funds, even in the course of a cross-border activity, has to observe the rules of his or her home Bar. The lawyer needs to be aware of questions which arise where the rules of more than one Member State may be applicable, especially where the lawyer is established in a Host State under the Lawyers Establishment Directive.

Commentary on Article 3.9 – Professional Indemnity Insurance

Article 3.9.1 reflects a recommendation, also adopted by the CCBE in Brussels in November 1985, on the need for all lawyers in the Community to be insured against the risks arising from professional negligence claims against them.

Article 3.9.2 deals with the situation where insurance cannot be obtained on the basis set out in Article 3.9.1.

Commentary on Article 4.1 – Rules of Conduct in Court

This provision applies the principle that a lawyer is bound to comply with the rules of the court or tribunal before which the lawyer practises or appears.

Commentary on Article 4.2 – Fair Conduct of Proceedings

This provision applies the general principle that in adversarial proceedings a lawyer must not attempt to take unfair advantage of his or her opponent. The lawyer must not, for example, make contact with the judge without first informing the lawyer acting for the opposing party or submit exhibits, notes or documents to the judge without communicating them in good time to the lawyer on the other side unless such steps are permitted under the relevant rules of procedure. To the extent not prohibited by law a lawyer must not divulge or submit to the court any proposals for settlement of the case made by the other party or its lawyer without the express consent of the other party's lawyer. See also on Article 4.5 below.

Commentary on Article 4.3 – Demeanour in Court

This provision reflects the necessary balance between respect for the court and for the law on the one hand and the pursuit of the client's best interest on the other.

Commentary on Article 4.4 – False or Misleading Information

This provision applies the principle that the lawyer must never knowingly mislead the court. This is necessary if there is to be trust between the courts and the legal profession.

Commentary on Article 4.5 – Extension to Arbitrators etc.

This provision extends the preceding provisions relating to courts to other bodies exercising judicial or quasi-judicial functions.

Commentary on Article 5.1 – Corporate Spirit of the Profession

These provisions, which are based on statements in the Declaration of Perugia, emphasise that it is in the public interest for the legal profession to maintain a relationship of trust and cooperation between its members. However, this cannot be used to justify setting the interests of the profession against those of justice or of clients (see also on Article 2.7).

Commentary on Article 5.2 – Co-operation among Lawyers of Different Member States

This provision also develops a principle stated in the Declaration of Perugia with a view to avoiding misunderstandings in dealings between lawyers of different Member States.

Commentary on Article 5.3 – Correspondence between Lawyers

In certain Member States communications between lawyers (written or by word of mouth) are normally regarded as to be kept confidential as between the lawyers. This means that the content of these communications cannot be disclosed to others, cannot normally be passed to the lawyers' clients, and at any event cannot be produced in court. In other Member States, such consequences will not follow unless the correspondence is marked as "confidential".

In yet other Member States, the lawyer has to keep the client fully informed of all relevant communications from a professional colleague acting for another party, and marking a letter as "confidential" only means that it is a legal matter intended for the recipient lawyer and his or her client, and not to be misused by third parties.

In some states, if a lawyer wishes to indicate that a letter is sent in an attempt to settle a dispute, and is not to be produced in a court, the lawyer should mark the letter as "without prejudice".

These important national differences give rise to many misunderstandings. That is why lawyers must be very careful in conducting cross-border correspondence.

Whenever a lawyer wants to send a letter to a professional colleague in another Member State on the basis that it is to be kept confidential as between the lawyers, or that it is "without prejudice", the lawyer should ask in advance whether the letter can be accepted on that basis. A lawyer wishing that a communication should be accepted on such a basis must express that clearly in the communication or in a covering letter.

A lawyer who is the intended recipient of such a communication, but who is not in a position to respect, or to ensure respect for, the basis on which it is to be sent, must inform the sender immediately so that the communication is not sent. If the communication has already been received, the recipient must return it to the sender without revealing its contents or referring to it in any way; if the recipient's national law or rules prevent the recipient from complying with this requirement, he or she must inform the sender immediately.

Commentary on Article 5.4 – Referral Fees

This provision reflects the principle that a lawyer should not pay or receive payment purely for the reference of a client, which would risk impairing the client's free choice of lawyer or the client's interest in being referred to the best available service. It does not prevent fee-sharing arrangements between lawyers on a proper basis (see also on Article 3.6 above).

In some Member States lawyers are permitted to accept and retain commissions in certain cases provided: a) the client's best interests are served, b) there is full disclosure to the client and c) the client has consented to the retention of the commission. In such cases the retention of the commission by the lawyer represents part of the lawyer's remuneration for the service provided to the client and is not within the scope of the prohibition on referral fees which is designed to prevent lawyers making a secret profit.

Commentary on Article 5.5 – Communication with Opposing Parties

This provision reflects a generally accepted principle, and is designed both to promote the smooth conduct of business between lawyers and to prevent any attempt to take advantage of the client of another lawyer.

Commentary on Article 5.6 – Change of Lawyer

Article 5.6 dealt with change of lawyer. It was deleted from the Code on 6 December 2002.

Commentary on Article 5.7 – Responsibility for Fees

These provisions substantially reaffirm provisions contained in the Declaration of Perugia. Since misunderstandings about responsibility for unpaid fees are a common cause of difference between lawyers of different Member States, it is important that a lawyer who wishes to exclude or limit his or her personal obligation to be responsible for the fees of a foreign colleague should reach a clear agreement on this at the outset of the transaction.

Commentary on Article 5.8 – Continuing Professional Development

Keeping abreast of developments in the law is a professional obligation. In particular it is essential that lawyers are aware of the growing impact of European law on their field of practice.

Commentary on Article 5.9 – Disputes amongst Lawyers in Different Member States

A lawyer has the right to pursue any legal or other remedy to which he or she is entitled against a colleague in another Member State. Nevertheless it is desirable that, where a breach of a rule of professional conduct or a dispute of a professional nature is involved, the possibilities of friendly settlement should be exhausted, if necessary with the assistance of the Bars or Law Societies concerned, before such remedies are exercised.

The European Communities (Services of Lawyers) Order 1978

European Communities (Services of Lawyers) Order 1978

SI 1978/1910

Made 20th December 1978

Authority: European Communities Act 1972, s 2(2)

Citation and commencement

1

This Order may be cited as the European Communities (Services of Lawyers) Order 1978 and shall come into operation on 1st March 1979.

Interpretation

2

In this Order, unless the context otherwise requires—

"advocate", "barrister" and "solicitor" mean, in relation to any part of the United Kingdom, a person practising in that part as an advocate, barrister or solicitor as the case may be;

"country of origin", in relation to a European lawyer, means the country or countries in which he is established;

"the Directive" means the European Communities Council Directive No. 77/249/EEC to facilitate the effective exercise by lawyers of freedom to provide services;

"European lawyer" means a person entitled to pursue his professional activities in a state in column 1 under the designation referred to in column 2—

State	Designation(s)
Austria	Rechtsanwalt
Belgium	Avocat/Advocaat
Bulgaria	Адвокат [advokat]
Croatia	Odvjetnik/Odvjetnica
Cyprus	Δικηγόρος [dikhgoros]
Czech Republic	Advokát
Denmark	Advokat
Estonia	Vandeadvokaat
Finland	Asianajaja/Advokat
France	Avocat
Germany	Rechtsanwalt

Hellenic Republic	Δικηγόρος [dikhgoros]
Hungary	Ügyvéd
Iceland	Lögmaður
Republic of Ireland	Barrister/solicitor
Italy	Avvocato
Latvia	Zverinâts advokâts
Liechtenstein	Rechtsanwalt
Lithuania	Advokatas
Luxembourg	Avocat-avoué
Malta	Avukat/Prokuratur Legali
Netherlands	Advocaat
Norway	Advokat
Poland	Adwokat/Radca prawny
Portugal	Advogado
Romania	Avocat
Slovakia	Advokát/Komercný právnik
Slovenia	Odvetnik/Odvetnica
Spain	Abogado/Advocat/Avogado/Abokatu
Sweden	Advokat
Switzerland	Avocat/Advokat/Rechtsanwalt/Anwalt/ Fürsprecher/Fürsprech/Avvocato

"own professional authority", in relation to a European lawyer, means an authority entitled to exercise disciplinary authority over him in his member State of origin.

3

(1) The Interpretation Act 1978 shall apply to this Order as it applies to subordinate legislation made after the commencement of that Act.

(2) Unless the context otherwise requires, any reference in this Order to a numbered article or to the Schedule is a reference to an article of, or the Schedule to, this Order.

Purpose of Order

4

The provisions of this Order shall have effect for the purpose of enabling a European lawyer to pursue his professional activities in any part of the United Kingdom by providing, under the conditions specified in or permitted by the Directive, services otherwise reserved to advocates, barristers and solicitors; and services which may be so provided are hereafter in this Order referred to as services.

Representation in legal proceedings

5

No enactment or rule of law or practice shall prevent a European lawyer from providing any service in relation to any proceedings, whether civil or criminal, before any court, tribunal or public authority (including appearing before and addressing the court, tribunal or public authority) by reason only that he is not an advocate, barrister or solicitor; provided that throughout he is instructed with, and acts in conjunction with, an advocate, barrister or solicitor who is entitled to practise before the court, tribunal or public authority concerned and who could properly provide the service in question.

6

Nothing in this Order shall enable a European lawyer:—

(a) if he is established in practice as a barrister in the Republic of Ireland, to provide in the course of any proceedings any service which could not properly be provided by an advocate or barrister;

(b) if he is instructed with and acts in conjunction with an advocate or barrister in any proceedings, to provide in the course of those proceedings, or of any related proceedings, any service which an advocate or barrister could not properly provide;

(c) if he is instructed with and acts in conjunction with a solicitor in any proceedings, to provide in the course of those proceedings, or of any related proceedings, any service which a solicitor could not properly provide.

7

A European lawyer in salaried employment who is instructed with and acts in conjunction with an advocate or barrister in any proceedings may provide a service on behalf of his employer in those proceedings only in so far as an advocate or barrister in such employment could properly do so.

Drawing of documents, etc not related to legal proceedings

8

No enactment or rule of law or practice shall prevent a European lawyer from drawing or preparing for remuneration:—

(i) in England, Wales or Northern Ireland, an instrument relating to personal estate, or

(ii) in Scotland, a writ relating to moveable property,

by reason only that he is not an advocate, barrister or solicitor.

9

Nothing in this Order shall entitle a European lawyer to draw or prepare for remuneration any instrument, or in Scotland any writ:—

(i) creating or transferring an interest in land; or

(ii) for obtaining title to administer the estate of a deceased person.

Legal aid

10

Services may be provided by a European lawyer by way of legal advice and assistance or legal aid under the enactments specified in Part 1 of the Schedule; and references to counsel and solicitors in those and any other enactments relating to legal advice and assistance or legal aid shall be construed accordingly.

Title and description to be used by European lawyers

11

In providing any services, a European lawyer shall use the professional title and description applicable to him in his country of origin, expressed in the language or one of the languages of that country, together with the name of the professional organisation by which he is authorised to practise or the court of law before which he is entitled to practise in that country.

Power to require a European lawyer to verify his status

12

A competent authority may at any time request a person seeking to provide any services to verify his status as a European lawyer.

13

Where a request has been made under article 12, the person to whom it is made shall not, except to the extent (if any) allowed by the competent authority making the request, be entitled to provide services in the United Kingdom until he has verified his status as a European lawyer to the satisfaction of that authority.

14

For the purposes of articles 12 and 13, a competent authority is:—

(a) where the services which the person concerned seeks to provide are reserved to advocates or barristers, or in any case where the person concerned claims to be a barrister established in practice in the Republic of Ireland, the Senate of the Inns of Court and the Bar, the Faculty of Advocates, or the Benchers of the Inn of Court of Northern Ireland, according to the part of the United Kingdom concerned; or

(b) where sub-paragraph (a) does not apply, the Law Society, the Law Society of Scotland, or the Incorporated Law Society of Northern Ireland, according to the part of the United Kingdom concerned; or

(c) in any case, any court, tribunal or public authority before which the person concerned seeks to provide services.

Professional misconduct

15

(1) A complaint may be made to a disciplinary authority that a European lawyer providing any services has failed to observe a condition or rule of professional conduct referred to in article 4 of the Directive and applicable to him.

(2) Where a complaint is made under paragraph (1), the disciplinary authority concerned shall consider and adjudicate upon it in accordance with the same procedure, and subject to the same rights of appeal, as apply in relation to an advocate, barrister or solicitor (as the case may be) over whom that authority has jurisdiction.

(3) For the purposes of this article and article 16, a disciplinary authority is:—

(a) where the services in question are reserved to advocates or barristers, or in any case where the person whose conduct is in question is established in practice as a barrister in the Republic of Ireland, an authority having disciplinary jurisdiction over advocates or barristers (as the case may be) in the part of the United Kingdom concerned;

(b) where sub-paragraph (a) does not apply, an authority having disciplinary jurisdiction over solicitors in the part of the United Kingdom concerned.

16

(1) Where a disciplinary authority finds that a European lawyer against whom a complaint has been made under article 15(1) has committed a breach of a condition or a rule of professional conduct mentioned in that article, that authority:—

(a) shall report that finding to the European lawyer's own professional authority; and

(b) may, if it thinks fit, direct him not to provide services in the United Kingdom, except to such extent and under such conditions (if any) as the disciplinary authority may specify in the direction.

(2) A disciplinary authority may at any time, if it thinks fit, vary, cancel or suspend the operation of a direction given by it under paragraph (1)(b).

17

A European lawyer in respect of whom a direction is made under article 16(1)(b) shall not be entitled to provide services in the United Kingdom except as allowed by the direction.

Modification of enactments

18

(1) Without prejudice to the generality of articles 5 and 8, the enactments specified in Part 2 of the Schedule (being enactments which reserve the provision of certain services to advocates, barristers, solicitors and other qualified persons) shall be construed subject to those articles.

(2) Notwithstanding anything in the Solicitors (Scotland) Act 1980, the Solicitors Act 1974 or the Solicitors (Northern Ireland) Order 1976, references to unqualified persons, however expressed, in the enactments specified in Part 3 of the Schedule (being enactments relating to unqualified persons acting as solicitors) shall not include a European lawyer providing services within the meaning of this Order.

(3) Nothing in section 33 of the Solicitors (Scotland) Act 1980 shall prevent a European lawyer from recovering any remuneration or expenses to which that section applies by reason only that he is not qualified as a solicitor.

SCHEDULE

Article 10

PART 1
ENACTMENTS RELATING TO THE PROVISION OF LEGAL ADVICE AND ASSISTANCE AND LEGAL AID

Legal Aid and Advice Act (Northern Ireland) 1965 (c. 8).

Legal Aid (Scotland) Act 1986 (c 47).

Legal Advice and Assistance Act 1972 (c. 50).

Legal Aid, Advice and Assistance (Northern Ireland) Order 1981 (SI No 228 (NI 8)).

Access to Justice Act 1999 (c 22).

Financial Services and Markets Act 2000 (c 8).

Legal Aid, Sentencing and Punishment of Offenders Act 2012 (c 10).

PART 2
ENACTMENTS RESERVING THE PROVISION OF SERVICES TO ADVOCATES, BARRISTERS, SOLICITORS, ETC

Article 18(1)

Solicitors (Scotland) Act 1980 (c 46), section 32.

Magistrates' Courts (Northern Ireland) Order 1981, article 164(1).

County Courts (Northern Ireland) Order 1980, article 50.

Solicitors Act 1974 (c. 47), sections 20, 22 [and 23].

Solicitors (Northern Ireland) Order 1976 (SI No. 582 (NI 12)), articles 19, 23.

PART 3
ENACTMENTS RELATING TO UNQUALIFIED PERSONS ACTING AS SOLICITORS

Article 18(2)

Solicitors (Scotland) Act 1980 (c 46), section 26.

Solicitors Act 1974 (c. 47), section 25(1).

Solicitors (Northern Ireland) Order 1976 (SI No. 582 (NI 12)), articles 25(1), 27.

APPENDIX 5

The European Communities (Lawyer's Practice) Regulations 2000

European Communities (Lawyer's Practice) Regulations 2000

SI 2000/1119

Made 8th April 2000

Laid 19th April 2000

Coming into force in accordance with regulation 1

The Lord Chancellor, being a Minister designated for the purposes of section 2(2) of the European Communities Act 1972 in relation to matters relating to the practice of the profession of lawyer, in exercise of the powers conferred on him by that section, makes the following Regulations—

PART 1
INTRODUCTORY

1 Citation, commencement and transitional provisions

(1) These Regulations may be cited as the European Communities (Lawyer's Practice) Regulations 2000 and shall come into force on 22nd May 2000*, except for regulations 21 and 22, which shall come into force on 22nd November 2000*.

(2) Where, on 22nd May 2000, a European lawyer is practising professional activities under his home professional title on a permanent basis in England and Wales or Northern Ireland or commences such practice by 21st November 2000, he shall apply to be registered in accordance with regulation 16 by 21st November 2000 where he intends to continue to practise those activities on a permanent basis after that date.

(3) On or after 22nd November 2000, a European lawyer shall not practise as referred to in paragraph (2) without being registered in accordance with regulation 16, unless he was already practising before that date and has made an application for registration which has not been determined.

(4) In paragraphs (3) and (5), an application for registration shall, as at a particular date, be taken not to have been determined if as at that date the applicant—

(a) has not received a rejection of his application and the period for such a rejection or a deemed rejection has not yet expired; or

(b) is appealing against a rejection of the application (including a deemed rejection) and the appeal has not been determined.

(5) Regulations 21(1)(b) and 22 shall not apply to a European lawyer who satisfies all the following conditions—

(a) immediately before 22nd November 2000 he was practising on a permanent basis in any part of the United Kingdom;

(b) before 22nd November 2000 he applied for registration to any of the barristers' professional bodies or solicitors' professional bodies, or to the Faculty of Advocates or the Law Society of Scotland; and

(c) as at the date in question his application for registration had not been determined.

[NOTES

***Modification**

As from 16 September 2004 the Regulations were extended by SI 2004/1628 to cover Cyprus, the Czech Republic, Estonia, Hungary, Iceland, Latvia, Liechtenstein, Lithuania, Malta, Norway, Poland, Slovenia, Slovakia or Switzerland.

As from 11 February 2008 the Regulations were extended by SI 2008/81 to cover Bulgaria or Romania.

As from 25 July 2014 the Regulations were extended by SI 2013/1605 to cover Croatia.

2 Interpretation

(1) In these Regulations, unless the context otherwise requires—

"the 1974 Act" means the Solicitors Act 1974;

"appeal body" means the body or person specified in relation to that profession in Schedule 1;

"barrister" means, in relation to England and Wales or Northern Ireland, a person who is a barrister of England and Wales or Northern Ireland, as the case may be;

"barristers' professional bodies" means the Inns of Court and the General Council of the Bar of England and Wales and the Executive Council of the Inn of Court of Northern Ireland;

"competent authority", in relation to England and Wales and Northern Ireland, means any of the bodies designated as competent authorities by regulation 4 to undertake the activities required by the Directive set out in that regulation;

"the Directive" means the European Communities Parliament and Council Directive No 98/5/EC to facilitate practice of the profession of lawyer on a permanent basis in certain States other than the State in which the professional qualification was obtained;

"European lawyer" has the meaning given in paragraphs (2) and (3);

"home State" means the State in paragraph (4) in which a European lawyer acquired his authorisation to pursue professional activities and, if he is authorised in more than one of those States, it shall mean any of those States;

"home professional title" means, in relation to a European lawyer, the professional title or any of the professional titles specified in relation to his home State in paragraph (4) under which he is authorised in his home State to pursue professional activities;

"Irish barrister" means a European lawyer who is authorised in the Republic of Ireland to pursue professional activities under the professional title of barrister and whose home State is the Republic of Ireland;

"Irish solicitor" means a European lawyer who is authorised in the Republic of Ireland to pursue professional activities under the professional title of solicitor and whose home State is the Republic of Ireland;

"limited liability partnership" has the meaning given by section 1(2) of the Limited Liability Partnerships Act 2000;

"member of a limited liability partnership" shall be construed in accordance with section 4 of the Limited Liability Partnerships Act 2000;

"member of the professional body" means a practising solicitor or barrister, as the case may be;

"Qualification Regulations" means the European Communities (Recognition of Professional Qualifications) Regulations 2007;

"registered European lawyer" means a European lawyer who is registered with a professional body in accordance with regulation 17 and whose registration has not been withdrawn or suspended;

"professional body" means, subject to regulation 16, any of the solicitors' professional bodies or the barristers' professional bodies;

"solicitor" means, in relation to England and Wales or Northern Ireland, a person who is a solicitor of England and Wales or Northern Ireland, as the case may be;

"solicitors' professional bodies" means the Law Society and the Law Society of Northern Ireland.

(2) In these Regulations, "European lawyer" means a person who is—

(a) a national of the United Kingdom or of a State listed in paragraph (4);

(b) authorised in any of the States listed in paragraph (4) to pursue professional activities under any of the professional titles appearing in that paragraph; and

(c) subject to paragraph (3), not a solicitor or barrister or, under the law of Scotland, a solicitor or advocate.

(3) Where a person is a European lawyer registered with more than one of the following—

(a) the solicitors' professional bodies or the barristers' professional bodies, or

(b) the Law Society of Scotland or the Faculty of Advocates,

and subsequently acquires the title used by members of one of those bodies, then notwithstanding paragraph (2)(c), that person shall continue to fall within the definition of a European lawyer in relation to that other professional body for the period that he remains registered with that other professional body.

(4) The States and professional titles referred to in the definition of European lawyer in paragraph (2) are as follows—

State	**Professional title(s)**
Belgium	Avocat/Advocaat/Rechtsanwalt
Denmark	Advokat
Germany	Rechtsanwalt
Greece	Δικηγόρος [dikegóros]
Spain	Abogado/Advocat/Avogado/Abokatu
France	Avocat
Republic of Ireland	Barrister/Solicitor
Italy	Avvocato
Luxembourg	Avocat
Netherlands	Advocaat
Austria	Rechtsanwalt
Portugal	Advogado
Finland	Asianajaja/Advokat
Sweden	Advokat
Switzerland	Avocat/Advokat/Rechtsanwalt/Anwalt/Fürsprecher/ Fürsprech/Avvocato

Iceland	Lögmaður
Liechtenstein	Rechtsanwalt
Norway	Advokat
Czech Republic	Advokát
Estonia	Vandeadvokaat
Cyprus	Δικηγόρος [dikhgóros]
Latvia	Zverinâts advokâts
Lithuania	Advokatas
Hungary	Ügyvéd
Malta	Avukat/Prokuratur Legali
Poland	Adwokat/Radca prawny
Slovenia	Odvetnik/Odvetnica
Slovakia	Advokát/Komercný právnik
Bulgaria	Адвокат [advokat]
Romania	Avocat
Croatia	Odvjetnik/Odvjetnica

(5) Unless the context otherwise requires, any reference in these Regulations to a numbered regulation, Part or Schedule is a reference to a regulation or Part of, or a Schedule to, these Regulations.

3 Purpose of Regulations

(1) The purpose of these Regulations is to implement the Directive in England and Wales and Northern Ireland.

(2) The provisions of these Regulations shall have effect for the purposes of facilitating the practice of the profession of lawyer on a permanent basis by a European lawyer in England and Wales and Northern Ireland.

(3) The provisions of these Regulations shall not affect the provision of services by lawyers within the meaning of the European Communities (Services of Lawyers) Order 1978.

4 Competent authorities

The bodies listed in column 2 of Schedule 2 shall be designated as the competent authorities for the purposes of—

(a) receiving applications for registration by European lawyers under Part III of these Regulations;

(b) receiving applications from registered European lawyers for entry into the profession of solicitor or barrister;

(c) the regulation of registered European lawyers registered with them; and

(d) the provision of certificates attesting to the registration of Solicitors or barristers registered with them.

5 Exchange of information

(1) In order to facilitate the application of the Directive and to prevent its provisions from being misapplied, a professional body may supply to or receive from—

(a) another professional body;

(b) the Faculty of Advocates or the Law Society of Scotland; or

(c) an authority in any of the States listed in regulation 2(4) which has been designated by that State under the Directive as a competent authority in that State,

any information relating to a European lawyer or to any person with whom he jointly practises.

(2) Subject to paragraph (1), a professional body shall preserve the confidentiality of any information received in accordance with paragraph (1) relating to a European lawyer or to any person with whom he jointly practises.

(3) A competent authority in England and Wales or Northern Ireland shall provide a certificate attesting to the registration of a solicitor or barrister registered with it and his authorisation to practise when requested to do so by that solicitor or barrister or by a competent authority in a State listed in regulation 2(4).

PART II
PRACTICE OF PROFESSIONAL ACTIVITIES BY A REGISTERED EUROPEAN LAWYER

6 Practice of professional activities

(1) Subject to the provisions of these Regulations, a registered European lawyer shall be entitled to carry out under his home professional title any professional activity that may lawfully be carried out by a member of the professional body with which he is registered and any enactment or rule of law or practice with regard to the carrying out of professional activities by members of that professional body shall be interpreted and applied accordingly.

(2) A registered European lawyer who is in salaried employment may carry out professional activities under his home professional title to the same extent that an employed member of the professional body with which he is registered may do so.

7 Title and description to be used by a registered European lawyer

(1) Where a registered European lawyer is engaged in—

(a) any professional activity authorised by the professional organisation in his home State which gave him the authorisation to practise; or

(b) any professional activity that may be carried out by a member of the professional body with which he is registered,

he shall comply with the requirements set out in paragraph (2).

(2) The requirements referred to in paragraph (1) are that a registered European lawyer shall—

(a) use his home professional title expressed in an official language of his home State in a manner which avoids confusion with the title of solicitor, barrister or advocate;

(b) indicate the professional organisation by which he is authorised to practise or the court of law before which he is entitled to practise in that State; and

(c) indicate the professional body with which he is registered in the United Kingdom.

8 Joint practice

A registered European lawyer may carry out professional activities under his home professional title as part of a joint practice—

(a) to the same extent and in the same manner as a member of the professional body with which he is registered may do so, with—

(i) a member of the professional body with which he is registered;

(ii) a registered European lawyer who is registered with the same professional body; or

(iii) any other person permitted by the professional body with which he is registered; or

(b) with another European lawyer who is practising on a permanent basis under his home professional title in that registered European lawyer's home State.

9 Name of joint practice

(1) Subject to paragraph (2), where a registered European lawyer is a member of a joint practice in his home State, he may use the name of that practice with his home professional title when practising as a registered European lawyer.

(2) Rules of conduct of the professional body with which a registered European lawyer is registered may prohibit the use by him of the name of a joint practice to the extent that—

(a) that name is also used by persons who are not European lawyers or solicitors of any part of the United Kingdom; and

(b) those rules prohibit members of that professional body from using that name.

10 Notification of joint practice

(1) Where a European lawyer is a member of a joint practice in his home State, he shall inform the professional body with which he intends to register and provide it with the following information—

(a) the name of the joint practice;

(b) his place of business;

(c) the name and place of business of any member of his joint practice;

(d) any other information about the joint practice requested by the professional body.

(2) A European lawyer shall notify that professional body of any changes in the information whether before or after registration.

11 Representation in legal proceedings

(1) Subject to paragraph (2), no enactment or rule of law or practice shall prevent a registered European lawyer from pursuing professional activities relating to the representation of a client in any proceedings before any court, tribunal or public authority (including addressing the court, tribunal or public authority) only because he is not a solicitor or barrister.

(2) In proceedings referred to in paragraph (1), where the professional activities in question may (but for these Regulations) be lawfully provided only by a solicitor, barrister or other qualified person, a registered European lawyer shall act in conjunction with a solicitor or barrister who is entitled to practise before the court, tribunal or public authority concerned and who could lawfully provide those professional activities.

(3) The solicitor or barrister referred to in paragraph (2) shall, where necessary, be answerable to the court, tribunal or public authority concerned.

(4) Paragraph (2) does not apply to professional activities relating to the representation of a client in proceedings before the Asylum and Immigration Tribunal or the Asylum Support Tribunal, or any tribunal hearing an appeal from those tribunals.

12 Property transactions

A registered European lawyer is not entitled, by virtue of regulation 6(1), to prepare for remuneration any instrument creating or transferring an interest in land unless he has a home professional title obtained in Denmark, the Republic of Ireland, Finland, Sweden, Iceland, Liechtenstein, Norway, the Czech Republic, Cyprus, Hungary or Slovakia.

13 Probate

A registered European lawyer is not entitled, by virtue of regulation 6(1), to prepare for remuneration any instrument for obtaining title to administer the estate of a deceased person unless he has a home professional title obtained in Denmark, Germany, the Republic of Ireland, Austria, Finland, Sweden, Iceland, Liechtenstein, Norway, Cyprus or Slovakia.

14 Legal aid

A registered European lawyer may provide professional activities by way of legal advice and assistance or legal aid under the enactments specified in Part 1 of Schedule 3 and references to a solicitor, counsel or legal representative in those and any other enactments relating to legal advice and assistance or legal aid shall be interpreted accordingly.

PART III
REGISTRATION

15 Establishment and maintenance of registers of European lawyers

Each professional body shall establish and maintain a register of registered European lawyers.

16 Application to be entered on a register

(1) Subject to regulation 18, a European lawyer who wishes to pursue professional activities under his home professional title on a permanent basis in England and Wales or Northern Ireland shall apply to be entered on the register maintained by a professional body.

(2) A European lawyer who wishes to register with a professional body in accordance with paragraph (1) shall provide the professional body with a certificate confirming his registration with the competent authority in each home State under whose home professional title he intends to practise.

(3) A professional body may require that the certificate referred to in paragraph (2) shall not have been issued more than three months before the date of the application under this regulation.

(4) An application for registration under this regulation shall comply with any applicable regulations made by the relevant professional body and be accompanied by the appropriate fee.

(5) Subject to regulation 18, a European lawyer may apply to be entered on the registers maintained by more than one professional body.

(6) In this regulation, "professional body" includes the Law Society of Scotland and the Faculty of Advocates.

17 Registration by professional body

(1) Subject to regulation 18, a professional body shall enter on its register the name of a European lawyer who applies to it in accordance with regulation 16.

(2) Where a professional body registers a European lawyer in accordance with paragraph (1), it shall inform the competent authority in the home State of the registration.

18 Restrictions on registration

(1) A European lawyer shall not be registered at the same time both with one of the solicitors' professional bodies and with one of the barristers' professional bodies.

(2) An Irish solicitor shall not be entered on a register maintained under regulation 15 by any of the barristers' professional bodies.

(3) An Irish barrister shall not be entered on a register maintained under regulation 15 by any of the solicitors' professional bodies.

(4) A European lawyer registered with the Law Society of Scotland shall not be entered on a register maintained under regulation 15 by any of the barristers' professional bodies.

(5) A European lawyer registered with the Faculty of Advocates shall not be entered on a register maintained under regulation 15 by any of the solicitors' professional bodies.

19 Time limit for decision and notification by professional body

(1) A professional body shall consider an application for registration under regulation 16 as soon as is reasonably practicable, and shall notify the European lawyer of its decision, and if the application is rejected or granted subject to conditions, the reasons upon which the rejection or the imposition of conditions is based, within four months of receipt of an application complying with regulation 16(2) and (4).

(2) Where the professional body fails to take a decision and notify the European lawyer within four months in accordance with paragraph (1), it shall be deemed to have taken a decision to reject his application and to have notified it to him on the last day of that period.

(3) Where a professional body withdraws or suspends a registration, it shall notify the European lawyer of its decision and of the reasons upon which the withdrawal or suspension is based.

20 Appeal by European lawyer

(1) Within three months of the notification to him of the professional body's decision, or later with the permission of the appeal body, the European lawyer may appeal against the decision to the appeal body specified in Schedule 1.

(2) An appeal body may, for the purpose of determining any appeal under this Part—

(a) order the professional body to register the European lawyer;

(b) refuse the appeal; or

(c) remit the matter to the professional body with such directions as the appeal body sees fit.

(3) The appeal body shall give reasons for its decision.

21 Offence of pretending to be a registered European lawyer

(1) A person who is not registered as a European lawyer in any part of the United Kingdom (including a person whose registration has been suspended) and—

(a) wilfully pretends to be a registered European lawyer or takes or uses any name, title, designation or description implying that he is a registered European lawyer; or

(b) subject to paragraph (2), carries on professional activities under one of the professional titles listed in regulation 2(4) or under any name, designation or description implying that he is entitled to pursue those activities under one of those professional titles;

shall be guilty of an offence and liable on summary conviction to a fine not exceeding the fourth level on the standard scale.

(2) Paragraph (1)(b) shall not apply to a person who satisfies any of the following conditions—

(a) he is not a national of the United Kingdom or of any of the States listed in regulation 2(4);

(b) he is a solicitor or barrister or, under the law of Scotland, a solicitor or advocate; or

(c) he is providing services within the meaning of the European Communities (Services of Lawyers) Order 1978 at the time his activities fall within paragraph (1)(b).

22 Costs and fees of an unregistered European lawyer

Where a European lawyer is carrying on professional activities under his home professional title in England and Wales or Northern Ireland but is not registered as a European lawyer in any part of the United Kingdom (including a person whose registration has been suspended), any costs or fees in respect of those activities shall not be recoverable by him or any other person.

23 Evidence of registration

Any certificate purporting to be signed by an officer of a professional body and stating that a person—

(a) is, or is not, registered with that professional body; or

(b) was, or was not, registered with that professional body during a period specified in the certificate,

shall, unless the contrary is proved, be evidence of that fact and be taken to have been so signed.

24 Publication of names of registered European lawyers

(1) Where a professional body publishes the names of solicitors or barristers registered with it, it shall also publish the names of any European lawyers registered with it.

(2) In this regulation, "publishes" or "publish" includes the provision of information to a legal publisher.

PART IV
REGULATION AND DISCIPLINE

25 Rules of professional conduct applicable

Where a registered European lawyer is practising under his home professional title in the United Kingdom, he shall be subject to the same rules of professional conduct as a member of the professional body with which he is registered, and if he is registered with more than one, he shall be subject to the rules of professional conduct of all the professional bodies with which he is registered.

26 Disciplinary proceedings applicable

(1) Where a registered European lawyer fails to comply with the rules of professional conduct to which he is subject under regulation 25, he shall be subject to the same rules of procedure, penalties and remedies as a member of the professional body with which the European lawyer is registered and shall, if appropriate, be subject to disciplinary proceedings brought by an appropriate authority.

(2) Any sanction against a registered European lawyer in relation to disciplinary proceedings may include withdrawal or suspension of his registration.

(3) The appropriate authority shall give reasons for its decision.

(4) In this regulation, an appropriate authority means—

(a) where the registered European lawyer is registered with one of the solicitors' professional bodies, an authority having disciplinary jurisdiction over solicitors in England and Wales or Northern Ireland, as the case may be;

(b) where the registered European lawyer is registered with one of the barristers' professional bodies, an authority having disciplinary jurisdiction over barristers in England and Wales or Northern Ireland, as the case may be;

(c) where the registered European lawyer is registered with more than one of the solicitors' professional bodies or the barristers' professional bodies, an authority having disciplinary jurisdiction over solicitors or barristers, as the case may be, in England and Wales or Northern Ireland.

27 Disciplinary proceedings against a registered European lawyer

(1) Where a professional body intends to begin disciplinary proceedings against a registered European lawyer, it shall—

(a) inform the competent authority in his home State of the intention to begin those proceedings and furnish it with all the relevant details;

(b) co-operate with that authority throughout those proceedings; and

(c) inform that authority of the decision reached in those proceedings, including the decision in any appeal, as soon as practicable after the decision is given.

(2) Subject to paragraph (3), where the competent authority in the registered European lawyer's home State withdraws his authorisation to practise under the home professional title either temporarily or permanently, his registration with the professional body shall be automatically withdrawn to the same extent.

(3) Where a registered European lawyer is authorised to practise under a home professional title in two or more home States, his registration shall be withdrawn in accordance with paragraph (2) only if his authorisation to practise under a home professional title has been withdrawn in all those home States.

(4) Where there is an appeal against a decision in disciplinary proceedings against a registered European lawyer, the body responsible for hearing the appeal shall afford the competent authority in the registered European lawyer's home State an opportunity to make representations in relation to that appeal.

28 Disciplinary proceedings against a solicitor or barrister

Where a professional body intends to begin disciplinary proceedings against a solicitor or barrister practising in a State listed in regulation 2(4), it shall inform the competent authority in that State of—

(a) the intention to begin those proceedings and furnish it with all the relevant details; and

(b) the decision reached in those proceedings, including the decision in any appeal, as soon as practicable after the decision is given.

PART V
ENTRY INTO THE PROFESSION OF SOLICITOR OR BARRISTER

29 Application by registered European lawyer

(1) Where a registered European lawyer applies to the professional body where he has been registered to become a solicitor or barrister, as the case may be, and that professional body requires him to pass an aptitude test under regulation 26(a) of the Qualification Regulations, he may apply to the professional body for an exemption from that requirement on the grounds that he falls within paragraph (2) or (3) of this regulation.

(2) A person falls within this paragraph if—

(a) he is a European lawyer and has been registered with that professional body for at least three years; and

(b) he has for a period of at least three years effectively and regularly pursued in England and Wales or Northern Ireland, professional activities under his home professional title in the law of England and Wales or Northern Ireland, as the case may be.

(3) A person falls within this paragraph if—

(a) he is a European lawyer and has been registered with that professional body for at least three years; and

(b) he has for a period of at least three years effectively and regularly pursued in England and Wales or Northern Ireland professional activities under his home professional title; and

(c) he has for a period of less than three years effectively and regularly pursued in England and Wales or Northern Ireland, professional activities under his home professional title in the law of England and Wales or Northern Ireland, as the case may be.

30 Decision by professional body

(1) Subject to paragraph (3), the professional body shall grant an exemption applied for under regulation 29 if it considers that the requirements under paragraph (2) or (3) of regulation 29 have been met.

(2) The registration of a registered European lawyer shall cease from the date he is granted entry into the profession of solicitor or barrister.

(3) The professional body may refuse to grant an exemption if it considers that the registered European lawyer would be unfit to practise as a solicitor or barrister.

31 Evidence in support of application for exemption under regulation 29(2)

(1) Where a registered European lawyer makes an application under paragraph (2) of regulation 29, he shall provide the professional body with any relevant information and documents which it may reasonably require.

(2) The professional body may verify the effective and regular nature of the professional activity pursued and may, if necessary, request the registered European lawyer to provide, orally or in writing, clarification of, or further details on, the information and documents referred to in paragraph (1).

32 Evidence in support of application for exemption under regulation 29(3)

(1) Where a registered European lawyer makes an application under paragraph (3) of regulation 29, he shall provide the professional body with any relevant information and documents it may reasonably require.

(2) When deciding whether to grant an application under paragraph (3) of regulation 29, the professional body shall take into account the professional activities the registered European lawyer has pursued during the period he has been registered and any knowledge and professional experience he has gained of, and any training he has received in, the law of any part of the United Kingdom and the rules of professional conduct of the profession concerned.

(3) Subject to paragraph (4), in the case of an application under paragraph (3) of regulation 29, the professional body shall assess and verify the registered European lawyer's effective and regular professional activity and his capacity to continue the activity he has pursued at an interview.

(4) Where a professional body believes that an interview is unnecessary and intends to grant an application under paragraph (3) of regulation 29, it may dispense with that requirement.

33 Meaning of "effectively and regularly pursued"

For the purposes of regulations 29 to 32 activities shall be regarded as effectively and regularly pursued if they are actually exercised without any interruption other than those resulting from the events of everyday life.

34 Time limit for decision and notification by professional body

(1) A professional body shall consider an application under regulation 29 as soon as is reasonably practicable, and shall notify the applicant of its decision and, if the application is rejected, the reasons for the rejection, within four months of receipt of all the relevant documents.

(2) Where the professional body fails to take a decision and notify the registered European lawyer within four months in accordance with paragraph (1), it shall be deemed to have taken a decision to reject his application and to have notified it to him on the last day of that period.

35 Appeal by registered European lawyer

(1) Within three months of the notification to him of the professional body's decision, or later with the permission of the appeal body, the registered European lawyer may appeal against the decision to the appeal body specified in Schedule 1.

(2) An appeal body may, for the purpose of determining any appeal under this Part—

(a) give the exemption and the authorisation to enter into the profession of solicitor or barrister, as the case may be;

(b) refuse the appeal; or

(c) remit the matter to the professional body with such directions as the appeal body sees fit.

(3) The appeal body shall give reasons for its decision.

36 Practice under the title of solicitor or barrister

(1) This regulation applies where a registered European lawyer ("the lawyer") is granted entry into the profession of solicitor or barrister.

(2) Subject to paragraph (3), the lawyer shall be entitled to continue to practise in England and Wales or Northern Ireland, as the case may be, under his home professional title, and to use his home professional title, expressed in an official language of his home State, alongside the title of solicitor or barrister, provided that he continues to be authorised in his home State to pursue professional activities under that title.

(3) For the purposes of rules of professional conduct, including those relating to disciplinary and complaints procedures, the lawyer's continuing practice in the United Kingdom under his home professional title shall be deemed to form part of his practice as a solicitor or barrister, and those rules shall apply to his practice under his home professional title as they do to his practice as a solicitor or barrister.

(4) Where this regulation applies, a lawyer's registration in accordance with regulation 17 with the professional body whose title he has acquired shall cease from the date he is entitled to use that title.

(5) Paragraph (4) shall not affect any registration the lawyer may have in another part of the United Kingdom.

PART VI
SUPPLEMENTARY PROVISIONS

37 Modification of enactments

(1) The enactments specified in Part 2 of Schedule 3 (being enactments which reserve certain activities to solicitors, barristers and other qualified persons) shall be interpreted subject to regulations 6, 11, 12 and 13.

(2) References to unqualified persons, however expressed, in the enactments specified in Part 3 of Schedule 3 (being enactments relating to unqualified persons acting as solicitors) shall not include a registered European lawyer pursuing professional activities within the meaning of these Regulations.

(3) Schedule 4 (extension of enactments (England and Wales)) shall apply in relation to the registration of European lawyers with the Law Society.

(4) Schedule 5 (extension of enactments (Northern Ireland)) shall apply in relation to the registration of European lawyers with the Law Society of Northern Ireland.

Irvine of Lairg, C

Dated 8th April 2000

SCHEDULE 1
Appeals Concerning Registration as a European Lawyer, Exemption from Regulation 26(a) of the Qualification Regulations and Entry into the Profession of Solicitor or Barrister

Regulations 2, 20 and 35

Column 1 **Profession**	*Column 2* **Appeal Body**
Solicitor (England and Wales)	The High Court
Solicitor (Northern Ireland)	The Lord Chief Justice of Northern Ireland
Barrister (England and Wales)	The High Court
Barrister (Northern Ireland)	The Executive Council of the Inn of Court of Northern Ireland

SCHEDULE 2
Competent Authorities

Regulation 4

Column 1 **Profession**	*Column 2* **Professional Body**
Solicitor (England and Wales)	The Law Society
Solicitor (Northern Ireland)	The Law Society of Northern Ireland
Barrister (England and Wales)	The Inns of Court and the General Council of the Bar of England and Wales
Barrister (Northern Ireland)	The Executive Council of the Inn of Court of Northern Ireland

SCHEDULE 3
Modification of Enactments

PART 1
ENACTMENTS RELATING TO THE PROVISION OF LEGAL ADVICE AND ASSISTANCE AND LEGAL AID

Regulation 14

Legal Aid, Advice and Assistance (Northern Ireland) Order 1981.

Legal Aid Act 1988.

Access to Justice Act 1999.

Financial Services and Markets Act 2000.

Legal Aid, Sentencing and Punishment of Offenders Act 2012.

PART 2
ENACTMENTS RESERVING CERTAIN ACTIVITIES TO SOLICITORS, BARRISTERS AND OTHER QUALIFIED PERSONS

Regulation 37(1)

Solicitors (Northern Ireland) Order 1976, articles 19, 23 and 24.

PART 3
ENACTMENTS RELATING TO UNQUALIFIED PERSONS ACTING AS SOLICITORS

Regulation 37(2)

Solicitors (Northern Ireland) Order 1976, articles 25(1) and 27.

SCHEDULE 4
Extension of Enactments in Relation to the Registration of European Lawyers with the Law Society

Regulation 37(3)

1 (1) The power to make regulations under section 2 of the Solicitors Act 1974 shall also be exercisable in relation to registered European lawyers.

(2) The power to make regulations under section 28(1)(c) to (d) of that Act shall also be exercisable in relation to registered European lawyers as it is in relation to solicitors, subject to the modifications specified in the Table and subject to paragraph 7(1A).

(2A) Section 28(3B) to (3G) of the 1974 Act has effect with respect to registered European lawyers as it has effect with respect to solicitors, subject to the modifications specified in the Table and subject to paragraph 7(1A).

(3) The power to make rules under—

(a) sections 31, 32, 33A, 34, 36 and 37 of the Solicitors Act 1974; and

(b) section 9 of the Administration of Justice Act 1985,

shall also be exercisable in relation to registered European lawyers.

2 Any of the powers referred to in paragraph 1 may be exercised so as to make different provision with respect to registered European lawyers.

3–6 [*repealed*]

7 (1) Subject to sub-paragraph (1A), the provisions of sections 1B, 9, 10, 10A, 11, 13, 13ZA, 13ZB, 13A, 13B, 15, 16, 17, 17A, 17B, 18 and 84 of the 1974 Act shall apply to registered European lawyers as they apply to solicitors subject to the modifications specified in the Table.

(1A) An appeal by a European lawyer in respect of the following decisions of the Law Society is to be made under regulation 20 and not under section 13 or 13B(7) of the 1974 Act or under regulations made under section 28(3D) of the 1974 Act—

(a) refusal of initial registration;

(b) grant of initial registration whilst refusing sole practitioner endorsement;

(c) grant of initial registration subject to a condition;

(d) refusal to renew a registration;

(e) failure to take a decision on an application for initial registration within the statutory time limit;

(f) withdrawal or revocation of a registration;

(g) suspension of a registration.

(2) Sections 31(2), 32(3) and (4), 33, 33A, 34(6) and (9), 34A, 34B, 38, 40, 44B, 44BA, 44BC, 44C, 44D, 44E, 56(1)(f), (2) and (4) to (7), 57 to 75, 81, 81A and 83 of the 1974 Act shall also apply to registered European lawyers as they apply to solicitors subject to the modifications specified in the Table.

(2A) The following provisions of the 1974 Act have effect as follows—

(a) in section 34(10) the reference to subsection (9) is to be read as including a reference to that subsection as it has effect by virtue of sub-paragraph (2);

(b) section 56(1)(a) to (e) to the extent necessary to give effect to section 56(1)(f) as it has effect by virtue of sub-paragraph (2).

(3) Sections 41, 42, 43 and 44 of the 1974 Act shall apply to registered European lawyers as they apply to solicitors subject to the modifications specified in the Table.

(4) Section 85 of the 1974 Act (bank accounts) shall apply to a registered European lawyer and to the partner of a registered European lawyer as it applies to a solicitor.

8 (1) Subject to sub-paragraph (1A), sections 36 and 36A of the 1974 Act shall apply to registered European lawyers as they apply to solicitors.

(1A) The Society may make different provision with respect to registered European lawyers, and European lawyers making an application for initial registration, from the provision made with respect to solicitors.

9 Section 35 of, and Schedule 1 to, the Solicitors Act 1974 shall apply to registered European lawyers as they apply to solicitors, and for that purpose—

(aa) reference to the roll is to be read as a reference to the register of European lawyers;.

(ab) reference to a solicitor suspended from practice is to be read as a reference to a European lawyer whose registration is suspended;

(ac) in paragraph 1(1)(k) of Schedule 1 to the 1974 Act, reference to a person acting as a solicitor when he did not have a practising certificate which was in force is to be read as a reference to a European lawyer or registered European lawyer who has committed an offence under regulation 21 of these Regulations;

(b) references to a solicitor's practising certificate shall be interpreted as references to a registered European lawyer's registration;

(c) reference to a sole solicitor is to be read as a reference to a sole practitioner.

10 Sections 46(10)(c), 47, 48, 49, 50(2), 50(3), 51, 52, 53 and 55 of the Solicitors Act 1974 shall apply to registered European lawyers as they apply to solicitors subject to the modifications specified in the Table.

11 Part XX of the Financial Services and Markets Act 2000, including the definition of "members" in section 325(2), has effect in relation to registered European lawyers as it has in relation to solicitors.

12 For the purposes of section 391 of the Insolvency Act 1986 and the Insolvency Practitioners (Recognised Professional Bodies) Order 1986, registered European lawyers and their partners shall be deemed to be—

(a) part of the solicitors' profession; and

(b) subject to the Law Society's rules in the practice of their profession.

13 Section 142 of the County Courts Act 1984 shall apply to registered European lawyers as it applies to solicitors.

14 (1) Section 89 of the Courts and Legal Services Act 1990 shall be amended as follows.

(2) In subsection (9), the following shall be substituted for the definition of "multi-national partnership"—

""multi-national partnership" means a partnership whose members consist of one or more registered foreign lawyers and one or more other lawyers as permitted by rules made under section 31 of the Solicitors Act 1974;"

15 [*repealed*]

16 [*repealed*]

17 In the Estate Agents Act 1979 the reference to a practising solicitor in section 1(2)(a) (which exempts solicitors from that Act) shall be interpreted as including a reference to a registered European lawyer and the partner of a registered European lawyer, providing professional services in accordance with rules made under section 31 of the Solicitors Act 1974 or section 9 of the Administration of Justice Act 1985.

18 [*repealed*]

19 In the Rehabilitation of Offenders Act 1974 (Exceptions) Order 1975 the reference to "solicitor" in Part I of Schedule 1 to the Order shall be interpreted as including reference to a registered European lawyer.

20 The Solicitors (Non-Contentious Business) Remuneration Order 1994 and any other order made under section 56 of the 1974 Act shall apply to registered European lawyers as it applies to solicitors.

21 Registered European lawyers shall be treated as if they were officers of the Supreme Court and shall be subject to the inherent jurisdiction of that court in like manner and to the same extent as if they were solicitors.

22 (1) References in the Charter to solicitors shall be deemed to include references to registered European lawyers.

(2) In this paragraph "the Charter" has the same meaning as it has in section 87(1) of the Solicitors Act 1974.

23 [*repealed*]

24 (1) The provisions of sections 40 and 43 of the Administration of Justice Act 1985 apply to registered European lawyers as they apply to solicitors, and for this purpose the reference to a person's solicitor in section 40(1) is to be read as a reference to a registered European lawyer acting for a person.

(2) In Schedule 2 to that Act the provisions of paragraphs 7, 9(3), 10(3), 18A(2), 18A(3), 20, 21(1) and 25(1) apply to registered European lawyers as they apply to solicitors, subject to the following modifications—

- (a) in paragraphs 9(3), 10(3) and 21(1) reference to the roll is to be read as a reference to the register of European lawyers;
- (b) in paragraph 18A(2)(c) reference to a person who is not a solicitor is to be read as a reference to a person who is neither a solicitor nor a registered European lawyer;.
- (c) in paragraph 21(1)(b) reference to suspension from practice as a solicitor is to be read as a reference to a European lawyer's suspension from the register of European lawyers.

Provision of the 1974 Act	*Modification*
Section 1B	Reference to a sole solicitor is to be read as a reference to a sole practitioner.
Section 1B(1)(a)	Reference to a practising certificate in force is to be read as a reference to a European lawyer's registration.
Section 1B(1)(b)	Reference to a certificate is to be read as a reference to a European lawyer's registration.
	Reference to a sole solicitor endorsement is to be read as a reference to a sole practitioner endorsement.
Section 9(1)	Reference to a person whose name is on the roll is to be read as a reference to a European lawyer, as defined by regulation 2(1) to (4) of these Regulations.
	Reference to the issuing of a practising certificate is to be read as a reference to initial registration or renewal of registration in the register of European lawyers.
Section 9(2)	Reference to a sole solicitor endorsement is to be read as a reference to a sole practitioner endorsement.
Section 9(4)(a)	Reference to a practising certificate is to be read as a reference to a European lawyer's registration.
Section 10(1) to (4)	Reference to the issuing of a practising certificate is to be read as a reference to initial registration or renewal of registration in the register of European lawyers.
	Reference to suspension from practice is to be read as a reference to suspension from the register of European lawyers.
Section 10(4)(a)	Reference to a sole solicitor endorsement is to be read as a reference to a sole practitioner endorsement.
	Reference to a sole solicitor is to be read as a reference to a sole practitioner.

Section 10(5)	Reference to a practising certificate is to be read as a reference to a European lawyer's registration.
Section 10A	Reference to solicitors who hold practising certificates is to be read as a reference to registered European lawyers.
Section 10A(2)(b)	Reference to a sole solicitor endorsement is to be read as a reference to a sole practitioner endorsement.
Section 11(1)	Reference to the issuing of a practising certificate is to be read as a reference to initial registration or renewal of registration.
Section 11(3)	Reference to a practising certificate is to be read as a reference to a European lawyer's registration.
Section 11(3)(b)	Reference to a practising certificate not having been issued since the Society became aware of the failure is to be read as a reference to a registration in the register of European lawyers not having been entered or renewed since the Society became aware of the failure.
Section 13	Section 13 is to be read as if subsection (1)(a) were omitted.
Section 13(1)(b) and (4)(b) and (f)	Reference to a sole solicitor endorsement or endorsement is to be read as a reference to a sole practitioner endorsement.
	Reference in section 13(1)(b) to an application for a solicitor endorsement being refused is not to be read as a reference to an application for initial registration including a sole solicitor endorsement.
Section 13(1)(c) and (4)(b) to (f)	Reference to the issuing of a practising certificate is to be read as a reference to renewal of registration.
	Reference to a practising certificate or certificate is to be read as a reference to a registration in the register of European lawyers.
Section 13(2)	Reference to a person who holds a practising certificate is to be read as a person who is registered in the register of European lawyers.
Section 13(3)	Reference to any application under section 9 is to be read as any application for renewal of registration in the register of European lawyers.
Section 13ZA(1)	Reference to a practising certificate being in force (a "current certificate") is to be read as a reference to a registered European lawyer's registration.
Section 13ZA(1), (2), (5) and (8)(b)	Reference to a sole solicitor endorsement or endorsement is to be read as a reference to a sole practitioner endorsement.
Section 13ZA(3)	Reference to suspension from practice as a sole solicitor is to be read as a reference to suspension of a sole practitioner endorsement.
Section 13ZA(2), (5), (6)(b) and (8)(c)	Reference to a practising certificate is to be read as a reference to a registered European lawyer's registration.
Section 13ZB	Reference to a sole solicitor endorsement or endorsement is to be read as a reference to a sole practitioner endorsement.

Section 13A(1), (2) and (7)(b)	Reference to a practising certificate being in force (a "current certificate") is to be read as a reference to a European lawyer's registration.
Section 13A(2)(a)	Reference to a sole solicitor endorsement is to be read as a reference to a sole practitioner endorsement.
Section 13A(9)	Reference to a solicitor who holds a practising certificate is to be read as a European lawyer who is registered in the register of European lawyers.
Section 13B(1) and (8)(b)	References to a practising certificate or the appellant's certificate are to be read as references to a registered European lawyer's registration.
	Reference to a sole solicitor endorsement is to be read as a reference to a sole practitioner endorsement.
Section 13B(6)	Reference to a solicitor's suspension from practice or from practice as a sole solicitor is to be read as a reference to a European lawyer's suspension from the register of European lawyers or suspension of a sole practitioner endorsement.
Section 15	Reference to a practising certificate is to be read as a reference to a European lawyer's registration.
	Reference in subsection (1) to suspension from practice is to be read as a reference to a European lawyer's suspension from the register of European lawyers.
Section 16	Reference to a practising certificate or certificate is to be read as a reference to a registration in the register of European lawyers.
	Reference to a solicitor's suspension from practice or suspension is to be read as reference to the suspension of a European lawyer's registration.
	Reference in subsections (1) and (3) to expiry of a certificate is to be read as expiry of a European lawyer's registration.
Section 17	Reference to suspension of a solicitor's practising certificate is to be read as reference to the suspension of a European lawyer's registration.
	Reference to a note against a solicitor's name on the roll is to be read as reference to a note against a European lawyer's name on the register of European lawyers.
Section 17A	Reference to a sole solicitor endorsement is to be read as a reference to a sole practitioner endorsement.
	Reference to suspension from practice as a sole solicitor is to be read as a reference to a European lawyer's suspension from practice as a sole practitioner.
Section 17B	Reference to suspension of a sole solicitor endorsement is to be read as a reference to suspension of a sole practitioner endorsement.
	Reference to a note against a solicitor's name on the roll is to be read as reference to a note against a European lawyer's name on the register of European lawyers.

Section 18	References to the register kept under section 10A are to be read as a reference to the register of European lawyers.
	Subsection (1) is to be read as if reference to an extract from the roll were omitted.
	Section 18 is to be read as if subsection (2)(a) were omitted.
Section 28(1)(c) to (d)	Reference in subsection (1)(c) to a practising certificate is to be read as a reference to a European lawyer's registration.
	Reference in subsection (1)(ca) to a sole solicitor endorsement is to be read as a reference to a sole practitioner endorsement.
	Reference in subsection (1)(d) to the register kept under section 10A is to be read as a reference to the register of European lawyers.
Section 28(3B) to (3G)	Reference to a practising certificate is to be read as a reference to a European lawyer's registration.
	Reference to a sole solicitor endorsement is to be read as a reference to a sole practitioner endorsement.
	Reference in subsection (3B)(d) and (e) to the issuing of a practising certificate is to be read as a reference to initial registration or renewal of registration.
	Reference in subsection (3B)(f) to a sole solicitor endorsement being made after a practising certificate was issued is to be read as a reference to a sole practitioner endorsement being made after registration in the register of European lawyers.
	Subsection (3B)(i) is to be read as if reference to replacement were omitted.
	Reference in subsection (3B)(k) to solicitors who hold practising certificates is to be read as reference to registered European lawyers.
	Reference in subsection (3C) to the register under section 10A is to be read as a reference to the register of European lawyers.
Section 41	Reference to a solicitor is to be read as to include a reference to a registered European lawyer.
	Reference in subsections (1)(a) and (4)(a) to the roll is to be read as to include a reference to the register of European lawyers.
	Reference in subsections (1)(b) and (4)(b) to suspension from practising as a solicitor is to be read as to include a reference to suspension from the register of European lawyers.
	Reference in subsection (1)(c) to a practising certificate being suspended is to be read as to include a reference to a European lawyer's registration being suspended.
	Reference in subsection (1B) to the "employed solicitor" is not to be read as a reference to an employed European lawyer.

Section 42	In subsection (1) reference to a person who is disqualified from practising as a solicitor by reason of a fact mentioned in paragraphs (a) to (c) is to be read as to include a reference to a European lawyer whose name has been struck off the register of European lawyers or whose registration in that register is suspended.
Section 43	In section 43(1) reference to a person who is not a solicitor is to be read as a reference to a person who is neither a solicitor nor a registered European lawyer.
Section 44	Reference to section 43(2) is to be read as to include a reference to that section as it has effect by virtue of these Regulations.
Section 47	Reference to the roll is to be read as reference to the register of European lawyers.
	Reference in section 47(1)(d) and (2)(b) and (e) to suspension from practice is to be read as a reference to suspension from the register of European lawyers.
	Reference in section 47(1)(ea) and (2)(bb) and (ea) to suspension from practice as a sole solicitor is to be read as a reference to a European lawyer's suspension from practice as a sole practitioner.
	Reference in section 47(2)(ba) to a sole solicitor endorsement is to be read as a reference to a sole practitioner endorsement.
	Reference in section 47(2A)(a) to another solicitor is to be read as to include a reference to a solicitor or a registered European lawyer.
	Reference in section 47(2B) to a firm of solicitors is to be read as a reference to a firm of solicitors and/or registered European lawyers.
	Reference to an employee who is not a solicitor is to be read as a reference to an employee who is neither a solicitor nor a registered European lawyer
Section 51	Reference in section 51(1) and (3)(b) to the striking off of a name from the roll is to be read as reference to striking a European lawyer's name from the register of European lawyers.
Section 52	Reference to the striking off of a name from the roll is to be read as reference to striking a European lawyer's name from the register of European lawyers.
Section 53	Reference to the striking off of a name from the roll is to be read as reference to striking a European lawyer's name from the register of European lawyers.
	Reference to suspension from practice is to be read as a reference to suspension from the register of European lawyers.
	Reference to a note of the order on the roll is to be read as reference to a note on the register of European lawyers.
Section 55	Reference to the striking off of a name from the roll is to be read as reference to striking a European lawyer's name from the register of European lawyers.

Section 84	Reference to a solicitor who has in force, or who has applied for, a practising certificate is to be read as a reference to a European lawyer who is registered or who has applied for registration in the register of European lawyers.
	Reference in subsection (3) to a practising solicitor is to be read as a reference to a registered European lawyer.

SCHEDULE 5
Extension of Enactments in Relation to the Registration of European Lawyers with the Law Society of Northern Ireland

Regulation 37(4)

1 (1) The power to make rules and regulations under article 75 of the Solicitors (Northern Ireland) Order 1976 shall also be exercisable in relation to registered European lawyers.

(2) The power to make regulations under articles 6, 26, 26A, 33, 34, 35, 61 and 63 shall also be exercisable in relation to registered European lawyers.

2 The provisions of articles 7, 8, 10, 11, 13 and 14 to 18 of that Order shall apply to registered European lawyers as they apply to solicitors, except that—

(a) references to a solicitor's practising certificate shall be interpreted as references to a registered European lawyer's registration; and

(b) references to the roll shall be interpreted as references to the register of European lawyers.

3 Articles 27, 28, 29, 32, 36 to 60, 62, 64A to 71H, 72A, 77 and 78 of, and Schedules 1, 1A and 2 to, that Order shall apply to registered European lawyers as they apply to solicitors except that—

(a) references to a solicitor's practising certificate shall be interpreted as references to a registered European lawyer's registration; and

(b) references to the roll shall be interpreted as references to the register of European lawyers.

4 Article 51 of the County Courts (Northern Ireland) Order 1980 shall apply to registered European lawyers as it applies to solicitors.

5 In the Estate Agents Act 1979 the reference to a practising solicitor in section 1(2)(a) (which exempts solicitors from that Act) shall be interpreted as including a reference to a registered European lawyer, and the partner of a registered European lawyer providing professional services in accordance with article 26 of the Solicitors (Northern Ireland) Order 1976.

6 In the Rehabilitation of Offenders (Northern Ireland) Order 1978 the references to "solicitor" in the Order shall be interpreted as including reference to a registered European lawyer.

7 The Solicitors Remuneration Order (Northern Ireland) 1977 shall apply to registered European lawyers as it applies to solicitors.

8 Registered European lawyers shall be treated as if they were officers of the Supreme Court of Northern Ireland and shall be subject to the inherent jurisdiction of that court in like manner and to the same extent as if they were solicitors.

APPENDIX 6

SRA warning notices, and Law Society advice

[Law Society copyright. *Please note that warning notices listed as 'Pending review' were written and issued before the introduction of the SRA Handbook on 6 October 2011 and may refer to regulatory material that is no longer in effect. For further information, please contact Professional Ethics.*]

Fraudulent financial arrangements

[Issued by the Solicitors Regulation Authority. Last updated April 2009. *Pending review*]

The Solicitors Regulation Authority takes strong action against those it regulates who appear to facilitate fraud.

Your obligations are set out in rule 1 of the Solicitors' Code of Conduct 2007.

Avoid dubious financial arrangements

You must ensure that you do not become involved in dubious financial arrangements or investment schemes. Failure to observe our warnings could lead to disciplinary action, criminal prosecution or both.

Schemes are formulated by fraudsters to prey upon the wealthy, greedy or vulnerable. They often sound "too good to be true" and almost always are.

Warning signs

- The promise of unrealistically high returns
- Deals forming part of larger deals involving millions, or billions of pounds, dollars or other currencies
- Any advance fee payable to secure future lending or to buy into an "investment" process
- Trading in apparent banking instruments such as Promissory Notes or Standby Letters of Credit to provide returns for non banking investors
- Confusing and complex transactions involving misleading descriptions or ill defined terminology, such as "grand master collateral commitment"
- Vague reference to humanitarian or charitable aims
- The need for secrecy to protect the scheme, particularly to prevent proper checks
- Use of faxed or easily forged documents often from offshore companies or from financial institutions abroad

Why involve you?

The fraudster wants to be associated with the legitimacy and respectability which, as a person or firm regulated by the SRA, you provide by:

- endorsing the arrangements by acting as the fraudster's legal adviser or banker
- providing correspondence to the fraudster's company or third parties
- "securing" the transaction with an undertaking from you
- opening bank accounts, awaiting receipt of funds or using your client account
- referring to your insurance or to the Compensation Fund.

If you do not understand the documents or a transaction in which you are involved, you must ask questions to satisfy yourself that it is proper for you to act. Why have you been approached? Do you have any expertise in this area of law? If you are not wholly satisfied as to the propriety of the transaction, you must refuse to act.

To report to us on a confidential basis, contact our Fraud and Confidential Intelligence Bureau on 01926 439673 or 0845 850 0999 or email redalert@sra.org.uk.

For advice, contact our Professional Ethics helpline [see **www.sra.org.uk/contact-us**].

Money laundering

[Issued by the Solicitors Regulation Authority. Last updated April 2009. *Pending review*]

The Solicitors Regulation Authority is determined to pursue those it regulates who are involved in money laundering.

Your obligations are set out in the Solicitors' Code of Conduct 2007, particularly rules 1 and 4, the Solicitors' Accounts Rules, the Proceeds of Crime Act 2002, the Terrorism Act 2000, and the Money Laundering Regulations 2007.

You must ensure that you do not facilitate laundering even when money does not pass through your firm's accounts. Failure to observe our warnings can lead to disciplinary action, criminal prosecution, or both.

Warning signs

Unusual payment requests

- Payments from a third party where you cannot verify the source of the funds
- Receipts of cash and requests for payments by cash
- Money transfers where there is a variation between the account holder/signatory
- Payments to unrelated third parties
- Litigation settlements which are reached too easily.

Unusual instructions

- Instructions outside the normal pattern of your business
- Instructions changed without a reasonable explanation
- Transactions that take an unusual turn
- Movement of funds between accounts, institutions or jurisdictions without reason.

Use of your client account

- Never accept instructions to act as a banking facility, particularly if you do not undertake any related legal work – be aware of note (ix) to rule 15 of the Solicitors' Accounts Rules 1998.
- Be wary if you are instructed to do legal work, receive substantial funds into your client account, but the instructions are later cancelled and you are asked to send the money to a third party or perhaps to your client.

Suspect territory

- Check official sources about suspect territories and sanctions.
- Be wary of funds moved around without a logical explanation.

Loss making transaction

- Instructions potentially leading to financial loss without logical explanation, particularly where your client seems unconcerned.

Legislation may require you to make an official disclosure to the Serious Organised Crime Agency (SOCA), PO Box 8000, London, SE11 5EN, call **020 7238 8282**, or send an email by registering on the secure site at www.ukciu.gov.uk/saroline.aspx. You will not commit the offence of "tipping off" by reporting a matter to the SRA. To report to us on a confidential basis, contact our Fraud and Confidential Intelligence Bureau on **01926 439673 or 0345 850 0999** or email **redalert@sra.org.uk**.

For conduct advice, contact our Professional Ethics helpline.

For general queries about good-practice anti-money laundering compliance, contact the Law Society's Practice Advice Service on 0870 606 2522 (9:00–17:00 Monday to Friday) or refer to www.lawsociety.org.uk/moneylaundering.

Undertakings

[Issued by the Solicitors Regulation Authority. Last updated April 2009. *Pending review*]

The SRA takes breaches of undertakings very seriously.

Your obligations are set out in rules 1, 5.01 and 10.05 of the Solicitors' Code of Conduct 2007 and its guidance.

Many transactions depend on the use of undertakings enabling you to negotiate and conduct your client's business successfully.

Where you give an undertaking

Those placing reliance on it will expect you to fulfil it. Ensure your undertakings are:

- Specific
- Measurable
- Agreed
- Realistic

- Timed.

A breach of undertaking can lead to a disciplinary finding and costs direction.

Undertakings you give are also summarily enforceable by the High Court. Be aware that you do not become exposed to a liability within the excess of your firm's insurance.

Where you accept an undertaking

Ensure that in doing so your client's position is protected and you are not exposed to a breach.

If you are a regulated person or firm

- Be clear about who can give undertakings.
- Ensure all staff understand they need your client's agreement.
- Be clear about how compliance will be monitored.
- Maintain a central record to ensure and monitor compliance.
- Prescribe the manner in which undertakings may be given.
- Prepare standard undertakings, where possible, with clear instructions that any departure be authorised in accordance with supervision and management responsibilities.
- Adopt a system that ensures terms are checked by another fee-earner.
- Confirm oral undertakings (given or received) in writing.
- Copy each undertaking and attach it to the relevant file; label the file itself.
- Ensure all staff understand the undertakings they give when using the Law Society's formulae for exchange of contracts and its code for completion by post.

To report to us on a confidential basis, contact our Fraud and Confidential Intelligence Bureau on **01926 439673 or 0345 850 0999** or email redalert@sra.org.uk.

For advice, contact our Professional Ethics helpline.

Equality and diversity

[Issued by the Solicitors Regulation Authority May 2010. *Pending review*]

The SRA takes compliance with the principles of equality and diversity very seriously.

Rule 6 of the Solicitors' Code of Conduct 2007 and general law lay down your equality and diversity obligations. The SRA expects you to meet those obligations. You must treat everyone fairly and must not breach your conduct or legal duties.

When we visit your firm, we expect you to demonstrate this by

- having arrangements in place to demonstrate your compliance with the principles of equality and diversity (as currently set out in rule 6),
- making your policy available for consideration by the SRA,
- providing examples of how your policy is implemented.

What you need to do

If you are a regulated person or firm

- Ensure that you do not discriminate on the grounds of race, sex, sexual orientation, religion or belief, age or disability.
- Ensure that disabled employees or clients are not placed at a substantial disadvantage in comparison with others and make reasonable adjustments.
- Adopt and implement a policy that ensures a safe working environment, free from harassment and bullying.
- Provide training and challenge discriminatory behaviour.
- Ensure your management systems comply with rule 6.
- Ensure all staff are aware of your policy and comply with it.
- Challenge inappropriate behaviour.

If you are recruiting or interviewing

- Remember your obligations not to discriminate either in the process or when interviewing for any position.
- Ensure your processes are fair, transparent and comply with your obligations, even when using agencies.

Complying with the law

If a court or tribunal finds you have committed an unlawful act of discrimination, that is likely to lead to an SRA investigation and could lead to disciplinary proceedings before the Solicitors Disciplinary Tribunal.

Your obligations are set out in rules 1, 5.01 and 6 of the Solicitors' Code of Conduct and its guidance and in legislation including, but not confined to, the Sex Discrimination Act 1975, the Race Relations Act 1976 and the Disability Discrimination Acts 1995 and 2005

The Equality Act 2010 which comes into force in October 2010 prohibits unlawful discrimination on the grounds of age, disability, gender reassignment, marriage and civil partnership, pregnancy and maternity, race, religion or belief, sex or sexual orientation.

For conduct advice, contact our Professional Ethics helpline.

Stamp duty land tax schemes

[Issued by the Solicitors Regulation Authority February 2012]

We are concerned about the promotion or facilitation of stamp duty land tax schemes.

This warning notice is for anyone who is or is considering becoming involved in the promotion or facilitation of schemes the purpose of which is to avoid or reduce stamp duty land tax. We are particularly concerned with schemes involving residential properties, but this notice may be helpful in relation to schemes involving any type of property. This notice does not form part of the SRA Handbook, but the SRA may have regard to it when exercising its regulatory functions.

The Principles

If you are or are considering becoming involved in the implementation or promotion of a stamp duty land tax (SDLT) scheme, you should consider whether you can comply with the Principles in the SRA Handbook. Whilst all the Principles may be relevant, some require particular attention:

- integrity,
- independence,
- best interests of the client,
- behaving in a way that maintains the trust the public places in you and the provision of legal services.

What is a stamp duty land tax scheme?

A SDLT scheme is a scheme which is designed to reduce or eliminate the correct level of stamp duty payable on a property. Generally, buyers of residential property are required to pay stamp duty land tax when they spend more than £125,000 on a residential property. The tax is charged at between 1 per cent and 5 per cent of the value of the residential property.

Warnings by HM Revenue and Customs

HM Revenue and Customs (HMRC) has warned that "where HMRC find property sale arrangements that have been artificially structured to avoid paying the correct amount of SDLT these will be actively challenged, through the courts where appropriate". HMRC has also warned that, in general, these schemes do not genuinely provide the savings their promoters claim. *The Times* newspaper has reported that the loss to the HMRC "is conservatively estimated at £500 million but some tax specialists believe that the true figures could be more than £1 billion". If HMRC is successful in challenging an SDLT scheme, buyers could be liable to pay the whole of the SDLT plus interest and potentially a penalty.

Why are the Principles relevant?

Whilst buyers of property are free to use honest and proper tax planning to mitigate their tax liability, there are a number of risks and misconceptions surrounding SDLT schemes. If you are asked to promote or implement a SDLT scheme, buyers will place reliance on you to act with integrity, independently, and to consider whether an SDLT scheme is in their interests.

Even if a buyer is aware of the risks and would like to use an SDLT scheme, you should take care to act in a way that maintains the trust the public places in you and the provision of legal services. This is particularly important with SDLT schemes where significant fees can be made from the implementation of a scheme but which may, in view of the warnings by HMRC, result in financial loss to buyers and HMRC.

Enforcement action

In view of the level of concern on the part of HMRC and the fundamental importance of integrity in the provision of legal advice, we are likely to look very closely at the conduct of any firm that is actively involved in these schemes.

We are taking action in a number of cases. In a recent case that came before the Solicitors Disciplinary Tribunal (SDT), a solicitor was fined £15,000 and ordered to pay £30,000 costs.

There was also a finding that there had been a lack of integrity. There are further cases due before the SDT which may result in more substantial penalties.

We are aware that a number of firms are taking corrective action such as ceasing to promote SDLT schemes, informing buyers that independent legal advice may be needed as well as ensuring lenders are aware of all the details of the SDLT scheme.

Factors to consider to help you decide if a SDLT scheme is in the interests of your clients

Below is a list of some of the factors which may be relevant in deciding if a SDLT scheme is in the interests of your client(s).

The SDLT scheme

- SDLT schemes are constantly changing and are usually very complex, bearing in mind what purchasers want to achieve. HMRC publish information on schemes which have been discredited;
- Be wary of claims by promoters of SDLT schemes that the scheme is backed by a "robust counsel's opinion". Based on what we have seen, we warn that you must check that the opinion
  - is genuine,
  - has not been tampered with,
  - is up to date, and
  - specifically covers the scheme which is being promoted.
- Bear in mind that reliance on counsel's opinion is not necessarily a defence to allegations of breaches of the Principles, and such a position is substantially weaker if the opinion has not been obtained by you for the particular client and the transaction in which you are acting;
- Be wary of claims that the SDLT scheme is approved by HMRC. Be aware that disclosure of the scheme to HMRC, and the issue of a scheme reference number by HMRC, is not confirmation the scheme is backed by HMRC;
- Be aware that HMRC can currently challenge SDLT schemes up to four years after the effective date of the transaction and this can be extended if there has been a careless or deliberate error in the submission of the SDLT return;
- Consider carrying out due diligence on the promoter of the SDLT scheme. If the promoter claims they will repay the fee charged for implementing the scheme, robustly check how realistic this is, bearing in mind that HMRC has four years to challenge the scheme. If the promoter is unable to repay the fee, the buyer may look to you to reimburse them;
- If the SDLT scheme is based on a supposed "no win no fee" basis said to be backed by insurance, robustly check that the policy is suitable and relevant to the purchasers circumstances.

The buyers

- Make sure that you have properly considered all the clients' interests and that no client will be disadvantaged by the scheme;
- Ensure that you account to the buyer for any benefit received by you, and disclose any referral arrangement connected to the scheme.

The lender

- If you act for a lender as well as the buyer, robust consideration needs to be given to whether the scheme could prejudice the interests of the lender. It is our view that it is likely to be very important to ensure that the lender is fully informed that the property is subject to an SDLT scheme with sufficient detail of how the scheme operates. Recent findings by the SDT would support this approach.

These schemes also carry significant risks for you. If you knowingly provide information in support of a tax return that is incorrect, HMRC could impose a penalty on you of £3,000 per submission.

For further advice on the application of the Principles in relation to stamp duty land tax avoidance schemes, please contact our Ethics helpline.

Bogus law firms and identity theft

[Issued by the Solicitors Regulation Authority 26 March 2012]

1. There are serious and continuing risks to the public arising from the activities of criminals and criminal gangs who are setting up bogus law firms or bogus branch offices of genuine law firms with the intention, usually, of stealing mortgage loans. This warning notice provides information about the threat and advice about how to protect yourself and others from it.
2. We are deploying our resources to mitigate the risk in various ways including rigorous authorisation processes, use of intelligence, urgent investigation, removal of records from Find a solicitor and publication of warnings.
3. It is important to bear in mind, however, that we do not regulate the people who are perpetrating these frauds and our powers over them are relatively limited. However, in one case where sufficient evidence was available, we obtained a injunction against an individual preventing him from having anything to do with any law firm in the future. If we obtain sufficient evidence to take such steps in any case, then we will do so.
4. It is important to share some of the indicators of these frauds to maximise the chances of prevention.
5. If you become suspicious about a law firm for any reason, please contact our Red Alert Line (0345 850 0999 or email redalert@sra.org.uk) as a matter of extreme urgency since some frauds are carried out very quickly.
6. Bear in mind that you may come across these frauds in different contexts. Of course, you must keep an eye on any indication that your firm is being targeted or its name being used improperly. If you discover this, you should contact the SRA and your insurers, including consideration of legal action such as by way of injunction either to stop misleading statements or to freeze assets if money has gone missing. If there is any evidence of a crime having been committed, you should also inform the Police.
7. There are risks to you and your firm. For example, in *Lloyds TSB Bank PLC v Markandan and Uddin* [2012] EWCA Civ 65 the firm that was said to be the victim of the fraud was still held liable for breach of trust in paying away mortgage monies.
8. Some practical things you can do:
    a. Search your firm's name on the internet from time to time, since that might bring up a false office—it may be worth considering doing the same with the names of some of your partners or staff;
    b. Check your firm and individual details on the Law Society's Find a solicitor web page—in case someone has misused your name to set up a false office;

c. Be alert to suspicious incidents such as transactions that others seem to think your firm is dealing with when you are not;

d. Look out for alerts and warnings on the SRA website about bogus firms.

9. Law firms dealing with conveyancing transactions or other work also sometimes become suspicious of firms on the other side and again it is important that such suspicions are reported and acted upon immediately.

10. Some examples of **factors giving rise to suspicion** are[1]

- errors in letterheading—in one case the bogus office had letterheading which misspelt the name of the town in which it was supposedly based;
- no landline telephone number—note that numbers beginning with 07 are mobile telephone numbers;
- inconsistent telephone or fax numbers with those usually used by the firm;
- telephone calls being diverted to a call-back service;
- a firm apparently based in serviced offices;
- email addresses using generic email accounts—most law firms have addresses incorporating the name of their firm; if in doubt, check the genuine law firm's website to identify its contact email address. You may well notice a difference;
- sudden appearance in your locality of a firm with no obvious connection to the area, probably not interacting with other local firms at all;
- a firm appearing to open a branch office a considerable distance from its head office for no obvious reason;
- a firm based in one part of the country supposedly having a bank account in another part of the country—this is a strong indicator and has been seen several times;
- a client account apparently overseas—this is a breach of rule 13.4 of the SRA Accounts Rules and is a major red flag;
- a strange or suspicious bank account name—such as the account not being in the name of the law firm you are supposedly dealing with either at all or by some variation.

11. If you become concerned, you should consider checking some of the above points yourself. Because of the possibility of the theft of the identity of a genuine solicitor, it is worth trying to speak to the solicitor concerned. For example, if the solicitor is supposedly at one particular office but is also based at a head office of the firm, you could speak to the head office preferably after verifying its genuine nature, perhaps by contact with the senior partner.

12. You should check the Find a solicitor website since there are sometimes bogus law firms which have not sought registration with the SRA and will not appear there; but bear in mind also that the nature of identity theft is that fraudsters may have obtained some form of registration by fraudulent misstatement to the SRA and therefore an entry on Find a solicitor should not be taken as verification that the firm is genuine.

13. Do not assume that the SRA or the Police can take direct steps to protect your firm. We each will do what we can although we will be focused on fraud prevention and you must not exclude the possibility of urgently seeking an injunction particularly if you are in possession of the most direct evidence and indeed if action is required very urgently. In such circumstances, we will seek to assist as much as we properly can in light of the evidence and any order of the court.

NOTES

1. These do not necessarily individually establish a serious problem but are factors to be considered.

Land banking schemes

[Issued by the Solicitors Regulation Authority September 2012]

This warning notice is for anyone who is involved or who is considering acting for clients involved in the promotion or facilitation of investment schemes which involve selling plots of land to investors on the basis of prospective planning permission.

Whilst this notice does not form part of the Solicitors Regulation Authority's (SRA) Handbook, the SRA may have regard to it when exercising its regulatory functions.

The issue

The SRA is aware that there are a number of fraudulent investment schemes. These are typically where agricultural, brownfield or other blighted land is acquired at low cost and divided into plots for sale to investors. Investors are informed that the land will soar in value once planning permission is obtained. However, as the land will usually be on a green belt or protected site, the land is unlikely to obtain planning permission or achieve the value intimated by the operator, resulting in the investor paying an inflated price for the land. This practice is sometimes known as "land banking".

In a recent case prosecuted by The Financial Services Authority (FSA), it was estimated that investors paid up to £32 million for land, when the actual value of the land was in the region of £3 million. The Financial Services Authority (FSA) estimate that the loss to investors through land banking schemes, is in the region of £200 million since 2006. Some schemes are run as 'collective investment schemes' and should be, but are rarely, authorised by the FSA.

The Principles

You should be aware that as a regulated individual or firm, you or your firm may be used by operators of land banking schemes to provide credibility to the scheme. You may also be asked to facilitate their operation by registering transfers of the individual plots and dealing with the proceeds of their sale. If you are involved or are considering becoming involved in a land banking scheme you should consider if you can comply with the Principles in the SRA Handbook and in particular:

Principle 2 – act with integrity;

Principle 3 – not allow your independence to be compromised;

Principle 4 – act in the best interests of each client;

Principle 6 – behave in a way that maintains the trust the public places in you and the provision of legal services;

Principle 8 – run your business or carry out you role in the business effectively and in accordance with proper governance and sound financial an risk management principles.

As land banking schemes may require you to deal with unrepresented investors, the outcomes in chapter 11 of the SRA Code of Conduct 2011 ("the Code") – relations with third parties – will also be relevant.

Complying with the Principles

To comply with the Principles it is important that you and your firm are able to identify land banking schemes and manage the risks associated with such schemes. Ensuring that you and everyone in your firm is aware of the following should assist with this:

FSA warnings: The FSA has released multiple warnings which detail how land banking schemes work and how you can protect yourself. You should consider these warnings and in particular the warning entitled Land banking 3 January 2007.

Misleading statements: Land banking schemes are often promoted on the basis that planning permission is imminent or that a well known company is about to buy the land. The SRA is aware that forged Land Registry letters and Land Registry estate plan approval letters have been used as evidence that planning permission is available when this is not the case. Also the obtaining of planning permission may be in the control of a management company which may have no intention of applying for planning permission.

If you are acting for the operator of a scheme you must ensure any information passed to third parties is not misleading. In such circumstances you must achieve O(11.1) – a requirement not to take unfair advantage of a third party.

Operators: Operators of land banking schemes are often based overseas, making it difficult for an investor to recover funds invested in a scheme or for enforcement action to be taken against the operator. Operators may also attempt to conceal the original value of the land by inter-company transactions which inflate the original purchase price.

Investors: Investors in land banking schemes may be unrepresented or based overseas and may be unaware of the risks involved in land banking schemes. Some investors may be investing their life savings in schemes or may have been induced into investing in a scheme on the basis they will be protected because you or your firm is regulated. In such circumstances, again, you must achieve O(11.1) (a requirement that you do not take unfair advantage of third parties on your client's behalf).

If you are acting for an investor in a landbanking scheme you must comply with Principle 4 (i.e. act in your client's best interests) and achieve the outcomes in Chapter 1 of the Code (you and your client). In particular, O(1.2) requires you to provide services to your in a manner which protects their interests in their matter, and O(1.5) makes it clear that the service you provide to clients must be competent, delivered in a timely manner and take account of your clients' needs and circumstances. This requires you to discuss with and advise clients of the risks and to ensure they understand all the relevant issues.

Please take extra care if it is envisaged that your retainer is to be limited in nature, for example it excludes providing advice to clients or is solely restricted to the registration of the properties. Before agreeing to act in these circumstances you should consider whether it is necessary to carry out due diligence in relation to the scheme in order to avoid unwittingly becoming involved in a fraudulent scheme. In particular Outcome 9.1 contains a requirement that your independence and your professional judgement are not prejudiced by virtue of any arrangement with another person. Outcome 9.2 makes it clear that you must ensure that your clients' interests are protected regardless of the interests of an introducer or fee sharer or your interest in receiving referrals. Outcome 9.3 makes it clear that you should ensure that; clients are in a position to make informed decisions about how to pursue their matter.

Collective investment schemes: Some land banking schemes are deliberately structured as 'collective investment schemes' (CIS) to prevent investors making their own enquiries and applications for planning permission. A CIS is an arrangement that enables a number of investors to pool their assets and have these professionally managed by an independent manager. Problems may be encountered because of the need for consent from all plot holders or the managing agent before an application for planning permission, which may never be given. A CIS must be authorised by the FSA. The definition of a CIS can be found in section 235 of the Financial Services and Markets Act 2000 and you should consider whether a scheme which has not been authorised by the FSA might fall within that definition.

Handling investor funds: The promoters of Land banking schemes will often require you or your firm to hold investor funds in your client account. There are specific outcomes in chapter

11 of the SRA Code of Conduct 2011 in relation to undertakings. They may also ask you to pay the proceeds of sale to unconnected third parties, who may be based off shore, or purchase high value assets on behalf of the company, its members or directors in which case consideration should also be given to compliance with Rule 14.5 of the SRA Accounts Rules 2011 (the prohibition on providing banking facilities through your client account) – and compliance with your obligations under the Money Laundering Regulations and related legislation.

Enforcement action

Whilst the SRA is committed to working constructively with firms, the SRA will take enforcement action against individuals or firms that fail to address the issues and risks associated with land banking schemes. The FSA are also investigating and prosecuting operators and those associated with land banking schemes.

The Solicitors Disciplinary Tribunal have recently prosecuted two cases involving solicitors in land banking schemes which were found to be collective investment schemes. These cases are Stephen Peter David Murrell who was struck off the roll and ordered to pay costs in the region of £42,000 and Ian David Campbell Smith who was fined £10,000 and ordered to pay costs in the sum of £25,000.

Further assistance

If you require further assistance with understanding your obligations in relation to land banking schemes please contact the Ethics Helpline [0370 606 25 77].

Advance fee fraud warning for firms

[Advice article by the Law Society 24 August 2011]

The Serious Organised Crime Agency (SOCA) has issued an updated warning in its recent e-newsletter, Payback Times, about the vulnerability of law firms to advanced fee fraud.

The methodology

Law firms have been approached to act for foreign nationals in relation to a personal injury or contractual dispute in the UK.

Shortly after instruction, cheques for substantial sums are received, purportedly as an out of court settlement.

These cheques have later turned out to be fraudulent or stolen, with some firms suffering losses where they have forwarded on payments before the cheques have cleared.

In many cases the purported client has also provided false identification details.

Action to take

Where you receive instructions from a client who is unusual for your firm, remember to always ask the question: why are you instructing me?

While litigation is not covered by the Money Laundering Regulations, it can be used to facilitate fraud and money laundering. Ensure that your fee earners know the warning signs, including unexpectedly quick settlements.

Read more on the warning signs of laundering through litigation [www.lawsociety.org.uk/Advice/Articles/Laundering-in-litigation/]

If you receive a stolen cheque, you will have the existing proceeds of crime. In this case you will need to consider making a suspicious activity report (SAR) to SOCA under section 332 of the Proceeds of Crime Act. You may also wish to make a separate crime report directly to the Police or the National Fraud Authority, as a SAR is not a crime report.

If you receive a fraudulent cheque, you are likely to be in possession of the instrument of a crime, rather than its proceeds, unless funds have already been drawn down against the cheque. If there are no existing proceeds of crime, you do not need to make a suspicious activity report, but should consider making a crime report directly to the Police or the National Fraud Authority.

You would also consider terminating the retainer to protect your firm from the fraud and to avoid being utilised in perpetrating the fraud on others.

Read more about the advice from SOCA in the recent edition of Payback Times

Get access to our money laundering reporting officer (MLRO) only forum to read other alerts from SOCA and previous editions of Payback Times by emailing us at antimoneylaundering@lawsociety.org.uk.

Debt recovery work and relationships with debt recovery businesses

[Issued by the Solicitors Regulation Authority. Last updated 11 June 2013]

This warning notice provides information about some regulatory issues which might arise in connection with debt recovery work including arrangements between firms and debt recovery companies. This notice does not set out an exhaustive list of all regulatory issues which might arise in this context, nor is it a substitute for the provisions of the SRA Handbook. It is the sole responsibility of regulated persons to ensure full compliance with the SRA Handbook at all times. The SRA may have regard to this notice when exercising its regulatory functions.

What are our principal concerns?

You must at all times comply with the SRA Principles and achieve the Outcomes set out in the SRA Code of Conduct 2011 ("the Code"). We are concerned about the conduct of some firms involved in debt recovery and the arrangements firms have in place with debt recovery companies. These include:

- arrangements by which a debt recovery business is effectively carrying out reserved legal activities, such as conducting litigation, as if it is entitled to do so;
- misleading or aggressive correspondence on the firm's letter headed paper which is sent by the firm or by a debt recovery business;
- letters before action on the firm's notepaper being sent without adequate supervision;
- firms putting their independence at risk by the nature of the arrangements with and/or their reliance upon a debt recovery company.

It is important that all work done in the name of your firm can properly be said to have been done by, or under, the effective and proper supervision of a regulated person. We will always look at the substance rather than the form of your relationship with a debt recovery business.

The SRA will look closely at your conduct if you make unjustified claims against a third party. An assertion that you were acting in the "*best interests*" of your client is not an answer to the making of an improper demand. You must not engage in business practices which are deceitful, oppressive or otherwise unfair or improper.

We expect you to accurately and openly represent your authority/status in all communications, and to convey in those communications the correct legal position with regard to debts and the debt recovery process.

The unlawful conduct of litigation

There are certain types of legal services ("reserved legal activities") that only regulated persons who are authorised to do so can undertake on behalf of clients. The reserved legal activities are as set out in the Legal Services Act 2007 ("LSA") S12 (1) and Schedule 2 and include:

- The exercise of a right of audience; and
- The conduct of litigation.

It is a criminal offence for a person to carry on a reserved legal activity unless that person is entitled to carry on the relevant activity (LSA s14 (1)).

A person is entitled to carry out reserved legal activities only if they are an authorised person (as defined under the LSA s18) or an exempt person (as defined under the LSA s19).

It is also a criminal offence for a person to wilfully pretend to be entitled to carry on any reserved legal activity when they are not entitled to do so, or for a person to take or use any name, title or description with the intention of falsely implying they are entitled to carry on a reserved legal activity (LSA s17 (1)).

Therefore you will need to satisfy yourself that you are not allowing a debt recovery business to conduct legal services which are reserved legal activities, because this may be unlawful.

The LSA Schedule 2 paragraph 4 defines the conduct of litigation as:

a. the issuing of proceedings before any court in England and Wales;

b. the commencement, prosecution and defence of such proceedings; and

c. the performance of any ancillary functions in relation to such proceedings.

Understanding whether an activity falls within the scope of "conducting litigation" is informed by both statute and case law.

If you enter into arrangements with debt recovery companies you are responsible for ensuring you are not party to an unlawful arrangement which allows the debt recovery company, for example, to use your name to conduct litigation.

In allowing a debt recovery business to carry out reserved legal activities, you may also breach one or more of the SRA Principles.

Outsourcing work to a debt collection business

If you outsource part of the work to a debt collection business, you must ensure that you achieve the Outcomes in Chapter 7 of the Code (Management of your business) and in particular, Outcomes (7.7) to (7.10).

You must ensure that any activities conducted in your name or on your behalf by a debt recovery business are not undertaken in a way which takes unfair advantage of others. For example, by making demands for payment from a third party for sums (such as the costs of a letter of claim) which are not legally recoverable from that party or making aggressive or misleading demand for repayment.

Independence

When entering into an agreement with a debt recovery business, you must ensure that the terms and substance of the arrangement do not compromise your independence. A relationship with a debt recovery business which enables it to have control over the supervision of cases and/or the direction and management of a firm is likely to compromise the firm's independence.

Examples of situations where your independence may be at risk under an arrangement with a debt recovery business include:

- Financial dependency;
- Contractual conditions which cede control;
- Giving access to confidential information;
- A non-arm's length relationship which suggests that the firm is more akin to a subsidiary rather than an independent law firm; and
- Fee sharing arrangements beyond that allowed in Chapter 9 of the Code.

Fee sharing and referrals

If you enter an arrangement for a debt collection business to refer clients to your firm, you must achieve the Outcomes in Chapter 9 of the Code. The arrangement must not compromise your independence and professional judgment, for example, by relinquishing control of the work to the debt collection business.

You should not enter into an arrangement which is clearly not in the best interests of your clients or which compromises your ability to act in the best interests of your clients. An example of this would be an arrangement which requires you to pay monies recovered from the debtor to the debt collection business rather than to your client.

The claimant will be your client and you must ensure that you achieve the Outcomes in Chapter 1 of the Code (You and your client). For example, failing to confirm the client's instructions at the outset of the retainer, or relying on the instructions of the debt collection business where the client has not directly authorised this, may put you at risk in respect of the Outcomes.

Enforcement action

Whilst the SRA is committed to working constructively with firms, the SRA will take enforcement action against regulated persons who fail to address the issues and risks associated with debt recovery work.

The Solicitors Disciplinary Tribunal has recently heard two cases brought by the SRA against solicitors involved with debt recovery work.

In the first, case the Tribunal found that the nature of the solicitor's arrangement with a debt recovery company was wholly irresponsible', and had resulted in a breach of his regulatory duties. In particular, the referral arrangement had compromised the solicitors independence and ability to act in the best interests of clients. The Tribunal were particularly concerned with a feature of the solicitor's arrangement which had facilitated the conduct of litigation by the debt recovery company when it was not permitted to do reserved legal activities. The arrangement had also given the misleading impression to opposing parties and the Court that the solicitor was responsible for conducting litigation which in fact was being conducted by the debt recovery company. Of further concern to the Tribunal was the fact that opposing parties received letters from the solicitor which could have been perceived as threatening in their demands for payment, and which contained misleading and inaccurate statements. The solicitor was ordered to pay a fine of £40,000 and costs of £35,000.

In the second case, the Tribunal decided that the solicitor's relationship with a debt recovery business compromised his integrity and his independence. The arrangement in this case meant that the solicitor had recklessly misled the court by facilitating the conduct of litigation by the debt recovery company. It also gave the misleading impression that the solicitor was responsible for conducting litigation which was actually being dealt with by the debt recovery company. The Tribunal commented that they considered this a very serious case and the Solicitor was ordered to pay a fine of £15,000 and costs of £50,000.

Further guidance

The Office of Fair Trading (OFT) has issued guidance on appropriate standards of behaviour to all businesses engaged in the recovery of consumer credit debts.

The OFT has granted a group consumer credit licence to the Law Society (managed by the SRA) which covers consumer credit work carried out by regulated persons. The SRA is responsible for ensuring that regulated persons comply with their obligations in consumer credit work. If appropriate the SRA may decide to refer a regulated person to the OFT if it is concerned about non-compliance with the OFT's guidance. The OFT can be minded to vary a group licence to exclude a member from the group as set out in sections 28 and 31 of the Consumer Credit Act 1974.

The SRA may also consider placing conditions on your practising certificate or registration. Some conditions restrict your ability to practise, and others outline steps you must follow.

Further guidance on the application of the SRA Principles and the Code can be obtained from our Ethics Helpline [0370 606 2577].

High-yield investment fraud

[Issued by the Solicitors Regulation Authority. Last updated 10 September 2013]

This warning notice is for anyone who is involved in, or is considering acting for clients involved in, the promotion or facilitation of financial arrangements that appear dubious.

Law firms have been targeted in the past by fraudsters promoting high-yield investment schemes which have proved to be ineffective and often fraudulent. Practitioners must not become involved in schemes that appear dubious or bear the hallmarks of possible fraud.

Economic pressures on law firms can lead to difficulty in obtaining work or finance and there is temptation to act in financial schemes either for fees or to make a promised profit. After a period of some years in which law firms were rarely involved in such schemes, the SRA is seeing a substantial increase in them again.

It is important always to bear in mind that a scheme that appears to be too good to be true is usually fraudulent. This notice sets out some factors that indicate there may be a fraud.

Whilst this notice does not form part of the SRA Handbook, the SRA may have regard to it when exercising its regulatory functions.

The Principles

It is your duty to ensure you do not become involved in potentially fraudulent financial arrangements. Failure to observe warnings from the SRA could lead to disciplinary action or criminal prosecution. Attempts to limit your involvement, particularly by a purportedly "limited retainer" are ineffective in protecting you if you simply should not become involved.

If you are, or are considering, becoming involved in any financial arrangement, you must consider whether you can comply with the Principles in the SRA Handbook. Whilst all the Principles may be relevant, some require particular attention:

- integrity
- independence
- best interests of the client
- behaving in a way that maintains the trust the public places in you and the provision of legal services.

What are high-yield investment frauds?

Frauds vary and fraudsters learn to avoid red flag phrases. Firms need to ensure that they understand the proposed scheme and that it makes logical and legal sense. Fraudsters use meaningless terminology but also use genuine terms to mask their frauds. It is important to assess the overall proposal and, if a genuine term is used, to check robustly whether it is being used in the correct context. Some common descriptions have included:

- High yield investment schemes
- Prime bank instrument schemes
- Private placement schemes.

Arrangements are formulated by fraudsters to prey upon vulnerable and sometimes wealthy people or companies. Those in need of money are often the most at risk. These schemes are often highly sophisticated confidence tricks, which involve lawyers facilitating what is essentially a fraud. Some schemes involve the movement of large sums of money and are a combination of a fraud—usually with the intention of stealing the "investment"—and the laundering of criminal proceeds by mixing them into other money transfers.

Common characteristics

It is your duty to ensure you comply with your professional obligations and exercise proper caution in considering any involvement in a scheme involving the "investment" of money or the transfer of funds that are presented to you. The following is a non-exhaustive list of common characteristics of fraudulent financial arrangements.

- Very high rate of return and disproportionate rewards, often within a short time frame—this is also a common characteristic in Ponzi schemes which involve payments to investors from subsequent investors rather than from any 'profit' earned by the individual or organisation running the fraudulent operation
- Very large sums of money said to be involved or required for "entry" to the "programme"
- Confusing and complex transactions with obscure descriptions
- Unusual currencies
- Prime Bank Guarantees (PBGs), Promissory Notes or Letters of Credit being offered or being the 'product' underpinning the finance
- Obscure "security" such as famous paintings or speculative international developments
- Opinions or letters from law firms or others that support the scheme but do not make sense or are empty of genuine content
- Security being offered to "investors" includes an undertaking from a law firm or that money will be held by a law firm—sometimes including reference to indemnity insurance or the Compensation Fund
- Security to be issued by an obscure or offshore bank that is difficult to contact—particularly if there is pressure not to contact the bank (or any other person) on (what are in fact spurious) confidentiality grounds
- Poorly drafted documentation
- Overwhelming amount of documents supposedly explaining the transaction; or a lack of any coherent explanation of the investment
- Suggestions that the scheme is supported by or operates under the auspices of a major international body (e g IMF, UN, Federal Reserve or Bank of England)
- Large projects that are difficult to verify e g financing of a project in distant jurisdiction where it hard to verify its genuineness
- The need for speed and great confidentiality to secure the deal – usually intended to prevent proper due diligence
- Unusual letters from genuine banks (that often turn out to be forged or provided by a rogue employee)—contact the bank's fraud prevention office for verification.

Promoters operating these scams engage the assistance of law firms for a number of reasons. The involvement of lawyers and their firms:

- Lends credibility to the scheme
- Enables promoters to offer a false sense of security based on the existence of compulsory insurance and the alleged safety net of the Compensation Fund
- Provides promoters with access to client accounts which can be utilised for the transfer of funds
- Enables promoters to make use of solicitors' undertakings as a means of appearing to give investors security
- Enables promoters to abuse legal professional privilege.

Types of legal services that promoters might request include:

- Moving monies through client account
- Advising on and drafting documents and/or contracts that have little genuine content
- Marketing and promoting the fraudulent scheme to attract investors
- Adding credibility to the fraudulent scheme by attending meetings, engaging in correspondence or providing undertakings
- Certifying or verifying documentation
- Use of the lawyer's office address and facilities.

Complying with the Principles

To comply with the Principles it is important that you and your firm are able to identify fraudulent or dubious financial arrangements and manage the associated risks.

The promoters of fraudulent arrangements will often want you or your firm to hold 'investor funds' in your client account (see Rule 14.5 of the SRA Accounts Rules 2011). You must not allow money to move through your accounts or an account you control unless you are doing so in the context of a genuine transaction about which you are providing legal services. Bear in mind also that the money may be the proceeds of the defrauding of the investors.

There are specific outcomes in chapter 11 of the SRA Code of Conduct 2011 in relation to undertakings.

If you are approached you must ensure that you comply with your obligations under the Money Laundering Regulations and related legislation.

Do not assume that because you are not acting for investors that you owe no duties as a matter of professional conduct. Not only must you avoid facilitating a fraud, monies sent by investors may well be subject to implied trust obligations particularly if the scheme is fraudulent.

Investors may be unrepresented or based overseas and may be unaware of the risks involved in financial arrangements or may have been induced in a scheme on the basis they will be protected because you or your firm is regulated. Whilst your client may be the promoter of the arrangement, you must not forget your public obligations as a lawyer and your overriding duty to act in the public interest.

How do I reduce the risk of fraud?

- Do not act if you have any doubts about the propriety of the transaction; or about how or why it is structured in a particular way.
- Never act if you do not fully understand the transaction, if it does not make sense or if you are essentially just providing a facility for the transfer of money.
- Do not be blinded by apparent involvement in high value international transactions sometimes including promises of or actual international travel or meetings since it is part of the psychological approach to fraud to impress the victim or professional who will facilitate the fraud.
- Always verify properly the identity of who you are dealing with.
- Bear in mind that Ponzi schemes involve the payment of "profits" at first—by using the funds of other investors—and so "evidence" that a scheme "works" is part of the fraud.
- Ensure that proper due diligence is performed before accepting any funds into your client account—be extremely wary of any scheme which requires the depositing of any substantial sums on money with you particularly if you are to be paid for doing very

little. Do not hold money in your client account (or any other account) for clients you know little about or who you are not providing legal advice to in relation to the transaction for which you are expected to hold money.

- Why you? Be particularly careful if you are asked to act in an area outside of your usual expertise. A small firm asked to act in an international financial transaction is at severe risk.
- Use of documentation – beware of any scheme which requires you to send details of your bank, client account or blank letterheads. Such information may be used to make unauthorised payments from your client account.
- Undertakings – do not give any form of undertaking to guarantee a financial obligation unless you are acting in a transaction you fully understand and you are fully secure in having funds to meet the obligation.

SRA action

Whilst we are committed to working constructively with firms and practitioners, we will take enforcement action against those that fail to address the issues and risks associated with dubious financial arrangements.

We have seen a number of solicitors and firms who have become involved in fraudulent schemes, some as investors and some as participators of the fraud, each with the intention of gaining an extra funds for the firm that could be used to run the practice, whether that be through the payment of a success fee for participation in the fraud or through profits arising from the scheme.

A defence based on ignorance or lack of understanding of the transactions involved is considered weak. Turning a blind eye to the suspicious features of a scheme or failing to verify the promoter's true intentions can constitute dishonesty.

Further assistance

If you require further assistance with understanding your obligations in relation to high yield investment schemes please contact the Ethics Helpline.

If you have evidence of one of these schemes or are concerned that you have been approached or have become involved, please contact your SRA supervisor.

If you are already involved and become concerned, urgently contact the SRA Fraud and Confidential Intelligence Bureau: call 0345 850 0999 or email redalert@sra.org.uk.

Referral fees, LASPO and the SRA Principles

[Issued by the Solicitors Regulation Authority. Last updated 11 October 2013]

Who is this guidance relevant to?

This warning notice is relevant to all practitioners who have referral arrangements for personal injury work. It reminds practitioners of the need, when entering into such arrangements, to consider not only whether they may be in breach of the ban in the Legal Aid, Sentencing and Punishment of Offenders Act 2012 (LASPO), but whether they are able to comply with their regulatory obligations, in particular the SRA Principles and the Outcomes in the SRA Code of Conduct 2011 ("the Code").

Whilst this notice does not form part of the SRA Handbook, the SRA may have regard to it when exercising its regulatory functions.

Our concerns

We know that the ban on referral fees has raised difficult issues in relation to its application and interpretation. We are also aware that, because of the wording of LASPO, it is possible for firms to have arrangements that involve the introduction of personal injury work without being in breach of LASPO. We are concerned, however, that in setting up arrangements in a way that does not breach LASPO, firms are failing to consider their wider duties to their clients and others, and in doing so may be breaching the Principles or failing to achieve the Outcomes. Examples include:

- agreeing with an introducer to deduct money from clients' damages;
- inappropriate outsourcing of work to introducers;
- referrals to other service providers which are not in the best interests of clients;
- failure to properly advise clients about the costs and how their claim should be funded; and
- lack of transparency about the arrangement.

The Principles

The most relevant Principles in relation to referral arrangements are that you must

1. uphold the rule of law and the proper administration of justice;
2. act with integrity;
3. not allow your independence to be compromised;
4. act in the best interests of each client;
5. provide a proper standard of service to your clients; and
6. behave in a way that maintains the trust the public places in you and in the provision of legal services.

The Outcomes

As well as the outcomes requiring practitioners to comply with LASPO (outcomes 6.4 and 9.8), chapters 6 and 9 of the Code include outcomes in connection with referrals to and by your firm, dealing with issues such as independence, transparency and the best interests of clients. These will apply in respect of any referral to or by your firm that is not prohibited by LASPO. You will also need to ensure that you achieve the outcomes relating to issues such as client care, conflict of interests, confidentiality and publicity.

Deductions from clients' damages

Some claims management companies ("CMCs") are seeking to charge clients a proportion of their damages in return for being referred to a suitable law firm and/or for other claims management services. In some cases firms are being asked, as part of their agreement with the CMC, to deduct these payments from the client's damages or even to forward the client's damages to the CMC. This type of arrangement can pose various risks to your ability to comply with the Principles.

Firstly, where the arrangement is not in the interests of your client, you will need to consider whether your ability to advise the client about the agreement they have entered into will be impaired by your relationship with the introducer. The Solicitors Disciplinary Tribunal has on a number of occasions criticised solicitors for failing to give such advice to their clients and for acting where their own commercial interests in a referral arrangement conflict with the interests of the client.

Money can only be deducted from a client's damages with the client's informed consent. Sending a client's damages to a third party introducer would also require the client's consent, but is unlikely ever to be in the client's interests.

In addition, this type of arrangement could place the introducer in breach of LASPO and you should not enter into any arrangement that would assist a third party to breach the legislation.

Outsourcing/paying for services

Some firms have arrangements that involve the introducer carrying out a certain amount of work on the client's matter and the firm paying the introducer for carrying out this work.

Provided the payment is for a genuine service and is reasonable in all the circumstances, such a payment may not breach LASPO. However, before entering into such an arrangement, you will need to consider carefully whether it is appropriate for the introducer to be carrying out such work. Failure to do so may compromise your ability to act in the best interests of your clients or to provide a proper standard of service. The work may, for example, include advising the client on the appropriate means of funding their matter, explaining and signing the client up to a conditional fee agreement or damages-based agreement. You have a duty to ensure that your clients receive sufficient information to make informed decisions about their matter and the way it will be handled. In our view, outsourcing this work, or relying on a third party to provide the necessary information to the client, represents a significant risk to your ability to achieve the relevant outcomes.

Inappropriate referrals

It has been suggested that some firms and introducers are arranging for clients to purchase insurance, medical reports or other products or services at inflated prices so that the firm or introducer will receive a higher commission. In some cases the firm may have an interest in the business providing the product or service. The receipt of such commissions, either by you or another person, may put you in breach of section 56(2) of LASPO. Also, where you refer your client to another service provider, the referral must be in the client's best interests and must not compromise your independence and you are required to account to the client for any financial benefit you receive as a result of their instructions. (See the outcomes in Chapters 1 and 6 of the Code.) Even if the client has been sold these products or service before instructing your firm you should be careful to ensure that you are not facilitating arrangements that are detrimental to clients' interests.

You should also consider whether any requirement by an introducer to use a particular provider compromises your independence or your ability to comply with the relevant outcomes (as well as whether your agreement to do so may amount to consideration and therefore a payment which breaches LASPO).

Funding and fee agreements

There have been suggestions that some firms are not discussing with clients the options for funding their claim and in particular that they are not exploring whether the client has insurance that would cover their legal costs, so that the firm can charge an uplift on their fees. It is important that clients are aware of, and understand, the options for funding their claim and any fee agreement they enter into with you. (See, for example, outcomes 1.1, 1.12 and 1.13 and indicative behaviours 1.13, 1.14, 1.15 and 1.17.)

Transparency

Clients need to be in a position to make informed decisions about any referral to a firm and about how their matter will be dealt with. Some introducers and firms have set up complex arrangements in order to ensure they do not breach LASPO, for example by ensuring it is the client, rather than the third party introducer, who provides information to the firm about a potential claim. If you are involved in such an arrangement, you need to be careful to ensure that the client is not misled about who they are dealing with and who is providing particular services. You will also need to achieve outcomes 9.3 and 9.4 and tell the client about any financial arrangement you have with the introducer.

Enforcement action

Whilst we are committed to working constructively with firms and practitioners, we will take enforcement action against those that fail to address the issues and risks associated with referral arrangements, particularly where those arrangements are detrimental to the interests of clients.

Further help

If you require further assistance in relation to your referral arrangements contact the Ethics Helpline.

Employed solicitors: publicity and information provided to third parties

[Issued by the Solicitors Regulation Authority. Last updated 8 July 2014]

Status

This warning notice does not form part of the Solicitors Regulation Authority (SRA) Handbook. However, the SRA will have regard to it when exercising its regulatory functions.

Who is this warning notice relevant to?

In-house/employed solicitors

Our concerns

There have been a number of complaints from the public regarding misleading information contained in letters and in letterheads, of some in-house solicitors. These complaints arise as a result of in-house solicitors giving the impression, through the wording contained in letters, through the use of business names by in-house solicitors, by the description of their regulatory status and by their contact details that they are an independent firm of solicitors or other legal services firm.

Overall, these approaches appear to be attempts to give the impression to a third party that an external agency or firm has been instructed to take legal action, up to and including, court proceedings.

These complaints have arisen most commonly in debt collection or enforcement matters where solicitors are employed in-house by the organisation seeking to recover the debt.

Further concern has been caused by complaints of solicitors having taken unfair advantage of a third party's lack of legal knowledge, particularly in debt collecting matters, where the third party is unrepresented.

The SRA Principles

The SRA Principles are mandatory and apply to all solicitors and to those acting under their supervision. The following SRA Principles are of particular relevance to this issue.

- Principle 2 – You must act with integrity
- Principle 6 – You must behave in a way that maintains the trust the public places in you and in the provision of legal services

SRA Mandatory Outcomes

The Outcomes in the SRA Code of Conduct 2011 are mandatory and describe what firms and individuals are expected to achieve in order to comply with the relevant SRA Principles. However, they are not an exhaustive list of the application of all the Principles.

The following Outcomes are of particular relevance to this issue.

- O(8.1) – your publicity in relation to your firm or in house practice or for any other business is accurate and not misleading, and is not likely to diminish the trust the public places in you and in the provision of legal services.
- O(8.4) – clients and the public have appropriate information about you, your firm and how you are regulated.
- O(11.1) – you do not take unfair advantage of third parties in either your professional or personal capacity.

Regulatory action

Failure to comply with this warning notice will lead to regulatory action. Regulatory action may also be necessary because of misconduct that has already taken place.

Our expectations

All solicitors must act with integrity and maintain the trust the public places in them and in the provision of legal services. We expect that all publicity and information regarding your position, as an in house/employed solicitor, is compliant with the Principles and relevant Outcomes in the SRA Code of Conduct 2011.

We have reviewed a number of complaints and a range of letters sent by solicitors employed within financial (and similar) institutions to pursue debts or other outstanding sums of money. We consider that, through a range of approaches, attempts are being made to mislead third parties (invariably individual debtors) that their case has been referred by the organisation owed money to an independent law firm to pursue the debt, notably the "naming" of in-house legal teams in the style of independent law firms.

We consider that such approaches do not meet the requirements of Principles 2 and 6 and of Outcomes 8.1, 8.4 and 11.1.

Letterheads must be clear as to the organisation employing you and you must not give any impression that you are part of an independent law firm or firm of solicitors or an independent solicitor.

Any contact details should ensure the third party is aware who they are contacting whether you directly, the in-house legal department or other staff of your employer.

Any correspondence from you, or sent under your supervision, must indicate your individual status as a solicitor regulated by the SRA but must not seek to give any impression that the organisation which employs you is regulated by the SRA.

Overall, the obligation on you is to take positive steps to ensure that third parties are clear about your status and relationship with the organisation seeking recovery of the debt.

In considering any complaints or regulatory action the SRA will consider whether the Principles are being complied with and Outcomes being met. We will consider the overall impact on the third party of information provided in the letterhead, the body of the correspondence and in the references made to regulatory status. In particular we will consider whether the totality of the information provided makes the solicitor's status clear or whether it gives a false impression and may mislead.

Further help

If solicitors require further help, they can call or email the SRA Ethics helpline.

APPENDIX 7

Council for Licensed Conveyancers Code of Conduct

[The Code is reproduced with the kind permission of the CLC. For the latest updates to the material, please see www.conveyancer.org.uk.]

Council for Licensed Conveyancers Code of Conduct

[6 October 2011]

Introduction

This *Code of Conduct* was made in accordance with s.20 of the *Administration of Justice Act 1985* and s.83 of the *Legal Services Act 2007*.

All individuals and bodies regulated by the *CLC* must comply with this Code and its associated *regulatory arrangements*. In this Code "you" refers to individuals and bodies (and the employees and managers within them) regulated by the *CLC*. You must not permit anyone else to act or fail to act in such a way as to amount to a breach of this Code. Your main driver should be the delivery of positive *client outcomes*. The Code comprises *principles* and *specific requirements*, which taken together deliver positive *Outcomes* for your *Clients* and, particularly in relation to *Overriding Principle* 6, for others you deal with.

To effectively secure the protection of, and the provision of choice for, the consumer of legal services, you must at all times comply with the following *Overriding Principles*:

1. Act with independence and integrity;
2. Maintain high standards of work;
3. Act in the best interests of your *Clients*;
4. Comply with your duty to the court;
5. Deal with regulators and ombudsmen in an open and co-operative way;
6. Promote equality of access and service.

These are underpinned by *principles* of behaviour which must be demonstrated and *specific requirements* which must be complied with in order that the *Overriding Principles* are supported.

Disciplinary proceedings may be taken against you if the *CLC* believes there has been a breach of this Code, meaning that *clients* do not receive the standard of legal services they should reasonably expect to receive. The *CLC's* response will be informed by the *CLC's* Regulatory and *Enforcement* Policies.

In exceptional circumstances the *CLC* may waive a provision, or provisions, of the *regulatory arrangements* for an individual, body or circumstance for a particular purpose, or purposes, and with the *conditions* specified in the waiver.

Overriding Principle 1. Act with independence and integrity

Outcomes – you must deliver the following *Outcomes*:

1.1 *Clients* receive good quality independent information, representation and advice;

1.2 *Clients* receive an honest and lawful service;

1.3 *Client money* is kept separately and safely.

Principles – delivery of these *Outcomes* requires you to act in a principled way:

(a) You do not allow your independence to be compromised.

(b) You act honestly, professionally and decently.

(c) You do not conduct yourself in a manner which may result in a breach of the law nor in any other manner which may bring the legal profession into disrepute.

(d) You *carry on Reserved Legal Activity* only through a person entitled to *carry on* that activity.

(e) You do not give false or misleading information relating to the provision of *Regulated Services*.

(f) You do not allow fee arrangements to prejudice your independence or professional judgement.

(g) You do not conduct business under a misleading name.

(h) You keep *Client money* safe.

(i) You do not publicise your business through unsolicited communications in person or by telephone.

(j) Your advertising is clear, accurate and fair.

(k) You keep *Client money* entirely separate from your money or the money of the entity.

(l) You do not take unfair advantage of any person, whether or not a *Client* of the business.

Specific Requirements – you must also comply with the following *specific requirements*:

(m) You comply with *anti-money laundering and prevention of financing terrorism legislation*.

(n) When acting as a *CLC* licensee, you accept instructions only to act in a matter which is regulated by the *CLC*.

(o) All business *communications*, websites and office premises display information confirming the entity is regulated by the *CLC* and the names of the *Managers* (identifying those who are *Authorised Persons*).

Overriding Principle 2. Maintain high standards of work

Outcomes – you must deliver the following *Outcomes*:

2.1 *Clients* are provided with a high standard of legal services;

2.2 *Client* matters are dealt with using care, skill and diligence;

2.3 Appropriate *arrangements*, resources, procedures, skills and commitment are in place to ensure *Clients* always receive a high standard of service.

Principles – delivery of these *Outcomes* requires you to act in a principled way:

(a) You provide the level of service appropriate for, and agreed with, the *Client.*

(b) You keep your skills and legal knowledge up-to-date.

(c) You ensure all individuals within the entity are competent to do their work.

(d) You supervise and regularly check the quality of work in *Client* matters.

(e) You comply fully with any undertaking given by you.

(f) You *systematically* identify and mitigate risks to the business and to *Clients.*

(g) You promote ethical practice and compliance with regulatory requirements.

(h) You enable staff to raise concerns which are acted on appropriately.

(i) You maintain proper governance, management, supervision, financial, and risk management *arrangements* and *controls.*

(j) You administer oaths, affirmations and declarations properly.

(k) You deliver services in accordance with timetables reasonably agreed with the *Client.*

Specific Requirements – you must also comply with the following *specific requirements*:

(l) *Control* of an entity is from a permanent fixed address in England or Wales.

(m) A *Manager* who is an *Authorised Person* is responsible for ensuring that all of the entity's *employees* are properly supervised.

(n) You make provision for alternative supervision *arrangements* in case of illness, accident or other unforeseen event.

(o) You maintain proper records to evidence your *arrangements* and *controls* and how they are applied.

Overriding Principle 3. Act in the best interests of your Clients

Outcomes – you must deliver the following *Outcomes*:

3.1 Each *Client's* best interests are served;

3.2 *Clients* receive advice appropriate to their circumstances;

3.3 *Clients* have the information they need to make informed decisions;

3.4 *Clients* are aware of any referral arrangements and that they are consistent with your responsibilities both to them and to the *CLC*;

3.5 *Clients* are aware of any limitation or any condition resulting from your relationship with another party;

3.6 *Clients'* affairs are treated confidentially (except as required or permitted by law or with the *Client's* consent).

Principles – delivery of these *Outcomes* requires you to act in a principled way:

(a) You only accept instructions and act in relation to matters which are within your professional competence.

(b) You keep the interests of the *Client* paramount (except as required by the law or the *CLC's regulatory arrangements*).

(c) You do not act for a *Client* where you judge it is not in their best interests for you to do so.

(d) You do not accept instructions from a person nor continue to act for a *Client* whose interests conflict directly with your own, the entity's, or another *Client*.

(e) You disclose *client* information only as the *Client* has instructed (or as required by the *CLC's regulatory arrangements* or by law), keeping effective records of any disclosures you make.

(f) You only recommend a particular person, business or product when it is in the best interests of the *Client*.

(g) You cease acting in a matter if the *Client* so instructs or, in the absence of such instructions where it is reasonable to do so.

(h) You provide the *Client* with information which is accurate, useful and appropriate to the particular *Client*.

(i) You only provide *Regulated Services* whilst you have *CLC*-approved *professional indemnity insurance* in force.

(j) You provide the *Client* with all relevant information relating to any fee arrangements or fee changes.

(k) You advise *Clients* of the name and status of the person dealing with their matter and the name of the person responsible for overall supervision.

(l) You consult *Clients* on key decisions in a timely way.

(m) You *promptly* advise *Clients* of any significant changes to projected *costs*, timelines and strategies.

Specific Requirements – you must also comply with the following *specific requirements*:

(n) Where the entity represents parties with different interests in any transaction each party is at all times represented by different *Authorised Persons* conducting themselves in the matter as though they were members of different entities.

(o) You ensure there are adequate indemnity arrangements in respect of *claims* made against you for work carried out by you after you have ceased to practise by *purchasing professional indemnity insurance* for a minimum of 6 years from the expiry of the period of *professional indemnity insurance* stated in your evidence of insurance or policy document.

(p) If you seek to exclude or limit liability, you do so only to the extent that such exclusion or limitation is above the minimum level of cover provided by *CLC*-approved *professional indemnity insurance*; you must obtain the written informed consent of the *Client* for such exclusion or limitation to be effective.

(q) When offering and providing services which are not regulated by the *CLC*, you advise your *Client* of this and inform them in writing that the activity is not covered by *CLC*-approved *professional indemnity insurance* or the *CLC*-administered *Compensation Fund*.

(r) Before or when accepting instructions, you inform *Clients* in writing of the terms on which the instructions are accepted, a complete, accurate estimate of fees and *disbursements* to be charged and if and when they are likely to change.

(s) You *promptly* inform the *Client* in writing of the existence and amount of any sum payable (whether directly or indirectly) as a result of receipt of that *Client's* instructions.

(t) With the exception of *disbursements*, you do not delay completion because fees are outstanding to you.

(u) You discuss and agree with the *Client* how *costs* will be paid, whether directly by the *Client*, by public funding, through an insurance policy or otherwise.

Overriding Principle 4. Comply with your duty to the court

Note: this Principle will only be applicable if the *CLC's* application to regulate *advocacy* and *litigation* services is successful

Outcomes – you must deliver the following *Outcomes*:

4.1 You act in the interests of justice;

4.2 You act in good faith towards *Clients*.

Principles – delivery of these *Outcomes* requires you to act in a principled way:

(a) You promote and protect the *client's* best interests.

(b) You do not compromise your professional standards or independence.

(c) You assist the court in the administration of justice.

(d) You do not knowingly or recklessly mislead or deceive the court, or allow the court to be misled.

(e) You ensure that the Court is informed of all relevant decisions and legislative provisions (whether this has a favourable or unfavourable effect on the case you are advancing).

(f) You comply with any Court Order (unless an application for a stay is pending or the Order has been revoked by the Court).

(g) You advise your *Client* to comply with Court Orders and of the consequences of failing to do so.

(h) You properly protect sensitive evidence.

(i) You safeguard the well being of children and other vulnerable persons.

Specific Requirement – you must also comply with the following specific requirement:

(j) You ensure that the court is made aware of any relevant legal or factual matters which are likely to have a material effect on the outcome of the proceedings.

Overriding Principle 5. Deal with regulators and ombudsmen in an open and co-operative way

Outcome – you must deliver the following *Outcome*:

5.1 You act in accordance with your regulatory responsibilities.

Principles – delivery of these *Outcomes* requires you to act in a principled way:

(a) You are open and honest in your dealings with us.

(b) You comply with the *CLC Code of Conduct* and the *CLC's* other *regulatory arrangements*.

(c) You comply *promptly* and fully with a *CLC* direction or request.

(d) You comply with any *authorisation*, *permission* or *condition* endorsed on your *licence*, *Recognised Body Certificate* or *Licensed Body Licence*.

(e) You co-operate with any *CLC* investigation.

(f) You co-operate with any *Legal Ombudsman* investigation.

(g) You comply *promptly* and fully with any *Legal Ombudsman* Order.

(h) You co-operate with other regulators and ombudsmen.

Specific Requirements – you must also comply with the following *specific requirements*:

(i) You make the *Compensation Fund* contribution determined by the *CLC*.

(j) You *systematically* identify, monitor and manage risks to the delivery of this Code's *outcomes*.

(k) You *promptly* notify insurers in writing of any facts or matters which may give rise to a *claim* under *CLC*-approved *professional indemnity insurance*.

(l) You *promptly* notify the *CLC* in writing of any facts or matters which may give rise to a *claim* under its *Compensation Fund*.

(m) As a *CLC* licensee operating in an entity regulated by another regulator you must comply with that regulator's regulations at all times in a way which is reasonably consistent with this Code.

(n) You obtain permission from the *CLC* before offering *Reserved legal activities*:

- as a new business;
- in an entity regulated by another *Approved Regulator*, or
- through a entity with a *Manager* who is not a *Licensed Conveyancer*.

(o) You notify the *CLC* of any material breach of this Code, whether by you, the entity or any other person.

(p) You notify the *CLC* of a change as set out in the *CLC's* Notification Code.

Overriding Principle 6. Promote equality of access and service.

Outcomes – you must deliver the following *Outcomes*:

6.1 The service is accessible and responsive to the needs of individual *Clients*, including those who are vulnerable;[1]

6.2 No-one – *Client*, *employee*, colleague, job applicant, trainee or other party – you deal with feels discriminated[2] against (whether directly or indirectly), victimised or harassed;

6.3 You accept responsibility where the service you provide is not of the expected standard and provide appropriate redress for the *Client* where necessary;

6.4 Handling of *complaints* takes proper account of *Clients'* individual needs, including those who are vulnerable;

6.5 *Complaints* are dealt with impartially and comprehensively.

Principles – delivery of these *Outcomes* requires you to act in a principled way:

(a) You comply with *Equalities legislation*.

(b) You make reasonable adjustments to prevent persons with disabilities from being placed at a substantial disadvantage.

(c) You provide equal opportunities for all partners, *employees* or applicants in employment and training.

(d) You make all reasonable efforts to ensure your service is accessible and responsive to *Clients*, including those with vulnerabilities.

(e) The *complaints* procedure is clear, well-publicised and free.

(f) You treat *complaints* seriously and provide appropriate redress options.

(g) You deal with *complaints* fairly and within 28 days.

(h) You identify and address systemic *Client Complaints* issues.

Specific Requirements – you must also comply with the following *specific requirements*:

(i) Any allegation of (direct or indirect) discrimination, victimisation and harassment is investigated thoroughly, resulting, where appropriate, in disciplinary action.

(j) From the outset you advise *Clients* in writing of their right to make a complaint, how to make it, to whom, and the timeframes involved.

(k) You advise *Clients* in writing of their right to have their *complaint* escalated to the *Legal Ombudsman* and provide them with contact details and timeframes of that body.

(l) You keep a record of *complaints* received and any action taken as a result.

Notes

1 A *Client* may be vulnerable because of a range of characteristics, including (but not limited to): basic skills: literacy and numeracy; complexity and confusion: difficulty of accessing and understanding large amounts of information; disability or other impairment; mental health issues; distress or sudden change in circumstances e.g. bereavement, divorce, illness or loss of employment; low income; age; caring responsibilities; limited knowledge of, or limited skills in, use of English; balance of power: lack of competition and or choice; or inexperience or lack of knowledge of a particular subject. Vulnerability can only be assessed on a case-by-case basis.

2 On the grounds of age, disability, gender reassignment, marital and civil partnership status, pregnancy and maternity, race, religion or faith, sex or sexual orientation.

APPENDIX 8

The Money Laundering Regulations 2007

[With consolidated amendments to 1 April 2014.]

Money Laundering Regulations 2007

SI 2007/2157

Made 24th July 2007

Laid before Parliament 25th July 2007

Coming into force 15th December 2007

The Treasury are a government department designated for the purposes of section 2(2) of the European Communities Act 1972 in relation to measures relating to preventing the use of the financial system for the purpose of money laundering;

The Treasury, in exercise of the powers conferred on them by section 2(2) of the European Communities Act 1972 and by sections 168(4)(b), 402(1)(b), 417(1) and 428(3) of the Financial Services and Markets Act 2000, make the following Regulations:

PART 1
GENERAL

1 Citation, commencement etc

(1) These Regulations may be cited as the Money Laundering Regulations 2007 and come into force on 15th December 2007.

(2) These Regulations are prescribed for the purposes of sections 168(4)(b) (appointment of persons to carry out investigations in particular cases) and 402(1)(b) (power of the Authority to institute proceedings for certain other offences) of the 2000 Act.

(3) The Money Laundering Regulations 2003 are revoked.

2 Interpretation

(1) In these Regulations—

"the 2000 Act" means the Financial Services and Markets Act 2000;

"Annex I financial institution" has the meaning given by regulation 22(1);

"auction platform" has the meaning given by regulation 3(13A);

"auditor", except in regulation 17(2)(c) and (d), has the meaning given by regulation 3(4) and (5);

"authorised person" means a person who is authorised for the purposes of the 2000 Act;

"the Authority" means the Financial Conduct Authority;

"beneficial owner" has the meaning given by regulation 6;

"bill payment service provider" means an undertaking which provides a payment service enabling the payment of utility and other household bills;

"business relationship" means a business, professional or commercial relationship between a relevant person and a customer, which is expected by the relevant person, at the time when contact is established, to have an element of duration;

"the capital requirements directive" means Directive 2013/36/EU of the European Parliament and of the Council of 26 June 2013 relating to the activity of credit institutions and the prudential supervision of credit institutions and investment firms, amending Directive 2002/87/EC and repealing Directives 2006/48/EC and 2006/49/EC;

"the capital requirements regulation" means Regulation (EU) 575/2013 of the European Parliament and of the Council of 26 June 2013 on prudential requirements for credit institutions and investment firms and amending Regulation (EU) No 648/2012;

"cash" means notes, coins or travellers' cheques in any currency;

"casino" has the meaning given by regulation 3(13);

"the Commissioners" means the Commissioners for Her Majesty's Revenue and Customs;

"credit institution" has the meaning given by regulation 3(2);

"customer due diligence measures" has the meaning given by regulation 5;

"DETI" means the Department of Enterprise, Trade and Investment in Northern Ireland;

"the electronic money directive" means Directive 2009/110/EC of the European Parliament and of the Council of 16th September 2009 on the taking up, pursuit and prudential supervision of the business of electronic money institutions;

"electronic money institution" has the meaning given by regulation 2(1) of the Electronic Money Regulations 2011;

"the emission allowance auctioning regulation" means Commission Regulation (EU) No 1031/2010 of 12 November 2010 on the timing, administration and other aspects of auctioning of greenhouse gas emission allowances pursuant to Directive 2003/87/EC of the European Parliament and of the Council establishing a scheme for greenhouse gas emission allowances trading within the Community;

"estate agent" has the meaning given by regulation 3(11);

"external accountant" has the meaning given by regulation 3(7);

"financial institution" has the meaning given by regulation 3(3);

"firm" means any entity, whether or not a legal person, that is not an individual and includes a body corporate and a partnership or other unincorporated association;

"high value dealer" has the meaning given by regulation 3(12);

"the implementing measures directive" means Commission Directive 2006/70/EC of 1st August 2006 laying down implementing measures for the money laundering directive;

"independent legal professional" has the meaning given by regulation 3(9);

"insolvency practitioner", except in regulation 17(2)(c) and (d), has the meaning given by regulation 3(6);

"the life assurance consolidation directive" means Directive 2002/83/EC of the European Parliament and of the Council of 5th November 2002 concerning life assurance;

"local weights and measures authority" has the meaning given by section 69 of the Weights and Measures Act 1985 (local weights and measures authorities);

"the markets in financial instruments directive" means Directive 2004/39/EC of the European Parliament and of the Council of 12th April 2004 on markets in financial instruments;

"money laundering" means an act which falls within section 340(11) of the Proceeds of Crime Act 2002;

"the money laundering directive" means Directive 2005/60/EC of the European Parliament and of the Council of 26th October 2005 on the prevention of the use of the financial system for the purpose of money laundering and terrorist financing;

"money service business" means an undertaking which by way of business operates a currency exchange office, transmits money (or any representations of monetary value) by any means or cashes cheques which are made payable to customers;

"nominated officer" means a person who is nominated to receive disclosures under Part 7 of the Proceeds of Crime Act 2002 (money laundering) or Part 3 of the Terrorism Act 2000 (terrorist property);

"non-EEA state" means a state that is not an EEA state;

"notice" means a notice in writing;

"occasional transaction" means a transaction (carried out other than as part of a business relationship) amounting to 15,000 euro or more, whether the transaction is carried out in a single operation or several operations which appear to be linked;

"ongoing monitoring" has the meaning given by regulation 8(2);

"payment services" has the meaning given by regulation 2(1) of the Payment Services Regulations 2009;

"person who has a qualifying relationship with a PRA-authorised person" is to be read with section 415B(4) of the 2000 Act;

"the PRA" means the Prudential Regulation Authority;

"PRA-authorised person" has the meaning given in section 2B(5) of the 2000 Act;

"regulated market"—

(a) within the EEA, has the meaning given by point 14 of Article 4(1) of the markets in financial instruments directive; and

(b) outside the EEA, means a regulated financial market which subjects companies whose securities are admitted to trading to disclosure obligations which are contained in international standards and are equivalent to the specified disclosure obligations;

"relevant person" means a person to whom, in accordance with regulations 3 and 4, these Regulations apply;

"the specified disclosure obligations" means disclosure requirements consistent with—

(a) Article 6(1) to (4) of Directive 2003/6/EC of the European Parliament and of the Council of 28th January 2003 on insider dealing and market manipulation;

(b) Articles 3, 5, 7, 8, 10, 14 and 16 of Directive 2003/71/EC of the European Parliament and of the Council of 4th November 2003 on the prospectuses to be published when securities are offered to the public or admitted to trading;

(c) Articles 4 to 6, 14, 16 to 19 and 30 of Directive 2004/109/EC of the

European Parliament and of the Council of 15th December 2004 relating to the harmonisation of transparency requirements in relation to information about issuers whose securities are admitted to trading on a regulated market; or

(d) EU legislation made under the provisions mentioned in sub-paragraphs (a) to (c);

"supervisory authority" in relation to any relevant person means the supervisory authority specified for such a person by regulation 23;

"tax adviser" (except in regulation 11(3)) has the meaning given by regulation 3(8);

"telecommunication, digital and IT payment service provider" means an undertaking which provides payment services falling within paragraph 1(g) of Schedule 1 to the Payment Services Regulations 2009;

"terrorist financing" means an offence under—

(a) section 15 (fund-raising), 16 (use and possession), 17 (funding arrangements), 18 (money laundering) or 63 (terrorist finance: jurisdiction) of the Terrorism Act 2000;

(b) paragraph 7(2) or (3) of Schedule 3 to the Anti-Terrorism, Crime and Security Act 2001 (freezing orders);

(c) [*repealed*]

(d) regulation 10 of the Al-Qaida (Asset-Freezing) Regulations 2011; or

(e) section 11, 12, 13, 14, 15 or 18 of the Terrorist Asset-Freezing etc Act 2010 (offences relating to the freezing of funds etc of designated persons);

"trust or company service provider" has the meaning given by regulation 3(10).

(2) In these Regulations, references to amounts in euro include references to equivalent amounts in another currency.

(3) Unless otherwise defined, expressions used in these Regulations and the money laundering directive have the same meaning as in the money laundering directive and expressions used in these Regulations and in the implementing measures directive have the same meaning as in the implementing measures directive.

3 Application of the Regulations

(1) Subject to regulation 4, these Regulations apply to the following persons acting in the course of business carried on by them in the United Kingdom ("relevant persons")—

(a) credit institutions;

(b) financial institutions;

(c) auditors, insolvency practitioners, external accountants and tax advisers;

(d) independent legal professionals;

(e) trust or company service providers;

(f) estate agents;

(g) high value dealers;

(h) casinos.

(1A) Regulations 2, 20, 21, 23, 24, 35 to 42, and 44 to 48 apply to an auction platform acting in the course of business carried on by it in the United Kingdom, and such an auction platform is a relevant person for the purposes of those provisions.

(2) "Credit institution" means—

(a) a credit institution as defined in Article 4(1)(1) of the capital requirements regulation; or

(b) a branch (within the meaning of Article 4(1)(17) of that regulation) located in an EEA state of an institution falling within sub-paragraph (a) (or an equivalent institution whose head office is located in a non-EEA state) wherever its head office is located,

when it accepts deposits or other repayable funds from the public or grants credits for its own account (within the meaning of the banking consolidation directive), or when it bids directly in auctions in accordance with the emission allowance auctioning regulation on behalf of its clients.

(3) "Financial institution" means—

(a) an undertaking, including a money service business, when it carries out one or more of the activities listed in points 2 to 12, 14 and 15 of Annex 1 to the capital requirements directive (the relevant text of which is set out in Schedule 1 to these Regulations), other than—

(i) a credit institution;

(ii) an undertaking whose only listed activity is as a creditor under an agreement which—

(aa) falls within section 12(a) of the Consumer Credit Act 1974 (debtor-creditor-supplier agreements),

(bb) provides fixed sum credit (within the meaning given in section 10 of the Consumer Credit Act 1974 (running-account credit and fixed-sum credit)) in relation to the provision of services, and

(cc) provides financial accommodation by way of deferred payment or payment by instalments over a period not exceeding 12 months;

(iii) an undertaking whose only listed activity is trading for own account in one or more of the products listed in point 7 of Annex 1 to the capital requirements directive where the undertaking does not have a customer,

and, for this purpose, "customer" means a third party which is not a member of the same group as the undertaking;

(b) an insurance company duly authorised in accordance with the life assurance consolidation directive, when it carries out activities covered by that directive;

(c) a person, other than a person falling within Article 2 of the markets in financial instruments directive, whose regular occupation or business is the provision to other persons of an investment activity on a professional basis, when providing or performing investment services or activities (within the meaning of that directive) or when bidding directly in auctions in accordance with the emission allowance auctioning regulation on behalf of clients;

(ca) a person falling within Article 2(1)(i) of the markets in financial instruments directive, when bidding directly in auctions in accordance with the emission allowance auctioning regulation on behalf of clients of the person's main business;

(d) a collective investment undertaking, when marketing or otherwise offering its units or shares;

(e) an insurance intermediary as defined in Article 2(5) of Directive 2002/92/EC of the European Parliament and of the Council of 9th December 2002 on insurance mediation, with the exception of a tied insurance intermediary as mentioned in Article 2(7) of that Directive, when it acts in respect of contracts of long-term insurance within the meaning given by article 3(1) of, and Part II of Schedule 1 to, the Financial Services and Markets Act 2000 (Regulated Activities) Order 2001;

(f) a branch located in an EEA state of a person referred to in sub-paragraphs (a) to (e) (or an equivalent person whose head office is located in a non-EEA state), wherever its head office is located, when carrying out any activity mentioned in sub-paragraphs (a) to (e);

(g) the National Savings Bank;

(h) the Director of Savings, when money is raised under the auspices of the Director under the National Loans Act 1968.

(4) "Auditor" means any firm or individual who is a statutory auditor within the meaning of Part 42 of the Companies Act 2006 (statutory auditors), when carrying out statutory audit work within the meaning of section 1210 of that Act.

(5) Before the entry into force of Part 42 of the Companies Act 2006 the reference in paragraph (4) to—

(a) a person who is a statutory auditor shall be treated as a reference to a person who is eligible for appointment as a company auditor under section 25 of the Companies Act 1989 (eligibility for appointment) or article 28 of the Companies (Northern Ireland) Order 1990; and

(b) the carrying out of statutory audit work shall be treated as a reference to the provision of audit services.

(6) "Insolvency practitioner" means any person who acts as an insolvency practitioner within the meaning of section 388 of the Insolvency Act 1986 (meaning of "act as insolvency practitioner") or article 3 of the Insolvency (Northern Ireland) Order 1989.

(7) "External accountant" means a firm or sole practitioner who by way of business provides accountancy services to other persons, when providing such services.

(8) "Tax adviser" means a firm or sole practitioner who by way of business provides advice about the tax affairs of other persons, when providing such services.

(9) "Independent legal professional" means a firm or sole practitioner who by way of business provides legal or notarial services to other persons, when participating in financial or real property transactions concerning—

(a) the buying and selling of real property or business entities;

(b) the managing of client money, securities or other assets;

(c) the opening or management of bank, savings or securities accounts;

(d) the organisation of contributions necessary for the creation, operation or management of companies; or

(e) the creation, operation or management of trusts, companies or similar structures,

and, for this purpose, a person participates in a transaction by assisting in the planning or execution of the transaction or otherwise acting for or on behalf of a client in the transaction.

(10) "Trust or company service provider" means a firm or sole practitioner who by way of business provides any of the following services to other persons—

(a) forming companies or other legal persons;

(b) acting, or arranging for another person to act—

(i) as a director or secretary of a company;

(ii) as a partner of a partnership; or

(iii) in a similar position in relation to other legal persons;

(c) providing a registered office, business address, correspondence or administrative address or other related services for a company, partnership or any other legal person or arrangement;

(d) acting, or arranging for another person to act, as—

(i) a trustee of an express trust or similar legal arrangement; or

(ii) a nominee shareholder for a person other than a company whose securities are listed on a regulated market,

when providing such services.

(11) "Estate agent" means—

(a) a firm; or

(b) sole practitioner,

who, or whose employees, carry out estate agency work, when in the course of carrying out such work.

(11A) For the purposes of paragraph (11) "estate agency work" is to be read in accordance with section 1 of the Estate Agents Act 1979 (estate agency work), but for those purposes references in that section to disposing of or acquiring an interest in land are (despite anything in section 2 of that Act) to be taken to include references to disposing of or acquiring an estate or interest in land outside the United Kingdom where that estate or interest is capable of being owned or held as a separate interest.

(12) "High value dealer" means a firm or sole trader who by way of business trades in goods (including an auctioneer dealing in goods), when he receives, in respect of any transaction, a payment or payments in cash of at least 15,000 euros in total, whether the transaction is executed in a single operation or in several operations which appear to be linked.

(13) "Casino" means the holder of a casino operating licence and, for this purpose, a "casino operating licence" has the meaning given by section 65(2) of the Gambling Act 2005 (nature of licence).

(13A) "Auction platform" means a platform which auctions two-day spot or five-day futures, within the meanings given by Article 3(4) and (5) of the emission allowance auctioning regulation, when it carries out activities covered by that regulation.

(14) In the application of this regulation to Scotland, for "real property" in paragraph (9) substitute "heritable property".

4 Exclusions

(1) These Regulations do not apply to the following persons when carrying out any of the following activities—

(a) a society registered under the Industrial and Provident Societies Act 1965, when it—

(i) issues withdrawable share capital within the limit set by section 6 of that Act (maximum shareholding in society); or

(ii) accepts deposits from the public within the limit set by section 7(3) of that Act (carrying on of banking by societies);

(b) a society registered under the Industrial and Provident Societies Act (Northern Ireland) 1969, when it—

(i) issues withdrawable share capital within the limit set by section 6 of that Act (maximum shareholding in society); or

(ii) accepts deposits from the public within the limit set by section 7(3) of that Act (carrying on of banking by societies);

(c) a person who is (or falls within a class of persons) specified in any of paragraphs 2 to 23, 25 to 38 or 40 to 49 of the Schedule to the Financial Services and Markets Act 2000 (Exemption) Order 2001, when carrying out any activity in respect of which he is exempt;

(ca) a local authority within the meaning given in article 3 of the Financial Services and Markets Act 2000 (Regulated Activities) Order 2001, when carrying on an activity which would be a regulated activity for the purposes of the Financial Services and Markets Act 2000 but for article 72G of that Order;

(d) a person who was an exempted person for the purposes of section 45 of the Financial Services Act 1986 (miscellaneous exemptions) immediately before its repeal, when exercising the functions specified in that section;

(e) a person whose main activity is that of a high value dealer, when he engages in financial activity on an occasional or very limited basis as set out in paragraph 1 of Schedule 2 to these Regulations; or

(f) a person, when he prepares a home report.

(2) These Regulations do not apply to a person who falls within regulation 3 solely as a result of his engaging in financial activity on an occasional or very limited basis as set out in paragraph 1 of Schedule 2 to these Regulations.

(3) Parts 2 to 5 of these Regulations do not apply to—

(a) the Auditor General for Scotland;

(b) the Auditor General for Wales;

(c) the Bank of England;

(d) the Comptroller and Auditor General;

(e) the Comptroller and Auditor General for Northern Ireland;

(f) the Official Solicitor to the Supreme Court, when acting as trustee in his official capacity;

(g) the Treasury Solicitor.

(4) In paragraph (1)(f), "home report" means the documents prescribed for the purposes of section 98, 99(1) or 101(2) of the Housing (Scotland) Act 2006.

PART 2
CUSTOMER DUE DILIGENCE

5 Meaning of customer due diligence measures

"Customer due diligence measures" means—

(a) identifying the customer and verifying the customer's identity on the basis of documents, data or information obtained from a reliable and independent source;

(b) identifying, where there is a beneficial owner who is not the customer, the beneficial owner and taking adequate measures, on a risk-sensitive basis, to verify his identity so that the relevant person is satisfied that he knows who the beneficial owner is, including, in the case of a legal person, trust or similar legal arrangement, measures to understand the ownership and control structure of the person, trust or arrangement; and

(c) obtaining information on the purpose and intended nature of the business relationship.

6 Meaning of beneficial owner

(1) In the case of a body corporate, "beneficial owner" means any individual who—

(a) as respects any body other than a company whose securities are listed on a regulated market, ultimately owns or controls (whether through direct or indirect ownership or control, including through bearer share holdings) more than 25% of the shares or voting rights in the body; or

(b) as respects any body corporate, otherwise exercises control over the management of the body.

(2) In the case of a partnership (other than a limited liability partnership), "beneficial owner" means any individual who—

(a) ultimately is entitled to or controls (whether the entitlement or control is direct or indirect) more than a 25% share of the capital or profits of the partnership or more than 25% of the voting rights in the partnership; or

(b) otherwise exercises control over the management of the partnership.

(3) In the case of a trust, "beneficial owner" means—

(a) any individual who is entitled to a specified interest in at least 25% of the capital of the trust property;

(b) as respects any trust other than one which is set up or operates entirely for the benefit of individuals falling within sub-paragraph (a), the class of persons in whose main interest the trust is set up or operates;

(c) any individual who has control over the trust.

(4) In paragraph (3)—

"specified interest" means a vested interest which is—

(a) in possession or in remainder or reversion (or, in Scotland, in fee); and

(b) defeasible or indefeasible;

"control" means a power (whether exercisable alone, jointly with another person or with the consent of another person) under the trust instrument or by law to—

(a) dispose of, advance, lend, invest, pay or apply trust property;

(b) vary the trust;

(c) add or remove a person as a beneficiary or to or from a class of beneficiaries;

(d) appoint or remove trustees;

(e) direct, withhold consent to or veto the exercise of a power such as is mentioned in sub-paragraph (a), (b), (c) or (d).

(5) For the purposes of paragraph (3)—

(a) where an individual is the beneficial owner of a body corporate which is entitled to a specified interest in the capital of the trust property or which has control over the trust, the individual is to be regarded as entitled to the interest or having control over the trust; and

(b) an individual does not have control solely as a result of—

(i) his consent being required in accordance with section 32(1)(c) of the Trustee Act 1925 (power of advancement);

(ii) any discretion delegated to him under section 34 of the Pensions Act 1995 (power of investment and delegation);

(iii) the power to give a direction conferred on him by section 19(2) of the Trusts of Land and Appointment of Trustees Act 1996 (appointment and retirement of trustee at instance of beneficiaries); or

(iv) the power exercisable collectively at common law to vary or extinguish a trust where the beneficiaries under the trust are of full age and capacity and (taken together) absolutely entitled to the property subject to the trust (or, in Scotland, have a full and unqualified right to the fee).

(6) In the case of a legal entity or legal arrangement which does not fall within paragraph (1), (2) or (3), "beneficial owner" means—

(a) where the individuals who benefit from the entity or arrangement have been determined, any individual who benefits from at least 25% of the property of the entity or arrangement;

(b) where the individuals who benefit from the entity or arrangement have yet to be determined, the class of persons in whose main interest the entity or arrangement is set up or operates;

(c) any individual who exercises control over at least 25% of the property of the entity or arrangement.

(7) For the purposes of paragraph (6), where an individual is the beneficial owner of a body corporate which benefits from or exercises control over the property of the entity or arrangement, the individual is to be regarded as benefiting from or exercising control over the property of the entity or arrangement.

(8) In the case of an estate of a deceased person in the course of administration, "beneficial owner" means—

(a) in England and Wales and Northern Ireland, the executor, original or by representation, or administrator for the time being of a deceased person;

(b) in Scotland, the executor for the purposes of the Executors (Scotland) Act 1900.

(9) In any other case, "beneficial owner" means the individual who ultimately owns or controls the customer or on whose behalf a transaction is being conducted.

(10) In this regulation—

"arrangement", "entity" and "trust" means an arrangement, entity or trust which administers and distributes funds;

"limited liability partnership" has the meaning given by the Limited Liability Partnerships Act 2000.

7 Application of customer due diligence measures

(1) Subject to regulations 9, 10, 12, 13, 14, 16(4) and 17, a relevant person must apply customer due diligence measures when he—

(a) establishes a business relationship;

(b) carries out an occasional transaction;

(c) suspects money laundering or terrorist financing;

(d) doubts the veracity or adequacy of documents, data or information previously obtained for the purposes of identification or verification.

(2) Subject to regulation 16(4), a relevant person must also apply customer due diligence measures at other appropriate times to existing customers on a risk-sensitive basis.

(3) A relevant person must—

(a) determine the extent of customer due diligence measures on a risk-sensitive basis depending on the type of customer, business relationship, product or transaction; and

(b) be able to demonstrate to his supervisory authority that the extent of the measures is appropriate in view of the risks of money laundering and terrorist financing.

(4) Where—

(a) a relevant person is required to apply customer due diligence measures in the case of a trust, legal entity (other than a body corporate) or a legal arrangement (other than a trust); and

(b) the class of persons in whose main interest the trust, entity or arrangement is set up or operates is identified as a beneficial owner,

the relevant person is not required to identify all the members of the class.

(5) Paragraph (3)(b) does not apply to the National Savings Bank or the Director of Savings.

8 Ongoing monitoring

(1) A relevant person must conduct ongoing monitoring of a business relationship.

(2) "Ongoing monitoring" of a business relationship means—

(a) scrutiny of transactions undertaken throughout the course of the relationship (including, where necessary, the source of funds) to ensure that the transactions are consistent with the relevant person's knowledge of the customer, his business and risk profile; and

(b) keeping the documents, data or information obtained for the purpose of applying customer due diligence measures up-to-date.

(3) Regulation 7(3) applies to the duty to conduct ongoing monitoring under paragraph (1) as it applies to customer due diligence measures.

9 Timing of verification

(1) This regulation applies in respect of the duty under regulation 7(1)(a) and (b) to apply the customer due diligence measures referred to in regulation 5(a) and (b).

(2) Subject to paragraphs (3) to (5) and regulation 10, a relevant person must verify the identity of the customer (and any beneficial owner) before the establishment of a business relationship or the carrying out of an occasional transaction.

(3) Such verification may be completed during the establishment of a business relationship if—

(a) this is necessary not to interrupt the normal conduct of business; and

(b) there is little risk of money laundering or terrorist financing occurring,

provided that the verification is completed as soon as practicable after contact is first established.

(4) The verification of the identity of the beneficiary under a life insurance policy may take place after the business relationship has been established provided that it takes place at or before the time of payout or at or before the time the beneficiary exercises a right vested under the policy.

(5) The verification of the identity of a bank account holder may take place after the bank account has been opened provided that there are adequate safeguards in place to ensure that—

(a) the account is not closed; and

(b) transactions are not carried out by or on behalf of the account holder (including any payment from the account to the account holder),

before verification has been completed.

10 Casinos

(1) A casino must establish and verify the identity of—

(a) all customers to whom the casino makes facilities for gaming available—

(i) before entry to any premises where such facilities are provided; or

(ii) where the facilities are for remote gaming, before access is given to such facilities; or

(b) if the specified conditions are met, all customers who, in the course of any period of 24 hours—

(i) purchase from, or exchange with, the casino chips with a total value of 2,000 euro or more;

(ii) pay the casino 2,000 euro or more for the use of gaming machines; or

(iii) pay to, or stake with, the casino 2,000 euro or more in connection with facilities for remote gaming.

(2) The specified conditions are—

(a) the casino verifies the identity of each customer before or immediately after such purchase, exchange, payment or stake takes place, and

(b) the Gambling Commission is satisfied that the casino has appropriate procedures in place to monitor and record—

(i) the total value of chips purchased from or exchanged with the casino;

(ii) the total money paid for the use of gaming machines; or

(iii) the total money paid or staked in connection with facilities for remote gaming,

by each customer.

(3) In this regulation—

"gaming", "gaming machine", "remote operating licence" and "stake" have the meanings given by, respectively, sections 6(1) (gaming & game of chance), 235 (gaming machine), 67 (remote gambling) and 353(1) (interpretation) of the Gambling Act 2005;

"premises" means premises subject to—

(a) a casino premises licence within the meaning of section 150(1)(a) of the Gambling Act 2005 (nature of licence); or

(b) a converted casino premises licence within the meaning of paragraph 65 of Part 7 of Schedule 4 to the Gambling Act 2005 (Commencement No 6 and Transitional Provisions) Order 2006;

"remote gaming" means gaming provided pursuant to a remote operating licence.

11 Requirement to cease transactions etc

(1) Where, in relation to any customer, a relevant person is unable to apply customer due diligence measures in accordance with the provisions of this Part, he—

(a) must not carry out a transaction with or for the customer through a bank account;

(b) must not establish a business relationship or carry out an occasional transaction with the customer;

(c) must terminate any existing business relationship with the customer;

(d) must consider whether he is required to make a disclosure by Part 7 of the Proceeds of Crime Act 2002 or Part 3 of the Terrorism Act 2000.

(2) Paragraph (1) does not apply where a lawyer or other professional adviser is in the course of ascertaining the legal position for his client or performing his task of defending or representing that client in, or concerning, legal proceedings, including advice on the institution or avoidance of proceedings.

(3) In paragraph (2), "other professional adviser" means an auditor, accountant or tax adviser who is a member of a professional body which is established for any such persons and which makes provision for—

(a) testing the competence of those seeking admission to membership of such a body as a condition for such admission; and

(b) imposing and maintaining professional and ethical standards for its members, as well as imposing sanctions for non-compliance with those standards.

12 Exception for trustees of debt issues

(1) A relevant person—

(a) who is appointed by the issuer of instruments or securities specified in paragraph (2) as trustee of an issue of such instruments or securities; or

(b) whose customer is a trustee of an issue of such instruments or securities,

is not required to apply the customer due diligence measure referred to in regulation 5(b) in respect of the holders of such instruments or securities.

(2) The specified instruments and securities are—

(a) instruments which fall within article 77 or 77A of the Financial Services and Markets Act 2000 (Regulated Activities) Order 2001; and

(b) securities which fall within article 78 of that Order.

13 Simplified due diligence

(1) A relevant person is not required to apply customer due diligence measures in the circumstances mentioned in regulation 7(1)(a), (b) or (d) where he has reasonable grounds for believing that the customer, transaction or product related to such transaction, falls within any of the following paragraphs.

(2) The customer is—

(a) a credit or financial institution which is subject to the requirements of the money laundering directive; or

(b) a credit or financial institution (or equivalent institution) which—

(i) is situated in a non-EEA state which imposes requirements equivalent to those laid down in the money laundering directive; and

(ii) is supervised for compliance with those requirements.

(3) The customer is a company whose securities are listed on a regulated market subject to specified disclosure obligations.

(4) The customer is an independent legal professional and the product is an account into which monies are pooled, provided that—

(a) where the pooled account is held in a non-EEA state—

(i) that state imposes requirements to combat money laundering and terrorist financing which are consistent with international standards; and

(ii) the independent legal professional is supervised in that state for compliance with those requirements; and

(b) information on the identity of the persons on whose behalf monies are held in the pooled account is available, on request, to the institution which acts as a depository institution for the account.

(5) The customer is a public authority in the United Kingdom.

(6) The customer is a public authority which fulfils all the conditions set out in paragraph 2 of Schedule 2 to these Regulations.

(7) The product is—

(a) a life insurance contract where the annual premium is no more than 1,000 euro or where a single premium of no more than 2,500 euro is paid;

(b) an insurance contract for the purposes of a pension scheme where the contract contains no surrender clause and cannot be used as collateral;

(c) a pension, superannuation or similar scheme which provides retirement benefits to employees, where contributions are made by an employer or by way of deduction from an employee's wages and the scheme rules do not permit the assignment of a member's interest under the scheme (other than an assignment permitted by section 44 of the Welfare Reform and Pensions Act 1999 (disapplication of restrictions on alienation) or section 91(5)(a) of the Pensions Act 1995 (inalienability of occupational pension)); or

(d) electronic money, within the meaning of Article 2(2) of the electronic money directive, where—

(i) if the device cannot be recharged, the maximum amount stored in the device is no more than 250 euro or, in the case of electronic money used to carry out payment transactions within the United Kingdom, 500 euro; or

(ii) if the device can be recharged, a limit of 2,500 euro is imposed on the total amount transacted in a calendar year, except when an amount of 1,000 euro or more is redeemed in the same calendar year by the electronic money holder (within the meaning of Article 11 of the electronic money directive).

(8) The product and any transaction related to such product fulfils all the conditions set out in paragraph 3 of Schedule 2 to these Regulations.

(9) The product is a child trust fund within the meaning given by section 1(2) of the Child Trust Funds Act 2004.

(10) The product is a junior ISA within the meaning given by regulation 2B of the Individual Savings Account Regulations 1998.

14 Enhanced customer due diligence and ongoing monitoring

(1) A relevant person must apply on a risk-sensitive basis enhanced customer due diligence measures and enhanced ongoing monitoring—

(a) in accordance with paragraphs (2) to (4);

(b) in any other situation which by its nature can present a higher risk of money laundering or terrorist financing.

(2) Where the customer has not been physically present for identification purposes, a relevant person must take specific and adequate measures to compensate for the higher risk, for example, by applying one or more of the following measures—

(a) ensuring that the customer's identity is established by additional documents, data or information;

(b) supplementary measures to verify or certify the documents supplied, or requiring confirmatory certification by a credit or financial institution which is subject to the money laundering directive;

(c) ensuring that the first payment is carried out through an account opened in the customer's name with a credit institution.

(3) A credit institution ("the correspondent") which has or proposes to have a correspondent banking relationship with a respondent institution ("the respondent") from a non-EEA state must—

(a) gather sufficient information about the respondent to understand fully the nature of its business;

(b) determine from publicly-available information the reputation of the respondent and the quality of its supervision;

(c) assess the respondent's anti-money laundering and anti-terrorist financing controls;

(d) obtain approval from senior management before establishing a new correspondent banking relationship;

(e) document the respective responsibilities of the respondent and correspondent; and

(f) be satisfied that, in respect of those of the respondent's customers who have direct access to accounts of the correspondent, the respondent—

(i) has verified the identity of, and conducts ongoing monitoring in respect of, such customers; and

(ii) is able to provide to the correspondent, upon request, the documents, data or information obtained when applying customer due diligence measures and ongoing monitoring.

(4) A relevant person who proposes to have a business relationship or carry out an occasional transaction with a politically exposed person must—

(a) have approval from senior management for establishing the business relationship with that person;

(b) take adequate measures to establish the source of wealth and source of funds which are involved in the proposed business relationship or occasional transaction; and

(c) where the business relationship is entered into, conduct enhanced ongoing monitoring of the relationship.

(5) In paragraph (4), "a politically exposed person" means a person who is—

(a) an individual who is or has, at any time in the preceding year, been entrusted with a prominent public function by—

(i) a state other than the United Kingdom;

(ii) an EU institution; or

(iii) an international body,

including a person who falls in any of the categories listed in paragraph 4(1)(a) of Schedule 2;

(b) an immediate family member of a person referred to in sub-paragraph (a), including a person who falls in any of the categories listed in paragraph 4(1)(c) of Schedule 2; or

(c) a known close associate of a person referred to in sub-paragraph (a), including a person who falls in either of the categories listed in paragraph 4(1)(d) of Schedule 2.

(6) For the purpose of deciding whether a person is a known close associate of a person referred to in paragraph (5)(a), a relevant person need only have regard to information which is in his possession or is publicly known.

15 Branches and subsidiaries

(1) A credit or financial institution must require its branches and subsidiary undertakings which are located in a non-EEA state to apply, to the extent permitted by the law of that state, measures at least equivalent to those set out in these Regulations with regard to customer due diligence measures, ongoing monitoring and record-keeping.

(2) Where the law of a non-EEA state does not permit the application of such equivalent measures by the branch or subsidiary undertaking located in that state, the credit or financial institution must—

(a) inform its supervisory authority accordingly; and

(b) take additional measures to handle effectively the risk of money laundering and terrorist financing.

(3) In this regulation "subsidiary undertaking"—

(a) except in relation to an incorporated friendly society, has the meaning given by section 1162 of the Companies Act 2006 (parent and subsidiary undertakings) and, in relation to a body corporate in or formed under the law of an EEA state other than the United Kingdom, includes an undertaking which is a subsidiary undertaking within the meaning of any rule of law in force in that state for purposes connected with implementation of the European Council Seventh Company Law Directive 83/349/EEC of 13th June 1983 on consolidated accounts;

(b) in relation to an incorporated friendly society, means a body corporate of which the society has control within the meaning of section 13(9)(a) or (aa) of the Friendly Societies Act 1992 (control of subsidiaries and other bodies corporate).

(4) Before the entry into force of section 1162 of the Companies Act 2006 the reference to that section in paragraph (3)(a) shall be treated as a reference to section 258 of the Companies Act 1985 (parent and subsidiary undertakings).

16 Shell banks, anonymous accounts etc

(1) A credit institution must not enter into, or continue, a correspondent banking relationship with a shell bank.

(2) A credit institution must take appropriate measures to ensure that it does not enter into, or continue, a corresponding banking relationship with a bank which is known to permit its accounts to be used by a shell bank.

(3) A credit or financial institution carrying on business in the United Kingdom must not set up an anonymous account or an anonymous passbook for any new or existing customer.

(4) As soon as reasonably practicable on or after 15th December 2007 all credit and financial institutions carrying on business in the United Kingdom must apply customer due diligence measures to, and conduct ongoing monitoring of, all anonymous accounts and passbooks in existence on that date and in any event before such accounts or passbooks are used.

(5) A "shell bank" means a credit institution, or an institution engaged in equivalent activities, incorporated in a jurisdiction in which it has no physical presence involving meaningful decision-making and management, and which is not part of a financial conglomerate or third-country financial conglomerate.

(6) In this regulation, "financial conglomerate" and "third-country financial conglomerate" have the meanings given by regulations 1(2) and 7(1) respectively of the Financial Conglomerates and Other Financial Groups Regulations 2004.

17 Reliance

(1) A relevant person may rely on a person who falls within paragraph (2) (or who the relevant person has reasonable grounds to believe falls within paragraph (2)) to apply any customer due diligence measures provided that—

(a) the other person consents to being relied on; and

(b) notwithstanding the relevant person's reliance on the other person, the relevant person remains liable for any failure to apply such measures.

(2) The persons are—

(a) a credit or financial institution which is an authorised person;

(aa) [*repealed*];

(b) a relevant person who is—

(i) an auditor, insolvency practitioner, external accountant, tax adviser or independent legal professional; and

(ii) supervised for the purposes of these Regulations by one of the bodies listed in Schedule 3;

(c) a person who carries on business in another EEA state who is—

(i) a credit or financial institution, auditor, insolvency practitioner, external accountant, tax adviser or independent legal professional;

(ii) subject to mandatory professional registration recognised by law; and

(iii) supervised for compliance with the requirements laid down in the money laundering directive in accordance with section 2 of Chapter V of that directive; or

(d) a person who carries on business in a non-EEA state who is—

(i) a credit or financial institution (or equivalent institution), auditor, insolvency practitioner, external accountant, tax adviser or independent legal professional;

(ii) subject to mandatory professional registration recognised by law;

(iii) subject to requirements equivalent to those laid down in the money laundering directive; and

(iv) supervised for compliance with those requirements in a manner equivalent to section 2 of Chapter V of the money laundering directive.

(3) In paragraph (2)(c)(i) and (d)(i), "auditor" and "insolvency practitioner" includes a person situated in another EEA state or a non-EEA state who provides services equivalent to the services provided by an auditor or insolvency practitioner.

(4) Nothing in this regulation prevents a relevant person applying customer due diligence measures by means of an outsourcing service provider or agent provided that the relevant person remains liable for any failure to apply such measures.

(5) In this regulation, "financial institution" excludes—

(a) any money service business;

(b) any authorised payment institution, EEA authorised payment institution or small payment institution (within the meaning of the Payment Services Regulations 2009) which provides payment services mainly falling within paragraph 1(f) of Schedule 1 to those Regulations; and

(c) any electronic money institution or EEA authorised electronic money institution (within the meaning of the Electronic Money Regulations 2011) which provides payment services mainly falling within paragraph 1(f) of Schedule 1 to the Payment Services Regulations 2009.

18

[*Repealed*]

PART 3
RECORD-KEEPING, PROCEDURES AND TRAINING

19 Record-keeping

(1) Subject to paragraph (4), a relevant person must keep the records specified in paragraph (2) for at least the period specified in paragraph (3).

(2) The records are—

(a) a copy of, or the references to, the evidence of the customer's identity obtained pursuant to regulation 7, 8, 10, 14 or 16(4);

(b) the supporting records (consisting of the original documents or copies) in respect of a business relationship or occasional transaction which is the subject of customer due diligence measures or ongoing monitoring.

(3) The period is five years beginning on—

(a) in the case of the records specified in paragraph (2)(a), the date on which—

(i) the occasional transaction is completed; or

(ii) the business relationship ends; or

(b) in the case of the records specified in paragraph (2)(b)—

(i) where the records relate to a particular transaction, the date on which the transaction is completed;

(ii) for all other records, the date on which the business relationship ends.

(4) A relevant person who is relied on by another person must keep the records specified in paragraph (2)(a) for five years beginning on the date on which he is relied on for the purposes of regulation 7, 10, 14 or 16(4) in relation to any business relationship or occasional transaction.

(5) A person referred to in regulation 17(2)(a) or (b) who is relied on by a relevant person must, if requested by the person relying on him within the period referred to in paragraph (4)—

(a) as soon as reasonably practicable make available to the person who is relying on him any information about the customer (and any beneficial owner) which he obtained when applying customer due diligence measures; and

(b) as soon as reasonably practicable forward to the person who is relying on him copies of any identification and verification data and other relevant documents on the identity of the customer (and any beneficial owner) which he obtained when applying those measures.

(6) A relevant person who relies on a person referred to in regulation 17(2)(c) or (d) (a "third party") to apply customer due diligence measures must take steps to ensure that the third party will, if requested by the relevant person within the period referred to in paragraph (4)—

(a) as soon as reasonably practicable make available to him any information about the customer (and any beneficial owner) which the third party obtained when applying customer due diligence measures; and

(b) as soon as reasonably practicable forward to him copies of any identification and verification data and other relevant documents on the identity of the customer (and any beneficial owner) which the third party obtained when applying those measures.

(7) Paragraphs (5) and (6) do not apply where a relevant person applies customer due diligence measures by means of an outsourcing service provider or agent.

(8) For the purposes of this regulation, a person relies on another person where he does so in accordance with regulation 17(1).

20 Policies and procedures

(1) A relevant person must establish and maintain appropriate and risk-sensitive policies and procedures relating to—

(a) customer due diligence measures and ongoing monitoring;

(b) reporting;

(c) record-keeping;

(d) internal control;

(e) risk assessment and management;

(f) the monitoring and management of compliance with, and the internal communication of, such policies and procedures,

in order to prevent activities related to money laundering and terrorist financing.

(2) The policies and procedures referred to in paragraph (1) include policies and procedures—

(a) which provide for the identification and scrutiny of—

(i) complex or unusually large transactions;

(ii) unusual patterns of transactions which have no apparent economic or visible lawful purpose; and

(iii) any other activity which the relevant person regards as particularly likely by its nature to be related to money laundering or terrorist financing;

(b) which specify the taking of additional measures, where appropriate, to prevent the use for money laundering or terrorist financing of products and transactions which might favour anonymity;

(c) to determine whether a customer is a politically exposed person;

(d) under which—

(i) an individual in the relevant person's organisation is a nominated officer under Part 7 of the Proceeds of Crime Act 2002 and Part 3 of the Terrorism Act 2000;

(ii) anyone in the organisation to whom information or other matter comes in the course of the business as a result of which he knows or suspects or has reasonable grounds for knowing or suspecting that a person is engaged in money laundering or terrorist financing is required to comply with Part 7 of the Proceeds of Crime Act 2002 or, as the case may be, Part 3 of the Terrorism Act 2000; and

(iii) where a disclosure is made to the nominated officer, he must consider it in the light of any relevant information which is available to the relevant person and determine whether it gives rise to knowledge or suspicion or reasonable grounds for knowledge or suspicion that a person is engaged in money laundering or terrorist financing.

(3) Paragraph (2)(d) does not apply where the relevant person is an individual who neither employs nor acts in association with any other person.

(4) A credit or financial institution and an auction platform must establish and maintain systems which enable it to respond fully and rapidly to enquiries from financial investigators accredited under section 3 of the Proceeds of Crime Act 2002 (accreditation and training), persons acting on behalf of the Scottish Ministers in their capacity as an enforcement authority under that Act, officers of Revenue and Customs or constables as to—

(a) whether it maintains, or has maintained during the previous five years, a business relationship with any person; and

(b) the nature of that relationship.

(5) A credit or financial institution and an auction platform must communicate where relevant the policies and procedures which it establishes and maintains in accordance with this regulation to its branches and subsidiary undertakings which are located outside the United Kingdom.

(5A) A relevant person who is an issuer of electronic money must appoint an individual to monitor and manage compliance with, and the internal communication of, the policies and procedures relating to the matters referred to in paragraph (1)(a) to (e), and in particular to—

(a) identify any situations of higher risk of money laundering or terrorist financing;

(b) maintain a record of its policies and procedures, risk assessment and risk management including the application of such policies and procedures;

(c) apply measures to ensure that such policies and procedures are taken into account in all relevant functions including in the development of new products, dealing with new customers and in changes to business activities; and

(d) provide information to senior management about the operation and effectiveness of such policies and procedures at least annually.

(6) In this regulation—

"politically exposed person" has the same meaning as in regulation 14(4);

"subsidiary undertaking" has the same meaning as in regulation 15.

21 Training

A relevant person must take appropriate measures so that all relevant employees of his are—

(a) made aware of the law relating to money laundering and terrorist financing; and

(b) regularly given training in how to recognise and deal with transactions and other activities which may be related to money laundering or terrorist financing.

PART 4
SUPERVISION AND REGISTRATION

Interpretation

22 Interpretation

(1) In this Part—

"Annex I financial institution" means any undertaking which falls within regulation 3(3)(a) other than—

(a) [*repealed*];

(b) a money service business;

(c) an authorised person;

(d) a bill payment service provider; or

(e) a telecommunication, digital and IT payment service provider;

"recognised investment exchange" has the same meaning as in section 285 of the 2000 Act (exemption for recognised investment exchanges and clearing houses).

(2) [*repealed*]

Supervision

23 Supervisory authorities

(1) Subject to paragraph (2), the following bodies are supervisory authorities—

(a) the Authority is the supervisory authority for—

(i) credit and financial institutions which are authorised persons but not excluded money service businesses;

(ii) trust or company service providers which are authorised persons;

(iii) Annex I financial institutions;

(iv) electronic money institutions;

(v) auction platforms;

(vi) credit unions in Northern Ireland;

(vii) recognised investment exchanges;

(b) [*repealed*];

(c) each of the professional bodies listed in Schedule 3 is the supervisory authority for relevant persons who are regulated by it;

(d) the Commissioners are the supervisory authority for—

(i) high value dealers;

(ii) money service businesses which are not supervised by the Authority;

(iii) trust or company service providers which are not supervised by the Authority or one of the bodies listed in Schedule 3;

(iv) auditors, external accountants and tax advisers who are not supervised by one of the bodies listed in Schedule 3;

(v) bill payment service providers which are not supervised by the Authority;

(vi) telecommunication, digital and IT payment service providers which are not supervised by the Authority.

(e) the Gambling Commission is the supervisory authority for casinos;

(f) DETI is the supervisory authority for—

(i) [*repealed*];

(ii) insolvency practitioners authorised by it under article 351 of the Insolvency (Northern Ireland) Order 1989;

(g) the Secretary of State is the supervisory authority for insolvency practitioners authorised by him under section 393 of the Insolvency Act 1986 (grant, refusal and withdrawal of authorisation).

(2) Where under paragraph (1) there is more than one supervisory authority for a relevant person, the supervisory authorities may agree that one of them will act as the supervisory authority for that person.

(3) Where an agreement has been made under paragraph (2), the authority which has agreed to act as the supervisory authority must notify the relevant person or publish the agreement in such manner as it considers appropriate.

(4) Where no agreement has been made under paragraph (2), the supervisory authorities for a relevant person must cooperate in the performance of their functions under these Regulations.

(5) For the purposes of this regulation, a money service business is an "excluded money service business" if it is an authorised person who has permission under the 2000 Act which relates to or is connected with a contract of the kind mentioned in paragraph 23 or paragraph 23B of Schedule 2 to that Act (credit agreements and contracts for hire of goods) but does not have permission to carry on any other kind of regulated activity.

(6) Paragraph (5) must be read with—

(a) section 22 of the 2000 Act,

(b) any relevant order under that section, and

(c) Schedule 2 to that Act.

24 Duties of supervisory authorities

(1) A supervisory authority must effectively monitor the relevant persons for whom it is the supervisory authority and take necessary measures for the purpose of securing compliance by such persons with the requirements of these Regulations.

(1A) The Authority, when carrying out its supervisory functions in relation to an auction platform—

(a) must effectively monitor the auction platform's compliance with—

(i) the customer due diligence requirements of Articles 19 and 20(6) of the emission allowance auctioning regulation;

(ii) the monitoring and record keeping requirements of Article 54 of the emission allowance auctioning regulation; and

(iii) the notification requirements of Article 55(2) and (3) of the emission allowance auctioning regulation; and

(b) may monitor the auction platform's compliance with regulations 20 and 21 of these Regulations.

(2) A supervisory authority which, in the course of carrying out any of its functions under these Regulations, knows or suspects that a person is or has engaged in money laundering or terrorist financing must promptly inform the National Crime Agency.

(3) A disclosure made under paragraph (2) is not to be taken to breach any restriction, however imposed, on the disclosure of information.

(4) The functions of the Authority under these Regulations shall be treated for the purposes of Parts 1, 2 and 4 of Schedule 1ZA to the 2000 Act (the Financial Conduct Authority) as functions conferred on the Authority under that Act.

(5) The functions of the PRA under these Regulations shall be treated for the purposes of Parts 1, 2 and 4 of Schedule 1ZB to the 2000 Act (the Prudential Regulation Authority) as functions conferred on the PRA under that Act.

24A Disclosure by supervisory authorities

(1) A supervisory authority may disclose to another supervisory authority information it holds relevant to its functions under these Regulations, provided the disclosure is made for purposes connected with the effective exercise of the functions of either supervisory authority under these Regulations.

(2) Information disclosed to a supervisory authority under paragraph (1) may not be further disclosed by that authority, except—

- (a) in accordance with paragraph (1);
- (aa) by the Authority to the PRA, where the information concerns a PRA-authorised person or a person who has a qualifying relationship with a PRA-authorised person;
- (b) with a view to the institution of, or otherwise for the purposes of, any criminal or other enforcement proceedings; or
- (c) as otherwise required by law.

Registration of high value dealers, money service businesses and trust or company service providers

25 Duty to maintain registers

(1) The Commissioners must maintain registers of—

- (a) high value dealers;
- (b) money service businesses for which they are the supervisory authority;
- (c) trust or company service providers for which they are the supervisory authority;
- (d) bill payment service providers for which they are the supervisory authority; and
- (e) telecommunication, digital and IT payment service providers for which they are the supervisory authority.

(2) The Commissioners may keep the registers in any form they think fit.

(3) The Commissioners may publish or make available for public inspection all or part of a register maintained under this regulation.

26 Requirement to be registered

(1) A person in respect of whom the Commissioners are required to maintain a register under regulation 25 must not act as a—

- (a) high value dealer;
- (b) money service business;

(c) trust or company service provider;

(d) bill payment service provider; or

(e) telecommunication, digital and IT payment service provider,

unless he is included in the register.

(2) Paragraph (1) and regulation 29 are subject to the transitional provisions set out in regulation 50.

27 Applications for registration in a register maintained under regulation 25

(1) An applicant for registration in a register maintained under regulation 25 must make an application in such manner and provide such information as the Commissioners may specify.

(2) The information which the Commissioners may specify includes—

(a) the applicant's name and (if different) the name of the business;

(b) the nature of the business;

(c) the name of the nominated officer (if any);

(d) in relation to a money service business or trust or company service provider—

(i) the name of any person who effectively directs or will direct the business and any beneficial owner of the business; and

(ii) information needed by the Commissioners to decide whether they must refuse the application pursuant to regulation 28.

(3) At any time after receiving an application and before determining it, the Commissioners may require the applicant to provide, within 21 days beginning with the date of being requested to do so, such further information as they reasonably consider necessary to enable them to determine the application.

(4) If at any time after the applicant has provided the Commissioners with any information under paragraph (1) or (3)—

(a) there is a material change affecting any matter contained in that information; or

(b) it becomes apparent to that person that the information contains a significant inaccuracy,

he must provide the Commissioners with details of the change or, as the case may be, a correction of the inaccuracy within 30 days beginning with the date of the occurrence of the change (or the discovery of the inaccuracy) or within such later time as may be agreed with the Commissioners.

(5) The obligation in paragraph (4) applies also to material changes or significant inaccuracies affecting any matter contained in any supplementary information provided pursuant to that paragraph.

(6) Any information to be provided to the Commissioners under this regulation must be in such form or verified in such manner as they may specify.

28 Fit and proper test

(1) The Commissioners must refuse to register an applicant as a money service business or trust or company service provider if they are satisfied that—

(a) the applicant;

(b) a person who effectively directs, or will effectively direct, the business or service provider;

(c) a beneficial owner of the business or service provider; or

(d) the nominated officer of the business or service provider,

is not a fit and proper person with regard to the risk of money laundering or terrorist financing.

(2) [*Repealed*]

(3) [*Repealed*]

29 Determination of applications under regulation 27

(1) Subject to regulation 28, the Commissioners may refuse to register an applicant for registration in a register maintained under regulation 25 only if—

(a) any requirement of, or imposed under, regulation 27 has not been complied with;

(b) it appears to the Commissioners that any information provided pursuant to regulation 27 is false or misleading in a material particular; or

(c) the applicant has failed to pay a charge imposed by them under regulation 35(1).

(2) The Commissioners must within 45 days beginning either with the date on which they receive the application or, where applicable, with the date on which they receive any further information required under regulation 27(3), give the applicant notice of—

(a) their decision to register the applicant; or

(b) the following matters—

(i) their decision not to register the applicant;

(ii) the reasons for their decision;

(iii) the right to a review under regulation 43A; and

(iv) the right to appeal under regulation 43.

(3) The Commissioners must, as soon as practicable after deciding to register a person, include him in the relevant register.

30 Cancellation of registration in a register maintained under regulation 25

(1) The Commissioners must cancel the registration of a money service business or trust or company service provider in a register maintained under regulation 25(1) if, at any time after registration, they are satisfied that he or any person mentioned in regulation 28(1)(b), (c) or (d) is not a fit and proper person within the meaning of regulation 28.

(2) The Commissioners may cancel a person's registration in a register maintained by them under regulation 25 if, at any time after registration—

(a) it appears to them that any condition in regulation 29(1) is met; or

(b) the person has failed to comply with any requirement of a notice given under regulation 37.

(2A) The Commissioners may cancel the registration of a money service business in a register maintained under regulation 25(1)(b) where the money service business—

(a) is providing a payment service in the United Kingdom, or is purporting to do so;

(b) is not included in the register of payment service providers maintained by the Authority under regulation 4(1) of the Payment Service Regulations 2009; and

(c) is not a person mentioned in paragraphs (c) to (h) of the definition of a payment service provider in regulation 2(1) of the Payment Services Regulations 2009, or a person to whom regulation 3) or 121 of those Regulations applies.

(3) Where the Commissioners decide to cancel a person's registration they must give him notice of—

(a) their decision and, subject to paragraph (4), the date from which the cancellation takes effect;

(b) the reasons for their decision;

(c) the right to a review under regulation 43A; and

(d) the right to appeal under regulation 43.

(4) If the Commissioners—

(a) consider that the interests of the public require the cancellation of a person's registration to have immediate effect; and

(b) include a statement to that effect and the reasons for it in the notice given under paragraph (3),

the cancellation takes effect when the notice is given to the person.

Requirement to inform the authority

31 Requirement on authorised person to inform the Authority

(1) An authorised person whose supervisory authority is the Authority must, before acting as a money service business or a trust or company service provider or within 28 days of so doing, inform the Authority that he intends, or has begun, to act as such.

(2) Paragraph (1) does not apply to an authorised person who—

(a) immediately before 15th December 2007 was acting as a money service business or a trust or company service provider and continues to act as such after that date; and

(b) before 15th January 2008 informs the Financial Services Authority that he is or was acting as such.

(3) Where an authorised person whose supervisory authority is the Authority ceases to act as a money service business or a trust or company service provider, he must immediately inform the Authority.

(4) Any requirement imposed by this regulation is to be treated as if it were a requirement imposed by or under the 2000 Act.

(5) Any information to be provided to the Authority under this regulation must be in such form or verified in such manner as it may specify.

Registration of Annex I financial institutions, estate agents etc

32 Power to maintain registers

(1) The supervisory authorities mentioned in paragraph (2), (3) or (4) may, in order to fulfil their duties under regulation 24, maintain a register under this regulation.

(2) The Authority may maintain a register of Annex I financial institutions.

(3) [*repealed*]

(4) The Commissioners may maintain registers of—

(a) auditors;

(b) external accountants; and

(c) tax advisers,

who are not supervised by the Secretary of State, DETI or any of the professional bodies listed in Schedule 3.

(5) Where a supervisory authority decides to maintain a register under this regulation, it must take reasonable steps to bring its decision to the attention of those relevant persons in respect of whom the register is to be established.

(6) A supervisory authority may keep a register under this regulation in any form it thinks fit.

(7) A supervisory authority may publish or make available to public inspection all or part of a register maintained by it under this regulation.

33 Requirement to be registered

Where a supervisory authority decides to maintain a register under regulation 32 in respect of any description of relevant persons and establishes a register for that purpose, a relevant person of that description may not carry on the business or profession in question for a period of more than six months beginning on the date on which the supervisory authority establishes the register unless he is included in the register.

34 Applications for and cancellation of registration in a register maintained under regulation 32

(1) Regulations 27, 29 (with the omission of the words "Subject to regulation 28" in regulation 29(1)) and 30(2), (3) and (4) apply to registration in a register maintained by the Commissioners under regulation 32 as they apply to registration in a register maintained under regulation 25.

(2) Regulation 27 applies to registration in a register maintained by the Authority under regulation 32 as it applies to registration in a register maintained under regulation 25 and, for this purpose, references to the Commissioners are to be treated as references to the Authority.

(3) The Authority may refuse to register an applicant for registration in a register maintained under regulation 32 only if—

(a) any requirement of, or imposed under, regulation 27 has not been complied with;

(b) it appears to the Authority that any information provided pursuant to regulation 27 is false or misleading in a material particular; or

(c) the applicant has failed to pay a charge imposed by the Authority under regulation 35(1).

(4) The Authority must, within 45 days beginning either with the date on which it receives an application or, where applicable, with the date on which it receives any further information required under regulation 27(3), give the applicant notice of—

(a) its decision to register the applicant; or

(b) the following matters—

(i) that it is minded not to register the applicant;

(ii) the reasons for being minded not to register him; and

(iii) the right to make representations to it within a specified period (which may not be less than 28 days).

(5) The Authority must then decide, within a reasonable period, whether to register the applicant and it must give the applicant notice of—

(a) its decision to register the applicant; or

(b) the following matters—

(i) its decision not to register the applicant;

(ii) the reasons for its decision; and

(iii) the right to appeal under regulation 44(1)(b).

(6) The Authority must, as soon as reasonably practicable after deciding to register a person, include him in the relevant register.

(7) The Authority may cancel a person's registration in a register maintained by them under regulation 32 if, at any time after registration—

(a) it appears to them that any condition in paragraph (3) is met; or

(b) the person has failed to comply with any requirement of a notice given under regulation 37.

(8) Where the Authority proposes to cancel a person's registration, it must give him notice of—

(a) its proposal to cancel his registration;

(b) the reasons for the proposed cancellation; and

(c) the right to make representations to it within a specified period (which may not be less than 28 days).

(9) The Authority must then decide, within a reasonable period, whether to cancel the person's registration and it must give him notice of—

(a) its decision not to cancel his registration; or

(b) the following matters—

(i) its decision to cancel his registration and, subject to paragraph (10), the date from which cancellation takes effect;

(ii) the reasons for its decision; and

(iii) the right to appeal under regulation 44(1)(b).

(10) If the Authority—

(a) considers that the interests of the public require the cancellation of a person's registration to have immediate effect; and

(b) includes a statement to that effect and the reasons for it in the notice given under paragraph (9)(b),

the cancellation takes effect when the notice is given to the person.

(11) In paragraphs (3) and (4), references to regulation 27 are to be treated as references to that paragraph as applied by paragraph (2) of this regulation.

Financial provisions

35 Costs of supervision

(1) The Authority and the Commissioners may impose charges—

(a) on applicants for registration;

(b) on relevant persons supervised by them.

(2) Charges levied under paragraph (1) must not exceed such amount as the Authority or the Commissioners (as the case may be) consider will enable them to meet any expenses reasonably incurred by them in carrying out their functions under these Regulations or for any incidental purpose.

(3) Without prejudice to the generality of paragraph (2), a charge may be levied in respect of each of the premises at which a person carries on (or proposes to carry on) business.

(4) The Authority must pay to the Treasury any amounts received by the Financial Services Authority during the financial year beginning with 1st April 2012 year by way of penalties imposed under regulation 42 after deducting any amounts the Financial Services Authority has, prior to 1st April 2013, applied towards expenses incurred by it in carrying out its functions under these Regulations or for any incidental purpose.

(4A) The Authority must in respect of the financial year beginning with 1st April 2013 and each subsequent financial year pay to the Treasury any amounts received by it during the year by way of penalties imposed under regulation 42.

(4B) The Treasury may give directions to the Authority as to how the Authority is to comply with its duties under paragraphs (4) and (4A).

(4C) The directions may in particular—

(a) specify the time when any payment is required to be made to the Treasury, and

(b) require the Authority to provide the Treasury at specified times with information relating to penalties that the Authority has imposed under regulation 42.

(4D) The Treasury must pay into the Consolidated Fund any sums received by them under this regulation.

(5) In paragraph (2), "expenses" in relation to the Authority includes expenses incurred by a local weights and measures authority or DETI pursuant to arrangements made for the purposes of these Regulations with the Authority—

(a) by or on behalf of the authority; or

(b) by DETI.

PART 5
ENFORCEMENT

Powers of designated authorities

36 Interpretation

In this Part—

"designated authority" means—

(a) the Authority; and

(b) the Commissioners;

(c) [*repealed*]

(d) [*repealed*]

"officer", except in regulations 40(3), 41 and 47 means—

(a) an officer of the Authority, including a member of the Authority's staff or an agent of the Authority;

(b) an officer of Revenue and Customs; or

(c) [*repealed*]

(d) a relevant officer;

(e) [*repealed*]

"recorded information" includes information recorded in any form and any document of any nature;

"relevant officer" means—

(a) in Great Britain, an officer of a local weights and measures authority;

(b) in Northern Ireland, an officer of DETI acting pursuant to arrangements made with the Authority for the purposes of these Regulations.

37 Power to require information from, and attendance of, relevant and connected persons

(1) An officer may, by notice to a relevant person or to a person connected with a relevant person, require the relevant person or the connected person, as the case may be—

(a) to provide such information as may be specified in the notice;

(b) to produce such recorded information as may be so specified; or

(c) to attend before an officer at a time and place specified in the notice and answer questions.

(2) For the purposes of paragraph (1)—

(a) "relevant person" includes a person whom a designated authority believes, or has reasonable grounds to suspect, is or has at any time been a relevant person; and

(b) a person is connected with a relevant person if the person is, or has at any time been, in relation to the relevant person, a person listed in Schedule 4 to these Regulations.

(3) An officer may exercise powers under this regulation only if the information sought to be obtained as a result is reasonably required in connection with the exercise by the designated authority for whom he acts of its functions under these Regulations.

(4) Where an officer requires information to be provided or produced pursuant to paragraph (1)(a) or (b)—

(a) the notice must set out the reasons why the officer requires the information to be provided or produced; and

(b) such information must be provided or produced—

(i) before the end of such reasonable period as may be specified in the notice; and

(ii) at such place as may be so specified.

(5) In relation to information recorded otherwise than in legible form, the power to require production of it includes a power to require the production of a copy of it in legible form or in a form from which it can readily be produced in visible and legible form.

(6) The production of a document does not affect any lien which a person has on the document.

(7) A person may not be required under this regulation to provide or produce information or to answer questions which he would be entitled to refuse to provide, produce or answer on grounds of legal professional privilege in proceedings in the High Court, except that a lawyer may be required to provide the name and address of his client.

(8) Subject to paragraphs (9) and (10), a statement made by a person in compliance with a requirement imposed on him under paragraph (1)(c) is admissible in evidence in any proceedings, so long as it also complies with any requirements governing the admissibility of evidence in the circumstances in question.

(9) In criminal proceedings in which a person is charged with an offence to which this paragraph applies—

(a) no evidence relating to the statement may be adduced; and

(b) no question relating to it may be asked,

by or on behalf of the prosecution unless evidence relating to it is adduced, or a question relating to it is asked, in the proceedings by or on behalf of that person.

(10) Paragraph (9) applies to any offence other than one under—

(a) section 5 of the Perjury Act 1911 (false statements without oath);

(b) section 44(2) of the Criminal Law (Consolidation) (Scotland) Act 1995 (false statements and declarations); or

(c) Article 10 of the Perjury (Northern Ireland) Order 1979 (false unsworn statements).

(11) In the application of this regulation to Scotland, the reference in paragraph (7) to—

(a) proceedings in the High Court is to be read as a reference to legal proceedings generally; and

(b) an entitlement on grounds of legal professional privilege is to be read as a reference to an entitlement on the grounds of confidentiality of communications—

(i) between a professional legal adviser and his client; or

(ii) made in connection with or in contemplation of legal proceedings and for the purposes of those proceedings.

38 Entry, inspection without a warrant etc

(1) Where an officer has reasonable cause to believe that any premises are being used by a relevant person in connection with his business or professional activities, he may on producing evidence of his authority at any reasonable time—

(a) enter the premises;

(b) inspect the premises;

(c) observe the carrying on of business or professional activities by the relevant person;

(d) inspect any recorded information found on the premises;

(e) require any person on the premises to provide an explanation of any recorded information or to state where it may be found;

(f) in the case of a money service business or a high value dealer, inspect any cash found on the premises.

(2) An officer may take copies of, or make extracts from, any recorded information found under paragraph (1).

(3) Paragraphs (1)(d) and (e) and (2) do not apply to recorded information which the relevant person would be entitled to refuse to disclose on grounds of legal professional privilege in proceedings in the High Court, except that a lawyer may be required to provide the name and address of his client and, for this purpose, regulation 37(11) applies to this paragraph as it applies to regulation 37(7).

(4) An officer may exercise powers under this regulation only if the information sought to be obtained as a result is reasonably required in connection with the exercise by the designated authority for whom he acts of its functions under these Regulations.

(5) In this regulation, "premises" means any premises other than premises used only as a dwelling.

39 Entry to premises under warrant

(1) A justice may issue a warrant under this paragraph if satisfied on information on oath given by an officer that there are reasonable grounds for believing that the first, second or third set of conditions is satisfied.

(2) The first set of conditions is—

(a) that there is on the premises specified in the warrant recorded information in relation to which a requirement could be imposed under regulation 37(1)(b); and

(b) that if such a requirement were to be imposed—

(i) it would not be complied with; or

(ii) the recorded information to which it relates would be removed, tampered with or destroyed.

(3) The second set of conditions is—

(a) that a person on whom a requirement has been imposed under regulation 37(1)(b) has failed (wholly or in part) to comply with it; and

(b) that there is on the premises specified in the warrant recorded information which has been required to be produced.

(4) The third set of conditions is—

(a) that an officer has been obstructed in the exercise of a power under regulation 38; and

(b) that there is on the premises specified in the warrant recorded information or cash which could be inspected under regulation 38(1)(d) or (f).

(5) A justice may issue a warrant under this paragraph if satisfied on information on oath given by an officer that there are reasonable grounds for suspecting that—

(a) an offence under these Regulations has been, is being or is about to be committed by a relevant person; and

(b) there is on the premises specified in the warrant recorded information relevant to whether that offence has been, or is being or is about to be committed.

(6) A warrant issued under this regulation shall authorise an officer—

(a) to enter the premises specified in the warrant;

(b) to search the premises and take possession of any recorded information or anything appearing to be recorded information specified in the warrant or to take, in relation to any such recorded information, any other steps which may appear to be necessary for preserving it or preventing interference with it;

(c) to take copies of, or extracts from, any recorded information specified in the warrant;

(d) to require any person on the premises to provide an explanation of any recorded information appearing to be of the kind specified in the warrant or to state where it may be found;

(e) to use such force as may reasonably be necessary.

(7) Where a warrant is issued by a justice under paragraph (1) or (5) on the basis of information on oath given by an officer of the Authority, for "an officer" in paragraph (6) substitute "a constable".

(8) In paragraphs (1), (5) and (7), "justice" means—

(a) in relation to England and Wales, a justice of the peace;

(b) in relation to Scotland, a justice within the meaning of section 307 of the Criminal Procedure (Scotland) Act 1995 (interpretation);

(c) in relation to Northern Ireland, a lay magistrate.

(9) In the application of this regulation to Scotland, the references in paragraphs (1), (5) and (7) to information on oath are to be read as references to evidence on oath.

40 Failure to comply with information requirement

(1) If, on an application made by—

(a) a designated authority; or

(b) a local weights and measures authority or DETI pursuant to arrangements made with the Authority—

(i) by or on behalf of the authority; or

(ii) by DETI,

it appears to the court that a person (the "information defaulter") has failed to do something that he was required to do under regulation 37(1), the court may make an order under this regulation.

(2) An order under this regulation may require the information defaulter—

(a) to do the thing that he failed to do within such period as may be specified in the order;

(b) otherwise to take such steps to remedy the consequences of the failure as may be so specified.

(3) If the information defaulter is a body corporate, a partnership or an unincorporated body of persons which is not a partnership, the order may require any officer of the body corporate, partnership or body, who is (wholly or partly) responsible for the failure to meet such costs of the application as are specified in the order.

(4) In this regulation, "court" means—

(a) in England and Wales and Northern Ireland, the High Court or the county court;

(b) in Scotland, the Court of Session or the sheriff court.

41 Powers of relevant officers

(1) A relevant officer may only exercise powers under regulations 37 to 39 pursuant to arrangements made with the Authority—

(a) by or on behalf of the local weights and measures authority of which he is an officer ("his authority"); or

(b) by DETI.

(2) Anything done or omitted to be done by, or in relation to, a relevant officer in the exercise or purported exercise of a power in this Part shall be treated for all purposes as having been done or omitted to be done by, or in relation to, an officer of the Authority.

(3) Paragraph (2) does not apply for the purposes of any criminal proceedings brought against the relevant officer, his authority, DETI or the Authority, in respect of anything done or omitted to be done by the officer.

(4) A relevant officer shall not disclose to any person other than the Authority and his authority or, as the case may be, DETI information obtained by him in the exercise of such powers unless—

(a) he has the approval of the Authority to do so; or

(b) he is under a duty to make the disclosure.

Civil penalties, review and appeals

42 Power to impose civil penalties

(1) A designated authority may impose a penalty of such amount as it considers appropriate on a person (except an auction platform) who fails to comply with any requirement in regulation 7(1), (2) or (3), 8(1) or (3), 9(2), 10(1), 11(1), 14(1), 15(1) or (2), 16(1), (2), (3) or (4), 19(1), (4), (5) or (6), 20(1), (4) or (5), 21, 26, 27(4) or 33.

(1A) A designated authority may impose a penalty of such amount as it considers appropriate on an auction platform which fails to comply with–

(a) the customer due diligence requirements of Article 19 or 20(6) of the emission allowance auctioning regulation;

(b) the monitoring and record keeping requirements of Article 54 of the emission allowance auctioning regulation; or

(c) regulation 20(1), (4) or (5) or 21 of these Regulations;

(1B) A designated authority may impose a penalty of such amount as it considers appropriate on a person who fails to comply with any requirement of a notice given under regulation 37(1).

(1C) In paragraphs (1), (1A) and (1B), "appropriate" means effective, proportionate and dissuasive.

(2) The designated authority must not impose a penalty on a person under paragraph (1), (1A) or (1B) where there are reasonable grounds for it to be satisfied that the person took all reasonable steps and exercised all due diligence to ensure that the requirement would be complied with.

(3) In deciding whether a person has failed to comply with a requirement of these Regulations, the designated authority must consider whether he followed any relevant guidance which was at the time—

(a) issued by a supervisory authority or any other appropriate body;

(b) approved by the Treasury; and

(c) published in a manner approved by the Treasury as suitable in their opinion to bring the guidance to the attention of persons likely to be affected by it.

(4) In paragraph (3), an "appropriate body" means any body which regulates or is representative of any trade, profession, business or employment carried on by the person.

(4A) Where the Authority proposes to impose a penalty under this regulation on a PRA-authorised person or on a person who has a qualifying relationship with a PRA-authorised person, it must consult the PRA.

(5) Where the Commissioners decide to impose a penalty under this regulation, they must give the person notice of—

(a) their decision to impose the penalty and its amount;

(b) the reasons for imposing the penalty;

(c) the right to a review under regulation 43A; and

(d) the right to appeal under regulation 43.

(6) Where the Authority or DETI proposes to impose a penalty under this regulation, it must give the person notice of—

(a) its proposal to impose the penalty and the proposed amount;

(b) the reasons for imposing the penalty; and

(c) the right to make representations to it within a specified period (which may not be less than 28 days).

(7) The Authority or DETI, as the case may be, must then decide, within a reasonable period, whether to impose a penalty under this regulation and it must give the person notice of—

(a) its decision not to impose a penalty; or

(b) the following matters—

(i) its decision to impose a penalty and the amount;

(ii) the reasons for its decision; and

(iii) the right to appeal under regulation 44(1)(b).

(8) A penalty imposed under this regulation is payable to the designated authority which imposes it.

43 Appeals against decisions of the Commissioners

(1) This regulation applies to decisions of the Commissioners made under—

(za) regulation 28, to the effect that a person is not a fit and proper person;

(a) regulation 29, to refuse to register an applicant;

(b) regulation 30, to cancel the registration of a registered person; and

(c) regulation 42, to impose a penalty.

(2) Any person who is the subject of a decision to which this regulation applies may appeal to the tribunal in accordance with regulation 43F.

(3) The provisions of Part 5 of the Value Added Tax Act 1994 (appeals), subject to the modifications set out in paragraph 1 of Schedule 5 to these Regulations, apply in respect of appeals to a tribunal made under this regulation as they apply in respect of appeals made to the tribunal under section 83 (appeals) of that Act.

(4) A tribunal hearing an appeal under paragraph (2) has the power to—

(a) quash or vary any decision of the supervisory authority, including the power to reduce any penalty to such amount (including nil) as it thinks proper, and

(b) substitute its own decision for any decision quashed on appeal.

(5) The modifications in Schedule 5 have effect for the purposes of appeals made under this regulation.

(6) For the purposes of appeals under this regulation, the meaning of "tribunal" is as defined in section 82 of the Value Added Tax Act 1994.

43A Offer of review

(1) The Commissioners must offer a person (P) a review of a decision that has been notified to P if an appeal lies under regulation 43 in respect of the decision.

(2) The offer of the review must be made by notice given to P at the same time as the decision is notified to P.

(3) This regulation does not apply to the notification of the conclusions of a review.

43B Review by the Commissioners

(1) The Commissioners must review a decision if—

(a) they have offered a review of the decision under regulation 43A, and

(b) P notifies the Commissioners accepting the offer within 30 days from the date of the document containing the notification of the offer.

(2) But P may not notify acceptance of the offer if P has already appealed to the tribunal under regulation 43F.

(3) The Commissioners shall not review a decision if P has appealed to the tribunal under regulation 43F in respect of the decision.

43C Extensions of time

(1) If under regulation 43A, the Commissioners have offered P a review of a decision, the Commissioners may within the relevant period notify P that the relevant period is extended.

(2) If notice is given the relevant period is extended to the end of 30 days from—

(a) the date of the notice, or

(b) any other date set out in the notice or a further notice.

(3) In this regulation "relevant period" means—

(a) the period of 30 days referred to in regulation 43B(1)(b), or

(b) if notice has been given under paragraph (1) that period as extended (or as most recently extended) in accordance with paragraph (2).

43D Review out of time

(1) This regulation applies if—

(a) the Commissioners have offered a review of a decision under regulation 43A, and

(b) P does not accept the offer within the time allowed under regulation 43B(1)(b) or 43C(2).

(2) The Commissioners must review the decision under regulation 43B if—

(a) after the time allowed, P notifies the Commissioners in writing requesting a review out of time,

(b) the Commissioners are satisfied that P had a reasonable excuse for not accepting the offer or requiring review within the time allowed, and

(c) the Commissioners are satisfied that P made the request without unreasonable delay after the excuse had ceased to apply.

(3) The Commissioners shall not review a decision if P has appealed to the tribunal under regulation 43F in respect of the decision.

43E Nature of review etc

(1) This regulation applies if the Commissioners are required to undertake a review under regulation 43B or 43D.

(2) The nature and extent of the review are to be such as appear appropriate to the Commissioners in the circumstances.

(3) For the purpose of paragraph (2), the Commissioners must, in particular, have regard to steps taken before the beginning of the review—

(a) by the Commissioners in reaching the decision, and

(b) by any person in seeking to resolve disagreement about the decision.

(4) The review must take account of any representations made by P at a stage which gives the Commissioners a reasonable opportunity to consider them.

(5) The review may conclude that the decision is to be—

(a) upheld,

(b) varied, or

(c) cancelled.

(6) The Commissioners must give P notice of the conclusions of the review and their reasoning within—

(a) a period of 45 days beginning with the relevant date, or

(b) such other period as the Commissioners and P may agree.

(7) In paragraph (6) "relevant date" means—

(a) the date the Commissioners received P's notification accepting the offer of a review (in a case falling within regulation 43A), or

(b) the date on which the Commissioners decided to undertake the review (in a case falling within regulation 43D).

(8) Where the Commissioners are required to undertake a review but do not give notice of the conclusions within the time period specified in paragraph (6), the review is to be treated as having concluded that the decision is upheld.

(9) If paragraph (8) applies, the Commissioners must notify P of the conclusion which the review is treated as having reached.

43F Bringing of appeals against decisions of the Commissioners

(1) An appeal under regulation 43 is to be made to the tribunal before—

(a) the end of the period of 30 days beginning with the date of the document notifying the decision to which the appeal relates, or

(b) if later, the end of the relevant period (within the meaning of regulation 43C).

(2) But that is subject to paragraphs (3) to (5).

(3) In a case where the Commissioners are required to undertake a review under regulation 43B—

(a) an appeal may not be made until the conclusion date, and

(b) any appeal is to be made within the period of 30 days beginning with the conclusion date.

(4) In a case where the Commissioners are requested to undertake a review in accordance with regulation 43D—

(a) an appeal may not be made—

(i) unless the Commissioners have notified P as to whether or not a review will be undertaken, and

(ii) if the Commissioners have notified P that a review will be undertaken, until the conclusion date;

(b) any appeal where sub-paragraph (a)(ii) applies is to be made within the period of 30 days beginning with the conclusion date;

(c) if the Commissioners have notified P that a review will not be undertaken, an appeal may be made only if the tribunal gives permission to do so.

(5) In a case where regulation 43E(8) applies, an appeal may be made at any time from the end of the period specified in regulation 43E(6) to the date 30 days after the conclusion date.

(6) An appeal may be made after the end of the period specified in paragraph (1), (3)(b), (4)(b) or (5) if the tribunal gives permission to do so.

(7) In this regulation "conclusion date" means the date of the document notifying the conclusions of the review.

44 Appeals

(1) A person may appeal from a decision by—

(a) [*repealed*]

(b) the Authority or DETI under regulation 34 or 42.

(2) An appeal from a decision by—

(a) [*repealed*]

(b) the Authority is to the Upper Tribunal;

(c) [*repealed*]

(d) DETI is to the High Court.

(3) [*repealed*]

(4) The provisions of Part 9 of the 2000 Act (hearings and appeals), subject to the modifications set out in paragraph 2 of Schedule 5, apply in respect of appeals to the Upper Tribunal made under this regulation as they apply in respect of references made to that Tribunal under that Act.

(5) [*repealed*]

(6) [*repealed*]

(7) [*repealed*]

(8) The modifications in Schedule 5 have effect for the purposes of appeals made under this regulation.

Criminal offences

45 Offences

(1) A person (except an auction platform) who fails to comply with any requirement in regulation 7(1), (2) or (3), 8(1) or (3), 9(2), 10(1), 11(1)(a), (b) or (c), 14(1), 15(1) or (2), 16(1), (2), (3) or (4), 19(1), (4), (5) or (6), 20(1), (4) or (5), 21, 26, 27(4) or 33 is guilty of an offence and liable—

(a) on summary conviction, to a fine not exceeding the statutory maximum;

(b) on conviction on indictment, to imprisonment for a term not exceeding two years, to a fine or to both.

(1A) An auction platform which fails to comply with the customer due diligence requirements of Article 19 or 20(6) of the emission allowance auctioning regulation, the monitoring and record keeping requirements of Article 54 of that regulation, or regulation 20(1), (4) or (5) or 21 of these Regulations, is guilty of an offence and liable—

(a) on summary conviction, to a fine not exceeding the statutory maximum;

(b) on conviction on indictment, to imprisonment for a term not exceeding two years, to a fine or to both.

(2) In deciding whether a person has committed an offence under paragraph (1) or (1A), the court must consider whether he followed any relevant guidance which was at the time—

(a) issued by a supervisory authority or any other appropriate body;

(b) approved by the Treasury; and

(c) published in a manner approved by the Treasury as suitable in their opinion to bring the guidance to the attention of persons likely to be affected by it.

(3) In paragraph (2), an "appropriate body" means any body which regulates or is representative of any trade, profession, business or employment carried on by the alleged offender.

(4) A person is not guilty of an offence under this regulation if he took all reasonable steps and exercised all due diligence to avoid committing the offence.

(5) Where a person is convicted of an offence under this regulation, he shall not also be liable to a penalty under regulation 42.

46 Prosecution of offences

(1) Proceedings for an offence under regulation 45 may be instituted by—

(a) order of the Commissioners;

(b) [*repealed*];

(c) a local weights and measures authority;

(d) DETI;

(e) the Director of Public Prosecutions; or

(f) the Director of Public Prosecutions for Northern Ireland.

(2) Proceedings for an offence under regulation 45 may be instituted only against a relevant person or, where such a person is a body corporate, a partnership or an unincorporated association, against any person who is liable to be proceeded against under regulation 47.

(3) Where proceedings under paragraph (1) are instituted by order of the Commissioners, the proceedings must be brought in the name of an officer of Revenue and Customs.

(4) [*repealed*]

(5) [*repealed*]

(6) A local weights and measures authority must, whenever the Authority requires, report in such form and with such particulars as the Authority requires on the exercise of its functions under these Regulations.

(7) Where the Commissioners investigate, or propose to investigate, any matter with a view to determining—

(a) whether there are grounds for believing that an offence under regulation 45 has been committed by any person; or

(b) whether such a person should be prosecuted for such an offence,

that matter is to be treated as an assigned matter within the meaning of section 1(1) of the Customs and Excise Management Act 1979.

(8) Paragraphs (1) and (3) to (6) do not extend to Scotland.

(9) In its application to the Commissioners acting in Scotland, paragraph (7)(b) shall be read as referring to the Commissioners determining whether to refer the matter to the Crown Office and Procurator Fiscal Service with a view to the Procurator Fiscal determining whether a person should be prosecuted for such an offence.

47 Offences by bodies corporate etc

(1) If an offence under regulation 45 committed by a body corporate is shown—

(a) to have been committed with the consent or the connivance of an officer of the body corporate; or

(b) to be attributable to any neglect on his part,

the officer as well as the body corporate is guilty of an offence and liable to be proceeded against and punished accordingly.

(2) If an offence under regulation 45 committed by a partnership is shown—

(a) to have been committed with the consent or the connivance of a partner; or

(b) to be attributable to any neglect on his part,

the partner as well as the partnership is guilty of an offence and liable to be proceeded against and punished accordingly.

(3) If an offence under regulation 45 committed by an unincorporated association (other than a partnership) is shown—

(a) to have been committed with the consent or the connivance of an officer of the association; or

(b) to be attributable to any neglect on his part,

that officer as well as the association is guilty of an offence and liable to be proceeded against and punished accordingly.

(4) If the affairs of a body corporate are managed by its members, paragraph (1) applies in relation to the acts and defaults of a member in connection with his functions of management as if he were a director of the body.

(5) Proceedings for an offence alleged to have been committed by a partnership or an unincorporated association must be brought in the name of the partnership or association (and not in that of its members).

(6) A fine imposed on the partnership or association on its conviction of an offence is to be paid out of the funds of the partnership or association.

(7) Rules of court relating to the service of documents are to have effect as if the partnership or association were a body corporate.

(8) In proceedings for an offence brought against the partnership or association—

(a) section 33 of the Criminal Justice Act 1925 (procedure on charge of offence against corporation) and Schedule 3 to the Magistrates' Courts Act 1980 (corporations) apply as they do in relation to a body corporate;

(b) section 70 (proceedings against bodies corporate) of the Criminal Procedure (Scotland) Act 1995 applies as it does in relation to a body corporate;

(c) section 18 of the Criminal Justice (Northern Ireland) Act 1945 (procedure on charge) and Schedule 4 to the Magistrates' Courts (Northern Ireland) Order 1981 (corporations) apply as they do in relation to a body corporate.

(9) In this regulation—

"officer"—

(a) in relation to a body corporate, means a director, manager, secretary, chief executive, member of the committee of management, or a person purporting to act in such a capacity; and

(b) in relation to an unincorporated association, means any officer of the association or any member of its governing body, or a person purporting to act in such capacity; and

"partner" includes a person purporting to act as a partner.

PART 6
MISCELLANEOUS

48 Recovery of charges and penalties through the court

Any charge or penalty imposed on a person by a supervisory authority under regulation 35(1) or 42(1) is a debt due from that person to the authority, and is recoverable accordingly.

49 Obligations on public authorities

(1) The following bodies and persons must, if they know or suspect or have reasonable grounds for knowing or suspecting that a person is or has engaged in money laundering or terrorist financing, as soon as reasonably practicable inform the National Crime Agency—

(a) the Auditor General for Scotland;

(b) the Auditor General for Wales;

(c) the Authority;

(d) the Bank of England;

(e) the Comptroller and Auditor General;

(f) the Comptroller and Auditor General for Northern Ireland;

(g) the Gambling Commission;

(h) [*repealed*]

(i) the Official Solicitor to the Supreme Court;

(j) the Pensions Regulator;

(ja) the PRA;

(k) the Public Trustee;

(l) the Secretary of State, in the exercise of his functions under enactments relating to companies and insolvency;

(m) the Treasury, in the exercise of their functions under the 2000 Act;

(n) the Treasury Solicitor;

(o) a designated professional body for the purposes of Part 20 of the 2000 Act (provision of financial services by members of the professions);

(p) a person or inspector appointed under section 65 (investigations on behalf of Authority) or 66 (inspections and special meetings) of the Friendly Societies Act 1992;

(q) an inspector appointed under section 49 of the Industrial and Provident Societies Act 1965 (appointment of inspectors) or section 18 of the Credit Unions Act 1979 (power to appoint inspector);

(r) an inspector appointed under section 431 (investigation of a company on its own application), 432 (other company investigations), 442 (power to investigate company ownership) or 446D (appointment of replacement inspectors) of the Companies Act 1985;

(s) a person or inspector appointed under section 55 (investigations on behalf of Authority) or 56 (inspections and special meetings) of the Building Societies Act 1986;

(t) a person appointed under section 167 (appointment of persons to carry out investigations), 168(3) or (5) (appointment of persons to carry out investigations in particular cases), 169(1)(b) (investigations to support overseas regulator) or 284 (power to investigate affairs of a scheme) of the 2000 Act, or under regulations made under section 262(2)(k) (open-ended investment companies) of that Act, to conduct an investigation; and

(u) a person authorised to require the production of documents under section 447 of the Companies Act 1985 (Secretary of State's power to require production of documents), Article 440 of the Companies (Northern Ireland) Order 1986 or section 84 of the Companies Act 1989 (exercise of powers by officer).

(2) A disclosure made under paragraph (1) is not to be taken to breach any restriction on the disclosure of information however imposed.

49A Disclosure by the Commissioners

(1) The Commissioners may disclose to the Authority information held in connection with their functions under these Regulations if the disclosure is made for the purpose of enabling or assisting the Authority to discharge any of its functions under the Payment Services Regulations 2009 or the Electronic Money Regulations 2011.

(2) Information disclosed to the Authority under subsection (1) may not be disclosed by the Authority or any person who receives the information directly or indirectly from the Authority except-—

(a) to, or in accordance with authority given by, the Commissioners;

(b) with a view to the institution of, or otherwise for the purposes of, any criminal proceedings;

(c) with a view to the institution of any other proceedings by the Authority, for the purposes of any such proceedings instituted by the Authority, or for the purposes of any reference to the Tribunal under the Payment Services Regulations 2009; or

(d) in the form of a summary or collection of information so framed as not to enable information relating to any particular person to be ascertained from it.

(3) Any person who discloses information in contravention of subsection (2) is guilty of an offence and liable—

(a) on summary conviction, to imprisonment for a term not exceeding three months, to a fine not exceeding the statutory maximum, or to both;

(b) on conviction on indictment, to imprisonment for a term not exceeding two years to a fine, or to both.

(4) It is a defence for a person charged with an offence under this regulation of disclosing information to prove that they reasonably believed

(a) that the disclosure was lawful; or

(b) that the information had already and lawfully been made available to the public.

50 Transitional provisions: requirement to be registered

(1) Regulation 26 does not apply to an existing money service business, an existing trust or company service provider, an existing high value dealer, an existing bill payment service provider or an existing telecommunication, digital and IT payment service provider until—

(a) where it has applied in accordance with regulation 27 before the specified date for registration in a register maintained under regulation 25(1) (a "new register")—

(i) the date it is included in a new register following the determination of its application by the Commissioners; or

(ii) where the Commissioners give it notice under regulation 29(2)(b) of their decision not to register it, the date on which the Commissioners state that the decision takes effect or, where a statement is included in accordance with paragraph (3)(b), the time at which the Commissioners give it such notice;

(b) in any other case, the specified date.

(2) The specified date is—

(a) in the case of an existing money service business, 1st February 2008;

(b) in the case of an existing trust or company service provider, 1st April 2008;

(c) in the case of an existing high value dealer, the first anniversary which falls on or after 1st January 2008 of the date of its registration in a register maintained under regulation 10 of the Money Laundering Regulations 2003.

(d) in the case of an existing bill payment service provider or an existing telecommunication, digital and IT payment service provider, 1st March 2010.

(3) In the case of an application for registration in a new register made before the specified date by an existing money service business, an existing trust or company service provider, an existing high value dealer, an existing bill payment service provider or an existing telecommunication, digital and IT payment service provider, the Commissioners must include in a notice given to it under regulation 29(2)(b)—

(a) the date on which their decision is to take effect; or

(b) if the Commissioners consider that the interests of the public require their decision to have immediate effect, a statement to that effect and the reasons for it.

(4) In the case of an application for registration in a new register made before the specified date by an existing money services business or an existing trust or company service provider, the Commissioners must give it a notice under regulation 29(2) by—

(a) in the case of an existing money service business, 1st June 2008;

(b) in the case of an existing trust or company service provider, 1st July 2008; or

(c) where applicable, 45 days beginning with the date on which they receive any further information required under regulation 27(3).

(5) In this regulation—

"existing bill payment service provider" and "existing telecommunication, digital and IT payment service provider" mean a bill payment service provider or a telecommunication, digital and IT payment service provider carrying on business in the United Kingdom immediately before 1st November 2009;

"existing money service business" and an "existing high value dealer" mean a money service business or a high value dealer which, immediately before 15th December 2007, was included in a register maintained under regulation 10 of the Money Laundering Regulations 2003;

"existing trust or company service provider" means a trust or company service provider carrying on business in the United Kingdom immediately before 15th December 2007.

51 Minor and consequential amendments

Schedule 6, which contains minor and consequential amendments to primary and secondary legislation, has effect.

Signatory text

Alan Campbell

Frank Roy

Two Lords Commissioners of Her Majesty's Treasury

24th July 2007

SCHEDULE 1
Activities Listed in Points 2 to 12, 14 and 15 of Annex 1 to the Capital Requirements Directive

Regulation 3(3)(a)

2 Lending including, inter alia: consumer credit, mortgage credit, factoring, with or without recourse, financing of commercial transactions (including forfeiting).

3 Financial leasing.

4 Payment services as defined in Article 4(3) of Directive 2007/64/EC of the European Parliament and of the Council of 13 November 2007 on payment services in the internal market.

5 Issuing and administering other means of payment (including travellers' cheques and bankers' drafts) insofar as this activity is not covered by point 4.

6 Guarantees and commitments.

7 Trading for own account or for account of customers in:

(a) money market instruments (cheques, bills, certificates of deposit, etc);

(b) foreign exchange;

(c) financial futures and options;

(d) exchange and interest-rate instruments; or

(e) transferable securities.

8 Participation in securities issues and the provision of services related to such issues.

9 Advice to undertakings on capital structure, industrial strategy and related questions and advice as well as services relating to mergers and the purchase of undertakings.

10 Money broking.

11 Portfolio management and advice.

12 Safekeeping and administration of securities.

14 Safe custody services.

15 Issuing electronic money.

SCHEDULE 2
Financial Activity, Simplified Due Diligence and Politically Exposed Persons

Regulations 4(1)(e) and (2),
13(6) and (8) and 14(5)

Financial activity on an occasional or very limited basis

1 For the purposes of regulation 4(1)(e) and (2), a person is to be considered as engaging in financial activity on an occasional or very limited basis if all the following conditions are fulfilled—

(a) the person's total annual turnover in respect of the financial activity does not exceed £64,000;

(b) the financial activity is limited in relation to any customer to no more than one transaction exceeding 1,000 euro, whether the transaction is carried out in a single operation, or a series of operations which appear to be linked;

(c) the financial activity does not exceed 5% of the person's total annual turnover;

(d) the financial activity is ancillary and directly related to the person's main activity;

(e) the financial activity is not the transmission or remittance of money (or any representation of monetary value) by any means;

(f) the person's main activity is not that of a person falling within regulation 3(1)(a) to (f) or (h);

(g) the financial activity is provided only to customers of the person's main activity and is not offered to the public.

Simplified due diligence

2 For the purposes of regulation 13(6), the conditions are—

(a) the authority has been entrusted with public functions pursuant to the Treaty on European Union, the Treaty on the Functioning of the European Union or EU secondary legislation;

(b) the authority's identity is publicly available, transparent and certain;

(c) the activities of the authority and its accounting practices are transparent;

(d) either the authority is accountable to an EU institution or to the authorities of an EEA state, or otherwise appropriate check and balance procedures exist ensuring control of the authority's activity.

3 For the purposes of regulation 13(8), the conditions are—

(a) the product has a written contractual base;

(b) any related transaction is carried out through an account of the customer with a credit institution which is subject to the money laundering directive or with a credit institution situated in a non-EEA state which imposes requirements equivalent to those laid down in that directive;

(c) the product or related transaction is not anonymous and its nature is such that it allows for the timely application of customer due diligence measures where there is a suspicion of money laundering or terrorist financing;

(d) the product is within the following maximum threshold—

  (i) in the case of insurance policies or savings products of a similar nature, the annual premium is no more than 1,000 euro or there is a single premium of no more than 2,500 euro;

(ii) in the case of products which are related to the financing of physical assets where the legal and beneficial title of the assets is not transferred to the customer until the termination of the contractual relationship (whether the transaction is carried out in a single operation or in several operations which appear to be linked), the annual payments do not exceed 15,000 euro;

(iii) in all other cases, the maximum threshold is 15,000 euro;

(e) the benefits of the product or related transaction cannot be realised for the benefit of third parties, except in the case of death, disablement, survival to a predetermined advanced age, or similar events;

(f) in the case of products or related transactions allowing for the investment of funds in financial assets or claims, including insurance or other kinds of contingent claims—

(i) the benefits of the product or related transaction are only realisable in the long term;

(ii) the product or related transaction cannot be used as collateral; and

(iii) during the contractual relationship, no accelerated payments are made, surrender clauses used or early termination takes place.

Politically exposed persons

4 (1) For the purposes of regulation 14(5)—

(a) individuals who are or have been entrusted with prominent public functions include the following—

(i) heads of state, heads of government, ministers and deputy or assistant ministers;

(ii) members of parliaments;

(iii) members of supreme courts, of constitutional courts or of other high-level judicial bodies whose decisions are not generally subject to further appeal, other than in exceptional circumstances;

(iv) members of courts of auditors or of the boards of central banks;

(v) ambassadors, chargés d'affaires and high-ranking officers in the armed forces; and

(vi) members of the administrative, management or supervisory bodies of state-owned enterprises;

(b) the categories set out in paragraphs (i) to (vi) of sub-paragraph (a) do not include middle-ranking or more junior officials;

(c) immediate family members include the following—

(i) a spouse;

(ii) a partner;

(iii) children and their spouses or partners; and

(iv) parents;

(d) persons known to be close associates include the following—

(i) any individual who is known to have joint beneficial ownership of a legal entity or legal arrangement, or any other close business relations, with a person referred to in regulation 14(5)(a); and

(ii) any individual who has sole beneficial ownership of a legal entity or legal arrangement which is known to have been set up for the benefit of a person referred to in regulation 14(5)(a).

(2) In paragraph (1)(c), "partner" means a person who is considered by his national law as equivalent to a spouse.

SCHEDULE 3
Professional Bodies

Regulations 17(2)(b), 23(1)(c) and 32(4)

PART 1

1 Association of Accounting Technicians

2 Association of Chartered Certified Accountants

3 Association of International Accountants

4 Association of Taxation Technicians

5 Chartered Institute of Management Accountants

6 Chartered Institute of Public Finance and Accountancy

7 Chartered Institute of Taxation

8 Council for Licensed Conveyancers

9 Faculty of Advocates

10 Faculty Office of the Archbishop of Canterbury

11 General Council of the Bar

12 General Council of the Bar of Northern Ireland

13 Insolvency Practitioners Association

14 Institute of Certified Bookkeepers

15 Institute of Chartered Accountants in England and Wales

16 Institute of Chartered Accountants in Ireland

17 Institute of Chartered Accountants of Scotland

18 Institute of Financial Accountants

19 International Association of Book-keepers

20 Law Society

21 Law Society of Northern Ireland

22 Law Society of Scotland

SCHEDULE 4
Connected Persons

Regulation 37(2)

Corporate bodies

1 If the relevant person is a body corporate ("BC"), a person who is or has been—

(a) an officer or manager of BC or of a parent undertaking of BC;

(b) an employee of BC;

(c) an agent of BC or of a parent undertaking of BC.

Partnerships

2 If the relevant person is a partnership, a person who is or has been a member, manager, employee or agent of the partnership.

Unincorporated associations

3 If the relevant person is an unincorporated association of persons which is not a partnership, a person who is or has been an officer, manager, employee or agent of the association.

Individuals

4 If the relevant person is an individual, a person who is or has been an employee or agent of that individual.

SCHEDULE 5
Modifications in Relation to Appeals

Regulation 44(8)

PART 1
PRIMARY LEGISLATION

The Value Added Tax Act 1994 (c 23)

1 Part 5 of the Value Added Tax Act 1994 (appeals) is modified by omitting sections 83A to 84, 85A and 85B.

The Financial Services and Markets Act 2000 (c 8)

2 Part 9 of the 2000 Act (hearings and appeals) is modified as follows—

(a) in the application of sections 133 to 133B to any appeal commenced before the coming into force of section 55 of the Consumer Credit Act 2006, for all the references to "the Authority", substitute "the Authority or the OFT (as the case may be)";

(aa) in section 133(7A), after paragraph (n), insert—

"(o) a decision to impose a penalty under regulation 42 of the Money Laundering Regulations 2007.

(b) [*repealed*]

(c) in section 133A omit subsections (1), (2), (3) and (5); and

(d) in section 133A(4) for "decision notice" in both places where it occurs substitute "notice under regulation 34(5) or (9) or 42(7) of the Money Laundering Regulations 2007".

PART 2

[repealed]

SCHEDULE 6
Minor and Consequential Amendments

Regulation 51

PART 1
PRIMARY LEGISLATION

The Value Added Tax Act 1994 (c 23)

1 In section 83 of the Value Added Tax Act 1994 (appeals), omit paragraph (zz).

The Northern Ireland Act 1998 (c 47)

2 In paragraph 25 of Schedule 3 to the Northern Ireland Act 1998 (reserved matters), for "2003" substitute "2007".

The Criminal Justice and Police Act 2001 (c 16)

3 In Part 1 of Schedule 1 to the Criminal Justice and Police Act 2001 (powers of seizure to which section 50 of the 2001 Act applies), after paragraph 73I insert—

"THE MONEY LAUNDERING REGULATIONS 2007

73J The power of seizure conferred by regulation 39(6) of the Money Laundering Regulations 2007 (entry to premises under warrant).".

PART 2
SECONDARY LEGISLATION

The Independent Qualified Conveyancers (**Scotland**) **Regulations 1997**

4 Regulation 28 of the Independent Qualified Conveyancers (Scotland) Regulations 1997 is revoked.

The Executry Practitioners (**Scotland**) **Regulations 1997**

5 Regulation 26 of the Executry Practitioners (Scotland) Regulations 1997 is revoked.

The Cross-Border Credit Transfers Regulations 1999

6 In regulation 12(2) of the Cross-Border Credit Transfers Regulations 1999, for "2003" substitute "2007".

The Terrorism Act 2000 (**Crown Servants and Regulators**) **Regulations 2001**

7 In regulation 2 of the Terrorism Act 2000 (Crown Servants and Regulators) Regulations 2001, in the definition of "relevant business", for "has the meaning given by regulation 2(2) of the Money Laundering Regulations 2003" substitute "means an activity carried on in the course of business by any of the persons listed in regulation 3(1)(a) to (h) of the Money Laundering Regulations 2007".

The Representation of the People (**England and Wales**) **Regulations 2001**

8 In regulation 114(3)(b) of the Representation of the People (England and Wales) Regulations 2001, for "2003" substitute "2007".

The Representation of the People (Scotland) Regulations 2001

9 In regulation 113(3)(b) of the Representation of the People (Scotland) Regulations 2001, for "2003" substitute "2007".

The Financial Services and Markets Act 2000 (Regulated Activities) Order 2001

10 In article 72E(9) of the Financial Services and Markets Act 2000 (Regulated Activities) Order 2001, for "2003" substitute "2007".

The Proceeds of Crime Act 2002 (Failure to Disclose Money Laundering: Specified Training) Order 2003

11 In article 2 of the Proceeds of Crime Act 2002 (Failure to Disclose Money Laundering: Specified Training) Order 2003, for "regulation 3(1)(c)(ii) of the Money Laundering Regulations 2003" substitute "regulation 21 of the Money Laundering Regulations 2007".

The Public Contracts (Scotland) Regulations 2006

12 In regulation 23(1)(f) of the Public Contracts (Scotland) Regulations 2006, for "2003" substitute "2007".

The Utilities Contracts (Scotland) Regulations 2006

13 In regulation 26(1)(f) of the Utilities Contracts (Scotland) Regulations 2006, for "2003" substitute "2007".

The Public Contracts Regulations 2006

14 In regulation 23(1)(e) of the Public Contracts Regulations 2006, for "2003" substitute "2007".

The Utilities Contracts Regulations 2006

15 In regulation 26(1)(e) of the Utilities Contracts Regulations 2006, for "2003" substitute "2007".

APPENDIX 9

SRA policy statement on publication of regulatory and disciplinary decisions

[Last updated July 2014.]

Publication of regulatory and disciplinary decisions

Introduction

1. The Solicitors Regulation Authority (SRA) publishes regulatory decisions when it considers it to be in the public interest to do so.
2. In developing this policy we have had regard to the principles of good regulation:
   - Proportionality
   - Accountability
   - Consistency
   - Transparency
   - Targeting
3. Publishing our regulatory decisions wherever possible is an important contribution to ensuring that what we do is transparent. It informs users of legal services, and helps others to hold us accountable by helping them to assess whether we are acting proportionately and consistently.

Decisions that may be published

4. It is not practicable to list all possible decisions that may or may not be published. In deciding whether a decision not listed in this paragraph should be disclosed, the SRA will apply the criteria set out below. Regulatory decisions that may be published include:
   - Decisions to impose fines and rebukes – in accordance with the SRA (Disciplinary Procedure) Rules in force from time to time;
   - The imposition of controls, such as conditions on practising certificates or on entities we have licensed when they are first imposed or materially varied (and continuing the current policy of disclosing conditions on enquiry);
   - The bringing of proceedings before the Solicitors Disciplinary Tribunal (SDT) once the Tribunal has certified a prima facie case. In exceptional cases, we may publish the fact of a referral to the SDP prior to certification by the SDT if we consider it is in the public interest for us to do so;
   - Regulatory Settlement Agreements unless otherwise stated in the Agreement;

APPENDIX 9

- Intervention decisions and the legal basis for the decision;
- Decisions to revoke recognition of entities we have licensed;
- Decisions to approve the employment of people who are subject to section 43 of the Solicitors Act 1974 or of struck off or suspended solicitors;
- Refusals to issue a practising certificate;
- Suspensions of practising certificate by way of bankruptcy or High Court Order.

5. The nature of the decision to publish in the public interest will vary depending on the decision. Publishing a rebuke or fine requires a statutory decision to publish and the circumstances are prescribed in the SRA (Disciplinary Proceedings) Rules 2011. In contrast, decisions to intervene have long been published as an essential part of informing clients that their law firm has been closed down. Similarly, bringing a case before the SDT, once a case has been certified, will lead to a public hearing, and controls, such as practising certificate conditions are already publicly available to telephone enquirers. Accordingly, whilst each decision in these circumstances will be taken on its own merits, it is expected that decisions will be published unless we consider that one or more of the factors at paragraph 9 below would make such publication inappropriate.

6. Decisions will not generally be published when they are the subject of an outstanding internal appeal or appeal to the High Court or to the SDT.

7. Intervention decisions and the legal basis for the decision will generally be published even if there is an application to the High Court for the intervention notice to be withdrawn.

Criteria for publication

8. Factors which support a decision to publish include:
   - The importance of transparency in the SRA's decision-making processes;
   - The importance of providing information about regulatory action against regulated persons to enable, for example:
     - Clients or prospective clients to make informed choices about whom to instruct;
     - Clients and others to decide whether behaviour of concern should be reported to the SRA;
   - The need to maintain public confidence in the provision of legal services by demonstrating what regulatory action is being or has been taken and why.
   - The circumstances leading to the regulatory or disciplinary decision are matters of legitimate public interest or arise from facts that may affect a number of clients or other persons or relate to the administration of justice.

9. Factors which support a decision not to publish include:
   - Potential damage to the underlying purpose of a Settlement or Issue Agreement, such as where substantial redress may be provided to clients or others but there is a risk of prejudicing the position of the solicitors or others in related litigation or potential claims;
   - Inability to publish without:
     - disclosing someone's confidential or legally privileged information;
     - disclosing someone's confidential medical condition or treatment;
     - prejudicing legal proceedings or legal, regulatory or disciplinary investigations;

  - a significant risk of breaching someone's rights under Article 8 of the European Convention on Human Rights.
- In all the circumstances the impact of publication on the regulated person would be disproportionate.

These factors are not exhaustive and do not prevent the SRA from taking into account other factors that it considers to be relevant.

10. Published information will usually be limited to a short statement of the decision with brief factual details such as the basis of the sanction imposed, the reasons for imposition of conditions, or the basis of a referral to the SDT. Regulatory Settlement Agreements will normally be published in full.

11. Decisions will normally be published promptly but we retain the discretion to publish them or parts of them at a later time. This may be necessary, for example, if an investigation or prosecution is sensitive, such as where there is a risk of prejudice to other proceedings or regulatory activity.

12. Other decision or information may be published if the SRA considers it in the public interest to do so. For example, in relation to an investigation giving rise to significant public concern, it may be in the public interest to disclose the fact that we are investigating how the investigation is progressing or its outcome, including that it has concluded without an adverse finding against the regulated person.

13. Information about internal decisions, such as the imposition of conditions which are not otherwise in the public domain will be removed from our website three years after publication unless we consider that there are public interest reasons not to do so. Disqualification decisions or referrals to the SDT that result in strike off or suspension will remain on the website until the period of the suspension has ended or a successful application is made for the disqualification, indefinite suspension or strike off to be lifted.

14. Decisions may be amended or removed from our website where we consider that publication is no longer necessary in the public interest. We will, for example, update the summary of allegations to be made at the SDT in a particular case when the SDT has accepted amendment or withdrawal and that means the summary is materially inaccurate.

NOTES:

1. Reference to "regulated person" includes solicitors, licensed and recognised bodies, recognised sole practitioners and all persons who may be affected by the SRA's decisions such as Registered European Lawyers, Registered Foreign Lawyers, employees, non-lawyer managers, authorised role holders and unadmitted persons subjected to investigation or application pursuant to section 43 of the Solicitors Act 1974.

2. Reference to "investigation" includes all disciplinary and regulatory applications, investigations and prosecutions.

3. Reference to "SRA" or "we" in this statement includes all those exercising delegated decision-making powers.

APPENDIX 10

Regulators' Code

Regulators' Code

This Code was laid before Parliament in accordance with section 23 of the Legislative and Regulatory Reform Act 2006 ("the Act"). Regulators whose functions are specified by order under section 24(2) of the Act must have regard to the Code when developing policies and operational procedures that guide their regulatory activities. Regulators must equally have regard to the Code when setting standards or giving guidance which will guide the regulatory activities of other regulators. If a regulator concludes, on the basis of material evidence, that a specific provision of the Code is either not applicable or is outweighed by another relevant consideration, the regulator is not bound to follow that provision, but should record that decision and the reasons for it.

1. Regulators should carry out their activities in a way that supports those they regulate to comply and grow

1.1 Regulators should avoid imposing unnecessary regulatory burdens through their regulatory activities[1] and should assess whether similar social, environmental and economic outcomes could be achieved by less burdensome means. Regulators should choose proportionate approaches to those they regulate, based on relevant factors including, for example, business size and capacity.

1.2 When designing and reviewing policies, operational procedures and practices, regulators should consider how they might support or enable economic growth for compliant businesses and other regulated entities[2], for example, by considering how they can best:

- understand and minimise negative economic impacts of their regulatory activities;
- minimising the costs of compliance for those they regulate;
- improve confidence in compliance for those they regulate, by providing greater certainty; and
- encourage and promote compliance.

1.3 Regulators should ensure that their officers have the necessary knowledge and skills to support those they regulate, including having an understanding of those they regulate that enables them to choose proportionate and effective approaches.

1.4 Regulators should ensure that their officers understand the statutory principles of good regulation[3] and of this Code, and how the regulator delivers its activities in accordance with them.

2. Regulators should provide simple and straightforward ways to engage with those they regulate and hear their views

2.1 Regulators should have mechanisms in place to engage those they regulate, citizens and others to offer views and contribute to the development of their policies and service standards. Before changing policies, practices or service standards, regulators should consider the impact on business and engage with business representatives.

2.2 In responding to non-compliance that they identify, regulators should clearly explain what the non-compliant item or activity is, the advice being given, actions required or decisions taken, and the reasons for these. Regulators should provide an opportunity for dialogue in relation to the advice, requirements or decisions, with a view to ensuring that they are acting in a way that is proportionate and consistent.

This paragraph does not apply where the regulator can demonstrate that immediate enforcement action is required to prevent or respond to a serious breach or where providing such an opportunity would be likely to defeat the purpose of the proposed enforcement action.

2.3 Regulators should provide an impartial and clearly explained route to appeal against a regulatory decision or a failure to act in accordance with this Code. Individual officers of the regulator who took the decision or action against which the appeal is being made should not be involved in considering the appeal. This route to appeal should be publicised to those who are regulated.

2.4 Regulators should provide a timely explanation in writing of any right to representation or right to appeal. This explanation should be in plain language and include practical information on the process involved.

2.5 Regulators should make available to those they regulate, clearly explained complaints procedures, allowing them to easily make a complaint about the conduct of the regulator.

2.6 Regulators should have a range of mechanisms to enable and regularly invite, receive and take on board customer feedback, including, for example, through customer satisfaction surveys of those they regulate[4].

3. Regulators should base their regulatory activities on risk

3.1 Regulators should take an evidence based approach to determining the priority risks in their area of responsibility, and should allocate resources where they would be most effective in addressing those priority risks.

3.2 Regulators should consider risk at every stage of their decision-making processes, including choosing the most appropriate type of intervention or way of working with those regulated; targeting checks on compliance; and when taking enforcement action.

3.3 Regulators designing a risk assessment framework[5], for their own use or for use by others, should have mechanisms in place to consult on the design with those affected, and to review it regularly.

3.4 Regulators, in making their assessment of risk, should recognise the compliance record of those they regulate, including using earned recognition approaches and should consider all available and relevant data on compliance, including evidence of relevant external verification.

3.5 Regulators should review the effectiveness of their chosen regulatory activities in delivering the desired outcomes and make any necessary adjustments accordingly.

4. Regulators should share information about compliance and risk

4.1 Regulators should collectively follow the principle of "collect once, use many times" when requesting information from those they regulate.

4.2 When the law allows, regulators should agree secure mechanisms to share information with each other about businesses and other bodies they regulate, to help target resources and activities and minimise duplication.

5. Regulators should ensure clear information, guidance and advice is available to help those they regulate meet their responsibilities to comply

5.1 Regulators should provide advice and guidance that is focused on assisting those they regulate to understand and meet their responsibilities. When providing advice and guidance, legal requirements should be distinguished from suggested good practice and the impact of the advice or guidance should be considered so that it does not impose unnecessary burdens in itself.

5.2 Regulators should publish guidance, and information in a clear, accessible, concise format, using media appropriate to the target audience and written in plain language for the audience.

5.3 Regulators should have mechanisms in place to consult those they regulate in relation to the guidance they produce to ensure that it meets their needs.

5.4 Regulators should seek to create an environment in which those they regulate have confidence in the advice they receive and feel able to seek advice without fear of triggering enforcement action.

5.5 In responding to requests for advice, a regulator's primary concerns should be to provide the advice necessary to support compliance, and to ensure that the advice can be relied on.

5.6 Regulators should have mechanisms to work collaboratively to assist those regulated by more than one regulator. Regulators should consider advice provided by other regulators and, where there is disagreement about the advice provided, this should be discussed with the other regulator to reach agreement.

6. Regulators should ensure that their approach to their regulatory activities is transparent

6.1 Regulators should publish a set of clear service standards, setting out what those they regulate should expect from them.

6.2 Regulators' published service standards should include clear information on:

a) how they communicate with those they regulate and how they can be contacted;

b) their approach to providing information, guidance and advice;

c) their approach to checks on compliance[6], including details of the risk assessment framework used to target those checks as well as protocols for their conduct, clearly setting out what those they regulate should expect;

d) their enforcement policy, explaining how they respond to non-compliance;

e) their fees and charges, if any. This information should clearly explain the basis on which these are calculated, and should include an explanation of whether compliance will affect fees and charges; and

f) how to comment or complain about the service provided and routes to appeal.

6.3 Information published to meet the provisions of this Code should be easily accessible, including being available at a single point[7] on the regulator's website that is clearly signposted, and it should be kept up to date.

6.4 Regulators should have mechanisms in place to ensure that their officers act in accordance with their published service standards, including their enforcement policy.

6.5 Regulators should publish, on a regular basis, details of their performance against their service standards, including feedback received from those they regulate, such as customer satisfaction surveys, and data relating to complaints about them and appeals against their decisions.

1 The term 'regulatory activities' refers to the whole range of regulatory options and interventions available to regulators.

2 The terms 'business or businesses' is used throughout this document to refer to businesses and other regulated entities.

3 The statutory principles of good regulation can be viewed in Part 2 (21) on page 12: http://www.legislation.gov.uk/ukpga/2006/51/pdfs/ukpga_20060051_en.pdf.

4 The Government will discuss with national regulators a common approach to surveys to support benchmarking of their performance.

5 The term 'risk assessment framework' encompasses any model, scheme, methodology or risk rating approach that is used to inform risk-based targeting of regulatory activities in relation to individual businesses or other regulated entities.
6 Including inspections, audit, monitoring and sampling visits, and test purchases.
7 This requirement may be satisfied by providing a single web page that includes links to information published elsewhere.

APPENDIX 11

Legal Ombudsman Scheme Rules

[The Legal Ombudsman Scheme Rules are reproduced with the kind permission of the Legal Ombudsman. For the latest updates to the material, please see www.legalombudsman.org.uk.]

[Last updated 1 February 2013]

Legal Ombudsman Scheme Rules

1 Introduction and definitions

Contents

1.1
- These scheme rules are about *complaints* made from 6 October 2010 to *authorised persons* including legal practitioners and others, authorised in England and Wales.
- They explain which *complaints* are covered by the *Legal Ombudsman* and how it will deal with them.
- This version includes amendments that apply to complaints referred to the Legal Ombudsman from 1 February 2013 (chapters 1 to 5) and from 1 April 2013 (chapter 6).

1.2 Parliament, in the *Act*:

- created the Legal Services Board (to oversee *Approved Regulators*) and the Office for Legal Complaints (to establish the *Legal Ombudsman*);
- gave the Lord Chancellor power to make orders, including orders modifying who would be able to bring a *complaint* to the *Legal Ombudsman*;
- gave the Legal Services Board power to set requirements for the rules of *Approved Regulators* about how *authorised persons* handle *complaints*[1] and cooperate with an *ombudsman*;[2] and
- gave the Office for Legal Complaints power to make rules affecting which *complaints* can be handled by the *Legal Ombudsman* and how those *complaints* will be handled.

1.3 These scheme rules include:

- a summary of relevant provisions in the *Act*, as modified by an order made by the Lord Chancellor (though it is the *Act* and the order themselves that count);
- a summary of requirements on complaint-handling made by the Legal Services Board under the powers given to it by the *Act*; and
- rules made by the Office for Legal Complaints under the powers given to it by the *Act*.

The endnotes identify the section of the *Act* that is being summarised, or under which an order, requirement or rule has been made; and which are the rules made by the Office of Legal Complaints for the Legal Ombudsman.

1.4 This book also includes some general guidance. There are six chapters –

1: Introduction and definitions:

- contents of this book;
- meaning of words that are underlined [italicised].

2: Who can complain about what:

- who can complain;
- what they can complain about.

3: What *authorised persons* must do:

- dealing with *complaints* themselves;
- cooperating with the *Legal Ombudsman*.

4: When *complaints* can be referred to the *Legal Ombudsman*:

- after complaining to the *authorised person*;
- time limit from act/omission;
- *ombudsman* extending time limits.

5: How the *Legal Ombudsman* deals with *complaints*:

- first contact;
- grounds for dismissal;
- referring a *complaint* to court;
- referring to another *complaints* scheme;
- related *complaints*;
- informal resolution and investigation;
- evidence;
- procedural time limits;
- hearings;
- determinations and awards by an *ombudsman*;
- acceptance/rejection of determinations;
- publication;
- enforcement.

6: Case fees payable by *authorised persons*.

Meaning of words that are underlined [italicised]

1.5 The *Act* means the Legal Services Act 2007.

1.6 *Complaint* means an oral or written expression of dissatisfaction which:

(a) alleges that the complainant has suffered (or may suffer) financial loss, distress, inconvenience or other detriment; and

(b) is covered by chapter two (who can complain about what).[3]

1.7 *Authorised person* means:

(a) someone authorised, in England and Wales, to carry out a *reserved legal activity*[4] at the time of the relevant act/omission or covered under section 129 of the *Act*,[5] including:

- alternative business structures (licensed under part 5 of the *Act*);
- barristers;
- costs lawyers;
- chartered legal executives;
- licensed conveyancers;
- notaries;
- patent attorneys;
- probate practitioners;
- registered European lawyers;
- solicitors;
- trade mark attorneys; and

(b) (under section 131 of the *Act*) includes:

- a business that is responsible for an act/omission of an employee; and
- a partnership that is responsible for an act/omission of a partner.[6]

1.8 *Approved Regulator* means a regulator approved under schedule 4 of the *Act*, including:

- the Association of Chartered Certified Accountants (for reserved probate activities);
- the Association of Costs Lawyers, through the Costs Lawyer Standards Board;
- the Bar Council, through the Bar Standards Board (for barristers);
- the Chartered Institute of Patent Attorneys, through the Intellectual Property Regulation Board;
- the Council for Licensed Conveyancers;
- the Institute of Chartered Accountants in Scotland (for reserved probate activities);
- the ILEX Professional Standards, through the Chartered Institute of Legal Executives;
- the Institute of Trade Mark Attorneys, through the Intellectual Property Regulation Board;
- the Law Society, through the Solicitors Regulation Authority;
- the Master of the Faculties (for notaries); and
- the Legal Services Board (but only for any alternative business structures it licenses directly).

1.9 *Legal Ombudsman* means the ombudsman scheme established by the Office for Legal Complaints.

1.10 *Ombudsman* means:

(a) any ombudsman from the *Legal Ombudsman*;[7] and

(b) any *Legal Ombudsman* staff member to whom an *ombudsman* has delegated the relevant functions (but an *ombudsman* cannot delegate the functions of determining a *complaint* or of dismissing or discontinuing it for any of the reasons under paragraph 5.7).[8]

1.11 *Party* includes:

(a) a complainant (covered by chapter two);

(b) an *authorised person* (covered by chapter two) against whom the *complaint* is made;

(c) an *authorised person* (covered by chapter five) whom an *ombudsman* treats as a joint respondent to a *complaint*.[9]

1.12 *Public body* means any government department, local authority or any other body constituted for the purposes of the public services, local government or the administration of justice.[10]

1.13 *Reserved legal activity* (as defined in schedule 2 of the *Act*) means:

(a) exercising a right of audience;

(b) conducting litigation;

(c) reserved instrument activities;

(d) probate activities;

(e) notarial activities; or

(f) administration of oaths.

2 Who can complain about what

Who can complain

2.1 A complainant must be one of the following:[11]

(a) an individual;

(b) a business or enterprise that was a micro-enterprise (European Union definition) when it referred the complaint to the *authorised person*;[12]

(c) a charity that had an annual income net of tax of less than £1 million when it referred the complaint to the *authorised person*;

(d) a club/association/organisation, the affairs of which are managed by its members/a committee/a committee of its members, that had an annual income net of tax of less than £1 million when it referred the complaint to the *authorised person*;

(e) a trustee of a trust that had an asset value of less than £1 million when it referred the complaint to the *authorised person*; or;

(f) a personal representative or beneficiary of the estate of a person who, before he/she died, had not referred the complaint to the *Legal Ombudsman*.

For (e) and (f) the condition is that the services to which the complaint relates were provided by the respondent to a person –

(a) who has subsequently died; and

(b) who had not by his or her death referred the complaint to the ombudsman scheme.

2.2 If a complainant who has referred a *complaint* to the *Legal Ombudsman* dies or is otherwise unable to act, the *complaint* can be continued by:[13]

(a) anyone authorised by law (for example:

- the executor of a complainant who has died; or
- someone with a lasting power of attorney from a complainant who is incapable); or

(b) the residuary beneficiaries of the estate of a complainant who has died.[14]

2.3 A complainant must not have been, at the time of the act/omission to which the *complaint* relates:

(a) a *public body* (or acting for a *public body*) in relation to the services complained about; or

(b) an *authorised person* who procured the services complained about on behalf of someone else.[15] [16]

2.4 For example, where the *complaint* is about a barrister who was instructed by a solicitor on behalf of a consumer, the consumer can complain to the *ombudsman* but the solicitor cannot.

2.5 A complainant can authorise someone else in writing (including an *authorised person*) to act for the complainant in pursuing a *complaint*, but the *Legal Ombudsman* remains free to contact the complainant direct where it considers that appropriate.[17]

What they can complain about

2.6 The *complaint* must relate to an act/omission by someone who was an *authorised person* at that time[18] but:

(a) an act/omission by an employee is usually treated also as an act/omission by their employer, whether or not the employer knew or approved;[19] and

(b) an act/omission by a partner is usually treated also as an act/omission by the partnership, unless the complainant knew (at the time of the act/omission) that the partner had no authority to act for the partnership.[20]

2.7 The act/omission does not have to:

(a) relate to a *reserved legal activity*;[21] nor

(b) be after the *Act* came into force[22] (but see the time limits in chapter four).

2.8 The *complaint* must relate to services which the *authorised person*:

(a) provided to the complainant; or

(b) provided to another *authorised person* who procured them on behalf of the complainant; or

(c) provided to (or as) a personal representative/trustee where the complainant is a beneficiary of the estate/trust;[23] or

(d) offered, or refused to provide, to the complainant.[24]

2.9 A *complaint* is not affected by any change in the membership of a partnership or other unincorporated body.[25]

2.10 Where *authorised person* A ceases to exist and B succeeds to the whole (or substantially the whole) of A's business:

(a) acts/omissions by A become acts/omissions of B;[26] and

(b) *complaints* already outstanding against A become *complaints* against B[27]

unless an *Ombudsman* decides that this is, in his/her opinion, not fair and reasonable in all the circumstances of the case.

3 What authorised persons must do

Dealing with complaints themselves

3.1 *Authorised persons* including legal practitioners and others must comply with their *Approved Regulator's* rules on handling *complaints*, including any requirements specified by the Legal Services Board.[28]

3.2 The Legal Services Board has required that:

(a) *authorised persons* tell all clients in writing at the time of engagement, or existing clients at the next appropriate opportunity that they can complain, how and to whom this can be done;

(b) this must include that they can complain to the *Legal Ombudsman* at the end of the *authorised person's* complaints process, the timeframe for doing so and full details of how to contact the *Legal Ombudsman*; and

(c) *authorised persons* tell all clients in writing at the end of the *authorised person's* complaints process that they can complain to the *Legal Ombudsman*, the timeframe for doing so and full details of how to contact the *Legal Ombudsman*.

3.3 The Legal Services Board expects that regulation of complaint-handling procedures by *Approved Regulators* will:

(a) give consumers confidence that:

- effective safeguards will be provided; and
- complaints will be dealt with comprehensively and swiftly, with appropriate redress where necessary;

(b) provide processes that are:

- convenient and easy to use (in particular for those that are vulnerable or have disabilities);
- transparent, clear, well-publicised, free and allow *complaints* to be made by any reasonable means;
- prompt and fair, with decisions based on sufficient investigation of the circumstances, and (where appropriate) offer a suitable remedy.

Cooperating with the Legal Ombudsman

3.4 *Authorised persons* must comply with their *Approved Regulator*'s rules on cooperating with an *ombudsman*, including any requirements specified by the Legal Services Board.[29]

4 When complaints can be referred to the Legal Ombudsman

After complaining to the authorised person

4.1 Ordinarily, a complainant cannot use the *Legal Ombudsman* unless the complainant has first used the *authorised person's* complaints procedure (referred to in chapter three).[30]

Time limit from authorised person's final response

4.2 But a complainant can use the *Legal Ombudsman* if:[31]

(a) the *complaint* has not been resolved to the complainant's satisfaction within eight weeks of being made to the *authorised person*; or

(b) an *ombudsman* considers that there are exceptional reasons to consider the *complaint* sooner, or without it having been made first to the *authorised person*; or

(c) where an *ombudsman* considers that in-house resolution is not possible due to irretrievable breakdown in the relationship between an *authorised person* and the person making the *complaint*.

4.3 For example, an *ombudsman* may decide that the *Legal Ombudsman* should consider the *complaint* where the authorised person has refused to consider it, or where delay would harm the complainant.

4.4 (a) This time limit applies only if the *authorised person's* written response to a *complaint* included prominently:

- an explanation that the *Legal Ombudsman* was available if the complainant remained dissatisfied;
- full contact details for the *Legal Ombudsman*; and
- a warning that the *complaint* must be referred to the *Legal Ombudsman* within six months of the date of the written response;

(b) If (but only if) the conditions in (a) are satisfied, a complainant must ordinarily refer the *complaint* to the *Legal Ombudsman* within six months of the date of that written response.

Time limit from act/omission

4.5 Ordinarily:

(a) the act or omission, or when the complainant should reasonably have known there was cause for complaints, must have been after 5 October 2010; and

(b) the complainant must refer the *complaint* to the *Legal Ombudsman* no later than:

– six years from the act/omission; or

– three years from when the complainant should reasonably have known there was cause for complaint.[32]

4.6 In relation to 4.5(b):

(a) where a complaint is referred by a personal representative or beneficiary of the estate of a person who, before he/she died, had not referred the complaint to the *Legal Ombudsman*, the period runs from when the deceased should reasonably have known there was cause for complaint; and

(b) when the complainant (or the deceased) should reasonably have known there was a cause for complaint will be assessed on the basis of the complainant's (or the deceased's) own knowledge, disregarding what the complainant (or the deceased) might have been told if he/she had sought advice.

Ombudsman extending time limits

4.7 If an *ombudsman* considers that there are exceptional circumstances, he/she may extend any of these time limits to the extent that he/she considers fair.[33]

4.8 For example, an *Ombudsman*:

(a) might extend a time limit if the complainant was prevented from meeting the time limit as a result of serious illness; and

(b) is likely to extend a time limit where the time limit had not expired when the complainant raised the *complaint* with the *authorised person*.

5 How the Legal Ombudsman will deal with complaints[34]

5.1 The *Legal Ombudsman* may require a complainant to complete its complaint form.[35]

5.2 In the case of a partnership (or former partnership), it is sufficient for the *Legal Ombudsman* to communicate with any partner (or former partner).[36]

First contact

5.3 Unless:

(a) the *authorised person* has already had eight weeks to consider the *complaint*; or

(b) the *authorised person* has already issued a written response to the *complaint*; or

(c) an *ombudsman* considers that there are exceptional reasons;

the *Legal Ombudsman* will:

(a) refer the *complaint* to the *authorised person*;

(b) notify the complainant; and

(c) explain why to both of them.[37]

5.4 If the *authorised person* claims that all or part of the *complaint*:

(a) is not covered by the Legal Ombudsman under chapter two; or

(b) is out-of-time under chapter four; or

(c) should be dismissed under paragraph 5.7;

an *ombudsman* will give all *parties* an opportunity to make representations before deciding.[38]

5.5 Otherwise, if an *ombudsman* considers that all or part of the *complaint*:

(a) may not be covered by the *Legal Ombudsman* under chapter two; or

(b) may be out-of-time under chapter four; or

(c) should be dismissed under paragraph 5.7;

the *ombudsman* will give the complainant an opportunity to make representations before deciding.[39]

5.6 The *ombudsman* will then give the complainant and the *authorised person* his/her decision and the reasons for it.[40]

Grounds for dismissing or discontinuing a complaint[41]

5.7 An *ombudsman* may (but does not have to) dismiss or discontinue all or part of a *complaint* if, in his/her opinion:

(a) it does not have any reasonable prospect of success, or is frivolous or vexatious; or

(b) the complainant has not suffered (and is unlikely to suffer) financial loss, distress, inconvenience or other detriment; or

(c) the *authorised person* has already offered fair and reasonable redress in relation to the circumstances alleged by the complainant and the offer is still open for acceptance; or

(d) the complainant has previously complained about the same issue to the *Legal Ombudsman* or a predecessor complaints scheme (unless the *ombudsman* considers that material new evidence, likely to affect the outcome, only became available to the complainant afterwards); or

(e) a comparable independent complaints (or costs-assessment) scheme or a court has already dealt with the same issue; or

(f) a comparable independent complaints (or costs-assessment) scheme or a court is dealing with the same issue, unless those proceedings are first stayed (by the agreement of all parties or by a court order) so that the *Legal Ombudsman* can deal with the issue; or

(g) it would be more suitable for the issue to be dealt with by a court, by arbitration or by another complaints (or costs-assessment) scheme;[42] or

(h) the issue concerns an *authorised person's* decision when exercising a discretion under a will or trust; or

(i) the issue concerns an *authorised person's* failure to consult a beneficiary before exercising a discretion under a will or trust, where there is no legal obligation to consult;

(j) the issue involves someone else who has not complained and the *ombudsman* considers that it would not be appropriate to deal with the issue without their consent; or

(k) it is not practicable to investigate the issue fairly because of the time which has elapsed since the act/omission; or

(l) the issue concerns an act/omission outside England and Wales and the circumstances do not have a sufficient connection with England and Wales;[43] or

(m) the *complaint* is about an *authorised person's* refusal to provide a service and the complainant has not produced evidence that the refusal was for other than legitimate or reasonable reasons; or

(n) there are other compelling reasons why it is inappropriate for the issue to be dealt with by the *Legal Ombudsman*.

Referring a complaint to court

5.8 Exceptionally (at the instance of an *ombudsman*) where the *ombudsman* considers that:

(a) resolution of a particular legal question is necessary in order to resolve a dispute; but

(b) it is not more suitable for the whole dispute to be dealt with by a court;

the *ombudsman* may (but does not have to) refer that legal question to court.[44]

5.9 Exceptionally, (at the instance of an *authorised person*) where:

(a) the *authorised person* requests, and also undertakes to pay the complainant's legal costs and disbursements on terms the *ombudsman* considers appropriate; and

(b) an *ombudsman* considers that the whole dispute would be more suitably dealt with by a court as a test case between the complainant and the *authorised person*;

the *ombudsman* may (but does not have to) dismiss the *complaint*, so that a court may consider it as a test case.[45]

5.10 By way of example only, in relation to a test case (at the instance of an *authorised person*) the *ombudsman* might require an undertaking in favour of the complainant that, if the complainant or the *authorised person* starts court proceedings against the other in respect of the *complaint* in any court in England and Wales within six months of the *complaint* being dismissed, the *authorised person* will:

(a) pay the complainant's reasonable costs and disbursements (to be assessed if not agreed on an indemnity basis);

(b) pay these in connection with the proceedings at first instance and also any subsequent appeal made by the *authorised person*; and

(c) make interim payments on account if and to the extent that it appears reasonable to do so.

5.11 Factors the *ombudsman* may take into account in considering whether to refer a legal question to court, or to dismiss a *complaint* so that it may be the subject of a test case in court, include (but are not limited to):

(a) any representations made by the *authorised person* or the complainant;

(b) the stage already reached in consideration of the dispute.

(c) how far the legal question is central to the outcome of the dispute;

(d) how important or novel the legal question is in the context of the dispute;

(e) the remedies that a court could impose;

(f) the amount at stake; and

(g) the significance for the *authorised person* (or similar *authorised persons*) or their clients.[46]

Referring to another complaints scheme

5.12 An *ombudsman* may refer a *complaint* to another complaints scheme if:

(a) he/she considers it appropriate; and

(b) the complainant agrees.[47]

5.13 If an *ombudsman* refers a *complaint* to another complaints scheme, the *ombudsman* will give the complainant and the *authorised person* reasons for the referral.[48]

Arrangements for assistance

5.14 The *Legal Ombudsman* may make such arrangements as it considers appropriate (which may include paying fees) for *Approved Regulators* or others to provide assistance to an *ombudsman* in the investigation or consideration of a *complaint.*[49]

Related complaints

5.15 The *Legal Ombudsman* may:

(a) tell a complainant that a related *complaint* could have been brought against some other *authorised person*;[50] or

(b) treat someone else who was an *authorised person* at the time of the act/omission as a joint respondent to the *complaint.*[51]

5.16 Where two or more *complaints* against different *authorised persons* relate to connected circumstances:

(a) the *Legal Ombudsman* may investigate them together, but an *ombudsman* will make separate determinations;[52] and

(b) the determinations may require the *authorised persons* to contribute towards the overall redress in the proportions the *ombudsman* considers appropriate.[53]

Informal resolution

5.17 The *Legal Ombudsman* will try to resolve *complaints* at the earliest possible stage, by whatever means it considers appropriate – including informal resolution.[54]

5.18 If a *complaint* is settled, abandoned or withdrawn, an *ombudsman* will tell both the complainant and the *authorised person*.[55]

Investigation

5.19 If the *Legal Ombudsman* considers that an investigation is necessary, it will:

(a) ensure both *parties* have been given an opportunity of making representations;

(b) send the *parties* a recommendation report (which the *Act* calls an 'assessment'), with a time limit for response; and

(c) if any *party* indicates disagreement within that time limit, arrange for an *ombudsman* to issue a final decision (which the *Act* calls a 'determination').[56]

5.20 If neither *party* indicates disagreement within that time limit, the *Legal Ombudsman* may treat the *complaint* as resolved by the recommendation report.[57]

Evidence

5.21 An apology will not of itself be treated as an admission of liability.[58]

5.22 An *ombudsman* cannot require anyone to produce any information or document or give any evidence which that person could not be compelled to produce in High Court civil proceedings, and the following provisions are subject to this.[59]

5.23 An *ombudsman* may give directions on:

(a) the issues on which evidence is required; and

(b) the way in which evidence should be given.[60]

5.24 An *ombudsman* may:

(a) take into account evidence from *Approved Regulators* or the Legal Services Board;

(b) take into account evidence from other third parties;

(c) treat any finding of fact in disciplinary proceedings against the *authorised person* as conclusive;

(d) include/exclude evidence that would be inadmissible/admissible in court;

(e) accept information in confidence where he/she considers that is both necessary and fair;[61]

(f) make a determination on the basis of what has been supplied;

(g) draw inferences from any *party's* failure to provide information requested; and

(h) dismiss a *complaint* if the complainant fails to provide information requested.[62]

5.25 An *ombudsman* may require a *party* to attend to give evidence and produce documents at a time and place specified by the *ombudsman*.[63]

5.26 An *ombudsman* may require a *party* to produce any information or document that the *ombudsman* considers necessary for the determination of a *complaint*.[64]

5.27 An *ombudsman* may:

(a) specify the time within which this must be done;

(b) specify the manner or form in which the information is to be provided; and

(c) require the person producing the document to explain it.[65]

5.28 If the document is not produced, an *ombudsman* may require the relevant *party* to say, to the best of his/her knowledge and belief, where the document is.[66]

5.29 If an *authorised person* fails to comply with a requirement to produce information or a document, the *ombudsman*:

(a) will tell the relevant *Approved Regulator*;

(b) may require that *Approved Regulator* to tell the *ombudsman* what action it will take; and

(c) may report any failure by that *Approved Regulator* to the Legal Services Board.[67]

5.30 Subject to this, if any *party* fails to comply with a requirement to produce information or a document, the *ombudsman* may enforce the requirement through the High Court.[68]

Procedural time limits

5.31 An *ombudsman* may fix (and may extend) a time limit for any stage of the investigation, consideration and determination of a *complaint*.[69]

5.32 If any *party* fails to comply with such a time limit, the *ombudsman* may:

(a) proceed with the investigation, consideration and determination;

(b) draw inferences from the failure;

(c) where the failure is by the complainant, dismiss the *complaint*; or

(d) where the failure is by the *authorised person*, include compensation for any inconvenience caused to the complainant in any award.[70]

Hearings

5.33 An *ombudsman* will only hold a hearing where he/she considers that the *complaint* cannot be fairly determined without one. In deciding whether (and how) to hold a hearing, the *ombudsman* will take account of article 6 in the European Convention on Human Rights.[71]

5.34 A *party* who wishes to request a hearing must do so in writing, setting out:

(a) the issues he/she wishes to raise; and

(b) (if appropriate) any reasons why the hearing should be in private;

so the *ombudsman* may consider whether:

(a) the issues are material;

(b) a hearing should take place; and

(c) any hearing should be in public or private.[72]

5.35 A hearing may be held by any means the *ombudsman* considers appropriate in the circumstances, including (for example) by phone.[73]

Determinations and awards by an ombudsman

5.36 An *ombudsman* will determine a *complaint* by reference to what is, in his/her opinion, fair and reasonable in all the circumstances of the case.[74]

5.37 In determining what is fair and reasonable, the *ombudsman* will take into account (but is not bound by):

(a) what decision a court might make;

(b) the relevant *Approved Regulator's* rules of conduct at the time of the act/omission; and

(c) what the *ombudsman* considers to have been good practice at the time of the act/omission.[75]

5.38 The *ombudsman*'s determination may contain one or more of the following directions to the *authorised person* in favour of the complainant:[76]

(a) to apologise;

(b) to pay compensation of a specified amount for loss suffered;

(c) to pay interest on that compensation from a specified time;[77]

(d) to pay compensation of a specified amount for inconvenience/distress caused;

(e) to ensure (and pay for) putting right any specified error, omission or other deficiency;

(f) to take (and pay for) any specified action in the interests of the complainant;

(g) to pay a specified amount for costs the complainant incurred in pursuing the *complaint*;[78] [79]

(h) to limit fees to a specified amount.

5.39 As a complainant does not usually need assistance to pursue a *complaint* with the *Legal Ombudsman*, awards of costs are likely to be rare.

5.40 If the determination contains a direction to limit fees to a specified amount, it may also require the *authorised person* to ensure that:[80]

(a) all or part of any amount paid is refunded;

(b) interest is paid on that refund from a specified time;[81]

(c) all or part of the fees are remitted;

(d) the right to recover the fees is waived, wholly or to a specified extent; or

(e) any combination of these.

5.41 An *ombudsman* will set (and may extend) a time limit for the *authorised person* to comply with a determination (and may set different time limits for the *authorised person* to comply with different parts of a determination).[82]

5.42 Any interest payable under the determination will be at the rate:

(a) specified in the determination; or

(b) (if not specified) at the rate payable on High Court judgment debts.[83]

5.43 There is a limit of £50,000 on the total value that can be awarded by the determination of a *complaint* in respect of:[84]

(a) compensation for loss suffered;

(b) compensation for inconvenience/distress caused;

(c) the reasonable cost of putting right any error, omission or other deficiency; and

(d) the reasonable cost of any specified action in the interests of the complainant.

5.44 If (before or after the determination is issued) it appears that the total value will exceed £50,000, an *ombudsman* may direct which part or parts of the award are to take preference.[85]

5.45 That limit does not apply to:

(a) an apology;

(b) interest on specified compensation for loss suffered;[86]

(c) a specified amount for costs the complainant incurred in pursuing the *complaint*;

(d) limiting fees to a specified amount; or

(e) interest on fees to be refunded.

Acceptance/rejection of determinations

5.46 The determination will:[87]

(a) be in writing, signed by the *ombudsman*;

(b) give reasons for the determination; and

(c) require the complainant to notify the *ombudsman*, before a specified time, whether the complainant accepts or rejects the determination.

5.47 The *ombudsman* may require any acceptance or rejection to be in writing, but will have regard to any reason why the complainant may be unable to use writing.[88]

5.48 The *ombudsman* will send copies of the determination to the *parties* and the relevant *Approved Regulator*.[89]

5.49 If the complainant tells the *ombudsman* that he/she accepts the determination, it is binding on the *parties* and final.[90]

5.50 Once a determination becomes binding and final, neither *party* may start or continue legal proceedings in respect of the subject matter of the *complaint*.

5.51 If the complainant does not tell the *ombudsman* (before the specified time) that he/she accepts the determination, it is treated as rejected unless:

(a) the complainant tells the *ombudsman* (after the specified time) that he/she accepts the determination; and

(b) the complainant has not previously told the *ombudsman* that he/she rejects the determination; and

(c) the *ombudsman* is satisfied that there are sufficient reasons why the complainant did not respond in time.[91]

5.52 If the complainant did not respond before the specified time, the *ombudsman* will notify the *parties* and the relevant *Approved Regulator* of the outcome, describing the provisions concerning late acceptance that are set out above.[92]

5.53 If the complainant accepts or rejects the determination, the *ombudsman* will notify the *parties* and the relevant Approved Regulator of the outcome.[93]

5.54 If a determination is rejected (or treated as rejected) by the complainant, it has no effect on the legal rights of any *party*.

Publication

5.55 The *Legal Ombudsman* may publish a report of its investigation, consideration and determination of a *complaint*. The report will not name (or otherwise identify) the complainant, unless the complainant agrees.[94]

Enforcement

5.56 A binding and final determination can be enforced through the High Court or a county court by the complainant.[95]

5.57 A binding and final determination can also be enforced through the High Court or a county court by an *ombudsman*, if:

(a) the complainant agrees; and

(b) the *ombudsman* considers it appropriate in all the circumstances.[96]

5.58 A court which makes an enforcement order must tell the *Legal Ombudsman*, and then an *ombudsman*:

(a) will tell the relevant *Approved Regulator*;

(b) may require that *Approved Regulator* to tell the *ombudsman* what action it will take; and

(c) may report any failure by that *Approved Regulator* to the Legal Services Board.[97]

Misconduct

5.59 If (at any stage after the *Legal Ombudsman* receives a *complaint*) an *ombudsman* considers that the *complaint* discloses any alleged misconduct about which the relevant *Approved Regulator* should consider action against the *authorised person*, the *ombudsman*:

(a) will tell the relevant *Approved Regulator*;

(b) will tell the complainant that the *Approved Regulator* has been told;

(c) may require that *Approved Regulator* to tell the *ombudsman* what action it will take; and

(d) may report any failure by that *Approved Regulator* to the Legal Services Board.[98]

5.60 If an *ombudsman* considers that an authorised person has failed to cooperate with the *Legal Ombudsman*, the *ombudsman*:

(a) will tell the relevant *Approved Regulator*;

(b) may require that *Approved Regulator* to tell the *ombudsman* what action it will take; and

(c) may report any failure by that *Approved Regulator* to the Legal Services Board.[99]

5.61 An *ombudsman*, the *Legal Ombudsman* and members of its staff will disclose to a *Approved Regulator* any information that it requests in order to investigate alleged misconduct or to fulfil its regulatory functions, so far as an *ombudsman* considers that the information:

(a) is reasonably required by the *Approved Regulator*; and

(b) has regard to any right of privacy of any complainant or third party involved (including rights of confidentiality or rights under the Data Protection Act 1998 or the Human Rights Act 1998).[100]

6 Case fees payable by authorised persons

6.1 A *complaint* is potentially chargeable unless:

(a) it is out of jurisdiction; or

(b) it is dismissed or discontinued under paragraph 5.7.[101]

6.2 [Rule 6.2 removed with effect from 1 April 2013][102]

6.3 A case fee is payable by the business/partnership or individual *authorised person* for every potentially chargeable *complaint* when it is closed unless:

(a) the *complaint* was:

- abandoned or withdrawn; or
- settled, resolved or determined in favour of the authorised person; and

(b) the *ombudsman* is satisfied that the *authorised person* took all reasonable steps, under his/her complaints procedures, to try to resolve the *complaint*.[103]

6.4 The case fee is £400 for all chargeable *complaints.*[104]

6.5 The remaining costs of running the *Legal Ombudsman* are covered by a levy on *Approved Regulators* by the Legal Services Board.[105]

6.6 There is no charge to complainants.

1. Section 112.
2. Section 145.
3. To distinguish complaints about service from those which relate solely to professional misconduct.
4. Sections 12 and 129.
5. This section covers the equivalent practitioners before the commencement of the Act.
6. [OLC rule] Sections 133(8) and 147(7).
7. Section 122(5).
8. Section 134.
9. [OLC rule]. Where it is apparent that another legal practitioner was also involved. Section 133(3)(c).
10. Section 128(7).
11. Individuals are covered under section 128(3). The others are covered under the Legal Services Act 2007 (Legal Complaints)(Parties) Order 2010 made by the Lord Chancellor.
12. Defined in European Commission Recommendation 2003/361/EC – broadly a business or enterprise with fewer than 10 employees and turnover or assets not exceeding €2 million.
13. [OLC rule] Section 132(4).
14. To save their having to take out a grant of representation if one is not otherwise required.
15. Section 128(5).
16. The Lord Chancellor can exclude others under section 130.
17. [OLC rule] Section 133(1).
18. Section 128(1) part.
19. Section 131(1).
20. Section 131(2) and (3).
21. Section 128(1) part.
22. Section 125(2).
23. Section 128(4).
24. The Lord Chancellor can include others under section 130.
25. Section 132(1).
26. [OLC rule] Section 132(2).
27. [OLC rule] Section 132(3).
28. Section 112(2)
29. Section 145.
30. Section 126(1).
31. [OLC rule] Section 126(3).
32. [OLC rule].
33. [OLC rule] Section 133(2)(b).
34. Section 133(1).
35. [OLC rule] This gives the Ombudsman service the right to require a complaint form, but does not oblige it to do so.
36. [OLC rule] To make it clear that the Ombudsman service does not have to communicate with each partner individually.
37. [OLC rule] Section 135.
38. [OLC rule] Section 133(1).
39. [OLC rule] Section 133(1).
40. Section 135.
41. [OLC rule] Section 133(3)(a).
42. Where a complaint is about professional negligence or judgement, the OLC will consider (on a case-by-case basis) whether the issue is one that the OLC can deal with or whether the issue would be better dealt with in court.
43. [OLC rule] For example, a French client wishes to complain about advice on French law given in France by a French lawyer who is also qualified in England and Wales.
44. [OLC rule].
45. Paragraph 5.9 only applies if the legal practitioner so requests. The idea is that, in suitable cases, the legal practitioner can go to court, provided the complainant's legal costs are met. In other circumstances, an Ombudsman cannot force a legal practitioner to pay the complainant's costs of going to court.
46. [OLC rule].
47. [OLC rule] Section 133(3)(b).
48. [OLC rule] Section 135.
49. Schedule 15, paragraph 18.
50. Where it is apparent that the complaint was made against the wrong legal practitioner.
51. [OLC rule] Where it is apparent that another legal practitioner was also involved. Section 133(3)(c).
52. There need to be separate determinations because of the £30,000 limit.
53. [OLC rule].
54. [OLC rule].
55. Section 135.
56. [OLC rule].
57. [OLC rule].

58. [OLC rule] To ensure legal practitioners are not discouraged from saying 'sorry'.
59. Sections 133(5) and 147(6).
60. [OLC rule].
61. Including, but not limited to, information which is "restricted information" under section 151.
62. [OLC rule].
63. [OLC rule] Section 133(3)(e).
64. Section 147(1) and (3).
65. Section 147(2) and (4).
66. Section 147(5).
67. Section 148.
68. Section 149.
69. [OLC rule].
70. [OLC rule].
71. [OLC rule].
72. [OLC rule].
73. [OLC rule]. The OLC has not exercised the power in section 133(3)(g) enabling it to make a rule about the OLC awarding expenses in connection with attending a hearing.
74. Section 137(1).
75. [OLC rule] Section 133(3)(f).
76. Section 137(2).
77. Section 137(4)(b).
78. [(g) is OLC rule] Section 133(3)(h).
79. The OLC has not exercised the power under section 133(3)(i) to make a rule requiring any party who has behaved unreasonably to pay costs to the Legal Ombudsman.
80. Section 137(2)(b)(ii).
81. Section 137(4)(b).
82. [OLC rule].
83. [OLC rule] Section 137(4).
84. Section 138(1) and (2). The Lord Chancellor can increase the limit under section 139.
85. [OLC rule].
86. Section 138(3).
87. Section 140(1) and (2).
88. [OLC rule].
89. Section 140(3).
90. Section 140(4).
91. [(c) is OLC rule] Section 140(5) and (6).
92. Section 140(7) and (8).
93. Section 140(7).
94. Section 150.
95. Section 141.
96. [OLC rule] Section 141(5).
97. Section 142.
98. Section 143.
99. Section 146.
100. [OLC rule] Section 144(1).
101. [OLC rule].
102. [OLC rule].
103. [OLC rule].
104. [OLC rule].
105. Sections 173 and 174.

APPENDIX 12

The Solicitors (Disciplinary Proceedings) Rules 2007 with Solicitors Disciplinary Tribunal practice directions and policy/practice note

[The practice directions are reproduced with the kind permission of the Solicitors Disciplinary Tribunal. For the latest updates to the material, please see www.solicitorstribunal.org.uk.]

Solicitors (Disciplinary Proceedings) Rules 2007

SI 2007/3588

Made 14th December 2007

Coming into force 14th January 2008

The Solicitors Disciplinary Tribunal in exercise of the powers conferred upon them by section 46 of the Solicitors Act 1974 hereby make the following Rules:

In accordance with section 46 of that Act the Master of the Rolls concurs with the making of these Rules.

APPENDIX 12

PART 1
INTRODUCTION

1 Citation and Commencement

These Rules may be cited as the Solicitors (Disciplinary Proceedings) Rules 2007 and shall come into force on 14th January 2008.

2 Interpretation

(1) In these Rules—

"the Act" means the Solicitors Act 1974;

"applicant" means a person making an application;

"application" means an application made under these Rules;

"case to answer" means an arguable or prima facie case;

"clerk" means any clerk to the Tribunal appointed under Rule 3 (including the Clerk);

"the Clerk" means the clerk to the Tribunal who is in office at the date these Rules come into force, or the clerk subsequently appointed under Rule 3(5);

"Division" means a division of three members of the Tribunal appointed for the hearing of an application or any matter connected with an application;

"the Law Society" includes any duly constituted committee of the Law Society or any body or person exercising delegated powers of the Law Society;

"respondent" means any party to an application other than the applicant;

"recognised body" has the same meaning as in section 9 of the Administration of Justice Act 1985;

"the Roll" means the Roll of Solicitors kept by the Law Society under section 6 of the Act;

"solicitor members" and "lay members" have the same meanings as in section 46 of the Act;

"Statement" means a written statement (including a witness statement) containing a statement of truth;

"the Tribunal" means the Solicitors Disciplinary Tribunal and where a Division has been appointed for the hearing of an application or any matter connected with it, includes a Division.

(2) References in these Rules to solicitors include, where appropriate, former solicitors.

(3) References in these Rules to registered foreign lawyers are references to lawyers whose names are entered in the register of foreign lawyers maintained under section 89 of the Courts and Legal Services Act 1990 and include, where appropriate, those who have ceased to be registered in that register or whose registration has been suspended.

(4) References in these Rules to registered European lawyers are references to lawyers whose names are entered in the register of registered European lawyers maintained by the Law Society under regulation 15 of the European Communities (Lawyer's Practice) Regulations 2000 and include, where appropriate, those who have ceased to be registered in that register or whose registration has been suspended.

PART 2
CONSTITUTION

3 President, Vice-Presidents and Clerk

(1) The President of the Tribunal holding office immediately before the date on which these rules come into force shall continue to hold office until the Tribunal's annual general meeting next following 30th April 2009.

(2) Subject to paragraph (1), the Tribunal, by a simple majority, shall appoint one of the solicitor members to be its President to hold office for a period of 3 years and the person so appointed may be re-appointed for a further period not exceeding 3 years.

(3) The Tribunal, by a simple majority, shall appoint one solicitor member and one lay member to be its Vice-Presidents to hold office for such period or periods not exceeding 3 years as the Tribunal shall think fit and to exercise such functions as are exercisable under these rules by the President as he may direct.

(4) The Tribunal shall meet not less than once in each calendar year and shall publish an annual report, a copy of which shall be delivered to the Master of the Rolls and the Law Society.

(5) The Tribunal shall appoint a Clerk to the Tribunal.

(6) The Tribunal may also appoint other clerks, including clerks appointed to deal with a particular case or cases.

(7) A clerk appointed by the Tribunal under this rule shall be a solicitor or barrister of not less than 10 years standing.

(8) A clerk shall vacate his office if—

(a) in the Tribunal's opinion (with which the Master of the Rolls agrees) he is physically or mentally incapable of performing his duties; or

(b) he retires; or

(c) he is removed from office by a resolution of the Tribunal approved by the Master of the Rolls.

(9) The Clerk shall be responsible to the Tribunal for the administration of the Tribunal in an efficient manner and, for so long as he shall be remunerated by the Law Society, shall be regarded as seconded to the Tribunal.

(10) The services of a clerk may be provided to the Tribunal through a body independent of the Law Society and that body may employ him on such terms (including remuneration and pension provision) as the Tribunal shall think fit.

(11) The Tribunal may prescribe the duties to be performed by the clerks or for which they shall be responsible and those duties shall include arrangements for—

(a) the submission of applications for certification of a case to answer;

(b) making pre-listing arrangements including directions of an administrative nature;

(c) listing of and attendance at hearings;

(d) securing a record of hearings (by tape recording or other means);

(e) advising the Tribunal on matters of law or procedure as may be necessary or expedient;

(f) preparing summaries of allegations, evidence and submissions for inclusion in the Tribunal's detailed findings;

(g) drawing orders and findings and filing them with the Law Society;

(h) the general supervision of other clerks and the Tribunal's administration and staff; and

(i) maintaining records and collecting statistics required by the Tribunal.

4 Constitution of Divisions

Subject to rules 6(1) and 6(3), a Division shall be constituted for the hearing of any application or matter relating to an application. Two of the Division members shall be solicitor members and one shall be a lay member and (unless the President shall determine otherwise) a solicitor member shall act as Chairman.

PART 3
APPLICATIONS

5 Applications in respect of solicitors, recognised bodies, registered European lawyers and registered foreign lawyers

(1) An application to the Tribunal in respect of any allegation or complaint made in respect of a solicitor, a recognised body, a registered European lawyer or a registered foreign lawyer shall be in the form of Form 1 in the Schedule to these Rules.

(2) The application shall be supported by a Statement setting out the allegations and the facts and matters supporting the application and each allegation contained in it.

(3) The application, the Statement and any documents exhibited with them shall be delivered to the Clerk together with 5 additional copies and a further copy for any second or further respondent.

6 Certification of a case to answer

(1) An application made under Rule 5 shall be considered by a solicitor member, who shall certify whether there is a case to answer.

(2) Paragraph (3) applies if—

(a) the solicitor member is minded not to certify that there is a case to answer; or

(b) in his opinion, the case is one of doubt or difficulty.

(3) If this paragraph applies, the application shall be considered by a panel of three members of the Tribunal, at least one of whom shall be a solicitor member and one a Lay member.

(4) If a solicitor member or a panel decides not to certify that a case to answer is established in accordance with this rule, the application shall be dismissed without formal order unless any party to the proceedings requires otherwise.

(5) If it is certified that there is a case to answer, a clerk shall serve the application, the Statement and any documents exhibited with them on each respondent in accordance with rule 10.

7 Supplementary statements

(1) The applicant may file supplementary Statements with the Clerk containing additional facts or matters on which the applicant seeks to rely or further allegations and facts or matters in support of the application. Any supplementary Statement containing further allegations against the respondent shall be treated as though it were an application for the purposes of rules 5(3) and 6(1), (2), (3) and (5).

(2) Without prejudice to any further application which may be made, no supplementary Statement shall, unless by order of the Tribunal, be filed later than 12 months after the date of the Application or less than 30 days before the date fixed for the hearing of the application.

8 Applications by the Law Society against solicitors' employees

(1) An application made by the Law Society for an order under section 43(2) of the Act shall be in the form of Form 2 in the Schedule to these rules.

(2) In a case where the Law Society has applied to the Tribunal for an order under section 43(2) of the Act, the solicitor, recognised body, or registered European lawyer by or for whose benefit the respondent is employed or remunerated—

(a) may also be named or joined as a respondent to the application; and

(b) shall be joined as a respondent if the Tribunal so direct.

(3) The provisions of rules 5(2) and (3) and 6(1) to (5) shall apply to every application made under section 43(2) of the Act.

(4) An application for a review of an order made under section 43(3) of the Act shall be in the form of Form 3 in the Schedule to these Rules.

(5) Every application under section 43(3) of the Act shall be served on the Law Society and the Law Society shall file with the Clerk a Statement setting out the facts and matters on which it relied in making the order under Section 43(2) of the Act.

9 Other Applications

(1) This rule applies to applications made to the Tribunal under section 47 of the Act—

(a) by a former solicitor seeking restoration to the Roll;

(b) by a person seeking restoration to the register of European lawyers or the register of foreign lawyers if his name has been removed from either register;

(c) by a solicitor, registered foreign lawyer or registered European lawyer seeking the termination of an indefinite period of suspension from practice imposed by the Tribunal.

(2) An application to which this rule applies shall be made in the form of Form 4 in the Schedule to these Rules.

(3) The Law Society shall be a respondent to every application to which this rule applies.

(4) The applicant shall serve on the Law Society—

(a) a copy of the application; and

(b) a Statement in support of the application.

(5) Every application to which this rule applies shall be advertised by the applicant once in the Law Society's Gazette and once in a newspaper circulating in the area of the applicant's former practice.

(6) Any person may, no later than 10 days before the hearing date of an application to which this rule applies, serve on the Tribunal and the parties to the application notice of his intention to oppose the grant of the application and the Tribunal may allow that person to appear before the Tribunal at the hearing of the application, call evidence and make representations upon which the Tribunal may allow him to be cross-examined.

PART 4
PROCEDURE AND RULES OF EVIDENCE

10 Service of documents

(1) Any application, Statement or other document required to be served under rules 6(5), 8(5) and 9(4) shall be served—

(a) personally; or

(b) by sending by guaranteed delivery post or other guaranteed and acknowledged delivery to the last known place of business or abode of the person to be served; and

(c) in such other manner as the Tribunal may direct.

(2) Any Statement, notice or document other than one which is required to be served in accordance with paragraph (1) may be served in accordance with that paragraph.

(3) In the case of a solicitor, any Statement, notice or other document required to be served under these rules may be served—

(a) by leaving it at the address shown as his place of business in the register kept by the Law Society under section 9 of the Act; or

(b) by any of the methods mentioned in paragraphs (a) to (d) of rule 6.2(1) of the Civil Procedure Rules 1998 as they may be modified, amended or replaced.

(4) Any application, Statement, notice or other document served in accordance with paragraph (1) shall be deemed served on the second working day following the day on which it is delivered, posted or transmitted.

(5) An application, Statement, notice or other document delivered to the last known place of business or abode of the person to be served may be regarded by the Tribunal as duly served if it is satisfied that it is reasonable to expect that the application, Statement, notice or other document has been received by or brought to the attention of the person to be served.

(6) If the Tribunal requires the advertisement of any proceedings under these Rules, it may regard that advertisement as service for the purposes of these Rules.

11 Directions

(1) A clerk may give any directions deemed necessary or appropriate for the hearing of any matter brought before the Tribunal.

(2) Without prejudice to paragraph (1), directions may be made about documentation, inspection, Statements, skeleton arguments and the place or time of any hearing.

(3) A clerk may appoint a time and place for the review of the progress of the matter and shall notify the parties of the date, time and place of any such review.

(4) A clerk may refer to the Tribunal any matter for a decision or directions and the Tribunal may itself or on the application of any party make an order on such terms as to the Tribunal shall appear just—

(a) to give consent to the withdrawal of an application or allegation in respect of which a case to answer has been certified;

(b) to adjourn any hearing listed for directions or for a substantive hearing;

(c) to agree to the amendment of any application or allegation or the correction of any matter;

(d) to make any directions which shall appear necessary or appropriate to secure the timely hearing of the matter.

(5) Any hearing under this rule shall be held in public unless rules 12(5) or (6) apply.

(6) No application or allegation in respect of which a case to answer has been certified may be withdrawn without the consent of the Tribunal.

12 Listing

(1) Unless the Tribunal has made directions in respect of the hearing, a clerk shall appoint a date for the hearing by the Tribunal and shall give notice of the date to the parties. The hearing shall not, unless all the parties have agreed or the Tribunal has so ordered, take place sooner than the expiry of a period of 42 days beginning with the date of service of the notice appointing the date of the hearing.

(2) A clerk shall arrange for the hearing date to be published in the Daily Cause List of the High Court.

(3) Subject to paragraphs (5) and (6) every hearing shall take place in public.

(4) Any party to an application and any person who claims to be affected by it may seek an order from the Tribunal that the hearing or part of it be conducted in private on the grounds of—

(a) exceptional hardship; or

(b) exceptional prejudice,

to a party, a witness or any person affected by the application.

(5) If it is satisfied that those grounds are met, the Tribunal shall conduct the hearing or part of it in private and make such order as shall appear to it to be just and proper.

(6) The Tribunal may, before or during a hearing, direct that the hearing or part of it be held in private if—

(a) the Tribunal is satisfied that it would have granted an application under paragraph (4) had one been made; or

(b) in the Tribunal's view a hearing in public would prejudice the interests of justice.

13 Evidence: general

(1) Subject to the following provisions of this rule, the Civil Evidence Act 1968, and the Civil Evidence Act 1995 shall apply in relation to proceedings before the Tribunal in the same manner as they apply in relation to civil proceedings.

(2) Any notice given under the provisions of the Acts mentioned in paragraph (1) shall be given no later than 21 days before the date fixed for the hearing of an application.

(3) Any counter-notice shall be given no later than 10 days before the date fixed for the hearing.

(4) No later than 28 days before the date fixed for the hearing of an application, the applicant may, by written notice, require any other party to the application to indicate to him, no later than the date on which the period of 14 days from the date of the giving of the notice expires, which of any facts set out in the Statement submitted in support of the application are in dispute.

(5) Failure to reply to such a notice shall be material only in relation to the question of costs.

(6) Any party to an application may, by written notice, not later than nine days before the date fixed for the hearing, request any other party to agree that any document may be admitted as evidence.

(7) If any other party desires to challenge the authenticity of a document which is the subject of paragraph (6), he shall no later than the date on which the period of six days beginning with the date on which the notice was served, give notice that he does not agree to the admission of the document and that he requires that its authenticity be proved at the hearing.

(8) If the recipient of a notice given under paragraph (6) does not give a notice in response within the period mentioned in paragraph (7), he shall be deemed to have admitted the document unless otherwise ordered by the Tribunal.

(9) A party to an application may, pursuant to Section 46(11) of the Act, require the attendance at the hearing of any person or the production of any document relevant to the proceedings and any summons for that purpose shall be in the form of Form 5 in the Schedule to these Rules.

(10) At the discretion of the Tribunal, the strict rules of evidence shall not apply at a hearing before the Tribunal.

14 Written evidence

(1) The Tribunal may in its discretion, in respect of a whole case or of any particular fact or facts, proceed and act upon evidence given by Statement.

(2) Every Statement upon which any party proposes to rely shall be filed with the Clerk and served on all other parties to the application in question no later than 21 days before the date fixed for the hearing of the application together with a notice in the form of Form 6 in the Schedule to these Rules.

(3) Any party on whom a notice has been served under paragraph (2) and who requires the attendance, at the hearing, of the witness in question shall, no later than 9 days before the date of the hearing require, in writing, the other party to produce the witness at the hearing.

(4) If no party requires the attendance of a witness in accordance with the provisions of this rule, the Tribunal may accept the Statement in question in evidence.

(5) If a witness who has been required to attend a hearing in accordance with the provisions of this Rule fails to do so, the onus shall be on the party seeking to rely on the Statement of that witness to show why the Statement should be accepted in evidence.

(6) If any party intends to call as a witness any person who has not produced a Statement, he must, no later than 10 days before the date fixed for the hearing, notify the Clerk and any

other party to the proceedings of his intention and forthwith serve a copy of a written proof of evidence on the other party and lodge five copies of the proof with the Clerk.

15 Previous findings of record

(1) In any proceedings before the Tribunal which relate to the decision of another court or tribunal, the following rules shall apply if it is proved that the decision relates to the relevant party to the application.

(2) A conviction for a criminal offence may be proved by the production of a certified copy of the certificate of conviction relating to the offence and proof of a conviction shall constitute evidence that the person in question was guilty of the offence. The findings of fact upon which that conviction was based shall be admissible as conclusive proof of those facts save in exceptional circumstances.

(3) The finding of and penalty imposed by any tribunal in or outside England and Wales exercising a professional disciplinary jurisdiction may be proved by producing a certified copy of the order, finding or note of penalty in question and the findings of fact upon which the finding in question was based shall be admissible as proof but not conclusive proof of the facts in question.

(4) The judgment of any civil court in any jurisdiction may be proved by producing a certified copy of the judgment and the findings of fact upon which that judgment was based shall be admissible as proof but not conclusive proof of those facts.

16 Hearings and Findings

(1) The hearing of an application shall take place at such time and place as shall be considered by the Tribunal to be appropriate and convenient.

(2) If the Tribunal is satisfied that notice of the hearing was served on the respondent in accordance with these Rules, the Tribunal shall have power to hear and determine an application notwithstanding that the Respondent fails to attend in person or is not represented at the hearing.

(3) At the conclusion of the hearing, the Tribunal shall make a finding as to whether any or all of the allegations in the application have been substantiated whereupon a clerk shall inform the Tribunal whether in any previous disciplinary proceedings before the Tribunal allegations were found to have been substantiated against the Respondent.

(4) The Respondent shall be entitled to make submissions by way of mitigation in respect of any sanction (including any order for costs) which the Tribunal may impose.

(5) The Tribunal may announce its decision and make an order at the conclusion of the hearing or may reserve its decision for announcement at a later date. In either case the announcement shall be made in public and in either case the Tribunal shall as soon as is practicable deliver to the applicant and to the respondent its detailed written findings which shall include its reasons and conclusions upon the evidence before it.

17 The Order

(1) An order made under rule 16(5) shall be signed by a member of the Tribunal upon the announcement of the decision and shall, subject to paragraph (2) be filed forthwith with the Law Society.

(2) The Tribunal may suspend the filing of the Order if it appears to the Tribunal that there is good reason to do so, in which event the Order shall not take effect (including any suspension from practice) until it is filed with the Law Society.

PART 5
MISCELLANEOUS

18 Costs

(1) The Tribunal may make such order as to costs as the Tribunal shall think fit including an order—

(a) disallowing costs incurred unnecessarily; or

(b) that costs be paid by any party judged to be responsible for wasted or unnecessary costs, whether arising through non compliance with time limits or otherwise.

(2) The Tribunal may order that any party bear the whole or a part or a proportion of the costs.

(3) The amount of costs to be paid may either be fixed by the Tribunal or be subject to detailed assessment by a Costs Judge.

(4) The Tribunal may also make an order as to costs under this Rule—

(a) where any application or allegation is withdrawn or amended;

(b) where no allegation of misconduct (including an application under Section 43 of the Solicitors Act) is proved against a respondent.

19 Re-hearing where respondent neither appears nor is represented

(1) At any time before the filing of the Tribunal's Order with the Law Society under rule 17 or before the expiry of the period of 14 days beginning with the date of the filing of the order, the respondent may apply to the Tribunal for a re-hearing of an application if—

(a) he neither attended in person nor was represented at the hearing of the application in question; and

(b) the Tribunal determined the application in his absence.

(2) An application for a re-hearing under this Rule shall be made in the form of Form 7 in the Schedule to these Rules and shall be supported by a Statement setting out the facts upon which the applicant wishes to rely.

(3) If satisfied that it is just so to do, the Tribunal may grant the application upon such terms, including as to costs, as it thinks fit. The re-hearing shall be held before a Division of the Tribunal comprised of different members from those who heard the original application.

20 Adjournment for Law Society to investigate

In the case of an application by a person other than the Law Society, the Tribunal may, before or after certification of a case to answer, adjourn the matter for a period not exceeding 3 months to enable the Law Society to carry out its own investigations and—

(a) if it thinks fit, initiate its own application; or

(b) by agreement with the applicant, undertake the application.

21 Miscellaneous

(1) Subject to the provisions of these Rules, the Tribunal may regulate its own procedure.

(2) The Tribunal may dispense with any requirements of these Rules in respect of notices, Statements, witnesses, service or time in any case where it appears to the Tribunal to be just so to do.

(3) The Tribunal (or a panel of Tribunal members consisting of not less than 5 members of whom not less than 2 shall be lay members) may give such notices or make such directions concerning the practices or procedures of the Tribunal as are consistent with these Rules and as shall seem appropriate.

(4) The Tribunal shall promulgate notices or directions given or made under paragraph (3) under the authority of the President. Practice Directions in force prior to the date on which these Rules come into force shall remain in full force and effect after that date.

(5) Where the Tribunal has made a finding based solely upon the certificate of conviction for a criminal offence which is subsequently quashed the Tribunal may, on the application of the Law Society or the respondent to the application in respect of which the finding arose, revoke its finding and make such order as to costs as shall appear to be just in the circumstances.

22 Revocation

The Solicitors (Disciplinary Proceedings) Rules 1994 are revoked.

23 Transitional provision

These Rules shall not apply to proceedings in which an Application is made before the date on which these rules came into force and those proceedings shall be subject to the Solicitors (Disciplinary Proceedings) Rules 1994 as if they had not been revoked.

Signed by authority of the Solicitors' Disciplinary Tribunal and approved by the Master of the Rolls

Anthony Isaacs

President

Sir Anthony Clarke

Master of the Rolls

14th December 2007

SCHEDULE

FORM 1

Rule 5(1)

FORM OF APPLICATION in respect of existing and former Solicitors, Registered Foreign Lawyers, Registered European Lawyers, and Incorporated Solicitors Practices.

Number ....

IN THE MATTER of the Solicitors Act 1974 (as amended)

.... Applicant

.... Respondent

I, ... of ....

APPLY [on behalf of (1)] that (2)

of..

be required to answer the allegations contained in the Statement which accompanies this Application and that such Order be made as the Tribunal shall think right.

SIGNED by the Applicant ....

whose address for service is

....

....

....

Dated

Notes:

1. Applicants making an application on behalf of a third party, e.g. the Law Society should so state.

2. Add the full names of the Respondent and his address or last known abode or last known place or places of business and his status as an existing or former Solicitor, registered European lawyer, registered foreign lawyer or Recognised Body (Incorporated Solicitors Practice).

3. An application may also be made in this form that a direction made by the Law Society in relation to inadequate professional services be made enforceable as if contained in an Order of the High Court.

FORM 2

Rule 8(1)

FORM OF APPLICATION in respect of a person who is or was employed or remunerated by a Solicitor, Registered European Lawyer or Recognised Body.

Number ....

IN THE MATTER OF The Solicitors Act 1974 and the Solicitors (Disciplinary Proceedings) Rules 2007

I ....

APPLY on behalf of The Law Society that an Order under Section 43 of the Solicitors Act 1974 (as amended) be made by the Tribunal directing that as from a date to be specified in such Order, no Solicitor, Recognised Body or registered European lawyer shall, employ or remunerate

....

who is or was employed or remunerated by .... ,

except in accordance with permission in writing granted by The Law Society or that such other Order might be made as the Tribunal should think right.

Dated ....

.... Applicant
Address of Applicant

FORM 3

Rule 8(4)

FORM of APPLICATION to review or revoke an Order made under Section 43 of the Solicitors Act 1974 (as amended) by The Law Society or the Tribunal with respect to a person who is or was employed or remunerated by a Solicitor, Recognised Body or Registered European lawyer.

Number ....

IN THE MATTER OF the Solicitors Act 1974 (as amended) and the Solicitors (Disciplinary Proceedings) Rules 2007

To: the Solicitors' Disciplinary Tribunal and to The Law Society

I, ... of ....

APPLY to the Tribunal for a [REVIEW][REVOCATION] of the Order made against me dated

(a copy of which is attached to this application)

Dated: ....

Signed: ....

Address: ....

....

....

Notes:

1. This Form should be used in respect of a person who is not a Solicitor or registered European lawyer and who has been made the subject of an Order under Section 43 of the Solicitors Act 1974 (as amended) by the Law Society and who (a) seeks a review of the Order or (b) seeks a revocation of the Order. It should be accompanied by a Statement setting out the grounds for such a review or revocation and attached to it should be a copy of the Order in question.

2. This Form should be served on the Tribunal and contemporaneously on The Law Society.

FORM 4

Rule 9(2)

FORM of APPLICATION for restoration to the Roll of Solicitors or Register of Foreign or European Lawyers; or

FORM of APPLICATION by a solicitor, Registered Foreign Lawyer or Registered European Lawyer who has been suspended from practice indefinitely by order of the Tribunal for an order to bring the suspension to an end

Number............................

IN THE MATTER OF the Solicitors Act 1974 (as amended) and the Solicitors (Disciplinary Proceedings) Rules 2007

I, ... of ....

was admitted as a Solicitor of the Supreme Court of Judicature* registered as a registered European lawyer*/registered foreign lawyer

on ....

* By an Order of the Solicitors Disciplinary Tribunal dated .... a true copy of which is attached to this application, I was struck off the Roll/Register of European/ Foreign Lawyers* and—

(1) I APPLY that my name be restored to the Roll/Register* of European/ Foreign Lawyers;

(2) I undertake to advertise this Application in accordance with the Rules.

* By an Order of the Solicitors Disciplinary Tribunal dated .... a true copy of which is attached to this application, my right to practise was the subject of an order of suspension from practise for an indefinite period and I APPLY that a date be fixed for the ending of such indefinite period of suspension.:

* delete as appropriate

Dated: ....

Signed
....

Note: This Form must be served on the Clerk to the Solicitors Disciplinary Tribunal and contemporaneously upon The Law Society accompanied by a Statement in support of the Application.

FORM 5

Rule 13(9)

WITNESS SUMMONS

Number.............................

IN THE MATTER OF the Solicitors Act 1974

AND IN THE MATTER OF

....

To

You are summoned to attend at the Solicitors' Disciplinary Tribunal at (Tribunal address)

on .... of .... at .... (am)(pm)

(and each following day of the hearing until the Tribunal tells you that you are no longer required.)

☐ to give evidence in respect of the above application

☐ to produce the following document(s) (*give details*)

The sum of £ is paid or offered to you with this summons. This is to cover your travelling expenses to and from the Tribunal and includes an amount by way of compensation for loss of time.

This summons was issued on the application of the applicant(respondent) or the applicant's (respondent's) solicitor whose name, address and reference number is:

Do not ignore this summons

If you were offered money for travel expenses and compensation for loss of time, at the time it was served on you, you must—

- attend the Tribunal on the date and time shown and/or produce documents as required by the summons; and
- take an oath or affirm as required for the purposes of answering questions about your evidence or the documents you have been asked to produce.

In the High Court, disobeyance of a witness summons is a contempt of court and you may be fined or imprisoned for contempt. You may also be liable to pay any wasted costs that arise because of your non-compliance.

If you wish to set aside or vary this witness summons, you make an application to the Court.

FORM 6

Rule 14(2)

FORM of NOTICE to accompany Statement of Evidence

Number........................

IN THE MATTER OF the Solicitors Act 1974 and the Solicitors Disciplinary Proceedings Rules 2007

AND IN THE MATTER OF

....

TAKE NOTICE that the applicant/respondent proposes to rely upon the statement(s) listed below, copies of which are served herewith.

If you wish any person who has made one of these statements to be required to attend the hearing as a witness you must, not less than 9 days before the date set down for the hearing of the application, notify me and the Clerk to the Tribunal to that effect. In the event of your failure to do so the Tribunal may accept the statement in question in evidence.

LIST

Date of Statement	Name of Person who made the Statement
1.	
2.	
3.	

Date: ....

Signed: ....

Address: ....

FORM 7

Rule 19(2)

FORM of APPLICATION for a Rehearing

Number: ....

IN THE MATTER OF the Solicitors Act 1974 and the Solicitors Disciplinary Proceedings Rules 2007

AND IN THE MATTER OF

....

Number of Tribunal case in respect of which a rehearing is requested ....

I APPLY under Rule 19(2) of the Solicitors (Disciplinary Proceedings) Rules 2007 that the abovementioned case be reheard by the Tribunal. The facts upon which I rely in support of this application are set out below:

(*set out here full details of the facts on which the applicant for a rehearing relies and include the reasons why the person applying for the rehearing did not appear or was not represented before the Tribunal at the earlier hearing and set out all matters which he wishes to place before the Tribunal in mitigation or otherwise*).

Dated: ....

Signature: ....

Address: ....

Solicitors Disciplinary Tribunal practice directions

Practice Direction No. 1

The Tribunal direct that generally pursuant to Rule 7(1)(iii) it will consider an Application and Statement or Affidavit pursuant to Rules 4 and 6 to have been properly served if an enquiry agent has established the address of the Respondent by enquiry and/or observation and leaves the appropriate papers at that address.

Practice Direction No. 2

Dated: 25th February 1996

Amended: 27th November 2002

Re: Disclosure/Discovery

Where directions are sought as to disclosure or discovery of documents, the Tribunal will adopt the view that material should be disclosed which could be seen on a sensible appraisal by the Applicant:-

(i) to be relevant or possibly relevant to an issue in the case;

(ii) to raise or possibly raise a new issue whose existence is not apparent from the evidence the Applicant proposes to use, and which would or might assist the Respondent in fully testing the Applicant's case or in adducing evidence in rebuttal;

(iii) to hold out a real (as opposed to a fanciful) prospect of providing a lead on evidence which goes to (i) or (ii).

There may be exceptional circumstances in which the Tribunal, balancing the interest in disclosure of a document against a competing public interest such as a specific and compelling need for confidentiality, may decide not to order disclosure of a document which falls within (i) (ii) or (iii) above.

Practice Direction No. 3

An application for a rehearing made pursuant to Rule 25 of the Solicitors (Disciplinary Proceedings) Rules 1994 will normally be heard in public in open court before a division of the Tribunal of different constitution from that which heard the matter in respect of which a rehearing is sought. It will be only in exceptional circumstances that the Tribunal will exercise its discretion in favour of a private hearing.

Dated this 5th day of March 1998

On behalf of the Tribunal

(signed) G. B. Marsh

President

Practice Direction No. 4

The Tribunal that direct that generally pursuant to Rule 7(1)(ii)(iii) it will consider an Application and Statement or Affidavit pursuant to Rules 4 and 6 to have been properly served if it has been sent using the Royal Mail's Special Delivery system in place of first class post with Recorded Delivery and Advice of Delivery.

Dated this 29th day of January 2001

(signed) G. B. Marsh

President

Practice Direction No. 5

Inference To Be Drawn Where Respondent Does Not Give Evidence

The Tribunal has taken careful note of the obiter dicta of the President of the Queen's Bench Division (Sir John Thomas) at paragraphs 25 and 26 of the Judgment in *Muhammed Iqbal v Solicitors Regulation Authority* [2012] EWHC 3251 (Admin). In the words of the President, "ordinarily the public would expect a professional man to give an account of his actions". The Tribunal directs for the avoidance of doubt that, in appropriate cases where a Respondent denies some or all of the allegations against him (regardless of whether it is alleged that he has been dishonest), and/or disputes material facts, and does not give evidence or submit himself to cross-examination, the Tribunal shall be entitled to take into account the position that the Respondent has chosen to adopt as regards the giving of evidence when reaching its decision in respect of its findings. This direction applies regardless of the fact that the Respondent may have provided a written signed statement to the Tribunal.

Dated this 4th day of February 2013

Signed on behalf of the Tribunal

Andrew Spooner

President

Practice Direction No. 6

Practice Direction on Case Management for First Instance Proceedings

1. The following Practice Direction is intended to give guidance to Applicants and Respondents appearing before the Solicitors Disciplinary Tribunal ("the Tribunal"). It is not intended to replace or vary The Solicitors (Disciplinary Proceedings) Rules 2007 ("SDPR") and is made by the Tribunal's Policy Committee under Rule 21(3) SDPR, and promulgated under the authority of the President under Rule 21(4) SDPR. It applies to cases certified by the Tribunal as showing a case to answer after 25 October 2013 and is subject to review by the Tribunal from time to time.

2. The Overriding Objective when managing all cases brought before the Tribunal is to ensure that they are dealt with justly:

   2.1 To determine allegations brought against Respondents;

   2.2 To deal fairly with Applicants and Respondents, their representatives and others appearing before the Tribunal;

   2.3 To deal with cases efficiently and expeditiously;

2.4 To ensure that all relevant evidential material is available to the Tribunal in a timely fashion and accessible format throughout the proceedings and at the final hearing;

2.5 To deal with matters proportionally;

2.6 To deal with matters in accordance with the Tribunal's duty to be independent, impartial and transparent.

3. It is the duty of every party actively to assist the Tribunal and its administrative staff in fulfilling the Overriding Objective.

4. Following receipt of an application ("the Application") and a worst-case scenario time estimate by the Tribunal and following certification by it of a case to answer, Standard Directions in the attached format will be sent to the parties, with dates completed by the Clerk to the Tribunal or by a Deputy Clerk to the Tribunal on the Clerk's instructions. In cases where the worst-case scenario time estimate provided by the Applicant is two days or more, a date will be provided in the Standard Directions for a Case Management Hearing ("CMH"). The CMH will take place either at the Tribunal's offices or by means of telephone conference call no sooner than 42 days after the deemed date of service of the proceedings. The CMH may be conducted by either a three-member Tribunal or by the Clerk or a Deputy Clerk. At the CMH, Directions using the Standard Directions as a starting point will be made as deemed appropriate after considering submissions from the parties and the specific issues in the case.

5. An application by a party to vary the Standard Directions must be made by email or post to the Tribunal, copied at the same time to every other party, within 21 days of the date of the Standard Directions.

6. All parties must ensure that, when documents upon which a party intends to rely are served on another party (including Answers, Statements (other than Statements and supporting documents under Rules 5, 7 and 8 which are served by the Tribunal's administrative office) and supporting documents), four copies of the documents are filed with the Tribunal in hard copy format at the same time. Any party who wishes to refer to a document at a hearing must ensure that he or she has sufficient copies available for every other party, the three members of the Tribunal, the clerk to the hearing and the witness. Bundles of documents must be clearly photocopied and paginated.

7. Pursuant to the Overriding Objective, the Respondent shall file at the Tribunal and serve on every other party an Answer to the Application stating which allegations (if any) are admitted and which (if any) are denied, by the date specified in the Standard Directions, which will be before the date fixed for a CMH where applicable. If any of the allegations are denied, the Answer must set out the reasons for the denial. The Respondent shall also file at the Tribunal and serve on every other party all documents on which the Respondent intends to rely at the substantive hearing by the date specified in the Standard Directions. The provision of an Answer by the Respondent will provide the Tribunal with a better understanding of the Respondent's case and assist in determining the Directions which should be given and accurately identifying the realistic amount of time required for the substantive hearing.

8. If a Respondent fails to comply with the Direction to file and serve an Answer, or any party fails to comply with any other Direction made by the Tribunal or by the Clerk/Deputy Clerk on its behalf, it will be open to the Tribunal at the substantive hearing:

8.1 To draw such adverse inference from this failure as it considers appropriate and/or

8.2 To direct that no evidence (either oral or in writing) which has not been filed and served as directed shall be adduced without leave of the Tribunal and/or

8.3 To make an adverse costs order in default of compliance, which may be ordered to be paid immediately to the other party.

9. If by the date specified in the Standard Directions, the Respondent fails to file and serve an Answer to the Application, a CMH will be listed to take place before a three-member Tribunal at which all parties must attend, and at which the Tribunal will consider:

   9.1 The reason(s) for the Respondent's failure to file and serve an Answer and what, if any, further Directions the Tribunal should make;

   9.2 Any Directions proposed by the parties;

   9.3 Setting a date for the substantive hearing and giving appropriate Directions in that regard;

   9.4 The Tribunal may exercise its discretion to hoid the CMH by telephone.

10. Attached to this Practice Direction are detailed examples of the Standard Directions that may be made. These are not intended to be exhaustive, nor may all be appropriate in every case. The particular circumstances of a case may result in other Directions being given.

11. So far as is reasonably practicable, cases will be allocated to a Deputy Clerk, supported by the Tribunal's Case Management Team, who will jointly monitor the progress of the case towards the substantive hearing. If parties request further Directions from the Tribunal, the request will be considered by the Deputy Clerk with case management responsibilities under the supervision of the Clerk at first instance. In such circumstances it will be the duty of the party seeking further Directions to make an application without delay. If the time estimate for the substantive hearing changes before the date by which the parties must file their Certificates of Readiness, the parties must immediately notify the Clerk of the revised time estimate with reasons and whether or not it has been agreed by all other parties.

12. No less than 28 days before the substantive hearing, all parties must file at the Tribunal and serve on every other party a Certificate of Readiness confirming that they are ready for the substantive hearing; stating what, if any, further Directions are required; and confirming that the time estimate of the final hearing is the same as was anticipated when Standard Directions were issued or at any subsequent CMH, or otherwise providing a revised time estimate. If on receipt of the Certificates of Readiness the Deputy Clerk with case management responsibilities considers after consultation with the Clerk that a further CMH is required, or, if one or more Certificates of Readiness have not been filed and served 28 days before the substantive hearing, a CMH date will be fixed at short notice which may be directed to take place by telephone rather than at the Tribunal's offices so that any further Directions can be made. Failure by a party to file and serve a Certificate of Readiness by the deadline specified in Standard Directions will not delay the substantive hearing which will proceed on the date fixed.

13. If at the substantive hearing the Respondent wishes his or her means to be taken into consideration by the Tribunal in relation to possible sanctions and/or costs, he/she shall by no later than the date specified in the Standard Directions file at the Tribunal and serve on every other party a Statement of Means including full details of assets (including, but not limited to, property)/income/outgoings supported by documentary evidence. Any failure to comply with this requirement may result in the Tribunal drawing such inference as it considers appropriate, and the Tribunal will be entitled to determine the sanction and/or costs without regard to the Respondent's means. A failure to comply may also cause the consideration of the Respondent's means to be adjourned by the Tribunal to a later date which may result in an increase in costs.

14. Any party seeking an Order for Costs against another party at an interim hearing shall file with the Tribunal and serve on the relevant party a schedule of costs no later than 48 hours before the hearing in respect of which the costs order is sought.

15. Any party seeking an Order for Costs against another party at a substantive hearing shall file with the Tribunal and serve on the relevant party a schedule of costs no later than 5 working days before the hearing in respect of which the costs order is sought.

16. Any application for an adjournment of a CMH or substantive hearing must be made as soon as the circumstances justifying an adjournment are known to the party making the application. The application will be considered on its merits by the Tribunal, or in limited circumstances the Clerk, both of whom will pay due regard to the Tribunal's Policy/Practice Note on Adjournments in force at the time the application for an adjournment is made.

17. Respondents are required to inform the Tribunal of their postal address, e-mail address, home, office and mobile telephone numbers and of any changes to that information as soon as possible after they come into effect. Any failure to comply with this requirement may result in an interim or substantive hearing proceeding in the absence of the Respondent.

Dated this 22nd day of October 2013

Signed on behalf of the Tribunal

Andrew Spooner

President

Solicitors Disciplinary Tribunal – Standard Directions

Standard Directions for First Instance Proceedings

IMPORTANT NOTES TO STANDARD DIRECTIONS

Applications by the parties (by agreement or otherwise) to vary the standard directions below, including applications to vary the fixed substantive hearing date, must be made by email or post to the Tribunal, copied to every other party, within 21 calendar days of the date of this document.

All parties must ensure that, when documents upon which a party intends to rely are served on another party, four copies of the documents are filed with the Tribunal in hard copy format at the same time.

Standard Directions

The Tribunal Orders that the parties prepare for the substantive hearing of this case as follows:

1. The case be listed for substantive hearing on [insert date, time and place] based on the worst-case scenario time estimate of [insert time estimate] provided by the Applicant/Applicant's legal representatives. **OR**

   A Case Management Hearing/Case Management Conference Call will take place on [insert date, time [and place]] with a time estimate of [insert time estimate] before the [Tribunal/Clerk/Deputy Clerk].

2. The Respondent(s) shall file at the Tribunal and serve on every other party an Answer to the Applicant's Rule [5, 7, 8] Statement by [4.00pm on [insert date 28 days after date of service of proceedings]]. The Answer must state which of the allegations (if any) are admitted and which (if any) are denied. In respect of any which are denied, the Answer must set out the reasons for the denial.

3. The Respondent(s) shall file at the Tribunal and serve on every other party all

documents on which the Respondent(s) intend(s) to rely at the substantive hearing by [4.00pm on [insert date 28 days after date of service of proceedings]].

4. The Applicant may, if so advised, file at the Tribunal and serve on every other party a Reply to the Answer by [4.00pm on [insert date 14 days after date of service of Answer]].

5. The Applicant shall file at the Tribunal and serve on every other party any documents not included in the Rule [5, 7, 8] Statement on which he relies by [4.00pm on [insert date 14 days after date of service of Answer]].

6. The Applicant and Respondent shall file at the Tribunal and serve on every other party the witness statements of any witnesses upon whose evidence they intend to rely at the substantive hearing and whose statement has not already been served by [4.00pm on [insert date]].

7. Each party to notify the other(s) of the names of any witnesses whom they wish to attend the hearing for cross-examination by no later than [4.00pm on [insert date]].

8. Rule 13 SDPR makes general provisions in relation to Evidence. Subject to the provisions in Rule 13, the Civil Evidence Act 1968 and the Civil Evidence Act 1995 apply to these proceedings in the same manner as they apply to civil proceedings. Rule 13(2) SDPR provides for the giving of notices under those Acts. Any Notice under Rule 13(2) SDPR shall be filed at the Tribunal and served on every other party by no later than [4.00pm on [insert date no later than 21 days before the date fixed for the hearing of an application]]. Rule 13 (3) SDPR provides for the giving of counter-notices under those Acts. Any Counter-Notice under Rule 13(3) SDPR shall be filed at the Tribunal and served on every other party by no later than [4.00pm on [insert date no later than 10 days before the date fixed for the hearing of an application]].

9. Each party must file at the Tribunal and serve on every other party a completed Certificate of Readiness on the attached form by no later than [4.00pm on [insert date 28 days before the date fixed for the hearing of an application].

10. If there remains a dispute about disclosure of documents or witness statements which cannot be resolved between the parties, either party is at liberty to apply to the Tribunal for further Directions.

11. If at the substantive hearing the Respondent wishes his or her means to be taken into consideration by the Tribunal in relation to possible sanctions and/or costs, he/she shall by no later than [4.00pm on [insert date 28 days before the date fixed for the hearing of the application]] file at the Tribunal and serve on every other party a Statement of Means including full details of assets (including, but not limited to, property)/income/outgoings supported by documentary evidence. Any failure to comply with this requirement may result in the Tribunal drawing such inference as it considers appropriate, and the Tribunal will be entitled to determine the sanction and/or costs without regard to the Respondent's means. A failure to comply may also cause the consideration of the Respondent's means to be adjourned by the Tribunal to a later date which may result in an increase in costs.

12. Any party seeking an Order for Costs against another party at an interim hearing shall file with the Tribunal and serve on the relevant party a schedule of costs not less than 48 hours before the hearing in respect of which the costs order is sought.

13. Any party seeking an Order for Costs against another party at a substantive hearing shall file with the Tribunal and serve on the relevant party a schedule of costs not less than 5 working days before the hearing in respect of which the costs order is sought.

14. The Applicant to serve a draft hearing bundle index on every other party by [4.00pm on [insert date]].

15. The parties to agree the content of the hearing bundle by [4.00pm on [insert date]].

16. Four copies of the agreed paginated hearing bundle must be filed at the Tribunal by [4.00pm on [insert date]], unless the documents to be relied upon have been exhibited to the Statement in support of the Application or to any witness statement or affidavit filed at the Tribunal.
17. Where a party wishes to rely upon skeleton arguments and authorities, they shall be filed at the Tribunal and served on every other party by [4.00pm on [insert date]].
18. [Insert other Directions e.g. expert evidence, disclosure]
19. Costs in the Application
20. Liberty to apply

Dated: [insert date]

[CASE HEADING AS IN PROCEEDINGS]

CERTIFICATE OF READINESS

NAME OF PARTY FILING CERTIFICATE:

DATE CERTIFICATE FILED AT TRIBUNAL:

1. I confirm that I sent a copy of this Certificate of Readiness and all documents attached to every other party on (please provide date below):

   DATE:

2. I confirm that I have complied with those Directions which require action by me and that I am ready for the final hearing (please place X in one box below):

YES	
NO	

If you have answered "No" – state the number(s) of the direction(s) with which you have yet to comply and the date by which this will be done. Please use an additional sheet if necessary.

Number of Direction(s) **Date by Which You Will Comply**

3. Do you require any further Directions (please place X in one box below):

YES	
NO	

If you have answered "Yes" – attach to this Certificate your application for further Directions with supporting documents (if applicable) and a draft of the Order sought.

4. How many witnesses will be giving evidence on your behalf at the final hearing?

5. Please provide the name, nature of advocate and contact details below of the person who will be presenting your case at the substantive hearing?

NAME:

COUNSEL OR SOLICITOR: CONTACT DETAILS:

Address:

Preferred Telephone Number:

Preferred Email Address:

Other contact details as applicable:

6. Has the time estimate for the final hearing changed?

YES	
NO	

If you have answered "Yes" please answer the questions below, using an additional sheet if necessary:

a) what are the reasons for this?

b) have you informed the Tribunal and, if so, when?

c) how long do you think the hearing will take?

d) have you agreed the new time estimate with every other party?

e) if not, why not?

SIGNED:

NAME OF SIGNATORY:

PARTY REPRESENTED (IF APPLICABLE):

DATE:

Solicitors Disciplinary Tribunal policy/practice note

Adjournments

(1) The following practice note is to give guidance to Applicants and Respondents who seek an adjournment of a hearing the date of which has been fixed.

(2) Applications for an adjournment made more than 21 days before the hearing date should be made by letter to the Clerk. The letter should

- (a) Indicate the full reasons why an adjournment is being sought
- (b) Provide any documentary evidence in support e.g. medical reports
- (c) State whether the other party to the proceedings supports or opposes the application for an adjournment

(3) The Tribunal will be reluctant to agree to an adjournment unless the request is supported by both parties or, if it is not, the reasons appear to the Tribunal to be justifiable because not to grant an adjournment would result in injustice to the person seeking the adjournment.

(4) The following reasons will NOT generally be regarded as providing justification for an adjournment:

(a) **The Existence of Other Proceedings**

The existence or possibility of criminal proceedings unless the criminal proceedings relate to the same or substantially the same underlying facts as form the basis of the proceedings before the Tribunal AND there is a genuine risk that the proceedings before the Tribunal may 'muddy the waters of justice' so far as concerns the criminal proceedings. Proceedings which are not imminent will not usually meet this criterion. Civil proceedings are even less likely to do so.

(b) **Lack of Readiness**

The lack of readiness on the part of either the Applicant or Respondent or any claimed inconvenience or clash of engagements whether professional or person.

(c) **Ill-health**

The claimed medical condition of the Applicant or Respondent unless this is supported by a reasoned opinion of an appropriate medical adviser. A doctor's certificate issued for social security and statutory sick pay purposes only or other certificate merely indicating that the person is unable to attend for work is unlikely to be sufficient.

(d) **Inability to Secure Representation**

The inability of the Respondent for financial or other reasons to secure the services of a representative at the hearing or financial reasons for the non attendance of the Respondent.

(5) The Tribunal accepts that there may be reasons why an application for an adjournment needs to be made within a three week period before the date which has been fixed for the Hearing. Except for cases where the reason for the adjournment application has genuinely arisen at a very late stage, the Tribunal will expect the Respondent to support a late application for adjournment with a statement of truth as to the reasons for the sought adjournment.

(6) Where the guidance given in this Practice Note is not followed, Applicants and Respondents will appreciate that the Tribunal may, in its discretion and in appropriate cases, order costs to be paid by either or both parties regardless of the outcome of the substantive proceedings.

(7) The Clerk to the Tribunal may agree to the adjournment of a matter if the application is made at least three weeks before the scheduled hearing date and she is satisfied that the adjournment is made in one of the circumstances referred to in this practice note. The Clerk may in any case where she considers it right either seek the approval of the Chairman of the Tribunal or list the matter for an adjournment hearing before a division of the Tribunal sitting in public. The Clerk will endeavour to list the adjournment hearing on a date before that fixed for the substantive hearing.

(8) Those appearing before the Tribunal should be conscious of the need to ensure that cases are heard with reasonable expedition so that the interests of the Public as well as the Profession can be protected. The efficient and timely determination of cases before the Tribunal will usually be in the best interests of all concerned and the Tribunal will always need to be convinced that the interests of justice in any particular cases will be best served by agreeing to an adjournment. **The Tribunal can (and does, therefore, in appropriate cases) exercise its right under the Rules to reject an application for an adjournment and proceed with a substantive hearing on the date which has been previously fixed. The Rules provide that such a hearing may take place in the absence of the Respondent.**

(9) Every application for adjournment will be considered on its own merits and this practice note is made to provide assistance as to matters which the Tribunal will regard as relevant to any such application, and to identify matters which in the experience of the Tribunal are frequently relied upon in support of applications but which, save in

exceptional circumstances, the Tribunal does not currently regard, and would in the future be similarly unlikely to regard as persuasive in themselves.

Anthony Isaacs
President

APPENDIX 13

The Solicitors Disciplinary Tribunal (Appeals and Amendment) Rules 2011

[With consolidated amendments, including correction slip issued 18 January 2013. For details see **www.solicitorstribunal.org.uk/constitution-and-procedures/appeals**]

Solicitors Disciplinary Tribunal (Appeals and Amendment) Rules 2011

SI 2011/2346

Made 22nd September 2011

Coming into force 1st October 2011

The Solicitors Disciplinary Tribunal in exercise of the powers conferred upon it by section 46 of the Solicitors Act 1974 as applied by paragraph 14C(2) of Schedule 2 to the Administration of Justice Act 1985 and section 44E(2) of the Solicitors Act 1974 and following the approval of the Legal Services Board makes the following Rules:

PART 1
INTRODUCTORY

1 Citation, commencement and application

(1) These Rules may be cited as the Solicitors Disciplinary Tribunal (Appeals and Amendment) Rules 2011 and shall come into force on 1st October 2011.

(2) These Rules (except rule 30) apply in relation to—

- (a) appeals to the Tribunal under paragraph 14C of Schedule 2 to the Administration of Justice Act 1985;
- (b) appeals to the Tribunal under section 44E of the 1974 Act (appeals against disciplinary action under section 44D); and
- (c) appeals to the Tribunal in respect of decisions made by the Society which are appealable under Part 5 of the 2007 Act or the Society's licensing rules and which, by virtue of article 4(1) of the Legal Services Act 2007 (Appeals from Licensing Authority Decisions) (No.2) Order 2011 are appeals which may be heard and determined by the Tribunal.

2 Interpretation

In these Rules—

"the 1974 Act" means the Solicitors Act 1974;

"the 2007 Act" means the Legal Services Act 2007;

"the 2007 rules" means the Solicitors (Disciplinary Proceedings) Rules 2007;

"appeal" means a Schedule 2 appeal, a section 44E appeal or a licensing appeal;

"appellant" means—

(a) a person who makes an appeal to the Tribunal; or

(b) a person added or substituted as an appellant under rule 13(1);

"the Board" means the Legal Services Board;

"clerk" has the same meaning as in the 2007 rules;

a "licensing appeal" means an appeal of the type mentioned in rule 1(2)(c);

"Panel" means a panel appointed under rule 3 for the hearing of an appeal or any matter connected with an appeal;

"party" means the appellant or the respondent;

"practice direction" means a practice direction made under rule 10;

"the President" means the President of the Tribunal, appointed under rule 3 of the 2007 rules;

"respondent" means—

(a) the person who made the decision in respect of which an appeal is made; or

(b) a person added or substituted as a respondent under rule 13(1);

a "Schedule 2 appeal" means an appeal of the type mentioned in rule 1(2)(a);

a "section 44E appeal" means an appeal of the type mentioned in rule 1(2)(b);

"the Society" means the Law Society and includes any duly constituted committee of the Law Society or any body or person exercising delegated powers of the Law Society;

"the Society's licensing rules" means licensing rules made by the Society under section 83 of the 2007 Act (licensing rules);

"solicitor members" and "lay members" have the same meanings as in section 46 of the 1974 Act;

a "Stay" means a prohibition on the respondent implementing the decision in respect of which an appeal is made;

"the Tribunal" means the Solicitors Disciplinary Tribunal and where a Panel has been appointed for the hearing of an appeal or any matter connected with it, includes a Panel.

PART 2
CONSTITUTION OF APPEAL PANELS

3 Composition of panel

(1) A Panel of at least three members of the Tribunal shall be appointed by the Tribunal for the hearing of any appeal.

(2) Unless the President otherwise directs, the majority of the Panel members shall be solicitor members.

4 Appointment of chairman

The chairman of each Panel shall be appointed by the Tribunal and (unless the President determines otherwise) shall be a solicitor member.

5 Delegation

(1) The duties to be performed by the clerks shall, in addition to the duties listed in rule 3(11) of the 2007 rules, include—

(a) appointing panels under rule 3(1);

(b) appointing a chairman of a Panel under rule 4; and

(c) giving directions under rules 9, 13 and 19(1).

(2) Paragraph (1) is without prejudice to rule 3(11) of the 2007 rules.

(3) No later than the date on which expires the period of 14 days beginning with the date on which the Tribunal sends notice to a party of a decision made by a clerk in exercise of functions of a judicial nature under paragraph (1), that party may send an application in writing to the Tribunal for that decision to be considered afresh by a Panel or a single solicitor member.

(4) The following powers of the Tribunal may be exercised by a single solicitor member—

(a) giving directions under rules 9, 13,14(2), (4) and (5), 15 and 19(1);

(b) taking action under rule 11(2)(a) and (b);

(c) making a decision under rule 14(1);

(d) giving consent under rule 16(2).

PART 3
APPEAL PROCEDURE

6 Notice of appeal

(1) An appellant must start proceedings for an appeal by sending or delivering a notice of appeal to the Tribunal.

(2) In the case of a Schedule 2 appeal, the notice of appeal must be sent or delivered so that it is received by the Tribunal no later than the date on which expires the period of 28 days beginning with the date on which the appellant was notified in writing of the decision in question under paragraph 14B(4) of Schedule 2 to the Administration of Justice Act 1985.

(3) In the case of a section 44E appeal, the notice of appeal must be sent or delivered so that it is received by the Tribunal no later than the date on which expires the period of 28 days beginning with the date on which the appellant was notified in writing of the decision in question under section 44D(4) of the 1974 Act.

(4) The notice of appeal must set out—

(a) the name and address of the appellant;

(b) the name and address of the appellant's representative (if any);

(c) an address where documents for the appellant may be sent or delivered;

(d) the basis on which the appellant has standing to start proceedings before the Tribunal;

(e) the name and address of the respondent;

(f) details of the decision or act to which the proceedings relate;

(g) the result the appellant is seeking;

(h) the grounds on which the appellant relies;

(ha) any application for an order for a Stay, if the appellant is allowed to make such an application under the Society's licensing rules;

(i) whether the appellant would be content for the case to be dealt with without a hearing if the Tribunal considers it appropriate; and

(j) any further information or documents required by a practice direction.

(4A) In the case of a licensing appeal made under the Society's licensing rules, if no time limit for the making of an appeal is prescribed under those rules, the notice of appeal must be sent or delivered so that it is received by the Tribunal no later than the date on which expires the period of 28 days beginning with the date on which the appellant was notified in writing of the decision which is the subject of the appeal.

(5) The appellant must send or deliver with the notice of appeal a copy of any written record of the decision in respect of which the appeal is made, and any statement of reasons for that decision that the appellant has or can reasonably obtain.

(6) The appellant must send or deliver three additional copies of the notice of appeal and any accompanying documents to the Tribunal at the same time as the appellant sends or delivers the notice of appeal to the Tribunal.

(7) The appellant must send or deliver a copy of the notice of appeal and any accompanying documents to the respondent at the same time as the appellant sends or delivers the notice of appeal to the Tribunal.

7 Response to notice of appeal

(1) The respondent must send or deliver to the Tribunal a response to the notice of appeal so that it is received no later than the date on which expires the period of 28 days beginning with the date on which the respondent received the notice of appeal.

(2) The response must set out at least—

(a) the name and address of the respondent;

(b) the name and address of the respondent's representative (if any);

(c) an address where documents for the respondent may be sent or delivered;

(d) any further information or documents required by a practice direction or a direction given under these Rules; and

(e) whether the respondent would be content for the case to be dealt with without a hearing if the Tribunal considers it appropriate.

(3) The response must include a statement as to whether the respondent opposes the appellant's case and, if so, any grounds for such opposition which are not contained in another document sent or delivered with the response.

(4) The respondent must send or deliver with the response—

(a) a copy of any written record of the decision, in respect of which the appeal is made, and any statement of reasons for that decision, that the appellant did not send or deliver with the notice of appeal and the respondent has or can reasonably obtain; and

(b) any documents relied upon by the respondent in making the decision in respect of which the appeal is made and which the respondent considers are relevant to the appeal.

(5) If the respondent sends or delivers the response to the Tribunal later than the time required by paragraph (1) or by any extension of time under rule 9(2)(a), the response must include a request for an extension of time and the reason why the response was not sent or delivered in time.

(6) The respondent must send or deliver three additional copies of the response and any accompanying documents to the Tribunal at the same time as the respondent sends or delivers the response to the Tribunal.

(7) The respondent must send or deliver a copy of the response and any accompanying documents to the appellant at the same time as it sends or delivers the response to the Tribunal.

8 Appellant's reply

(1) The appellant may send or deliver to the Tribunal—

(a) a reply to the respondent's response; and

(b) any additional documents relied upon by the appellant in the reply.

(2) Any reply and additional documents must be sent or delivered to the Tribunal so that they are received no later than the date on which expires the period of 14 days beginning with the date on which the appellant received the notice from the respondent.

(3) If the appellant sends or delivers a reply to the Tribunal later than the time required by paragraph (2) or by any extension of time under rule 9(2)(a) the reply must include a request for an extension of time and the reason why the reply was not sent or delivered in time.

(4) The appellant may send or deliver with the reply a list of documents on which the appellant relies in support of the appeal, and which the appellant did not send or deliver with the notice of appeal.

(5) The appellant must send or deliver three additional copies of the reply and any accompanying documents to the Tribunal at the same time as the appellant sends or delivers the reply to the Tribunal.

(6) The appellant must send or deliver a copy of any reply and any accompanying documents to the respondent at the same time as the appellant sends or delivers the reply to the Tribunal.

(7) If the appellant has sent or delivered a list of documents under paragraph (4), the appellant must within 7 days of receiving a request from the respondent or the Tribunal—

(a) send or deliver to the respondent or Tribunal a copy of any document specified in the list (and in the case of the Tribunal, any additional copies of the document requested by the Tribunal, up to a maximum of four in number); or

(b) make such document available to the respondent or Tribunal to read or copy.

9 Directions and case management

(1) The Tribunal may give a direction in relation to the conduct or disposal of appeal proceedings at any time, including a direction amending, suspending or setting aside an earlier direction.

(2) In particular, and without restricting the general powers in paragraph (1) and rule 18, the Tribunal may—

(a) extend or shorten the time for complying with any rule, practice direction or direction, unless such extension or shortening would conflict with a provision of another enactment (or of any rule made under another enactment) containing a time limit;

(b) consolidate or hear together two or more sets of proceedings or parts of proceedings raising common issues, or treat a case as a lead case (whether under rule 15 or otherwise);

(ba) hear any application for an Order or a Stay;

(c) permit or require a party to amend a document;

(d) permit or require a party or another person to provide documents, information or submissions which are relevant to the proceedings to the Tribunal or a party;

(e) deal with an issue in the proceedings as a preliminary issue;

(f) hold a hearing to consider any matter, including a case management issue;

(g) decide the form of any hearing;

(h) adjourn or postpone a hearing;

(i) require a party to produce a bundle for a hearing;

(j) require a party to provide a skeleton argument;

(k) decide the place and time of any hearing;

(l) make requirements about documentation and inspection:

(m) stay proceedings;

(n) suspend the effect of its own decision pending the determination by the High Court of an application for permission to appeal against, and any appeal of, that decision.

(3) A clerk may appoint a time and place for the review of the progress of the matter and shall notify the parties of the date, time and place of any such review.

(4) A clerk may refer to the Tribunal any matter for a decision or directions and the Tribunal may itself or on the application of any party make a decision on such terms as to the Tribunal shall appear just—

(a) to adjourn any hearing listed for directions or for a substantive hearing;

(b) to agree to the amendment of any document or the correction of any matter;

(c) to make any directions which shall appear necessary or appropriate to secure the timely hearing of the appeal.

(5) Any hearing under this rule shall be held in public unless rule 23(2) or (3) applies.

10 Practice directions

(1) The Tribunal (or a panel of Tribunal members consisting of not less than 5 members of whom no fewer than 2 shall be lay members) may give such notices or make such directions concerning the practices or procedures of the Tribunal as are consistent with these Rules and as shall seem appropriate.

(2) The Tribunal shall promulgate notices or directions given or made under paragraph (1) under the authority of the President.

11 Failure to comply with rules, practice directions or tribunal directions

(1) An irregularity resulting from a failure to comply with any provision of these Rules, a practice direction or a direction given under these Rules does not of itself render void the appeal or any step taken in the appeal.

(2) If a party has failed to comply with a requirement in these Rules, a practice direction or a direction given under these Rules, the Tribunal may take such action as the Tribunal considers just, which may include—

(a) waiving the requirement;

(b) requiring the failure to be remedied;

(c) exercising its power under rule 12;

(d) otherwise barring or restricting a party's participation in the appeal.

(3) The Tribunal may not bar or restrict a party's participation in the appeal under paragraph (2)(d) without first giving the party an opportunity to make representations in relation to the proposed action.

12 Striking out a party's case

(1) The Tribunal must strike out the whole or a part of an appeal if the Tribunal does not have jurisdiction in relation to the appeal or that part of it.

(2) The Tribunal may strike out the whole or a part of an appeal if—

(a) the appellant has failed to comply with a direction given under these Rules which stated that failure by the appellant to comply with the direction could lead to the striking out of the appeal or part of it;

(b) the appellant has failed to co-operate with the Tribunal to such an extent that the Tribunal cannot deal with the appeal fairly and justly; or

(c) the Tribunal considers there is no reasonable prospect of the appellant's case, or part of it, succeeding.

(3) The Tribunal may not strike out the whole or a part of the appeal under paragraph (1) or (2)(b) or (c) without first giving the appellant an opportunity to make representations in relation to the proposed striking out.

(4) If the appeal, or part of it, has been struck out under paragraph (2)(a), the appellant may apply for the appeal, or part of it, to be reinstated.

(5) An application under paragraph (4) must be made in writing and received by the Tribunal no later than the date on which expires the period of 28 days beginning with the date on which the Tribunal sent notification of the striking out to the appellant.

(6) This rule applies to a respondent as it applies to an appellant except that—

(a) a reference to the striking out of the whole or a part of the appeal is to be read as a reference to the striking out of the whole or a part of the response to the appeal; and

(b) a reference to an application for the reinstatement of an appeal which has been struck out is to be read as a reference to an application for the reinstatement of a response to an appeal which has been struck out.

13 Addition, substitution and removal of parties

(1) The Tribunal may give a direction adding, substituting or removing a party as an appellant or a respondent.

(2) If the Tribunal gives a direction under paragraph (1) it may give such consequential directions as it considers appropriate.

(3) A person who is not a party may apply to the Tribunal to be added or substituted as a party.

(4) If a person who is entitled to be a party to an appeal by virtue of another enactment applies to be added as a party, and any conditions applicable to that entitlement have been satisfied, the Tribunal must give a direction adding that person as a respondent or, if appropriate, as an appellant.

14 Prevention of disclosure or publication of documents and information

(1) The Tribunal may make a decision prohibiting the disclosure or publication of—

(a) specified documents or information relating to any appeal proceedings; or

(b) any matter likely to lead members of the public to identify any person whom the Tribunal considers should not be identified.

(2) The Tribunal may give a direction prohibiting the disclosure of a document or information to a person if—

(a) the Tribunal is satisfied that such disclosure would be likely to cause that person or some other person serious harm; and

(b) the Tribunal is satisfied, having regard to the interests of justice, that it is proportionate to give such a direction.

(3) If a party ("the first party") considers that the Tribunal should give a direction under paragraph (2) prohibiting the disclosure of a document or information to another party ("the second party"), the first party must—

(a) exclude the relevant document or information from any documents that will be sent or delivered to the second party; and

(b) send or deliver to the Tribunal the excluded document or information, and the reason for its exclusion, so that the Tribunal may decide whether the document or information should be disclosed to the second party or should be the subject of a direction under paragraph (2).

(4) If the Tribunal gives a direction under paragraph (2) which prevents disclosure to a party who has appointed a representative, the Tribunal may give a direction that the documents or information be disclosed to that representative if the Tribunal is satisfied that—

(a) disclosure to the representative would be in the interests of the party; and

(b) the representative will act in accordance with paragraph (5).

(5) Documents or information disclosed to a representative in accordance with a direction under paragraph (4) must not be disclosed either directly or indirectly to any other person without the Tribunal's consent.

(6) The Tribunal may, on its own initiative or on the application of a party, give a direction that certain documents or information must or may be disclosed to the Tribunal on the basis that the Tribunal will not disclose such documents or information to other persons, or specified other persons.

(7) A party making an application for a direction under paragraph (6) may withhold the relevant documents or information from other parties until the Tribunal has granted or refused the application.

(8) Unless the Tribunal considers that there is good reason not to do so, the Tribunal must send notice that a party has made an application for a direction under paragraph (6) to each other party.

(9) The Tribunal must conduct proceedings and record its decision and reasons appropriately so as not to undermine the effect of a decision made under paragraph (1) or a direction given under paragraph (2) or (6).

15 Lead cases

(1) This rule applies if—

(a) two or more appeals have been started before the Tribunal;

(b) in each such appeal the Tribunal has not made a decision finally disposing of all issues in the proceedings; and

(c) the appeals give rise to common or related issues of fact or law.

(2) The Tribunal may give a direction—

(a) specifying one or more appeals falling under paragraph (1) as a lead case or lead cases; and

(b) staying the other appeals falling under paragraph (1) ("the related cases").

(3) When the Tribunal makes a decision in respect of the common or related issues—

(a) the Tribunal must send or deliver a copy of that decision to each party in each of the related appeals; and

(b) subject to paragraph (4), that decision shall be binding on each of those parties.

(4) No later than the date on which expires the period of 28 days beginning with the date on which the Tribunal sent or delivered a copy of the decision to a party under paragraph (3)(a), that party may apply in writing for a direction that the decision does not apply to, and is not binding on the parties to, a particular related appeal.

(5) The Tribunal must give directions in respect of appeals which are stayed under paragraph (2)(b), providing for the disposal of or further directions in those appeals.

(6) If the lead case or cases lapse or are withdrawn before the Tribunal makes a decision in respect of the common or related issues, the Tribunal must give directions as to—

(a) whether another appeal or other appeals are to be specified as a lead case or lead cases; and

(b) whether any direction affecting the related appeals should be set aside or amended.

16 Withdrawal

(1) Subject to paragraph (2), an appellant may give notice of the withdrawal of its appeal, or any part of it, and the respondent may do likewise in respect of its case against the appeal—

(a) at any time before a hearing to consider the disposal of the appeal (or, if the Tribunal disposes of the appeal without a hearing, before that disposal), by sending or delivering to the Tribunal a written notice of withdrawal; or

(b) orally at a hearing.

(2) Notice of withdrawal will not take effect unless the Tribunal consents to the withdrawal, which may be given subject to such order relating to costs as the Tribunal shall think fit.

(3) A party which has withdrawn its appeal or case against the appeal may apply to the Tribunal for the appeal or case to be reinstated.

(4) An application under paragraph (3) must be made in writing and be received by the Tribunal no later than the date on which expires the period of 28 days beginning with—

(a) the date on which the Tribunal received the notice under paragraph (1)(a); or

(b) the date of the hearing at which the appeal or case was withdrawn orally under paragraph (1)(b).

(5) The Tribunal must notify each party in writing of a withdrawal under this rule.

17 Consent orders

(1) The Tribunal may, at the request of the parties and only if it considers it appropriate, make a consent order disposing of the appeal proceedings and making such other appropriate provision as the parties have agreed.

(2) Despite any other provision of these Rules, the Tribunal need not hold a hearing before making an order under paragraph (1), or provide reasons for the order.

18 General powers of Tribunal

(1) Subject to the provisions of these Rules, the Tribunal may regulate its own procedure.

(2) The Tribunal may dispense with any requirements of these Rules in respect of notices, statements or other documents, witnesses, service or time in any case where it appears to the Tribunal to be just so to do.

19 Disclosure, evidence and submissions

(1) Without restriction on the general powers in rule 9 and 18, the Tribunal may give directions in relation to an appeal as to—

(a) the exchange between parties of lists of documents which are relevant to the appeal, or relevant to particular issues, and the inspection of such documents;

(b) the provision by parties of statements of agreed matters;

(c) issues on which it requires evidence or submissions;

(d) the nature of the evidence or submissions it requires;

(e) whether the parties are permitted or required to provide expert evidence, and if so whether the parties must jointly appoint a single expert to provide such evidence;

(f) any limit on the number of witnesses whose evidence a party may put forward, whether in relation to a particular issue or generally;

(g) the manner in which any evidence or submissions are to be provided, which may include a direction for them to be given—

(i) orally at a hearing; or

(ii) by written submissions or witness statement; and

(h) the time at which any evidence or submissions are to be sent or delivered.

(2) The Tribunal may—

(a) admit evidence whether or not—

(i) the evidence would be admissible in a civil trial in the United Kingdom; or

(ii) the evidence was available to a previous decision maker; or

(b) exclude evidence that would otherwise be admissible where—

(i) the evidence was not provided within the time allowed by a direction given under these Rules or a practice direction;

(ii) the evidence was otherwise provided in a manner that did not comply with a direction given under these Rules or a practice direction; or

(iii) it would otherwise be unfair, disproportionate or unnecessary in the interests of justice to admit the evidence.

(3) The Tribunal may consent to a witness giving, or require any witness to give, evidence on oath, and may administer an oath for that purpose.

20 Written evidence

(1) The Tribunal may in its discretion, in respect of a whole case or of any particular fact or facts, proceed and act upon evidence given by Statement.

(2) Every Statement upon which any party proposes to rely shall be sent or delivered to the clerk and to all other parties no later than 21 days before the date fixed for the hearing of the appeal together with a notice in the form of Form 1 in the Schedule.

(3) Any party on whom a notice has been served under paragraph (2) and who requires the attendance, at the hearing, of the witness in question shall, no later than 9 days before the date of the hearing require, in writing, the other party to produce the witness at the hearing.

(4) If no party requires the attendance of a witness in accordance with the provisions of this rule, the Tribunal may accept the Statement in question in evidence.

(5) If any party intends to call as a witness any person who has not produced a Statement, he must, no later than 10 days before the date fixed for the hearing, notify the clerk and any other party to the proceedings of his intention and forthwith send or deliver a copy of a written proof of evidence to the other party and lodge five copies of the proof with the clerk.

(6) In this rule, "Statement" means a written statement (including a witness statement) containing a statement that the party putting forward or making the Statement believes the facts stated in the Statement are true.

21 Decision with or without a hearing

(1) The Tribunal must hold a hearing before making a decision which disposes of proceedings unless—

(a) each party has consented to the matter being determined without a hearing; and

(b) the Tribunal is satisfied that it can properly determine the issues without a hearing.

(2) Despite anything to the contrary in these Rules, if the Tribunal holds a hearing to consider a preliminary issue, and following the disposal of that preliminary issue no further issue remains to be determined, the Tribunal may dispose of the proceedings without holding any further hearing.

22 Listing of appeal hearing

(1) Unless the Tribunal has made directions in respect of the hearing of an appeal, a clerk shall appoint a date for the hearing by the Tribunal and shall give notice of the date to the parties.

(2) The hearing shall not, unless all the parties have agreed or the Tribunal has so ordered, take place sooner than the date on which expires the period of 28 days beginning with the date of service of the notice appointing the date of the hearing.

23 Public or private hearings

(1) Subject to paragraphs (2) and (3) every appeal hearing shall take place in public.

(2) Any party and any person who claims to be affected by an appeal may seek a decision from the Tribunal that the hearing or part of it be conducted in private on the grounds of—

(a) exceptional hardship; or

(b) exceptional prejudice,

to a party, a witness or any person affected by the appeal.

(3) If it is satisfied that those grounds are met, the Tribunal shall conduct the hearing or part of it in private and make such decision as shall appear to it to be just and proper.

(4) The Tribunal may, before or during a hearing, direct that the hearing or part of it be held in private if—

(a) the Tribunal is satisfied that it would have granted an application under paragraph (2) had one been made; or

(b) in the Tribunal's view a hearing in public would prejudice the interests of justice.

(5) The Tribunal may give a direction excluding from any hearing, or part of it—

(a) any person whose conduct the Tribunal considers is disrupting or is likely to disrupt the hearing;

(b) any person whose presence the Tribunal considers is likely to prevent another person from giving evidence or making submissions freely;

(c) any person who the Tribunal considers should be excluded in order to give effect to the requirement at rule 14(9); or

(d) any person where the purpose of the hearing would be defeated by the attendance of that person.

(6) The Tribunal may give a direction excluding a witness from a hearing until that witness gives evidence.

24 Decisions

(1) The Tribunal may announce a decision orally at a hearing of or relating to an appeal or may reserve its decision for announcement at a later date. In either case the announcement shall be made in public.

(2) Subject to rule 14(9), the Tribunal must provide to each party as soon as reasonably practicable after making a decision which finally disposes of all issues in the proceedings—

(a) an order stating the Tribunal's decision;

(b) written reasons for the decision; and

(c) notification of any right of appeal against the decision and the time within which, and manner in which, such right of appeal may be exercised.

(3) The Tribunal may provide written reasons for any decision to which paragraph (2) does not apply.

(4) An order under paragraph (2)(a) shall be signed by a member of the Tribunal upon the announcement of the decision and shall, subject to paragraph (5), be filed forthwith with the Society.

(5) The Tribunal may suspend the filing of an order under paragraph (2)(a) if it appears to the Tribunal that there is good reason to do so, in which event the decision shall not take effect until the order is filed with the Society.

(6) Subject to rule 14(9), the Tribunal may publicise a decision in such manner as it thinks fit.

25 Re-hearing where a party neither appears nor is represented

(1) At any time before the date on which expires the period of 14 days beginning with the date on which an order was provided to the party under rule 24(2), a party may apply to the Tribunal for a re-hearing of an appeal if—

(a) he neither attended in person nor was represented at the hearing of the appeal in question; and

(b) the Tribunal determined the appeal in his absence.

(2) An application for a re-hearing under this rule shall be made in the form of Form 2 in the Schedule and shall be supported by a statement setting out the facts upon which the applicant wishes to rely.

(3) If satisfied that it is just so to do, the Tribunal may grant the application upon such terms, including as to costs, as it thinks fit. The re-hearing shall be held before a Panel comprised of different members from those who heard the original appeal.

PART 4
MISCELLANEOUS

26 Sending and delivery of documents

(1) Any document to be sent or delivered to the Tribunal or to a party under these Rules, a practice direction or a direction given under these Rules must be—

(a) sent by pre-paid first class post or by document exchange, or delivered by hand, to the address specified for the proceedings;

(b) sent by fax (in the case of documents to be sent or delivered to the Tribunal, to the number specified for the proceedings); or

(c) sent or delivered by such other method as the Tribunal may permit or direct.

(2) Subject to paragraph (3), if a party provides a fax number, email address or other details for the electronic transmission of documents to them, that party must accept delivery of documents by that method.

(3) If a party informs the Tribunal and all other parties that a particular form of communication, other than pre-paid post or delivery by hand, should not be used to send or deliver documents to that party, that form of communication must not be so used.

(4) If the Tribunal or a party sends a document to a party or the Tribunal by email or any other electronic means of communication, the recipient may request that the sender send or deliver a hard copy of the document to the recipient. The recipient must make such a request as soon as reasonably practicable after receiving the document electronically.

(5) The Tribunal and each party may assume that the address provided by a party or its representative is and remains the address to which documents should be sent or delivered until receiving written notification to the contrary.

(6) If a document submitted to the Tribunal is not written in English, it must be accompanied by an English translation.

27 Calculating time

(1) An act required by these Rules, a practice direction or a direction given under these Rules to be done on or by a particular day must be done by 5pm on that day.

(2) If the time specified by these Rules, a practice direction or a direction given under these Rules for doing any act ends on a day other than a working day, the act is done in time if it is done on the next working day.

(3) In this rule "working day" means any day except a Saturday or Sunday, Christmas Day, Good Friday or a bank holiday under section 1 of the Banking and Financial Dealings Act 1971.

28 Representatives

(1) A party may appoint a representative (whether a legal representative or not) to represent that party in the proceedings.

(2) If a party appoints a representative, that party (or the representative if the representative is a legal representative) must send or deliver to the Tribunal written notice of the representative's name and address, together with a copy of the notice.

(3) A party who sends or delivers a notice under paragraph (2) must, at the same time, send or deliver a copy of the notice to the other party.

(4) Anything permitted or required to be done by a party under these Rules, a practice direction or a direction given under these Rules may be done by the representative of that party, except signing a witness statement.

(5) A person who receives due notice of the appointment of a representative—

(a) must send or deliver to the representative any document which, at any time after the appointment, is required to be sent or delivered to the represented party, and need not send or deliver that document to the represented party; and

(b) may assume that the representative is and remains authorised as such until they receive written notification that this is not so from the representative or the represented party.

(6) At a hearing a party may be accompanied by another person whose name and address has not been notified under paragraph (2) but who, with the permission of the Tribunal, may act as a representative or otherwise assist in presenting the party's case at the hearing.

(7) Paragraphs (2) to (5) do not apply to a person who accompanies a party under paragraph (6).

(8) In this rule "legal representative" means a person who, for the purposes of the 2007 Act, is an authorised person in relation to an activity which constitutes the exercise of a right of audience or the conduct of litigation within the meaning of that Act, an advocate or solicitor in Scotland or a barrister or solicitor in Northern Ireland.

29 Costs

(1) The Tribunal may, at any stage of an appeal, make such order as to costs as the Tribunal shall think fit, including an order—

(a) disallowing costs incurred unnecessarily; or

(b) that costs be paid by any party judged to be responsible for wasted or unnecessary costs, whether arising through failure to comply with time limits or otherwise.

(2) The Tribunal may order that any party bear the whole or a part or a proportion of the costs.

(3) The amount of costs to be paid may either be fixed by the Tribunal or be subject to detailed assessment by a Costs Judge.

(4) The Tribunal may also make an order as to costs under this rule where any appeal is withdrawn or amended.

30 Amendment of 2007 rules

(1) The 2007 rules are amended as follows.

(2) In Form 6 in the Schedule, for "21 days" substitute "9 days".

Signed by authority of the Solicitors Disciplinary Tribunal

Jeremy Barnecutt

President

Solicitors Disciplinary Tribunal

22nd September 2011

SCHEDULE
FORMS

Rules 20(2) and 25(2)

FORM 1

FORM of NOTICE to accompany Statement of Evidence

Number ....

IN THE MATTER OF the Solicitors Disciplinary Tribunal (Appeals and Amendment) Rules 2011

AND IN THE MATTER OF

....

TAKE NOTICE that the [appellant][respondent] proposes to rely upon the statement(s) listed below, copies of which are served herewith.

If you wish any person who has made one of these statements to be required to attend the hearing as a witness you must, not less than 9 days before the date set down for the hearing of the appeal, notify me and the Clerk to the Tribunal to that effect. In the event of your failure to do so the Tribunal may accept the statement in question in evidence.

LIST

Date of Statement	Name of Person who made the Statement
1.	
2.	
3.	

Date: ....

Signed: ....

Address: ....

FORM 2

FORM of APPLICATION for a Rehearing

Number ....

IN THE MATTER OF the Solicitors Disciplinary Tribunal (Appeals and Amendment) Rules 2011

AND IN THE MATTER OF

....

Number of Tribunal case in respect of which a rehearing is requested ....

I APPLY under Rule 25(1) of the Solicitors Disciplinary Tribunal (Appeals and Amendment) Rules 2011 that the above-mentioned case be reheard by the Tribunal. The facts upon which I rely in support of this application are set out below:

(set out here full details of the facts on which the applicant for a rehearing relies and include the reasons why the person applying for the rehearing did not appear or was not represented before the Tribunal at the earlier hearing and set out all matters which he wishes to place before the Tribunal in mitigation or otherwise).

Dated: ....

Signature: ....

Address: ....

APPENDIX 14

Solicitors Disciplinary Tribunal guidance note on sanctions

[Reproduced with the kind permission of the Solicitors Disciplinary Tribunal. Issued by the SDT September 2013]

Guidance note on sanctions

Introduction

This Guidance Note consists of a distillation of current Solicitors Disciplinary Tribunal ("the Tribunal") sanctioning principles brought together in one document. Every case is fact-specific, and this Guidance Note consists of guidelines only; it is not intended in any way to fetter the discretion of the Tribunal when deciding sanction. The exercise of its powers and the imposition of sanctions are matters solely for determination by the Tribunal. The purpose of this Guidance Note is to assist the parties, the public and the profession in understanding the Tribunal's decision-making process.

The Tribunal is the statutory tribunal responsible for adjudicating upon applications and complaints made under the provisions of the Solicitors Act 1974 (as amended) ("the Act").

It is the function of the Tribunal to protect the public from harm, to maintain public confidence in the profession and to preserve the reputation of the solicitors' profession for honesty, probity, trustworthiness, independence and integrity.

The Tribunal deals with an infinite variety of cases. Prescriptive, detailed guidelines for sanctions in individual cases are neither practicable nor appropriate. The Tribunal adopts broad guidance. Its focus is to establish the seriousness of the misconduct and, from that, to determine a fair and proportionate sanction.

Section A: Principles and procedure

Sanctions and orders available to the Tribunal

Solicitors

1. The Tribunal's jurisdiction and powers on an application are set out in Section 47 of the Act and include:
   - the imposition of a reprimand
   - the imposition of a financial penalty payable to HM Treasury
   - suspension from practice indefinitely or for a specified period
   - striking off the Roll of Solicitors

2. The Tribunal is not restricted as to the number or combination of sanctions which it may impose.

3. Other orders which the Tribunal can make in respect of solicitors or former solicitors include:

   - no order
   - restrictions upon the way in which a solicitor can practise
   - termination of a period of suspension
   - restoration to the Roll following strike off
   - costs

Solicitors' employees

4. By Section 43 of the Act the Tribunal has a limited jurisdiction to deal with misconduct by those who are not admitted but are employed or remunerated by solicitors. The powers which the Tribunal may exercise in respect of such individuals are:

   - to make no order
   - to make an order prohibiting, save with the prior consent of the regulator, any solicitor from employing the person to whom the order relates

Purpose of sanctions

5. The case of *Bolton v The Law Society* [1994] 1 WLR 512 sets out the fundamental principle and purposes of the imposition of sanctions by the Tribunal:

> "Any solicitor who is shown to have discharged his professional duties with anything less than complete integrity, probity and trustworthiness must expect severe sanctions to be imposed upon him by the Solicitors Disciplinary Tribunal."

> "… a penalty may be visited on a solicitor … in order to punish him for what he has done and to deter any other solicitor tempted to behave in the same way …"

> "… to be sure that the offender does not have the opportunity to repeat the offence; and"

> "… the most fundamental of all: to maintain the reputation of the solicitors' profession as one in which every member, of whatever standing, may be trusted to the ends of the earth … a member of the public … is ordinarily entitled to expect that the solicitor will be a person whose trustworthiness is not, and never has been, seriously in question. Otherwise, the whole profession, and the public as a whole, is injured. A profession's most valuable asset is its collective reputation and the confidence which that inspires." (Sir Thomas Bingham, then Master of the Rolls)

Human rights, equality and diversity

6. The Tribunal is a "public authority" for the purposes of the Human Rights Act 1998, and it seeks to uphold and promote the principles of the European Convention on Human Rights in accordance with the Act. In deciding what sanction, if any, to impose the Tribunal should have regard to the principle of proportionality, weighing the interests of the public with those of the practitioner. The interference with the solicitor's right to practice must be no more than necessary to achieve the Tribunal's purpose in imposing sanctions. Reasons should be given for the sanction imposed, and the decision should usually be pronounced publicly.

The Tribunal is committed to promoting equality, diversity and inclusion in carrying out all its functions. It values and embraces difference and individuality in its staff, those who work on its behalf and the public it serves. It aims to ensure that its processes and procedures are fair, objective and transparent and free from unlawful discrimination. Promoting equality is also a requirement under current and emerging equality legislation. Everyone who is acting for the Tribunal and Tribunal Members are expected to adhere to the spirit and letter of this legislation.

Common procedural issues affecting sanction

Admission, but dispute as to facts

7. A respondent may admit the alleged misconduct, but dispute particular details. Where the dispute is such that it would materially affect sanction, the Tribunal decides the factual basis upon which sanction will be based.

8. The Tribunal adopts the principle established in *R v Newton* [1983] Crim LR 198, and will only impose sanction upon a respondent where the particular misconduct is either admitted by, or proved against him.

9. If at a hearing to establish the facts on which sanction is to be based (a "Newton hearing"), the respondent fails to adduce evidence in support of facts exclusively within his knowledge, this will entitle the Tribunal to draw such inference from that failure as it might see fit – *R v Underwood* [2005] 1 Cr.App.R. 13.

10. Once the factual basis has been established, the respondent will have the opportunity to make representations as to the level of sanction to be imposed before the Tribunal makes its final decision.

Multiple/Alternative Allegations

11. Multiple allegations involving essentially the same wrongdoing committed concurrently, drafted in the alternative, or numerous similar examples of wrong-doing committed over a period of time, sometimes come before the Tribunal. When some or all of such allegations are found proved, it may be disproportionate and unjust to impose a sanction for each matter. In such a situation the Tribunal may in respect of matters found proved:

- impose a sanction, determined by the totality of the misconduct, which is specified as being in respect of all those matters; or
- impose a sanction on the more serious allegation/s, and make no separate order (or sanction) in respect of other more minor matters.

Sanction for each separate and distinct allegation

12. Where distinct and separate allegations are either admitted or proved, the Tribunal may:

- impose a particular sanction (determined by the totality of the misconduct) specified as being in respect of all matters; or
- determine the individual seriousness of each separate and distinct proven allegation, and the appropriate sanction in respect of each. Sanctions imposed will be proportionate to the totality of the misconduct.

Section B: Determining sanction

Assessing seriousness

13. The Tribunal will assess the seriousness of the misconduct in order to determine which sanction to impose. Seriousness is determined by a combination of factors, including:

- the respondent's culpability for their misconduct
- the harm caused by the respondent's misconduct
- the existence of any aggravating factors
- the existence of any mitigating factors

Culpability

14. The level of culpability will be influenced by such factors as (but not limited to):
    - the respondent's motivation for the misconduct
    - whether the misconduct arose from actions which were planned or spontaneous
    - the extent to which the respondent acted in breach of a position of trust
    - the extent to which the respondent had direct control of or responsibility for the circumstances giving rise to the misconduct
    - respondent's level of experience and harm caused

Harm

15. In determining harm, the Tribunal will assess:
    - the impact of the respondent's misconduct upon the public and the reputation of the profession. The greater the extent of the respondent's departure from the "complete integrity, probity and trustworthiness" expected of a solicitor, the greater the harm to the profession's reputation
    - the extent of the harm that was intended or might reasonably foreseeably have been caused by the respondent's misconduct

Aggravating Factors

16. Factors that aggravate the seriousness of the misconduct include (but are not limited to):
    - dishonesty where alleged and proved.
    - misconduct involving the commission of a criminal offence, not limited to dishonesty
    - misconduct which was deliberate and calculated or repeated
    - misconduct continuing over a period of time
    - taking advantage of a vulnerable person
    - concealment of wrongdoing
    - misconduct where the respondent knew or ought reasonably to have known that the conduct complained of was in material breach of obligations to protect the public and the reputation of the profession
    - previous disciplinary matter(s) before the Tribunal where allegations were found proved

Mitigating Factors

17. Factors that mitigate the seriousness of the misconduct itself include (but are not limited to):

- misconduct resulting from deception or otherwise by a third party (including the client)
- the timing of and extent to which any loss arising from the misconduct is made good by the respondent
- whether the respondent voluntarily notified the regulator of the facts and circumstances giving rise to misconduct
- whether the misconduct was either a single episode, or one of very brief duration in a previously unblemished career
- genuine insight
- open and frank admissions at an early stage and/or degree of cooperation with the investigating body

NOTE: Matters of purely personal mitigation are of no relevance in determining the seriousness of the misconduct. However, they will be considered by the Tribunal when determining the fair and proportionate sanction (see below, paragraphs 44 and 45).

Particular sanctions

18. Having determined the seriousness of the misconduct, the Tribunal will assess whether to make an order, and if so, which sanction to impose.

No Order

19. The Tribunal may conclude that, having regard to all the circumstances, and where the Tribunal has concluded that the level of seriousness of the misconduct or culpability of the respondent is low, that it would be unfair or disproportionate to impose a sanction. In such circumstances, the Tribunal may decide not to impose a sanction, save for an order for costs.

Reprimand

20. A Reprimand will be imposed where the Tribunal has determined that the seriousness of the respondent's misconduct justifies a sanction at the lowest level and that the protection of the public and the reputation of the profession does not require a greater sanction.

21. Relevant factors may include:
    - the respondent's culpability is low
    - there is no identifiable harm caused to any individual
    - the risk of any such harm was negligible
    - the likelihood of future misconduct of a similar nature or any misconduct is very low
    - evidence of genuine insight
    - minor breaches of regulation not dealt with under the Solicitors Regulation Authority's own disciplinary jurisdiction

Fine

22. A Fine will be imposed where the Tribunal has determined that the seriousness of the misconduct is such that a Reprimand will not be a sufficient sanction, but neither the protection of the public nor the protection of the reputation of the profession justifies Suspension or Strike Off.

Level of Fine

23. The Tribunal will consider the following in determining the appropriate level of Fine or combination of Fines to be imposed:

- there is no limit to the level of Fine the Tribunal may impose. In deciding the level of Fine, the Tribunal will consider all the circumstances of the case, including aggravating and mitigating factors. The Tribunal will fix the Fine at a level which reflects the seriousness of and is proportionate to the misconduct
- the respondent shall be entitled to adduce evidence that the ability to pay a Fine is limited by his means

24. In the absence of evidence of limited means, the Tribunal is entitled to assume that the respondent's means are such that he/she can pay the Fine which the Tribunal decides is appropriate.

25. Fines are payable to HM Treasury, which is responsible for enforcing payment.

Restriction Order

26. The Tribunal, exercising its wide power to "make such order as it may think fit", may if it deems it necessary to protect the public, impose restrictions in the form of conditions upon the way in which a solicitor continues to practise. If the conditions are for an indefinite period it must be part of the order that the solicitor subject to the condition(s) has liberty to apply to the Tribunal to vary or discharge the conditions. Any breach of conditions imposed by the Tribunal would be a disciplinary offence which would generally merit a separate penalty. See in particular *Ebhogiaye v Solicitors Regulation Authority* [2013] EWHC 2445 (Admin).

27. Restricted practice will only be ordered if necessary to ensure the protection of the public and the reputation of the profession from future harm by the respondent.

28. A Restriction Order may be for either a finite or an indefinite period.

29. If the Tribunal makes an order for an indefinite period, it will specify as part of the order that the respondent may apply to it to vary or rescind the restrictions either at any time or after the elapse of a defined period.

Suspension

30. Suspension from the Roll will be the appropriate penalty where the Tribunal has determined that:

- the seriousness of the misconduct is such that neither a Reprimand nor a Fine is a sufficient sanction or in all the circumstances appropriate
- there is a need to protect both the public and the reputation of the profession from future harm from the respondent by removing his/her ability to practise, but
- neither the protection of the public nor the protection of the reputation of the profession justifies striking off the Roll
- public confidence in the profession demands no lesser sanction
- professional performance, including a lack of sufficient insight by the respondent, is such as to call into question the continued ability to practise appropriately

31. Suspension from the Roll, and thereby from practice, reflects serious misconduct.

32. Suspension can be for a fixed term or for an indefinite period. A term of suspension can itself be temporarily suspended.

Suspended Term of Suspension

33. Where the Tribunal concludes that the seriousness of the misconduct justifies suspension from the Roll, but it is satisfied that:

- by imposing a Restriction Order, the risk of harm to the public and the public's confidence in the reputation of the profession is proportionately constrained; and
- the combination of such an Order with a period of pending Suspension provides adequate protection

the Tribunal may suspend that period of suspension for so long as the Restriction Order remains in force.

Fixed Term of Suspension

34. Having concluded that the respondent should be immediately removed from practice, but that the protection of the public and the protection of the reputation of the profession do not require that he/she be struck off the Roll, the Tribunal will fix a term of suspension of such length both to punish and deter whilst being proportionate to the seriousness of the misconduct.

35. The Tribunal can also impose a staged order with a fixed term of suspension followed by a period of restricted practice under a Restriction Order.

Indefinite Suspension

36. Indefinite Suspension marks the highest level of misconduct that can appropriately be dealt with short of striking off the Roll. In deciding that an indefinite period of suspension is the fair and proportionate sanction, the Tribunal will have formed the view that:

- the seriousness of the misconduct is so high that striking off is the most appropriate sanction; but
- the presence of truly compelling and exceptional personal mitigation makes that course of action unjust; and/or
- there is a realistic prospect that the respondent will recover or respond to retraining so that he/she no longer represents a material risk of harm to the public or to the reputation of the profession

Striking Off the Roll of Solicitors

37. Where the Tribunal has determined that:

- the seriousness of the misconduct is at the highest level, such that a lesser sanction is inappropriate; and
- the protection of the public and/or the protection of the reputation of the profession requires it

the Tribunal will strike a solicitor's name off the Roll of Solicitors.

Dishonesty

38. The most serious misconduct involves dishonesty, whether or not leading to criminal proceedings and criminal penalties. A finding that an allegation of dishonesty has been proved will almost invariably lead to striking off, save in exceptional circumstances.

Absence of Dishonesty

39. Striking off can be appropriate in the absence of dishonesty where, amongst other things;

- the seriousness of the misconduct is itself very high; and
- the departure by the respondent from the required standards of integrity, probity and trustworthiness is very serious.

40. In such cases, the Tribunal will have regard to the overall facts of the misconduct, and in particular the effect that allowing the respondent's name to remain on the Roll will have upon the public's confidence in the reputation of the profession. See in particular *Solicitors Regulation Authority v Emeana, Ijewere and Ajanaku* [2013] EWHC 2130 (Admin).

Misappropriation of client funds falling short of Dishonesty

41. The Tribunal regards the breach of the heavy obligation to safeguard clients' money, which is quite distinct from the solicitor's duty to act honestly, as extremely serious.

42. The dishonest misappropriation of client funds will invariably lead to strike off.

43. Strike off can be appropriate in the absence of dishonesty. Where a respondent's failure properly to monitor clients' money leads to its misappropriation or misuse by others, such a serious breach of the obligation could warrant striking off.

> "... the tribunal had been at pains to make the point, which was a good one, that the solicitors' accounts rules existed to afford the public maximum protection against the improper and unauthorised use of their money and that, because of the importance attached to affording that protection and assuring the public that such protection was afforded, an onerous obligation was placed on solicitors to ensure that those rules were observed." (Lord Bingham LCJ in *Weston v Law Society* [1998] Times, 15th July)

Personal mitigation

44. Before finalising sanction, consideration will be given to any particular personal mitigation advanced by or on the respondent's behalf. The Tribunal will have regard to the following principles:

> "Because orders made by the tribunal are not primarily punitive, it follows that considerations which would ordinarily weigh in mitigation of punishment have less effect on the exercise of this jurisdiction than on the ordinary run of sentences imposed in criminal cases. It often happens that a solicitor appearing before the tribunal can adduce a wealth of glowing tributes from his professional brethren. He can often show that for him and his family the consequences of striking off or suspension would be little short of tragic. Often he will say, convincingly, that he has learned his lesson and will not offend again.
>
> ... All these matters are relevant and should be considered. But none of them touches the essential issue, which is the need to maintain among members of the public a well-founded confidence that any solicitor whom they instruct will be a person of unquestionable integrity, probity and trustworthiness. Thus it can never be an objection to an order of suspension in an appropriate case that the solicitor may be unable to re-establish his practice when the period of suspension is past. If that proves, or appears, likely to be so the consequence for the individual and his family may be deeply unfortunate and unintended. But it does not make suspension the wrong order if it is otherwise right. The reputation of the profession is more important than the fortunes of any individual member. Membership of a profession brings many benefits, but that is a part of the price." (*Bolton* above)

45. Particular matters of personal mitigation that may be relevant and may serve to reduce the nature of the sanction, and/or its severity include:

- that the misconduct arose at a time when the respondent was affected by a physical or mental illness that affected his ability to conduct himself to the standards of the reasonable solicitor. Such mitigation should be supported by medical evidence from a suitably qualified practitioner
- that the respondent was an inexperienced practitioner and was inadequately supervised by his employer
- that the respondent made prompt admissions and demonstrated full cooperation with the regulator

Section C: Other powers of the Tribunal

Application for termination of a period of suspension

46. The length of the period of suspension is determined by the seriousness of misconduct, and the potential for harm to the public and the reputation of the profession.

47. Indefinite Suspension can only be revoked by the Tribunal upon the application of the respondent. In considering any such application, the Tribunal will need to be satisfied that revocation of suspension would not adversely affect the reputation of the profession nor be contrary to the interests of the public.

48. Any application for the lifting of an Indefinite Suspension, or early termination of a fixed term, must be supported by evidence of changed circumstances that justify the application.

49. Although suspension is one step below the ultimate sanction of strike off, the factors considered by the Tribunal will be similar to those listed below in relation to restoration to the Roll.

Application for restoration to the Roll

50. The Tribunal has power to restore to the Roll the name of a former solicitor whose name has been struck from it. An application in such a case must be supported by a statement setting out:
    - details of the original order of the Tribunal leading to strike off
    - details of the applicant's employment and training history since the Tribunal's order of strike off
    - details of the applicant's intentions as to and any offers of employment within the profession in the event that the application is successful

51. An application for restoration is not an appeal against the original decision to strike off. The Tribunal's function when considering an application for restoration is to determine whether an applicant has established that he/she is now a fit and proper person to have their name restored to the Roll.

52. In considering any application for restoration to the Roll, the Tribunal will have regard to the following factors:
    - the period which has elapsed since the order of strike off was made. Save in the most exceptional circumstances an application for restoration to the Roll within six years of the original strike off is likely to be regarded by the Tribunal as premature
    - evidence of rehabilitation. This will usually require detailed evidence of substantial and satisfactory employment within the profession in the period since strike off

- the applicant's future employment intentions and whether another solicitor would be willing to employ the applicant within a practice in the event that the applicant's name is restored to the Roll
- the extent to which the applicant has repaid any losses sustained by others as a result of the applicant's original misconduct, including any fines and cost orders made by the Tribunal. The applicant must be in a position to demonstrate that he/she has made a sustained effort to meet any such liability
- a criminal conviction recorded against an applicant involving dishonesty or a finding of dishonesty by the Tribunal can constitute an almost insurmountable obstacle to a successful application for restoration

Section D: Costs

53. The Tribunal has the power to make such order as to costs as it thinks fit, including the payment by any party of costs or a contribution towards costs of such amount (if any) as the Tribunal may consider reasonable (Section 47 of the Act). Such costs are those arising from or ancillary to proceedings before it.

54. The Tribunal may make an order for the payment of a fixed amount of costs. This will be the usual order of the Tribunal where the parties are in agreement as to the liability for, and the amount of, those costs. Otherwise, the Tribunal will determine liability for costs, and either summarily assess those costs itself or refer the case for detailed assessment by a Costs Judge.

Costs against Respondent: allegations admitted/proved

General considerations

55. The Tribunal, in considering the respondent's liability for the costs of the applicant, will have regard to the following principles, drawn from *R v Northallerton Magistrates Court, ex parte Dove* (1999) 163 JP 894:

    - it is not the purpose of an order for costs to serve as an additional punishment for the respondent, but to compensate the applicant for the costs incurred by it in bringing the proceedings
    - any order imposed must never exceed the costs actually and reasonably incurred by the applicant

56. Before making any order as to costs, the Tribunal will give the respondent the opportunity to adduce financial information and make submissions:

> "If a solicitor wishes to contend that he is impecunious and cannot meet an order for costs, or that its size should be confined, it will be up to him to put before the Tribunal sufficient information to persuade the Tribunal that he lacks the means to meet an order for costs in the sum at which they would otherwise arrive … where a solicitor admits the disciplinary charges brought against him, and who therefore anticipates the imposition of a sanction upon him, it should be incumbent upon him before the hearing to give advance notice to the SRA and to the Tribunal that he will contend either that no order for costs should be made against him, or that it should be limited in amount by reason of his own lack of means. He should also supply to the SRA and to the Tribunal, in advance of the hearing, the evidence upon which he relies to support that contention" (*Solicitors Regulation Authority v Davis and McGlinchey* [2011] EWHC 232 (Admin) per Mitting J and *Agyeman v Solicitors Regulation Authority* [2012] EWHC 3472 (Admin)).

57. Where the Tribunal decides that the respondent is, notwithstanding his limited means,

properly liable for the applicant's costs (either in full or in part) and is satisfied that there is a reasonable prospect that, at some time in the future, his/her ability to pay those costs will improve, it may order the respondent to meet those costs but direct that such order is not to be enforced without leave of the Tribunal.

58. Such an order may be appropriate where the respondent adduces evidence of current absence of income and capital or a total, but temporary, dependence upon state benefits.

Costs against Respondent: some allegations not proved

59. Where the respondent is partially successful in defending the allegations pursued by the applicant, in considering the respondent's liability for costs the Tribunal will have regard to the following factors:

- the reasonableness of the applicant in pursuing an allegation on which it was unsuccessful
- the manner in which the applicant pursued the allegation on which it was unsuccessful and its case generally
- the reasonableness of the allegation, that is, was it reasonable for the applicant to pursue the allegation in all the circumstances
- the extra costs in terms of preparation for trial, witness statements and documents and so on, taken up by pursuing the allegation upon which the applicant was unsuccessful
- the extra Tribunal time taken in considering the unsuccessful allegation
- the extent to which the allegation was inter-related in terms of evidence and argument with those allegations in respect of which the applicant was successful
- the extra costs borne by the respondent in defending an allegation which was not found to be proved
- the Tribunal may award costs against a respondent even if it makes no finding of misconduct, "if having regard to his conduct or to all the circumstances, or both, the Tribunal shall think fit" (Rule 18 of the Solicitors (Disciplinary Proceedings) Rules 2007).

Costs against Applicant

60. The starting point adopted by the Tribunal in considering whether costs should be awarded against the regulator (where that is the applicant in a particular case) is:

> "In respect of costs, the exercise of its regulatory function placed the Law Society in a wholly different position from that of a party to ordinary civil litigation. Unless a complaint was improperly brought or, for example, had proceeded as a "shambles from start to finish", when the Law Society was discharging its responsibilities as a regulator of the profession, an order for costs should not ordinarily be made against it on the basis that costs followed the event." (per Laws LJ, *Baxendale-Walker v The Law Society* [2007] EWCA Civ 233):

61. Where a respondent seeks to pursue an application for costs against the regulator, the Tribunal will have regard to the following principles:

- an order that the applicant pay a successful respondent's costs on the grounds that costs follow the event should not ordinarily be made on that basis alone
- there is no assumption that such an order will automatically follow
- "to expose a regulator to the risk of an adverse costs order simply because it

properly brought proceedings which were unsuccessful might have a chilling effect upon its regulatory function" *Baxendale-Walker*, above

62. In addition, the Tribunal will consider the balance to be struck between:

- the financial prejudice to the successful respondent in the particular circumstances if an order for costs is not made in his/her favour; and
- "the need for a regulator to make and stand by honest, reasonable and apparently sound decisions made in the public interest without fear of exposure to undue financial prejudice if unsuccessful" (Per Bingham CJ, *Bradford MDC v Booth* (2000) 164 JP 485 DC)

APPENDIX 15

Extracts from the Solicitors Act 1974

[With consolidated amendments to 1 April 2013]

Solicitors Act 1974

1974 CHAPTER 47

An Act to consolidate the Solicitors Acts 1957 to 1974 and certain other enactments relating to solicitors

[31st July 1974]

BE IT ENACTED by the Queen's most Excellent Majesty, by and with the advice and consent of the Lords Spiritual and Temporal, and Commons, in this present Parliament assembled, and by the authority of the same, as follows:—

PART I
RIGHT TO PRACTISE AS SOLICITOR

Qualifications and training

1 Qualifications for practising as solicitor

No person shall be qualified to act as a solicitor unless—

(a) he has been admitted as a solicitor, and

(b) his name is on the roll, and

(c) he has in force a certificate issued by the Society in accordance with the provisions of this Part authorising him to practise as a solicitor (in this Act referred to as a "practising certificate").

1A Practising certificates: employed solicitors

A person who has been admitted as a solicitor and whose name is on the roll shall, if he would not otherwise be taken to be acting as a solicitor, be taken for the purposes of this Act to be so acting if he is employed in connection with the provision of any legal services—

(a) by any person who is qualified to act as a solicitor;

(b) by any partnership at least one member of which is so qualified;

(c) by a body recognised under section 9 of the Administration of Justice Act 1985 (incorporated practices); or

(d) by any other person who, for the purposes of the Legal Services Act 2007, is an authorised person in relation to an activity which is a reserved legal activity (within the meaning of that Act).

1B Restriction on practice as sole solicitor

(1) Rules under section 31 (rules as to professional practice etc) must provide that a solicitor may not practise as a sole solicitor unless he has in force—

(a) a practising certificate, and

(b) an endorsement of that certificate by the Society authorising him to practise as a sole solicitor (a "sole solicitor endorsement").

(2) The rules may provide that, for the purposes of the rules and this Act, a solicitor is not to be regarded as practising as a sole solicitor in such circumstances as may be prescribed by the rules.

(3) The rules must prescribe the circumstances in which a solicitor may be regarded by the Society as suitable to be authorised to practise as a sole solicitor.

13 Appeals etc in connection with the issue of practising certificates

(1) A person who makes an application under section 9 may appeal to the High Court against—

(a) a decision to refuse the application for a practising certificate,

(b) if the application included an application for a sole solicitor endorsement, a decision to refuse the application for the endorsement, or

(c) a decision to impose a condition on a practising certificate issued in consequence of the application.

(2) A person who holds a practising certificate subject to a condition within section 10(4)(b) may appeal to the High Court against any decision by the Society to refuse to approve the taking of any step for the purposes of that condition.

(3) The Society may make rules which provide, as respects any application under section 9 that is neither granted nor refused by the Society within such period as may be specified in the rules, for enabling an appeal to be brought under this section in relation to the application as if it had been refused by the Society.

(4) On an appeal under subsection (1), the High Court may—

(a) affirm the decision of the Society,

(b) direct the Society to make a sole solicitor endorsement on the applicant's practising certificate and to issue that certificate subject to such conditions (if any) as the High Court may think fit,

(c) direct the Society to issue a certificate to the applicant free from conditions or subject to such conditions as the High Court may think fit,

(d) direct the Society not to issue a certificate,

(e) if a certificate has been issued, by order suspend it,

(f) if the certificate has been endorsed with a sole solicitor endorsement, by order suspend the endorsement, or

(g) make such other order as the High Court thinks fit.

(5) On an appeal under subsection (2), the High Court may—

(a) affirm the decision of the Society,

(b) direct the Society to approve the taking of one or more steps for the purposes of a condition within section 10(4)(b), or

(c) make such other order as the High Court thinks fit.

(6) In relation to an appeal under this section the High Court may make such order as it thinks fit as to payment of costs.

(7) The decision of the High Court on an appeal under subsection (1) or (2) shall be final.

13ZA Application to practise as sole practitioner while practising certificate in force

(1) A solicitor whose practising certificate for the time being in force (his "current certificate") does not have a sole solicitor endorsement, may apply to the Society for such an endorsement.

(2) For the purposes of subsection (1) a practising certificate with a sole solicitor endorsement which is suspended is to be treated as having such an endorsement.

(3) A solicitor may not apply under subsection (1) if he is suspended from practice as a sole solicitor.

(4) An application must be—

(a) made in accordance with regulations under section 28, and

(b) accompanied by any fee payable under section 13ZB in respect of the endorsement applied for.

(5) Where a sole solicitor endorsement is granted to an applicant of a prescribed description, the applicant's practising certificate shall have effect subject to any conditions prescribed in relation to applicants of that description.

"Prescribed" means prescribed by regulations under section 28(3B)(f).

(6) A person who makes an application under this section may appeal to the High Court against—

(a) a decision to refuse the application, or

(b) a decision to impose a condition on a practising certificate in accordance with subsection (5).

(7) The Society may by rules make provision, as respects any application under this section that is neither granted nor refused by the Society within such period as may be specified in the rules, for enabling an appeal to be brought under this section in relation to the application as if it had been refused by the Society.

(8) On an appeal under this section the High Court may—

(a) affirm the decision of the Society,

(b) direct the Society to grant a sole solicitor endorsement,

(c) direct that the applicant's practising certificate is to have effect subject to such conditions (if any) as the High Court thinks fit, or

(d) make such other order as the High Court thinks fit.

(9) In relation to an appeal under this section the High Court may make such order as it thinks fit as to payment of costs.

(10) The decision of the High Court on an appeal under this section shall be final.

13ZB Fee payable on making of sole solicitor endorsement

(1) Before a sole solicitor endorsement is granted under section 13ZA, there must be paid to the Society in respect of the endorsement a fee of such amount as the Society may from time to time determine.

(2) Different fees may be specified for different categories of applicant and in different circumstances.

(3) If a fee payable under this section would not otherwise be a practising fee for the purposes of section 51 of the Legal Services Act 2007, it is to be treated for the purposes of that section as such a fee.

(4) In subsection (3) "practising fee" has the meaning given by that section.

13A Imposition of conditions while practising certificates are in force

(1) Subject to the provisions of this section, the Society may in the case of any solicitor direct that his practising certificate for the time being in force (his "current certificate") shall have effect subject to such conditions as the Society may think fit.

(2) The power conferred by subsection (1) is exercisable in relation to a solicitor at any time during the period for which the solicitor's current certificate is in force if—

(a) under section 13ZA the Society grants a sole solicitor endorsement, or

(b) it appears to the Society that the case is of a prescribed description.

(3) "Prescribed" means prescribed by regulations under section 28.

(6) A solicitor in whose case a direction is given under this section may appeal to the High Court against the decision of the Society.

(7) On an appeal under subsection (6), the High Court may—

(a) affirm the decision of the Society; or

(b) direct that the appellant's current certificate shall have effect subject to such conditions as the High Court thinks fit; or

(c) by order revoke the direction; or

(d) make such other order as it thinks fit.

(7A) The decision of the High Court on an appeal under subsection (6) shall be final.

(8) Subsections (4) and (5) of section 10 apply for the purposes of subsection (1) of this section as they apply for the purposes of that section.

(9) A solicitor who holds a practising certificate subject to a condition imposed under subsection (1) which prohibits that solicitor from taking any steps specified in the condition, except with the approval of the Society, may appeal to the High Court against any decision by the Society to refuse to approve the taking of any step for the purposes of that condition.

(10) On an appeal under subsection (9), the High Court may—

(a) affirm the decision of the Society,

(b) direct the Society to approve the taking of one or more steps for the purposes of the condition, or

(c) make such other order as the High Court thinks fit.

(11) The decision of the High Court on an appeal under subsection (9) shall be final.

(12) In relation to an appeal under this section the High Court may make such order as it thinks fit as to payment of costs.

13B Suspension of practising certificates where solicitors convicted of fraud or serious crime

(1) Where—

(a) a solicitor has been convicted of—

(i) an offence involving dishonesty or deception; or

(ii) an indictable offence; and

(b) the Society has made an application to the Tribunal under section 47 with respect to him, the Society may direct that any practising certificate or sole solicitor endorsement of his which is for the time being in force be suspended.

(2) Any such suspension shall be for such period, not exceeding six months, as the Society shall specify in the direction.

(3) If, before the specified period expires—

- (a) the Tribunal determines the Society's application;
- (b) the conviction is quashed or set aside; or
- (c) the Society withdraws its application to the Tribunal,

the suspension shall cease to have effect.

(4) Where the specified period comes to an end without any of the events mentioned in subsection (3) having occurred, the Society may direct that the suspension be continued for such period, not exceeding six months, as it shall specify in the direction.

(5) A suspension under this section may only be extended once under subsection (4).

(6) Nothing in this section is to be taken as in any way affecting the Tribunal's power to suspend a solicitor from practice or from practice as a sole solicitor.

(7) A solicitor in whose case a direction is given under subsection (1) or (4) may appeal to the High Court against the direction within one month of being notified of it.

(8) In an appeal under subsection (7), the High Court may—

- (a) affirm the suspension;
- (b) direct that the appellant's certificate or sole solicitor endorsement shall not be suspended, but that the appellant's certificate shall have effect subject to such conditions as the High Court thinks fit;
- (c) by order revoke the direction; or
- (d) make such other order as it thinks fit.

(9) In relation to an appeal under subsection (7) the High Court may make such order as it thinks fit as to payment of costs.

(10) The decision of the High Court on an appeal under subsection (7) shall be final.

15 Suspension of practising certificates

(1) The making by the Tribunal or by the court of an order suspending a solicitor from practice shall operate, and an adjudication in bankruptcy of a solicitor or the making of a debt relief order (under Part 7A of the Insolvency Act 1986) in respect of a solicitor shall operate immediately, to suspend any practising certificate of that solicitor for the time being in force.

(1A) Where the power conferred by paragraph 6(1), 6A(1) or 9(1) of Schedule 1 has been exercised in relation to a solicitor by virtue of paragraph 1(1)(a)(i), (aa), (c) (so far as it applies to rules made by virtue of section 31 or 32) or (e) of that Schedule, the exercise of that power shall operate immediately to suspend any practising certificate of that solicitor for the time being in force.

(1B) Subsection (1A) does not apply if, at the time when the power referred to there is exercised, the Society directs that subsection (1A) is not to apply in relation to the solicitor concerned.

(1C) If, at the time when the power referred to in subsection (1A) is exercised, the Society gives a direction to that effect, the solicitor concerned may continue to act in relation to any matter specified in the direction as if his practising certificate had not been suspended by virtue of subsection (1A), but subject to such conditions (if any) as the Society sees fit to impose.

(2) For the purposes of this Act, a practising certificate shall be deemed not to be in force at any time while it is suspended.

16 Duration of suspension of practising certificates

(1) Where a practising certificate is suspended, it expires on such date as may be prescribed by regulations under section 28.

(2) The suspension of a practising certificate by virtue of section 15(1) by reason of an adjudication in bankruptcy shall terminate if the adjudication is annulled and an office copy of the order annulling the adjudication is served on the Society.

(2A) The suspension of a practising certificate by virtue of section 15(1) by reason of the making of a debt relief order shall terminate—

(a) if the debt relief order is revoked on the ground mentioned in section 251L(2)(c) or (d) of the Insolvency Act 1986 and a copy of the notice provided to the debtor under Rule 5A.16 of the Insolvency Rules 1986 is served on the Society or the debt relief order is revoked by the court under section 251M(6)(e) of that Act and a copy of the court order is served on the Society;

(b) if the debt relief order is revoked and a period of one year has elapsed beginning with the effective date of that order.

(3) Where a solicitor's practising certificate is suspended—

(a) by an order under section 13(4); or

(b) by virtue of section 15(1) by reason of his adjudication in bankruptcy or the making of a debt relief order (under Part 7A of the Insolvency Act 1986) in respect of him; or

(c) by virtue of section 15(1) by reason of his suspension from practice and the period of his suspension from practice expires before the date on which his certificate will expire,

(d) by virtue of section 15(1A)

the solicitor may at any time before the certificate expires (and, in the case of adjudication in bankruptcy, while the adjudication remains unannulled) apply to the Society to terminate the suspension.

(4) On an application under subsection (3), the Society may in its discretion—

(a) by order terminate the suspension either unconditionally or subject to such conditions as the Society may think fit; or

(b) refuse the application.

(5) If on an application by a solicitor under subsection (3) the Society refuses the application or terminates the suspension subject to conditions, the solicitor may appeal against the decision of the Society to the High Court, which may—

(a) affirm the decision; or

(b) terminate the suspension either unconditionally or subject to such conditions as it may think fit.

(6) In relation to an appeal under subsection (5) the High Court may make such order as it thinks fit as to payment of costs.

(7) The decision of the High Court on an appeal under subsection (5) shall be final.

17 Publicity in relation to suspension of practising certificates

(1) Where a solicitor's practising certificate is suspended by an order under section 13(4), or by virtue of section 15(1) by reason of his adjudication in bankruptcy, the Society shall forthwith cause notice of that suspension to be published and a note of it to be entered against the name of the solicitor on the roll.

(2) Where any such suspension of a practising certificate as is mentioned in subsection (1) is terminated under section 16(2), (4) or (5), the Society shall forthwith cause a note of that termination to be entered against the name of the solicitor on the roll and, if so requested in writing by the solicitor, a notice of it to be published.

17A Suspension of sole solicitor endorsement

(1) The making by the Tribunal or by the court of an order suspending a solicitor from practice as a sole solicitor shall operate to suspend any sole solicitor endorsement of that solicitor for the time being in force.

(2) For the purposes of this Act, a sole solicitor endorsement shall be deemed not to be in force at any time while it is suspended.

(3) Subsection (2) is subject to section 13ZA(2).

17B Duration and publicity of suspension of sole solicitor endorsement

(1) Where a sole solicitor endorsement is suspended, it expires on such date as may be prescribed by regulations under section 28.

(2) Where a solicitor's sole solicitor endorsement is suspended—

(a) by an order under section 13(4), or

(b) by virtue of section 17A(1) in circumstances where the period of that suspension expires before the date on which his endorsement will expire,

the solicitor may at any time before the endorsement expires apply to the Society to terminate the suspension.

(3) Section 16(4) to (7) apply in relation to an application under subsection (2) as they apply in relation to an application under section 16(3).

(4) Where a solicitor's sole solicitor endorsement is suspended by an order under section 13(4) or by virtue of section 17A(1), the Society shall forthwith cause notice of that suspension to be published and a note of it to be entered against the name of the solicitor on the roll.

(5) Where any suspension is terminated by virtue of section 16(4) or (5), as applied by subsection (3) of this section, the Society shall forthwith cause a note of that termination to be entered against the name of the solicitor on the roll and, if so requested in writing by the solicitor, a notice of it to be published.

Supplementary

28 Regulations

(1) The Society may make regulations about the following matters, namely—

(a) admission as a solicitor;

(b) the keeping of the roll;

(c) practising certificates;

(ca) sole solicitor endorsements and applications for them;

(d) the keeping of the register under section 10A.

(2) (*repealed*)

(3) (*repealed*)

(3A) Regulations about the keeping of the roll may (among other things)—

(za) make provision about the form in which the roll is to be kept and the manner in which entries are to be made, altered and removed;

(a) provide for the Society, at such intervals as may be specified in the regulations, to enquire of solicitors of any class so specified whether they wish to have their names retained on the roll;

(b) require solicitors of any such class, at such intervals as aforesaid, to pay to the Society a fee in respect of the retention of their names on the roll of such amount as may be prescribed by the regulations;

(c) authorise the Society to remove from the roll the name of any solicitor who—

(i) fails to reply to any enquiry made in pursuance of paragraph (a) or to pay any fee payable by virtue of paragraph (b), or

(ii) replies to any such enquiry by indicating that he does not wish to have his name retained on the roll;

(d) authorise the Society to remove from the roll the name of any solicitor who has died;

(e) require the information on the roll to be made available to the public;

(f) specify the manner in which information is to be made so available and require it to be made so available during office hours and without charge.

(3B) Regulations about practising certificates or sole solicitor endorsements may (among other things)—

(a) prescribe the form and manner in which applications for, or relating to, practising certificates or sole solicitor endorsements are to be made;

(b) prescribe information which must be included in or accompany such applications;

(c) make provision about time limits for dealing with such applications, and confer on a person power to extend or bring forward such a time limit in prescribed circumstances;

(d) prescribe the requirements which applicants for practising certificates must satisfy before they may be issued with a practising certificate;

(e) prescribe descriptions of applicants, and conditions in relation to them, for the purposes of section 10(2) (circumstances in which practising certificates must be issued subject to prescribed conditions);

(f) prescribe descriptions of applicants, and conditions in relation to them, for the purposes of section 13ZA(5) (circumstances in which a practising certificate endorsed with a sole solicitor endorsement after it was issued must be made subject to prescribed conditions);

(g) prescribe circumstances for the purposes of section 10(3) (circumstances in which application may be refused etc in the public interest);

(h) make provision about when conditions imposed on practising certificates take effect (including provision conferring power on the Society to direct that a condition is not to have effect until the conclusion of any appeal in relation to it);

(i) make provision for the commencement, duration, replacement, withdrawal and expiry of practising certificates or sole solicitor endorsements;

(j) prescribe circumstances for the purposes of section 13A(2) (circumstances in which conditions can be imposed during period of practising certificate);

(k) require solicitors who hold practising certificates to notify the Society of such matters as may be prescribed, at such times, or in such circumstances as may be prescribed.

(3C) Regulations about the keeping of the register under section 10A may (among other things)—

(a) make provision about the form in which the register is to be kept and the manner in which entries are to be made, altered and removed;

(b) require information of a specified kind to be included in entries in the register;

(c) require information (or information of a specified description) on the register to be made available to the public;

(d) specify the manner in which it is to be made so available and require it to be made so available during office hours and without charge.

(3D) Regulations under this section may make provision for appeals to the High Court against decisions made by the Society under the regulations.

(3E) In relation to an appeal under regulations made by virtue of subsection (3D), the High Court may make such order as it thinks fit as to payment of costs.

(3F) The decision of the High Court on such an appeal shall be final.

(3G) Regulations under this section may—

(a) provide for a person to exercise a discretion in dealing with any matter;

(b) include incidental, supplementary and consequential provision;

(c) make transitory or transitional provision and savings;

(d) make provision generally or only in relation to specified cases or subject to specified exceptions;

(e) make different provision for different cases.

(4) [*repealed*]

(5) [*repealed*]

PART II
PROFESSIONAL PRACTICE, CONDUCT AND DISCIPLINE OF SOLICITORS AND CLERKS

Practice rules

31 Rules as to professional practice, conduct and discipline

(1) Without prejudice to any other provision of this Part the Society may make rules for regulating in respect of any matter the professional practice, conduct, fitness to practise and discipline of solicitors and for empowering the Society to take such action as may be appropriate to enable the Society to ascertain whether or not the provisions of rules made, or of any code or guidance issued, by the Society are being, or have been, complied with.

(1A) The powers conferred on the Society by subsection (1) include power to make, in relation to solicitors, provision of a kind which the Society would be prohibited from making but for section 157(5)(c) of the Legal Services Act 2007 (exception from prohibition on approved regulators making provision for redress).

(2) If any solicitor fails to comply with rules made under this section, any person may make a complaint in respect of that failure to the Tribunal.

(3) [*repealed*]

(4) [*repealed*]

Accounts etc

32 Accounts rules and trust accounts rules

(1) The Society shall make rules—

- (a) as to the opening and keeping by solicitors of accounts at banks or with building societies for money within subsection (1A);
- (aa) as to the operation by solicitors of accounts kept by their clients or other persons at banks or with building societies or other financial institutions;
- (b) as to the keeping by solicitors of accounts containing information as to money received, held or paid by them for or on account of their clients or other persons (including money received, held or paid under a trust); and
- (c) empowering the Society to take such action as may be necessary to enable it to ascertain whether or not the rules are being, or have been, complied with;

(1A) The money referred to in subsection (1) is money (including money held on trust) which is received, held or dealt with for clients or other persons.

(2) (*repealed*)

(3) If any solicitor fails to comply with rules made under this section, any person may make a complaint in respect of that failure to the Tribunal.

(4) The Society shall be at liberty to disclose a report on or information about a solicitor's accounts obtained in the exercise of powers conferred by rules made under subsection (1) for use in investigating the possible commission of an offence by the solicitor or any of his employees and for use in connection with any prosecution of the solicitor or any of his employees consequent on the investigation.

(5) Rules under this section may specify circumstances in which solicitors or any class of solicitors are exempt from the rules or a part of the rules.

(6) [*repealed*]

33 Interest on clients' money

(1) Rules under section 32 may require a solicitor to pay interest, or sums in lieu of and equivalent to interest, to a client, any other person or any trust, for whom the solicitor holds money.

(2) The cases in which a solicitor may be required by the rules to act as mentioned in subsection (1) may be defined, among other things, by reference to the amount of any sum received or the period for which it is or is likely to be retained or both.

(3) Except as provided by the rules, a solicitor is not liable to account to any client, other person or trust for interest received by the solicitor on money held at a bank or building society in an account which is for money received or held for, or on account of—

- (a) the solicitor's clients, other persons or trusts, generally, or
- (b) that client, person or trust, separately.

(4) Rules under section 32 may—

(a) prescribe the circumstances in which a solicitor may make arrangements to limit or exclude an obligation imposed on the solicitor by rules made by virtue of this section, and

(b) prescribe the requirements to be met by and in relation to those arrangements.

33A Inspection of practice bank accounts etc

(1) The Society may make rules empowering the Society to require a solicitor to produce documents relating to any account kept by him at a bank or with a building society—

(a) in connection with his practice; or

(b) in connection with any trust of which he is or formerly was a trustee,

for inspection by a person appointed by the Society pursuant to the rules.

(2) The Society shall be at liberty to disclose information obtained in exercise of the powers conferred by rules made under subsection (1) for use in investigating the possible commission of an offence by the solicitor and for use in connection with any prosecution of the solicitor consequent on the investigation.

34 Accountants' reports

(1) The Society may make rules requiring solicitors to provide the Society with reports signed by an accountant (in this section referred to as an "accountant's report") at such times or in such circumstances as may be prescribed by the rules.

(2) The rules may specify requirements to be met by, or in relation to, an accountant's report (including requirements relating to the accountant who signs the report).

(6) If any solicitor fails to comply with the provisions of any rules made under this section, a complaint in respect of that failure may be made to the Tribunal by or on behalf of the Society.

(7) *(repealed)*

(8) *(repealed)*

(9) Where an accountant, during the course of preparing an accountant's report—

(a) discovers evidence of fraud or theft in relation to money held by a solicitor for a client or any other person (including money held on trust) or money held in an account of a client of a solicitor, or an account of another person, which is operated by the solicitor, or

(b) obtains information which the accountant has reasonable cause to believe is likely to be of material significance in determining whether a solicitor is a fit and proper person to hold money for clients or other persons (including money held on trust) or to operate an account of a client of the solicitor or an account of another person,

the accountant must immediately give a report of the matter to the Society.

(10) No duty to which an accountant is subject is to be regarded as contravened merely because of any information or opinion contained in a report under subsection (9).

Sole solicitors

34A Employees of solicitors

(1) Rules made by the Society may provide for any rules made under section 31, 32, 33A or 34 to have effect in relation to employees of solicitors with such additions, omissions or other modifications as appear to the Society to be necessary or expedient.

(2) If any employee of a solicitor fails to comply with rules made under section 31 or 32, as they have effect in relation to the employee by virtue of subsection (1), any person may make a complaint in respect of that failure to the Tribunal.

(3) If any employee of a solicitor fails to comply with rules made under section 34, as they have effect in relation to the employee by virtue of subsection (1), a complaint in respect of that failure may be made to the Tribunal by or on behalf of the Society.

34B Employees of solicitors: accounts rules etc

(1) Where rules made under section 32(1) have effect in relation to employees of solicitors by virtue of section 34A(1), section 85 applies in relation to an employee to whom the rules have effect who keeps an account with a bank or building society in pursuance of such rules as it applies in relation to a solicitor who keeps such an account in pursuance of rules under section 32.

(2) Subsection (3) applies where rules made under section 32—

(a) contain any such provision as is referred to in section 33(1), and

(b) have effect in relation to employees of solicitors by virtue of section 34A(1).

(3) Except as provided by the rules, an employee to whom the rules are applied is not liable to account to any client, other person or trust for interest received by the employee on money held at a bank or building society in an account which is for money received or held for, or on account of—

(a) clients of the solicitor, other persons or trusts, generally, or

(b) that client, person or trust, separately.

(4) Subsection (5) applies where rules made under section 33A(1) have effect in relation to employees of solicitors by virtue of section 34A(1).

(5) The Society may disclose a report on or information about the accounts of any employee of a solicitor obtained in pursuance of such rules for use—

(a) in investigating the possible commission of an offence by the solicitor or any employees of the solicitor, and

(b) in connection with any prosecution of the solicitor or any employees of the solicitor consequent on the investigation.

(6) Where rules made under section 34 have effect in relation to employees of solicitors by virtue of section 34A(1), section 34(9) and (10) apply in relation to such an employee as they apply in relation to a solicitor.

Intervention in solicitor's practice, Compensation Fund and professional indemnity

35 Intervention in solicitor's practice

The powers conferred by Part II of Schedule 1 shall be exercisable in the circumstances specified in Part I of that Schedule.

Restrictions on employment of certain persons

41 Employment by solicitor of person struck off or suspended

(1) No solicitor shall, except in accordance with a written permission granted under this section, employ or remunerate in connection with his practice as a solicitor any person who to his knowledge is disqualified from practising as a solicitor by reason of the fact that—

(a) his name has been struck off the roll, or

(b) he is suspended from practising as a solicitor, or

(c) his practising certificate is suspended while he is an undischarged bankrupt.

(1A) No solicitor shall, except in accordance with a written permission granted under this section, employ or remunerate in connection with his practice as a solicitor any person if, to his knowledge, there is a direction in force under section 47(2)(g) in relation to that person.

(1B) Where—

(a) a solicitor ("the employed solicitor") is employed by another solicitor in accordance with a written permission granted under this section, and

(b) the employed solicitor is disqualified from practising as a solicitor by reason of a fact mentioned in subsection (1)(b) or (c),

section 20(1) does not apply in relation to anything done by the employed solicitor in the course of that employment.

(2) The Society may grant a permission under this section for such period and subject to such conditions as the Society thinks fit.

(3) A solicitor aggrieved by the refusal of the Society to grant a permission under subsection (2), or by any conditions attached by the Society to the grant of any such permission, may appeal to the High Court which may—

(a) confirm the refusal or the conditions, as the case may be; or

(b) grant a permission under this section for such period and subject to such conditions as it thinks fit.

(4) If any solicitor acts in contravention of this section or of any conditions subject to which a permission has been granted under it, the Tribunal or, as the case may be, the High Court may—

(a) order that his name be struck off the roll,

(b) order that he be suspended from practice for such period as the Tribunal or court thinks fit, or

(c) make such other order in the matter as it thinks fit.

(4A) In relation to an appeal under subsection (3) the High Court may make such order as it thinks fit as to payment of costs.

(4B) The decision of the High Court on an appeal under subsection (3) shall be final.

(5) [*repealed*]

42 Failure to disclose fact of having been struck off or suspended

(1) Any person who, while he is disqualified from practising as a solicitor by reason of the fact that—

(a) his name has been struck off the roll, or

(b) he is suspended from practising as a solicitor, or

(c) his practising certificate is suspended while he is an undischarged bankrupt,

seeks or accepts employment by a solicitor in connection with that solicitor's practice without previously informing him that he is so disqualified shall be guilty of an offence and liable on summary conviction to a fine not exceeding level 3 on the standard scale.

(1A) Any person—

(a) with respect to whom a direction is in force under section 47(2)(g); and

(b) who seeks or accepts employment by a solicitor in connection with that solicitor's practice without previously informing him of the direction, shall be guilty of an offence and liable on summary conviction to a fine not exceeding level three on the standard scale.

(2) Notwithstanding anything in the Magistrates' Courts Act 1980, proceedings under this section may be commenced at any time before the expiration of six months from the first discovery of the offence by the prosecutor, but no such proceedings shall be commenced except by, or with the consent of, the Attorney General.

43 Control of solicitors' employees and consultants

(1) Where a person who is or was involved in a legal practice but is not a solicitor—

(a) has been convicted of a criminal offence which is such that in the opinion of the Society it would be undesirable for the person to be involved in a legal practice in one or more of the ways mentioned in subsection (1A), or

(b) has, in the opinion of the Society, occasioned or been a party to, with or without the connivance of a solicitor, an act or default in relation to a legal practice which involved conduct on his part of such a nature that in the opinion of the Society it would be undesirable for him to be involved in a legal practice in one or more of the ways mentioned in subsection (1A),

the Society may either make, or make an application to the Tribunal for it to make, an order under subsection (2) with respect to that person.

(1A) A person is involved in a legal practice for the purposes of this section if the person—

(a) is employed or remunerated by a solicitor in connection with the solicitor's practice;

(b) is undertaking work in the name of, or under the direction or supervision of, a solicitor;

(c) is employed or remunerated by a recognised body;

(d) is employed or remunerated by a manager or employee of a recognised body in connection with that body's business;

(e) is a manager of a recognised body;

(f) has or intends to acquire an interest in such a body.

(2) An order made by the Society or the Tribunal under this subsection is an order which states one or more of the following—

(a) that as from the specified date—

(i) no solicitor shall employ or remunerate, in connection with his practice as a solicitor, the person with respect to whom the order is made,

(ii) no employee of a solicitor shall employ or remunerate, in connection with the solicitor's practice, the person with respect to whom the order is made,

(iii) no recognised body shall employ or remunerate that person, and

(iv) no manager or employee of a recognised body shall employ or remunerate that person in connection with the business of that body,

except in accordance with a Society permission;

(b) that as from the specified date no recognised body or manager or employee of such a body shall, except in accordance with a Society permission, permit the person with respect to whom the order is made to be a manager of the body;

(c) that as from the specified date no recognised body or manager or employee of such a body shall, except in accordance with a Society permission, permit the person with respect to whom the order is made to have an interest in the body.

(2A) The Society may make regulations prescribing charges to be paid to the Society by persons who are the subject of an investigation by the Society as to whether there are grounds for the Society—

(a) to make an order under subsection (2), or

(b) to make an application to the Tribunal for it to make such an order.

(2B) Regulations under subsection (2A) may—

(a) make different provision for different cases or purposes;

(b) provide for the whole or part of a charge payable under the regulations to be repaid in such circumstances as may be prescribed by the regulations.

(2C) Any charge which a person is required to pay under regulations under subsection (2A) is recoverable by the Society as a debt due to the Society from the person.

(3) Where an order has been made under subsection (2) with respect to a person by the Society or the Tribunal—

(a) that person or the Society may make an application to the Tribunal for it to be reviewed, and

(b) whichever of the Society and the Tribunal made it may at any time revoke it.

(3A) On the review of an order under subsection (3) the Tribunal may order—

(a) the quashing of the order;

(b) the variation of the order; or

(c) the confirmation of the order;

and where in the opinion of the Tribunal no prima facie case for quashing or varying the order is shown, the Tribunal may order its confirmation without hearing the applicant.

(4) The Tribunal, on the hearing of any application under this section, may make an order as to the payment of costs by any party to the application.

(5) Orders made under subsection (2) by the Society, or made, varied or confirmed under this section by the Tribunal and filed with the Society, may be inspected during office hours without payment.

(5A) In this section—

"manager", in relation to a recognised body, has the same meaning as it has in relation to a body in the Legal Services Act 2007 (see section 207 of that Act);

"recognised body" means a body recognised under section 9 of the Administration of Justice Act 1985;

"specified date" means such date as may be specified in the order;

"Society permission" means permission in writing granted by the Society for such period and subject to such conditions as the Society may think fit to specify in the permission.

(5B) A person has an interest in a recognised body for the purposes of this section if the person has an interest in that body within the meaning of Part 5 of the Legal Services Act 2007 (see sections 72 and 109 of that Act).

(6) (*repealed*)

(7) For the purposes of this section an order discharging a person absolutely or conditionally in respect of an offence shall, notwithstanding anything in section 14 of the Powers of Criminal Courts (Sentencing) Act 2000, be deemed to be a conviction of the offence for which the order was made.

44 Offences in connection with orders under section 43(2)

(1) It is an offence for a person in respect of whom there is in force an order under section 43(2) which contains provision within section 43(2)(a)—

(a) to seek or accept any employment or remuneration from a solicitor, or an employee of a solicitor, in connection with the practice carried on by that solicitor without previously informing the solicitor or employee of the order;

(b) to seek or accept any employment or remuneration from a recognised body, or a manager or employee of a recognised body, in connection with that body's business, without previously informing the body, or manager or employee, of the order.

(1A) It is an offence for a person in respect of whom there is in force an order under section 43(2) which contains provision within section 43(2)(b) to seek or accept a position as a manager of a recognised body, without previously informing that body of the order.

(1B) It is an offence for a person in respect of whom there is in force an order under section 43(2) which contains provision within section 43(2)(c) to seek or accept an interest in a recognised body from any person, without previously informing that person and (if different) the recognised body of the order.

(1C) A person guilty of an offence under subsection (1), (1A) or (1B) is liable on summary conviction to a fine not exceeding level 3 on the standard scale.

(2) Where an order under section 43(2) is in force in respect of a person, then, if any solicitor knowingly acts in contravention of that order or of any conditions subject to which permission for the taking of any action has been granted under it, a complaint in respect of that contravention may be made to the Tribunal by or on behalf of the Society.

(3) Any document purporting to be an order under section 43(2) and to be duly signed in accordance with section 48(1) shall be received in evidence in any proceedings under this section and be deemed to be such an order without further proof unless the contrary is shown.

(4) Notwithstanding anything in the Magistrates' Courts Act 1980, proceedings under subsection (1) may be commenced at any time before the expiration of six months from the first discovery of the offence by the prosecutor, but no such proceedings shall be commenced, except with the consent of the Director of Public Prosecutions, by any person other than the Society or a person acting on behalf of the Society.

(5) In this section—

"manager" has the same meaning as in section 43;

"recognised body" means a body recognised under section 9 of the Administration of Justice Act 1985;

and for the purposes of subsection (1B) a person seeks or accepts an interest in a recognised body if the person seeks or accepts an interest which if it were obtained by the person would result in the person having an interest in that body within the meaning of Part 5 of the Legal Services Act 2007 (see sections 72 and 109 of that Act).

Examination of files

44A

[*repealed*]

44B Provision of information and documents by solicitors etc

(1) The Society may by notice require a person to whom this section applies—

(a) to provide information, or information of a description, specified in the notice, or

(b) produce documents, or documents of a description, specified in the notice.

(2) This section applies to—

(a) a solicitor;

(b) an employee of a solicitor;

(c) a recognised body;

(d) an employee or manager of, or a person with an interest in, a recognised body.

(3) The Society may give a notice under this section only if it is satisfied that it is necessary to do so for the purpose of investigating—

(a) whether there has been professional misconduct by a solicitor;

(b) whether a solicitor, or an employee of a solicitor, has failed to comply with any requirements imposed by or by virtue of this Act or any rules made by the Society;

(c) whether a recognised body, or any of its managers or employees has failed to comply with any requirement imposed by or by virtue of the Administration of Justice Act 1985 or any rules made by the Society and applicable to the body, manager or employee by virtue of section 9 of that Act;

(d) whether there are grounds for making, or making an application to the Tribunal for it to make, an order under section 43(2) with respect to a person who is or was involved in a legal practice (within the meaning of section 43(1A)).

(4) A notice under this section—

(a) may specify the time and place at which, and manner and form in which, the information is to be provided or document is to be produced;

(b) must specify the period within which the information is to be provided or the document produced;

(c) may require the information to be provided or document to be produced to the Society or to a person specified in the notice.

(5) The Society may pay to any person such reasonable costs as may be incurred by that person in connection with the provision of any information, or production of any document, by that person pursuant to a notice under this section.

(6) Paragraphs 9(3) and (4) and 13, 15 and 16 of Schedule 1 apply in relation to the powers to obtain information conferred by this section, but for this purpose—

(a) paragraph 9 of that Schedule has effect as if—

(i) in sub-paragraph (3) for "such documents" there were substituted "information to which a notice given to him under section 44B applies",

(ii) in that sub-paragraph for "sub-paragraph (1)" there were substituted "the notice", and

(iii) in sub-paragraph (4) for "produce" (in the first place) to the end there were substituted "provide information pursuant to a notice under section 44B to provide the information to any person appointed by the Society at such time and place as may be specified in the order.", and

(b) the reference to the solicitor or his personal representative in paragraph 13 of that Schedule is to be construed as a reference to the person to whom the notice was given under this section.

(7) Paragraphs 9 (other than sub-paragraphs (1) and (3)), 12, 13, 15 and 16 of Schedule 1 apply in relation to the powers to obtain documents conferred by this section as they apply in relation to the powers conferred by paragraph 9(1) of that Schedule, except that for this purpose—

(a) any reference in paragraph 9 of that Schedule to a person appointed, or to a requirement, under sub-paragraph (1) of that paragraph is to be construed as a reference to a person appointed, or to a requirement to produce documents, under this section,

(b) any reference in that paragraph to any such documents as are mentioned in paragraph 9(1) of that Schedule is to be construed as a reference to any documents to which a notice under this section applies,

(c) the references to the solicitor or his firm in paragraph 9(5) and (6) of that Schedule, and the reference to the solicitor or personal representative in paragraph 9(7) of that Schedule, are to be construed as references to the person to whom the notice was given under this section, and

(d) the reference in paragraph 9(12) of that Schedule to the Society is to be construed as including a reference to a person specified under subsection (4)(c).

(8) Where powers conferred by Part 2 of Schedule 1 to the 1974 Act are exercisable in relation to a person within paragraph (a), (b), (c) or (d) of subsection (2), they continue to be so exercisable after the person has ceased to be a person within the paragraph in question.

(9) In this section—

"manager" has the same meaning as in the Legal Services Act 2007 (see section 207 of that Act);

"recognised body" means a body recognised under section 9 of the Administration of Justice Act 1985;

and the reference to a person who has an interest in a recognised body is to be construed in accordance with sections 72 and 109 of the Legal Services Act 2007.

44BA Power to require explanation of document or information

(1) The Society may, by notice, require a person to whom a notice is given under section 44B (or a representative of the person) to attend at a time and place specified in the notice to provide an explanation of any information provided or document produced pursuant to the notice.

(2) The Society may pay to any person such reasonable costs as may be incurred by that person in connection with that person's compliance with a requirement imposed under subsection (1).

(3) Paragraphs 9(3) and (4) and 13, 15 and 16 of Schedule 1 apply in relation to a notice under this section, except that for this purpose—

(a) paragraph 9 of that Schedule has effect as if—

(i) in sub-paragraph (3) for "having" to "sub-paragraph (1)" there were substituted "refuses, neglects or otherwise fails to comply with a requirement under section 44BA(1)", and

(ii) in sub-paragraph (4) for "produce" (in the first place) to the end there were substituted "provide an explanation of any information provided or document produced pursuant to a notice under section 44B (or a representative of such a person) to attend at a time and place specified in the order to provide an explanation of any information so provided or document so produced.", and

(b) the reference to the solicitor or his personal representative in paragraph 13 of that Schedule is to be construed as a reference to the person to whom the notice was given under this section.

44BB Provision of information and documents by other persons

(1) The High Court, on the application of the Society, may order a person to whom section 44B does not apply—

(a) to provide information, or information of a description, specified in the notice, or

(b) to produce documents, or documents of a description, specified in the notice.

(2) The High Court may make an order under this section only if it is satisfied—

(a) that it is likely that the information or document is in the possession or custody of, or under the control of, the person, and

(b) that there is reasonable cause to believe that the information or document is likely to be of material significance to an investigation into any of the matters mentioned in section 44B(3)(a) to (d).

(3) An order under this section may direct the Society to pay to a person specified in the order such reasonable costs as may be incurred by that person in connection with the provision of any information, or production of any document, by that person pursuant to the order.

(4) Section 44B(4) applies in relation to an order under this section as it applies in relation to a notice under section 44B.

(5) Paragraphs 9(5A) and (7) to (12), 12, 13, 15 and 16 of Schedule 1 apply in relation to an order under this section as they apply in relation to an order under paragraph 9(4) of that Schedule, except that for this purpose—

(a) the reference to the solicitor or personal representative in paragraph 9(7) of that Schedule is to be construed as a reference to the person in respect of whom the order under this section is made,

(b) the reference in paragraph 9(12) of that Schedule to the Society is to be read as including a reference to a person specified under section 44B(4)(c) (as applied by subsection (4) of this section), and

(c) the reference to the solicitor or his personal representative in paragraph 13 of that Schedule is to be construed as a reference to the person to whom the notice was given under this section.

44BC Information offences

(1) It is an offence for a person who knows or suspects an investigation into any of the matters mentioned in section 44B(3)(a) to (d) is being or is likely to be conducted—

(a) to falsify, conceal, destroy or otherwise dispose of a document which the person knows or suspects is or would be relevant to the investigation, or

(b) to cause or permit the falsification, concealment, destruction or disposal of such a document.

(2) In proceedings for an offence under subsection (1) it is a defence for the accused to show that the accused had no intention of concealing facts disclosed by the documents from the person conducting the investigation.

(3) It is an offence for a person, in purported compliance with a requirement imposed on the person under section 44B, 44BA or 44BB—

(a) to provide information which the person knows to be false or misleading in a material particular, or

(b) recklessly to provide information which is false or misleading in a material particular.

(4) A person who is guilty of an offence under subsection (1) or (3) is liable—

(a) on summary conviction, to imprisonment for a term not exceeding 12 months or a fine not exceeding the statutory maximum, or both;

(b) on conviction on indictment, to imprisonment for a term not exceeding 2 years or a fine, or both.

(5) In relation to an offence under subsection (1) or (3) committed before the commencement of section 154(1) of the Criminal Justice Act 2003 the reference in subsection (4)(a) to 12 months is to be read as a reference to 6 months.

Costs of investigations

44C Power to charge for costs of investigations

(1) The Society may make regulations prescribing charges to be paid to the Society by solicitors who are the subject of a discipline investigation.

(2) A "discipline investigation" is an investigation carried out by the Society into—

(a) possible professional misconduct by a solicitor, or

(b) a failure or apprehended failure by a solicitor to comply with any requirement imposed by or by virtue of this Act or any rules made by the Society.

(3) Regulations under this section may—

(a) make different provision for different cases or purposes;

(b) provide for the whole or part of a charge payable under the regulations to be repaid in such circumstances as may be prescribed by the regulations.

(4) Any charge which a solicitor is required to pay under regulations under this section is recoverable by the Society as a debt due to the Society from the solicitor.

(5) This section (other than subsection (2)(a)) applies in relation to an employee of a solicitor as it applies in relation to a solicitor.

Disciplinary powers of the Society

44D Disciplinary powers of the Society

(1) This section applies where the Society is satisfied—

(a) that a solicitor or an employee of a solicitor has failed to comply with a requirement imposed by or by virtue of this Act or any rules made by the Society, or

(b) that there has been professional misconduct by a solicitor.

(2) The Society may do one or both of the following—

(a) give the person a written rebuke;

(b) direct the person to pay a penalty not exceeding £2,000.

(3) The Society may publish details of any action it has taken under subsection (2)(a) or (b), if it considers it to be in the public interest to do so.

(4) Where the Society takes action against a person under subsection (2)(b), or decides to publish under subsection (3) details of any action taken under subsection (2)(a) or (b), it must notify the person in writing that it has done so.

(5) A penalty imposed under subsection (2)(b) does not become payable until—

(a) the end of the period during which an appeal against the decision to impose the penalty, or the amount of the penalty, may be made under section 44E, or

(b) if such an appeal is made, such time as it is determined or withdrawn.

(6) The Society may not publish under subsection (3) details of any action under subsection (2)(a) or (b)—

(a) during the period within which an appeal against—

(i) the decision to take the action,

(ii) in the case of action under subsection (2)(b), the amount of the penalty, or

(iii) the decision to publish the details,

may be made under section 44E, or

(b) if such an appeal has been made, until such time as it is determined or withdrawn.

(7) The Society must make rules—

(a) prescribing the circumstances in which the Society may decide to take action under subsection (2)(a) or (b);

(b) about the practice and procedure to be followed by the Society in relation to such action;

(c) governing the publication under subsection (3) of details of action taken under subsection (2)(a) or (b);

and the Society may make such other rules in connection with the exercise of its powers under this section as it considers appropriate.

(8) Before making rules under subsection (7), the Society must consult the Tribunal.

(9) A penalty payable under this section may be recovered as a debt due to the Society, and is to be forfeited to Her Majesty.

(10) The Lord Chancellor may, by order, amend paragraph (b) of subsection (2) so as to substitute for the amount for the time being specified in that paragraph such other amount as may be specified in the order.

(11) Before making an order under subsection (10), the Lord Chancellor must consult the Society.

(12) An order under subsection (10) is to be made by statutory instrument subject to annulment in pursuance of a resolution of either House of Parliament.

(13) This section is without prejudice to any power conferred on the Society or any other person to make an application or complaint to the Tribunal.

44E Appeals against disciplinary action under section 44D

(1) A person may appeal against—

(a) a decision by the Society to rebuke that person under section 44D(2)(a) if a decision is also made to publish details of the rebuke;

(b) a decision by the Society to impose a penalty on that person under section 44D(2)(b) or the amount of that penalty;

(c) a decision by the Society to publish under section 44D(3) details of any action taken against that person under section 44D(2)(a) or (b).

(2) Subsections (9)(b), (10)(a) and (b), (11) and (12) of section 46 (Tribunal rules about procedure for hearings etc) apply in relation to appeals under this section as they apply in relation to applications or complaints, except that subsection (11) of that section is to be read as if for "the applicant" to "application)" there were substituted "any party to the appeal".

(3) Rules under section 46(9)(b) may, in particular, make provision about the period during which an appeal under this section may be made.

(4) On an appeal under this section, the Tribunal has power to make such order as it thinks fit, and such an order may in particular—

(a) affirm the decision of the Society;

(b) revoke the decision of the Society;

(c) in the case of a penalty imposed under section 44D(2)(b), vary the amount of the penalty;

(d) in the case of a solicitor, contain provision for any of the matters mentioned in paragraphs (a) to (d) of section 47(2);

(e) in the case of an employee of a solicitor, contain provision for any of the matters mentioned in section 47(2E);

(f) make such provision as the Tribunal thinks fit as to payment of costs.

(5) Where by virtue of subsection (4)(e) an order contains provision for any of the matters mentioned in section 47(2E)(c), section 47(2F) and (2G) apply as if the order had been made under section 47(2E)(c).

(6) An appeal from the Tribunal shall lie to the High Court, at the instance of the Society or the person in respect of whom the order of the Tribunal was made.

(7) The High Court shall have power to make such order on an appeal under this section as it may think fit.

(8) Any decision of the High Court on an appeal under this section shall be final.

(9) This section is without prejudice to any power conferred on the Tribunal in connection with an application or complaint made to it.

45

[*repealed*]

Disciplinary proceedings before Solicitors Disciplinary Tribunal

46 Solicitors Disciplinary Tribunal

(1) Applications and complaints made by virtue of any provision of this Act shall be made, except so far as other provision is made by this Act or by any regulations under it, to the tribunal known as the "Solicitors Disciplinary Tribunal".

(2) The Master of the Rolls shall appoint the members of the Tribunal.

(3) The Tribunal shall consist—

(a) of practising solicitors of not less than ten years' standing (in this section referred to as "solicitor members"); and

(b) of persons who are neither solicitors nor barristers (in this section referred to as "lay members").

(4) A member of the Tribunal shall hold and vacate his office in accordance with the terms of his appointment and shall, on ceasing to hold office, be eligible for re-appointment.

(5) The Tribunal may pay its members such remuneration, fees or allowances as it may determine with the approval of the Legal Services Board.

(5A) The Tribunal may do anything calculated to facilitate, or incidental or conducive to, the carrying out of any of its functions.

(6) (*repealed*)

(7) (*repealed*)

(8) (*repealed*)

(9) The Tribunal may make rules—

(a) empowering the Tribunal to elect a solicitor member to be its president; and

(b) about the procedure and practice to be followed in relation to the making, hearing and determination of applications and complaints (including provision about the composition of the Tribunal).

(10) Without prejudice to the generality of subsection (9)(b), rules made by virtue of that paragraph may in particular—

(a) empower the president of the Tribunal to appoint a chairman for the hearing and determination of any application or complaint;

(b) provide that, if the president does not appoint a chairman, a solicitor member shall act as chairman; and

(c) provide, in relation to any application or complaint relating to a solicitor, that, where in the opinion of the Tribunal no prima facie case in favour of the applicant or complainant is shown in the application or complaint, the Tribunal may make an order refusing the application or dismissing the complaint without requiring the solicitor to whom it relates to answer the allegations and without hearing the applicant or complainant.

(11) For the purposes of any application or complaint made to the Tribunal under this Act, the Tribunal may administer oaths, and the applicant or complainant and any person with respect to whom the application or complaint is made (or, in the case of an application under section 47(1)(b), any of the parties to the application) may issue writs of subpoena ad testificandum and duces tecum, but no person shall be compelled under any such writ to produce any document which he could not be compelled to produce on the trial of an action.

(12) The power to make rules conferred by subsection (9) shall be exercisable by statutory instrument, and the Statutory Instruments Act 1946 shall apply to a statutory instrument containing such rules in like manner as if the rules had been made by a Minister of the Crown.

46A Funding of the Tribunal

(1) The Tribunal must submit to the Society in respect of each year a budget for the year approved by the Legal Services Board.

(2) A budget for a year is a statement of the amount of money which the Tribunal estimates is required to enable it to meet all of its expenditure in that year (having regard to any amounts received but not spent in previous years).

(3) Before approving a statement for the purposes of subsection (1) the Legal Services Board must consult the Society.

(4) The budget for a year must be submitted to the Society under subsection (1) no later than the date in the preceding year specified by the Society for the purposes of this subsection.

(5) Before specifying a date for this purpose the Society must consult the Tribunal.

(6) The amount specified in a budget submitted under subsection (1) must be paid by the Society to the Tribunal—

(a) in such instalments and at such times as may be agreed between the Society and the Tribunal, or

(b) in the absence of such agreement, before the beginning of the year to which the budget relates.

(7) The Society may pay the Tribunal such other amounts as the Society considers appropriate.

(8) In this section "year" means a calendar year.

47 Jurisdiction and powers of Tribunal

(1) Any application—

(a) to strike the name of a solicitor off the roll;

(b) to require a solicitor to answer allegations contained in an affidavit;

(c) to require a former solicitor whose name has been removed from or struck off the roll to answer allegations contained in an affidavit relating to a time when he was a solicitor;

(d) by a solicitor who has been suspended from practice for an unspecified period, by order of the Tribunal, for the termination of that suspension;

(e) by a former solicitor whose name has been struck off the roll to have his name restored to the roll;

(ea) by a solicitor who has been suspended from practice as a sole solicitor for an unspecified period, by order of the Tribunal, for the termination of that suspension;

(f) by a former solicitor in respect of whom a direction has been given under subsection (2)(g) to have his name restored to the roll,

shall be made to the Tribunal; but nothing in this subsection shall affect any jurisdiction over solicitors exercisable by the Master of the Rolls, or by any judge of the High Court, by virtue of section 50.

(2) Subject to subsections (2E) and (3) and to section 54, on the hearing of any application or complaint made to the Tribunal under this Act, other than an application under section 43, the Tribunal shall have power to make such order as it may think fit, and any such order may in particular include provision for any of the following matters—

(a) the striking off the roll of the name of the solicitor to whom the application or complaint relates;

(b) the suspension of that solicitor from practice indefinitely or for a specified period;

(ba) the revocation of that solicitor's sole solicitor endorsement (if any);

(bb) the suspension of that solicitor from practice as a sole solicitor indefinitely or for a specified period;

(c) the payment by that solicitor or former solicitor of a penalty, which shall be forfeit to Her Majesty;

(d) in the circumstances referred to in subsection (2A), the exclusion of that solicitor from criminal legal aid work (either permanently or for a specified period);

(e) the termination of that solicitor's unspecified period of suspension from practice;

(ea) the termination of that solicitor's unspecified period of suspension from practice as a sole solicitor;

(f) the restoration to the roll of the name of a former solicitor whose name has been struck off the roll and to whom the application relates;

(g) in the case of a former solicitor whose name has been removed from the roll, a direction prohibiting the restoration of his name to the roll except by order of the Tribunal;

(h) in the case of an application under subsection (1)(f), the restoration of the applicant's name to the roll;

(i) the payment by any party of costs or a contribution towards costs of such amount as the Tribunal may consider reasonable.

(2A) An order of the Tribunal may make provision for the exclusion of a solicitor from criminal legal aid work as mentioned in subsection (2)(d) where the Tribunal determines that there is good reason for doing so arising out of—

(a) his conduct, including conduct in the capacity of agent for another solicitor, in connection with the provision for any person of services provided under arrangements made for the purposes of Part 1 of the Legal Aid, Sentencing and Punishment of Offenders Act 2012; or

(b) his professional conduct generally.

(2B) Where the Tribunal makes any such order as is referred to in subsection (2A) in the case of a solicitor who is a member of a firm of solicitors, the Tribunal may, if it thinks fit, order that any other person who is for the time being a member of the firm shall be excluded (either permanently or for a specified period) from criminal legal aid work.

(2C) The Tribunal shall not make an order under subsection (2B) unless an opportunity is given to him to show cause why the order should not be made.

(2D) Any person excluded from criminal legal aid work by an order under this section may make an application to the Tribunal for an order terminating his exclusion.

(2E) On the hearing of any complaint made to the Tribunal by virtue of section 34A(2) or (3), the Tribunal shall have power to make one or more of the following—

(a) an order directing the payment by the employee to whom the complaint relates of a penalty to be forfeited to Her Majesty;

(b) an order requiring the Society to consider taking such steps as the Tribunal may specify in relation to that employee;

(c) if that employee is not a solicitor, an order which states one or more of the matters mentioned in paragraphs (a) to (c) of section 43(2);

(d) an order requiring the Society to refer to an appropriate regulator any matter relating to the conduct of that employee.

(2F) Subsections (1) to (1C), (3) and (4) of section 44 apply in relation to an order under subsection (2E)(c) as they apply in relation to an order under section 43(2).

(2G) Section 44(2), paragraph 16(1)(d) and (1A)(d) of Schedule 2 to the Administration of Justice Act 1985 and paragraph 15(3A) of Schedule 14 to the Courts and Legal Services Act 1990 apply in relation to an order under subsection (2E)(c) as they apply in relation to an order under section 43(2).

(2H) For the purposes of subsection (2E)(d) an "appropriate regulator" in relation to an employee means—

(a) if the employee is an authorised person in relation to a reserved legal activity (within the meaning of the Legal Services Act 2007), any relevant approved regulator (within the meaning of that Act) in relation to that employee, and

(b) if the employee carries on activities which are not reserved legal activities (within the meaning of that Act), any body which regulates the carrying on of such activities by the employee.

(3) On proof of the commission of an offence with respect to which express provision is made by any section of this Act, the Tribunal shall, without prejudice to its power of making an order as to costs, impose the punishment, or one of the punishments, specified in that section.

(3A) Where, on the hearing of any application or complaint under this Act, the Tribunal is satisfied that more than one allegation is proved against the person to whom the application or complaint relates it may impose a separate penalty (by virtue of subsection (2)(c)) with respect to each such allegation.

(3B) For the avoidance of doubt, nothing in this section permits the Tribunal to make an order requiring redress to be made in respect of any act or omission of any person.

(3C) In this section "criminal legal aid work" means the provision under arrangements made for the pur-poses of Part 1 of the Legal Aid, Sentencing and Punishment of Offenders Act 2012 of—

(a) advice or assistance described in section 13 or 15 of that Act, or

(b) representation for the purposes of criminal proceedings.

(4) [*repealed*]

(5) [*repealed*]

(6) [*repealed*]

47A

[*repealed*]

48 Orders of Tribunal

(1) An order of the Tribunal shall be filed with the Society, and a statement of the Tribunal's findings, signed by the chairman or by some other member of the Tribunal authorised by him in that behalf, shall either be prefaced to the order or added to the file containing the order as soon as may be after the order has been made.

(2) Where an order which has been filed includes provision for any of the matters referred to in paragraphs (a) to (i) of section 47(2), the Society—

(a) shall cause a note of the effect of the order to be entered on the roll against the name of the solicitor or former solicitor with respect to whom the application or complaint was made; and

(b) except where it only makes provision for matters referred to in paragraph (e), (ea), (f), (h) or (i) of section 47(2), shall forthwith upon filing the order cause a notice stating its effect to be published.

(3) Any file kept by the Society under this section may be inspected during office hours without payment.

(4) An order which has been filed shall be treated, for the purpose of enforcement, as if it had been made by the High Court.

(5) In the case of orders of the Tribunal under section 44E, the reference in subsection (2)(a) to the application or complaint is to be read as a reference to the Tribunal's order.

49 Appeals from Tribunal

(1) An appeal from the Tribunal shall lie to the High Court.

(2) Subject to subsection (3) and to section 43(5) of the Administration of Justice Act 1985, an appeal shall lie at the instance of the applicant or complainant or of the person with respect to whom the application or complaint was made.

(3) An appeal against an order under section 43(3A) shall lie only at the instance of the person with respect to whom the order was made, and an appeal against an order under section 47 excluding any person or persons from criminal legal aid work (as defined in that section) shall lie only at the instance of any person so excluded.

(4) The High Court shall have power to make such order on an appeal under this section as it may think fit.

(5) Subject to any rules of court, on an appeal against an order made by virtue of rules under section 46(10)(c) without hearing the applicant or complainant, the court—

(a) shall not be obliged to hear the appellant, and

(b) may remit the matter to the Tribunal instead of dismissing the appeal.

(6) Any decision of the High Court—

(a) on an application under section 43(3) or 47(1)(d), (e), (ea) or (f), or

(b) against an order under section 43(3A),

shall be final.

(6) [*repealed*]

49A Appeals to the Tribunal instead of the High Court

(1) The Society may, with the approval of the Tribunal, make rules which provide that in such circumstances as may be prescribed by the rules an appeal under any of the provisions listed in subsection (2) lies to the Tribunal and not to the High Court.

(2) Those provisions are—

(a) section 8(4);

(b) section 13A(6);

(c) section 16(5);

(d) section 28(3D);

(e) section 41(3);

(f) paragraph 14 of Schedule 14 to the Courts and Legal Services Act 1990 (foreign lawyers: appeals against conditions or refusals).

(3) Any decision of the Tribunal on an appeal by virtue of rules made under this section shall be final.

Disciplinary proceedings before Senior Courts

50 Jurisdiction of Senior Courts over solicitors

(1) Any person duly admitted as a solicitor shall be an officer of the Senior Courts.

(2) Subject to the provisions of this Act, the High Court, the Crown Court and the Court of Appeal respectively, or any division or judge of those courts, may exercise the same jurisdiction in respect of solicitors as any one of the superior courts of law or equity from

which the Senior Courts were constituted might have exercised immediately before the passing of the Supreme Court of Judicature Act 1873 in respect of any solicitor, attorney or proctor admitted to practise there.

(3) An appeal shall lie to the Court of Appeal from any order made against a solicitor by the High Court or the Crown Court in the exercise of its jurisdiction in respect of solicitors under subsection (2).

51 Procedure upon certain applications to High Court

(1) Where an application to strike the name of a solicitor off the roll or to require a solicitor to answer allegations contained in an affidavit is made to the High Court, then, subject to section 54, the following provisions of this section shall have effect in relation to that application.

(2) The court shall not entertain the application except on production of an affidavit proving that the applicant has served on the Society fourteen clear days' notice of his intention to make the application, together with copies of all affidavits intended to be used in support of the application.

(3) The Society may appear by counsel on the hearing of the application and any other proceedings arising out of or in reference to the application, and may apply to the court—

(a) to make absolute any order nisi which the court may have made on the application;

(b) to make an order that the name of the solicitor be struck off the roll; or

(c) to make such other order as the court may think fit.

(4) The court may order the costs of the Society of or relating to any of the matters mentioned in subsections (2) and (3) to be paid by the solicitor against whom, or by the person by whom, the application was made, or was intended to be made, or partly by one and partly by the other of them.

Disciplinary proceedings—general

54 Restrictions on powers to strike names off roll

(1) No solicitor shall be liable to have his name struck off the roll on account of any failure to comply with the requirements with respect to persons seeking admission as solicitors of any training regulations or on account of any defect in his admission and enrolment, unless—

(a) the application to strike his name off the roll is made within twelve months of the date of his enrolment; or

(b) fraud is proved to have been committed in connection with the failure or defect.

(2) No solicitor shall be liable to have his name struck off the roll by reason only—

(a) that a solicitor who undertook a training responsibility for him under training regulations neglected or omitted to take out a practising certificate; or

(b) that the name of a solicitor who undertook such a responsibility for a period has been removed from or struck off the roll after the end of that period.

55 Applications to require solicitor to answer allegations

For the avoidance of doubt it is hereby declared that an application by any person to require a solicitor to answer allegations contained in an affidavit, whether that application is made to the Tribunal or to the High Court, may be treated as an application to strike the name of that solicitor off the roll on the grounds of the matters alleged.

SCHEDULE 1
Intervention in Solicitor's Practice

Section 35

PART I
CIRCUMSTANCES IN WHICH SOCIETY MAY INTERVENE

1 (1) Subject to sub-paragraph (2), the powers conferred by Part II of this Schedule shall be exercisable where—

(a) the Society has reason to suspect dishonesty on the part of—

(i) a solicitor, or

(ii) an employee of a solicitor, or

(iii) the personal representatives of a deceased solicitor,

in connection with that solicitor's practice or former practice or in connection with any trust of which that solicitor is or formerly was a trustee or that employee is or was a trustee in his capacity as such an employee;

(aa) the Society has reason to suspect dishonesty on the part of a solicitor ("S") in connection with—

(i) the business of any person of whom S is or was an employee, or of any body of which S is or was a manager, or

(ii) any business which is or was carried on by S as a sole trader;

(b) the Society considers that there has been undue delay on the part of the personal representatives of a deceased solicitor who immediately before his death was practising as a sole solicitor in connection with that solicitor's practice or in connection with any trust;

(c) the Society is satisfied that a solicitor has failed to comply with rules made by virtue of section 31, 32 or 37(2)(c);

(d) a solicitor has been adjudged bankrupt or has made a composition or arrangement with his creditors;

(e) a solicitor has been committed to prison in any civil or criminal proceedings;

(ee) the Society is satisfied that a sole solicitor is incapacitated by illness, injury or accident to such an extent as to be unable to attend to his practice;

(f) a solicitor lacks capacity (within the meaning of the Mental Capacity Act 2005) to act as a solicitor and powers under sections 15 to 20 or section 48 of that Act are exercisable in relation to him; or

(g) the name of a solicitor has been removed from or struck off the roll or a solicitor has been suspended from practice;

(h) the Society is satisfied that a solicitor has abandoned his practice;

(i) the Society is satisfied that a sole solicitor is incapacitated by age to such an extent as to be unable to attend to his practice;

(j) any power conferred by this Schedule has been exercised in relation to a sole solicitor by virtue of sub-paragraph (1)(a) and he has acted as a sole solicitor within the period of eighteen months beginning with the date on which it was so exercised;

(k) the Society is satisfied that a person has acted as a solicitor at a time when he did not have a practising certificate which was in force;

(l) the Society is satisfied that a solicitor has failed to comply with any condition, subject to which his practising certificate was granted or otherwise has effect, to the effect that he may act as a solicitor only—

(i) in employment which is approved by the Society in connection with the imposition of that condition;

(ii) as a member of a partnership which is so approved;

(iii) as a manager of a body recognised by the Society under section 9 of the Administration of Justice Act 1985 and so approved; or

(iv) in any specified combination of those ways;

(m) the Society is satisfied that it is necessary to exercise the powers conferred by Part 2 of this Schedule (or any of them) in relation to a solicitor to protect—

(i) the interests of clients (or former or potential clients) of the solicitor or his firm, or

(ii) the interests of the beneficiaries of any trust of which the solicitor is or was a trustee.

(1A) In sub-paragraph (1) "manager" has the same meaning as in the Legal Services Act 2007 (see section 207 of that Act).

(2) [*repealed*]

2 On the death of a sole solicitor paragraphs 6 to 8 shall apply to the client accounts of his practice.

3 The powers conferred by Part II of this Schedule shall also be exercisable, subject to paragraphs 5(4) and 10(9), where—

(a) the Society is satisfied that there has been undue delay—

(i) on the part of a solicitor in connection with any matter in which the solicitor or his firm is or was acting on behalf of a client or with any trust, or

(ii) on the part of an employee of a solicitor in connection with any trust of which the employee is or was a trustee in his capacity as such an employee; and

(b) the Society by notice in writing invites the solicitor to give an explanation within a period of not less than 8 days specified in the notice; and

(c) the solicitor fails within that period to give an explanation which the Society regards as satisfactory; and

(d) the Society gives notice of the failure to the solicitor and (at the same or any later time) notice that the powers conferred by Part II of this Schedule are accordingly exercisable.

4 (1) Where the powers conferred by Part II of this Schedule are exercisable in relation to a solicitor, they shall continue to be exercisable after his death or after his name has been removed from or struck off the roll.

(2) The references to the solicitor or his firm in paragraphs 5(1), 6(2) and (3), 6A, 8, 9(1), (5) and (6) and 10(2) and (7) include, in any case where the solicitor has died, references to his personal representatives.

PART II
POWERS EXERCISABLE ON INTERVENTION

Money

5 (1) The High Court, on the application of the Society, may order that no payment shall be made without the leave of the court by any person (whether or not named in the order) of any money held by him (in whatever manner and whether it was received before or after the making of the order) on behalf of the solicitor or his firm.

(2) No order under this paragraph shall take effect in relation to any person to whom it applies unless the Society has served a copy of the order on him (whether or not he is named in it) and, in the case of a bank or other financial institution, has indicated at which of its branches the Society believes that the money to which the order relates is held.

(3) A person shall not be treated as having disobeyed an order under this paragraph by making a payment of money if he satisfies the court that he exercised due diligence to ascertain whether it was money to which the order related but nevertheless failed to ascertain that the order related to it.

(4) This paragraph does not apply where the powers conferred by this Part of this Schedule are exercisable by virtue of paragraph 3.

6 (1) Without prejudice to paragraph 5, if the Society passes a resolution to the effect that any sums of money to which this paragraph applies, and the right to recover or receive them, shall vest in the Society, all such sums shall vest accordingly (whether they were received by the person holding them before or after the Society's resolution) and shall be held by the Society on trust to exercise in relation to them the powers conferred by this Part of this Schedule and subject thereto and to rules under paragraph 6B upon trust for the persons beneficially entitled to them.

(2) This paragraph applies—

(a) where the powers conferred by this paragraph are exercisable by virtue of paragraph 1, to all sums of money held by or on behalf of the solicitor or his firm in connection with:

  (i) his practice or former practice,

  (ii) any trust of which he is or formerly was a trustee, or

  (iii) any trust of which a person who is or was an employee of the solicitor is or was a trustee in the person's capacity as such an employee;

(b) where they are exercisable by virtue of paragraph 2, to all sums of money in any client account; and

(c) where they are exercisable by virtue of paragraph 3, to all sums of money held by or on behalf of the solicitor or his firm in connection with the trust or other matter in connection with which the Society is satisfied there has been undue delay as mentioned in sub-paragraph (a) of that paragraph.

(3) The Society shall serve on the solicitor or his firm and on any other person having possession of sums of money to which this paragraph applies a certified copy of the Council's resolution and a notice prohibiting the payment out of any such sums of money.

(4) Within 8 days of the service of a notice under sub-paragraph (3), the person on whom it was served, on giving not less than 48 hours' notice in writing to the Society and (if the notice gives the name of the solicitor instructed by the Society) to that solicitor, may apply to the High Court for an order directing the Society to withdraw the notice.

(5) If the court makes such an order, it shall have power also to make such other order with respect to the matter as it may think fit.

(6) If any person on whom a notice has been served under sub-paragraph (3) pays out sums of money at a time when such payment is prohibited by the notice, he shall be guilty of an offence and liable on summary conviction to a fine not exceeding level 3 on the standard scale.

6A (1) Without prejudice to paragraph 5, if the Society passes a resolution to the effect that any rights to which this paragraph applies shall vest in the Society, those rights shall vest accordingly.

(2) This paragraph applies to any right to recover or receive debts due to the solicitor or his firm in connection with his practice or former practice.

(3) Any sums recovered by the Society by virtue of the exercise of rights vested under sub-paragraph (1) shall vest in the Society and shall be held by it on trust to exercise in relation to them the powers conferred by this Part of this Schedule and, subject to those powers and to rules under paragraph 6B, upon trust for the persons beneficially entitled to them.

(4) The Society shall serve on the solicitor or his firm, and any person who owes a debt to which the order applies, a certified copy of the Society's resolution.

6B (1) The Society may make rules governing its treatment of sums vested in it under paragraph 6 or 6A(3).

(2) The rules may in particular make provision in respect of cases where the Society, having taken such steps to do so as are reasonable in all the circumstances of the case, is unable to trace the person or persons beneficially entitled to any sum vested in the Society under paragraph 6 or 6A(3) (including provision which requires amounts to be paid into or out of compensation funds (within the meaning of section 36A)).

7 (1) If the Society takes possession of any sum of money to which paragraph 6 or 6A(3) applies, the Society shall pay it into a special account in the name of the Society or of a person nominated on behalf of the Society, or into a client account of a solicitor nominated on behalf of the Society, and any such person or solicitor shall hold that sum on trust to permit the Society to exercise in relation to it the powers conferred by this Part of this Schedule and subject thereto and to rules under paragraph 6B on trust for the persons beneficially entitled to it.

(2) A bank or other financial institution at which a special account is kept shall be under no obligation to ascertain whether it is being dealt with properly.

8 Without prejudice to paragraphs 5 to 7, if the High Court is satisfied, on an application by the Society, that there is reason to suspect that any person

(a) holds money on behalf of the solicitor or his firm, or

(b) has information which is relevant to identifying any money held by or on behalf of the solicitor or his firm,

the court may require that person to give the Society information as to any such money and the accounts in which it is held.

Documents

9 (1) The Society may give notice to the solicitor or his firm requiring the production or delivery to any person appointed by the Society at a time and place to be fixed by the Society—

(a) where the powers conferred by this Part of this Schedule are exercisable by virtue of paragraph 1, of all documents in the possession or under the control of the solicitor or his firm in connection with his practice or former practice or with any trust of which the solicitor is or was a trustee; and

(b) where they are exercisable by virtue of paragraph 3, of all documents in the possession or under the control of the solicitor or his firm in connection with the trust or other matters of which the Society is satisfied (whether or not they relate also to other matters).

(2) The person appointed by the Society may take possession of any such documents on behalf of the Society.

(3) Except in a case where an application has been made to the High Court under sub-paragraph (4), if any person having possession or control of any such documents refuses, neglects or otherwise fails to comply with a requirement under sub-paragraph (1), he shall be guilty of an offence and liable on summary conviction to a fine not exceeding level 3 on the standard scale.

(4) The High Court, on the application of the Society, may order a person required to produce or deliver documents under sub-paragraph (1) to produce or deliver them to any person appointed by the Society at such time and place as may be specified in the order, and authorise him to take possession of them on behalf of the Society.

(5) If on an application by the Society the High Court is satisfied that there is reason to suspect that documents in relation to which the powers conferred by sub-paragraph (1) are exercisable have come into the possession or under the control of some person other than the solicitor or his firm, the court may order that person to produce or deliver the documents to any person appointed by the Society at such time and place as may be specified in the order and authorise him to take possession of them on behalf of the Society.

(5A) In the case of a document which consists of information which is stored in electronic form, a requirement imposed by a notice under sub-paragraph (1) or an order under sub-paragraph (4) or (5), is a requirement to produce or deliver the information in a form in which it is legible or from which it can readily be produced in a legible form.

(6) On making an order under this paragraph, or at any later time, the court, on the application of the Society, may authorise a person appointed by the Society to enter any premises (using such force as is reasonably necessary) to search for and take possession of—

(a) any documents to which the order relates;

(b) any property—

   (i) in the possession of or under the control of the solicitor or his firm, or

   (ii) in the case of an order under sub-paragraph (5), which was in the possession or under the control of such a person and has come into the possession or under the control of the person in respect of whom the order is made,

which the Society reasonably requires for the purpose of accessing information contained in such documents, and to use property obtained under paragraph (b) for that purpose.

(7) The Society, on taking possession of any documents or other property under this paragraph, shall serve upon the solicitor or personal representatives and upon any other person from whom they were received on the Society's behalf or from whose premises they were taken a notice that possession has been taken on the date specified in the notice.

(8) Subject to sub-paragraph (9) a person upon whom a notice under sub-paragraph (7) is served, on giving not less than 48 hours notice to the Society and (if the notice gives the name of the solicitor instructed by the Society) to that solicitor, may apply to the High Court for an order directing the Society to deliver the documents or other property to such person as the applicant may require.

(9) A notice under sub-paragraph (8) shall be given within 8 days of the service of the Society's notice under sub-paragraph (7).

(10) Without prejudice to the foregoing provisions of this Schedule, the Society may apply to the High Court for an order as to the disposal or destruction of any documents or other property in its possession by virtue of this paragraph or paragraph 10.

(11) On an application under sub-paragraph (8) or (10), the Court may make such order as it thinks fit.

(12) Except so far as its right to do so may be restricted by an order on an application under sub-paragraph (8) or (10), the Society may take copies of or extracts from any documents in its possession by virtue of this paragraph or paragraph 10 and require any person to whom it is proposed that such documents shall be delivered, as a condition precedent to delivery, to give a reasonable undertaking to supply copies or extracts to the Society.

Mail and other forms of communication

10 (1) The High Court, on the application of the Society, may from time to time make a communications redirection order.

(2) A communications redirection order is an order that specified communications to the solicitor or his firm are to be directed, in accordance with the order, to the Society or any person appointed by the Society.

(3) For the purposes of this paragraph—

- (a) "specified communications" means communications of such description as are specified in the order;
- (b) the descriptions of communications which may be so specified include—
  - (i) communications in the form of a postal packet;
  - (ii) electronic communications;
  - (iii) communications by telephone.

(4) A communications redirection order has effect for such time not exceeding 18 months as is specified in the order.

(5) Where a communications redirection order has effect, the Society or the person appointed by the Society may take possession or receipt of the communications redirected in accordance with the order.

(6) Where a communications redirection order is made, the Society must pay to—

- (a) in the case of an order relating to postal packets, the postal operator concerned, and
- (b) in any other case, the person specified in the order,

the like charges (if any) as would have been payable for the redirection of the communications to which the order relates if the addressee had permanently ceased to occupy or use the premises or other destination of the communications and had applied to the postal operator or the specified person (as the case may be) to redirect the communications to him as mentioned in the order.

(7) The High Court may, on the application of the Society, authorise the Society, or a person appointed by it, to take such steps as may be specified in the order in relation to any website purporting to be or have been maintained by or on behalf of the solicitor or his firm if the High Court is satisfied that the taking of those steps is necessary to protect the public interest or the interests of clients (or potential or former clients) of the solicitor or his firm.

(8) In this paragraph "postal operator" and "postal packet" have the meaning given by section 27 of the Postal Services Act 2011.

(9) This paragraph does not apply where the powers conferred by this Part of this Schedule are exercisable by virtue of paragraph 3.

Trusts

11 (1) If the solicitor or his personal representative is a trustee of a trust, the Society may apply to the High Court for an order for the appointment of a new trustee in substitution for him.

(2) The Trustee Act 1925 shall have effect in relation to an appointment of a new trustee under this paragraph as it has effect in relation to an appointment under section 41 of that Act.

General

12 The powers in relation to sums of money, documents and other property conferred by this Part of this Schedule shall be exercisable notwithstanding any lien on them or right to their possession.

13 Subject to any order for the payment of costs that may be made on an application to the court under this Schedule, any costs incurred by the Society for the purposes of this Schedule, including, without prejudice to the generality of this paragraph, the costs of any person exercising powers under this Part of this Schedule on behalf of the Society, shall be paid by the Solicitor or his personal representatives and shall be recoverable from him or them as a debt owing to the Society.

13A(1) The High Court, on the application of the Society, may order a former partner of the solicitor to pay a specified proportion of the costs mentioned in paragraph 13.

(2) The High Court may make an order under this paragraph only if it is satisfied that the conduct (or any part of the conduct) by reason of which the powers conferred by this Part were exercisable in relation to the solicitor was conduct carried on with the consent or connivance of, or was attributable to any neglect on the part of, the former partner.

(3) In this paragraph "specified" means specified in the order made by the High Court.

14 Where an offence under this Schedule committed by a body corporate is proved to have been committed with the consent or connivance of, or to be attributable to any neglect on the part of, any director, manager, secretary or other similar officer of the body corporate or any person who was purporting to act in any such capacity, he, as well as the body corporate, shall be guilty of that offence and shall be liable to be proceeded against and punished accordingly.

15 Any application to the High Court under this Schedule may be disposed of in chambers.

16 The Society may do all things which are reasonably necessary for the purpose of facilitating the exercise of its powers under this Schedule.

APPENDIX 16

Extracts from the Administration of Justice Act 1985

[With consolidated amendments to 22 April 2014]

Administration of Justice Act 1985

1985 CHAPTER 61

An Act to make further provision with respect to the administration of justice and matters connected therewith; to amend the Solicitors Act 1974; to regulate the provision of solicitors' services in the case of incorporated practices; to regulate the provision of conveyancing services by persons practising as licensed conveyancers; to make further provision with respect to complaints relating to the provision of legal aid services; to amend the law relating to time limits for actions for libel and slander; and to make further provision with respect to arbitrations and proceedings in connection with European patents

[30th October 1985]

BE IT ENACTED by the Queen's most Excellent Majesty, by and with the advice and consent of the Lords Spiritual and Temporal, and Commons, in this present Parliament assembled, and by the authority of the same, as follows:–

Incorporated practices

9 Incorporated practices

(1) The Society may make rules—

(a) making provision as to the management and control of legal services bodies;

(b) prescribing the circumstances in which such bodies may be recognised by the Society as being suitable bodies to undertake the provision of any solicitor services or other relevant legal services;

(c) prescribing the requirements which (subject to any exceptions provided by the rules) must at all times be satisfied by bodies so recognised if they are to remain so recognised; and

(d) regulating the conduct of the affairs of such bodies.

(1A) Where the Society makes rules under subsection (1), it must by rules under subsection (1)(c) prescribe the requirement that (subject to any exceptions provided by the rules) recognised bodies must not provide services other than—

(a) solicitor services, or

(b) solicitor services and other relevant legal services.

(1B) "Relevant legal services" means—

(a) solicitor services, and

(b) where authorised persons other than solicitors or registered European lawyers are managers or employees of, or have an interest in, a recognised body, services of the kind provided by individuals practising as such authorised persons (whether or not those services involve the carrying on of reserved legal activities within the meaning of the Legal Services Act 2007).

(1C) The Society may by rules under this section provide that services specified, or of a description specified, in the rules are not to be treated as solicitor services or other relevant legal services.

(2) Rules made by the Society may also make provision—

(a) for the manner and form in which applications for recognition under this section, or for the renewal of such recognition, are to be made, and requiring such applications to be accompanied by a fee of such amount as the Society may from time to time determine;

(aa) for the manner and form in which other applications under the rules are to be made, and requiring such applications to be accompanied by a fee of such amount as the Society may from time to time determine;

(ab) requiring recognised bodies, or descriptions of recognised body, to pay periodical fees of such amount as the Society may from time to time determine;

(b) for regulating the names that may be used by recognised bodies;

(c) about the time when any recognition, or renewal of recognition, takes effect and the period for which it is (subject to the provisions made by or under this Part) to remain in force;

(d) for the suspension or revocation of any such recognition, on such grounds and in such circumstances as may be prescribed by the rules;

(e) about the effect on the recognition of a partnership or other unincorporated body ("the existing body") of any change in the membership of the existing body, including provision for the existing body's recognition to be transferred where the existing body ceases to exist and another body succeeds to the whole or substantially the whole of its business;

(ea) for the keeping by the Society of a register containing the names and places of business of all bodies which are for the time being recognised under this section, and such other information relating to those bodies as may be specified in the rules;

(eb) for information (or information of a specified description) on such a register to be made available to the public, including provision about the manner in which, and times at which, information is to be made so available;

(f) for rules made under any provision of the 1974 Act to have effect in relation to recognised bodies with such additions, omissions or other modifications as appear to the Society to be necessary or expedient;

(fa) about the education and training requirements to be met by managers and employees of recognised bodies;

(fb) for rules made under any provision of the 1974 Act to have effect in relation to managers and employees of recognised bodies with such additions, omissions or other modifications as appear to the Society to be necessary or expedient;

(fc) requiring recognised bodies to appoint a person or persons to monitor compliance, by the recognised body, its managers and its employees, with requirements imposed on them by or by virtue of this Act or any rules applicable to them by virtue of this section;

(g) *(repealed)*

(h) for the manner of service on recognised bodies of documents authorised or required to be served on such bodies under or by virtue of this Part.

(2A) If rules under this section provide for the recognition of legal services bodies which have one or more managers who are not legally qualified, the rules must make provision—

(a) for the recognition of such bodies to be suspended or revoked, on such grounds and in such circumstances as may be prescribed by the rules;

(b) as to the criteria and procedure for the Society's approving, as suitable to be a manager of a recognised body, an individual who is not legally qualified (and for the Society's withdrawing such approval).

(2B) Rules under this section may make provision for appeals to the High Court against decisions made by the Society under the rules—

(a) to suspend or revoke the recognition of any body;

(b) not to approve, as suitable to be the manager of a recognised body, an individual who is not legally qualified (or to withdraw such approval).

(2C) The rules may provide for appeals against decisions within subsection (2B)(b) to be brought by the individual to whom the decision relates (as well as the body).

(2D) In relation to an appeal under rules made by virtue of subsection (2B), the High Court may make such order as it thinks fit as to payment of costs.

(2E) The decision of the High Court on such an appeal shall be final.

(2F) Where the Society decides to recognise a body under this section it must grant that recognition subject to one or more conditions if—

(a) the case is of a kind prescribed for the purposes of this section by rules made by the Society, and

(b) the Society considers that it is in the public interest to do so.

(2G) While a body is recognised under this section, the Society—

(a) must direct that the body's recognition is to have effect subject to one or more conditions if—

(i) the case is of a prescribed kind, and

(ii) the Society considers that it is in the public interest to do so;

(b) may, in such circumstances as may be prescribed, direct that the body's recognition is to have effect subject to such conditions as the Society may think fit.

"Prescribed" means prescribed by rules made by the Society.

(2H) The conditions which may be imposed under subsection (2F) or (2G) include—

(a) conditions requiring the body to take specified steps that will, in the opinion of the Society, be conducive to the carrying on by the body of an efficient business;

(b) conditions which prohibit the body from taking any specified steps except with the approval of the Society;

(c) if rules under this section provide for the recognition of legal services bodies which have one or more managers who are not legally qualified, a condition that all the managers of the body must be legally qualified.

"Specified" means specified in the condition.

(2I) Rules made by the Society may make provision about when conditions imposed under this section take effect (including provision conferring power on the Society to direct that a condition is not to have effect until the conclusion of any appeal in relation to it).

(2J) Section 86A of the 1974 Act applies to rules under this section as it applies to rules under that Act.

(2K) Rules under this section may contain such incidental, supplemental, transitional or transitory provisions or savings as the Society considers necessary or expedient.

(3) Despite section 24(2) of the 1974 Act, section 20 of that Act (prohibition on unqualified person acting as solicitor) does not apply to a recognised body; and nothing in section 24(1) of that Act applies in relation to such a body.

(4) (*repealed*)

(5) A certificate signed by an officer of the Society and stating that any body is or is not, or was or was not at any time, a recognised body shall, unless the contrary is proved, be evidence of the facts stated in the certificate; and a certificate purporting to be so signed shall be taken to have been so signed unless the contrary is proved.

(6) Schedule 2 (which makes provision with respect to the application of provisions of the 1974 Act to recognised bodies and with respect to other matters relating to such bodies) shall have effect.

(7) Subject to the provisions of that Schedule, the Lord Chancellor may by order made by statutory instrument subject to annulment in pursuance of a resolution of either House of Parliament provide for any enactment or instrument passed or made before or in the same session as the Legal Services Act 2007 was passed and having effect in relation to solicitors to have effect in relation to recognised bodies with such additions, omissions or other modifications as appear to the Lord Chancellor to be necessary or expedient.

(8) In this section—

"the 1974 Act" means the Solicitors Act 1974;

"authorised person" means an authorised person in relation to an activity which is a reserved legal activity (within the meaning of the Legal Services Act 2007);

"the Society" has the meaning given by section 87(1) of the 1974 Act;

"legally qualified" and "legal services body" have the meaning given by section 9A;

"manager", in relation to a body, has the same meaning as in the Legal Services Act 2007 (see section 207 of that Act);

"recognised body" means a body for the time being recognised under this section;

"registered European lawyer" means a person who is registered with the Law Society under regulation 17 of the European Communities (Lawyers' Practice) Regulations 2000;

"solicitor services" means professional services such as are provided by individuals practising as solicitors or lawyers of other jurisdictions;

and a person has an interest in a body if the person has an interest in the body within the meaning of Part 5 of the Legal Services Act 2007 (see sections 72 and 109 of that Act).

(9) [*repealed*]

9A Legal services bodies

(1) For the purposes of section 9, a "legal services body" means a body (corporate or unincorporate) in respect of which—

(a) the management and control condition, and

(b) the relevant lawyer condition,

are satisfied.

(2) The management and control condition is satisfied if—

(a) at least 75% of the body's managers are legally qualified,

(b) the proportion of shares in the body held by persons who are legally qualified is at least 75%,

(c) the proportion of voting rights in the body which persons who are legally qualified are entitled to exercise, or control the exercise of, is at least 75%,

(d) all the persons with an interest in the body who are not legally qualified are managers of the body, and

(e) all the managers of the body who are not legally qualified are individuals approved by the Society as suitable to be managers of a recognised body.

(3) The Society may by rules under section 9 provide that, in relation to specified kinds of bodies, subsection (2) applies as if the references to 75% were to such greater percentage as may be specified (and different percentages may be specified for different kinds of bodies).

(4) The relevant lawyer condition is satisfied in relation to a body if at least one manager of the body is—

(a) a solicitor,

(b) a registered European lawyer, or

(c) a qualifying body.

(5) For that purpose a qualifying body is a body in respect of which—

(a) the management and control condition is satisfied,

(b) the relevant lawyer condition is satisfied by virtue of subsection (4)(a) or (b), and

(c) the services condition is satisfied.

(6) For the purposes of this section the following are legally qualified—

(a) an authorised person who is an individual;

(b) a registered foreign lawyer (within the meaning of section 89 of the Courts and Legal Services Act 1990 (c 41));

(c) a person entitled to pursue professional activities under a professional title to which the Directive applies in a state to which the Directive applies (other than the title of barrister or solicitor in England and Wales);

(d) an authorised person which is a body in respect of which—

(i) the services condition is satisfied, and

(ii) the management and control condition would be satisfied if the references in subsection (2) to persons who are legally qualified were to persons who are legally qualified by virtue of paragraphs (a) to (c);

(e) a body which provides professional services such as are provided by individuals who are authorised persons or lawyers of other jurisdictions, and in respect of which the management and control condition would be satisfied if the references in subsection (2) to persons who are legally qualified were to persons who are legally qualified by virtue of paragraphs (a) to (c).

(f) a legal partnership which—

(i) was in existence immediately before the commencement of this paragraph,

(ii) since that time has continued to be a partnership of the kind mentioned in rule 12.01(1)(b), 12.02(1)(b) or 12.04(1)(c)(i) of the pre-commencement conduct rules (framework of practice), and

(iii) has not, since that time, had a body corporate (other than a body within paragraph (g)) as a member;

(g) a body corporate which—

(i) was recognised under section 9 immediately before the commencement of this paragraph, and

(ii) has since that time continued to satisfy the requirements of rule 14.03(1) and 14.04(1) to (3) or the requirements of rule 14.05(1) to (3) of the pre-commencement conduct rules (restrictions on directors, owners etc of incorporated practices);

(h) a body which—

(i) is an authorised person and satisfies the services condition, or

(ii) provides professional services such as are provided by individuals who are authorised persons or lawyers of other jurisdictions,

and which satisfies the requirements of rules under subsection (6C).

(6A) For the purposes of subsection (6)(f), a partnership is to be treated as the same partnership despite a change in membership, if any person who was a member before the change remains a member.

(6B) For the purposes of subsection (6)(f) and (g), the references in the pre-commencement conduct rules to a recognised body are to be construed as references to a body which was recognised under section 9 immediately before the commencement of subsection (6)(f) and (g).

(6C) The Society must make rules for the purposes of paragraph (h) of subsection (6) prescribing the requirements relating to management and control which must be satisfied by or in relation to a body for it to fall within that paragraph.

(7) For the purposes of this section, the services condition is satisfied in relation to a body if the body provides only services which may be provided by a recognised body (having regard to rules under section 9(1A) and (1C)).

(8) For the purposes of this section—

"authorised person" has the same meaning as in section 9;

"the Directive" means Directive 98/5/EC of the European Parliament and the Council, to facilitate practice of the profession of lawyer on a permanent basis in a Member State other than that in which the qualification was obtained;

"legal partnership" means a partnership in which a solicitor, a registered European lawyer or a recognised body is permitted to practise by virtue of rules made under section 31 of the Solicitors Act 1974 (c 47), as those rules had effect immediately before the commencement of subsection (6)(f);

"manager", in relation to a body, has the meaning given by section 9;

"pre-commencement conduct rules" means rules under Part 2 of the Solicitors Act 1974 or section 9 of this Act, known as the Solicitors' Code of Conduct 2007, as those rules had effect immediately before the commencement of subsection (6)(f) and (g);

"recognised body" has the same meaning as in section 9 (subject to subsection (6B) above);

"registered European lawyer" has the same meaning as in section 9;

"shares" has the same meaning as for the purposes of Part 5 of the Legal Services Act 2007 (see sections 72 and 109 of that Act);

"the Society" has the meaning given by section 87(1) of the Solicitors Act 1974;

"specified" means specified in rules made by the Society;

and a person has an interest in a body if the person has an interest in the body for the purposes of section 9.

10 Penalty for pretending to be a body recognised under s 9

(1) A body shall not describe itself or hold itself out as a body for the time being recognised under section 9 unless it is so recognised.

(2) Any body which contravenes subsection (1) shall be guilty of an offence and liable on summary conviction to a fine not exceeding the fourth level on the standard scale.

(3) Where an offence under this section committed by a body corporate is proved to have been committed with the consent or connivance of or to be attributable to any neglect on the part of an officer of the body corporate, that officer (as well as the body corporate) is guilty of the offence and is liable to be proceeded against and punished accordingly.

(4) Where the affairs of a body corporate are managed by its members, subsection (3) applies in relation to the acts and defaults of a member in connection with the member's functions of management as it applies to an officer of the body corporate.

(5) Proceedings for an offence under this section alleged to have been committed by an unincorporated body are to be brought in the name of that body (and not in that of any of its members) and, for the purposes of any such proceedings, any rules of court relating to the service of documents have effect as if that body were a corporation.

(6) A fine imposed on an unincorporated body on its conviction of an offence under this section is to be paid out of the funds of that body.

(7) If an unincorporated body is charged with an offence under this section, section 33 of the Criminal Justice Act 1925 (c 86) and Schedule 3 to the Magistrates' Courts Act 1980 (c 43) (procedure on charge of an offence against a corporation) have effect in like manner as in the case of a corporation so charged.

(8) Where an offence under this section committed by an unincorporated body (other than a partnership) is proved to have been committed with the consent or connivance of, or to be attributable to any neglect on the part of, any officer of the body or any member of its governing body, that officer or member as well as the unincorporated body is guilty of the offence and liable to be proceeded against and punished accordingly.

(9) Where an offence under this section committed by a partnership is proved to have been committed with the consent or connivance of, or to be attributable to any neglect on the part of, a partner, that partner as well as the partnership is guilty of the offence and liable to be proceeded against and punished accordingly.

(10) In this section "officer", in relation to a body corporate, means—

(a) any director, secretary or other similar officer of the body corporate, or

(b) any person who was purporting to act in any such capacity.

SCHEDULE 2
Legal services practices: Supplementary Provisions

Section 9

Interpretation

1 (1) Subject to sub-paragraph (2), references in this Schedule to a recognised body are references to a body for the time being recognised under section 9 of this Act.

(2) References in this Schedule to a recognised body in relation to—

(a) a complaint (other than such a complaint as is mentioned in paragraph 16(1)(a));

(b) *(repealed)*

include references to a body that was recognised under section 9 of this Act at the time when the conduct to which the complaint relates took place.

(2A) References in this Schedule to a manager or employee of a recognised body, in relation to a complaint (other than such a complaint as is mentioned in paragraph 16(1A)(a)), include references to a person who was such a manager or employee at the time when the conduct to which the complaint relates took place.

(3) *(repealed)*

(4) In section 87(1) of the 1974 Act the definitions of "client", "contentious business" and "non-contentious business" shall apply for the purposes of—

(a) this Schedule; and

(b) any provision of the 1974 Act in so far as it has effect in relation to a recognised body by virtue of this Schedule,

as if for any reference to a solicitor there were substituted a reference to a recognised body.

(5) Subject to sub-paragraphs (4) and (6), any expression used in this Schedule which is also used in the 1974 Act has the same meaning as in that Act.

(6) In this Schedule—

"manager", in relation to a body, has the same meaning as in the Legal Services Act 2007 (see section 207 of that Act);

"registered European lawyer" has the same meaning as in section 9A;

"the 1974 Act" means the Solicitors Act 1974.

Appeal against refusal of Society to grant recognition etc

2 (1) A body may appeal to the High Court against—

(a) a decision to refuse an application by the body for recognition under section 9;

(b) a decision to impose a condition under subsection (2F) of that section on the body's recognition under that section;

(c) a decision to impose a condition under subsection (2G) of that section on the body's recognition under that section.

(2) A recognised body whose recognition is subject to a condition within section 9(2H)(b) may appeal to the High Court against any decision by the Society to refuse to approve the taking of any step for the purposes of that condition.

(3) Rules made by the Society may make provision, as respects any application for recognition that is neither granted nor refused by the Society within such period as may be specified in the rules, for enabling an appeal to be brought under this paragraph in relation to the application as if it had been refused by the Society.

(4) On an appeal under sub-paragraph (1)(a) or (b), the High Court may—

(a) affirm the decision of the Society,

(b) direct the Society to grant the body recognition under section 9 free from conditions or subject to such conditions as the High Court may think fit,

(c) direct the Society not to recognise the body,

(d) if the Society has recognised the body, by order suspend the recognition, or

(e) make such other order as the High Court thinks fit.

(5) On an appeal under sub-paragraph (1)(c), the High Court may—

(a) affirm the decision of the Society,

(b) direct that the body's recognition under section 9 is to have effect subject to such conditions as the High Court may think fit,

(c) by order revoke the direction given by the Society under section 9(2G), or

(d) make such other order as the High Court thinks fit.

(6) On an appeal under sub-paragraph (2), the High Court may—

(a) affirm the decision of the Society,

(b) direct the Society to approve the taking of one or more steps for the purposes of a condition within section 9(2H)(b), or

(c) make such other order as the High Court thinks fit.

(7) In relation to an appeal under this paragraph, the High Court may make such order as it thinks fit as to payment of costs.

(8) The decision of the High Court on an appeal under this paragraph is final.

Accounts rules

3 (1) This paragraph applies where rules made under section 32(1) of the 1974 Act are applied—

(a) to recognised bodies in accordance with section 9(2)(f) of this Act, or

(b) to managers or employees of such bodies in accordance with section 9(2)(fb) of this Act.

(2) The Society may disclose a report on or information about the accounts of a recognised body, or a manager or employee of a recognised body, obtained in pursuance of such rules for use—

(a) in investigating the possible commission of an offence by the body or any of its managers or employees, and

(b) in connection with any prosecution of the body or any of its managers or employees consequent on the investigation.

Interest on client's money

4 (1) Where rules made under section 32 of the 1974 Act and containing any such provision as is referred to in section 33(1) of that Act are applied to recognised bodies in accordance with section 9(2)(f) of this Act, then, except as provided by the rules, a recognised body is not liable to account to any client, other person or trust for interest received by the recognised body on money held at a bank or building society in an account which is for money received or held for, or on account of—

(a) clients of the recognised body, other persons or trusts, generally, or

(b) that client, person or trust separately.

(2) *[repealed]*

4ZA Where rules made under section 32 of the 1974 Act and containing any such provision as is referred to in section 33(1) of that Act are applied to managers or employees of recognised bodies in accordance with section 9(2)(fb), then, except as provided by the rules, a manager or employee to whom the rules are applied is not liable to account to any client, other person or trust for interest received by the manager or employee on money held at a bank or building society in an account which is for money received or held for, or on account of—

(a) clients of the recognised body, other persons or trusts, generally, or

(b) that client, person or trust, separately.

Inspection of bank accounts

4A (1) This paragraph applies where rules made under section 33A(1) of the 1974 Act are applied—

(a) to recognised bodies in accordance with section 9(2)(f) of this Act, or

(b) to managers or employees of such bodies in accordance with section 9(2)(fb) of this Act.

(2) The Society may disclose information about the accounts of a recognised body, or a manager or employee of a recognised body, obtained in pursuance of such rules for use—

(a) in investigating the possible commission of an offence by the body or any of its managers or employees, and

(b) in connection with any prosecution of the body or any of its managers or employees consequent on the investigation.

Accountant's reports

5 Where rules made under section 34 of the 1974 Act are applied to recognised bodies in accordance with section 9(2)(f), section 34(9) and (10) of that Act apply in relation to a recognised body as they apply in relation to a solicitor.

5A Where rules made under section 34 of the 1974 Act are applied to managers or employees of recognised bodies in accordance with section 9(2)(fb), section 34(9) and (10) of that Act apply in relation to a manager or employee to which the rules are applied as they apply in relation to a solicitor.

Compensation Fund

6 (1) Section 36 of the 1974 Act applies in relation to recognised bodies as if for paragraphs (a) and (b) of subsection (1) there were substituted—

"(a) an act or omission of a recognised body or former recognised body;

(b) an act or omission of a manager or employee, or former manager or employee, of a recognised body or former recognised body;

(2) Section 36A(2) and (3) of the 1974 Act applies in relation to recognised bodies as it applies in relation to solicitors.

Solicitor who is justice of the peace not to act in certain proceedings

7 In section 38 of the 1974 Act references to any partner of a solicitor shall be construed, in relation to a solicitor who is a manager of a recognised body, as references to any other solicitor who is a manager of that body.

8 (*repealed*)

Restriction on employment of person struck off roll or suspended

9 (1) Section 41 of the 1974 Act (except subsection (4)) shall apply to a recognised body (and any manager or employee of it) and its business as such as it applies to a solicitor and his practice as such.

(2) No recognised body (or manager or employee of such a body) may, except in accordance with a written permission granted by the Society under this paragraph, permit a person to whom sub-paragraph (3) applies to—

(a) be a manager of the body, or

(b) have an interest in the body;

and for this purpose a person has an interest in the body if he has an interest in the body within the meaning of Part 5 of the Legal Services Act 2007 (see sections 72 and 109 of that Act).

(3) This sub-paragraph applies to a person who to the knowledge of the recognised body (or, as the case may be, the manager or employee) is a person—

(a) who is disqualified from practising as a solicitor by reason of one of the facts mentioned in section 41(1)(a), (b) or (c) of the 1974 Act (name struck off the roll, suspension etc), or

(b) in respect of whom there is a direction in force under section 47(2)(g) of that Act (prohibition on restoration to roll).

(4) Permission granted for the purposes of sub-paragraph (2) may be granted for such period and subject to such conditions as the Society thinks fit.

(5) A person aggrieved by the refusal of the Society to grant permission under sub-paragraph (4), or by any conditions attached by the Society to the grant of any such permission may appeal to the High Court which may—

(a) confirm the refusal or the conditions, as the case may be, or

(b) grant a permission under this paragraph for such period and subject to such conditions as it thinks fit.

(6) In relation to an appeal under sub-paragraph (5) the High Court may make such order as it thinks fit as to payment of costs.

(7) The decision of the High Court on an appeal under sub-paragraph (5) is final.

Failure to disclose fact of having been struck off or suspended

10 (1) Section 42(1) and (1A) of the 1974 Act shall apply in relation to employment by a recognised body (or any manager or employee of such a body) in connection with its business as it applies in relation to employment by a solicitor in connection with his practice.

(2) It is an offence for a person ("P") to whom sub-paragraph (3) applies—

(a) to seek or accept from any person an interest in a recognised body, without previously informing that person (and, if different, the recognised body) that P is a person to whom that sub-paragraph applies, or

(b) to seek or accept a position as a manager of a recognised body, without previously informing that body that P is such a person.

(3) This sub-paragraph applies to a person—

(a) who is disqualified from practising as a solicitor by reason of one of the facts mentioned in section 41(1)(a), (b) or (c) of the 1974 Act (name struck off the roll, suspension etc), or

(b) in respect of whom there is a direction in force under section 47(2)(g) of that Act (prohibition on restoration to roll).

(4) A person guilty of an offence under sub-paragraph (2) is liable on summary conviction to a fine not exceeding level 3 on the standard scale.

(5) Subsection (2) of section 42 of the 1974 Act applies in relation to an offence under sub-paragraph (2) as it applies in relation to an offence under that section.

(6) For the purposes of sub-paragraph (2)(a) a person seeks or accepts an interest in a recognised body if the person seeks or accepts an interest which if it were obtained by the person would result in the person having an interest in that body within the meaning of Part 5 of the Legal Services Act 2007 (see sections 72 and 109 of that Act).

11 *(repealed)*

12 *(repealed)*

13 *(repealed)*

Information about suitability for recognition

14 (1) The Society may give a notice under this paragraph if it is satisfied that it is necessary to do so for the purpose of investigating whether—

(a) a recognised body continues to be suitable to be recognised under section 9, or

(b) a manager of a recognised body who is not legally qualified (within the meaning of section 9A) continues to be suitable to be a manager of a recognised body.

(2) A notice under this paragraph is a notice which requires a person within sub-paragraph (3)—

(a) to provide information, or information of a description, specified in the notice, or

(b) to produce documents, or documents of a description, specified in the notice.

(3) The persons are—

(a) the recognised body;

(b) an employee or manager of the recognised body;

(c) a person who has an interest in the recognised body (within the meaning of the Legal Services Act 2007 (see sections 72 and 109 of that Act)).

(4) For the purposes of this paragraph, section 44B(4) to (7) of the 1974 Act applies—

(a) in relation to a notice under this paragraph as if it were a notice under section 44B of that Act, and

(b) in relation to a person given a notice under this paragraph as if that person were a person given a notice under that section,

and references in subsections (6) and (7) of that section to powers conferred by that section are to be read as references to powers conferred by this paragraph.

(5) Where powers conferred by Part 2 of Schedule 1 to the 1974 Act are exercisable in relation to a person within paragraph (a), (b) or (c) of sub-paragraph (3), they continue to be so exercisable after the person has ceased to be a person within the paragraph in question.

(6) Section 44BA of the 1974 Act (power to require explanation of document or information) applies in relation to a notice under this paragraph and the person to whom such a notice is given as it applies in relation to a notice under section 44B of the 1974 Act and the person to whom such a notice is given.

(7) Subsection (1) of section 44BC of that Act (falsification of documents etc) applies in relation to an investigation of the kind mentioned in sub-paragraph (1) as it applies in relation to the investigations mentioned in that subsection, and subsections (2), (4) and (5) of that section apply accordingly.

(8) Subsection (3) of that section (provision of false information etc) applies in relation to a requirement imposed under this paragraph as it applies in relation to a requirement imposed by section 44B of that Act, and subsections (4) and (5) of that section apply accordingly.

Power to charge for costs of investigation

14A(1) The Society may make regulations prescribing charges to be paid to the Society by recognised bodies who are the subject of a discipline investigation.

(2) A discipline investigation is an investigation carried out by the Society into a failure or apprehended failure by a recognised body to comply with any requirement imposed by or by virtue of this Act or any rules applicable to it by virtue of section 9.

(3) Regulations under this paragraph may—

(a) make different provision for different cases or purposes;

(b) provide for the whole or part of a charge payable under the regulations to be repaid in such circumstances as may be prescribed by the regulations.

(4) Any charge which a recognised body is required to pay under regulations under this paragraph is recoverable by the Society as a debt due to the Society from the recognised body.

(5) This paragraph applies in relation to a manager or employee of a recognised body as it applies in relation to a recognised body.

Disciplinary powers of the Society

14B(1) This paragraph applies where the Society is satisfied that a recognised body, or a manager or employee of a recognised body, has failed to comply with a requirement imposed by or by virtue of this Act or any rules applicable to that person by virtue of section 9 of this Act.

(2) The Society may do one or both of the following—

(a) give the person a written rebuke;

(b) direct the person to pay a penalty not exceeding £2,000.

(3) The Society may publish details of any action it has taken under sub-paragraph (2)(a) or (b), if it considers it to be in the public interest to do so.

(4) Where the Society takes action against a person under sub-paragraph (2)(b), or decides to publish under sub-paragraph (3) details of such action under sub-paragraph (2)(a) or (b), it must notify the person in writing that it has done so.

(5) A penalty imposed under sub-paragraph (2)(b) does not become payable until—

(a) the end of the period during which an appeal against the decision to impose the penalty, or the amount of the penalty, may be made under paragraph 14C, or

(b) if such an appeal is made, such time as it is determined or withdrawn.

(6) The Society may not publish under sub-paragraph (3) details of any action under sub-paragraph (2)(a) or (b)—

(a) during the period within which an appeal against—

(i) the decision to take the action,

(ii) in the case of action under sub-paragraph (2)(b), the amount of the penalty, or

(iii) the decision to publish the details,

may be made under paragraph 14C, or

(b) if such an appeal has been made, until such time as it is determined or withdrawn.

(7) The Society must make rules—

(a) prescribing the circumstances in which the Society may decide to take action under sub-paragraph (2)(a) or (b);

(b) about the practice and procedure to be followed by the Society in relation to such action;

(c) governing the publication under sub-paragraph (3) of details of action taken under sub-paragraph (2)(a) or (b);

and the Society may make such other rules in connection with the exercise of its powers under this paragraph as it considers appropriate.

(8) Before making rules under sub-paragraph (7), the Society must consult the Tribunal.

(9) A penalty under this paragraph may be recovered as a debt due to the Society, and is to be forfeited to Her Majesty.

(10) The Lord Chancellor may, by order, amend paragraph (b) of sub-paragraph (2) so as to substitute for the amount for the time being specified in that paragraph such other amount as may be specified in the order.

(11) Before making an order under sub-paragraph (10), the Lord Chancellor must consult the Society.

(12) An order under sub-paragraph (10) is to be made by statutory instrument subject to annulment in pursuance of a resolution of either House of Parliament.

(13) This paragraph is without prejudice to any power conferred on the Society, or any other person, to make an application or complaint to the Tribunal.

14C(1) A person may appeal against—

(a) a decision by the Society to rebuke that person under paragraph 14B(2)(a) if a decision is also made to publish details of the rebuke;

(b) a decision by the Society to impose a penalty on that person under paragraph 14B(2)(b) or the amount of that penalty;

(c) a decision by the Society to publish under paragraph 14B(3) details of any action taken against that person under paragraph 14B(2)(a) or (b).

(2) Subsections (9)(b), (10)(a) and (b), (11) and (12) of section 46 of the 1974 Act (Tribunal rules about procedure for hearings etc) apply in relation to appeals under this paragraph as they apply in relation to applications or complaints, except that subsection (11) of that section is to be read as if for "the applicant" to "application)" there were substituted "any party to the appeal".

(3) Rules under section 46(9)(b) of the 1974 Act may, in particular, make provision about the period during which an appeal under this paragraph may be made.

(4) On an appeal under this paragraph, the Tribunal has power to make an order which—

(a) affirms the decision of the Society;

(b) revokes the decision of the Society;

(c) in the case of a penalty imposed under paragraph 14B(2)(b), varies the amount of the penalty;

(d) in the case of a recognised body, contains provision for any of the matters mentioned in paragraph 18(2);

(e) in the case of a manager or employee of a recognised body, contains provision for any of the matters mentioned in paragraph 18A(2);

(f) makes such provision as the Tribunal thinks fit as to payment of costs.

(5) Where, by virtue of sub-paragraph (4)(e), an order contains provision for any of the matters mentioned in sub-paragraph (2)(c) of paragraph 18A, sub-paragraphs (5) and (6) of that paragraph apply as if the order had been made under sub-paragraph (2)(c) of that paragraph.

(6) An appeal from the Tribunal shall lie to the High Court, at the instance of the Society or the person in respect of whom the order of the Tribunal was made.

(7) The High Court shall have power to make such order on an appeal under this paragraph as it may think fit.

(8) Any decision of the High Court on an appeal under this section shall be final.

(9) This paragraph is without prejudice to any power conferred on the Tribunal in connection with an application or complaint made to it.

15 *(repealed)*

Complaints to Tribunal with respect to recognised bodies

16 (1) The Tribunal shall have jurisdiction to hear and determine any of the following complaints made to it under this paragraph with respect to a recognised body, namely—

(a) a complaint that the body has (while a recognised body) been convicted by any court of a criminal offence which renders it unsuitable to be recognised under section 9 of this Act;

(b) a complaint that the body has failed to comply with any requirement imposed by or by virtue of this Act or with any rules applicable to it by virtue of section 9 of this Act;

(c) a complaint that the body has acted in contravention of section 41 of the 1974 Act or paragraph 9(2) of this Schedule or of any conditions subject to which a permission has been granted under section 41 of that Act or that paragraph of this Schedule; or

(d) a complaint that the body has knowingly acted in contravention of any such order as is mentioned in section 44(2) of the 1974 Act or of any conditions subject to which a permission has been granted under such an order.

(1A) The Tribunal shall have jurisdiction to hear and determine any of the following complaints made to it under this paragraph with respect to a manager or employee of a recognised body ("the relevant person")—

(a) a complaint that the relevant person has been convicted by any court of a criminal offence which renders that person unsuitable to be a manager or employee (or both) of a recognised body;

(b) a complaint that the relevant person has failed to comply with any requirement imposed by or by virtue of this Act or any rules applicable to the relevant person by virtue of section 9 of this Act;

(c) a complaint that the relevant person has acted in contravention of section 41 of the 1974 Act or paragraph 9(2) of this Schedule or of any conditions subject to which a permission has been granted under that section or for the purposes of paragraph 9(2) of this Schedule;

(d) a complaint that the relevant person has knowingly acted in contravention of an order under section 43(2) of the 1974 Act or of any conditions subject to which a permission has been granted under such an order.

(2) A complaint may be made to the Tribunal under this paragraph by any person.

Procedure on applications and complaints

17 In subsections (9) to (11) of section 46 of the 1974 Act—

(a) any reference to an application or complaint shall be construed as including a reference to any such application as is mentioned in paragraph 21(1) or any such complaint as is mentioned in paragraph 16(1) or (1A);

(b) any reference to an application or complaint made under that Act shall be construed as including a reference to any such application or complaint as aforesaid made under this Schedule; and

(c) in the case of subsection (10)(c), any reference to a solicitor shall be construed as including a reference to a recognised body or, in the case of such a complaint as is mentioned in paragraph 16(1A), to a manager or employee of such a body.

Powers of Tribunal with respect to recognised bodies

18 (1) Where on the hearing of any complaint made to it under this Schedule (other than paragraph 16(1A)) the Tribunal is satisfied that a recognised body—

(a) has been convicted as mentioned in paragraph (a) of paragraph 16(1); or

(b) has failed to comply with any requirement imposed by or by virtue of this Act or with any such rules as are mentioned in paragraph (b) of paragraph 16(1); or

(c) has acted as mentioned in paragraph (c) or (d) of that provision;

(d) [*repealed*]

the Tribunal may, if it thinks fit, make one or more of the orders referred to in sub-paragraph (2).

(2) Those orders are—

(a) an order revoking the recognition under section 9 of this Act of the body to which the complaint relates;

(b) an order directing the payment by that body of a penalty, to be forfeited to Her Majesty;

(c) an order requiring that body to pay the costs incurred in bringing against it the proceedings before the Tribunal or a contribution towards those costs, being a contribution of such amount as the Tribunal considers reasonable.

(2A) Where, on the hearing of any application or complaint made to it under this Schedule, the Tribunal is satisfied that more than one allegation is proved against the recognised body to whom the application or complaint relates, it may impose a separate penalty (by virtue of sub-paragraph (2)(b)) with respect to each such allegation.

(3) [*repealed*]

(4) [*repealed*]

18A(1) Where, on the hearing of any complaint made to it under paragraph 16(1A) of this Schedule, the Tribunal is satisfied that a manager or employee of a recognised body—

(a) has been convicted as mentioned in paragraph (a) of paragraph 16(1A),

(b) has failed to comply with any requirement imposed by or by virtue of this Act or any rules applicable to the relevant person by virtue of section 9 of this Act, or

(c) has acted as mentioned in paragraph (c) or (d) of paragraph 16(1A),

the Tribunal may, if it thinks fit, make one or more of the orders referred to in sub-paragraph (2).

(2) Those orders are—

(a) an order directing the payment by the relevant person of a penalty to be forfeited to Her Majesty;

(b) an order requiring the Society to consider taking such steps as the Tribunal may specify in relation to the relevant person;

(c) if the person is not a solicitor, an order which states one or more of the matters mentioned in sub-paragraph (3);

(d) an order requiring the Society to refer to an appropriate regulator any matter relating to the conduct of the relevant person.

(3) The matters referred to in sub-paragraph (2)(c) are—

(a) that as from the specified date—

(i) no solicitor or employee of a solicitor shall employ or remunerate, in connection with the practice carried on by that solicitor, the person with respect to whom the order is made, and

(ii) no recognised body, or manager or employee of such a body, shall employ or remunerate that person, in connection with the business of the recognised body,

except in accordance with a Society permission;

(b) that as from the specified date no recognised body or manager or employee of such a body shall, except in accordance with a Society permission, permit the person with respect to whom the order is made to be a manager of the body;

(c) that as from the specified date no recognised body or manager or employee of such a body shall, except in accordance with a Society permission, permit the person with respect to whom the order is made to have an interest in the body.

(4) For this purpose a person has an interest in a body if the person has an interest in the body within the meaning of Part 5 the Legal Services Act 2007 (see sections 72 and 109 of that Act).

(5) Subsections (1) to (1C), (3) and (4) of section 44 of the 1974 Act (offences in connection with orders under section 43(2) of that Act) apply in relation to an order under sub-paragraph (2)(c) as they apply in relation to an order under section 43(2) of that Act, except that references in those subsections to provision within section 43(2)(a), (b) or (c) of that Act are to be read as references to provision within sub-paragraph (3)(a), (b) or (c).

(6) Section 44(2) of the 1974 Act, paragraph 16(1)(d) and (1A)(d) of this Schedule and paragraph 15(3A) of Schedule 14 to the Courts and Legal Services Act 1990 apply in relation to an order under sub-paragraph (2)(c) as they apply in relation to an order under section 43(2) of the 1974 Act.

(7) For the purposes of sub-paragraph (2)(d) an "appropriate regulator" in relation to the relevant person means—

(a) if the person is an authorised person in relation to a reserved legal activity for the purposes of the Legal Services Act 2007, any relevant approved regulator (within the meaning of that Act) in relation to that person, and

(b) if the person carries on activities which are not reserved legal activities, any body which regulates the carrying on of such activities by the person.

19 (*repealed*)

Powers of Tribunal in respect of legal aid complaints

20 (1) Where the Tribunal makes any such order as is referred to in subsection (2A) of section 47 of the 1974 Act in the case of a solicitor who is a manager or employee of a recognised body, the Tribunal may, if it thinks fit, order that any solicitor who is for the time being a manager of that body shall be excluded (either permanently or for a specified period) from criminal legal aid work (as defined in that section).

(2) (*repealed*)

Revocation of recognition by reason of default by director

21 (1) Where—

(a) any order is made by the Tribunal under section 47 of the 1974 Act in the case of a manager of a recognised body; or

(b) an order is made by the High Court or the Court of Appeal that the name of a manager of a recognised body be struck off the roll or that such a manager be suspended from practice as a solicitor; or

(c) any such order as is mentioned in paragraph (a) or (b) is made in the case of a person employed by a recognised body and the act or omission constituting the ground on which the order was made was instigated or connived at by a manager of the recognised body or, if the act or omission was a continuing act or omission, a manager of the body had or reasonably ought to have had knowledge of its continuance,

the Tribunal may, on an application made with respect to the recognised body by or on behalf of the Society, by order revoke its recognition under section 9 of this Act.

(2) The Tribunal shall not take a case into consideration during any period within which proceedings by way of appeal may be brought which may result in sub-paragraph (1) being rendered inapplicable in that case, or while any such proceedings are pending.

(3) Any reference to a manager of a recognised body in any of paragraphs (a) to (c) of sub-paragraph (1) includes a reference to a person who was a manager of the body at the time of the conduct leading to the making of the order referred to in that paragraph.

(4) The reference in paragraph (c) of sub-paragraph (1) to a person employed by a recognised body includes a reference to a person who was so employed at the time of the conduct leading to the making of the order referred to in that paragraph.

Costs: general modification of provisions of Part III of 1974 Act

22 (1) In the provisions to which this paragraph applies—

(a) any reference to a solicitor or to a client of a solicitor shall be construed as including a reference to a recognised body or to a client of such a body; and

(b) any reference to a client's solicitor shall be construed as including a reference to any recognised body acting for a client.

(2) This paragraph applies to the following provisions of the 1974 Act (which relate to the remuneration of solicitors in respect of contentious and non-contentious business), namely—

section 56 (except subsections (1)(e) and (5));

sections 57 to 59;

section 60 (except subsection (5));

sections 61 and 62;

sections 64 and 65;

section 67;

section 69(1); and

sections 70 to 74.

Orders as to remuneration for non-contentious business

23 (1) In relation to an order under section 56 of the 1974 Act prescribing (by virtue of paragraph 22) general principles to be applied when determining the remuneration of recognised bodies in respect of non-contentious business, subsection (5) of that section shall have effect as if—

(a) in paragraph (a), for "the solicitor" there were substituted "the recognised body"; and

(b) in paragraph (d), the reference to the solicitor or any employee of the solicitor who is an authorised person were a reference to any manager or employee of the recognised body who is an authorised person.

(2) In this paragraph "authorised person" means a person who is an authorised person in relation to an activity which is a reserved legal activity, within the meaning of the Legal Services Act 2007 (see section 18 of that Act).

Effect of contentious business agreements

24 (1) This paragraph applies in relation to a contentious business agreement made between a recognised body and a client.

(2) A provision in the agreement that the body shall not be liable for the negligence of any of its managers or employees shall be void if the client is a natural person who, in entering that agreement, is acting for purposes which are outside his trade, business or profession.

(3) A provision in the agreement that the body shall be relieved from any responsibility to which it would otherwise be subject in the course of carrying on its business as a recognised body shall be void.

(4) A provision in the agreement that any manager of the body shall be relieved from any responsibility to which the manager would otherwise be subject in the course of the carrying on by the body of its business as a recognised body shall be void.

Effect on contentious business agreement of supervening incapacity of recognised body to act for client

25 (1) If, after some business has been done under a contentious business agreement made between a recognised body and a client but before the body has wholly performed it, the body ceases to be capable of wholly performing it by reason of one of the following events, namely—

(a) the body ceases (for any reason) to be a recognised body;

(b) a relevant insolvency event occurs in relation to the body; or

(c) the client terminates the retainer or employment of the body in favour of another recognised body or a solicitor (as, notwithstanding the agreement, he shall be entitled to do),

any party to, or the representative of any party to, the agreement may apply to the court, and the court shall have the same jurisdiction as to enforcing the agreement so far as it has been performed, or setting it aside, as the court would have had if the recognised body were still capable of wholly performing it.

(2) The court, notwithstanding that it is of the opinion that the agreement is in all respects fair and reasonable, may order the amount due in respect of business under the agreement to be ascertained by assessment, and in that case—

(a) the costs officer, in ascertaining that amount, shall have regard so far as may be to the terms of the agreement; and

(b) payment of the amount found by him to be due may be enforced in the same manner as if the agreement had been wholly performed.

(3) If in such a case as is mentioned in sub-paragraph (1)(c) an order is made for the assessment of the amount due to the recognised body in respect of the business done under the agreement, the court shall direct the costs officer to have regard to the circumstances under which the termination of the body's retainer or employment has taken place, and the costs officer, unless he is of the opinion that there has been no default, negligence, improper delay or other conduct on the part of any manager or employee of the body affording the client reasonable ground for terminating its retainer or employment, shall not allow to the body the full amount of the remuneration agreed to be paid to it.

(4) For the purposes of this paragraph a relevant insolvency event occurs in relation to a recognised body if—

(a) a resolution for a voluntary winding-up of the body is passed without a declaration of solvency under section 89 of the Insolvency Act 1986;

(b) the body enters administration within the meaning of paragraph 1(2)(b) of Schedule B1 to that Act;

(c) an administrative receiver within the meaning of section 251 of that Act is appointed;

(d) a meeting of creditors is held in relation to the body under section 95 of that Act (creditors' meeting which has the effect of converting a members' voluntary winding up into a creditors' voluntary winding up);

(e) an order for the winding up of the body is made.

Assessments with respect to contentious business

26 (1) Subject to the provisions of any rules of court, on every assessment of costs in respect of any contentious business done by a recognised body, the costs officer may—

(a) allow interest at such rate and from such time as he thinks just on money disbursed by the body for the client, and on money of the client in the possession of, and improperly retained by, the body or any manager or employee of the body; and

(b) in determining the remuneration of the body, have regard to the skill, labour and responsibility on the part of any authorised person, being a manager or employee of the body, which the business involved.

(2) In this paragraph "authorised person" means an authorised person, in relation to an activity which is a reserved legal activity, within the meaning of the Legal Services Act 2007.

Power of court to order delivery of bill of costs, etc.

27 Any jurisdiction—

(a) of the High Court to make any such orders as are referred to in subsection (1) of section 68 of the 1974 Act in relation to a solicitor (whether or not business has been done by him in the High Court); or

(b) of the county court or the family court to make any such orders as are referred to in subsection (2) of that section in relation to a solicitor,

shall be exercisable in like manner in relation to a recognised body.

Power of court to order recognised body to pay over clients' money

28 Any jurisdiction of the High Court to make, in the case of a solicitor who is acting or has acted as such for a client, an order requiring the payment or delivery up of, or otherwise relating to, money or securities which the solicitor has in his possession or control on behalf of the client shall be exercisable in like manner in the case of a recognised body which is acting or has acted as such for a client or any manager or employee of such a body.

Actions to recover costs

29 (1) Subsection (2A) of section 69 of the 1974 Act shall have effect in relation to a bill of costs delivered by a recognised body as if for paragraphs (a) and (b) there were substituted—

"(a) signed on behalf of the recognised body by any manager or employee of the body authorised by it to do so, or

(b) enclosed in, or accompanied by, a letter which is so signed and refers to the bill."

(2) Subsection (2E) of that section shall have effect in relation to such a bill as if for "the solicitor" there were substituted "the recognised body".

Power of Society to inspect files relating to certain proceedings

30 Section 83 of the 1974 Act shall apply in relation to proceedings which have been brought with respect to a recognised body for any of the following purposes, namely—

(a) for the winding-up of the body;

(b) for the appointment of an administrative receiver within the meaning of section 251 of the Insolvency Act 1986; or

(c) for the appointment of an administrator under Schedule B1 to the Insolvency Act 1986,

as it applies in relation to proceedings in bankruptcy which have been taken against a solicitor.

Bank accounts

31 Where rules made under section 32(1) of the 1974 Act are applied to recognised bodies in accordance with section 9(2)(f) of this Act, section 85 of the 1974 Act shall apply in relation to a recognised body which keeps an account with a bank or building society in pursuance of any such rules as it applies in relation to a solicitor who keeps such an account in pursuance of rules under section 32.

31A Where rules made under section 32(1) of the 1974 Act are applied to managers or employees in accordance with section 9(2)(fb) of this Act, section 85 of the 1974 Act shall apply in relation to a manager or employee to whom the rules are applied who keeps an account with a bank or building society in pursuance of any such rules as it applies in relation to a solicitor who keeps such an account in pursuance of rules under section 32.

Intervention by Society

32 (1) Subject to sub-paragraph (2), where—

(a) the Society is satisfied that a recognised body or a manager of such a body has failed to comply with any rules applicable to the body or manager by virtue of section 9 of this Act; or

(b) a person has been appointed receiver or manager of property of a recognised body; or

(c) a relevant insolvency event occurs in relation to a recognised body; or

(d) the Society has reason to suspect dishonesty on the part of any manager or employee of a recognised body in connection with—

(i) that body's business,

(ii) any trust of which that body is or was a trustee,

(iii) any trust of which the manager or employee is or was a trustee in his capacity as such a manager or employee, or

(iv) the business of another body in which the manager or employee is or was a manager or employee or the practice (or former practice) of the manager or employee; or

(e) the Society is satisfied that it is necessary to exercise the powers conferred by Part 2 of Schedule 1 to the 1974 Act (or any of them) in relation to a recognised body to protect—

(i) the interests of clients (or former or potential clients) of the recognised body,

(ii) the interests of the beneficiaries of any trust of which the recognised body is or was a trustee, or

(iii) the interests of the beneficiaries of any trust of which a person who is or was a manager or employee of the recognised body is or was a trustee in that person's capacity as such a manager or employee;

the powers conferred by Part II of Schedule 1 to the 1974 Act shall be exercisable in relation to the recognised body and its business in like manner as they are exercisable in relation to a solicitor and his practice.

(1A) For the purposes of this paragraph a relevant insolvency event occurs in relation to a recognised body if—

(a) a resolution for a voluntary winding-up of the body is passed without a declaration of solvency under section 89 of the Insolvency Act 1986;

(b) the body enters administration within the meaning of paragraph 1(2)(b) of Schedule B1 to that Act;

(c) an administrative receiver within the meaning of section 251 of that Act is appointed;

(d) a meeting of creditors is held in relation to the body under section 95 of that Act (creditors' meeting which has the effect of converting a members' voluntary winding up into a creditors' voluntary winding up);

(e) an order for the winding up of the body is made.

(2) [*repealed*]

33 The powers conferred by Part II of Schedule 1 to the 1974 Act shall also be exercisable as mentioned in paragraph 32(1) of this Schedule where—

(a) the Society is satisfied that there has been undue delay—

(i) on the part of a recognised body in connection with any matter in which it is or was acting on behalf of a client or with any trust of which it is or was a trustee, or

(ii) on the part of a person who is or was a manager or employee of a recognised body in connection with any trust of which the manager or employee is or was a trustee in his capacity as such a manager or employee;

(b) the Society by notice in writing invites the body to give an explanation within such period following the giving of the notice as may be specified in it, being a period of not less than eight days; and

(c) the body fails within that period to give an explanation which the Society regards as satisfactory; and

(d) the Society gives notice of the failure to the body and (at the same or any later time) notice that the powers conferred by Part II of Schedule 1 to the 1974 Act are accordingly exercisable in its case by virtue of this paragraph.

34 (1) Where the recognition of a body under section 9 of this Act—

(a) has been revoked in accordance with rules under that section or by an order of the Tribunal under this Schedule; or

(b) has expired and no further recognition of that body has been granted under that section,

the powers conferred by Part II of Schedule 1 to the 1974 Act shall be exercisable in relation to the body and its former business as a recognised body as they are exercisable in relation to a solicitor and his practice.

(2) Where the powers conferred by Part II of Schedule 1 to the 1974 Act are exercisable in relation to a recognised body in accordance with paragraph 32 or 33 of this Schedule they shall continue to be so exercisable after that body's recognition under section 9 of this Act has been revoked or has otherwise ceased to be in force.

35 In connection with the application of Part II of Schedule 1 to the 1974 Act for the purposes of this Schedule, in that Part of that Schedule—

(a) any reference to the solicitor or to his practice shall be construed as including a reference to the body in relation to which the powers conferred by that Part of that Schedule are exercisable by virtue of paragraph 32, 33 or 34(1) of this Schedule or to its business (or former business) as a recognised body;

(b) any reference to paragraph 1 of that Schedule shall be construed as including a reference to paragraph 32 or 34(1) of this Schedule;

(c) any reference to paragraph 3 of that Schedule shall be construed as including a reference to paragraph 33 of this Schedule;

(d) paragraph 6(2)(a) of that Schedule is to be construed as including a reference to sums of money held by or on behalf of the recognised body in connection with any trust of which a person who is or was a manager of the recognised body is or was a trustee in his capacity as such a manager;

(e) paragraph 9 of that Schedule is to be construed—

(i) as if sub-paragraph (1) included a reference to documents in the possession or under the control of the recognised body in connection with any trust of which a person who is or was a manager or employee of the recognised body is or was a trustee in his capacity as such a manager or employee, and

(ii) as applying to such a manager or employee and documents and property in his possession or under his control in connection with such a trust as it applies to a solicitor and documents and property in the possession or under the control of the solicitor;

(f) paragraph 11(1) of that Schedule is to be construed as including a power for the Society to apply to the High Court for an order for the appointment of a new trustee to a trust in substitution for a person who is a trustee, in his capacity as a manager or employee of the recognised body; and

(g) paragraph 13A of that Schedule is to be read as if the references to a former partner were references—

(i) in the case of a recognised body which is a partnership, to a former partner in the partnership, and

(ii) in any other case to a manager or former manager of the recognised body.

Privilege from disclosure etc.

36 (1) Where a recognised body acts as such for a client, any communication, document, material or information is privileged from disclosure in like manner as if the recognised body had at all material times been a solicitor acting for the client.

(2) Any enactment or instrument making special provision in relation to a solicitor or other legal representative as to the disclosure of information, or as to the production, seizure or removal of documents, with respect to which a claim to professional privilege could be maintained shall, with any necessary modifications, have effect in relation to a recognised body as it has effect in relation to a solicitor.

(3) In sections 748(4), 749 and 771(5) and (6) of the Income Tax Act 2007 and section 832(5) and (6) of the Corporation Tax Act 2010 any reference to a solicitor's client shall, in relation to a solicitor who is a manager or employee of a recognised body, be construed as a reference to a client of that body.

(4) This paragraph does not apply to a recognised body which holds a licence under Part 5 of the Legal Services Act 2007 (alternative business structures).

Modification of enactments relating to conveyancing etc.

37 In the following provisions, namely—

(a) sections 10(2), 48 and 182 of the Law of Property Act 1925;

(b) *(repealed)*

(c) section 12 of the Land Charges Act 1972;

(d) section 13 of the Local Land Charges Act 1975;

any reference to a solicitor shall be construed as including a reference to a recognised body, and any reference to a person's solicitor shall be construed as including a reference to a recognised body acting for that person.

APPENDIX 17

Extracts from the Courts and Legal Services Act 1990

[With consolidated amendments to 1 January 2010 and prospective amendments in section 89.]

Courts and Legal Services Act 1990

1990 CHAPTER 41

An Act to make provision with respect to the procedure in, and allocation of business between, the High Court and other courts; to make provision with respect to legal services; to establish a body to be known as the Lord Chancellor's Advisory Committee on Legal Education and Conduct and a body to be known as the Authorised Conveyancing Practitioners Board; to provide for the appointment of a Legal Services Ombudsman; to make provision for the establishment of a Conveyancing Ombudsman Scheme; to provide for the establishment of Conveyancing Appeal Tribunals; to amend the law relating to judicial and related pensions and judicial and other appointments; to make provision with respect to certain officers of the Supreme Court; to amend the Solicitors Act 1974; to amend the Arbitration Act 1950; to make provision with respect to certain loans in respect of residential property; to make provision with respect to the jurisdiction of the Parliamentary Commissioner for Administration in connection with the functions of court staff; to amend the Children Act 1989 and make further provision in connection with that Act; and for connected purposes

[1st November 1990]

BE IT ENACTED by the Queen's most Excellent Majesty, by and with the advice and consent of the Lords Spiritual and Temporal, and Commons, in this present Parliament assembled, and by the authority of the same, as follows:–

...

PART IV
SOLICITORS

89 Foreign lawyers: recognised bodies and partnerships with solicitors

(1) The Law Society shall maintain a register of foreign lawyers for the purposes of this section.

(2) A foreign lawyer who wishes to be registered under this section must apply to the Society in accordance with the requirements of Part I of Schedule 14.

(3) The power to make rules under—

(a) the following provisions of the Solicitors Act 1974—

(i) section 31 (professional practice, conduct and discipline);

(ii) section 32 (accounts and trust accounts);

(iii) section 34 (accountants' reports);

(iv) sections 36 and 36A (compensation grants); and

(v) section 37 (professional indemnity); and

(b) section 9 of the Administration of Justice Act 1985 (incorporated practices),

shall also be exercisable in relation to registered foreign lawyers.

(4) Subject to the provisions of Schedule 14, any such power may be exercised so as to make different provision with respect to registered foreign lawyers to the provision made with respect to solicitors.

(5) Subject to the provisions of Schedule 14, the Lord Chancellor may by order provide that any enactment or instrument—

(a) passed or made before or in the same Session as the Legal Services Act 2007 was passed;

(b) having effect in relation to solicitors; and

(c) specified in the order,

shall have effect with respect to registered foreign lawyers as it has effect with respect to solicitors.

(6) An order under subsection (5) may provide for an enactment or instrument to have effect with respect to registered foreign lawyers subject to such additions, omissions or other modifications as the Lord Chancellor sees fit to specify in the order.

(7) Subject to the provisions of Schedule 14, the Lord Chancellor may by order provide that any enactment or instrument—

(a) passed or made before or in the same Session as the Legal Services Act 2007 was passed;

(b) having effect in relation to recognised bodies; and

(c) specified in the order,

shall, in its application in relation to recognised bodies whose managers include one or more registered foreign lawyers, have effect with such additions, omissions or other modifications as the Lord Chancellor sees fit to specify in the order.

(8) Schedule 14 shall have effect for the purposes of supplementing this section.

(8A) Rules and regulations made by the Law Society under, or by virtue of, this section or Schedule 14 which are not regulatory arrangements within the meaning of the Legal Services Act 2007 are to be treated as such arrangements for the purposes of that Act.

(9) In this section and in Schedule 14—

"foreign lawyer" means a person who is not a solicitor or barrister but who is a member, and entitled to practise as such, of a legal profession regulated within a jurisdiction outside England and Wales;

"manager", in relation to a body, has the same meaning as in the Legal Services Act 2007 (see section 207 of that Act);

"multi-national partnership" means a partnership whose members consist of one or more registered foreign lawyers and one or more other lawyers as permitted by rules made under section 31 of the Solicitors Act 1974;

"recognised body" has the same meaning as in section 9 of the Administration of Justice Act 1985 (management and control by solicitors of incorporated practices); and

"registered foreign lawyer" means a foreign lawyer who is registered under this section.

SCHEDULE 14
Foreign Lawyers: Partnerships and Recognised Bodies

Section 89

PART I
REGISTRATION

General

1 In this Schedule—

"the Act of 1974" means the Solicitors Act 1974;

"the register" means the register maintained by the Society under section 89;

"registration" means registration in that register;

"the Society" means the Law Society; and

"the Tribunal" means the Solicitors Disciplinary Tribunal.

Application for registration

2 (1) An application for registration or for renewal of registration—

(a) shall be made to the Society in such form as the Society may prescribe; and

(b) shall be accompanied by such fee as the Society may, with the concurrence of the Legal Services Board, prescribe.

(2) Where such an application is duly made by a foreign lawyer, the Society may register the applicant if it is satisfied that the legal profession of which the applicant is a member is one which is so regulated as to make it appropriate for members of that profession to be managers of recognised bodies.

(3) *(repealed)*

(4) The Society may make regulations, with the concurrence of the Legal Services Board, with respect to—

(a) the keeping of the register (including the form of the register and the manner in which entries are to be made, altered or removed); and

(b) applications for registration or renewal of registration; and

(c) the making available to the public of the information contained in the register (including the manner in which, and hours during which, the information is to be made so available and whether the information is to be made available free of charge).

(5) [*repealed*]

2A (1) The Society may direct that a foreign lawyer's registration is to have effect subject to such conditions as the Society thinks fit to impose.

(2) A direction under sub-paragraph (1) may be given in respect of a foreign lawyer

(a) at the time he is first registered, or

(b) at any time when the registration has effect.

APPENDIX 17

Duration of registration

3 (1) Every registration shall have effect from the beginning of the day on which it is entered in the register.

(2) The Society may make regulations—

(a) prescribing the date ("the renewal date") by which each registered foreign lawyer must apply for his registration to be renewed; and

(b) requiring every entry in the register to specify the renewal date applicable to that registration.

(3) Any such regulations may—

(a) provide different renewal dates for different categories of registered foreign lawyer or different circumstances;

(b) provide for the Society to specify, in the case of individual registered foreign lawyers, different renewal dates to those prescribed by the regulations;

(c) make such transitional, incidental and supplemental provision in connection with any provision for different renewal dates as the Society considers expedient.

(4) Where a foreign lawyer is registered, the Society may cancel his registration if—

(a) the renewal date for his registration has passed but he has not applied for it to be renewed; or

(b) he has applied to the Society for it to be cancelled.

Evidence as to registration

4 Any certificate purporting to be signed by an officer of the Society and stating that a particular foreign lawyer—

(a) is, or is not, registered; or

(b) was registered during a period specified in the certificate,

shall, unless the contrary is proved, be evidence of that fact and be taken to have been so signed.

PART II
REGISTERED FOREIGN LAWYERS: SUPPLEMENTARY PROVISIONS

Intervention in practices

5 (1) In this paragraph "the intervention powers" means the powers conferred by Part II of Schedule 1 to the Act of 1974 (intervention in solicitors' practices) as modified by this Schedule or under section 89.

(2) Subject to sub-paragraphs (3) and (4), the intervention powers shall be exercisable in relation to a person who is or has been a registered foreign lawyer and the practice of the multi-national partnership of which he is or was a member as they are exercisable in relation to a solicitor and his practice.

(3) The intervention powers are only exercisable where—

(a) the Society has reason to suspect dishonesty on the part of the registered foreign lawyer, or on the part of an employee of the multi-national partnership, in connection with—

(i) the practice of that partnership; or

(ii) any trust of which the registered foreign lawyer is or was a trustee;

(b) in the case of a registered foreign lawyer who has died, the Society has reason to suspect dishonesty on the part of his personal representative, in connection with—

(i) the practice of the multi-national partnership; or

(ii) any trust of which the registered foreign lawyer was a trustee;

(ba) the Society has reason to suspect dishonesty on the part of the registered foreign lawyer ("L") in connection with—

(i) the business of any person of whom L is or was an employee, or of any body of which L is or was a manager, or

(ii) any business which is or was carried on by L as a sole trader;

(c) the Society is satisfied that the registered foreign lawyer has failed to comply with rules made under section 32 or 37(2)(c) of the Act of 1974;

(d) a bankruptcy order (as defined in paragraph 10(3)) has been made against him or he has made a composition or arrangement with his creditors;

(e) he has been committed to prison in any civil or criminal proceedings;

(ea) the Society is satisfied that he has abandoned his practice;

(f) he lacks capacity (within the meaning of the Mental Capacity Act 2005) to act as a registered foreign lawyer and powers under sections 15 to 20 or section 48 are exercisable in relation to him;

(g) his name has been struck off the register or his registration has been suspended or cancelled;

(h) he has purported to act as a member of a multi-national partnership at a time when he was not registered;

(i) the Society is satisfied that he has failed to comply with any condition, subject to which he is registered, to the effect that—

(i) he may only be a member of a partnership which is approved by the Society; or

(ii) he may only be a manager of a recognised body which is so approved; or

(iii) he may only be such a member or such a manager

(j) the Society is satisfied that it is necessary to exercise the intervention powers (or any of them) in relation to the registered foreign lawyer to protect—

(i) the interests of clients (or former or potential clients) of the registered foreign lawyer or the multi-national partnership, or

(ii) the interests of the beneficiaries of any trust of which the registered foreign lawyer is or was a trustee.

(4) *(repealed)*

(5) The intervention powers (other than those conferred by paragraphs 5 and 10 of Part II of Schedule 1 to the Act of 1974) shall also be exercisable where—

(a) the Society is satisfied that there has been undue delay on the part of a registered foreign lawyer in connection with—

(i) any matter in which he, or the multi-national partnership of which he is or was a member, was instructed on behalf of a client; or

(ii) any trust;

(b) the Society by notice invites the registered foreign lawyer to give an explanation within a period (of not less than 8 days) specified in the notice;

(c) the registered foreign lawyer fails within that period to give an explanation which the Society regards as satisfactory; and

(d) the Society gives notice of the failure to the registered foreign lawyer and notice that the intervention powers are accordingly exercisable.

(6) Where the intervention powers are exercisable in relation to a registered foreign lawyer, they shall continue to be exercisable—

(a) at any time when his registration is suspended;

(b) after his name has been struck off the register or his registration has been cancelled; or

(c) after his death.

(7) Part II of Schedule 1 to the Act of 1974 shall have effect in relation to the intervention powers exercisable by virtue of this Schedule, subject to—

(a) any express modifications made under section 89; and

(b) any modifications necessary in the light of this paragraph.

(8) For the purposes of this paragraph, Part II of Schedule 1 to the Act of 1974 shall be read with paragraph 4(2) of Part I of that Schedule.

(9) The notices required to be given by this paragraph must be in writing but need not be given at the same time.

(10) In this paragraph "manager", in relation to a recognised body, has the same meaning as in the Legal Services Act 2007 (see section 207 of that Act).

The Compensation Fund

6 Section 36 of the 1974 Act applies in relation to registered foreign lawyers as if for paragraphs (a) and (b) of subsection (1) there were substituted—

"(a) an act or omission of a registered foreign lawyer or former registered foreign lawyer;

(b) an act or omission of an employee or former employee of a registered foreign lawyer or former registered foreign lawyer;".

Contributions to the Fund

7 Section 36A(2) and (3) of the 1974 Act applies in relation to registered foreign lawyers as it applies in relation to solicitors.

Accountants' reports

8 Section 34 of the Act of 1974 applies in relation to registered foreign lawyers as it applies in relation to solicitors.

9 *(repealed)*

Effect of bankruptcy

10 (1) The registration of any foreign lawyer against whom a bankruptcy order is made shall be suspended on the making of that order.

(2) The suspension of any registration by reason of a bankruptcy order shall terminate if the order is annulled and an office copy of the order annulling it is served on the Society.

(3) In sub-paragraph (1), "bankruptcy order" includes any order which is not a bankruptcy order but which has the same, or a similar, effect under the law in force in any territory outside England and Wales.

Effect of disciplinary action

11 (1) Where a registered foreign lawyer is struck off, or suspended from practice, his registration shall be suspended.

(2) In sub-paragraph (1) "struck off" and "suspended from practice" mean—

(a) any action taken within the jurisdiction by reference to which the registered foreign lawyer is qualified to be registered; or

(b) where the registered foreign lawyer is qualified to be registered by reference to more than one jurisdiction, any action taken within any one of those jurisdictions,

which is the equivalent, respectively, of a solicitor being struck off the roll or suspended from practice under the Act of 1974.

Re-instatement of disciplined foreign lawyer

12 (1) Where a person's registration has been suspended by virtue of paragraph 11, it shall be revived—

(a) if his right to practise in the jurisdiction in question is restored; and

(b) a copy of the instrument restoring his right, certified to be a true copy by an officer of the appropriate court in the jurisdiction in question, or the professional body concerned, is served on the Society.

(2) Where a person whose registration is suspended by virtue of paragraph 11 applies to the Society for the suspension to be terminated, the Society may terminate it subject to such conditions, if any, as it thinks fit to impose.

Effective date of revived registration

13 Where a foreign lawyer's registration is revived (whether as the result of the termination of its suspension, restoration by order of the Tribunal or for any other reason), that revival shall take effect on such date, and subject to such conditions, as the Society may direct.

Appeal against conditions or refusals

14 (1) Any foreign lawyer may appeal to the High Court against—

(a) the refusal of the Society to register him or to renew his registration;

(b) the refusal of the Society to terminate the suspension of his registration on an application made by him under paragraph 12;

(c) the failure of the Society to deal with any application by him for registration, renewal of registration or the termination (under paragraph 12(2)) of a suspension within a reasonable time; or

(d) any condition imposed by the Society under paragraph 2A, 12(2) or 13; or

(e) a decision of the Society to remove his name from the register.

(2) *(repealed)*

(3) On an appeal under this paragraph, the High Court may make such order as it thinks fit.

(4) In relation to an appeal under this paragraph the High Court may make such order as it thinks fit as to payment of costs.

(5) The decision of the High Court on an appeal under this paragraph shall be final.

Jurisdiction and powers of Disciplinary Tribunal

15 (1) Subject to paragraph 16, section 46 of the Act of 1974 (Solicitors Disciplinary Tribunal) shall apply, with the necessary modifications, in relation to applications and complaints made by virtue of any provision of this Schedule as it applies in relation to applications and complaints made by virtue of any provision of that Act.

(2) Any application—

(a) to strike the name of a foreign lawyer off the register;

(b) to require a registered foreign lawyer to answer allegations in an affidavit;

(c) to suspend the registration of a foreign lawyer for a specified or indefinite period;

(d) by a foreign lawyer whose name has been struck off the register by order of the Tribunal to have his name restored to the register;

(e) by a foreign lawyer whose registration has been suspended for an indefinite period by order of the Tribunal for the termination of that suspension,

shall be made to the Tribunal.

(3) Any person who alleges that a registered foreign lawyer has failed to comply with any rule made under section 31, 32, 34, or 37 of the Act of 1974 may make a complaint to the Tribunal.

(3A) Any person who alleges that a registered foreign lawyer has knowingly acted in contravention of any order under section 43(2) of the Act of 1974 or of any conditions subject to which a permission has been granted under such an order may make a complaint to the Tribunal.

(4) On the hearing of any application or complaint made to the Tribunal with respect to a foreign lawyer, the Tribunal shall have power to make such order as it may think fit, and any such order may in particular include provision for any of the following matters—

(a) the striking off the register of the name of the foreign lawyer to whom the application or complaint relates;

(b) the suspension of that foreign lawyer's registration indefinitely or for a specified period;

(c) the payment by that foreign lawyer of a penalty, which shall be forfeit to Her Majesty;

(d) the termination of that foreign lawyer's unspecified period of suspension from registration;

(e) the restoration to the register of the name of a foreign lawyer which has been struck off the register;

(f) the payment by any party of costs or a contribution towards costs of such amount as the Tribunal may consider reasonable.

(5) [*repealed*]

Foreign lawyers assisting the Tribunal

16 (1) For the purposes of section 46 of the Act of 1974 (Solicitors Disciplinary Tribunal), the Tribunal may make rules providing for it to be assisted, in dealing with any application or complaint of a kind mentioned in paragraph 15, by a member of the legal profession in the jurisdiction by reference to which the foreign lawyer is or was qualified to be registered.

(2) Rules under sub-paragraph (1) shall not be made without the concurrence of the Legal Services Board.

(3) Subsection (12) of section 46 of the Act of 1974 (rules to be made by statutory instrument etc) shall apply to rules made under this paragraph as it applies to rules made under subsection (9) of that section.

Appeals from Tribunal

17 (1) An Appeal from the Tribunal shall lie to the High Court.

(2) The High Court shall have power to make such order on an appeal under this paragraph as it may think fit.

(3) Any decision of the High Court on an appeal in the case of an order on an application under paragraph 15(2)(d) or (e), or the refusal of any such application, shall be final.

APPENDIX 18

Extracts from the Legal Services Act 2007

[With consolidated amendments to 22 April 2014.]

Legal Services Act 2007

2007 CHAPTER 29

An Act to make provision for the establishment of the Legal Services Board and in respect of its functions; to make provision for, and in connection with, the regulation of persons who carry on certain legal activities; to make provision for the establishment of the Office for Legal Complaints and for a scheme to consider and determine legal complaints; to make provision about claims management services and about immigration advice and immigration services; to make provision in respect of legal representation provided free of charge; to make provision about the application of the Legal Profession and Legal Aid (Scotland) Act 2007; to make provision about the Scottish legal services ombudsman; and for connected purposes.

[30th October 2007]

Be it enacted by the Queen's most Excellent Majesty, by and with the advice and consent of the Lords Spiritual and Temporal, and Commons, in this present Parliament assembled, and by the authority of the same, as follows:—

PART 1
THE REGULATORY OBJECTIVES

1 The regulatory objectives

(1) In this Act a reference to "the regulatory objectives" is a reference to the objectives of—

(a) protecting and promoting the public interest;

(b) supporting the constitutional principle of the rule of law;

(c) improving access to justice;

(d) protecting and promoting the interests of consumers;

(e) promoting competition in the provision of services within subsection (2);

(f) encouraging an independent, strong, diverse and effective legal profession;

(g) increasing public understanding of the citizen's legal rights and duties;

(h) promoting and maintaining adherence to the professional principles.

(2) The services within this subsection are services such as are provided by authorised persons (including services which do not involve the carrying on of activities which are reserved legal activities).

(3) The "professional principles" are—

(a) that authorised persons should act with independence and integrity,

(b) that authorised persons should maintain proper standards of work,

(c) that authorised persons should act in the best interests of their clients,

(d) that persons who exercise before any court a right of audience, or conduct litigation in relation to proceedings in any court, by virtue of being authorised persons should comply with their duty to the court to act with independence in the interests of justice, and

(e) that the affairs of clients should be kept confidential.

(4) In this section "authorised persons" means authorised persons in relation to activities which are reserved legal activities.

...

PART 4
REGULATION OF APPROVED REGULATORS

Introductory

27 Regulatory and representative functions of approved regulators

(1) In this Act references to the "regulatory functions" of an approved regulator are to any functions the approved regulator has—

(a) under or in relation to its regulatory arrangements, or

(b) in connection with the making or alteration of those arrangements.

(2) In this Act references to the "representative functions" of an approved regulator are to any functions the approved regulator has in connection with the representation, or promotion, of the interests of persons regulated by it.

General duties of approved regulators

28 Approved regulator's duty to promote the regulatory objectives etc

(1) In discharging its regulatory functions (whether in connection with a reserved legal activity or otherwise) an approved regulator must comply with the requirements of this section.

(2) The approved regulator must, so far as is reasonably practicable, act in a way—

(a) which is compatible with the regulatory objectives, and

(b) which the approved regulator considers most appropriate for the purpose of meeting those objectives.

(3) The approved regulator must have regard to—

(a) the principles under which regulatory activities should be transparent, accountable, proportionate, consistent and targeted only at cases in which action is needed, and

(b) any other principle appearing to it to represent the best regulatory practice.

...

Regulatory conflict

52 Regulatory conflict with approved regulators

(1) The regulatory arrangements of an approved regulator must make such provision as is reasonably practicable to prevent regulatory conflicts.

(2) For the purposes of this section and section 53, a regulatory conflict is a conflict between—

(a) a requirement of the approved regulator's regulatory arrangements, and

(b) a requirement of the regulatory arrangements of another approved regulator.

(3) Subsection (4) applies where a body is authorised by an approved regulator ("the entity regulator") to carry on an activity which is a reserved legal activity.

(4) If a conflict arises between—

(a) a requirement of the regulatory arrangements of the entity regulator, in relation to the body authorised by the entity regulator or an employee or manager of the body ("an entity requirement"), and

(b) a requirement of the regulatory arrangements of another approved regulator in relation to an employee or manager of the body who is authorised by it to carry on a reserved legal activity ("an individual requirement"),

the entity requirement prevails over the individual requirement.

...

PART 5
ALTERNATIVE BUSINESS STRUCTURES

Introductory

71 Carrying on of activities by licensed bodies

(1) The provisions of this Part have effect for the purpose of regulating the carrying on of reserved legal activities and other activities by licensed bodies.

(2) In this Act "licensed body" means a body which holds a licence in force under this Part.

72 "Licensable body"

(1) A body ("B") is a licensable body if a non-authorised person—

(a) is a manager of B, or

(b) has an interest in B.

(2) A body ("B") is also a licensable body if—

(a) another body ("A") is a manager of B, or has an interest in B, and

(b) non-authorised persons are entitled to exercise, or control the exercise of, at least 10% of the voting rights in A.

(3) For the purposes of this Act, a person has an interest in a body if—

(a) the person holds shares in the body, or

(b) the person is entitled to exercise, or control the exercise of, voting rights in the body.

(4) A body may be licensable by virtue of both subsection (1) and subsection (2).

(5) For the purposes of this Act, a non-authorised person has an indirect interest in a licensable body if the body is licensable by virtue of subsection (2) and the non-authorised person is entitled to exercise, or control the exercise of, voting rights in A.

(6) In this Act "shares" means—

(a) in relation to a body with a share capital, allotted shares (within the meaning of the Companies Acts);

(b) in relation to a body with capital but no share capital, rights to share in the capital of the body;

(c) in relation to a body without capital, interests—

(i) conferring any right to share in the profits, or liability to contribute to the losses, of the body, or

(ii) giving rise to an obligation to contribute to the debts or expenses of the body in the event of a winding up;

and references to the holding of shares, or to a shareholding, are to be construed accordingly.

Licensing

84 Application for licence

(1) A licensing authority must determine any application for a licence which is made to it.

(2) The Board (acting in its capacity as a licensing authority) may determine an application for a licence which is made to it only if the applicant is entitled to make the application by virtue of a decision of the Board (acting otherwise than in its capacity as a licensing authority) under Schedule 12.

(3) A licensing authority may not grant an application for a licence unless it is satisfied that if the licence is granted the applicant will comply with its licensing rules.

(4) If the licensing authority grants an application for a licence, it must issue the licence as soon as reasonably practicable.

(5) The licence has effect from the date on which it is issued.

(6) References in this section to an application for a licence are to an application for a licence which is—

(a) made to a licensing authority by a licensable body, in accordance with the authority's licensing rules, and

(b) accompanied by the required application fee (if any).

85 Terms of licence

(1) A licence issued under section 84 must specify—

(a) the activities which are reserved legal activities and which the licensed body is authorised to carry on by virtue of the licence, and

(b) any conditions subject to which the licence is granted.

(2) If an order under section 106 has been made in relation to the licensed body, the licence must also specify the terms of the order.

(3) The licence may authorise the licensed body to carry on activities which are reserved legal activities only if the licensing authority is designated in relation to the reserved legal activities in question.

(4) A licence must be granted subject to the condition that—

(a) any obligation which may from time to time be imposed on the licensed body or a person within subsection (5) by or under the licensing authority's licensing rules is complied with, and

(b) any other obligations imposed on the licensed body or a person within that subsection by or under this or any other enactment (whether passed before or after this Act) are complied with.

(5) The persons mentioned in subsection (4) are the managers and employees of a licensed body, and non-authorised persons having an interest or an indirect interest, or holding a material interest, in the licensed body (in their capacity as such).

(6) A licence may be granted subject to such other conditions as the licensing authority considers appropriate.

(7) Those conditions may include conditions as to the non-reserved activities which the licensed body may or may not carry on.

(8) In this Part references to the terms of the licence are to the matters listed in subsections (1) and (2).

86 Modification of licence

(1) A licensing authority may modify the terms of a licence granted by it—

(a) if the licensed body applies to the licensing authority, in accordance with its licensing rules, for it to do so;

(b) in such other circumstances as may be specified in its licensing rules.

(2) If a licensed body is a body to which section 106 applies, the licensing authority may modify the terms of its licence in accordance with sections 106 and 107.

(3) A licensing authority modifies the terms of a licensed body's licence by giving the licensed body notice in writing of the modifications; and the modifications have effect from the time the licensing authority gives the licensed body the notice or such later time as may be specified in the notice.

(4) The licensing authority's power under this section is subject to—

(a) section 85(3) and (4), and

(b) licensing rules made under paragraph 6 of Schedule 11.

...

Regulation of licensed bodies

...

93 Information

(1) The relevant licensing authority in relation to a licensed body may by notice require a person within subsection (2)—

(a) to provide information, or information of a description, specified in the notice, or

(b) produce documents, or documents of a description, specified in the notice,

for the purpose of enabling the licensing authority to ascertain whether the terms of the licensed body's licence are being, or have been, complied with.

(2) The persons are—

(a) the licensed body;

(b) any manager or employee (or former manager or employee) of the licensed body;

(c) any non-authorised person who has an interest or an indirect interest, or holds a material interest, in the licensed body.

(3) A notice under subsection (1)—

(a) may specify the manner and form in which any information is to be provided;

(b) must specify the period within which the information is to be provided or the document produced;

(c) may require the information to be provided, or the document to be produced, to the licensing authority or to a person specified in the notice.

(4) The licensing authority may, by notice, require a person within subsection (2) (or a representative of such a person) to attend at a time and place specified in the notice to provide an explanation of any information provided or document produced under this section.

(5) The licensing authority may pay to any person such reasonable costs as may be incurred by that person in connection with—

(a) the provision of any information, or production of any document, by that person pursuant to a notice under subsection (1), or

(b) that person's compliance with a requirement imposed under subsection (4).

(6) The licensing authority, or a person specified under subsection (3)(c) in a notice, may take copies of or extracts from a document produced pursuant to a notice under subsection (1).

(7) For the purposes of this section and section 94, references to a licensed body include a body which was, but is no longer, a licensed body.

94 Enforcement of notices under section 93

(1) Where a person is unable to comply with a notice given to the person under section 93, the person must give the licensing authority a notice to that effect stating the reasons why the person cannot comply.

(2) If a person refuses or otherwise fails to comply with a notice under section 93, the licensing authority may apply to the High Court for an order requiring the person to comply with the notice or with such directions for the like purpose as may be contained in the order.

95 Financial penalties

(1) A licensing authority may, in accordance with its licensing rules, impose on a licensed body, or a manager or employee of a licensed body, a penalty of such amount as it considers appropriate.

(2) The amount must not exceed the maximum amount prescribed under subsection (3).

(3) The Board must make rules prescribing the maximum amount of a penalty which may be imposed under this section.

(4) Rules may be made under subsection (3) only with the consent of the Lord Chancellor.

(5) A penalty under this section is payable to the licensing authority.

(6) For the purposes of this section—

(a) references to a licensed body are to a body which was a licensed body at the time the act or omission in respect of which the penalty is imposed occurred, and

(b) references to a manager or employee of a licensed body are to a person who was a manager or employee of a licensed body at that time,

(whether or not the body subsequently ceased to be a licensed body or the person subsequently ceased to be a manager or employee).

(7) In sections 96 and 97 references to a "penalty" are to a penalty under this section.

96 Appeals against financial penalties

(1) A person on whom a penalty is imposed under section 95 may, before the end of such period as may be prescribed by rules made by the Board, appeal to the relevant appellate body on one or more of the appeal grounds.

(2) The appeal grounds are—

(a) that the imposition of the penalty is unreasonable in all the circumstances of the case;

(b) that the amount of the penalty is unreasonable;

(c) that it is unreasonable of the licensing authority to require the penalty imposed or any portion of it to be paid by the time or times by which it was required to be paid.

(3) On any such appeal, where the relevant appellate body considers it appropriate to do so in all the circumstances of the case and is satisfied of one or more of the appeal grounds, that body may—

(a) quash the penalty,

(b) substitute a penalty of such lesser amount as it considers appropriate, or

(c) in the case of the appeal ground in subsection (2)(c), substitute for any time imposed by the licensing authority a different time or times.

(4) Where the relevant appellate body substitutes a penalty of a lesser amount it may require the payment of interest on the substituted penalty at such rate, and from such time, as it considers just and equitable.

(5) Where the relevant appellate body specifies as a time by which the penalty, or a portion of the penalty, is to be paid a time before the determination of the appeal under this section it may require the payment of interest on the penalty, or portion, from that time at such rate as it considers just and equitable.

(6) A party to the appeal may appeal to the High Court on a point of law arising from the decision of the relevant appellate body, but only with the permission of the High Court.

(7) The High Court may make such order as it thinks fit.

(8) Except as provided by this section, the validity of a penalty is not to be questioned by any legal proceedings whatever.

97 Recovery of financial penalties

(1) If the whole or any part of a penalty is not paid by the time by which, in accordance with licensing rules, it is required to be paid, the unpaid balance from time to time carries interest at the rate for the time being specified in section 17 of the Judgments Act 1838 (c. 110).

(2) Where a penalty, or any portion of it, has not been paid by the time by which, in accordance with licensing rules, it is required to be paid and—

(a) no appeal relating to the penalty has been made under section 96 during the period within which such an appeal can be made, or

(b) an appeal has been made under that section and determined or withdrawn,

the licensing authority may recover from the person on whom the penalty was imposed, as a debt due to the licensing authority, any of the penalty and any interest which has not been paid.

(3) A licensing authority must pay into the Consolidated Fund any sum received by it as a penalty (or as interest on a penalty).

98 Referral of employees etc to appropriate regulator

(1) The relevant licensing authority may refer to an appropriate regulator any matter relating to the conduct of—

(a) an employee or manager of a licensed body;

(b) a person designated as a licensed body's Head of Legal Practice or Head of Finance and Administration.

(2) The licensing authority may also refer any matter relating to the conduct of such a person to the Board.

(3) Appropriate regulators are—

(a) if the person is an authorised person in relation to a reserved legal activity, any relevant approved regulator in relation to that person, and

(b) if the person carries on non-reserved activities, any person who exercises regulatory functions in relation to the carrying on of such activities by the person.

99 Disqualification

(1) A licensing authority may in accordance with its licensing rules disqualify a person from one or more of the activities mentioned in subsection (2) if—

(a) the disqualification condition is satisfied in relation to the person, and

(b) the licensing authority is satisfied that it is undesirable for the person to engage in that activity or those activities.

(2) The activities are—

(a) acting as Head of Legal Practice of any licensed body,

(b) acting as Head of Finance and Administration of any licensed body,

(c) being a manager of any licensed body, or

(d) being employed by any licensed body.

(3) The disqualification condition is satisfied in relation to a person if, in relation to a licensed body licensed by the licensing authority, the person (intentionally or through neglect)—

(a) breaches a relevant duty to which the person is subject, or

(b) causes, or substantially contributes to, a significant breach of the terms of the licensed body's licence.

(4) The relevant duties are—

(a) the duties imposed on a Head of Legal Practice by section 91,

(b) the duties imposed on a Head of Finance and Administration by section 92,

(c) the duties imposed by section 176 on regulated persons (within the meaning of that section), and

(d) the duty imposed on non-authorised persons by section 90.

100 Lists of disqualified persons

(1) The Board must keep lists of persons who are disqualified from—

(a) acting as Head of Legal Practice of any licensed body,

(b) acting as Head of Finance and Administration of any licensed body,

(c) being a manager of any licensed body, or

(d) being employed by any licensed body.

(2) A person is disqualified from acting in a way mentioned in subsection (1) if—

(a) the person has been disqualified from so acting by a licensing authority under section 99, and

(b) the disqualification continues in force.

(3) The disqualification ceases to be in force if the appropriate licensing authority so determines, on a review or otherwise, in accordance with licensing rules made under paragraph 23 of Schedule 11.

(4) The appropriate licensing authority is—

(a) the licensing authority which disqualified the person, or

(b) if the person was disqualified by an approved regulator which is no longer designated as a licensing authority, the successor licensing authority.

(5) The successor licensing authority is—

(a) the licensing authority which licenses the body in relation to which the disqualification condition (within the meaning of section 99) was satisfied in respect of the person, or

(b) if there is no such licensing authority, the licensing authority designated by the Board on an application by the disqualified person.

(6) The Board must publish the lists kept by it under subsection (1).

…

PART 6
LEGAL COMPLAINTS

Complaints procedures of authorised persons

112 Complaints procedures of authorised persons

(1) The regulatory arrangements of an approved regulator must make provision requiring each relevant authorised person—

(a) to establish and maintain procedures for the resolution of relevant complaints, or

(b) to participate in, or make arrangements to be subject to, such procedures established and maintained by another person,

and provision for the enforcement of that requirement.

(2) The provision made for the purposes of subsection (1) must satisfy such requirements as the Board may, from time to time, specify for the purposes of that subsection.

(3) In this section—

"relevant authorised person", in relation to an approved regulator, means a person in relation to whom the approved regulator is a relevant approved regulator;

"relevant complaint", in relation to a relevant authorised person, means a complaint which—

(a) relates to an act or omission of that person, and

(b) may be made under the scheme provided for by this Part

(4) The Board must publish any requirements specified by it for the purposes of subsection (2).

(5) This section applies in relation to the licensing rules of the Board as it applies in relation to the regulatory arrangements of an approved regulator except that subsection (3) has effect as if for the definition of "relevant authorised person" there were substituted—

"'relevant authorised person', in relation to the Board, means a person licensed by the Board under Part 5;".

Overview of the scheme

113 Overview of the scheme

(1) This Part provides for a scheme under which complaints which—

(a) relate to an act or omission of a person ("the respondent") in carrying on an activity, and

(b) are within the jurisdiction of the scheme (see section 125),

may be resolved quickly and with minimum formality by an independent person.

(2) Under the scheme—

(a) redress may be provided to the complainant, but

(b) no disciplinary action may be taken against the respondent.

(3) Section 157 prevents provision relating to redress being included in the regulatory arrangements of an approved regulator.

(4) But neither the scheme nor any provision made by this Part affects any power of an approved regulator to take disciplinary action.

(5) "Disciplinary action" means the imposition of sanctions, in respect of a breach of conduct rules or discipline rules, on a person who is an authorised person in relation to an activity which is a reserved legal activity.

Jurisdiction and operation of the ombudsman scheme

125 Jurisdiction of the ombudsman scheme

(1) A complaint which relates to an act or omission of a person ("the respondent") in carrying on an activity is within the jurisdiction of the ombudsman scheme if—

(a) the complaint is not excluded from the jurisdiction of the scheme by section 126, or by scheme rules made under section 127,

(b) the respondent is within section 128, and

(c) the complainant is within section 128 and wishes to have the complaint dealt with under the scheme.

(2) In subsection (1) references to an act or omission include an act or omission which occurs before the coming into force of this section.

(3) The right of a person to make a complaint under the ombudsman scheme, and the jurisdiction of an ombudsman to investigate, consider and determine a complaint, may not be limited or excluded by any contract term or by notice.

126 Complaints excluded because respondent's complaints procedures not used

(1) A complaint is excluded from the jurisdiction of the ombudsman scheme if the complainant has not first used the respondent's complaints procedures in relation to the complaint.

(2) The respondent's complaints procedures are the procedures established by the respondent, or which the respondent participates in or is subject to, in accordance with regulatory arrangements made in accordance with section 112.

(3) Scheme rules may provide that subsection (1) does not apply in specified circumstances.

127 Complaints excluded by scheme rules

(1) Scheme rules may make provision excluding complaints of a description specified in the rules from the jurisdiction of the ombudsman scheme.

(2) But they may not make provision excluding a complaint from the jurisdiction of the ombudsman scheme on the ground that it relates to a matter which has been or could be dealt with under the disciplinary arrangements of the respondent's relevant authorising body.

128 Parties

(1) The respondent is within this section if, at the relevant time, the respondent was an authorised person in relation to an activity which was a reserved legal activity (whether or not the act or omission relates to a reserved legal activity).

(2) The complainant ("C") is within this section if C—

(a) meets the first and second conditions, and

(b) is not excluded by subsection (5).

(3) The first condition is that C is—

(a) an individual, or

(b) a person (other than an individual) of a description prescribed by order made by the Lord Chancellor in accordance with a recommendation made under section 130.

(4) The second condition is that—

(a) the services to which the complaint relates were provided by the respondent to C;

(b) the services to which the complaint relates were provided by the respondent to an authorised person who procured them on C's behalf;

(c) the services to which the complaint relates were provided by the respondent—

(i) in the respondent's capacity as a personal representative or trustee, or

(ii) to a person acting as a personal representative or trustee,

and C is a beneficiary of the estate or trust in question; or

(d) C satisfies such other conditions, in relation to the services to which the complaint relates, as may be prescribed by order made by the Lord Chancellor in accordance with a recommendation made under section 130.

(5) C is excluded if, at the relevant time—

(a) C was an authorised person in relation to an activity which was a reserved legal activity and the services to which the complaint relates were procured by C on behalf of another person,

(b) C was a public body or was acting on behalf of such a body in relation to the services to which the complaint relates, or

(c) C was a person prescribed, or of a description prescribed, as excluded by order made by the Lord Chancellor in accordance with a recommendation made under section 130.

(6) In subsection (4)(b) "authorised person" means an authorised person in relation to any activity which is a reserved legal activity.

(7) In this section—

"public body" means any government department, local authority or other body constituted for purposes of the public services, local government or the administration of justice;

"relevant time", in relation to a complaint, means the time when the act or omission to which the complaint relates took place.

129 Pre-commencement acts and omissions

(1) For the purposes of section 128 a person is to be regarded as an authorised person in relation to an activity which is a reserved legal activity, at a time before section 125 comes into force, if the person was at that time—

(a) a person of the kind mentioned in paragraph 2(4) of Schedule 15,

(b) a body recognised under section 9 or 32 of the Administration of Justice Act 1985 (c. 61) (recognised bodies), or

(c) a legal partnership, a conveyancing partnership, a patent attorney body or a trade mark attorney body.

(2) In this section—

"conveyancing partnership" has the meaning given by paragraph 11(5) of Schedule 5;

"legal partnership" has the meaning given by paragraph 7(4) of that Schedule;

"patent attorney body" has the meaning given by paragraph 14(7) of that Schedule;

"trade mark attorney body" has the meaning given by paragraph 16(7) of that Schedule.

130 Orders under section 128

(1) An interested body may, at any time, recommend to the Lord Chancellor that the Lord Chancellor make an order under section 128(3)(b), (4)(d) or (5)(c).

(2) An interested body must, if requested to do so by the Lord Chancellor, consider whether or not it is appropriate to make a recommendation under subsection (1).

(3) An interested body must, before making a recommendation under subsection (1)—

(a) publish a draft of the proposed recommendation,

(b) invite representations regarding the proposed recommendation, and

(c) consider any such representations which are made.

(4) Where the Lord Chancellor receives a recommendation under subsection (1), the Lord Chancellor must consider whether to follow the recommendation.

(5) If the Lord Chancellor decides not to follow the recommendation, the Lord Chancellor must publish a notice to that effect which includes the Lord Chancellor's reasons for the decision.

(6) In this section "interested body" means—

(a) the OLC,

(b) the Board, or

(c) the Consumer Panel.

131 Acts and omissions by employees etc

(1) For the purposes of this Part and the ombudsman scheme, any act or omission by a person in the course of the person's employment is to be treated as also an act or omission by the person's employer, whether or not it was done with the employer's knowledge or approval.

(2) For the purposes of this Part and the ombudsman scheme, any act or omission by a partner in a partnership in the course of carrying on, in the usual way, business of the kind carried on by the partnership is to be treated as also an act or omission by the partnership.

(3) But subsection (2) does not apply if the partner had no authority to act for the partnership and the person purporting to rely on that subsection knew, at the time of the act or omission, that the partner had no such authority.

132 Continuity of complaints

(1) The ability of a person to make a complaint about an act or omission of a partnership or other unincorporated body is not affected by any change in the membership of the partnership or body.

(2) Scheme rules must make provision determining the circumstances in which, for the purposes of the ombudsman scheme, an act or omission of a person ("A") is, where A ceases to exist and another person ("B") succeeds to the whole or substantially the whole of the business of A, to be treated as an act or omission of B.

(3) Rules under subsection (2) must, in relation to cases where an act or omission of A is treated as an act or omission of B, make provision about the treatment of complaints under the ombudsman scheme which are outstanding against A at the time A ceases to exist.

(4) Scheme rules must make provision permitting such persons as may be specified in the rules to continue a complaint made by a person who has died or is otherwise unable to act; and for that purpose may modify references to the complainant in this Part and in scheme rules.

133 Operation of the ombudsman scheme

(1) Scheme rules must set out the procedure for—

- (a) the making of complaints under the ombudsman scheme, and
- (b) the investigation, consideration and determination of complaints by an ombudsman.

(2) Scheme rules—

- (a) must provide that a complaint is to be entertained under the ombudsman scheme only if the complainant has made the complaint under that scheme before the applicable time limit (determined in accordance with the scheme rules) has expired, and
- (b) may provide that an ombudsman may extend that time limit in specified circumstances.

(3) Scheme rules made under subsection (1) may (among other things) make provision—

- (a) for the whole or part of a complaint to be dismissed, in specified circumstances, without consideration of its merits;
- (b) for the reference of a complaint, in specified circumstances and with the consent of the complainant, to another body with a view to it being determined by that body instead of by an ombudsman;
- (c) for a person who, at the relevant time (within the meaning of section 128(7)) was an

authorised person in relation to an activity to be treated in specified circumstances, for the purposes of the scheme and this Part, as if that person were a co-respondent in relation to a complaint;

(d) about the evidence which may be required or admitted and the extent to which it should be oral or written;

(e) for requiring parties to the complaint to attend to give evidence and produce documents, and for authorising the administration of oaths by ombudsmen;

(f) about the matters which are to be taken into account in determining whether an act or omission was fair and reasonable;

(g) for an ombudsman, in such circumstances as may be specified, to award expenses to persons in connection with attendance at a hearing before an ombudsman;

(h) for an ombudsman to award costs against the respondent in favour of the complainant;

(i) for an ombudsman to award costs against the complainant or the respondent in favour of the OLC for the purpose of providing a contribution to resources deployed in dealing with the complaint, if in the ombudsman's opinion that person acted so unreasonably in relation to the complaint that it is appropriate in all the circumstances of the case to make such an award;

(j) for the purpose of facilitating the settlement of a complaint with the agreement of the parties to it;

(k) for specified persons to be notified of complaints, determinations and directions under the ombudsman scheme.

(4) The circumstances specified under subsection (3)(a) may include the following—

(a) the ombudsman considers the complaint or part to be frivolous or vexatious or totally without merit;

(b) the ombudsman considers that the complaint or part would be better dealt with under another ombudsman scheme, by arbitration or by other legal proceedings;

(c) the ombudsman considers that there has been undue delay in the making of the complaint or part, or the provision of evidence to support it;

(d) the ombudsman is satisfied that the matter which is the subject of the complaint or part has previously been dealt with under another ombudsman scheme, by arbitration or by other legal proceedings;

(e) the ombudsman considers that there are other compelling reasons why it is inappropriate for the complaint or part to be dealt with under the ombudsman scheme.

(5) No person may be required by scheme rules—

(a) to provide any information or give any evidence which that person could not be compelled to provide or give in evidence in civil proceedings before the High Court, or

(b) to produce any document which that person could not be compelled to produce in such proceedings.

(6) Scheme rules may authorise an ombudsman making an award of costs in accordance with rules within subsection (3)(h) or (i) to order that the amount payable under the award bears interest, from a time specified in or determined in accordance with the order, at a rate specified in or determined in accordance with the rules.

(7) An amount due under an award made in favour of a person by virtue of provision made under subsection (3)(g), (h) or (i) is recoverable as a debt due to that person.

(8) In this section—

"party", in relation to a complaint, means—

(a) the complainant,

(b) the respondent, and

(c) any other person who in accordance with scheme rules is to be regarded as a party to the complaint;

"specified" means specified in scheme rules.

134 Delegation of an ombudsman's functions

(1) An ombudsman may delegate to a member of the OLC's staff appointed under paragraph 13 of Schedule 15—

(a) any function of the ombudsman in relation to the making, investigation or consideration of a complaint;

(b) any other function conferred on the ombudsman by or by virtue of this Part.

(2) Nothing in subsection (1) applies to the following functions—

(a) the function of determining a complaint;

(b) the function of deciding that a complaint should be dismissed by virtue of rules under section 133(3)(a);

(c) the Chief Ombudsman's power to consent to the appointment of an assistant ombudsman under section 122;

(d) the duties imposed on the Chief Ombudsman by section 123 (Chief Ombudsman's report).

135 Notification requirements

(1) This section applies where a complaint—

(a) is excluded from the jurisdiction of the ombudsman scheme under section 126, or by virtue of scheme rules made under section 127;

(b) is dismissed, or referred to another body, by virtue of scheme rules;

(c) is settled, withdrawn or abandoned (or treated as withdrawn or abandoned by virtue of scheme rules).

(2) The ombudsman must notify—

(a) the complainant;

(b) the respondent;

(c) any relevant authorising body, in relation to the respondent, notified of the complaint in accordance with rules within section 133(3)(k),

and, in a case within subsection (1)(a) or (b), must give reasons for the exclusion, dismissal or referral.

136 Charges payable by respondents

(1) Scheme rules must require respondents, in relation to complaints under the ombudsman scheme, to pay to the OLC such charges as may be specified in the rules.

(2) The rules must provide for charges payable in relation to a complaint to be waived (or wholly refunded) where—

(a) the complaint is determined or otherwise resolved in favour of the respondent, and

(b) the ombudsman is satisfied that the respondent took all reasonable steps to try to resolve the complaint under the respondent's complaints procedures.

(3) The rules may make provision as to—

(a) the circumstances in which a complaint is to be treated as determined or otherwise resolved in favour of the respondent (which may include circumstances where a complaint is settled, withdrawn or abandoned (or treated as withdrawn or abandoned by virtue of scheme rules));

(b) matters to be taken into account by the ombudsman for the purposes of subsection (2)(b).

(4) The respondent's complaints procedures are the procedures established by the respondent, or which the respondent participates in or is subject to, in accordance with regulatory arrangements (or licensing rules of the Board) made in accordance with section 112.

(5) The rules may, among other things—

(a) provide for the OLC to reduce or waive a charge in such other circumstances as may be specified;

(b) set different charges for different stages of the proceedings on a complaint;

(c) provide for charges to be wholly or partly refunded in such other circumstances as may be specified;

(d) provide that if the whole or any part of a charge is not paid by the time by which it is required to be paid under the rules, the unpaid balance from time to time carries interest at the rate specified in, or determined in accordance with, the rules.

(6) Any charge which is owed to the OLC by virtue of rules made under this section may be recovered as a debt due to the OLC.

Determinations under the scheme

137 Determination of complaints

(1) A complaint is to be determined under the ombudsman scheme by reference to what is, in the opinion of the ombudsman making the determination, fair and reasonable in all the circumstances of the case.

(2) The determination may contain one or more of the following—

(a) a direction that the respondent make an apology to the complainant;

(b) a direction that—

(i) the fees to which the respondent is entitled in respect of the services to which the complaint relates ("the fees") are limited to such amount as may be specified in the direction, and

(ii) the respondent comply, or secure compliance, with such one or more of the permitted requirements as appear to the ombudsman to be necessary in order for effect to be given to the direction under sub-paragraph (i);

(c) a direction that the respondent pay compensation to the complainant of such an amount as is specified in the direction in respect of any loss which has been suffered by, or any inconvenience or distress which has been caused to, the complainant as a result of any matter connected with the complaint;

(d) a direction that the respondent secure the rectification, at the expense of the respondent, of any such error, omission or other deficiency arising in connection with the matter in question as the direction may specify;

(e) a direction that the respondent take, at the expense of the respondent, such other action in the interests of the complainant as the direction may specify.

(3) For the purposes of subsection (2)(b) "the permitted requirements" are—

(a) that the whole or part of any amount already paid by or on behalf of the complainant in respect of the fees be refunded;

(b) that the whole or part of the fees be remitted;

(c) that the right to recover the fees be waived, whether wholly or to any specified extent.

(4) Where—

(a) a direction is made under subsection (2)(b) which requires that the whole or part of any amount already paid by or on behalf of the complainant in respect of the fees be refunded, or

(b) a direction is made under subsection (2)(c),

the direction may also provide for the amount payable under the direction to carry interest from a time specified in or determined in accordance with the direction, at the rate specified in or determined in accordance with scheme rules.

(5) The power of the ombudsman to make a direction under subsection (2) is not confined to cases where the complainant may have a cause of action against the respondent for negligence.

138 Limitation on value of directions under the ombudsman scheme

(1) Where a determination is made under the ombudsman scheme in respect of a complaint, the total value of directions under section 137(2)(c) to (e) contained in the determination must not exceed £50,000.

(2) For this purpose the total value of such directions is the aggregate of—

(a) the amount of any compensation specified in a direction under subsection (2)(c) of section 137, and

(b) the amount of any expenses reasonably incurred by the respondent when complying with a direction under subsection (2)(d) or (e) of that section.

(3) For the purposes of determining that total value, any interest payable on an amount within subsection (2)(a) of this section, by virtue of section 137(4), is to be ignored.

139 Alteration of limit

(1) The Lord Chancellor may by order amend section 138(1) in accordance with a recommendation made by an interested body under subsection (2).

(2) An interested body may, at any time, recommend to the Lord Chancellor that section 138(1) should be amended so as to substitute the amount specified in the recommendation for the amount for the time being specified in that provision.

(3) An interested body must, if requested to do so by the Lord Chancellor, consider whether or not it is appropriate to make a recommendation under subsection (2).

(4) An interested body must, before making a recommendation under subsection (2)—

(a) publish a draft of the proposed recommendation,

(b) invite representations regarding the proposed recommendation, and

(c) consider any such representations which are made.

(5) Where the Lord Chancellor receives a recommendation under subsection (2), the Lord Chancellor must consider whether to follow the recommendation.

(6) If the Lord Chancellor decides not to follow the recommendation, the Lord Chancellor must publish a notice to that effect which includes the Lord Chancellor's reasons for the decision.

(7) In this section "interested body" means—

(a) the OLC,

(b) the Board, or

(c) the Consumer Panel.

140 Acceptance or rejection of determination

(1) When an ombudsman has determined a complaint the ombudsman must prepare a written statement of the determination.

(2) The statement must—

(a) give the ombudsman's reasons for the determination,

(b) be signed by the ombudsman, and

(c) require the complainant to notify the ombudsman, before a time specified in the statement ("the specified time"), whether the complainant accepts or rejects the determination.

(3) The ombudsman must give a copy of the statement to—

(a) the complainant,

(b) the respondent, and

(c) any relevant authorising body in relation to the respondent.

(4) If the complainant notifies the ombudsman that the determination is accepted by the complainant, it is binding on the respondent and the complainant and is final.

(5) If, by the specified time, the complainant has not notified the ombudsman of the complainant's acceptance or rejection of the determination, the complainant is to be treated as having rejected it.

(6) But if—

(a) the complainant notifies the ombudsman after the specified time that the determination is accepted by the complainant,

(b) the complainant has not previously notified the ombudsman of the complainant's rejection of the determination, and

(c) the ombudsman is satisfied that such conditions as may be prescribed by the scheme rules for the purposes of this subsection are satisfied,

the determination is treated as if it had never been rejected by virtue of subsection (5).

(7) The ombudsman must give notice of the outcome to—

(a) the complainant,

(b) the respondent, and

(c) any relevant authorising body in relation to the respondent.

(8) Where a determination is rejected by virtue of subsection (5), that notice must contain a general description of the effect of subsection (6).

(9) A copy of the determination on which appears a certificate signed by an ombudsman is evidence that the determination was made under the scheme.

(10) Such a certificate purporting to be signed by an ombudsman is to be taken to have been duly signed unless the contrary is shown.

(11) Neither the complainant nor the respondent, in relation to a complaint, may institute or continue legal proceedings in respect of a matter which was the subject of a complaint, after the time when a determination by an ombudsman of the complaint becomes binding and final in accordance with this section.

141 Enforcement by complainant of directions under section 137

(1) This section applies where—

(a) a determination is made in respect of a complaint under the ombudsman scheme,

(b) one or more directions are made under section 137(2), and

(c) the determination is final by virtue of section 140(4).

(2) An amount payable in accordance with—

(a) a direction under subsection (2)(b) of section 137 which requires that the whole or part of any amount already paid by or on behalf of the complainant in respect of the fees be refunded, or

(b) a direction under subsection (2)(c) of that section,

including any interest payable by virtue of subsection (4) of that section, is recoverable, if a court so orders on the application of the complainant or an ombudsman, as if it were payable under an order of that court.

(3) If the respondent fails to comply with any other direction under section 137(2), the complainant or an ombudsman may make an application to the court under this subsection.

(4) If, on an application under subsection (3), the court decides that the respondent has failed to comply with the direction in question, it may order the respondent to take such steps as the court directs for securing that the direction is complied with.

(5) An ombudsman may make an application under subsection (2) or (3) only in such circumstances as may be specified in scheme rules, and with the complainant's consent.

(6) If the court makes an order under subsection (2) on the application of an ombudsman, the ombudsman may in such circumstances as may be specified in scheme rules and with the complainant's consent recover the amount mentioned in that subsection on behalf of the complainant.

(7) In this section "court" means the High Court or the county court.

142 Reporting court orders made against authorised persons

(1) Where a court makes an order under section 141, it must give the OLC notice to that effect.

(2) Where the order is made against a person who is an authorised person in relation to any activity which is a reserved legal activity, the OLC must make arrangements to ensure that an ombudsman gives to each relevant authorising body, in relation to that person, a report which states that the order has been made.

(3) A report under subsection (2) may require the relevant authorising body to report to the ombudsman the action which has been or is to be taken by it in response to the report under subsection (2) and the reasons for that action being taken.

(4) If an ombudsman, having regard to any report produced by the relevant authorising body in compliance with a requirement imposed under subsection (3), or any failure to comply with such a requirement, considers—

(a) that there has been a serious failure by the relevant authorising body to discharge its regulatory functions, or

(b) if such a requirement has been imposed on the body on more than one occasion, that the relevant authorising body has persistently failed adequately to discharge its regulatory functions,

the ombudsman may make a report to that effect to the Board.

Reporting misconduct

143 Reporting possible misconduct to approved regulators

(1) This section applies where—

(a) an ombudsman is dealing, or has dealt, with a complaint under the ombudsman scheme, and

(b) the ombudsman is of the opinion that the conduct of the respondent or any other person in relation to any matter connected with the complaint is such that a relevant authorising body in relation to that person should consider whether to take action against that person.

(2) The ombudsman must give the relevant authorising body a report which—

(a) states that the ombudsman is of that opinion, and

(b) gives details of that conduct.

(3) The ombudsman must give the complainant a notice stating that a report under subsection (2) has been given to the relevant authorising body.

(4) A report under subsection (2) may require the relevant authorising body to report to the ombudsman the action which has been or is to be taken by it in response to the report and the reasons for that action being taken.

(5) The duty imposed by subsection (2) is not affected by the withdrawal or abandonment of the complaint.

(6) If an ombudsman, having regard to any report produced by the relevant authorising body in compliance with a requirement imposed under subsection (4), or any failure to comply with such a requirement, considers—

(a) that there has been a serious failure by the relevant authorising body to discharge its regulatory functions, or

(b) if such a requirement has been imposed on the body on more than one occasion, that the relevant authorising body has persistently failed adequately to discharge its regulatory functions,

the ombudsman may make a report to that effect to the Board.

Co-operation with investigations

144 Duties to share information

(1) Scheme rules must make provision requiring persons within subsection (3) to disclose to an approved regulator information of such description as may be specified in the rules, in such circumstances as may be so specified.

(2) The regulatory arrangements of an approved regulator must make provision requiring the approved regulator to disclose to persons within subsection (3) information of such description as may be specified in the arrangements, in such circumstances as may be so specified.

(3) The persons are—

(a) the OLC;

(b) an ombudsman;

(c) a member of the OLC's staff appointed under paragraph 13 of Schedule 15.

(4) Provision made under subsection (1) or (2) must satisfy such requirements as the Board may, from time to time, specify.

(5) In specifying requirements under subsection (4) the Board must have regard to the need to ensure that, so far as reasonably practicable—

(a) duplication of investigations is avoided;

(b) the OLC assists approved regulators to carry out their regulatory functions, and approved regulators assist with the investigation, consideration and determination of complaints under the ombudsman scheme.

(6) The Board must publish any requirements specified by it under subsection (4).

(7) The OLC must—

(a) before publishing under section 205(2) a draft of rules it proposes to make under subsection (1), consult each approved regulator to which the proposed rules apply, and

(b) when seeking the Board's consent to such rules under section 155, identify any objections made by an approved regulator to the rules and not withdrawn.

(8) An approved regulator must—

(a) consult the OLC before making provisions in its regulatory arrangements of the kind mentioned in subsection (2), and

(b) where an application is made for the Board's approval of such provisions, identify any objections made by the OLC to the provisions and not withdrawn.

(9) [*repealed*]

145 Duties of authorised persons to co-operate with investigations

(1) The regulatory arrangements of an approved regulator must make—

(a) provision requiring each relevant authorised person to give ombudsmen all such assistance requested by them, in connection with the investigation, consideration or determination of complaints under the ombudsman scheme, as that person is reasonably able to give, and

(b) provision for the enforcement of that requirement.

(2) The provision made for the purposes of subsection (1) must satisfy such requirements as the Board may, from time to time, specify for the purposes of that subsection.

(3) The Board must publish any requirements specified by it under subsection (2).

(4) In this section "relevant authorised person"—

(a) in relation to an approved regulator, has the same meaning as in section 112, and

(b) [*repealed*].

146 Reporting failures to co-operate with an investigation to approved regulators

(1) This section applies where an ombudsman is of the opinion that an authorised person has failed to give an ombudsman all such assistance requested by the ombudsman, in connection with the investigation, consideration or determination of a complaint under the ombudsman scheme, as that person is reasonably able to give.

(2) The ombudsman must give each relevant authorising body, in relation to that person, a report which—

(a) states that the ombudsman is of that opinion, and

(b) gives details of the failure.

(3) A report under subsection (2) may require the relevant authorising body to report to the ombudsman the action which has been or is to be taken by it in response to the report under that subsection and the reasons for that action being taken.

(4) The duty imposed by subsection (2) is not affected by the withdrawal or abandonment of the complaint.

(5) If an ombudsman, having regard to any report produced by the relevant authorising body in compliance with a requirement imposed under subsection (3), or any failure to comply with such a requirement, considers—

(a) that there has been a serious failure by the relevant authorising body to discharge its regulatory functions, or

(b) if such a requirement has been imposed on the body on more than one occasion, that the relevant authorising body has persistently failed adequately to discharge its regulatory functions,

the ombudsman may make a report to that effect to the Board.

(6) In this section "authorised person" means an authorised person in relation to any activity which is a reserved legal activity.

Information

147 Information and documents

(1) An ombudsman may, by notice, require a party to a complaint under the ombudsman scheme—

(a) to produce documents, or documents of a description, specified in the notice, or

(b) to provide information, or information of a description, specified in the notice.

(2) A notice under subsection (1) may require the information or documents to be provided or produced—

(a) before the end of such reasonable period as may be specified in the notice, and

(b) in the case of information, in such manner or form as may be so specified.

(3) This section applies only to information and documents the provision or production of which the ombudsman considers necessary for the determination of the complaint.

(4) An ombudsman may—

(a) take copies of or extracts from a document produced under this section, and

(b) [*repealed*]

(5) If a person who is required under this section to produce a document fails to do so, an ombudsman may require that person to state, to the best of that person's knowledge and belief, where the document is.

(6) No person may be required under this section—

(a) to provide any information which that person could not be compelled to provide or give in evidence in civil proceedings before the High Court, or

(b) to produce any document which that person could not be compelled to produce in such proceedings.

(7) In this section "party", in relation to a complaint, means—

(a) the complainant;

(b) the respondent;

(c) any other person who in accordance with the scheme rules is to be regarded as a party to the complaint.

148 Reporting failures to provide information or produce documents

(1) This section applies where an ombudsman is of the opinion that an authorised person has failed to comply with a requirement imposed under section 147(1).

(2) The ombudsman must give each relevant authorising body, in relation to that person, a report which—

(a) states that the ombudsman is of that opinion, and

(b) gives details of the failure.

(3) A report under subsection (2) may require the relevant authorising body to report to the ombudsman the action which has been or is to be taken by it in response to the report under that subsection and the reasons for that action being taken.

(4) The duty imposed by subsection (2) is not affected by the withdrawal or abandonment of the complaint in relation to which the requirement was imposed under section 147(1).

(5) If an ombudsman, having regard to any report produced by the relevant authorising body in compliance with a requirement imposed under subsection (3), or any failure to comply with such a requirement, considers—

(a) that there has been a serious failure by the relevant authorising body to discharge its regulatory functions, or

(b) if such a requirement has been imposed on the body on more than one occasion, that the relevant authorising body has persistently failed adequately to discharge its regulatory functions,

the ombudsman may make a report to that effect to the Board.

(6) In this section "authorised person" means an authorised person in relation to any activity which is a reserved legal activity.

149 Enforcement of requirements to provide information or produce documents

(1) This section applies where an ombudsman is of the opinion that a person ("the defaulter") has failed to comply with a requirement imposed under section 147(1).

(2) The ombudsman may certify the defaulter's failure to comply with the requirement to the court.

(3) Where an ombudsman certifies a failure to the court under subsection (2), the court may enquire into the case.

(4) If the court is satisfied that the defaulter has failed without reasonable excuse to comply with the requirement, it may deal with—

(a) the defaulter, and

(b) in the case of a body, any manager of the body,

as if that person were in contempt.

(5) Subsection (6) applies in a case where the defaulter is an authorised person in relation to any activity which is a reserved legal activity.

(6) The ombudsman ("the enforcing ombudsman") may not certify the defaulter's failure to the court until a report by that or another ombudsman has been made as required by section 148(2) and the enforcing ombudsman is satisfied—

(a) that each relevant authorising body to whom such a report was made has been given a reasonable opportunity to take action in respect of the defaulter's failure, and

(b) that the defaulter has continued to fail to provide the information or produce the documents to which the requirement under section 147 related.

(7) In this section "court" means the High Court.

150 Reports of investigations

(1) The OLC may, if it considers it appropriate to do so in any particular case, publish a report of the investigation, consideration and determination of a complaint made under the ombudsman scheme.

(2) A report under subsection (1) must not (unless the complainant consents)—

(a) mention the name of the complainant, or

(b) include any particulars which, in the opinion of the OLC, are likely to identify the complainant.

151 Restricted information

(1) Except as provided by section 152, restricted information must not be disclosed—

(a) by a restricted person, or

(b) by any person who receives the information directly or indirectly from a restricted person.

(2) In this section and section 152—

"restricted information" means information (other than excluded information) which is obtained by a restricted person in the course of, or for the purposes of, an investigation into a complaint made under the ombudsman scheme (including information obtained for the purposes of deciding whether to begin such an investigation or in connection with the settlement of a complaint);

"restricted person" means—

(a) the OLC,

(b) an ombudsman, or

(c) a person who exercises functions delegated under paragraph 22 of Schedule 15.

(3) For the purposes of subsection (2) "excluded information" means—

(a) information which is in the form of a summary or collection of information so framed as not to enable information relating to any particular person to be ascertained from it;

(b) information which at the time of the disclosure is or has already been made available to the public from other sources;

(c) information which was obtained more than 70 years before the date of the disclosure.

152 Disclosure of restricted information

(1) A restricted person may disclose restricted information to another restricted person.

(2) Restricted information may be disclosed for the purposes of the investigation in the course of which, or for the purposes of which, it was obtained.

(3) Section 151 also does not preclude the disclosure of restricted information—

(a) in a report made under—

(i) section 143(2) (report of possible misconduct to approved regulators),

(ii) section 146(2) (report of failure to co-operate with investigation),

(iii) section 148 (reporting failures to provide information or produce documents), or

(iv) section 150 (reports of investigations),

(b) for the purposes of enabling or assisting the Board to exercise any of its functions,

(c) to an approved regulator for the purposes of enabling or assisting the approved regulator to exercise any of its regulatory functions,

(d) with the consent of the person to whom it relates and (if different) the person from whom the restricted person obtained it,

(e) for the purposes of an inquiry with a view to the taking of any criminal proceedings or for the purposes of any such proceedings,

(f) where the disclosure is required by or by virtue of any provision made by or under this Act or any other enactment or other rule of law,

(g) to such persons (other than approved regulators) who exercise regulatory functions as may be prescribed by order made by the Lord Chancellor, for such purposes as may be so prescribed.

(4) Subsections (2) and (3) are subject to subsection (5).

(5) The Lord Chancellor may by order prevent the disclosure of restricted information by virtue of subsection (2) or (3) in such circumstances, or for such purposes, as may be prescribed in the order.

153 Data protection

In section 31 of the Data Protection Act 1998 (c. 29) (regulatory activity), after subsection (4B) (inserted by section 170) insert—

"(4C) Personal data processed for the purposes of the function of considering a complaint under the scheme established under Part 6 of the Legal Services Act 2007 (legal complaints) are exempt from the subject information provisions in any case to the extent to which the application of those provisions to the data would be likely to prejudice the proper discharge of the function."

Defamation

154 Protection from defamation claims

For the purposes of the law of defamation—

(a) proceedings in relation to a complaint under the ombudsman scheme are to be treated as if they were proceedings before a court, and

(b) the publication of any matter by the OLC under this Part is absolutely privileged.

PART 8
MISCELLANEOUS PROVISIONS ABOUT LAWYERS ETC

Duties of regulated persons

176 Duties of regulated persons

(1) A person who is a regulated person in relation to an approved regulator has a duty to comply with the regulatory arrangements of the approved regulator as they apply to that person.

(2) A person is a regulated person in relation to an approved regulator if the person—

(a) is authorised by the approved regulator to carry on an activity which is a reserved legal activity, or

(b) is not so authorised, but is a manager or employee of a person who is so authorised.

(3) This section applies in relation to the Board in its capacity as a licensing authority and its licensing rules, as it applies in relation to an approved regulator and its regulatory arrangements.

APPENDIX 19

Summary of reporting and similar obligations

[Law Society copyright. This material appeared as Chapter 8 in *Outcomes-Focused Regulation*, Andrew Hopper and Gregory Treverton-Jones, published by the Law Society, 2011.]

Summary of reporting and similar obligations

There are now so many obligations of this kind that it seems sensible and helpful to list them.

8.1 Statutory requirements

- Solicitors Act 1974, s.84: notification of a change in a solicitor's place of business;
- Legal Services Act 2007, Sched. 13, para. 21: notification by non-authorised persons (investors) who propose to acquire an interest in a licensed body (ABS) which would amount to a restricted interest (currently 10 per cent) or who have acquired such an interest must notify the proposal or the acquisition. Failure to do so is a criminal offence.

8.2 SRA requirements

8.2.1 Under the Code of Conduct

- O(10.2): providing information required by the SRA to deal with any application (such as for a practising certificate);
- O(10.3): prompt notification of any material changes to relevant information including serious financial difficulty, action taken by another regulator and serious failure to comply with or achieve the Principles, rules, outcomes and other requirements of the SRA Handbook;
- O(10.4): prompt reporting of serious misconduct by any person or firm authorised by the SRA, or any employee, manager or owner of any such firm (taking into account, where necessary, the duty of confidentiality to clients);
- O(10.5): ensuring that the SRA is in a position to assess whether any persons requiring prior approval are fit and proper at the point of approval and remain so;
- O(10.6): full co-operation with the SRA and the Legal Ombudsman at all times, including in relation to any investigation about a claim for redress;
- O(10.7): prohibition of any attempt to prevent anyone from providing information to the SRA or the Legal Ombudsman;
- O(10.8): prompt compliance with any written notice from the SRA;
- O(10.9): pursuant to any notice by the SRA the production of any documents; the

provision of all information and explanations requested; compliance with all requests from the SRA as to the form in which any documents held electronically are produced, and for photocopies of any documents to be taken, provided that they are in connection with the individual's practice or in connection with any trust of which he or she is, or formerly was, a trustee;

- O(10.11): when required by the SRA to investigate whether any person may have a claim for redress, acting promptly to do so, reporting to the SRA the outcome of the investigation and identifying the persons who may have a claim, notifying those persons about the possible claim, about the firm's complaints procedures and about the Legal Ombudsman (as well as dealing with the matter as if a complaint had been made);
- O(10.13): informing the SRA before a firm closes as part of the orderly wind-down of a firm ceasing to practise.

8.2.2 Under the SRA Authorisation Rules for Legal Services Bodies and Licensable Bodies

- Rule 3: notification of any change in information provided in an application for authorisation;
- Rule 8.5(c)(ii): report by a COLP of any material non-compliance as soon as reasonably practicable;
- Rule 8.5(e)(ii): report by a COFA of any material non-compliance as soon as reasonably practicable;
- Rule 8.7(a): provision of an annual information report containing such information as may be specified in the prescribed form by the prescribed date;
- Rule 8.7(c): notification of any changes to relevant information about the firm, its employees, managers or interest holders, including non-compliance with the Authorisation Rules and the conditions on its authorisation;
- Rule 8.7(d): immediate notification of any information which reasonably suggests that the firm has or may have provided the SRA with information which was or may have been false, misleading, incomplete or inaccurate, or has or may have changed in a materially significant way;
- Rule 8.8: notification by the sole surviving partner of a partnership in the event that they are the sole active partner by reason of the imprisonment or incapacity of, the imposition of relevant conditions on or abandonment of the practice by the other partner or partners;
- Rule 8.9: notification in similar circumstances by a legal services body of the loss of the sole remaining solicitor or REL whose role ensured the status of the body as a legal services body;
- Rule 8.10: notification in similar circumstances by a licensed body (ABS) of the loss of the sole remaining authorised individual whose role enabled the body to be a licensable body;
- Rule 18: notification that the firm ceases to have an approved COLP or COFA;
- Rule 23: notification of unforeseen temporary breach of conditions or eligibility criteria to be a legal services body or licensed body;
- Rule 24: notification of relevant changes in the composition of a partnership where temporary emergency recognition of a sole practitioner or new firm is required;
- Rule 25: applications for temporary emergency authorisations.

8.2.3 Under the SRA Practice Framework Rules

- Rule 18.1: any information and documentation relating to the composition and structure of the firm, or about its managers, employees or shareowners, as and when requested by the SRA;
- Rule 18.2: notification of any change to the firm's name, registered office or practising addresses, managers, members if it is a company, interest holders if it is a recognised body, owners if it is a licensed body, COLP or COFA;
- Rule 18.3: notification by an unlimited company of re-registration under the Companies Acts (the Companies Act 1985 and the Companies Act 2006) as a limited company;
- Rule 18.4: notification of a relevant insolvency event.

8.2.4 Under the SRA Accounts Rules

- Rule 35: strictly not a duty to inform, but to have a standard letter of engagement with reporting accountants enabling and requiring them to make a report to the SRA on discovery of relevant matters.

8.2.5 Under the SRA Practising Regulations

- Regulation 4.3: notification of a change in a firm's composition resulting in a solicitor or REL becoming a sole principal;
- Regulation 4.5: notification of the death of a recognised sole practitioner;
- Regulation 15.1: notification by a solicitor, REL or RFL if he or she:

(a) is committed to prison in civil or criminal proceedings;

(b) is charged with or convicted of an indictable offence;

(c) is made the subject of bankruptcy proceedings;

(d) makes a proposal for an individual voluntary arrangement or is a manager of a firm which makes a proposal for a company voluntary arrangement or a partnership voluntary arrangement under the Insolvency Act 1986;

(e) is admitted as:

(i) a member of a legal profession of a jurisdiction other than England and Wales;

(ii) a lawyer of England and Wales other than a solicitor;

(f) is made subject to disciplinary proceedings as:

(i) a member of a legal profession of a jurisdiction other than England and Wales; or

(ii) a lawyer of England and Wales other than a solicitor;

(g) becomes a manager of or acquires any interest in a firm which is a recognised body, or becomes a manager or owner of a firm which is a licensed body or an authorised non-SRA firm;

(h) sets up a sole practice as:

(i) a member of a legal profession of a jurisdiction other than England and Wales; or

(ii) a lawyer of England and Wales other than a solicitor;

(i) changes his or her name as shown on the register of holders of practising certificates, the register of European lawyers or the register of foreign lawyers, and must at the same time provide details of his or her new name.

A number of events or occurrences are reportable under more than one regulation, which does not indicate a completely integrated approach.

Where requirements are not referred to as 'immediate' or 'prompt' or 'as soon as reasonably practicable' and refer to the happening of a particular event, the obligation is generally to notify within seven days.

APPENDIX 20

Sources of help

[Law Society copyright. This material appeared as Chapter 19 in *The Solicitor's Handbook 2011*, Andrew Hopper and Gregory Treverton-Jones, published by the Law Society, 2011.]

What do you do when a letter arrives from the Solicitors Regulation Authority or Legal Ombudsman (LeO) with some kind of complaint, or if you are subject to a forensic investigation by the SRA, or if you face disciplinary proceedings? Where do you turn for assistance?

The first point to make is that doing nothing is not an option. Both the LeO and the SRA apply strict time limits; adjudications will be adverse if you do not provide your explanations – your side of the story – for the benefit of the adjudicator or ombudsman. Do not assume that you will be given extensions of time – any request for more time will have to be fully justified and will be considered on the premise that complying with the requirements of the regulator will be a matter of priority. At the other extreme, failing to appear at the Solicitors Disciplinary Tribunal in your own defence may be a terminal mistake.

Specialist assistance

In any matter of complexity or apparent seriousness it is desirable to obtain specialist assistance, and there are relatively few with the requisite expertise.

The ethics helpline formerly operated by the Law Society is now under the jurisdiction of the SRA. It is not known to what extent information received as a result of advice being sought will be treated as information about the person enquiring, for the purposes of regulatory action.

The **Solicitors' Assistance Scheme** is independent of the Law Society and SRA. Established in 1972, it now has some 80 members around the country available to give advice and assistance, not only on matters of professional regulation but also on partnership and employment issues, financial concerns and stress-related problems. The initial interview is without charge. They can be contacted via the helpline number on 020 7117 8811 and at **www.thesas.org.uk**.

Professional indemnity insurance no longer provides cover for the costs of defending disciplinary or regulatory proceedings.

LawCare is a confidential advisory and support service to help lawyers, their staff and their immediate families to deal with health problems, such as depression and addiction, and related emotional difficulties. The contact number for solicitors, law students and legal executives in England and Wales is 0800 279 6888. Their website is **www.lawcare.org.uk**.

The Law Society's **Practice Advice Service** is a dedicated support-line for solicitors, trainees and employees of law firms. It is staffed by a team of experienced solicitors who deal with enquiries using their own knowledge and a variety of information sources, as well as the experience of other specialists within the Law Society. They are able to assist with enquiries on legal practice in many areas including anti-money laundering; solicitors' costs; multi-party actions; conveyancing; conditional fee agreements; probate; and rights of audience in the

Crown Court. Advice by the Practice Advice Service does not constitute legal advice and cannot be relied upon as such. The contact number is 0870 606 2522 and e-mail **lib-pas@lawsociety.org.uk**.

Financial assistance

Less relevant to the regulatory context, but a potential source of financial assistance for those in need, is the **Solicitors Benevolent Association** (SBA) which is the principal nationwide charity for solicitors in England and Wales. The aim of the Association is to assist solicitors and their dependants who are in need. The SBA helps those suffering ill-health (typical examples are debilitating diseases such as multiple sclerosis, and mental conditions such as bipolar disorder and schizophrenia), accident victims, and those without work – for whatever reason. Most applicants are in receipt of state benefits. The Association's telephone number is 020 8675 6440, or see its website: **www.sba.org.uk**.

Index